KT-450-465

Tower Hamlets College
Learning Centre

127585

From All Points

American West in the Twentieth Century
Martin Ridge and Walter Nugent, eds.

FROM ALL POINTS

America's Immigrant West,
1870s–1952

Elliott Robert Barkan

THE LIBRARY
TOWER HAMLETS COLLEGE
POPLAR HIGH STREET
LONDON E14 0AF
Tel: 0207 510 7763

Indiana University Press / *Bloomington and Indianapolis*

This book is a publication of

Indiana University Press
601 North Morton Street
Bloomington, IN 47404-3797 USA

http://iupress.indiana.edu

Telephone orders 800-842-6796
Fax orders 812-855-7931
Orders by e-mail iuporder@indiana.edu

© 2007 by Elliott Robert Barkan
All rights reserved

No part of this book may be reproduced or utilized in any form or by any means,
electronic or mechanical, including photocopying and recording, or by any
information storage and retrieval system, without permission in writing from the
publisher. The Association of American University Presses' Resolution on Permissions
constitutes the only exception to this prohibition.

The paper used in this publication meets the minimum requirements of American
National Standard for Information Sciences—Permanence of Paper for Printed
Library Materials, ANSI Z39.48-1984.

Manufactured in the United States of America

Library of Congress Cataloging-in-Publication Data

Barkan, Elliott Robert.
From all points : America's immigrant West, 1870s–1952 / Elliott Robert Barkan.
p. cm.—(American West in the twentieth century)
Includes bibliographical references and index.
ISBN: 978-0-253-34851-7 (cloth : alk. paper)
1. Minorities—West (U.S.)—History. 2. Immigrants—West (U.S.)—History.
3. Pioneers—West (U.S.)—History. 4. West (U.S.)—Emigration and immigration—
History. 5. West (U.S.)—History. 6. West (U.S.)—Ethnic relations. 7. Pluralism
(Social sciences)—West (U.S.)—History. 8. Acculturation—West (U.S.)—History.
9. Racism—West (U.S.)—History. 10. West (U.S.)—Social conditions. I. Title.
F596.2.B37 2007
305.800978—dc22
2006032173

1 2 3 4 5 12 11 10 09 08 07

Order No:

Class: 973.91 BAR

Accession No: 127585

Type: 3 Weeks.

In memory of Libby Medrich (1909–2006), a woman of remarkable talents, humor, and love of life—as well as the mother of my beloved Bryn

CONTENTS

Photos appear after pages 154 and 346.

PREFACE

RICHARD WHITE, THE eminent historian of the American West, observed that just as people ignored garbage along trails, so Frederick Jackson Turner and his followers "eliminated from their history as so much human garbage most of the diverse peoples of the West . . . whose presence endangered their [thesis regarding the region's] homogeneity." Turner's memorable thesis included a discussion of the moving frontier as the site of the evolution of a composite American nationality based essentially on Protestant northern Europeans. However, so beguiling and persuasive was his 1893 essay that it created an interpretive "box" from which western historians and writers have been struggling to break free. Ninety years later, Frederick Luebke took western historians to task for treating "their subject as the story of an undifferentiated English-speaking majority." However, fifteen years later, he was lamenting, "European immigrants are the forgotten people of the American West." But that did not signify an adequate coverage of those "others," for when it came to the region's ethnic diversity, most works that were not focused on a specific group have been limited, one-dimensional, at best providing little more than a checklist of some ethnic peoples present. Although several authors in Gerald Nash and Richard Etulain's collection *Researching Western History: Topics in the Twentieth Century* (1997)—notably Roger Lotchin, Glenda Riley, and Robert Cherny—did address the larger reality, overall the remarkable array of immigrants in the West has been left, figuratively speaking, in the wings and rarely moved to center stage in the region's history.[1]

Notwithstanding the increasing appearance of individual works on Asian and Latino populations, Jews, and peoples from the Middle East (along with African Americans, and Native Americans), we would not be going far afield to modify Luebke's observation to conclude that, on several levels, "many groups of immigrants are still the forgotten people of the American West." News stories and discussions concerning, for example, undocumented aliens, amnesty, NAFTA, race relations, California's Proposition 187 (1994), and Arizona's Proposition 200 (2004) do not make it emphatically clear, as I earlier wrote, that "the vast achievements in the West in the 20th century were made possible principally because immigrant men and women and often their children provided much . . . of the labor"—frequently along with their material resources, creativity, and entrepreneurialism.[2]

At the beginning of the 20th century somewhat less than 10 percent of the nation's foreign born resided in the West.[3] By 1950, some 17.6 percent did so, and by 2000 nearly 47 percent. Put another way, 15.4 percent of the West's population in 1900 was foreign born compared with 13.5 percent in the rest of the nation. At the end of the century, 17.4 percent of westerners were immigrants as opposed to less than half that elsewhere (8.4 percent). Immigrants and their children have consistently comprised a significant portion of the West's population.

The principal objective of this book is to tell their story. It goes beyond accounts of one group or cohort of immigrants and explores the collective experiences of ethnic groups over time and place. Only in this way is it possible to show how, time and again, immigrants were critical to the growth of the region—economically, socially, and culturally. Some groups do stand out, usually by virtue of their greater numbers and economic roles, but only by examining the extraordinary array of peoples who have been present can the full measure of their impact be understood. In other words, the history of the West is a mosaic of rich hues and variations representing its myriad populations, with the edges of each blurring into one another as peoples met, worked in the same places, lived nearby and sometimes as neighbors, sent their children to the same schools, and gradually socialized, dated, and married across ethnic boundaries. Not all did so, of course, but many did, in the process sharing experiences, values, customs, and foods.

This is a narrative about peoples (not a people) and about the steady appearance of new groups under conditions that were continually evolving. All such newcomers have encountered the challenges of immigration, of occupying a new place and trying to adapt to new surroundings and new institutions. Not all adapted successfully, nor did all by any means integrate (much less assimilate), but many thousands of immigrants and especially children of immigrants did, while others left a mark on the West even when their stays were of short duration. At the same time, the struggles of old and new to co-exist have ultimately compelled communities from Hawai'i to Texas to accommodate to the unfolding multi-ethnic realities in their midst. It has not been only the newcomers who have had to adapt; the region's existing populations and institutions also have had to adjust to the new immigrants—be they new arrivals or transplants from elsewhere in the nation.

These stages are a core part of this narrative, for its broad perspective must necessarily contain within it both parallel and consecutive storylines, capturing the multiplicity of peoples and multiple locations. The narrative begins with the presence of the Chinese; *overlaps* with parallel streams of southern and eastern Europeans, Scandinavians, Mexicans, Canadians, Filipinos, and other Asians; *continues* with smaller streams of Europeans plus greater flows of Latinos from the Americas, a persisting influx from Canada, and new currents from across the Asian spectrum; and is *further reshaped* in recent decades by still newer immigrant populations from Africa and Western Asia. The story has not ended.

This narrative, therefore, does not focus just on Mexicans, Chinese, and Japanese, whose visibility has been considerable, their histories so prominent, and their mistreatment so glaring that they could not be ignored. Rather, a whole array of groups are incorporated, including Europeans—not all of whom have assimilated into mainstream society of the American West even now. Precisely because in many locations across the decades numerous foreign-born groups have been found living and working in rather close proximity to one another, we must approach this work as a story of many peoples—with combinations from Asia, the Pacific, Europe, and North America, along with, in places, African Americans, Native Americans, and Native Alaskans. In fact, on the eve of World War Two, more than one-third of the entire population of the West was made up of foreign-born and second-generation men, women, and children—referred to together as the "foreign stock." Most writers discussing the West have also by and large omitted (or skimmed over) the Pacific Northwest and almost entirely sidelined Hawai'i and Alaska. Yet, the role of these territories in western history has been immense, especially in western economic history. They cannot be omitted without doing a real injustice to the peoples of the West.

And the significance of their presence goes beyond the region's economic growth. That is why this cannot be a one-themed or one-people story. These immigrants and children of immigrants built communities, contributed to the region's culture, and contended with discrimination, the pressures and lure of Americanization, American culture, and the desirable passkey of whiteness; many gradually won acceptance and entered political arenas. For those reasons, among those who chose to remain and those who did not, their trials and tribulations, successes and failures, became integral parts of what emerges as the newer West of the late nineteenth and twentieth centuries. The history of the West is, most accurately, one of great diversity—diversity of groups and of the themes in their lives. Any history of the West without this rich diversity cannot do justice to the region. Moreover, the many dimensions and complexities of that history necessitate our using various tools of the social sciences. They are invaluable for analyzing the dynamics of what has occurred, along with identifying and highlighting patterns of ethnic continuity and change.

Besides the groups, it soon becomes evident that in order to tell these stories properly, one cannot speak only of groups and communities—with the inevitable need to generalize—for the full power of their stories emerges when we move on and examine the accounts of specific individuals, in effect putting names and faces on these histories. Narratives adapted from oral histories add much richness to the tales of immigrants and their children. A selection of such narratives follows the introduction as the prelude to this study and also begins each part (with still other narratives included in various chapters) because I wanted at the outset of each part to introduce, along with the themes and key events they represent, some of those persons who populated these stories, met the challenges, and experienced the successes and failures that came with migration and settlement.

Thus, a proper telling of the history of immigration in the late nineteenth and early twentieth centuries must necessarily be multi-ethnic, multi-disciplinary, and multi-themed. Only then can the true wealth of the West become evident: the wealth that is its peoples.

To accomplish this required several decisions. First, only a few works have adequately included the necessary immigration and census data one requires for a concrete, not anecdotal, portrait of these groups. Considerable use has been made of these resources to provide the factual framework for the immigration, settlement, and growth of these peoples. The tables are in the book's appendixes. Second, given the treatment of immigrants by state and federal authorities, with laws and court decisions fundamentally affecting their movements (their right to enter), their freedoms, their access to economic and educational opportunities, and even their right to citizenship—in other words, defining the borders and boundaries many would encounter—the story of these peoples must include relevant excerpts from key laws and court decisions that have so affected their lives. Many of these laws and decisions have either been omitted by others or presented in extremely abbreviated form.

Third, the story of immigration into the West involves so many peoples that it has been necessary to make choices. One was that many groups could not be included in depth, while some reappear in the different segments of the book because their histories and experiences span much of the history of the West (the Japanese, Mexicans, and Scandinavians being three prominent examples). The related choice was that the focus had to remain on immigrants and their children; Native Americans and African Americans appear here but could not be given their full due as important native-born groups among the peoples of the West, for that would have required a different (and longer) kind of book and a different focus.

Finally, for practical reasons this narrative begins in the 1870s, because the

Chinese Exclusion Act of 1882 is the essential point of departure for understanding the legal and social developments of the next 120-plus years. The present volume ends with the omnibus Immigration and Nationality Act of 1952, which not only carried forward the immigration system set in place a generation earlier but also included elements that, along with other measures recently passed, set the stage for the immigration revolution that would be underway by the mid-1960s. Those developments will constitute the planned second volume.

Across the nearly eight decades covered in this volume, the West underwent profound changes, and immigrants and the children of immigrants, though they too underwent changes, continued to be present in very large numbers and remained key players in the transformation of the region. Their personal stories throughout this book become important narratives capturing their experiences and reminding us of their varied social, cultural, political, and economic roles—their human capital—which should be at center stage for any full grasp of the twentieth-century West.

Lastly, why this focus on the West? Because so many have used the West to define the American character. Because so many have looked to it for inspiration, for role models, and even for cultural icons. Because so many have emulated aspects of it, even people in other countries. Because so many fiction and nonfiction authors have written about it. And because so few have fully understood it.

ACKNOWLEDGMENTS

ALTHOUGH THE FINAL VERSION of this book, and any errors that escaped our attention, remain my responsibility, I owe an enormous debt of gratitude to those who so generously agreed to reads portions of this manuscript, notably David Reimers, Leonard Dinnerstein, Barbara Posadas and Roland Guyotte, Rodolfo Acuña, Richard White, Diane Vecchio, Bryn Barkan, and especially my very supportive and patient editor, Walter Nugent—who assured me that even after his own book appeared in 1999, there was still much of the story of immigrants in the West yet to be told. Extremely generous with her amazing assistance has been Marian L. Smith, senior historian for the U.S. Citizenship & Immigration Services agency of the Department of Homeland Security, who in numerous instances provided me with invaluable immigration and naturalization reports and data, as has Michael Hoefer, director, Office of Immigration Statistics for the same agency. The staff at the archives and oral history collections at Baylor University, the University of Washington, the University of Oregon, the Oregon Historical Society, the Washington State Archives in Olympia, the Huntington Library, the Nordic Heritage Museum in Ballard, Washington, the Institute for Texas Cultures (ITC) in San Antonio, the Center for Oral and Public History at California State University, Fullerton, the Hawaiian Historical Society and the Bishop Museum of Honolulu, Carl Hallberg of Wyoming's Department of Parks and Cultural Resources, Tom Shelton of the ITC, as well as Warren Nishimoto, director of the Oral History Project at the University of Hawai'i, Honolulu, have all been wonderfully cooperative. My thanks also to Eugene Turner, professor of Geography, California State University, Northridge, for his prompt preparation of the map used here. Three other special statements of appreciation go to the outstanding inter-library loan staff at California State University, San Bernardino, who have done remarkable work in securing innumerable works that I required for this project, to Jane Curran for the fine copyediting job, and to Bob Sloan, editorial director, Indiana University Press, for his understanding, patience, support, and very valuable editorial comments.

And, there are some special words of thanks. Although this was not the book Martin Ridge originally wanted me to write (as co-editor of the Indiana series with Walt Nugent), when he began reading the first portions, he recognized that my strongest wish was to write a rather comprehensive narrative, not a textbook. He supported my choice, for which I am most grateful. He told me, however, that he might not live to see this book if I took too long. Well, it did take longer to complete than I planned, and I regret he did not live to see the finished volume. I thank you, Martin, for your vote of confidence.

Finally, once again, I thank my delightful wife, Bryn, who has shown exceptional fortitude while I remained single-mindedly focused on completing this project.

I dedicate this work to the many, many immigrants whom I have been fortunate enough to meet here in the American West, for they have shown me so much about the courage that it takes to pull up roots, to flee oppression, to start new lives in a strange land. Leaving Brooklyn was traumatic for me, but it does not compare to what the true immigrants have gone through so that they could reach this destination and contribute to the building of the American West.

NOTE ON TRANSLATION
AND TRANSLITERATION

NAMES OF JAPANESE AND Chinese immigrants appear both in traditional and Western order, depending their degree of acculturation; such "inconsistencies" were the norm in the early days of East Asian immigration. All translations into English are those used in the sources cited, as are the transliterations of non-English words.

FROM ALL POINTS

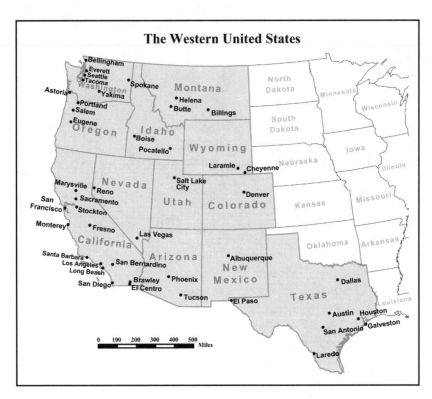

The Western United States

Alaska

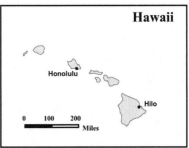

Hawaii

The American West: An Immigration Perspective

Defining Themes—The West, Westerners, and Whiteness

O VER A HALF CENTURY AGO, the historian Oscar Handlin began his great poetic saga *The Uprooted* with the now-famous remark, "Once I thought to write a history of the immigrants in America. Then I discovered that the immigrants *were* American history."[1] Unfortunately, most historians of the American West did not take to heart Handlin's reflection. Some might explain their omission by pointing out his incomplete vision and the peoples he overlooked. Most have been mesmerized by other tales from the frontiers and Far West. Some have included individual migrants, and some have focused on particular groups. But the romance, the aura, the myths, the sheer grandeur surrounding the story of "The West" have commonly veiled one vital "chamber" in the heart of that history. The Native Americans and natives are identified; the visionaries and villains, the victors and victims, are present. And yet, as the stories unfold into the twentieth century, only fleetingly—and far too often anonymously or as undifferentiated groups—has the cast of characters included the indispensable builders of the West: the immigrants.

This "truth" is not meant to dismiss or devalue the vital roles of the American-born pioneers, farmers, businessmen and women, entrepreneurs, capitalists, or later seekers and settlers and the like, or the central role of various levels of governments, or the obviously enormous impact of American technology and inventiveness, or the unique physical environment without whose vast resources all the rest would have been largely immaterial, or Native Americans who have been contributors and victims. Rather, it is to suggest that the American West is what it is—with all its created richness, diversity, and complexity—in great

1

measure because of the multitude of immigrants. Without them, the West as we know it could not have become the West as we have come to experience it.

From wherever they came, from all compass points, so many of these immigrant men and women and their children contributed their labor, talents, ingenuity, capital, inventiveness, risk taking, and commitment, thereby incalculably shaping that West: from the mines in Clifton-Morenci, Arizona, to the canneries in Alaska, from the railroads in Montana to the assembly plants in Silicon Valley and the sweatshops in Los Angeles, from Harlingen, Texas, to Hollywood to Honolulu. A generation of ethnic historians has now begun uncovering and detailing many invaluable chapters in this story, but too many still remain unrevealed, forgotten.[2]

The significance of immigration in the history of the twentieth-century American West is the story I wish to tell—a story of groups, of labor "gangs," of individual men and women, of those who remained and those who chose to move on or to return home. It is a story of peoples who have either been rendered invisible by historians and other western writers, or who have commonly been consigned to bit parts, scattered scenes—periodic moments in the historical spotlight. This volume is an effort to move them to center stage, to make them visible as a multi-ethnic presence across the region and over time, to number the numberless and name the nameless.

DEFINING THE WEST

What a "curious assortment of people!" was how Carey McWilliams captured tourists' reactions to Southern Californians in the 1940s.[3] No doubt it was the kind of remark newcomers might well have expressed in many parts of the West, long before McWilliams's work and ever since. Just about a half-century earlier the writer Frank Norris had observed about California, "As yet, we out here, on the fringe of the continent, are not a people, we are peoples—agglomeration rather than conglomerate. All up and down the coast, from Mexico to Oregon, are scattered 'little' Italys, 'little' Spains, 'little' Chinas, and even 'little' Russias—settlements, colonies, tiny groups of nationalities flung from the parent stock, but holding tightly to themselves, unwilling to mix and forever harking back to their native lands."[4] That 1897 statement suggests that some (perhaps many) of Norris's contemporaries were aware of the diversity in their relatively "new" region.[5]

For about the past quarter century the "New Historians" have been reexamining many of their predecessors' works on the West and, most prominently, the 1893 seminal essay by Frederick Jackson Turner on the frontier.[6] Turner's work reinforced the preoccupation with the nineteenth-century West, eventually prompting historian Gerald D. Nash's emphatic comment: "The West represented in the popular mind is a 19th century West that is no more. It was a passing phase in the process of western development." Brian Dippie put the alternative challenge most succinctly: "To effect a revision in western history one need simply move forward into the twentieth century." Indeed, historian Patricia Limerick emphasized the argument that even if historians were focused on frontiers, omitting the twentieth century—when far more people moved to the West than during the prior century—immersed them "in a conceptual fog."[7] This study follows through with their emphases, setting off from the late nineteenth century and concentrating on the myriad immigrant experiences in the twentieth-century West.

Where is the West? The issue of the perimeters of the American West is part of the long debate over whether there has ever been "A West."[8] Whatever unifying threads that historians have woven together into "A West," there have been flaws found or geographical areas omitted—because they were not part of the Mexican Cession, or were not beyond the 100th meridian, or were not arid enough, or were beyond 125 degrees longitude or 49 degrees latitude and therefore not contiguous with the rest of the United States—"the lower 48." Or perhaps the model suggested was seen as simply lacking the right mix of farm folk, ranchers, and Indians! To approach this from another perspective, John Findlay argued rather forcefully (or with tongue in cheek?) that labeling Oregon and Washington the Pacific Northwest was "a fishy proposition" because such a claim to regional consciousness was "dubious, artificial, and ever shifting"—the creation of outsiders. Of course, some would apply this line of reasoning to all of "the West" and declare that it, too, was similarly contrived. After all, was it a *place*, or was it real because the frontier *process* occurred there? Given the incredible diversity of variables, is any configuration of "A West" bound to be hopelessly fragmented? Or, on the other hand, is there actually a "connectedness" of sorts—"a series of interlocking relationships" tying the regional segments together—that has not always been apparent?[9]

Although the details of this complex, seemingly unending debate will not be revisited here, the "West" in this study is one that has been largely interconnected by the ebb and flows, the circulations of immigrants—settlers and sojourners—the foreigners who migrated to, from, and within the "Primary West" of New Mexico, Arizona, California, Oregon, Washington, Alaska, Hawai'i, and central, southern, and western Texas, as well as to, from, and within the "Secondary West" (or "Interior West"): Utah, Colorado, Wyoming, Montana, Idaho, and Nevada. The immigrant-related West, the focus of this book, consists of 14 states and territories, and the data presented here are based on the inclusion of all 14.[10]

But even with that definition, matters are not so simple. Any radical leap over to the twentieth century that ignored the prior years could trivialize vitally important patterns and precedents from the 1800s (and earlier). That could leave us in as much of a "conceptual fog" as that befalling those refusing to take their studies of the West beyond the 1890s. Moreover, the mystique of the West that took hold well before 1900 endured throughout the next century and even deepened thanks to the modern media. Walter Nugent, one of the foremost scholars of the West, cogently pointed out that in 1890 the region, with perhaps 5 percent of the American population, was to others elsewhere in the nation "an exotic place that was distant, unknown, dreamed about and mythified." And not only Europeans and Americans in the East had golden dreams about America, and not only the Chinese envisioned it as the Golden Mountain. "In America," prospective Japanese immigrants believed, "money was hanging from the trees and one could rake up treasure like fallen leaves."

The myths that the nineteenth-century West fueled—though frequently exaggerated—did endure and were "polestars" for twentieth-century migrants and immigrants. Among both of those populations people would celebrate the immense potential for economic rewards in the West and its beauty. Italians, for example, waxed euphoric, thinking of how northern California reminded them of Italy; Norwegians were thrilled when they saw Puget Sound looking much like their fjords. Many others were convinced about the curative powers of the West's climate. So lavish had the praises and fantasy images become that McWilliams was prompted to quote a rather humorous take on these boosters: "How intense everything is in Southern California! The fruit is so immense, the canyons so deep, the trees so big, the hills so high, the rain so wet, and the drought so dry!"[11]

Boosters throughout the West exclaimed with great hyperbole about their new communities. One real estate firm in the late 1880s claimed that San Diego had a population of 150,000—"only they are not all here yet!" Accounts of the West did draw a considerable diversity of peoples, one so rich that it has indeed become synonymous with the West—and not merely from eastern states or northern Europe. Historian Carl Abbott noted that the "hidden theme" of frontier history was that a blending of peoples had taken place in the West that was greater than along the East Coast. Patricia Limerick urged fellow historians to acknowledge that "the West was, in truth, a place of extraordinary convergence, one of the great meeting zones on the planet." This demographic phenomenon has also been labeled "cosmopolitanization," the fifth force shaping the West (along with aridity, reliance on federal funding and extractive industries, and the recency of the frontier experience). It has also been described quite eloquently as "a cornucopia of immigrants whose cultural heritage may be traced to Europe, Africa, or Asia but who sometimes arrived from farther north via Canada, from father west via the Pacific Islands, from farther south via Mexico and Latin America."

The challenge of the twentieth-century West is to recognize the dimensions of its multi-ethnicity and to fully incorporate that pluralism into the whole, unfolding story and not leave it as piecemeal inserts unintegrated into the larger history of the region. It has been emphasized that many of the early newcomers, such as the Irish, Cornish, Greeks, Italians, Basques, Germans, and Scandinavians, though fading, were "still making their presence felt in the modern West." Roger Lotchin posed a distinction between the West as a melting pot versus the region as the setting for exceptional multi-culturalism and enduring ethnicity, and he raised a most intriguing conundrum: The "Caucasian, white, Anglo" population had originally included Jews, Germans, Cornish, Irish, Canadians, Serbs, and others: "If they have not melted, that would indicate even more multi-cultural diversity" than the multi-culturalists were acknowledging. However, if these groups were no longer "Jewish, Midwestern, German, English, Canadian, Irish, Cornish, Basque," and so forth, then the melting pot worked. In that case "we must explain how the ethnics got into that container and, more importantly, in what condition they came out." His point: too many ethnic and eastern/southern/midwestern groups "have been relatively neglected" by western scholars.[12]

The neglect to which Lotchin refers—and which I address in this book— concerns not only the accounting of how many came and where they went but who came, why, and with what impact on their new destinations, on those already living there, and on the homelands left behind. How did the ethnic groups affect each other; to what extent have these ethnic groups persisted; and how has the core society been altered by the inclusion of such peoples? In the most basic sense, as historian Frederick Luebke put it, "An ethnic community should be studied holistically because its history emerges from the interaction of its culture with the environment of its new home." With that in mind, I plan to take the story one step further. Japanese immigrants referred to fellow migrants from the same village as *sonjin kai*, and Yukiko Kimura, in her history of the Issei (first-generation Japanese immigrants) in Hawai'i, pointed out that people from different prefectures were meeting for the first time in Hawai'i, and their initial encounters were not always cordial. "Open hostility" was often the outcome, and sometimes, as Okinawans discovered to their chagrin, the resulting social distance could endure for decades. Italians traditionally referred to those who lived beyond the sound of their village church bells (*campanilismo*) as *stranieri* (strangers), and that attitude was carried to America. Greeks commonly limited themselves to coffeehouses set up by kinsmen from the same immediate region in Greece, and Greek labor contractors also often gave preference in hiring to men from that same region, or island (as with Cretans).

Thus, the meeting of peoples in the West in the early stages frequently involved individuals and families from the same country who often had not yet developed any inclusive national identity or familiarity with those from other regions of that same country. Before there could be any melting pot, perhaps there would first have to be numerous smaller melting cups within which those with similar origins initially and individually engaged each other, as would take place in the many and varied labor pools, in the mines, logging camps, and railroad section crews, and among migrant farm laborers. They represent the stories not yet fully told.[13]

DEFINING WESTERNERS AND WHITENESS

From the last quarter of the nineteenth century until the Depression of the 1930s great surges of immigration took place into and across the Secondary and the Primary West (as defined above), including Alaska and Hawai'i. Where communities did not exist, it was often the immigrants who created them or played a part in nurturing them into towns and cities. As that great era of immigration was being phased out by the 1920s, new streams were already under way from Mexico and the Philippines (the latter having begun migrating to Hawai'i a decade earlier). After the Second World War, other immigration streams would start or resume, principally across the Primary West, their paths eased by a series of major legislative changes beginning in 1945.[14] From the vantage point of such immigration flows it is not a question of finding *the* common thread (or theme) more or less binding the western region together but of recognizing the whole, intricately woven tapestry of immigration found in the West. Men, women, and children from dozens of nations, legal and undocumented, provided the raw human fabric with which entrepreneurs—from farmers and ranchers to manufacturers and merchants—built the West in the twentieth century. These populations increased the region's "connection to the world's peoples," and no mere litany of nationalities can do justice to contributions of such magnitude.[15]

Of course, this story goes well beyond the economics. The majority of these multitudes of newcomers remained—or returned home only to migrate once more. They created extensive networks that channeled men, women, and teenagers to the waiting arms of friends, compatriots, relatives, and immediate family members. Men sought out spouses here or in their hometowns and villages. Newcomers built and rebuilt communities; formed extensive arrays of self-help and fraternal institutions, churches, and schools; acquired American citizenship; on occasion entered American political life; and often watched, at times with serious misgivings, as their American-born (as well as foreign-born but America-raised) children became more acculturated and more integrated than they were. All the while, immigrants continued to send hundreds of thousands of dollars to families left behind—until they either paid for their family members' passage to the United States, or, as their own roots took hold in the new land, gradually felt the grasp of the ties binding them to those distant homelands fall away.[16]

Yet, that sequence did not always go smoothly. Walls of opposition appeared, because, as vital as were the newcomers' economic roles—in fact, not infrequently in reaction to the immigrants' participation—native-born Americans, and even other immigrants who had earlier come most commonly from northern and western Europe responded to the newest strangers with anxieties, fear, and an intense, defensive nationalism. The newcomers were seen as the source of an array of *perceived* provocations (including various combinations of racial, social, cultural, religious, and economic dangers), and the resulting nativism generated an opposition that very much colored the history of immigration into the West—and that color was white: one's possession of it, or one's manifestation of some of it, or one's classification as devoid of it. Though layered with economic competitiveness and a determination to ensure that only American culture and institutions took root in the West, the preoccupation with whiteness implicitly centered on hierarchies of power and control in all spheres of western life.

This is not a matter of current perspectives reconfiguring behavior patterns one century ago, a hindsight view or mere re-interpretation of past patterns. Many were the references during the late nineteenth and early twentieth centuries to Americans who were white and immigrants who were not. They suggest that the issue was an important factor in inter-group relations flowing beneath the surface of the often frenzied West—and not infrequently roiling its surface. In fact, when attitudes, behaviors, and language of inter-group discourse shifted in the mid-twentieth century toward an explicitly greater acceptance of diversity, being white and possessing whiteness did not disappear but was incorporated into the intense debates over multi-culturalism. This contestation over whiteness, then, was not a passing fad; it was inseparable from group relations throughout the years of this study. It would become a barrier for many, an admission ticket for others. So prominent and persistent was the issue across the decades that it is essential here at the outset of this narrative to address the theme of whiteness in the West. The fate of many newcomers (along with Native Americans and African Americans) was tied so tightly to how they were "racially" identified—and not just as white but *how* white, if white at all—that it frequently determined whether they were welcomed or excluded, well treated or mistreated, equitably rewarded or simply exploited, tolerated, or killed.

An Englishman, a Major W. Shepherd, wrote a book on America in 1885 in which he observed that "The American does not like foreigners, but he tolerates their presence if they will follow his example and adopt his institutions; but to be a separatist, to live in small national colonies, to appear or behave differently to the accredited type, not to care for local topics or the politics of the saloon—these are all crimes which the American cannot allow."[17] Four decades later a Texas cotton grower, Frank Hoepner, commented that Mexicans do not try to assimilate, but the eastern Europeans do: "The Bohunks want to intermarry with whites. Yes, they're white, but they're not our kind of white." As scholars Neil Foley, Matthew Jacobson, and Peter Kolchin, among others, have emphasized, during the American colonial period one was black or white, essentially slave or free. White became a default category—if someone was not black, then he or she was white. The Naturalization Act of 1790 accorded citizenship to "a free white person," making it, in effect, an inclusive category for all who were not black, until other peoples arrived or were encountered.[18]

A half-century later, Mexicans were regarded as "mongrelized" and were grouped with blacks as "not whites." However, the 1848 Treaty of Guadalupe Hidalgo granted U.S. citizenship automatically to all Mexicans who remained for one year within the territories acquired by the United States from Mexico, a provision subsequently upheld in federal district court in Texas in 1897, based on the Mexicans' nationality rather than on any racial premise (*In re Rodriguez*, 81 F. 337 (1897), Dist. Ct, W.D. Texas). Although described by many Anglos as mongrelized greasers but legally classified as eligible for citizenship (even before those of African descent), were Mexicans then technically white but still something else—"not quite white" or "lesser white"? And how much did their presence in the Southwest with this marginal status affect perceptions of other still-marginal groups, such as the Greeks and Italians? Perhaps, in part, the latter were gradually perceived as "more white" as the number of "non-white" Mexicans in their communities and work places sharply increased—notwithstanding the legal nicety that the Mexicans could be naturalized.

The pattern of shifting perceptions had begun earlier. In the 1840s and 1850s the Irish were arriving in great numbers, with their Catholic religion awakening latent anti-Catholicism and with their poverty and illiteracy raising deep-seated misgivings about their "racial" status as whites. Quite rapidly, many Irish did come to understand that acceptance as Americans (achieving some higher social status) rested on not being perceived as black or anything else but white as well as on their not associating with any non-whites. They had to "establish their own whiteness, and thereby prove their Americanness."[19]

But could we not also say that the Irish example actually raised the opposite strategy as well? In other words, were these newcomers in reality being compelled to establish their Americanness in order to be accepted as whites (rather than vice versa), or was it simply a case, as Neil Foley put it, that "being American was synonymous with being white"? The Irish, who were legally white, also "became" white by, for example, (1) the behavioral and cultural changes they made in themselves; (2) their identification with the struggles of American workers for their rights and dignity as free workers; (3) their clear embrace of American political values and practices; and (4) their disassociation from blacks and adoption of Americans' anti-black prejudices. In other words, whiteness was not immutable, not unambiguous, but, rather, freighted with various meanings and shadings depending on time, place, and situational circumstances. The whole issue weighed heavily on many immigrants in the West who struggled for acceptance by mainstream Americans. For members of numerous groups their status, rights, and the opportunities available to them were part and parcel of where they were situated in this partially fluid "practice" of classification ("system" would imply more coherence and consistency than it had).

Of the three most serious implications, the first was that if groups could "acquire" whiteness, they could also lose it. This was the point Neil Foley made about the "'human debris' of whiteness" in Texas—the poor whites whose socio-economic status (and lack of land ownership), cultural impoverishment, and political powerlessness rendered them less white. In other words, not only were there different situations marked by "gradations of both whiteness and non-whiteness," but within the variegated nature of whiteness itself there were also gradations. In one scenario differences existed between groups and within groups, based on such factors as social class, economic activity, appearance, and behavioral and attitudinal characteristics. Some would meet the criteria, while, to use Gunther Peck's phrase, "their 'unwashed' brethren . . . remained nonwhite, emasculated and aliens in the eyes of most native-born Americans." In a second scenario, being settled in one place (namely, actually residing there) was considered an important attribute among white persons, although, like so much about this mode of identification, by itself it was no guarantee of a white status. However, among immigrant workers, Peck stressed, "Transience by contrast was almost always a marker of non-whiteness in the West in 1900." Peter La Chapelle provides another, more contemporary illustration of that attitude, regarding the Dust Bowl refugees of the 1930s. They "regressed in social phenotypic standing," he pointed out, from white to "not quite white," highlighting "California's anti-rural and anti-poor-white sentiment" and the "fluid, socially constructed" nature of whiteness.[20]

The second implication is that whiteness was clearly associated not just with appearance, values, and behavior but, most fundamentally, with power. Power and privilege. To cross the threshold noted above and to be recognized as white was to be accepted (on some to-be-determined level) as participating in that power (or hegemony) and having access to the "assets of whiteness" (voting, holding office, union participation, etc.), whereas to be designated as "not white" (or even "not quite white") was to be excluded from the privileges of whiteness, to be regarded as relatively disempowered, perhaps vulnerable, defenseless, even exploitable. One historian's somewhat offhand remark that "There is no obvious frontier except in the sense that in some places you run out of white people" could be taken as a rather Eurocentric perspective associating civilization just with whiteness or as representing an aspect of whiteness that was more than "who looks like us" in the dynamic state of Western society. This certainly could be seen when so many groups were arriving in the late nineteenth and early twentieth centuries. The explicit implication is that whiteness was indeed largely synonymous with power. I say "largely" because even with power as a core characteristic, whiteness was not monolithic. It was, to reiterate, internally hierarchical, and even that hierarchy varied in different places and at different times; it was scarcely a uniform category. But it remained a potent weapon of differentiation.

It has also been argued that race used in this manner was a way by which Americans organized labor (such as who would be admitted into unions and who would not), which could be applied in various other circumstances. Thus, Mexicans in multi-ethnic northern cities sought acceptance by claiming the status of being white, yet in Texas "even sympathetic whites typically saw Mexicans as unequal to European immigrants." In fact, the Mexican consul general there, Benito Rodriguez, pointed out during the 1920s that most Mexicans in Texas identified as *Americanos*, whereas "the people here refer to whites, Greeks, Italians, and Mexicans." In other words, the latter three were not (yet) a part of white America. Early in the 1900s Greeks in Utah were "thought to be lawless, dirty, lewd, and lazy, images that paralleled then current racial stereotypes of African Americans in the South," and such images rendered the Greeks "racially" nonwhite. By acculturating (becoming more Americanized), settling, and joining unions—in this case the Western Federation of Miners—and participating in other (non-ethnic, American) organizations, they were gradually recognized as having "become whitened members."[21] That did not erase all vestiges of nativism toward Greeks for quite some time, but they had at least taken a step off the sideline and into the white, American mainstream.

For others, Filipinos in particular, such efforts would not prove to have as whitening an effect, representing acceptance and inclusion, because the outreach was offset by perceptions of their behavior as overly assertive and their encounters with American women as intolerably "intimate" (e.g., dating and dancing in dime-a-dance halls). That triggered sexual fears, resentments, and then violence, followed by legislative barriers to intermarriage. Such experiences illustrate how the boundaries of whiteness could also be used to legally define insiders/outsiders notwithstanding the degree of a group's acculturation. Lacking the power and influence associated with whiteness left such immigrants vulnerable to abuse—in social relations, in the political sphere, and especially in domains of business and labor.

The third implication was that whiteness was inextricably tied to the acquisition of traits associated with the American character. While descriptions of the American "type" were "closely connected to the rights and practices of U.S. citizenship," in reality the act of acquiring citizenship—in the same manner as acquiring a "white" (namely, American) appearance—provided no assurance that this characteristic alone would qualify one to be recognized as white. Whiteness was clearly identified with power and with the attributes associated with "being" American. In other words, as central as having the right political values was to the possession of whiteness, it was actually the array of "American" qualities, behaviors, values, and appearance that together served as a critical standard in the ultimate measure of a person's whiteness. Thus, one U.S. senator, during the 1870 debate over what became the Fifteenth Amendment to the U.S. Constitution, implicitly defined an individual's whiteness as indicating, wrote Matthew Jacobson, "not only color but degree of freedom . . . , level of 'civilization' . . . , and devotion to Christianity." The senator from Nevada declared that to be more acceptable, the Chinese had to be "republicanized and Christianized."[22]

Many peoples who were initially rejected would later come to be defined as whites. Others were commonly held to be (more or less indefinitely) not-white. Just such a development confronted certain parvenu German Jews, too, only seven years after that debate in Congress, and it persisted throughout the last quarter of the nineteenth century and beyond. These German Jews may have been resented for their successes and mocked for their pretensions, but the re-emergence of anti-Semitism was part of the response which in some places expressed the view that such Jews did not meet the criteria of whiteness. Such a trend would adversely affect their public roles after 1900. In contrast, Portuguese laborers who migrated to Hawai'i and eventually settled there were certainly not put down for being parvenu but for having been former plantation workers (and *lunas*, the supervisors), who likewise did not qualify as haoles. The leaders among the islands' white population asserted themselves as the principal arbiters of Hawaiian society, and until 1940 the Portuguese were counted separately from "Other Caucasians" (but not in U.S. Census reports). For Leo Pap, who studied Portuguese migration to America, that illustrated how "the popular perception of physical traits [was] often inseparably tied to the perception of cultural-behavioral traits," which in turn long disqualified the Portuguese for the status of being white. In a similar vein Peck concluded his study of Italians in the Canadian West and Greeks and Mexicans in the U.S. West up to 1930 by noting that the Italians and Greeks no longer constituted non-white racial groups "in part because of the economic and political success of each group in North America." In other words, they had gradually met sufficient criteria to be regarded as whites, however fluid and inconsistent those standards were. In the West many ethnic groups would go from non-whiteness to "probationary whiteness" to full incorporation.[23] And that, too, added an important dimension to the history of the West.

Analyzing the episodes surrounding the Sleepy Lagoon murder of August 1942 and the Zoot Suit–Navy riots of June 1943, both in Los Angeles (covered in part 4), Eduardo Obregón Pagán provides a case study that is, in effect, a valuable synthesis related to the key points defining whiteness here. He begins by stressing, "Racial categories have not always been defined by an empirical reality but at times by a *perceived* reality. In other words, the racialization of an individual or group did not always correspond with skin pigmentation but drew from dominant ideas about behavior, clothing, music, culture, and symbols." Therefore, the status of whiteness, though tied to color and class, was "not entirely absolute and fixed . . . but relative and malleable enough to incorporate those whose talents, interests, or political and social affiliations supported those with full access to power." He sees the clashes of 1942 and 1943 as confrontations arising over social position, power, and privilege—"privileges based on . . . behavior, comportment, social connections, political views, and willingness to work with the powers that be." Those two episodes involved a matter of "a code of cultural behavior and social propriety. The relationship between power and behavior rested, in part, on a larger set of assumptions about social respectability and cultural propriety," which were considered essential attributes of whiteness. "For many Americans at mid-century, being 'white' . . . meant acting 'white,'" and opposite behaviors "were heavily racialized."[24]

And, what about those who were "racialized," classified as not-white? I would suggest that they were often so categorized because of their perceived "race" and because Americans believed that these newcomers saw their presence in the United States as temporary. In transnational terms, they were seen as continuing to focus their energies, interests, loyalties, and financial resources on their home country, while resisting significant accommodations to American culture, values, norms, and citizenship. Of course, an alternative view is that the migrants responded so negatively to the pressures to conform precisely because they were reacting to the way they were being perceived and treated by mainstream America. Or, their situation was some combination of action and reaction on both sides. Eventually, in many such groups that were initially marginalized, members did undergo shifts in their cultural behaviors and commitment to American institutions and values. They did decide to remain in America and gradually moved away from their tight, on-going transnational bonds with their homeland and toward more limited, more intermittent, more financially restricted ties to their homeland, which I have elsewhere labeled "translocal"—a status that I believe has been more commonplace than the more specifically defined transnationalism.[25] As more and more "settled in," the community transitioned from being an immigrant group (or transient migrant group) to an ethnic group. Many who underwent that change (and who were not racially ostracized) subsequently found themselves accorded a probationary white status and gradually more access to the American mainstream. That, too, would tend to distance such persons further from their homeland connections.

Let me summarize with Patricia Limerick's emphatic point, which follows from Pagán's, namely, "The West has in fact been a scene of intense struggles over power and hierarchy, not only between the races but also between classes, genders, and other groups within white society." Those groups closest to a white status are those that have been seen as most physically (racially) and culturally akin to Americans and as having explicitly demonstrated an interest in fitting into American society. They have incorporated key aspects of those behaviors, norms, and values of American society that have come to be identified as American—white American.

But there is one final implication for the critical pattern of inter-group relations in the West as outlined here. We now recognize that for a number of peoples in the American West the quest for whiteness was largely irrelevant— that is, it was scarcely a hurdle to be surmounted (notably for Canadians and Scandinavians); for many other newcomers it proved to be rather daunting yet by various measures attainable—precisely because of the fluid nature of whiteness (notably for Greeks and Armenians); and for still other groups in certain parts of the western region (and with no great consistency), the full status of whiteness remained quite elusive, or impermanent, and they often found themselves vulnerable and victimized (for example, for Mexicans, Filipinos, Japanese, and Chinese). Significant changes in their status frequently had to await the maturity of their second and third generations—if those modifications occurred at all. Any portrait of the West without this layered perspective remains decidedly two-dimensional.

THE PLAN FOR THIS VOLUME

To do justice to this elaborate, multi-dimensional, multi-group topic, the study has been divided into two parts. This volume covers from the mid-1870s to 1952. A planned second volume will examine the second half of the twentieth century and a few years beyond. An opening section of this volume, titled Prelude, presents a series of immigrant narratives based on oral histories that illustrate the diversity of peoples and themes that recur throughout this work. Part 1 treats the period between the mid-1870s and 1903. During that period, in response to the Chinese exclusion challenge, the foundations of immigration law, policy enforcement, and citizenship qualifications through the first half of the twentieth century were defined. We also see the growing diversity of immigration into the West, from Texas to Hawai'i to the Pacific Northwest, and the varied economic roles of immigrants that so exceptionally contribute to the growth of the West. The efforts to draw them into the labor movements repeatedly figure prominently in this period.

Part 2 carries us from 1903 to 1923, peak years of immigration, war, xenophobia, and Americanization programs, followed by disillusionment and collective fears regarding the millions of newcomers. Those fears were exploited by proponents of immigration restriction. They carried the day, ending relatively open immigration provisions and putting in place the first quota system. Citizenship and immigration "reforms" not only alienated some immigrant-sending nations but also intensified a major shift underway in the immigration patterns from the Americas.

Part 3, 1923–1941, details the major legislative and judicial actions that set in law the concept of aliens ineligible for citizenship, the parameters outlining illegal immigration, the deportation provisions regarding such persons, the National Origins system, and reforms in citizenship regarding women. The Great Depression followed, triggering the repatriation of Mexicans and then curbs on Filipino migration. Mounting labor struggles, new crises over European refugees, and the evolution of alien enemy policies up to the attack on Pearl Harbor—aggravating the political vulnerability of Japanese Americans —complete that period.

Part 4, 1942–1952, examines the Second World War, its impact on Japanese, Italians, and Germans, the evacuations and incarcerations, new measures affecting aliens, the vast war-related economic expansion in the West and its impact on working-class men and women, the clashes targeting Mexicans in Los Angeles, and the initiation of another temporary labor program with Mexico that, for the most part, persisted for over two decades. This final section then explores the postwar years, with their numerous economic, social, and political changes, culminating in major refugee legislation and the landmark omnibus immigration and security legislation of 1950–1952. These generated profound consequences for immigrants and others. We conclude these topics with the president's commission evaluating the 1952 legislation, laying out an agenda of needed reforms that were enacted by 1965, setting the stage for the next several decades of an immigration revolution. This volume ends with Dora Sanchez Treviño's life story, which began in the 1940s and encompasses the next half-century, providing a link between the narrative here and the developments that will unfold in volume 2.

FOUR CENTRAL THEMES

Ethnic diversity and its impact on the West is indeed at the heart of this narrative. And, while it is tempting to try to reduce the diversity of immigrant experiences to a common text of influx, impact, and accommodation, this account cannot be just one story of one place and one outcome. Instead, the book follows many groups—peoples lured by opportunities, by networks, and by hope—as they shaped and reshaped the twentieth-century West. The multidisciplinary, multi-ethnic approach used here will enable readers to examine quite contrasting experiences in different western settings. As the book follows these groups, it presents four themes: (1) the changes in who came and their migration prospects over time and across this space; (2) the changes in the economic development of the West that influenced and shaped the lives of the newcomers; (3) the changes in the laws, court decisions, government policies, patterns of citizenship, and the differing legal statuses; and (4) the changes in the broader modes of adaptation and accommodation among the immigrants and between immigrants and Americans.[26]

These patterns of change course through this narrative from beginning to end, engaging group after group. The four themes of change are central to establishing the unifying threads in western history beginning in the 1870s. They underscore the persistence of specific issues and demographic trends that identify the continuous presence and critical roles of immigrants in the twentieth-century West. Some of the more prominent groups change over time as they integrate or emigrate; others come on the scene, replacing prior peoples, taking over economic roles or confronting new demands and seizing new opportunities. The economy thus evolves, diversifies, matures; federal and state policies (including critical court decisions) likewise evolve, closing some doors and opening others; and cultural and social differences emerge in various parts of the West, affecting newcomers' economic prospects, the jobs they hold, and the strategies needed to integrate into the new environment (including, for example, accommodation of some values and practices, language, associations, and celebrations). The immigrants migrate, relocate, emigrate, and, if they remain, in some cases gradually assimilate. Consistently, how they have been received and how they have responded have been framed by the variables of racial and social class backgrounds, gender distributions, religious affiliations, acquired norms and values, and the group members' principal occupations and historical experiences—together with contemporary socio-economic conditions and prevailing public attitudes and policies. These factors provide the raw ingredients with which the newcomers and their children mold their place in the West—or find that place being shaped for them.

What makes all this relatively unique in the West? Notwithstanding the complex, distinctive, and changing mix of peoples present across the decades, as well as the different and evolving economic opportunity structures and federal regulations, these variables have generated enduring patterns of inter-group relations and have determined the instrumental roles that immigrants and their children have played (and continue to play) in the growth of the region. Because those persistent patterns, amid all the changes, are represented by the four themes that figure prominently throughout the period of this work, those themes are the cables linking the years, the peoples, the geographical sections of this narrative. Because they are persistent, they resurface throughout the book: America changed; the West changed; economies changed; laws changed; and migrant and immigrant groups were continually succeeded by newer arriving populations—but, invariably, the overriding, shaping themes essentially remained.

Changes in Who Came—and Migration Prospects
Streams of immigrants were present in California not long after gold was discovered in 1848 and the news had crisscrossed the globe, but we pick up the story in

the 1870s and 1880s, when the Chinese on the mainland became a target of workers' hostility and victims of political convenience. Their prevailing differentness enabled protestors to identify more closely with Americans as fellow whites defending the country against those unwilling or unable to adapt or assimilate. In Hawai'i, the Hawaiian Sugar Planters' Association (HSPA) came at the Chinese "problem" from a different angle. They feared their own vulnerability due to their growing dependency on a single block of imported workers, prompting them to halt the arrival of Chinese laborers and import Japanese and then Koreans (as well as contingents of Portuguese, Germans, Scandinavians, and Puerto Ricans). With a more diversified labor force, the HSPA hoped to render their workers less capable of collaborating against the plantation companies. Such targeting of groups perceived as social, cultural, economic, and even political threats would periodically reemerge, particularly against a variety of Asian peoples. Mexicans would also be singled out for such traumatic treatment during the mid-1910s, late 1920s, 1930s, and 1950s. Campaigns aimed at undocumented aliens likewise run through these decades. While enforcement agencies were being developed and refined and then enlarged to handle various kinds of challenges, the attention obscured the thousands of others from across Europe, Canada, and then Japan and the Philippines who were making their way to the West, with each generation adding layers of immigrants from largely previously untapped sending areas on the periphery of global capitalism. Their economic contributions would prove indispensable for the flourishing economy, especially as they gradually distributed themselves across the entire region.

With respect to who came and how these populations evolved over time, the reasons for migration, whatever the place of origin, become relevant here for assessing the long-term motives or migration goals and the prospects for acculturation and adaptation: Are they refugees bent on never returning to their homelands and therefore resigned (or committed) to fitting into the host society, or are they refugees fleeing war and other domestic turmoil who are rather more likely to go back when the disruptions or dangers end? Have the immigrants come for economic or other more finite objectives, which suggest that these individuals will limit their response to Americanization pressures, leaving or moving on once they succeed or fail in realizing those aims? Alternatively, have the migrants come with plans that change and a desire to return that dissolves—especially with the growth of the second generation—or did they arrive with aspirations to settle because there were few opportunities to succeed (or perhaps to survive) in their homeland? Ultimately, immigrants who came cannot be divorced from why they came, for the latter so affects which immigrants remained.

Changes in Economic Development
By the beginning of the twentieth century, thousands of immigrants with roots ranging from Mexico to Italy, Greece, and Japan were readily being hired to lay

and maintain railroads tracks and then urban electric railway systems. Concentrations of Swedes dominated logging and milling operations in the Pacific Northwest, while Norwegians, Chinese, and Italians took to the sea, and many other Scandinavians continued their farming and dairying operations from California to Washington State and Montana. Their compatriots and eventually Filipinos would labor in the salmon canneries. Many Mexican, southern European, and Japanese women soon took seasonal jobs in vegetable and fruit packinghouses; great numbers of southern and eastern European men, as well as Irish, Cornish, and Finns, still worked the mines from Wyoming and Colorado to Washington State; Mexicans continued to labor in the mining operations along the southern tier of states and soon provided invaluable labor during the cotton and sugar beet harvests (along with many Germans from Russia); and Basques carried on their trekking with the great flocks of sheep they herded across the open spaces of public lands in California, Nevada, Oregon, Idaho, and Wyoming. Along with these quite varied immigrant-dominated and second-generation-dominated enterprises overlapping the old century and first decades of the new century, one found Jewish entrepreneurs from Juneau, Seattle, Portland, San Francisco, and Los Angeles to Helena, Cheyenne, Waco, and Galveston. Clusters of Czechs, Poles, Italians, Germans, Portuguese, Greeks, Canadians, Japanese, Armenians, and Norwegians exemplified the great array of producers and businessmen rooted across the West—both the urban and rural West.

The many business venturers, sometimes accompanied by wives, were risk takers at the cutting edge of western development, establishing enterprises, stimulating commerce, providing goods and services to so many Americans and other immigrants engaged in a host of undertakings. Their commercial endeavors often laid the foundations for new communities, whereas their fellow countrymen and women, immigrant and second-generation men and women, moved into established urban centers, launching businesses, building factories, operating wholesale and retail market centers, even dry goods shops, serving as middlemen between producers and shippers, importers and exporters, or as providers of essential services in their local communities. During the first decades of the century, a number of them transplanted the still novel filmmaking industry to Hollywood and Culver City, California. New groups, with new industries, would strive to replicate such patterns, even as conditions around them profoundly changed and as growth and technology transformed infrastructures. In addition, twentieth-century wars imposed ever greater demands on western productivity, especially when key theaters of operation were increasingly located along the Pacific Rim. Here, too, immigrants and second-generation workers proved vital for success on the home fronts—urban and rural.[27]

So much of this was taking place simultaneously—with more immigrants arriving among those groups already present, newcomers pioneering their people's presence, many individuals arriving directly from their homelands, others transplanting from the Midwest and East Coast, still more crossing (often regularly back and forth) from Canada and Mexico, and others relocating within the region itself. Technological innovations eased the journeys, while generating countless urban and rural opportunities for employment. Literally and figuratively, new fields of endeavor were cultivated, and the availability of immigrants' labor was often the key to success. Actually, a vast array of enterprises remained highly dependent on the continued presence of immigrants. With many of them not so readily possessing sufficient capital to begin their own businesses or agricultural operations (or not so inclined), they would provide the cheaper—and often more mobile—labor. Many in business stressed that as markets became more national and global, the wage factor remained the one variable that could still be manipulated to ensure a profit and make their enterprises more competitive. But precisely because of that, workers quickly learned to organize and challenge owners and entrepreneurs, at times finding themselves engaged in clashes with anti-union forces (including strikebreakers)—from Everett, Washington, to Ludlow, Colorado, to Bisbee, Arizona, to the plantations on Oahu and Kaua'i.

Even with the differences within the western region, the dynamic economic mix for many of the decades included technological innovations, risk-taking enterprises, business expansions, agricultural and industrial diversification, expanding urbanization and then suburbanization, later massive federal expenditures, and the in-migration of changing combinations of immigrant populations. One must also remember that these diverse newcomers were consumers as well as producers, thus stimulating economies at both ends. Despite these transformations, the themes outlined here represent core processes of incorporation that have persisted over time.

Changes in Legislation and Political Conditions
The broad context shaping responses to, as well as the impact of, immigrants has two additional dimensions. First were the forces of necessity and opportunism propelling immigrant adventurers to depart from their homelands and then easing or obstructing their opportunities to maintain ties with their homeland and to return if they wished to do so. Second was the body of laws, decisions, and administrative procedures that evolved during these decades and that determined the ease of admission, the chances for family reunification, the freedom to leave and return, and the option to integrate politically and enjoy the rights of native-born Americans. The modern legal infrastructure began with the Page Law of 1875 and the series of Chinese Exclusion Acts between 1882 and 1904. Ground rules of eligibility for citizenship had been laid down several times between 1790 and 1870, but the immigration and naturalization laws were now considerably expanded and codified, the federal ad-

ministrative machinery was developed and refined, and key U.S. Supreme Court decisions about issues long in dispute were handed down between 1891 and 1924. The repeal of the Chinese Exclusion Acts in 1943, the rollback of the remaining restrictions on Asian eligibility for citizenship in 1946 and 1952, and the breakthrough in postwar refugee legislation (and presidential directives) between 1945 and 1953 would profoundly affect who could enter, how many, how easily, under what sponsorship, and with what standard ground rules for obtaining American citizenship. Meanwhile, the lesson of the Japanese American wartime cases, that the civil rights of immigrants and citizens could be adversely affected during times of national crises, was not lost on immigrants during the Cold War and again after 9/11.

While many legislative measures particularly impacted Asians, the quota laws—though steadily undermined by various legislative and presidential measures during the late 1940s and 1950s—remained in force until the mid-1960s, particularly affecting many Europeans and Asians seeking refugee and immigrant admission. However, the absence of such restrictive legislation applying to nations in the Western Hemisphere (beyond some standard requirements for all admissions) significantly influenced the extent of migration from the Americas. Furthermore, the special labor agreements during both world wars (mainly with Mexico) would be reenacted in 1951 during the Korean War. This Bracero Program lasted for the next 13 years. The consequences for the American West of this triple cocktail of immigration and naturalization laws, court decisions, and administrative regulations would be nothing short of revolutionary both before and after the Second World War.

Changes in Modes of Adaptation and Accommodation
Finally, and likewise paralleling all of the changes outlined here, a large percentage of the newcomers (roughly two-thirds) did choose to remain, even though they continued moving about the region. In so doing, they engaged in the processes of community building, creating a whole range of organizations and institutions that helped root them and the networks that facilitated their adjustment to American society and economy. All this was designed to ease their way in coping with circumstances ranging from discrimination and unemployment to homesickness and the preservation of homeland ties. But the longer they stayed and the more set they became with respect to remaining, the more likely they were to begin, or perhaps to accelerate, the next stages beyond acculturation, namely adaptation and accommodation.

In the nineteenth century and until the more recent settlement of, for example, significant numbers of Afghanis, Iraqis, and several Central American peoples, a sizable proportion of ethnic group members have undergone these measures, emulating their predecessors' patterns and adapting to (and integrating) new social, economic, political, and technological conditions, although usually adding their own cultural twists. Thus, as natives and newcomers came into contact, and boundaries were slowly breached and blurred, immigrants gradually contributed more of their customs, foods, celebrations, borrowed words, and family connections to the mélange of the broader communities. From Arabs to Wends, we see before us multiple generations of immigrants and their children in various stages of adjustment to American life, from those fiercely resistant to those eagerly pushing ahead with their patterns of incorporation, which, we have noted, have been experienced continually by most newly arriving peoples. The outcome? Distinctive, multi-ethnic combinations of groups and communities, native and immigrant. They have enriched the pluralistic character of the American West—from Texas's Lower Rio Grande Valley to Hawai'i's Big Island.

To be more precise in terms of both the individual and group, acculturation begins that adjustment process, and then, in overlapping fashion, the patterns of adaptation and accommodation gradually become more apparent. Adaptation here refers to an increasing shift of attention among immigrants to concerns in the new land (host society) and less involvement in the homeland (transitioning in my model from transnationalism to translocalism); less frequent conflict with, and/or rejection by, the mainstream society; more inter-ethnic contacts; increased participation by the second generation in organizational or community affairs; and adjustments, or cultural changes, by the ethnic institutions in an effort to maintain influence within their respective communities. However, along with the role that mainstream political institutions play in facilitating or modeling forms of civic participation as a key feature of that adaptation, David Tyack for one emphasizes the traditional role performed by public schools in inculcating American political and cultural values in the children of second and later generations.[28]

By the next stage, accommodation, the percentage of foreign born in the ethnic community declines as the second and even third generations become more numerous. The remaining immigrants now give more limited attention to homeland affairs; individuals' ethnic identification shifts more toward either a dual American/ethnic identity or to one of competing loyalties; and such persons become more involved in the larger society, or in non-ethnic organizations. There is a further reduction in the use of the native language and native language publications, or more English is introduced into daily speech, newspapers, church services, and organizations' proceedings. In this way, some institutions step up efforts to retain a hold on the American-born generations, while others become less viable. Finally, one witnesses more social mobility among group members and instances of inter-marriage.

However, two important factors must be emphasized. Where individuals and groups have chosen to move forward, they would gradually experience many of these stages, but in both past and present the rate of such change has consistently varied among groups and individuals. Moreover, these stages are neither linear nor inevitable (all will not traverse them and eventually assimilate), for there have always been those who have chosen not to advance far along this path, usually for cultural or religious reasons (e.g., Hasidic or other Orthodox Jews, Hutterites, and Molokans), or because they intend to return to their homeland. Such persons and communities may successfully engage American society economically but far less (or not at all) socially or culturally. The ethnic boundaries of such groups have rarely become more permeable.[29]

WHO'S IN? FINAL OBSERVATIONS

The principal objective of this study is not only to move the immigrants' role in the western economy to center stage but to move their broader experiences—their relations with the dominant society and with other groups—to center stage as well. In other words, I wish to take their story beyond their migration to the West and to examine their impact on the West and its impact on them and their children. However, it is obvious that it is not feasible to cover all 14 states equally, nor all groups equally. I emphasize key developments involving and affecting a wide variety of peoples in different parts of the West and reflecting the shifts in the origins of the immigrant and ethnic populations between the late nineteenth and (including the planned second volume) the early twenty-first centuries. Some groups certainly "melt" considerably during this time; others persist in various ways and to different extents, some symbolically, some substantively. Some groups have been revitalized by new waves of immigrants, although not uncommonly those newcomers—coming from different backgrounds and altered political and economic homeland settings—have quite often proven to be either irritants to old-timers or catalysts for significant changes within the ethnic communities.

Then there were the new groups that appeared on the scene, certainly replicating many of the processes and stages that earlier groups had gone through but also taking advantage of both the extraordinary opportunities that globalization and modern technology have been making available to immigrants and the political and social environment of greater toleration for diversity that has become part of the American ethos. Finally, in virtually all cases, government policies and international conditions and agreements are the intermediate variables influencing the feasibility of emigration, the ease of travel and admission, and the maintenance of on-going bonds with homelands.

In conclusion, the unifying theme here is that discussions of the growth of the West, federal programs and federal spending, aridity and water projects, the impact of extractive industries, and the consequences of world wars (among other themes) are certainly all relevant for understanding the history of this region, but the persistence over time of the patterns described in the previous paragraphs makes it clear that the transformation of the West during the twentieth century was inseparable from the on-going, though shifting, composition of its many immigrant peoples—even as those immigrant groups were themselves being transformed by their experiences throughout the West and even though they were not uniformly present across the region. As this book amply demonstrates, the history of the American West should not, and cannot, be separated from the many peoples who have journeyed there. Theirs was truly a migration from all points, due West, and their impact can be appreciated only by bringing their stories together in one narrative and at center stage in the region's history.

Our story thus begins a decade after the U.S. Civil War, a time of no great world conflagrations, continuing immigration from western Europe and China as well as the eve of the great waves of southern and eastern European and Japanese migrations, the era of sailing ships, the first steel-hulled steamships, and communication with most homelands largely by letters or via return visitors. At our halfway point (the end of this volume) we reach the years of more rapid airline travel, international telephone connections, television as the new mass media, and generally easier and multiple links between host and homelands. But those years also witnessed extensive transfers of refugee populations and all the tensions, dangers, and complications brought on by the Cold War. By the first years of the twenty-first century we find ourselves in the midst of the era of commuter jet travel, camcorder recordings, digital photography electronically transmitted, almost world-wide access to homelands, compatriots, and family via relatively inexpensive cell phones, phone cards, Internet connections, and other rapidly unfolding forms of virtually instant communications—and a post–Cold War rimless world of global trade and migrations. As was true 130 years before, this was a time of new challenges and a world of new opportunities.

Western Immigrant Experiences

T

   SUGIKI — A TERM MEANING "grafting," or "grafted tree" — has been used to describe the Japanese immigrant experience in America. Many immigrants in the twentieth-century American West would have agreed with that image of their encounters in the new land.[1] They could not expect their lives, cultures, and occupations to remain unchanged, yet they did not wish to give up all that was their tradition to become "American." They would, in a manner of speaking, negotiate the extent of the changes — of the cultural grafting. They would have to cope with emerging government immigration policies and bureaucracies; laws regulating admissions and citizenship; discrimination, stereotyping, and perhaps being defined as "not white"; economic exploitation, dual wage systems, harsh and dangerous working conditions; and pressures to keep moving in search of employment.

Most newcomers did not come as pioneers, breaking the soil where only Native Americans had trod before. Rather, most entered communities already taking shape in cities and towns, in mining centers, and, more slowly, in rural areas, such as in central and south Texas, northern Nevada, eastern Montana, and eastern Oregon. In patterns of step migration, large numbers of immigrants by the early 1900s had already lived and worked for a time elsewhere in the United States — for example, an estimated three-quarters of Swedes, Danes, and Norwegians heading for Washington State and Oregon. That would soon be as true for sizable numbers of Portuguese, Italians, Greeks, Armenians, and Mexicans entering the West. Until 1907 this pattern was akin to that of thousands of Chinese,

Japanese, and, in smaller numbers, Koreans (and, later, Filipino nationals), who relocated from Hawai'i to the mainland.

All this is no footnote to western history, for as the American Federation of Labor's publication *American Federalist* declared in 1894, there were three sources of the nation's wealth: "First—God. Second—Our form of government. Third—Our Immigrants." Throughout the period of 1876–1917, "some industries were impossible to conceive without their chief labor imports— Mexicans in southwestern metalliferos imports, the Chinese in railroad construction and maintenance, Slavs in meatpacking, or Jews in the needle trades."[2] San Francisco has been depicted as another Babel that included European workers of French, Italian, Portuguese, Greek, Irish, and German origins.[3] In eastern Washington Henry Villard was determined to funnel more efficiently the immigrants' travel on the Northern Pacific Railroad to job sites in need of workers. He hired a retired general, Thomas Tannett, to direct thousands of Irish to railroad jobs, Scandinavians to lumbering and logging opportunities, Italians to mines, and Germans to farmlands. The Palouse region in eastern Washington drew, among its many newcomers, Irish, Scots, Russian-born Germans, Swedes, Danes, English, Norwegians, and other Scandinavians from the Midwest.[4]

From the farmlands of south Texas to the plantations in Hawai'i, the canneries in Oregon and Alaska, and the factories in San Francisco, the transformation of the western economy into a full-fledged capitalist system rapidly integrating into the national and international market economies created a virtually insatiable demand for immigrant labor. That labor was expected to be temporary in character but ample in volume, cheap and exploitable but essentially "expendable" when not needed. From the mill towns to the mining towns, wrote historian David Montgomery, "immigrants and their children provided the overwhelming majority of industrial wage earners."[5] At the same time, it was often immigrant entrepreneurs who envisioned the market potential in the burgeoning worker populations, be that in the harbor towns or mining towns, or at crossroads that initially seemed to exist randomly in the midst of great rural expanses. The newcomers' stories put faces on these great anonymous forces shaping the West. Simply put, the twentieth-century American West is inseparable from the waves of immigrants who steadily entered the region and, with their hands, their feet, their ingenuity, their indefatigable energy, their sacrifices, their passions and fortitude, and sometimes their capital, helped make a reality of the promise of the West.

Setting the stage are the following eight vignettes from the late nineteenth and early twentieth centuries: a Japanese woman and men of Italian, Jewish, Japanese, Chinese, Norwegian, Armenian, Czech American, and Jewish American backgrounds. Their experiences varied, their degree of success varied, and their locations varied, but together they provide initial portraits of what it was like for newcomers of significantly different backgrounds to migrate to the West and to build a life there, as well as what life was like for the two American-born young men who also struggled to get ahead. We will encounter many more men and women in the pages that follow. These opening accounts provide a prelude, presenting newcomers' own tales of planting roots, overcoming adversities, and hoping to see those efforts bear fruit, especially for their children. The more they succeeded, the more it appeared that the region was taking shape and succeeding. Their stories—and many more could have readily been included—illustrate the themes that make up the unifying threads of this narrative.

Teiko Matsui was born in Japan in December 1896.[6] Twenty-four years later she was matched up with Masakazu Tomita and in February 1921 returned with him to his farm near Wapato, on the Yakima Indian Reservation in Washington State. She would express a lifetime of experiences and ordeals through her 31-syllable *tanka* poems. Gathering sagebrush roots for fuel and drawing water from an outside well, she had to cope with privations, isolation, and winters so cold in the house that "you could hear eggs in the kitchen cracking." Frosts covered the bedroom sheets at night. They labored to grow alfalfa, onions, tomatoes, beans, and melons, coping with the desert and the ever-present sand:

> Sagebrush desert to fertile plain
> A transformation, I hear,
> But when the windy season comes
> There's no transforming the sandstorm

In 1929 they moved to Sunnydale (near the future Seattle-Tacoma Airport), began a plant nursery, sustained the loss of a daughter, and converted to Christianity. Thirteen years later, war, relocation, and incarceration with their four children first at Tule Lake and then at Heart Mountain deprived the couple of all they had struggled for. Even more, fearing how authorities would view her writings in Japanese, Teiko burned all her poems. "Much of the poetic record of her life [up to that time] was wiped out," commented Gail Nomura. Teiko did resume her poetry in the camps, reflecting on conditions and the turmoil of being caught in "a war between the country of birth and the adopted country which had not accepted them as its own." She and Masakazu were on work release in Minnesota when the war's end was declared:

> Among whites jubilantly shouting
> "The war is over"
> My husband and I
> Cried throughout the night.

And then,

> For the first time in five years
> Letters are permitted to the home country
> Today I write only
> "We're safe."

Safe but compelled to start anew. They returned to Seattle, and Teiko obtained a job as a seamstress, working alongside women of other ethnic groups. Meanwhile, in their neighborhood they met Italians, who also struggled with their farms. She discovered a newfound community:

> In their hard work
> Italians are like we Japanese
> Daughters and wives, too
> Work all day in the fields.

Teiko and Masakazu shared the ordeals of farming, raising a family, making tough decisions, seeing children go off to college and start their own families, and then having to endure still another relocation in 1967 with the planned expansion of SeaTac Airport. They moved in with their daughter's family in Seattle. In the years that followed, Teiko would recall her "bitter ordeals" along with the pleasures of children and grandchildren. Writing in 1983, at 87 years of age, she looked upon "the seeds I planted" and penned this *tanka:*

> From my granddaughter in New York
> A letter in Japanese
> As I read it
> Tears of joy overflow.

Angelo Noce was born in Genoa in June 1847 and was brought to America by his parents three years later.[7] He obtained an education in California, became a court interpreter in Sacramento, and in 1870 a typesetter and member of the printer's union. During the next decade he helped establish the local philharmonic society and the Bersaglieri Mutual Benevolent Society and provided other assistance to Italians in San Francisco. At the end of that decade he moved on to Eureka, Nevada, where he became a notary public, applied for citizenship in 1882, and in that same year moved again. This time he relocated to Denver, where he obtained employment as a deputy county assessor in 1885, a deputy sheriff for Arapahoe County four years later, and in 1896 a clerk in Colorado's House of Representatives. He even tried his hand at starting an Italian weekly, *La Stella,* but there were still too few Italians to sustain it.

Back in the mid-1870s Noce had begun a campaign to get Cristofo Colombo honored, and in 1890, anticipating the quatercentenary of Columbus's arrival in the Americas, he tried to convince Denver officials to build a monument to Columbus. They declined, and for the next 15 years Noce labored to establish an honored recognition for Columbus. In January 1905, he persuaded Emmet Bromley, in the Colorado House, and then Casimero Barela, in the Colorado Senate, to introduce legislation making October 12 an official state holiday. Although the measure did not pass, Governor Jesse McDonald was receptive, and in both 1905 and 1906 he declared October 12 a legal holiday. Finally, on April 1, 1907, Noce saw the fruit of his 30-year effort when Governor Henry A. Buchtel signed the bill making Colorado the first state in the nation to establish Columbus Day as a legal state holiday. Six months later, 60-year-old Angelo Noce was made the grand marshal of Denver's Columbus Day parade on October 12, 1907.

Ephraim Zalman Hoffman was born in March 1894, near Lublin, in Russian-controlled Poland.[8] When he reached age 19, rather than go through with an arranged marriage to a wealthy older woman, he borrowed money from her and fled with a false passport, joining other Polish Jews bound for Galveston, Texas. He arrived in late September 1913, and the Jewish Immigrants' Information Bureau, established to assist Jews arriving in Galveston, sent him off to a job in the Fort Worth stockyards. When his false passport was detected, he was promptly fired. Sitting in the street, alone and crying, he was befriended by a German Jew, who offered him a waiter's job in his restaurant. Soon, Ephraim had saved enough money to go into the business of peddling "silks, dresses, and imported novelties"—by which time he had also acquired the nickname "Charlie." (He was told it was easier to remember than Ephraim.) However, his business partner apparently accepted too many payments from women customers in the form of "services," which doomed the business, based as it was largely on credit and cash flows.

It could also have ended their friendship except that his partner's future wife introduced Charlie to Sarah Bernstein, who had arrived from Russia via Galveston soon after Ephraim had. Her father, Chaim, had earlier journeyed to America, first trying his fortunes as a Hebrew teacher in New York City. Finding it earned him too little money, he migrated to Texas at the behest of a nephew, W. H. Novit. Novit had built up a successful business selling bananas in Gatesville, near Waco; they were shipped up by train from Galveston. Chaim joined Novit in the banana trade, setting himself up in Comanche, three train stops northwest of Gatesville. Novit soon had sufficient funds to bring over Sarah, who arrived in October 1913 with her cousin Sol Novit. After working for a time in Fort Worth and attending a women's college there, Sarah went to Gatesville, where she met up with the Novits, who introduced her to Charlie. They married in November 1915 and raised their family in Texas.

Ah Quinn's story is unusual enough to have merited him the title "One of San Diego's Founding Fathers."[9] Born in December 1848 in China, Quinn was taken to Guangzhou, where he attended missionary school. At the age of 20 he sailed to San Francisco, remaining there for six years and working as a cook and houseboy. He then joined his uncle, who operated a general store in Santa Barbara. Quinn eventually began working for a Judge Charles Huse, who befriended him and apparently inspired Quinn to begin wearing American clothes and following American customs. In 1877, after four years in Santa Barbara, he signed up as a cook with a company that operated a coal mine in Alaska. It was then that he cut off his queue and began what would become a 17-year diary—in English. He returned to San Francisco a year later, worked for two years there making use of his bilingual ability, and in 1880 journeyed to San Diego as a labor contractor. At that time there were 229 Chinese in San Diego out of a total population of 8,600. They were mostly laborers, service workers, merchants, and fishermen, along with only 8 women. The Chinese hired by Quinn helped build the railroad between San Bernardino and San Diego.

Shortly after his 33rd birthday, Quinn wed Sue Leong, from San Francisco, and they settled in San Diego, where he began acquiring properties, farmland, and a potato ranch, along with real estate and a business partnership. In the early years of the new century, Quinn continued to prosper, buying and selling properties—until February 1914, when he was killed at the age of 66 by a motorcyclist while crossing a street. At the funeral, this unofficial "Mayor of San Diego" had six Chinese and six American pallbearers, and he left an estate worth $50,000. He was the father of 12 children, 3 of whom wed Euro-Americans. Today, there are over 140 descendants of Ah Quinn and Sue Leong.

In 1872, when Peter Wigen was 19, his family migrated to Minnesota from Selbu, in the Trøndelag region of Norway.[10] A dozen years later, Peter wed his Selbu sweetheart, Beret Johnsdatter Kjosnes (called "Betsy" in America). In 1891 they were finally able to buy a 240-acre farm in Mower County, Minnesota, where they settled down for a decade, living modestly, raising a family, and working hard. And then Wigen came upon a January 18, 1901, issue of *Skandinaven*, with a letter written a month earlier by one Elias Molee, who had journeyed from Minnesota to La Crosse, which is between the Palouse and Snake Rivers in Washington State's southeastern Whitman County. Using no capitals in his script, Molee described the prairie lands as "suited for farming, cattle- and sheep raising," whereas the coastal region, with far more rain, was best for trade, lumbering, and fishing. It was December 29, Molee noted, and "we have no snow and the calves are hopping and dancing around . . . without extra fodder or shelter. . . . we are few and far between here, but people do not think it is an inconvenience to drive 10 or 15 miles for a visit. grass and horses are cheap; men and boys all have horses and deep saddles. . . . some Norwegians from iowa and wisconsin have come here. There are many free quarters and eighths [of land] again, and much cheap land can now be purchased for $5 or $6 per acre. we have too few girls here, but they will come."

Wigen was struck by the letter and found the description most appealing. But he was nearly 48 and decided to see this land first before uprooting his family. It was still January when he took the train to La Crosse. As his daughter later recalled, he arrived to find "the men walking around in their shirtsleeves. That sold him. He bought 800 acres of land, went back home to Minnesota, sold his dairy farm, and left for La Crosse in February." Within a year, two of his brothers sold their Minnesota holdings and joined Peter in the Palouse region. Before another year elapsed, 11 more Selbyggerne (natives of Selbu) in Minnesota etched the migration channel deeper. Others followed over the next two years, as news articles, letters, personal contacts, and visits promoted the new region. Then, in 1906, Betsy Wigen returned to Norway to visit Selbu and, based on her accounts, motivated a second stream of 25 persons to migrate directly from Norway to the Palouse. Others came to La Crosse from neighboring Norwegian communities and from other parts of that country, their numbers slacking off during World War One but resuming in the 1920s. Although Peter Wigen was by no means a wealthy man or a major community leader, by the time he died in 1923 he had initiated what became significant flows of Norwegians both from the Midwest and directly from Norway. And yet, a relative scarcity of available farm lands had soon become apparent, prompting some who went to the Palouse region to respond to promotional tours arranged by real estate agents and railroad companies. They turned to Canada and Colorado for farming opportunities. Nonetheless, the Wigens' impact remained quite considerable.

One other example where individuals sparked a larger migration early in the twentieth century, as did Peter and Betsy Wigen, involved the Seropian brothers — Hagop, Garabed, Simon, and half-brothers Kevork and Hovaness. They were Armenians who moved to California because one of them, Hagop (Jacob), needed a change in climate for health reasons.[11] They had already converted from the Armenian Apostolic Church to Protestantism, and fellow Congregationalists may have told them about Fresno and the better economic opportunities there. They arrived in 1881, bought farmland, and opened a general store, selling an odd assortment of goods that included candy, tobacco, and rugs. When the store burned down, they then tried peddling fruit. That evolved in classic fashion into a store selling fresh and dried fruits and eventually groceries. But it, too, failed, and they reopened it as a general food store that also shipped dried fruit, mostly up to Stockton. In 1898 they added a packinghouse, and six years later they incorporated and issued stock. Unfortunately, they were soon caught up in a struggle with the Guggenheim Packing Company and once more lost their business. After 20 years of successes and failures, each brother went his own way. But many other Armenians were drawn to Fresno by the Seropians' early presence. In 1910, there were nearly 3,800 in Fresno County.

Not unexpectedly, the children of immigrants carved their own streams and niches and made their own contributions, modest and great, as they sought to move closer to the mainstream. Charles Henry Chernosky was born New Year's Day of 1885 in the Rocky Creek community of Austin County, Texas.[12] In 1870, his father had come from Moravia (in what is today the Czech Republic). Charles's maternal grandparents had earlier fled the revolutions of 1848, and his Czech parents had wed in Texas in 1882. During his first 22 years Chernosky worked on the family farm before taking a job as a store clerk—until the devastation wrought by the great hurricane of September 8, 1900. He then went to business college, learned bookkeeping, and tried sales. On the advice of a teacher, he earned a law degree in June 1912. He opened a law office in Rosenberg and married Vlasta Fojt, who was also Czech American. In 1916, the 31-year-old Chernosky was elected county judge for Fort Bend County and reelected in 1918. Four years after leaving that position in 1920, he moved to Houston, where he continued his law practice. This account of Chernosky's life (written in 1934) illustrated his success in planting his feet in his ethnic community as well as in the mainstream. He was twice elected president of the Slavonic Benevolent Order of the State of Texas and in 1929 was appointed to the new Texas State Board of Education.

Twenty-nine years before Chernosky's birth, Mark Levy was born in New York City to German-born parents.[13] They moved across the country to Sacramento and established a business there until it was wrecked by a flood in 1861. When young Levy was ten he was already out selling fruit to workers on boats along the Sacramento River. Within three years he had a job in a commission house, where he remained employed for a dozen years. Then his brother informed him that there was no comparable commission house in the growing city of Portland, Oregon. Taking $800 he had saved, Levy moved to Portland and built a successful business that, for the 36 years until his death, grew along with the city. He, too, demonstrated his ability to progress at the same time that he stood astride both the ethnic and larger American societies, for he was long active in both Jewish and non-Jewish organizations, including Temple Beth Israel, the Concordia Club, and the Elks.

These eight stories (of Tomita, Noce, Hoffman, Quinn, Wigen, Seropian, Chernosky, and Levy) cover seven different ethnic groups in five western states and span from the mid-nineteenth to the mid-twentieth centuries. They represent many of the elements that characterize the immigrant experiences in the West. In so doing, they capture aspects of the four themes that link together the periods of this narrative. The tales of these immigrants and sons of immigrants, who migrated from western, eastern, and southern Europe and from Japan and China, certainly illustrate the diversity of those who migrated to the American West from abroad and from elsewhere in the nation. All eight were products of

(or shaped by) a west in the process of technological and economic modernization, with Quinn ironically becoming a victim of it, too. The late-nineteenth-
century era saw the growth and expansion of capitalism, the creation of transportation systems that knit the region together and the region to the nation and
world, along with the development of markets that gradually stretched from the
local to the global. These men and women shared the fruits of the regional
growth both as consumers and producers.[14]

On one level, these men and women became a farmer, merchant, shipper,
marketing middleman, labor contractor, entrepreneur, real-estate investor,
lawyer, and government official—a variety reflecting some of the range of occupations held by immigrants and their children. Many would move off into new
fields or, literally, resettle to farm new fields. Several of them were affected by
government policies, policies setting boundaries, affecting lives, even withholding political rights. Others had access to political, even electoral, opportunities and sought to take on roles influencing or implementing institutional
and governmental policies. All experienced different degrees of acculturation
and Americanization, particularly Noce, Quinn, and Chernosky. The latter
also exemplified the strides taken by many second-generation Americans toward incorporating themselves into American society. Consequently, most of
those who found an American environment that encouraged or welcomed further acculturation usually proved to be receptive to more accommodation and
more permeable ethnic borders.

But if, on that one level, these men and women present case studies of the
four themes, especially the efforts taken by the men from Italy (Noce) and
China (Quinn), there was also a second level that immigrants learned about all
too well, the more personal phase of their experiences. Consider how the Tom-
itas and Seropians struggled and at times were defeated or overwhelmed by factors beyond their control, such as war, fire, displacement by government, and
more powerful business foes. They were risk takers who had mixed successes,
just as Hoffman and Levy were risk takers who relocated to new communities.
And, while Levy did well in Portland, it is less likely that Hoffman did particularly well selling bananas in the small Texas town of Comanche. Noce and
Quinn had three parallels even though Noce's estate was unlikely to have
matched Quinn's: they both moved about considerably before finding an acceptable niche; they both embraced American culture to a remarkable degree;
and yet both retained clear ties to their traditional cultures. Finally, second-
generation Levy and second-generation Chernosky, both ambitious young
men, demonstrated a desire to balance their ethnic attachments and their
Americanization. Opportunities opened doors to politics and law for Chernosky just as the expansion of Portland provided commercial avenues for Levy.

In their modest ways, these eight men and women contributed to the
growth of their respective communities and also to the region's overall devel-

opment. Those communities were richer for the presence of such immigrant men and women and the children of immigrants. If, as historian Richard White declared, the West was "a land and people constantly in the midst of re-invention and reshaping," then these were the types of peoples who figured prominently in making that happen. They were, in effect, on the ground floor of the building of the West and, with each additional generation, could also be found on each new "floor" being constructed.[15] They and many others who appear in these pages reinforce a central conclusion: American entrepreneurs, growers, and investors could not, on their own, have built the West as we now know it in the absence of immigrant workers.

What sets the immigrant history of the West apart from that elsewhere in the country is its multiple dimensions and rich ethnic diversity. At the outset of our story, the West was an American region less populated, less settled, less developed, less institutionally complete than the East, and with fewer entrenched elites. It was still struggling to resolve the demands of those long native to those territories, Native Americans and Mexicans. The arrival of several distinct "racial" groups in a nation where race has been a principal preoccupation may also have drawn attention away from the streams of American, European, and Canadian migrants that continued to arrive in the West, keeping vibrant the region's remarkable multi-racial pluralism. Clearly, a major part of the continued "reshaping" of the West's population unquestionably involved the admission of new peoples, some racially apart, others of mixed race, and many who would not be identified as other than white. Rarely would we find such a striking convergence of peoples and experiences and a region that so richly benefited as the meeting place of many groups.

CONCLUSION

The long-standing American quest to create a unified society in a nation so diverse since its founding was most severely tested in the polyglot West. Populations had entered not just from Europe but increasingly from points across the world that were being transformed by the expanding global capitalist economy. Moreover, that test was taking place at the same time that Native Americans were experiencing some of their worst oppression in the Midwest and West, and Jim Crow was rapidly being legislated into place in the American South (while being informally tolerated in the West and directed at Asians and Mexicans). The deteriorating racial climate in the first decades of the century was the negative context of reception that would be encountered by a significant number of newcomers to the West.[16] Whether they came as sojourners—that is, temporary residents and workers—who subsequently determined to remain, or came with the intention of settling, these multitudes of new immigrant men and women and soon their growing number of offspring gradually became part of American society. Eventually, elements of their cultures penetrated the prevailing American culture, rural and urban, and, in time, the immigrants and their children became part of the fabric of western history.[17]

Indeed, whereas so many immigrant men and women lived the modest lives of Teiko and Masakazu Tomita or the Wigen family, others emerged from among the ordinary peoples and were extraordinary. Consider Simon Bamberger, an immigrant Jew and a Democrat, who became the first "Gentile" governor of the Republican- and Mormon-dominated state of Utah in 1917. Later on, men of modest backgrounds also rose up, such as Syrian American Victor Atiyeh (born in Portland in 1923), who was elected governor of Oregon in 1978—a state not often associated with immigrant leaders. Filipino American Benjamin Cayetano (born in Honolulu in 1939) attained the governorship of Hawai'i in 1994; Gary Locke (Chinese American), who served as governor of Washington State from 1996 to 2004, was the first Asian American governor on the mainland. Gradually, among Mexican Americans, too, men began to surmount negative public attitudes and win political office, including Senator Dennis Chavez (New Mexico), Congressmen Henry Gonzalez (Texas) and Edward Roybal (California), and Mayors Henry Cisneros (San Antonio) and, most recently, Antonio Villaraigosa (Los Angeles). But it has become commonplace for those writing about the American West to concentrate on Asian and Mexican examples, and although these have been vitally important groups, such a limited scope does a disservice to so many others. Too readily forgotten are the immigrants from Europe, the Middle East (western Asia), Central and South America, and other non-Asian, non-Latino homelands, all of whom became more and more visible as the century unfolded.

One other example illustrates the immigrants' perennial presence in tumultuous western scenes despite their historical invisibility. Major episodes get mentioned routinely but not always the ethnic origins of those involved. Consider the infamous Bisbee, Arizona, clash of July 1917. Sheriff Harry Wheeler, of Cochise County, and some 2,000 deputized men rounded up 1,186 men (strikers at the Bisbee copper mines and their supporters), transported them in boxcars across the state line to the desert town of Hermanas, New Mexico, and left them with no food, water, or shelter until they were rescued two days later by U.S. troops. Most sources do not detail who the nearly 1,200 were, but 984 of them were foreign born (of whom 269 were naturalized citizens). They represented 20 nationalities, mostly Mexican, but included 141 British, 179 Slavs, 82 Serbians, and some Germans and Austro-Hungarians.[18] The several strikes at Clifton-Morenci during the first two decades of the century (see part 2), climaxing with the deportations, provide corroboration for Richard White's conclusion that "A dual labor system based on race and the existence of minority groups with distinctive [unequal] legal relationships to the larger society have defined the American West."[19] It is the diversity of those peoples that we must no longer minimize.

Finally, even beyond the recognition of race or ethnicity, there remains one other dynamic element, namely the many roles performed by the women, those who, as Walter Nugent put it, "created homes as havens."[20] In good economic times they maintained their homes and frequently worked alongside the men on farms and in businesses. They took in boarders or provided meals to workers on farms and ranches. When the husbands went out on strike, when they were deported, when they had no jobs or only occasional and part-time ones, it was the wives and daughters who maintained the homes, sought employment, sometimes walked the picket lines, and expanded their productive and reproductive gender roles. They were very much a part of the changing West.

Furthermore, so much focusing on race robs us of still other rich stories, those capturing the region's vast multi-cultural panorama and the overlapping waves of newcomers forging communities. Within those communities, multiple generations were present at different stages of acculturation and adaptation and with differing degrees of attachment to their homelands. While adjusting to new laws and federal immigration and naturalization policies, many of the newcomers and new communities have not only replicated earlier patterns of ethnic incorporation but also capitalized on new technologies, new forms of transportation and communication, new areas of employment, and new modes of organization. Whether we speak of the 1870s, 1920s, 1970s, or early 2000s, immigrants and the children of immigrants continued to seek economic stability as they sought a balance between integrated, translocal, and transnational lifestyles. They gradually made those choices, doing so based more and more on the unifying elements within the host (or settlement) society rather than around homeland ties.

The concluding point of this Prelude? Discussions of groups must not be at the expense of the individuals, for those specific narrative portraits, as we see, can frequently convey in concrete, personal ways the dynamics only sketched on the broader group-oriented canvases. Similar accounts appear throughout this book for the same purpose, representing its unifying themes. They are part of the varied angles of vision employed here that, hopefully, will serve as reminders that the history of the American West is like a diamond—examining one facet alone, using one approach only, cannot reveal the beauty of the whole.

PART 1.

Laying the Groundwork

IMMIGRANTS AND IMMIGRATION LAWS,
OLD AND NEW, 1870s–1903

The era from approximately 1870 to 1900 represents a transitional period from Old West to New West. Historians Michael Malone and Richard Etulain describe the 1890s as a crossroads, a time of "change and continuity . . . [that] continued as a hallmark of the twentieth century West." That can be seen, they added, in the way that "the modern West blends pacesetting and imitative tendencies," which both "break *from* as well as adher[e] *to* the patterns of the nation at large."[1] Immigrants to this West had to make comparable choices—how strongly to hold on to their traditions or how far to move away from their past— and at what personal cost? We now recognize how, as the twentieth-century West ran its course, the immigrants' labor (and sometimes capital), skills, enterprise, resilience, fortitude, and cultural diversity contributed to the growth of the region and profoundly influenced its character, yet in the process these newcomers did not remain unchanged. Understanding their place in the West is a matter of appreciating that their contributions came with consequences for the immigrants, for western society, and, in policy terms, for the nation.

It is by now a common assertion that the late nineteenth century marked the beginning of the shift from the "Old" immigrants to the "New" immigrants, which in effect meant a swing in the preponderant numbers of those admitted from northern and western Europe to those from southern and eastern Europe. Of course, that emphasis detracted from the continued exodus from western Europe and virtually ignored the increasing rivulets of migrants from Mexico and Canada, the migration from China, and the emergence of Japan as the major Asian-sending nation. All this would particularly hold true for the West, for together with Americans relocating largely from the Midwest and East, immigrants were arriving from Europe and Asia, and some (uncertain) numbers were crisscrossing the Mexican and Canadian borders.

While a principal feature of these decades was certainly this pluralistic in-migration, it was the initial assertions of federal control over both admissions and naturalization procedures that truly set these years dramatically apart from the preceding ones, certainly as much as—perhaps even more than—those gradual changes in the origins of European immigrants. A sharp break was taking place, and such federal regulations affected groups heading to the West (Asians especially, who mostly settled and worked in the West). In fact, the federal government's novel immigration laws were a response to demands that it curb the entry of the Chinese and affirm concretely that such persons were ineligible for U.S. citizenship. It is that combination of diverse peoples, unprecedented policies, and the region's exceptional economic development that most emphatically draws our attention to the decades just prior to the new century.

It is also now clear that the completion of the conquest and subjugation of native peoples in the West during these years opened the way in dramatic fashion for the nation's continuing thrust outward beyond its coastal borders. The extended consequences of the annexation of Hawai'i and the occupation of the Philippines would be felt more heavily in the periods after 1903. Still, the expansionistic moves during this first era of our study reflected a new sense of the nation, a surge of nationalism and the widespread belief that the country shared the responsibility for carrying out the "White Man's Burden"—conveying civilization to the "less civilized." Concurrent with the nation's increasing boldness on the international stage was federal officials' determination that it was time to define American sovereignty explicitly through better control of its borders. The new and expanded guidelines for admission and citizenship, plus the opening of Ellis Island and the creation of a new immigration-related bureaucracy, were a part of this energized national consciousness. In a sense, these assertions of sovereignty and control over entry into the country and into its political communities set such important precedents and so directly affected the West that I would suggest that, in a manner of speaking, the twentieth-century West began during these decades beginning in 1875. By 1903 the closing gates confronted mainly the Chinese and several classes of other individuals but not on the basis of their race or nationality. Consequently, the skeletal framework of new federal regulations did not block most newcomers or slow the trends toward an ever-greater diversity of peoples in the West, so global was its attraction. But it did establish momentous precedents for additional controls and restrictions.

In terms of productivity and exports, the access to new national and international markets triggered more extensive mining, agricultural, maritime, and commercial enterprises in the West, which in turn created enormous opportunities in cities, on the land, and at sea and produced insatiable demands for workers. Although there would now be dramatic business cycles rattling these new economic conditions, Americans and foreigners alike continued to see the region as a land of great promise. For those who chose to migrate there and remained, the promised land meant a place where people could try their luck, test their skills, and begin anew. By the 1900s that powerful and magnetic image was already a given, and events to the contrary would only temper enthusiasm for a time. The economic recoveries seemed like new gold rushes (and actual ones did take place in the 1890s), new boom times, irresistibly attracting people from around the country and eventually from around the world.

Nevertheless, while race, regulation, and expansionism figure prominently on the broader level of prominent issues at that time—as our first three themes suggest—on another, quite personal, level—the fourth theme—there was an extensive amount of settlement as well as sojourning taking place among many immigrants throughout the West. In response to those ventures, the critical questions that arose for the immigrants were no less important to them than were the macro-level questions for the region's leaders. More mundane perhaps, but no less germane, for they recognized that at stake were their own futures: Would they fit in? Could they fit in? Did they wish to fit in? Would they remain, or would the demands of the homeland prevail? What were the viable options in terms of family, friends, and employment opportunities? Did the new federal laws represent a grave threat or a minimal nuisance? So much was new, unfamiliar, challenging, promising, but also scattered across vast expanses of land that were as novel as the peoples and cultures. And to an extent that mixture of responses applied, as well, to the migrants who had been living elsewhere in America before relocating. The many decisions newcomers faced would become part of the ongoing processes of continuity and change by individuals and then, collectively, by ethnic groups: the continuity of traditions versus the imperative for change created by life in the American West. What is more, the immigrants' stories paralleled many of the experiences challenging native-born Americans moving into the region. For so many and in so many ways, western history was the newcomers' experience writ large.

Thus, in terms of the peoples and policies, numerous outlines of the new century were set at this time, in the decades prior to 1903, and by then the West had become an established destination for migrants "from all points." The accounts of the following four individuals illustrate this, setting the stage for the experiences of four principal immigrant populations: Chinese, Scandinavians, Germans, and Mexicans.

CHAPTER ONE

Immigrant Stories from the West

*I*N 1873 OLAV AND Anne Ormbrek left their dairy farm in Høydalsmo, Norway, and migrated with their two sons to Odin, Minnesota.[1] There, Anne gave birth to a third son, and soon, in pioneer fashion, the family of five was on its way to Seattle in a covered wagon. Olav acquired a farm near Ballard (just northwest of today's downtown Seattle) and built his house and barn Norwegian style. About 14 years later their nephew, Gunnleik Ormbrek, who was at that time 19 or 20, migrated directly to his uncle's farm. He subsequently acquired American citizenship, changing his name to Gilbert because his cousin's name was also Gunnleik Ormbrek. By that time teenage Kari Fosberg had migrated from Norway to her uncle's farm in Washington's Central Valley (Kitsap County). She and Gilbert met and wed in 1896. Five years later they acquired a 40-acre farm in Woodinville, where Gilbert also worked as a sawyer in logging camps and lumber mills. By that time Anne was occupied raising their ten children.

Meanwhile, Olav and Anne's son Gunnleik, who had a dairy farm near his parents, married a woman from his Norwegian community; their son and grandson would continue to operate that farm. Gunnleik's brother Kjetil, however, disliked farming, moved south to Lewis County, wed a non-Norwegian, and also raised a family of ten children. The youngest brother, Eslek, wed a Norwegian woman but also shunned farming and went into the insurance business. Despite the occupational changes and the changes in some traditions, others certainly endured. Gilbert was active in the Norwegian Male Chorus of Seattle and played the Hardanger violin, as did his uncle and cousin Kjetil. Olav and his family helped establish the Bothell First Lutheran Church, while Eslek became a high-ranking Mason and was elected to the Bothell City Council.

For the Ormbreks, migration had multiple outcomes. The family settled in the West, but its members did not follow common paths. For those wishing to move away from the tradition of working the land, numerous opportunities offered an array of available options—some known, some previously unknown to those immigrants. Within this one family we see step migration (via Minnesota) and direct migration; marriage within the group and outside it; continuation with farming and the move into wholly different occupations; little said about homeland ties but various efforts to preserve elements of ethnicity. On several levels there is a story of continuity and change.

In 1872, the 29-year-old Anna Freudenthal married Isadore Elkan Solomon (known as I. E.) in Inowroclaw, Prussia, and they left the next day for Towanda, Pennsylvania, where I. E. began a livery service.[2] After four years of slow business and the birth of three children, Anna persuaded her husband to relocate to the Arizona Territory, where her cousins, Henry and Charles Lesinsky, were already in business as owners of the Longfellow Copper Mine. Along the Gila River, in eastern Arizona, I. E. started a charcoal business to supply the nearby Longfellow Mine. Living in a deteriorating adobe home, with no furniture or stove for months and with no domestic help, Anna struggled. Eventually, she ran the family store they started, raised a family that soon included six children, and, around this nucleus, helped establish the community of Solomonville, which subsequently became the seat of Graham County. Faced now with a continuous stream of friends, visitors, people coming for county business, and travelers going between Tucson and El Paso, Anna opened a hotel in 1880, which she supervised while continuing to operate the store. Aided by Chinese and Mexican help, she made the Solomon Hotel famous, in time supplying it with foods from their own orchard and ranch. By 1907, the marriage of their daughter was a major social event of the region.

Clearly, men alone did not build the West. Gender roles were modified, and men and women shared the risks. Mixed ethnic workforces were evident early on and in the humblest of enterprises, but while the composition of the labor force continued to change, hierarchies of workers persisted. In the comparatively unstructured West, opportunities abounded for those of modest means but with ambition and drive—where racial and ethnic barriers were not insurmountable. Many of those whose paths were not obstructed would then use their success as a stepping-stone to participation in the broader community and to even greater prominence.

Yoryis Zisimopoulos was born in Klepá, Roumeli, in central Greece, in the mid-1880s.[3] His father, Yiannis, a self-taught lawyer, struggled to feed his family.

Yoryis learned the shoemaker's trade, but the people of Klepá were too poor to buy his products. He headed for Alexandria, Egypt, in search of a job, sailing with "hundreds of Greeks, Arabs, a few blacks, East Indians, Turks, and Persians [who] were on their way to America."[4] Unsuccessful in Alexandria, Yoryis persuaded his father to borrow the equivalent of $23, and Yoryis departed for America in the fall of 1907. He began his American saga (unknowingly) as a strikebreaker in Pawtucket, Rhode Island. He soon quit, found a Greek coffeehouse in New York frequented by Roumeliot (people from his homeland region), and got a lead on a job in Oklahoma City, alongside Cretans digging vile-smelling sewer trenches. He soon moved on to Pueblo, Colorado, which "swarmed with Greeks." There, he briefly worked for the Colorado Fuel and Iron Company until molten steel fell on some men, instantly killing them. Immediately, Italians, Greeks, and Slavs were waiting to take their places.

After seeking in vain for work in Leadville, Colorado, he made his way to Salt Lake City and looked up Leonidas Skliris, a cunning labor agent known as the "Czar of the Greeks." But Skliris hired men mainly from his village, then from near Sparta, then Spartans, and, after them, villagers from his Greek agents' home communities. Relatives first, then relatives of relatives. Roumeliots did not qualify; Skliris hired non-Peloponnesians only if he needed strikebreakers. Yoryis, by now calling himself George Zeese, next found a job on a railroad section gang in Nebraska, alongside an Arab gang. Standing up to a Greek boss who was a bully, George became the boss of his group and for the next six years organized section gangs for various railroads, particularly in Idaho, where "thousands" of Greeks in Pocatello were seeking work. From Portola, California, to Gary, Indiana, and back to Rock Springs, Wyoming, up to Montana, and over to Idaho, George continually migrated in search of work. Then, tired of the struggle and ashamed of having sent home only $1,600 during the prior six years, George took up homesteading in Idaho, growing wheat. By this time, Emilia Papachristou, who had migrated from Greece to Salt Lake City, decided to move up to Pocatello. She was soon introduced to George, and on the first day they met he proposed and she accepted. They wed in May 1915.

Soon, a decade had elapsed since George's arrival in America. He had had 15 jobs, and even the homestead had been pulled out from under him. George now took his growing family to Helper, Utah, to try his luck running coffeehouses and cigar stores. In 1924 he and an educated young Greek acquired a grocery that proved to be the first of eleven Success Markets in Utah. George Zeese, impoverished immigrant from Klepá, Greece, eventually had a new six-room house and a growing business. He was invited to be a bank director and attended Republican Party conventions in Utah.

Like others described here, George's life was a remarkable blend of ethnic retention and cultural adaptation, of limited ties to his family in Greece and ultimately a significant measure of integration. Fortitude and ingenuity, net-

works and ethnic bonds, persistence and luck, a spouse who was an able partner, and still more persistence—all were invaluable assets that such migrants
as Zeese relied upon for long-term success. Newcomers to the West seized opportunities and, where not evident, they often created opportunities.

Chin Lung would agree. He came to the United States in 1882 and became a
successful merchant in Stockton, California, principally by developing enormously successful agricultural operations in the Sacramento Delta region.[5] In
1888, he returned to China and married Leong Kum Kew (married name
Leong Shee). After adjusting his status to that of merchant, as required by the
Chinese Exclusion Act of 1882, he was able to sponsor Leong to migrate in 1893.
The following year she gave birth to Chin Suey Kum. Over the next decade,
while Chin Lung worked in the Sacramento Delta area, Leong lived in San
Francisco, raising two girls and three boys. But she found America "inconve-
nient, alienating, and harried." Unhappy, she at last convinced Chin to take
the family back to China in 1904. There, Leong Shee changed from bound to
natural feet, converted to Christianity, learned to read and write, and lived out
her days in comfort. Chin chose to remain in America and made periodic trips
home, siring two more sons. Eventually, all five sons returned to the United
States with Chin, but the two daughters remained in China. Indeed, while
back in China, Chin Lung married off their first daughter, Chin Suey Kum, to
an herb doctor, Jew Yee Yuet. However, by marrying a foreigner ineligible for
U.S. citizenship, Suey Kum lost her own U.S. birthright citizenship. She and
her husband remained in China and had seven children; the eldest, Jew Law
Ying, was born in 1915.
    Leong's granddaughter, Jew Law Ying, could not claim derivative U.S. citi-
zenship since her American-born mother had lost her own. She could gain admission only if she herself were the wife of a U.S. citizen or a Chinese merchant. In 1937, wanting to come to America and escape the war in China, Jew
agreed to an arranged marriage with a Chinese immigrant living in California
whose legal status was that of a second-generation Chinese American. The
complexities of the Chinese immigration dilemma at that time are well revealed in the overlay of names that follows. When applying for entry into the
United States in 1941, Jew indicated the she was married to Yung Hin Sen, born
in 1903, the merchant son of Yung Ung and Won Shee. Actually, Yung Hin Sen
was really Tom Yip Jing, born in 1905 to Tom Fat Kwong (who had himself
been smuggled in from Mexico in 1911) and Lee Shee. Yung Hin Sen had been
admitted in 1921 as the (paper) son of Yung Ung and Won Shee. He now posed
as a merchant by paying $1,000 (borrowed from relatives) to invest in an import
company so that this poor gardener could pose as a salesman and partner of the
firm, obtain an affidavit to that effect signed by two whites, and thereby "legitimately" bring in his wife. Husband and wife were each asked about 100 questions

by inspectors before Jew Law Ying was admitted with her daughter in April 1941. Faced with the reality of her new situation, she was about to begin her own struggles.

By this time, Jew's grandfather, Chin Lung, had returned to China (1932) and was living with Leong Shee in Macao, where he had invested in numerous businesses, rental properties, and land. He died there in 1942; Leong Shee would live there 20 years more. Neither got to see their great-granddaughter, Tom Bak Fong, born in 1946 to Jew Law Yung and Yung Hin Sen (the name Tom was based on her father's real family name). The child grew up to become a historian and prominent author specializing in Chinese American women's history, Judy Yung (the name Yung was based on the family's "paper" name). As Judy Yung would later observe, many Chinese women like her great-grandmother and mother "did not find immigration a liberating experience." But they proved to be "the glue that held the family together," teaching their daughters "to be women warriors."[6]

If women were able to demonstrate the same durable qualities as such men as George Zeese, they could also respond as negatively to the new society as did so many male migrants, choosing to look to their homeland transnationally rather than to the new host society. But this, as with other choices, could prove permanently divisive. This account emphasizes that there was no one pattern and no one outcome—even at the individual family level. It also dramatizes one of the major themes running through the story of immigration into the West: men and women frequently went to great lengths and great deceits in order to enter the United States, and as the edifice of immigration and naturalization law and enforcement grew more complex and obstructive, prospective immigrants and citizens faced numerous hurdles. This was especially true for the Chinese because they were the first to be targeted for exclusion, setting precedents that would affect millions of newcomers thereafter. Many Chinese and others persisted and overcame a multitude of obstacles; still others abandoned their efforts, either not seeking admission (at any rate, not pursuing legal admission) or not applying for citizenship. Many chose not to remain in America. The Chin Lung family odyssey reminds us that a serious, racist component warped laws and policies well before 1900. In that respect, for decades there would be considerable continuity and only limited change.

These four vignettes highlight step migration and chain migration, networks and novel community building, cultural persistence and cultural change, endogamous ties and inter-marriage. We see women as well as men playing powerful decision-making, leadership, and economic roles, all the while raising families, adapting to new cultures, and serving as community builders. In most situations we find elements of both cultural continuity and change. Rarely could the immigrant community actually replicate *all* the components and securities of its traditional society. For some, there was the intense, ongoing transnational attachment to homeland and to families left behind. For others, there was a limited, periodic, translocal involvement; and for still others, a gradual disengagement from the land of their origins.[7]

The story of Leong Shee, her daughter, and her granddaughter demonstrates that immigration was not always an unmixed blessing, and that all newcomers did not hang on and endure in the new land. Many sought refuge or the customary comforts of their homeland. For them, the price of resettlement was too high—or it was a price they never intended to pay. On the one hand, most others, like the Ormbreks, Zeeses, and Solomons, eventually did overcome displacement and marginalization (or their children did). On the other hand, the Chinese regarded the exclusion legislation (1882–1904) as racist laws that compelled them to resort to elaborate strategies of evasion, deception, covert entries, and a complicated array of "paper" names. Whatever the rationale, the responses often involved a form of illegal immigration. In its many variations, such undocumented migration would progressively become one of the major issues in the history of immigration into the twentieth-century West.

CHAPTER TWO

The Draw of the Late-Nineteenth-Century West

*I*T IS THE DYNAMIC and quite remarkable series of transitions during this period that set the stage for the twentieth-century West. At the heart of these transitions were the following developments:

The end of the wars with Native Americans in the Southwest, together with the subordination, segregation, and disempowerment of many long-present Mexican and Mexican American communities, especially in Texas, Arizona, New Mexico, and California;

The federal reclamation programs (e.g., the 1902 Newlands Reclamation Act) and the continued growth of large agricultural and (on Hawai'i) plantation enterprises, along with 1.4 million homestead applications in the years 1862–1900;

The expansion of major mining operations, in particular for coal and copper and then oil;

The development, or growth, of many industries and businesses, such as fishing, canneries, packinghouses, sugar refineries, logging and mills, construction, and urban electric transportation systems (with many more soon to follow);

The major surges to the mainland by northern European immigrants along with greater numbers from southern and eastern Europe, Japan, and then Mexico (and several Asian groups to Hawai'i)—accompanying the western resettlement of large contingents of native-born white and black Americans;

Sufficient urban growth by 1880 to push the West's urban population past the national figure of 22.6 percent, followed by the proliferation of new communities during the 1880s and 1890s and thereafter;[1]

The completion of a web of transcontinental and regional railroads as well as coastal and international shipping companies, linking pools of labor with urban and extractive enterprises, and all of them with local, national, and international markets;

The enactment between 1875 and 1903 of precedent-setting laws and court decisions establishing or confirming federal control of immigration and naturalization; and

The revival of nativist hostilities and fears and, periodically, their violent expression directed against the Chinese and then against other Asians.

These sweeping developments signal a West moving—and being moved—in new directions that would certainly persist.[2] They also remind us that this was very much a transitional era.

In 1880, in 7 western states and territories, one-fourth to two-fifths of the population were foreign born, with Arizona and Nevada having the highest percentages (40 to 41 percent) and New Mexico and neighboring Texas the lowest (both around 7 percent). The percentage of foreign born in the total population of these "lower" 12 states and territories dropped slightly during the 1880s and 1890s (to 15.3 percent) due to the greater influx of Americans, but the actual *number* of foreign born rose by more than four-fifths. By 1900, one in nine immigrants lived in the West. Principally as a consequence of its mining communities, Montana had the highest percentage of foreign born—almost 28 percent (tables 1.1 and 1.2).

What was actually taking place in the West in the late 1800s and early 1900s that was related to the experiences of immigrants and the ways in which they would contribute to the region's growth? Finnish immigrant John Kuwala expressed it quite succinctly. Eighteen-year-old John migrated from Finland to Astoria, Oregon, where his uncle and sister lived. His reason for going? "I come to get a little butter on top of the bread."[3] Thousands like him journeyed to the American West to butter their bread. Many would find the butter, but many others would have agreed with a South Slav's definition of work as "a fight for daily bread."[4]

However, Kuwala's image of the region was of the kind that would create an irresistible lure for foreigners—and for native born, too. It was being disseminated by a plague of western promoters that descended upon late-nineteenth-century Europeans. These boosters were sponsored by railroads, by such growing urban centers as Seattle, Spokane, and Los Angeles, and by speculators hawking the magical qualities of the land and sun, including the "fact" that rain in the Pacific Northwest was not as bad as reported—it was "Preferable to Eastern Weather."[5] Agents sang praises to the local natural beauty, especially remarking on similarities to the old homelands. For Scandinavians it was deemed sufficient to refer to the northwest as the "Nordic Northwest." The Northern Pacific Railroad (NPRR) in the late 1880s sent 831 representatives to Great Britain and 124 more to Scandinavia and northern Europe. Such promoters urged readers and listeners to act at once, claiming that the choice lots were going fast. Boosters planted stories in local newspapers abroad, with letters from those who had already migrated. Communities were inundated with brochures and pamphlets issued by chambers of commerce, land companies, local governments, steamship lines, western newspapers, labor unions, the Mormon Church, and the major railroads. The NPRR alone, it was reported, sent 630,000–650,000 pieces of literature in seven languages to Great Britain, Sweden, Denmark, Holland, Switzerland, and Germany.

Even city directories were distributed to furnish evidence that people from the old country were indeed succeeding in the new one.[6] In effect, their message was "Surely _____ (fill in name of place) is 'the promised land,' 'the New Eden,' or 'the reconstructed Garden of Eden.'" One 1871 promotion claimed that Seattle was superior to San Francisco—when its 1870 population scarcely topped 1,100 and San Francisco's had already exceeded 149,500—because "the climate is better, the water healthier, Sound deeper, trees taller, rivers longer . . . [and the] Indians more brave and God-like."[7] Later, a promotional piece for Palouse County (in eastern Washington) depicted the idyllic conditions that supposedly existed there: "When once the sod is broken there are no weeds for the farmer to fight." Meanwhile, in the fall of 1875 the Washington Territorial government established a Board of Immigration (emulating several midwestern states), and within a year the board had answered 550 letters and distributed 4,000 pamphlets and 16,000 circulars and newspapers in Canada, the United States, and Europe.

In 1908 the journalist Ray Stannard Baker succinctly caught the theme linking these efforts: "The West was inevitable but the railroad was the instrument of its fate." Of course, thousands had made their way to the West before the Union Pacific and Central Pacific Railroads were joined in May 1869—by land or sea, or a combination of both.[8] But if the weave of immigrant trails created a fabric that overlay the western landscape, then one must acknowledge how thoroughly the transcontinental railroad systems reduced the isolation of numerous communities; linked cities, towns, seaports, agricultural and mining centers; provided many thousands of jobs directly and indirectly; enabled innumerable men, women, and families to reach new destinations more rapidly; and integrated the western economy more fully into the national economic structure, while it facilitated population explosions in new communities from the lower Rio Grande Valley to the Washington mill town of Everett.[9]

Concurrently with these developments was the completion of north-south rail lines in neighboring Mexico that eventually reached the border at El Paso and south of Tucson and San Antonio. Constructed mostly with U.S. investments, they would provide avenues for Mexican migration and employment that by the twentieth century would prove of immense economic value for the American West and Midwest. Eventually, they would have a profound impact on the West's society, culture, and politics. By 1890, north of the border, there were nearly 72,500 miles of railroad west of the Mississippi, furnishing enormous opportunities for Mexicans migrating northward. In fact, during the railroad-building boom of the 1880s, the railroads were, collectively, the largest employer of laborers (with 30 percent of workers toiling for them) and were continually in need of a reliable supply of labor. Although that high percentage would not be sustained as the economy expanded, the railroads would continue to be a major employer for at least four more decades and a major stimulus to other employment and business opportunities. Journeying from job to job across the West, immigrants provided most of the labor that built and maintained the region's railroads and then its urban electric railway systems.[10]

The historian Gerald Nash stressed that the image of the West in the twentieth century was, "above all, an urban rather than a rural" one. Like the railroads, "hectic" urbanization ran through much of the West's transition from Old to New, for "the most important American cities were founded by the 1890s." Indeed, between 1880 and 1900, the population of Los Angeles leaped by 807 percent, Denver's population by 275 percent, Salt Lake City's by 157 percent, and Seattle's by 2,183 percent. By that time a greater percentage of westerners lived in towns of 10,000 persons or more than did people in all the other sections of the country except the Northeast. In 1900, almost 31 percent of all westerners (but 54 percent of the white foreign born) were living in urban areas, with the railroads merging metropolitan regions (e.g., San Francisco had almost 342,800 persons and Denver about 133,900 in 1900). The major western cities, from Houston and Dallas to Portland and Seattle, had (or were about to have) substantial and complex economies, providing goods and services to their hinterlands, furnishing ever larger markets for agricultural produce (particularly from truck farmers), and serving as the intermediary hubs for the shipment of western products into national and international markets.[11]

Nevertheless, as urban or as metropolitan as some "images" of the West were presented, and as colorful and as economically prominent as they were becoming, immigration history and the commercial shipping and export records remind us that, at the beginning of the twentieth century, a clear majority of westerners still lived in small villages and in entirely rural locations. In 1890 both Arizona and New Mexico were still over 90 percent rural; Texas stood at 84 percent; and six other states reported between 63 and 73 percent rural populations (Washington, Utah, Wyoming, Nevada, Montana, and Oregon). California and Colorado recorded the lowest figures—yet still rural majorities (51 percent and 55 percent, respectively).[12]

Agriculture would continue to play a profoundly important role in the twentieth-century West, along with other extractive and rural industries. It constituted a parallel theme to that of urbanization, namely "ruralization"—including great swaths of industrial agriculture: From the wheat fields and huge sheep ranches in Washington and Oregon to the raisin, potato, rice, vegetable, fruit, and nut farmers and dairy producers in the California's Central Valley. From the ever-more extensive sugar beet farms in Colorado to the great cotton factories-in-the-fields just emerging in Arizona, California's Imperial Valley, and south Texas and west to Hawai'i's sugar and pineapple plantations. This ruralism also included the many truck farmers near the major cities across the West, who supplied them with arrays of fresh fruits and vegetables, not a few of which were introduced by the immigrants. Many of these agricultural enterprises were owned or operated by immigrants and their children (except for the large absentee corporate firms), and over time nearly all would be connected by the cyclical travels of the foreign-born migrant farm workers.

Indeed, all these developments meant that rural and urban workers were fast becoming part of a "monetized" economy and were approaching what historian Carlos Schwantes labeled the "wageworkers' frontier." They were confronting the realities of corporate capitalism. Many would find, particularly miners from Bisbee to Butte, that, in the face of rather brutal confrontations, their struggles for a living wage with a shorter work day, safer and healthier working conditions, stable employment, and union recognition would entail more prolonged and greater sacrifices.[13] Meanwhile, plantation workers in Hawai'i were coming to a similar realization by the early years of the twentieth century. Vulnerability to business cycles and fluctuating global markets—with their demand and pricing structures far removed from the workers (and even from many local owners and operators)—compounded the workers' insecurity and quest for job protection. All this meant that not only laborers were affected by these cyclical economic patterns. In communities large and small across the West, the uncertainties of wage work as well as the vagaries of initiating new business ventures also weighed heavily on the shoulders of enterprising immigrants and their families.

A critical outcome of these conditions, wrote historian David Montgomery, is that "chronic deflation and staggering cycles of boom and bust forced employers to undertake an intensive search for labor that was cheaper and could be more tightly controlled," labor that was "elastic," "inexhaustible," and of a "temporary character": in other words, immigrants, preferably immigrants from the periphery of the world's expanding capitalist economy; unskilled immigrants; docile immigrants unfamiliar with labor unions; immigrants who would tolerate both a dual wage system that favored white, native-born, and northern European workers along with quite marginal working conditions; immigrants who would be easily deportable if they became troublesome; temporary immigrant workers—sojourners most likely to return to their homeland, or at least to move on from the job site; and immigrants without families (with the exception of plantation workers, where managers promoted the establishment of families as a stabilizing factor). Unskilled, relatively uneducated, unattached, assumably unambitious immigrant workers would be the ideal solution to meet businesses' need for the most readily available, adjustable cost—labor pools that would be responsive to business revivals and readily removable during economic downturns.[14] To their chagrin, employers soon learned how quickly many immigrants came to understand the dynamics of the labor market and their need to combine their efforts in the fight for workers' rights. Others, however, were not as attuned to such organizational efforts, or were at too great a disadvantage in the workplace—too vulnerable—to take action (which could include a dependence upon company housing, company stores, and company credit).

Of course, employers did realize that immigrants varied considerably. Many immigrant workers came because they had to—for a host of political, economic, and social reasons. Many others, of different social classes, became part of the mass of refugees fleeing from political or economic oppression (Jews and Armenians; Greeks and Italians). Not uncommonly, many of the former had little intention of returning to their homeland. More among the latter saw conditions in their native land as salvageable, and with money earned in America they hoped to buy land there and return, or cover the costs for a sister's or daughter's dowry, or start a business, or fulfill some other economic objective. Still others, as Dino Cinel outlined, came with no clear, long-term objectives, often because they were young and had migrated for the adventure or to rejoin family members. Cultural factors played a role in determining the type of work the immigrants sought—be it in agriculture or construction; in fishing or logging, or canneries; with railroads or factories, or mines; or starting a business or working for one. Whatever the various choices, the earnings were often astonishing and irresistible, although the realities of the work itself, the cost of living, including, among other items, transportation to job sites and payoffs to foremen, padrones, and unions, frequently proved as astonishing.

The type of employment influenced how frequently immigrants—skilled or unskilled, artisan or entrepreneur—moved about. Or, newer, possibly better, opportunities were discovered elsewhere, and they went in pursuit of them. In making their decisions, perhaps the immigrants believed the promotional literature or the on-site agents, or more likely the testimonials appearing in native language publications or the letters from friends and family members. They believed that, as David Montgomery described it, "they could earn in one day in the United States what they could in five or six days at home." Moreover, even those already working in cities or on farms in the East and Midwest (e.g., Germans and Scandinavians) heard that farther west the situation was better, opportunities were more promising, the environment less harsh. And they migrated once more.

Consider the life of Julius Basinski, a life that embraced much of the frenetic pace of many Jewish adventurers (and other entrepreneurs) during this period. It offers insights into the lives of those who went West in search of their fortune — or at least more opportunities. Born in Germany in 1844, he fled to the United States at the age of 21 to avoid military service. After working for his uncle in New York City for four years, he bought a ticket to San Francisco and obtained 1,000 cigars on credit from two Jewish merchants. He traveled first to Ogden, Utah, sought the help of the banking firm Goldberg and Kissel, altered his itinerary, cashed in his ticket, and took a coach to Helena, Montana, arriving in February 1870. Having no idea how to start a business there, he met two clothing merchants, Jack and David Goldberg. The Goldbergs introduced him to a cigar dealer, who promptly bought the 1,000 cigars, leaving Basinski a $100 profit and orders for 25,000 more. Basinski then moved to a small mining town southwest of Helena, opened a candy and cigar store, and on Sundays carried goods to another mining camp. A group of Jewish merchants was now willing to extend him credit. He moved to Bozeman, Montana, and urged his two brothers to join him in the business, which he ultimately set up in yet another mining town.

Faced first with stiff competition and then the Panic of 1873 and the depression of the 1870s, Basinski survived by supplementing his business with peddling in several mining camps. When a huge fire engulfed Helena in early January 1874, the brothers rushed there and quickly sold $3,000 in merchandise. Then, hearing that the U.S. Army was to encamp at Fort Keogh, in Miles City, Basinski developed a scheme to float supplies to them down the Yellow River. He maintained that profitable business arrangement for 17 years, gradually expanding his stock, even to including photos of actresses. Successful at last, he reestablished a branch in Bozeman, became the town's first banker (he had the one safe), and finally, in 1885, got married at the age of 41 to Fanny Bruce, whom he met on a business trip to New York.[15]

Looking for more ventures despite three fires destroying his businesses during the 1880s, Basinski completely altered his enterprise and began to raise some 1,000 sheep. At age 50, he sold that business and moved to Tacoma, anticipating significant growth there as the terminus for the recently completed Northern Pacific Railroad. Indeed, his general merchandise store, the Tacoma Bazaar, did well. He also became active in the newly organized Temple Beth Israel in Tacoma. Not yet fully satisfied at age 63, he and Fanny moved to Wenatchee, Washington, where he bought a 27-acre orchard and made a profit raising apples. A dozen years later, in 1919, they moved to Portland to be near their children. In April 1926, Basinski died at the age of 81. Unfortunately, we do not know what Fanny thought of this amazingly peripatetic life, but she appears to have endured over 40 years of it with him.[16]

Most business venturers could not match Basinski's half century of entrepreneurial endeavors—from cigars to dry goods to sheep to apples—and his decades of survival in the Montana winters. But his story illustrates a number of factors that characterize many immigrants going to the West—some particularly applicable to business venturers, others to a broader spectrum of newcomers. The central factor is that Basinski was preeminently a risk taker. He began with little, was mentored by members of his ethnic group, eventually became successful, and was admitted into the elaborate networks of Jewish businessmen. With further achievements he acquired the capital that enabled him to expand his business, which also benefited from his years of total commitment, the help of family members, and credit extended to him by fellow Jews.

Basinski's strategies worked because he enjoyed the benefit of luck, location, and links—as well as timing and access to capital. As historian Earl Pomeroy put it, the Jewish immigrants "arrived at the right time, were in the right place, and had the right skill." Furthermore, resilient in the face of setbacks, Basinski continued to search out new business opportunities even at the age of 63. He was quick to recognize marketing voids and then step in to meet the needs of growing communities in this still plastic and rather open West. By diversifying his goods and business sites, his enterprises grew with those communities, and when they languished, he moved on. In addition to being resourceful, driven, and committed, Basinski learned a key component to making it in the West. He was settled upon settling. He saw his future in America, not in Germany, and therefore husbanded his profits and reinvested them. While doing that, he strengthened the breadth of his commercial reach by familiarizing himself with America and American culture. Finally, he integrated himself into American society but did not find it essential to do so by abandoning his ethnic roots. He married a Jewish woman and, when it was feasible, was active in a synagogue.[17]

The Butte Irish provide a contrasting example of the western immigrant experience. These miners were among the 6,600 Irish in Montana in 1890. David Emmons, in his brilliant study, presents a story that starkly contrasts with that of Julius Basinski and his brothers, highlighting the spectrum of immigrant responses to life and labor in the West. Emmons shows that many Irish regarded their migration to America as a type of forced exile and held on to their feelings of exile as fiercely as most did their hatred of England. (So sustained was that hatred that Irish workers were immensely shocked, dismayed, and angry when the United States entered the First World War as an ally of Great Britain.) Yet, few thought that returning to Ireland was a realistic option. Their future was in Butte—until economic conditions disrupted the stability they long enjoyed there.

The principal figure in Butte was Irish-born Marcus Daly. He was passionately Irish and an immensely successful mine operator. He bought the Anaconda silver mine in 1880 and soon realized its greater potential for producing copper. By 1895 one-fourth of the world's copper was coming from Butte. Daly favored Irish miners, protected them, and accommodated work schedules for various pro-Irish and pro-Ireland activities. His actions were "the single most important reason for the massive Irish immigration into Butte in the 1880s and

1890s." Many of these immigrants were "seasoned industrial workers" who had been employed elsewhere in America. However, Butte was actually a remarkably multi-ethnic set of sub-communities—Germans, Finns, Italians Austrians, English, and Irish. The English miners, mostly Cornish, outnumbered the Irish until the early 1900s, when the Irish were eventually able to dominate the hiring scene, with not a little help from Daly. He favored men from County Cork and those Irish who were most intent upon settling in Butte. For example, in 1894, out of the 5,534 miners he hired, 1,251 were Irish-born (nearly 23 percent) and hundreds more were Irish American; only 365 were English born.

Six years later, out of approximately 10,000 miners, 2,192 were Irish born and 1,397 were second-generation Irish American. By this time, Irish migration to Butte had become a self-sustaining "group migration," and the message to prospective emigrants was "Don't stop in the U.S., come right out to Butte." The Irish created a powerful enclave with the aid of their wives (there were 2,400 wives for the 5,200 men). It was a community knotted together by clubs, parish churches, schools, the union, and settled men with settled jobs. The Irish effectively dominated the local Catholic parishes and controlled much of the hiring through the Ancient Order of Hiberians (AOH) and the Robert Emmet Literary Society (RELA), the latter a radical, secretive organization many of whose members also belonged to the AOH. Through the AOH and RELA, the Irish also dominated much of Butte's political leadership and most of the elections. They had become "a labor aristocracy"—and by no means a democratic one. Ethnic divisions were pronounced, and lines were rarely crossed. Indeed, the Butte Miners' Union (BMU) newspaper in 1897 referred to southern European miners in Butte as "brutish, ignorant men," "three centuries behind northern Europeans in intelligence."[18]

Perhaps of even greater significance is that the Irish controlled the BMU, established in 1878. Its governing objective for 36 years was to prevent strikes and work stoppages that could jeopardize the security they so carefully protected, actions that could put them out on the road, returning them to the transiency they so deplored. For them, "security of position was often more important than opportunity for advancement." They valued communalism over individualism, predictability over risky confrontations. Their conservative commitment to the status quo at home and to independence in the homeland also diverted invaluable psychic, political, and financial resources, hampering their mobility in America. The Butte Irish were risk takers in leaving Ireland, but they then sought to reduce that risk with tight controls over their living and working environments. It was a strategy that worked for several decades. To their dismay they eventually discovered that in the new world of absentee corporate capitalism, those controls proved illusive.[19]

Many of the other 113,700 Irish in the West were not so rooted and would experience the challenges of a modernizing, urbanizing region. They remained transient, short-term workers in situations not unlike those of the Chinese. Chinese, Irish, and other immigrant workers traveled about the West with similar agendas. They worked on railroads, in mines, as city laborers (Irish), as farm laborers (Chinese), as longshoremen. They made money, sent remittances, paid off debts (such as the Chinese's credit-ticket costs for travel to America), and, if possible, returned home (most likely the Chinese).

Thomas Strain combined qualities of Basinski and Butte's Marcus Daly and reminds us that such men were exceptionally driven but not singular. Strain was born in Belfast, Ireland, in 1845 and was captivated by the tales of the California gold discoveries ("It was the fairy tale of Europe"). He worked with his father and siblings in William Strain and Sons, which specialized in photography and lithography. In 1873, he used his opposition to an Irish law requiring vaccinations for children as the excuse to migrate with his wife and five children. He was affluent enough to spend four years trying out various places to live in America, Cuba, and Jamaica, before going to Placentia, south of Los Angeles. "Tall, slender, aristocratic," with a lengthy full beard and strong demeanor, Strain bought land and on his own planted orange orchards. Then, employing Chinese and later Mexican workers, Strain turned to overseeing the construction of what was reputedly the first orange packing shed in Fullerton. Over time, this vegetarian and "fruitarian" acquired other land in California (and in Ireland, which he visited), oil wells, and coastal properties, including all of what has become the upscale Marina Del Rey. He continued to gather such successes until his death in the 1920s.[20]

How all this played out for immigrants who were most often confronting a new society and new culture in the late nineteenth century would be repeated among newcomers in the twentieth century. In one scenario, common to eastern and southern Europeans, men (mostly) first migrated in search of work in nearby communities and eventually in neighboring countries, as did many northern Italians. Migration to America was then one more rung in their ladder of step migration. In a second scenario immigrants had their initial immersion on America's East Coast or in the Midwest and then relocated to the West, as did many Scandinavians. In a third and quite common situation, the immigrants had little or no such migratory history, as was often the case with many Irish, Norwegians, Greeks, Chinese, or Japanese. Such individuals most likely were migrating between a traditional society, culture, and economy and a more rapidly evolving economy, unfamiliar society, and culture. In another variation, immigrant entrepreneurs came to the West either directly or in stages, starting businesses and, if not with their own capital, borrowing resources in order to carve their own niches in the West's economy. They often did so at the cutting edge of production or marketing, whether in merchandising, new crops, new technologies, or new media.

The culture that greeted these newcomers was, in varying degrees, novel due to its Anglo-American origins and language and to the still-plastic nature of many of its institutions. Notwithstanding friends, neighbors, or family members who accompanied them or were already there (often in ethnic enclaves or on the work gang of fellows from the same homeland), immigrants like George Zeese and Chin Lung could not entirely avoid some sense of uprooting, and, of course, the same was true for women. Others, like Thomas Strain, experienced far less marginality—even though they maintained homeland ties as he did—because of their social class and skills and a far narrower cultural gulf between their homeland's culture and the new land's.

A determination to return home and thereby resist making much accommodation could mitigate but not dissipate the cultural dissonance those newcomers initially experienced. Notwithstanding that, those who returned home quite likely brought back new skills, new expectations, or a taste for consumerism. These new values or simply new economic resources immediately marked them as *americano, amerikanski,* or the equivalent label.

Anne Ormbrek, Anna Solomon, Leong Shee, and Emilia Papachristou remind us that we will also encounter great numbers of female migrants, young single women seeking adventure or their own escape, or women coming to meet new spouses, or the considerable number who were joining or accompanying their husbands. In 1900, females made up 39 percent of the white foreign born in the West (but only about 11.7 percent of Asians were female). Most of these immigrant women remained in America, as did most men, but as Leong Shee demonstrates, women remigrated too, often to rejoin families, or because they could not or would not adapt to American life, or they preferred their traditional cultures.

It is true that the greater the similarities in culture, the less the culture shock a newcomer was likely to experience. Brits and Canadians migrating to the western states commonly experienced less stress than did those from a Polish or southern Italian rural area, or those from rural China or Mexico. Those who had undergone step migration had probably already endured some culture shock, marginalization, and pressures to make accommodations to a new society. Settling in the West, they were better able to acculturate and to adapt still further, I would argue, than was the case with many of the others arriving for the first time.[21]

Political and diplomatic conditions, the technology of international travel and communications, a combination of the newcomer's migration motives and extent of family left behind, the skills and resources brought to the new land (essentially the human capital), the quality of the various networks found here (the social capital), and the nature of the reception faced in the West—all shaped the immigrants' adjustment and strengthened or attenuated the homeland ties. Moreover, given that so many areas in the West in the late nineteenth century were, institutionally, still in their formative stages, the opportunities to gain acceptance and play a public role continued to be available. Last, among those who were more disengaged and had come with little or no intention of returning to their homeland (for example, Germans escaping Russian persecution and, later on, Armenians fleeing the Turkish genocide and Jews anxiously seeking visas to exit Nazi Germany), the determination to fit into western society was that much greater.

Whatever the scenario, several realities emerged. First, migration inescapably involved risk—risk of alienation; risk of failure; risk of injury or death in a strange, distant land. Many of the jobs set aside for the unskilled and semi-skilled immigrants were detrimental to their health and rife with danger. Second, newcomers were frequently conspicuous by virtue of their dress, behavior, language, religion, foods, "clannish" practices, and attachment to homelands. Many also differed from native-born Americans because of their short-term job goals, lack of job skills, and unfamiliarity with unions and the "sin" of strike-breaking. They were also untutored in democratic politics, committed to sending a goodly portion of their earnings home rather than investing them in America, and reluctant to apply for American citizenship. Third, many of those who migrated from countries regarded as on the periphery of emerging capitalism— that is, from much of the entire world outside western Europe—were more frequently viewed as marginal persons, nonwhite, inferior, and potential cultural and economic threats. Fourth, the late-nineteenth-century context of adaptation awaiting newcomers included an unstable economy, periods of high unemployment, corporate resistance to union organizing, capricious hiring and on-the-job practices (e.g., to foster a dual labor force and exploit workers), and an anxiety among Americans that reflected their uncertainty about the rapid socio-economic and cultural changes taking place.

At times, many Americans in the West were aroused to action against the new immigrants by incendiary newspaper editors, union leaders, and political figures—that is, by men (and sometimes by women) who were alarmed by the changes taking place or who had ulterior economic motives.[22] Their provocations frequently climaxed with conflict. The greater the cultural disparity, the greater the disparagement, and those who were vulnerable and powerless faced the threats of exclusion, expulsion, and even murder.[23] Despite it all, the immigrants kept coming. With varying degrees of intensity, the inter-group patterns such as we observe in Texas (e.g., segregation, exploitation, political manipulation)—where the foreign-born population increased 56 percent from 1880 to 1900 and then more than doubled by 1920—could be seen throughout the West.[24] But, elsewhere in the West some groups would for a time experience challenges to their place in the region. In other cases resentment lasted for extended periods.

CHAPTER THREE

Where in the West Were They?

T HE LATE-NINETEENTH-CENTURY WEST, celebrated for all of its exceptional combination of economic, environmental, and mythic qualities,
was especially distinct because it was the setting for a convergence of native-
born Anglo- or Euro-Americans, native-born African and Native American minorities, and immigrants from across the borders and from several continents,
a meeting of peoples that had profound consequences for the twentieth-
century West. That convergence is one of the most important ingredients in
the region's blend of continuity and change. And even though the spectrum
of the contact would range from relatively greater homogeneity in parts of Wyoming and Utah to the truly multi-racial amalgams of Texas, California, and
Hawai'i, it was the overall dynamics of this meeting of peoples that defined the
emerging West. So many of the grand developments upon which western historians have more commonly dwelled ultimately depended on this "foreign
stock"—from the arterial network of railroads to the urbanization, metropolitanization, modern ruralization (the agri-businesses), continued reliance on
extracted resources, and the diverse sectors of industrialization.

Nonetheless, there was a darker side to the coming together of diverse peoples. Americans' lingering ambivalence about the new immigrants' commitment to America periodically stirred up fears among the native born that American society was culturally vulnerable to centrifugal forces of what was perceived
to be too much diversity and that their workers were economically vulnerable
due to the abundant number of low-wage, non-union laborers. When the economy periodically faltered, as it did several times, and when the nation seemed to
be experiencing unusually rapid changes, as it did numerous times, Americans
laid the blame on the newly arrived "others." They rallied around nativist and

racist slogans, unfurling banners proclaiming that the nation was under siege. The lines of demarcation were drawn: Old West versus New West; old-stock Americans versus new-stock immigrants; old patterns of accommodation versus new groups and new patterns; old threats versus new strategies of coping; and even old economic practices versus new technologies, new products, new markets. This was the American West as it approached the twentieth century.

The 1890 census illustrates just how dispersed throughout the West the major immigrant nationalities were. The results enable us to see how migration routes spanning the region were already being carved by chain migrations, by groups' preferences for certain environments, and by the quest for employment. For example, the Germans are not usually thought of as a major immigration population in the West (as opposed to the Midwest) and yet, because of the considerable number of German communities in Texas (with 48,843 people) and California (61,472), they were actually the largest foreign-born ethnic population in the West (169,210; table 1.1).[1]

The Irish presence, on the other hand, is well known and long associated with parts of the West, particularly because of their mining community in Butte, Montana, and their active labor and political roles in San Francisco. The Irish were the second largest immigrant group in the West in 1890 (close to 113,700), with considerable numbers in most of the mainland western states and territories (excluding Alaska). Not surprisingly, their heaviest concentration was also in California (about 63,140), followed by the mining centers in Colorado (12,350). Their numbers did stretch from Texas (8,200) to Washington (7,800).[2] Unexpected is the considerable number of English. They constituted the third largest group of newcomers (more than 113,000), with somewhat over 35,450 in California and 20,900 in Utah, where many Mormon converts had been encouraged to "gather" (along with Welsh and Scots). In fact, the British (English, Cornish, Welsh, Northern Irish, and Scots), at nearly 154,000, were second only to the Germans. A related group, (mostly non-French) Canadians (78,350), was concentrated close to the Northwest border—particularly in Washington State.

It was the Chinese, however, who demonstrated a particularly strong determination to seek out work wherever possible and to persist even in the face of life-threatening violence. The 1882 Exclusion Act was a major blow to them, but there were nearly 96,200 foreign-born Chinese in 1890.[3] Over nine-tenths of them resided in the West, with over a thousand in each of 9 of the 13 states and territories, mostly in locations where mining had persisted. They had chosen to remain even when many eventually left the mines to pursue other occupations.[4] As with 11 of the 13 peoples in our sample, the largest number of Chinese was in California (over 71,060), but the second major concentration was in the Kingdom of Hawai'i, where they were the second most numerous population after

Hawaiians (16,750). Due to the economic prominence of Portland as well as of the salmon canneries on the Oregon side of the Columbia River (especially Astoria), it was there that one found the third largest number of foreign-born Chinese (9,460), nearly three times the population of Chinese in neighboring Washington.

One might conclude that certain immigrant populations were clustered in particular parts of the West because of networks and migration streams related to jobs and land. However, the heavy promotional campaigns following the completion of the NPRR to Tacoma, Washington, and the Oregon Short Line to Portland drew many immigrants from Great Britain, Germany, and Scandinavia.[5] In Colorado, a crossroad of several railroad lines, Denver was growing rapidly, and mining continued to flourish, all of which attracted many Canadians, British, Irish, Swedes, and Italians, among others. Meanwhile, the Mormon Church continued for another decade or so to urge converts "to gather in Zion," and that appeal (directive) drew most of the 26,760 British, 9,020 Danes, and nearly 6,000 Swedes reported in Utah in 1890.

The concentrations of Canadians and Mexicans reveal the expected consequences of contiguous homelands: 44 percent of Canadian immigrants were living in Montana, Idaho, Washington, and Oregon, and 89 percent of foreign-born Mexicans were in Texas, New Mexico, and Arizona. But, proximity was obviously not a variable shaping the settlement decisions of Scandinavians, who found the Pacific Northwest most attractive and most akin to their homelands. Organized promotions by Scandinavian pioneers and by ministers selected by Lutheran churches striving to start new communities began to lure many from the Midwest and directly from Scandinavia. By 1890 just over one-fourth of the West's Scandinavian immigrants lived in Washington, Oregon, and Idaho.

However, if the distribution of Scandinavian residents was already giving some indication of the future centers of their communities in Washington and Oregon, early figures illustrate the same pattern for several other peoples, too. Consider that of the 10,509 Portuguese reported in the West in 1890, almost 9,860 lived in California, most densely in Alameda County, on San Francisco Bay, and in the San Joaquin Valley. Another 12,700 were tabulated in the Kingdom of Hawai'i. Such was the situation with the Japanese. They had just begun migrating, and there were merely 1,668 foreign-born Japanese in the mainland West in 1890. Nearly three-fourths of them were in California and almost all the rest in Washington. By this time they were already the third largest non-Hawaiian group on the Islands (12,610). While many large-scale migrations from southern and eastern Europe were yet to accelerate in large numbers, the 27,000 Italians — nearly three-fifths of them in California — would be another link between the old and new migrations and would continue to be found predominantly in California. Accounting for the French in the American West is more difficult because of the lack of details in the census records. Some 19,600 French persons were present, including over 11,850 in California (notably in San Francisco) and 2,730 in Texas, where many had been drawn by Henri Castro's ambitious colonization scheme. Another newly present population could be found in Fresno County, where 360 Armenians were said to be living. Some violence against them had already occurred in the Ottoman Empire, although the worst massacres and large-scale expulsions by the Turks were still some years off. For decades, Fresno would become the foremost destination for Armenians heading to California.[6]

Finally, the one group whose impact far outweighed its numbers was the Jews. A survey done by a Jewish organization between 1876 and 1878 reported 21,465 Jews in the 11 western states (18,000 of them in California). A 1912 estimate put the population at that time at about 100,000, with most of the growth taking place after 1900, at which time the shift from predominantly German Jews to eastern European Jews was underway. Sephardic Jews were settling in Seattle in the early 1900s. Although most of these new immigrants located in the cities, or in places with mining and other commercial activities, the Jews could be found elsewhere in small numbers (such as the Auerbach brothers in Salt Lake City), or even just one family (recall the Solomons). Or even one man (notably, Basinski).[7]

CHAPTER FOUR

Targets of Racism
Chinese and Others on the Mainland and Hawai'i

T HE CHINATOWNS WERE ethnic enclaves, only more so. Such ethnic communities were not unique to the Chinese, but the degree of their concentration in the West by the beginning of the twentieth century was exceptional, as was the long-term gender imbalance that retarded the growth of more demographically even societies. Moreover, life within the Chinatown enclave was far from simple for most Chinese laborers. They were caught between indebtedness to the Chinese mercantile elite in the Chinese Consolidated Benevolent Association (CCBA)—also known as the Six Companies—and the Anglo- or Euro-Americans, who perceived the Chinese as both exploited pawns of business and direct threats because of their willingness to accept low-wage employment. As the movements against the Chinese spread well beyond California's borders (with Idaho being one of their few havens), the Chinese had little choice except to concentrate in marginal occupations shunned by most native-born whites, such as the vestiges of placer mines, service jobs, land reclamation, or intensive agriculture (truck farming)—or mercantile niches bypassed by most white Americans, including import/export firms and some manufacturing enterprises (e.g., cigar making).[1]

Where the Chinese were few in number in a community, they were often spared the worst conflicts, especially if they operated businesses or made some efforts to acculturate or interact with non-Chinese (as did Ah Quinn in the prelude). Wong Leung Ka arrived without family in Ogden, Utah, around 1880 and was one of just 33 Chinese there. He lived there for 46 years, returning to China only twice. He was a well-regarded merchant. His grocery store, Sin Lung Store, carried food items and imports, while upstairs were sleeping rooms that often became the refuge for unemployed Chinese. He died in 1927, age 69, shortly before his planned return to China to see his family for the third time. His two sons eventually came to America, and in time his grandchildren attended the University of Utah.

Meanwhile, in Idaho the Chinese equaled more than one-third of the population in 1870, including nearly three-fifths of the miners. Although their numbers thereafter declined, numerous individuals remained who were well accepted. Ah Choy was a freighter (transporter of goods) between 1862 and 1888. He learned English and was quite successful before returning to China. Another, known only as "Pie Biter," worked in the Idaho mines from 1878 to 1889, living on pies and whiskey. He was well known and was reported to have finally returned to China with $10,000 and 50 pies. Hong Sling came to Pocatello in the late 1880s as a cook for the superintendent of the Oregon Short Line. Besides doing court interpreting, he helped build the First Congregational Church and was one of the first supporters of the YMCA (Young Men's Christian Association). He went on to establish a successful restaurant in Chicago, prospered in shipping, and saw his son graduate from Harvard University.[2]

There were others, who sold vegetables, took in laundry, operated restaurants, did domestic work, or engaged in small businesses. They were rarely perceived as threats. However, Charles Crocker's praise of "the fidelity and industry" of the 12,000 Chinese who helped complete the Central Pacific Railroad and the later acknowledgment of the contributions of the 7,000 who labored on the NPRR were soon forgotten.[3] In the wake of the first flush of euphoria and speculation upon the completion of the new transcontinental links came the depression of the 1870s, followed by the collapse of several economic booms in the 1880s and then the Panic of 1893 and depression of the 1890s. All these set up recurrent waves of hard times and fierce job competition that prompted the search for scapegoats. Indeed, throughout many areas of the West negative attitudes toward the Chinese, long present and widespread, would turn remarkably bitter, inuring Americans to the victimization of the Chinese and their fate as targets of white fears and hostility.

Already by the 1840s stereotypes disseminated by missionaries had plagued the Chinese, but among the factors that aroused workers' antagonism toward them was their willingness to work for less than did white workers, their resistance (or indifference) to union membership, and their non-acculturating, sojourner mentality and behavior. Of course, their lack of political power and unfamiliarity with democratic political institutions (combined with their small numbers) reinforced the perceptions of them as nonwhites and made them a vulnerable and convenient target. That so many areas of the West during this time still possessed weak political, legal, and enforcement institutions and were often populated by relatively large numbers of young men (and far fewer women and families) only compounded the problems for the Chinese.

Moreover, the press frequently inflamed situations. In November 1870, a Missoula, Montana, paper referred to the Chinese as "this tapeworm [in] our entrails." They were accused of "taking bread out of the mouths of white men and women." Six years later, another paper in Missoula declared, notwithstanding the presumed superiority of whites, that the Chinese will "have the effect of arresting the progress of civilization of the American people." Recall, too, territorial governor James Ashley's remark that Montana needs "Norwegians, Swedes and Germans not Chinese"—"European immigrants that could properly intermarry with Americans." The Chinese sometimes found it difficult to find sanctuary where they could work unthreatened. Miners in Park City, Utah, seeking to boycott Chinese businesses, were more direct. They announced: "Shall the widows famish while the heathen Chinese feast? . . . Either the widows or the Chinese must go."

Many works have recounted the frequently negative and often violent experiences of the Chinese at this time, and we need not cover here such familiar ground except to note the way anti-Chinese hostility crescendoed into pathbreaking federal legislation. Although the Chinese leaders actually had numerous courtroom victories fighting discriminatory local ordinances and court decisions (particularly *Yick Wo v. Hopkins* [1886]), they had little success against federal legislation or the violence directed at them in many parts of the West. According to historian Shi Shan Henry Tsai, 55 anti-Chinese riots took place between 1871 and 1887, 36 of them in California.[4] They reflected the volatile mixture of economic frustrations, even desperation of whites, and the inflamed rhetoric of editors, labor spokesmen, and political leaders. Other immigrant groups, including Irish, Italian, English, Cornish, Austrian, and Slavic workers and miners, joined forces against the Chinese to deflect opposition from themselves.

The emergence of the Workingmen's Party in California in the late 1870s, its few election victories, and the revisions it promoted in the 1879 California Constitution against the hiring of Chinese on public-funded and public-works projects are only the more well-known political expressions of the anti-Chinese movement. The agitation against Chinese strikebreakers galvanized the attention of workers in the East, giving substance to the belief that the Chinese had become a national problem. A sign in the Colorado mining town of Leadville in 1879 succinctly captured the mounting hostility: "The Chinese Must Not Come." The *Rocky Mountain News* fanned the flames in nearby Denver by warning that the Chinese had ruined California and that Colorado was under threat. A demonstration on October 31, 1880, turned into a riot, and the lives of 34 Chinese were probably saved by 10 women working in Liz Preston's brothel who gave the men refuge.

Seeking to escape the job-related tensions following the completion of the transcontinental railroad, the decline in mining opportunities, economic downturns, and the overt hostility in many far-flung communities during the mid- to late-1870s, more than 12,000 Chinese concentrated in San Francisco by 1870, and over 21,700 in 1880.[5] Even there, the deteriorating climate could be sensed. During a smallpox episode in 1875–1876, as a result of which 400 white persons died, a city health officer declared that the cause was "the presence in our midst of 30,000 . . . unscrupulous, lying and treacherous Chinamen, who have disregarded our sanitary laws, concealed and are concealing their cases of small pox." The health officer declared that Chinatown was a "cancer" which should be condemned and removed.[6]

By 1880 thousands of the city's Chinese were shifting to small businesses, crafts, service work, and manufacturing, producing over two dozen consumer products. More than 2,100 operated laundries; another 2,440 were servants; and over 2,200 were merchants. The result, historian Sucheng Chan concluded, was that by the early 1900s, "rapid economic change, anti-Chinese discrimination, and finally Chinese exclusion rather than any inherent racial or cultural characteristics" had made the Chinese "into an urban mercantile and servile population."[7]

Of course, the Chinese story would dominate any account of this era in the West because they were the first major nonwhite, non-Christian, non-European sojourning migrant population. They were distinctive culturally, in their working and enclave-living patterns, and in the shared pride in their ancient heritage. Most maintained a physical appearance and attire (notably the queues) that openly underscored their sojourning mentality and resistance to substantial adaptation. They emphasized ties to their homeland, in particular the sending of remittances; and they deferred to the outsized role of the CCBA (the Six Companies), thereby compounding their subservient image.

These circumstances were the backdrop of the prolonged confrontation by whites that culminated in unprecedented federal actions: the 1875 Page Law, which prohibited both the importation of women for purposes of prostitution and the involuntary importation of individuals from Asia, targeting the Chinese;[8] the November 1880 Burlingame Treaty revision, which allowed the United States to "regulate, limit, or suspend" but "not absolutely prohibit [the] immigration of [Chinese] laborers"; and the Chinese Exclusion Act of May 6, 1882, which closed the door for a decade on the admission of Chinese laborers and expressly prohibited the naturalization of Chinese persons. That provision ended the efforts of lawyers for the Chinese who had argued that the vague term "white persons" could include "Mongolians," that is, the Chinese.[9]

The legislation did not end the violence. In September 1885, in a Rock Springs, Wyoming, mining area, misfortune in inter-racial labor conditions turned to inter-racial murder. White workers amassed for a multi-pronged attack on the living quarters of the Chinese, killing 28. Property losses amounted to some $147,000.[10] Less than two months later, riots broke out in Tacoma when a mob of some 500 people, led by the Sinophobic German immigrant mayor R. Jacob Weisbach, marched on the Chinese community of 700. They placed 200 on wagons and drove them out of town, while the others were put on a train.[11] Three months later, a Seattle crowd invaded its Chinese section and forced over 190 men to leave the city by ship; a week later another 110 were sent away. The Chinese population of King County (where Seattle is located) plummeted from 967 to 142.[12]

The hostility persisted. In the *Northwest Illustrated Monthly* (a NPRR publication) in May 1888, a mystified writer declared: "I firmly believe the Chinese a curse in any community in which they settle in large numbers, but . . . [to] the Eastern tourist the Chinese Quarter of Portland is a wondrous delight full of curiosities and surprises." Nevertheless, in the midst of the 1890s depression, tourism was not a particularly major draw, and another instance of inflammation of the editorial pen illustrated that the situation remained volatile. *El Fronterizo* (Tucson) declared in early August 1894, "the Chinaman is a fungus that lives in isolation, sucking the sap of the other plants." One should not be too surprised, then, at the experience Henry Lesinsky had had in eastern Arizona a decade earlier. He owned the Longfellow Mine and had hired Mexican miners, only to have them threatened by the Apaches. He responded by hiring Chinese, and in a short time one-fourth of the 400 workers were Chinese, which antagonized the Mexicans. However, his Scottish mining engineer, James Colquhon, had a revealing take on the situation: "If occasionally a few [Chinese] were killed no questions were asked, and the work went on as usual."[13]

The enactment of the various restrictions triggered an increase in illegal Chinese entries across the Canadian and then Mexican borders.[14] The foreign-born Chinese population in the West, which had risen by nearly 39,400 during the 1870s, plummeted by 34,700 during the 1890s. The Chinese reworked their occupations but could not escape opposition. More than 4,000 joined the Germans and Irish who made up half of the labor force in the salmon canneries along the Columbia River, and nearly 400 became fishermen. The latter soon faced increasing competition from the growing cadre of Sicilian fishermen, while the Columbia River Fishermen's Protective Association gradually forced out the self-employed Chinese. In the canneries the Chinese also encountered demands to limit their numbers, which then dropped from 4,000 in the 1880s to 500–600 by 1892 and 332 in 1900. It has also been estimated that between 1876 and 1906 over 78,400 Chinese worked on commercial ships traversing the Pacific. (In fact, in 1900 four-fifths of "American" seamen were foreign born.) Yet, the La Follette Act of 1915 imposed conditions that forced out most of the Chinese, primarily because of the English language requirement for crew members.[15]

Despite the violence and legislation, many Chinese immigrants continued their valuable economic endeavors. By 1880–1882, over 28,500 made up the principal farm worker population just in California, and another nearly 10,250 worked on plantations in Hawai'i. A growing number among them switched to truck farming, but because European immigrant farmers (particularly Italians, Germans, French, Irish, English, and Portuguese) had a lock on the areas near San Francisco and were displacing the Chinese, the latter focused their vegetable farming efforts in the Sacramento Delta and Sacramento Valley, while some transferred their operations to the Los Angeles area. It was in the arduous work of dredging the delta lands and farming there that the Chinese would secure for a time a strong presence, especially with their potato crops (in which Chin Lung played a major role) and later rice. They were also prominent in the construction and maintenance of the nearby Napa Valley vineyards.

Despite the turmoil the Chinese began to make some accommodations, but they still maintained community institutions, the Six Companies and the family and district associations. More merchants and other exempt classes of Chinese were establishing families, the noticeable start of a Chinese American generation.[16] Even so, the steady retreat to their sheltered Chinatown enclaves did not offset the stereotypes and violence. Nor do those antagonisms entirely explain their historical significance because what set the Chinese apart does not entirely explain the motives for action against them. In the final analysis, they were too few and too powerless to halt the hostility and repeated public assertions that they posed an unacceptable threat.

The many factors of action and perception crystallized into a profound watershed in American history, a distinct break from the past. Because the Chinese population was concentrated in the West, it was the western region that pressed the federal government hardest for unprecedented legislation, singling out for the first time a specific immigrant nationality and ethnic group for special legislative and judicial action. As a result, the West especially experienced the impact of the new policy developments. Moreover, even though the "problem" of the Chinese was not entirely resolved by the turn of the century, whites there expanded the anti-Chinese campaign into a broader anti-Asian movement. The new target would be the Japanese, as well as Chinese, and shortly thereafter would include Koreans, "Hindoos," and then Filipinos. Concurrent with these popular movements between the 1870s and 1900s were the tactics of racist journalists, opportunistic politicians, and well-known labor leaders.

The novel legislative, judicial, and administrative innovations gradually set the stage for the federal government's far more sweeping and more active role in regulating immigration and naturalization. The revolution in policy was apparent not only in the Page Law (March 3, 1875) and Exclusion Laws between 1882 and 1904 but also in the Immigration Act of March 3, 1891.[17] That legislation established the office of superintendent of immigration, increased federal supervision, spelled out inspection procedures, expanded the initial list of individual migrants who could be barred from admission, and provided for the return of illegal aliens. The Bureau of Immigration was created in August 1894.[18]

The first Chinese Exclusion Law (May 6, 1882) barred skilled and unskilled laborers (and miners) and, as noted, denied Chinese the right of naturalization. It provided for certificates and the registration of laborers who were departing the country so that they could be readmitted to the United States. The act of 1882 did not specifically bar the admission of wives of laborers, but in the summer of 1884 the law was so interpreted in *In re Ah Quan* and *The Case of the Chinese Wife* (Cheong Ah Moy). Wives would be excluded because, as the spouses of laborers arriving for the first time, they lacked laborers' *certificates of return* to America (or certificates of an exempt class, such as merchants' wives) and therefore were categorized as "laborers" prohibited from entering. Those decisions constituted a major blow to the growth of stable Chinese communities by seriously hampering most laborers from establishing families in America. Anti-miscegenation laws in many places also prohibited Chinese from marrying white women.[19]

The July 5, 1884, law defined Chinese merchants as not including "hucksters, peddlers, or those engaged in taking, drying, or otherwise preserving shell or other fish." The Scott Act (September 13, 1888) did, however, itemize "Classes Permitted to Enter": "Chinese officials, teachers, students, merchants, or travelers for pleasure or curiosity." It now limited the return of laborers (even those with certificates) to those with a wife, child, or parent in the United States or property or debts worth $1,000. But merely 18 days later, on October 1, 1888, the act was amended, terminating outright the further re-admission of *all* laborers whose return had previously been provided for. It has been estimated that some 20,000 laborers who had certificates of return and had gone to China temporarily were now prohibited from re-entering, including some 600 who were at sea when the law was amended. All U.S.-issued certificates were now void.

Seven months later, the U.S. Supreme Court, in *Chae Chan Ping v. United States* (May 13, 1889), reaffirmed the right of the U.S. government to exclude "foreigners of a different race . . . who will not assimilate with us," and it declared that "the power of exclusion of foreigners" was an inherent right of sovereignty. The Geary Act (May 5, 1892) extended the 1882 Exclusion Law for another decade and required all Chinese laborers to possess a *"certificate of residence."* They were given six months to obtain one, but extensive resistance compelled Congress to extend the time to obtain them (McCreary Amendment, November 3, 1893). As part of a continuing effort to combat fraud and evasion of the law, this latest measure defined laborers still more explicitly "to mean both skilled and unskilled manual laborers, including Chinese employed in mining, fishing, huckstering, peddling, laundrymen, or those engaged in taking, drying, or otherwise preserving shell or other fish." It also defined merchants as those ("and none other") who are "engaged in buying and selling merchandise, at a fixed place of business . . . in his name, and who . . . does not engage in . . . any manual labor." The law required, for what may have been the first time, that the certificates include certain personal information and a photograph. The Exclusion Act of April 29, 1902, once more extended the prohibition; that of April 27, 1904, banned the admission of Chinese laborers indefinitely.[20]

Although Chinese leaders invested heavily in some of the top lawyers of the day and filed some 50 cases challenging the new laws, the efforts were in vain. Another serious challenge concerned the citizenship rights of children who were born in the United States to parents ineligible for such citizenship. An 1884 case, *In re Look Tin Sing*, had apparently not resolved the issue. In *United States v. Wong Kim Ark* (March 28, 1898; 169 U.S. 649), a case whose centennial was actually celebrated in Chinese communities in 1998, the U.S. Supreme Court declared that, indeed, Wong, born in the United States, was a U.S. citizen based on Section One of the Fourteenth Amendment. That also meant that various provisions and requirements of the Exclusion Laws for people of the Chinese "race" did not apply to Chinese American citizens.[21]

There was, nevertheless, an additional wrinkle in this complex, unfolding story, one that would affect many Chinese immigrants and their children. On January 17, 1893, in the midst of the Exclusion Law controversy and the various court cases being filed by the Chinese, the white elite in Hawai'i launched a coup against the government of the kingdom, displaced the monarch, Queen Lili'uokalani, established the Republic of Hawai'i, and applied to the United States to annex the Hawaiian Islands. Although President Grover Cleveland recognized the republic, he had misgivings about the coup and withdrew the proposal for annexation. His successor, William McKinley, had no such qualms, and Hawai'i was annexed July 7, 1898. By the Organic Acts of April 30, 1900, citizens of Hawai'i became citizens of the United States, contract labor was banned, the Exclusion Laws were extended to the Hawaiian Islands, and the Chinese there were expressly forbidden to relocate to the mainland.[22]

Ten years earlier, in 1890, the Chinese had been the most numerous (non-Hawaiian) ethnic group on the Islands (16,752). By the end of the century the Japanese had surpassed the Chinese, for during that decade the Chinese population rose to 25,767 but that of the Japanese to 61,111.[23] The Portuguese were also catching up during the 1890s (increasing to 18,272)—mostly from Madeira and the Azores. The principal reason for the changing situation was the Hawaiian leadership's concern that the Chinese, who had been brought in as contract labor for the sugar plantations since mid-century, were now dominating the islands' labor market. The need to find a substitute (or supplement) for the Chinese was urgent due to the U.S.-Hawaiian Reciprocity Treaty in mid-1876, allowing for the duty-free exportation of sugar to the mainland.

Nonetheless, in 1883 the government placed a ceiling on Chinese immigration (at 2,400 per year) and then phased out the admission of Chinese contract laborers (permitting only merchants or other non-laborers), while—in a step toward fostering a split labor market—encouraging Japanese and Portuguese labor immigration.[24] Also, the Chinese were leaving the plantations either to farm on their own or, more commonly, go into business, mostly in Honolulu.

The hope that the decline in the number of Chinese laborers would be offset by the introduction of compliant Japanese suffered a setback when the recently arrived Japanese launched a protest strike and two dozen work stoppages and began deserting plantations and breaking their contracts. The Hawaiian Sugar Planters' Association (HSPA) recognized that it urgently needed to tap still other contract labor sources besides the Japanese—not just for the numbers but to offset the Japanese, too. (For example, the Portuguese population had increased, but they either tended to avoid remaining as laborers or were moved into supervisory positions as *lunas*.)[25]

During this period, planters were attempting to recruit various European groups, too, including 600 Scandinavians and nearly 1,400 Germans. However, the Scandinavians soon left for the mainland or returned home, while the Germans clustered on a plantation on Kauai—similar to the colonies established in Texas. Notwithstanding that small community, few other Germans joined them.[26] The fluid labor system would periodically involve serious labor unrest and a considerable outflow of workers to their own farms, or to the cities, or back to their homelands. With so many peoples in relatively close quarters, inter-group contact on and off the plantations was inevitable and cross-cultural exchanges unstoppable. By 1900, several hundred Chinese-Hawaiian marriages had taken place, and Chinese, Japanese, and Portuguese children were attending the Islands' public schools. In fact, an assessment made of the Chinese in the 1890s—that "A Chinaman. . . . remains a Chinaman as long as he lives and wherever he lives; he retains his Chinese dress; his habits; his methods; his religion"—failed to anticipate the kind of powerful assimilative effect of the Hawaiian society, culture, and values that was starting to become evident.[27]

The race-related developments during this quarter-century prior to 1900 marked a turning point in American history. The policies implemented against the Chinese strongly suggest that, given sufficient circumstances and provocation, when race confronted the U.S. Constitution, most often race won. That reality would persist for decades, and immigrants in the West would repeatedly be caught in the middle of the racial fray.[28] Although Hawai'i was in reality no racial paradise—least of all around 1900—compared to what was unfolding on the mainland it was indeed becoming its own kind of paradise in America's West.

CHAPTER FIVE

The Scandinavians and Step Migration

*E*THNIC MIXING, ACCULTURATION, and integration were taking place in the mainland West, but little of it was interracial in the late nineteenth century. Some of the most conspicuous examples of ethnic group adjustment were among Scandinavians in the Northwest, which has prompted many western historians to overlook or minimize their presence. Their relatively rapid incorporation would contrast rather sharply with the more limited (or slower) experiences of other groups already present and newer ones beginning to arrive at this time in larger numbers, such as the Portuguese, Italians, and Armenians in California, the Mexicans in Texas and Arizona, and the Greeks in Utah and Idaho. Most of these stories more fully emerge after 1900.

When John Toskey arrived in Moscow, Idaho Territory, he remarked, "We have now come to Norway." Writing in 1900, Thomas O. Stine described Washington State in terms that would melt a Scandinavian's heart:

> The fertility of the Pacific forest is something incredulous, the quantity and quality of lumber produced are astounding to all not familiar with the country. . . . In the State of Washington forests spread over thirteen million acres of land. . . . Sawmills and shingle factories are being busy the year round. . . . Mining is an important pursuit, rugged brows smile with independent richness. . . . The rolling prairies between the Rocky and Cascades are especially adapted for the raising of cereals. . . . Here and there meander silvery streams of clear water. . . . Irrigation is so easily practiced, and the crops thus raised are so enormous, may it be grain or fruit, that the eastern agriculturalist cannot conceive of our natural advantages.

Such descriptions were, said Leola Bergmann, "like tales of a fabled land"—
and they did draw Norwegians and other Scandinavians.[1]

In 1877 John Saether made his way from Norway to Palouse, in southeastern
Washington Territory, by first going to Wisconsin, then on to San Francisco,
up to Portland, and over to Palouse—all within about a year. P. N. Wogensen's
story was even more representative. Born in Denmark in June 1864, one of
seven children, he accompanied his family to Clinton, Iowa, in 1883. After four
years in a factory job, his father moved to Lincoln County, Minnesota, where
he farmed 160 acres until his death 15 years later. P. N. had learned the blacksmith trade in Denmark, which he pursued in Iowa. He, too, went to Minnesota but remained only a year before opening a shop in Watertown, South Dakota. Subsequently, he crossed back into Lincoln County and took over his
father's farm until 1910. Then, at age 46, he moved to Ferndale, Washington,
north of Bellingham and near Puget Sound, in Whatcom County. He was still
operating a farm and blacksmith shop there in the mid-1920s. In 1893 he had
wed Norwegian-born Thea Petersen, who had come with her family in 1867,
also to Iowa. Her family farmed in Iowa, Minnesota, and South Dakota, where
P. N. met Thea. They had seven children. The written account about P. N.,
who was an Adventist church member as well as a member of the Whatcom
County Poultry Association, described him as a "self-made man," strong and
alert, whose life was not "pretentious or exalted." Nevertheless, "he is recognized as one of the leading men of his locality."[2]

In an analysis I have done of 100 randomly selected, foreign-born persons described in Lottie Roth's two-volume history of Whatcom County (1926), which
is adjacent to the Canadian border, 76 had lived elsewhere in the United States
before relocating to Whatcom. My similar analysis of the 66 persons whose
lives were described by Thomas O. Stine in his 1900 study of Northwest Scandinavians found that 51 (77 percent) of them had likewise lived and worked in
other parts of the United States first.[3] That does not mean that the remaining
one-fourth were not at all like Charles Erholm, who grew up in Finland and, at
age 18, joined his older brother in Wisconsin but moved to Seattle the following
year (1887). Rather, many were akin to Andrew Erikson, who grew up in Sweden and, at age 25, migrated directly to Bellingham, where he resumed his job
as a logger. After all, as Finnish-born Hilma Salvon put it, some may have had
doubts in the first place about going to America, but, "When somebody sends
you a ticket from America—well, you go."[4]

In 1890, one-quarter of Washington State's population were foreign born,
and of that population nearly one-quarter were Scandinavian, while the British, Germans, and Canadians ranged from 17 percent to 19 percent. The four
groups comprised 77 percent of the foreign born. Thus, historian Jorgen
Dahlie's comment for 1910 was as true for 1890: "The native-born American in
Washington State was likely to find himself working side by side with Germans,

Canadians, Irishmen, Russians, or Austrians" as well as Scandinavians. In 1910 Seattle was 31 percent Scandinavian. In Oregon, where 18 percent were foreign born, only 13 percent were Scandinavian. Yet, the same four groups did represent three-fifths of that state's foreign born. In both states, the Scandinavian population would, over the next two decades, grow either more rapidly than the total state population (Oregon) or almost exactly at the same rate (Washington). Consequently, they remained numerically quite visible, and a large percentage were what Dahlie called "second stage immigrants," who had, as I noted, relocated mostly from the Midwest. Their integration was significantly more rapid, and Dahlie concluded that "a key to the Scandinavians' view of themselves is to be found in their belief that they were not newcomers to American ways, at least not in Washington": "Scandinavians were aggressively insistent on portraying themselves as good Americans."[5]

A more cynical view was expressed by a local teacher in Palouse in 1884. Regarding the many older students (close to her own age, in fact), "all they want" of our English language, she decided, "is just enough to read a little and make change." A Swedish editor of the period viewed matters quite differently. "What our countrymen find is that very few come directly to the west coast. The majority have gone through the beginning experience . . . , their 'greenhorn period,' in the East or Midwest and they speak, if not always correctly, the English language quite easily and read it with ease. In any question of use and customs they are already Americanized."[6]

Whatever the motives were, it appears that Scandinavians' assimilation almost from the outset has been taken for granted. The impression that they had completely melted into American society may actually reflect the great strides taken by many second-generation Scandinavians during the twentieth century. As one historian expressed it, "By 1920 the Nordics were either assimilated or on the path to assimilation." Certainly, the whiteness issue never arose with respect to Scandinavians. It has been suggested that Danes readily dispersed because they were culturally and racially akin to Americans and viewed as white. Most were fluent in English, and there was "strife and divisiveness within the Danish American community" that may have weakened ethnic community ties.[7] The cultural compatibility of Danes is supported by a study of the political acculturation of Nordics in Seattle and Ballard during the 1890s, which concluded that "the Danes were the most integrated (assimilated) into the general Seattle and Ballard communities." That conclusion was based on data measuring residential concentration, urbanization, extent of marriage with non-Danes, occupational distribution (including percent of employed housewives), percent naturalized, and percent registered to vote. In fact, in the same way that scarcity of land and a lack of agricultural opportunities, along with a desire to avoid military service, were homeland factors that stirred Norwegians to respond favorably to reports of high wages and employment opportunities in Washington, so the fact that Danes came from a country which had early on (in the 1870s) achieved the highest level of political participation in Europe could help explain their exceptional levels of naturalization and political mobilization.[8]

Although the Mormon leaders were determined not to permit exclusively Scandinavian colonies in Utah, by 1869 almost 10,850 Scandinavian converts had migrated to Utah, and they did not entirely forsake their roots. In 1872, they sent $10,000 home to pay for others to migrate; in 1883, $30,000 was sent just to Sweden. The Mormon Church tried to treat the Nordics as one people, but even among the missionaries differences emerged. In 1900, 1,337 Scandinavian missionaries went back to their respective homelands, including 130 Norwegians, 417 Swedes, and 516 Danes. By 1905 the subdivisions were conceded in a reorganization of that mission. Norway's achievement of full independence in 1905 and its renewed nationalism hastened the split. Even the Swedes by 1900 had begun to meet separately from the other Scandinavian Mormons, a measure of the persistence of ethnicity during the 1890s, when clubs and organizations were founded and the different groups began celebrating Old World holidays (such as Norway's *Syttende Mai*, May 17). For a time, there were Danish-Norwegian newspapers, *Utah Posten* and *Bikuben*, the latter supported by the Mormon Church. These efforts spawned musical, literary, and dramatic societies and separate social gatherings. Elsewhere, without the binding force of the Mormon Church, individual churches, mostly Lutheran, rather quickly arose among the different nationalities.[9]

In 1890, Rev. Bjug Harstad was sent from Minnesota by the Norwegian Evangelical Church to organize Lutherans in the Northwest. Out of those efforts would come Pacific Lutheran University, in Parkland (now Tacoma), Washington. He also journeyed to the Willamette Valley and Silverton, a budding Norwegian community near Salem, Oregon. He then encouraged one Ingebret Larson to migrate to Silverton from the Midwest to establish a church, which Larson did. His letters to the Norwegian press in North Dakota about Silverton were reprinted by other Norwegian papers, including his comments about the advantage of the coming railroad lines. Within a year, 27 families, including Albert Olsen, his family, three horses, and a dog, were making the journey by train. At about the same time, in 1890, Norwegian-born Andrew Olsen, age 21, came to Portland, moved on to Astoria, where the Columbia River meets the Pacific, worked as a fisherman, and in 1895 helped organize the Union Fisherman's Cooperative Packing Company. From an initial $18,000 investment, the firm grew to a value of a half-million dollars; by 1904 it was the largest salmon cannery in Astoria—sometimes canning 3,000 cases per day. Olsen was on the board of directors and became president of the company in 1914.[10]

Meanwhile, Danes were gathering in Petaluma, north of San Francisco, where they launched a massive egg-producing business. Others went to Fresno, where they established dairy farms and then created the Danish Creamery cooperative; to Humboldt, where they engaged in shipping, fishing, and ship-building; to several neighborhoods in San Francisco, establishing a variety of small businesses, a Scandinavian church in the "Little Denmark" district, and the newspaper *Bien*. Many journeyed to Portland and Junction City, in Oregon, to Tacoma, Seattle, and Enumclaw (east of Tacoma), in Washington, and on to the rural as well as mountain and mining communities in Montana. Social organizations were established, churches begun, and newspapers launched in most of these locations and many more after 1900.

In the late 1890s, Finns were moving into Astoria, which by 1905 contained the largest Finnish community west of the Mississippi.[11] Many were attracted to the Columbia River area because of opportunities for logging jobs, fishing, and farmlands and because they had heard about Finnish entrepreneur B. S. Seaborg (Sjöberg). In 1880, across the Columbia, in Ilwaco, Seaborg had established a cannery and sawmill, naming the cannery the Aberdeen Packing Company after the Scottish port town he admired. As with the small community further upriver, appropriately namely Deep River (described in part 2), many Finns, especially bachelors who were mostly fishermen and loggers, moved in here, as did about 30 Chinese who worked in the cannery. Some Finns brought wives and built homes there—always with saunas—and Finnish was still the common language in 1900. Indeed, "many a child . . . never learned a word of English until he started school, although he might already know how to read and write his parents' tongue." Seaborg was active in the community and was elected the first state senator from the area.[12] However, the cannery burned down in 1898 and was not rebuilt. For five years Finns brought their fish to Astoria's canneries, and then this small Washington community began to decline.[13]

In San Francisco in 1882, Finns had established the United Finnish Kaleva Brothers and Sisters, which would become one of the largest Finnish organizations in America. In fact, a second branch was formed in Astoria—as was a woman's auxiliary—and a third in Fort Bragg, north of the California coastal town of Mendocino. Nearly one-third of California's foreign-born Finns lived in the Mendocino area by 1900, as did about 11 percent up in Humboldt, near the Oregon state border. Key organizations, besides the Kaleva, included the Finnish Lutheran Church (first erected in San Francisco in 1890 and then in Astoria), temperance societies, a consumer co-op grocery, the Comrade Hall for the Finnish Socialist Club, the Finnish Brotherhood Lodge, and the Knights of Kaleva.[14] As we shall see, a similarly elaborate array of organizations and institutions would be created in Astoria as well.

Indeed, Scandinavian men and women established an array of institutions in most of their communities. Their rich organizational life attested to the continuing value to them of their national origins and homeland-rooted associations. The latter became the foundation of their ethnic communities. Even Icelanders would create such associations in Seattle. In addition to the Finnish organizations mentioned, male choruses—for example, the Norwegian Singing Societies and the Svenska Gleeklubben—were important in all their communities, as were the Sons of Norway, the Swedish Society (Svea), the Swedish Club, the Norwegian Workingmen's Society, the Norse Club, and numerous other ethnically distinct societies, including the Danish Brotherhood and Sisterhood lodges, the Swedes' Valhalla Lodge, and the Norwegians' Ancient Order of Vikings. Just in Seattle and neighboring Ballard between 1885 and 1900, over two dozen Swedish and Norwegian newspapers were begun as well as a Scandinavian one. During the same period at least 19 Scandinavian, Norwegian, and Swedish churches were also established.[15]

First-generation Scandinavians were eager to gain American acceptance but were not ready to entirely abandon their language, their church, or their desire to associate with one another and to celebrate homeland festivals as they had in the old country. With increasing frequency (and contrary to what one might have anticipated), they did so not in combined Scandinavian groups but in separate Norwegian, Swedish, Danish, Finnish, and occasionally Icelandic organizations. And yet, the various political organizations in the 1890s reveal a willingness of some among this first generation to get involved in the general community. Andrew Chilberg's life illustrates how Scandinavians, especially after 1900, rapidly bridged their two worlds and how his step migration from the Midwest facilitated the process for him.

Chilberg was born in Sweden in 1845 and migrated with his family to Iowa and then to Sacramento in 1863, after which he returned to work in Iowa as a teacher for several years. He relocated to Seattle in 1875 with his two brothers and went into the grocery business with them before branching off into insurance. Just three years after his arrival he was elected to the Seattle City Council. He became vice-consul for Sweden and Norway the following year—the first consul assigned to Seattle. He was elected county assessor in 1882, county treasurer in 1885, and was appointed president of the Scandinavian-American Bank in 1892. Four years later he was elected to the board of education and continued, as of his 85th year (1930), as both bank president and vice consul, at which point we last hear about him.[16]

CHAPTER SIX

The German Presence

OUR KNOWLEDGE OF SCANDINAVIANS is rather substantial compared with what is available on German immigrants in the West. In 1890, the Germans were the most numerous foreign-born population in the West (169,210), but their story has been rather overlooked in that region (as opposed to the Midwest (table 1.1). Consider the life of Arthur Breyman.[1] Born in Hannover in 1838, he arrived in America in 1855, following the death of his father. He was urged by his brother to journey to the Northwest. Sidetracked to Wisconsin for four years, he subsequently sailed around the horn to Oregon, where he met up with his two brothers. He went into business with them, saved money in order to open a dry goods business in a mining community and then in Salem, the state capital. There he married and became a leading merchant within five years. At that point, he invested in cattle and a merchandising business across the Cascade Mountains in eastern Oregon in Prineville. Eventually, he returned to Portland, where he soon acquired land and operated the Breyman Leather Company with his son (one of his five children). Breyman died shortly before his 80th birthday, in 1908.

Early migration; step migration; family ties; urban and rural living and urban and rural businesses; prominent, established, solid citizen and family man. The extent of Breyman's success may not have been experienced by most Germans, but his life touches on key components in the diversity among Germans in the American West.[2] They came early and continued coming; by the 1890s, as direct migration tapered off, others were relocating to Texas from Illinois, Iowa, Minnesota, and neighboring states. They were diverse in their origins, migrating from different parts of what became Germany in the early 1870s as well as from Austria, the German region of Switzerland, and the German communities in Russia. They were Lutheran, Catholic, Evangelical, and Jewish, along with a variety of smaller sects or none at all. The mid-century newcomers had been landowning middle-class farmers and artisans (plus some professionals), who tore up their roots because they believed Texas promised more opportunities than did the restricted conditions in Germany. From Texas to Washington and even Hawai'i, they settled in both urban and rural areas—and, in fact, they were already proportionally more concentrated in Texas cities by 1880 than other immigrants in that state.

Like the Scandinavians, the Germans established a great variety of fraternal, mutual aid, religious, recreational, musical, and athletic societies and newspapers, along with churches. They preserved their ethnicity and held their communities together, even among quite small groups, such as those on Moloka'i and Kaua'i. In many places their cultural influence at this time was considerable. Some individuals achieved great prominence in business and politics (Claus Spreckels especially) and many were content to acquire land and focus on their religious communities, particularly in Texas. Kathleen Conzen, writing about Germans in the Midwest, may have identified the underlying issue regarding the record of Germans in the West: "the defining contradiction of German Americans" is "that they ferociously [clung] to a group identity while at the same time assimilating almost without a trace into the American mainstream."[3]

Between 1832 and 1846 some 7,160 Germans had arrived in Texas via Galveston, and another 8,000 in 1847.[4] Thousands more then began arriving via New Orleans. A society for colonization in Texas had also been established in New York in 1839, and it directed some settlers to Texas. A company was established in 1845 to promote a wholly German community in Texas, near San Antonio, that would maintain "an unbroken connection between themselves and the old country." It was that plan which resulted in the establishment of New Braunfels, Fredericksburg, and numerous smaller, largely rural German communities in and near the Texas Hill Country, such as Boerne. Indeed, a "German Belt" of rural and urban settlements took shape, stretching from Galveston and Houston west to this central region surrounding and north of San Antonio. By 1883 it was estimated that about 40 percent of San Antonio was German, one-third of Austin, two-thirds of Dallas, and nearly all of Fredricksburg. Although the Germans had come from nearly a dozen different districts in the German region, more than half had migrated from Prussia, and many others from west central Germany (notably Hessen and Lower Saxony). That foreign-born population did level off at about 48,300 in 1900 and 44,900 in 1910, but— indicative of the stability of those communities—there were in 1910 close to 126,900 second-generation German Americans in Texas, predominantly where the foreign born also resided.[5]

By the early years of the new century it was estimated that between 75,000 and 100,000 persons of German extraction lived in south central and southwestern Texas. A 1907 report, with some exaggeration, indicated that many of those, especially in the area surrounding San Antonio, were retaining their language and identity: "German customs of life still hold sway. . . . [O]ne would see there probably the most thoroughly Germanized portion of the United States," with Comal and Gillepsie Counties (just to the north of San Antonio) in particular "almost entirely German in sentiment, in speech, and in methods of life." At that time, the 60,000 population of San Antonio was still about one-third German, numerous enough that many African Americans and Mexicans there spoke German. In addition, there were German Swiss colonies in Dallas, Galveston, and Houston as well as San Antonio. Throughout many parts of the state, therefore, the German Texans had their churches (mostly Lutheran), schools, turnverein (gymnastic clubs), and singing societies, along with 29 German-language newspapers, including the *San Antonio Zeitung* and the *New Braunfels Zeitung*.

During the same period as Germans were establishing sizeable settlements in Texas, others had been migrating into Utah and Colorado in two different patterns. Beginning in 1853, in response to Brigham Young's call for a "gathering in Zion," German converts to Mormonism began their journey to Utah from Germany as well as from the German region of Switzerland.[6] Until the mid-1880s the stream continued. At that time, beginning in August 1882, new federal laws to prohibit the admission of paupers complicated Mormon plans that migrants deposit their money with the church emigration office in Liverpool. Further complications arose with the March 1891 immigration law, which enumerated a fuller catalogue of inadmissible immigrants, including polygamists. In addition, the federal government seized Mormon Church assets (arising from the church-state controversy), some of which were funds to assist with migrants' transportation costs.

At the same time, the now-united German government enacted a variety of insurance and pension laws and guarantees of civil rights that together diluted some of the pressures to emigrate. Those developments, and Germany's law prohibiting the recruitment of emigrants, prompted the Church of the Latter Day Saints in the early 1900s to revise its policy and begin discouraging any "gathering" in Utah. It urged, instead, that converts remain in their native lands as the foundations of a world-wide church. Meanwhile, since the late 1850s non-Mormon Germans (including German Jews) had also been heading to Utah, drawn by opportunities in Salt Lake City, in the mining areas, and on the railroads. Newcomers were being attracted to similar opportunities in Denver and the Colorado mining communities. The completion of the transcontinental railroad in May 1869 accelerated the trend. Thus, the population of 871 Germans, Austrian, and Swiss in Utah and the 1,662 in Colorado in 1870, though a young and impermanent group, jumped considerably by 1900 to 7,524 and 22,439, respectively.

Another development by 1890 that significantly explains the prominence of Germans in Colorado (as well as in Kansas, Nebraska, and Washington) was Russia's revocation in 1871 of long-standing guarantees and protection to its German population—notably Volga and Black Sea German Russians. By 1873 they had begun migrating to the Plains states and by the 1880s into northern Colorado, especially Globeville—Globeville because the German Russians were quickly drawn to the opportunities in the rapidly expanding sugar beet industry (and even more so after the tariff exemptions on Hawaiian sugar were reversed in the 1890s). With earnings for a family of six laboring in the fields reaching $1,000 from just one season, these newcomers were rapidly able to acquire their own farms. Their peak immigration occurred after 1900.[7]

Germans had also been migrating to the West Coast since the first gold discoveries and early on became prominent members of the San Francisco community and many smaller mining communities. Glenna Matthews described San Francisco as "born cosmopolitan," given its early array of ethnic groups. Germans figured prominently in this—even to the surprising extent of the Know-Nothings nominating a German Catholic immigrant for mayor in 1854.[8] By 1870, Germans constituted 19 percent of the foreign born in San Francisco, exceeded only by the 35 percent who were of Irish background. In 1900, despite the sharp drop in foreign-born Irish during the 1890s, there were evidently still more second-generation Irish, for the figure for Irish foreign stock (first two generations) stood at 27 percent compared with 23 percent for the Germans.[9]

Although many Germans entered a wide variety of trades and became shopkeepers—including, for example, positions as butchers, bakers, clockmakers and watchmakers, and beer brewers—German Jews in San Francisco focused on an array of commercial endeavors, with some spectacular results, such as by Levi Strauss (clothing), the eight Seligman brothers (dry goods and then investment banking), Anthony Zellerbach (stationery and bag manufacturing), Aaron Fleishacker (manufacturing), Lewis Gerstle (stocks and Alaskan commerce), Adolf Sutro (mining and real estate), and Mary Ann and Isaac Magnin (merchandising, department store).[10] They would represent an extraordinary array of German Jews who spread throughout the West in the late 1800s and were among those to achieve remarkable successes, for example, Charles Ilfield and Henry Lesinsky in New Mexico; Michael Goldwater, William Zeckendorf, and Anna and I. E. Solomon in Arizona; Sam Kahn, the two Auerbach brothers, and Simon Bamberger in Utah; Harris Newmark in Los Angeles; Aaron Meier in Portland; the three Schwabacher brothers of Walla Walla and Seattle, Washington; and David Falk of Boise, Idaho.

Together with the Irish in the late nineteenth century, the Germans made up over half of the foreign stock population of San Francisco, yet occupationally the two were quite distinct. The Germans' occupational distribution in 1900 certainly well represented their particular urban endeavors. Germans made up one-ninth of the city's laborers (two-fifths were Irish); one-seventh of servants (one-fifth were Irish); about one-eighth of other blue-collar workers (one-third were Irish); but nearly one-sixth of the professionals, over one-quarter of the bankers, brokers, and tradespeople, and nearly that many of the boarding house, restaurant, and saloon owners and employees. Elsewhere in California, Germans were concentrated in agriculture, including their efforts to establish a number of agricultural colonies (such as in Anaheim and Fresno). A singular exception in ranching was Heinrich Alfred Kreiser (aka Henry Miller), who arrived in 1847 at age 19, began as a butcher in San Francisco, and, with Charles Lux, eventually established the Miller & Lux Land and Cattle Company. It accumulated one million acres in the San Joaquin Valley, including a strip one hundred miles long.[11]

That spread of activities would, as Arthur Breyman's story suggested, also be found in the Northwest, where Germans constituted almost 19 percent of the Oregon and Washington foreign-born population. They made up, in 1890, one-quarter of Spokane's foreign born, over one-fifth of Portland's, well over one-sixth of Tacoma's, and close to one-sixth of Seattle's (along with Austrians and German Swiss), plus the thousands living in the rural areas, especially in the eastern regions of the two states—enough to count for one-third of the population of several eastern Washington counties by the early 1900s. And, as in parts of the Interior West, German Russians flocked to that same agricultural region in Washington, particularly in Adams, Lincoln, and Whitman Counties. Finally, two German immigrants had an especially huge impact on this region, profoundly affecting the economy and the influx of immigrants: Frederick Weyerhaeuser acquired 900,000 acres from the NPRR in 1900, creating a vast logging empire, and Henry Villard proved to be exceptional in his work for the NPRR, extensively promoting migration to the Pacific Northwest.

Given the numbers and broad distribution of Germans, it is not surprising that a whole array of German institutions, newspapers, and churches were established in German centers across the West, and even in Hawai'i—and that held both for rural and urban communities. By contrast, most German Jews in the West would be found in urban centers, particularly San Francisco, Portland, Denver, and Salt Lake City. For example, 768 German Jews were identified in Portland in 1880 (up from 135 in 1860) and 2,200 in 1900, but there had also been considerable transience and population turnover among the less established (and usually younger) men. By the early 1900s there were an estimated 16,000 (predominantly German) Jews in San Francisco. Along with some Polish, English, and American ones, these Jews offer a case study of communal institution building, for they brought with them from Europe a tradition of survival by constructing self-contained community institutions. High holiday services (Rosh Hashanah and Yom Kippur) were held in 1849 in San Francisco, and within a year steps were taken to organize Congregation Sherith Israel. Congregation Emanu El, with a somewhat different orientation, was established at the same time, and in 1863 an orthodox congregation was founded. A Jewish cemetery had been quickly acquired, benevolent societies established, and a charter for a B'nai B'rith chapter was obtained in November 1855; by 1915 there were 20 chapters in California, 7 in Washington, 2 in Oregon, 2 in Montana, 1 each in Utah, Nevada, Idaho, and Arizona. In 1889 the Jewish community provided for the Hebrew Home for Aged Disabled.

The examples of the speed and extent of their organizing in San Francisco by both men and women had parallels in other major cities and on a more modest scale in smaller urban areas, too. For example, in response to the growing social hostility to Jews in Los Angeles, two community leaders responded in the early 1890s by establishing an elite social center of their own, the Concordia Club (now the Hillcrest Country Club). A more sweeping illustration across California was the growth of synagogues, which were also established in Los Angeles, Oakland, Stockton, Sacramento, and San Diego. One could find them in most other major western communities before 1900, from San Antonio and El Paso to Portland and Seattle.

Moreover, already in the nineteenth century, there were Jews (again, largely German Jews) active in local politics, and they were elected mayor in Butte, Boise, Astoria, Eugene, Portland, San Francisco, Sacramento, Seattle, Denver, Tombstone, Tucson, Phoenix, Santa Fe, and El Paso—among many others. In addition to those examples, Simon Bamberger's election in 1917 as the first non-Mormon, German Jewish governor of Utah (he was one of a number of German Jews elected governor, representative, and senator) also exemplifies what would become quite prevalent by the early twentieth century, namely German American and Jewish involvement in western politics.[12] That would gradually change, however, with the generations, the increased antisemitism, and the presence of more men of other backgrounds interested in politics. Still, in this earlier era the Jews' contribution to local western politics was substantial.

CHAPTER SEVEN

Proximity of Homeland
The Mexicans

*I*N THE WEST YOU WERE either a Native American or a migrant/immigrant, or a close descendant of one. The one exception unique to the West were those of Spanish or mestizo (mixed Indian-European race) origins who traced their roots in the American Southwest to those who moved into the region when that did not represent "crossing" into it. Don Juan de Oñate had arrived in 1598, and a dozen years later his successor established Santa Fe de Francisco, thus beginning what is now more than 400 years of continuous presence, predating permanent English, French, Swedish, and Dutch settlements in North America. The 1845 annexation of Texas and then the acquisition of the Mexican Cession—the latter an outcome of the Mexican-American War and the resulting Treaty of Guadalupe Hidalgo (1846–1848)—involved the addition of 918,000 square miles to the United States, plus 30,000 more in the 1853 Gadsden Purchase.

A border now existed, but it was a distinctive one given that it bisected a region where the culture, contacts, and trade had long moved readily north and south, such as along the Chihuahua Trail. An estimated 72,000–82,000 Spanish-speaking Mexican citizens were north of the new border in 1848.[1] This was a border, Linda Gordon wrote, "that made little social and economic difference during the next half century." What would be the relationship between those who chose to remain and those compatriots who afterward elected to migrate *al norte*? Gordon added, "There were no guards at the borders, no checking of papers, and indeed no one had papers; few residents knew exactly where the border was."[2]

This situation was, after all, not comparable to the U.S.-Canadian situation because Canadians in the West were not exploited, confined to enclaves, victims of on-going violence, nor bent on preserving a distinct subculture. Many of those of Mexican origin were holding on to traditions, especially in New Mexico, where they remained a majority until at least the fourth decade of the twentieth century. Border crossings were occurring at many points, from Brownsville to El Paso to Tucson, and *mexicanos* did encounter such communities and enclaves, with language, religion, and cultural practices that were quite familiar. Their numbers reaching the border accelerated in 1884 when the Mexican Central Railroad reached Ciudad Juarez, across from El Paso. Even before that, Manuel Gonzales observes, Arizona was a "haven for Sonorans," especially those fleeing the political turmoil there. Or consider Mariano Samaniego, who had come from Sonora with his widowed mother in the 1850s. He earned a college degree from St. Louis University, returned and built a freight business in Tucson during the 1870s, and expanded into ranching and mining. By the 1890s he was regarded as the foremost *patron* of the *tucsoneses*.[3]

On the one hand, relations with Canada—separated by a "boundary"— would evolve far more cordially after the War of 1812 than did those with Catholic, Spanish-speaking Mexico—separated by a "border." The distinction carried great weight when it came to the flow of immigrants and the enforcement of admission regulations, for the United States eventually felt compelled to guard the "border" in ways and for reasons more forcefully than it did its northern "boundary." Episodes like those involving Juan Cortina (1859–1860s) and Catarino Garza (1890s), both of whom sought to provoke cross-border military action against Anglo-Americans, had no parallels in the north and would be reawakened after 1900 by the radical plots of Ricardo Flores Magón (against the Mexican regime), El Plan de San Diego (1915), Pancho Villa's raid into New Mexico (1916), and the alleged conspiracy surrounding the Zimmerman Note (1915). These evoked periodic concerns about security along the border, sometimes provoking fierce retaliation by Americans. Those concerns persist, in various forms, even at the present time.[4]

On the other hand, the Southwest was not a place where two nations were separate and sharply discrete entities. Those borderlands were "an ecological whole"—"one of the world's great cultural borderlands." As early as 1825 a Mexican newspaper quite presciently predicted what would transpire along the borderlands: "Mexicans who live under poverty and ignorance on one side of the river cannot remain unaware of the fortunes enjoyed by citizens of the United States who live on the opposite bank." The whole magnetic force of the "proximity of homeland" would operate more forcefully here than in most other places precisely because the resident population was split and would develop parallel and inter-connected communities (socially, culturally, economically, and even politically) and because the same terrain extends across the international border, rendering any specific line virtually invisible for so many mi-grants, residents, and revolutionaries. For more militant activists, such a border was considered immaterial, if not to be intentionally breached.[5]

What we have, then, is an increasingly complex situation where the chief cultural and community components converge by the end of the century. In one respect, Anglo-Americans labored to come to terms with Mexican Americans —mixed-race Catholics who were now citizens of the United States by virtue of the 1848 treaty. Many of them also claimed to possess grants to immense amounts of lands in Texas, New Mexico, and California, which were generally held individually (or by families) but in New Mexico most often by the villages. Theoretically, the grants were protected by the articles of the 1848 treaty. None-theless, the *tejanos, californios,* and *nuevo mexicanos* had to figure out how to cope with an aggressive Anglo population rapidly entering their lands who pos-sessed a language, culture, religious orientation, legal system, political organi-zation, economic values, and racial attitudes that were largely alien to them.

In a second respect, it appears that in the early years, just before and after the U.S.-Mexican War, in California, Arizona (essentially Tucson), New Mexico, and parts of Texas along the Rio Grande, including El Paso, small numbers of Anglos did co-exist amicably with Latinos and frequently inter-married with them and collaborated in economic enterprises. The critical point appears to have come in the early 1880s with the arrival of the railroad and the explosive expansion of Anglo-American populations. These newcomers had no familiar-ity with the prior traditions of accommodation (aside from the animosities cul-tivated in Texas following its break away from Mexico). They rather rapidly came to see the Mexicans in significantly negative ways. That development eroded previous, friendlier relations. The stability of Latino communities across much of the Southwest was undermined by the economic aggressiveness of the Anglo-Americans, the serious setbacks for cattle ranching in the mid-1880s— due to changes in marketing patterns and severe deadly winter storms—the in-troduction of more large-scale cotton growing operations (expanded into Ari-zona and California after 1900), and the various strategies that for some time had been employed to siphon lands away from the longtime Latino owners. The one exception was some elites (*los ricos*), who managed to preserve a few collaborative alliances with the Anglo-Americans.

At the same time, increasing numbers of *mexicanos* (immigrants) began to walk or swim across the border, at first to work in the gold fields and later (espe-cially when the Mexican railroads were completed to the U.S. border) to work in the silver, copper, and other mines, or to seek jobs on the railroads and on the farms in Texas and then particularly on cotton farms in Arizona and California. The treatment accorded Mexican and Mexican American workers may have differed somewhat, but, increasingly, white Americans made little distinction between *mexicanos* and those Mexican American residents who had in 1848 chosen to remain north of the border in the Mexican Cession and thereby, as noted, become U.S. citizens.

Since there was no formal Border Patrol before 1924 and few formal procedures at the border, Mexican men and women crossed and re-crossed it with little regard to formalities.[6] The estimate of 8,600 recorded admissions between 1869 and 1899 cannot be considered an adequate measure of the bi-directional flow, especially since the 1890 census reported 75,740 Mexican-born persons in the West (out of 77,853 in the United States, or 97.3 percent), more than two-thirds of them in Texas. A decade later, the 1900 census recorded 100,676 in the West (out of 103,445).[7] Capitalism was now rapidly transforming the Mexican landscape, and numerous peasant farmers were either dispossessed or reduced to a marginal existence. Desperate, they and their families migrated in Mexico in search of jobs and then turned to the United States for employment. The pressures to adopt such long distance job strategies intensified in the years before the Mexican Revolution.[8]

Whether influenced by the Black Legend of the decadent, cruel Spanish in constructing their perceptions of Mexicans and Mexican Americans, or interpreting personal experiences or the fallout from the often bitter competition for the land and its mineral and other natural resources, the end result for Anglo-Americans was an array of negative depictions of Mexicans that corresponded to much that was expressed, for example, in Texas about African Americans or Native Americans. We see here early on that "most Texas whites viewed practically all Mexicans as unambiguously nonwhite" — "like the Chinese, a culturally and biologically inferior race" — and in Arizona "'Mexican' was a racial-ethnic not a national designation." Whites denied to Mexicans "the chance to become white"; they "made them non-white." And, by doing so, they effectively denied Mexicans equal opportunities to move ahead. For example, by 1856 in Santa Barbara, *californios* were already being described as "habitually and universally opposed to all progress whatsoever and . . . they look with decided disfavor upon every innovation." Although merely eight years had passed since the end of the war, they were chastised for making "little change in their habits, customs, tastes, or sympathies" — precisely the response that would disqualify them from whiteness.[9]

In 1873, the *californios* lost virtually all the elections for city and county positions in Santa Barbara, paralleling the shift taking place from a pastoral economy to an incipient capitalist one. Power and prerogative were switching hands, just as they had in Los Angeles, Arizona, parts of New Mexico, and Texas. Every strategy of coercion, legal manipulation, deception, and "retributive violence" was used to secure lands Anglos were unable to obtain by direct challenges to the Spanish- or Mexican-based claims. As indicated, with those massive property shifts and the corresponding deterioration in economic and political fortunes, especially in south Texas, many *tejanos* were reduced to landlessness, and they and the *mexicanos* entering the state were largely confined to farm labor employment—a floating pool of unskilled labor. White landowners in the 1890s even used a dual wage structure with Mexicans in order to displace black workers in the cotton fields with those perceived as more docile and manipulable.

A similar trend occurred in Southern California without as much violence. As European immigrants moved in, taking advantage of many commercial opportunities, the Latino population was gradually reduced to "part time, seasonal, migratory work," along with chronic unemployment. At the same time, the percentage of female-headed families increased, with more women and children compelled to seek employment. As Richard Griswold del Castillo summed up for Los Angeles, "During the American era [post-1848], the Mexican American occupational structure was stagnant, with little opportunity for significant upward mobility." Parallels to this would occur in Arizona once cotton production took hold in the Salt River Valley shortly before the First World War as it had shortly before in California's Imperial Valley. In New Mexico, however, the outcome was more varied and took place sooner, for that is where most of the original pre-1848 persons of Mexican origin had resided in the Southwest. One estimate for 1900 puts its population at 6,649 foreign born and 122,000 second- or later generation, for there had already been ten generations living there. The situation was more complex both because of the number of Spanish-descent persons and because a clear hierarchy existed in many villages, with power exercised by the elite, *los ricos.* Many of them were willing to collaborate with Anglos, who soon organized the Santa Fe Ring, led by Tom Catrón. *Los ricos* worked out a power-sharing formula and secured themselves in positions up to the governorship (Miguel A. Otero Jr. and later Octaviano Larrazolo) and even the U.S. Senate (Dennis Chavez, beginning in 1933). In a unique recognition of this reality, the state constitution was issued in Spanish and English, the only one in the United States.[10]

Unfortunately, lawyers and others still managed to gain control of huge portions of the New Mexico Territory, particularly members of the Ring. While sheep and cattle ranchers carried on a long battle for control of vast open lands in what was known as the Lincoln County War (until the early 1880s), Anglo land seekers were pushing into the Upper Rio Grande Valley. A most extreme episode involved the Maxwell Land Grant, which may originally have been anywhere between 32,000 and 97,000 acres. It was taken over by a foreign group, and by the time the Ring consolidated its control it had grown to 1.7 million acres—at the expense of many communities in Colfax County. Violent confrontations took place—with men killed and property and livestock destroyed—but to no avail. In April 1887 the land claims of the company were upheld in court. In northern San Miguel County resistance between 1889 and 1891 took the form of a vigilante group. Las Gorras Blancas (the White Caps) determined to cut fences and take other measures to stop the Las Vegas land grant from holding on to some 10,000 acres at the expense of the original occupants. Such resistance was also largely unsuccessful. Economic conditions deteriorated, and a new work strategy began to appear of village men migrating into Colorado, usually to work in the sugar beet fields, while leaving their wives to run family and village affairs in their absence.[11]

From Texas to California, denigration, intimidation, subordination, exploitation, and expropriation were used to subdue and control. Within those dynamics the trend was toward ever-greater segregation and separation of Anglos and Mexicans—in housing, jobs, churches, public accommodations, and schools. It was part of what has been called "Barrioization"—a combination of voluntary and involuntary withdrawal into their own Mexican/Mexican American communities.[12] Yet, the Mexicans and Mexican Americans were not without responses, for just as *nuevo mexicanos* struggled to preserve the integrity of their villages, so the others labored to create communities in which they could turn to *mutualistas* for help, such as Sociedad Mutualista Miguel Hidalgo (Brownsville, 1881), Sociedad Benevolencia Mexicana (San Antonio, 1875), and Sociedad Mutualista Mexicana "La Protectora" (El Paso, 1888). Women also organized a number of *mutualistas* in the 1890s, including Sociedad Josefa Ortíz de Domínguez (Laredo, 1890s) and such groups as Fiestas Patrias for organizing celebrations of Mexican holidays, notably September 16, Mexican Independence Day. Then, in Tucson, in response to a newly formed nativist organization (the American Protective Association), Mexican Americans founded La Alianza Hispano-Americana in January 1894, which went on to establish chapters throughout the Southwest and has continued to the present day to support civil rights efforts. *Mexicanos* and Mexican Americans also started up well over 100 newspapers across the Southwest, notably Carlos Velasco's *El Fronterizo* (1878–1914), also in Tucson.

Unlike other groups, however, these Latinos did not *at this time* establish as broad an array of community organizations as we observe within other immigrant communities, perhaps because many persons were migratory for months at a time, or because of the lack of organizational precedents, or because of the efforts made to Americanize the Catholic Church in the Southwest (which Bishop Jean-Baptiste Lamy and his successor Jean-Baptiste Salpointe attempted to do in New Mexico). The latter deprived the Mexican and Mexican American communities of that particularly important institutional leadership—a leadership most other immigrant communities received or fostered. The earlier scarcity of clergy in New Mexico had led to one exception, the formation of the Confraternity of Our Father, Jesus the Nazarene, commonly known as the Penitente Brotherhood. It was a lay organization that was prominent in the villages of northern New Mexico and provided some of the support and assistance usually available through mutualistas.[13]

While Mexican Americans sought to define an identity, as the Hispanos had carved out in New Mexico, *mexicanos* continued to see themselves as Mexican, mostly unwilling to entertain the idea of adopting American citizenship. "I will never change my citizenship," a *mexicano* told an interviewer, "for that would be to deny the mother who has brought me into the world."[14] But what about those who had become, or wished to be, naturalized? Were those mixed-race persons actually citizens, and if so, were the Mexican immigrants therefore entitled to apply for citizenship should they wish to? The century may have ended with the Anglo-Americans viewing Mexican Americans once again with suspicion during the Spanish-American War, but, a year before, a vitally important court decision put to rest the nagging issue concerning Mexicans' eligibility for U.S. citizenship.

The debate over the whiteness of Mexicans represented one important facet of the contentious but inconsistent issues regarding who could qualify for the power and privileges of white, mainstream American membership. Two Anglo politicians in San Antonio challenged one Ricardo Rodriguez's right to vote on the grounds that he was an Indian Mexican. Consequently, they contended, he was not white and therefore not a citizen entitled to vote. On May 3, 1897, in the West District Court in Texas, Judge Thomas S. Maxey settled the matter of *In re Rodriguez*. He wrote that the intent of the 1790 law regarding free white persons versus blacks and Indians was not the issue here, nor the scientific question of whether Rodriguez was white or not. Was a Mexican citizen residing in the United States (and meeting the requirements) eligible for U.S. citizenship (and, therefore, the right to vote)? The Texas Constitution had conferred the right of citizenship on resident Mexicans, and the joint resolution of Congress admitting Texas granted U.S. citizenship to all citizens of Texas.

Judge Maxey then cited Article VIII of the 1848 Treaty of Guadalupe Hidalgo, in which it was stated that all Mexicans who chose to remain in the territory given to the United States and who had not expressly retained their Mexican citizenship during the one-year interim period "shall be considered to have elected to become citizens of the United States." In Article IX, all such Mexicans were to be guaranteed "the enjoyment of all rights of citizens of the United States according to the principles of the Constitution." In effect, Maxey asserted, the treaty makes "citizens of all grades, combinations, and colors"—"all Mexicans, without discrimination as to color." He affirmed that, at a time when only "free white persons" were entitled to U.S. citizenship, the 1848 treaty gave the mixed-race population of Mexicans that privilege hitherto associated exclusively with whiteness. White racial stereotypes regarding Mexicans and Mexican Americans were immaterial.[15]

The unique dynamics of race and class in the late-nineteenth-century Southwest centered around the layers of Latino generations where conditions of economic competition and violence were present along with elements of cultural rejuvenation, organizational precedents, and models of labor activism brought across the border by the streams of *mexicanos*, especially during the last 15 years of the 1800s. Surviving *tejanos, californios,* and *nuevo mexicanos* were thus pulled oppositely by arriving Anglos and *mexicanos*. While there would be no one outcome between the patterns of accommodation and resistance, the much greater influx of non-Latinos steadily reduced the leverage of Mexican Americans in most locations. Even in New Mexico, where their majority numbers endured longest, the manipulation by political machines and the intervention by the federal government, with both claiming lands long held by the villages, weakened the economic stability of all but the most elite. Such economic and political decline, combined with recurrent episodes of violence, especially in Texas and New Mexico, and the proletarianization of many Latino workers would be visible in various communities across the Southwest even before the century's end. Manuel Gonzales concludes, as have others, that "many attitudes today are products of the trials and tribulations endured" before 1900.[16] And all this was taking place before the economic and political crises south of the border and the resulting mass migration radically altered conditions in much of the Southwest—and then well beyond it.

CHAPTER EIGHT

In the Year 1903

A SERIES OF EVENTS set 1903 apart as a major nexus between the continuities of the late nineteenth century and the further changes about to unfold in the twentieth. First, in late February the newly formed Japanese-Mexican Labor Association struck against sugar beet growers in Oxnard, California, because of the efforts of the growers, through their new Western Agricultural Contracting Company, to control the hiring of workers, the withholding of salaries, and the workers' use of the company store.[1] The workers prevailed. The two groups joined in establishing the Sugar Beet and Farm Laborers Union of Oxnard and sought American Federation of Labor (AFL) affiliation. But AFL president Samuel Gompers refused to admit the Japanese, and the Mexicans declined to proceed alone. "We refuse any other kind of charter, except one which will wipe out race prejudices and recognize our fellow workers as being good as ourselves."

In April of that year, having organized La Union Federal Mexicana (the Mexican Federal Union), 700 Mexicans commenced a strike against Henry Huntington's Pacific Electric Railway in Los Angeles when he refused their demands for a pay raise. The Los Angeles Merchants and Manufacturers Association, determined to preserve Los Angeles as an open-shop city, recruited Mexican strikebreakers from El Paso. Despite support from the AFL, San Francisco's Union Labor Party mayor, Eugene Schmitz, and the Los Angeles Council of Labor, the strike failed because Anglo workers would not back the Mexican workers by walking off their jobs as they had promised to do.

In early June 1903, between 1,200 and 1,500 Mexican and Italian miners walked off their jobs against mine owners in Clifton, Arizona. The owners had responded to an eight-hour work law passed by the state legislature by cutting wages 10 percent. In a classic case of a split wage scale, two-thirds of the Mexican miners had been earning less than 30 cents per hour, compared to one-fifth of the Italians and less than one percent of the Euro-American workers. Eighty to ninety percent of the strikers were Mexicans from Jalisco, Michoacán, Guanajuato, Aguascalientes, and Zacatecas—soon to become among the principal sending states of Mexico. They shut down the mines in Clifton, Morenci, and Metcalf. A number of Mexicans had leadership experience through their *mutualistas*, and there were hundreds of Mexican miners who were not transient but were stable homeowners; in fact, over one-fifth of the voters in Clifton-Morenci were Mexican. When additional demands were made regarding work conditions and hiring practices, the Arizona Rangers were sent in to intimidate the strikers. They responded by marching 2,000 strong. But the march—and the strike—were cut short by a torrential downpour on June 9 that flooded the canyon in which Clifton stood, killing 50 persons.

About six months later, in November 1903, in Carbon County, Utah, where Finns, Italians, Slavs, and Austrians worked in the coal mines, the men decided to follow a coal miners' strike in Pennsylvania and one in Colorado begun three days earlier (which also involved Italians). They called for a work stoppage of their own against the Utah Fuel Company in order to address certain grievances and win recognition of the United Mine Workers (UMW). Italians led the way, but the company denied any grievances existed concerning hours, wages, company store policies, company cheating at the scales, or union recognition. It fired the workers and evicted them from the company housing in December. Nearly 630 men joined the UMW, while the company sought public sympathy by whipping up nativist fears against such foreign miners. The National Guard was summoned, but many of them were soon sympathetic to the strikers.

Some 1,200 strikers had joined the union by the time the Italian consul, Dr. Guiseppe Cuneo, arrived from Denver at the behest of the company. He did not voice support for the strikers. A Salt Lake City paper attacked them as "an alien class, ignorant in most cases, unlettered." In late December the company reopened its mine but hired only those rejecting the union. Mostly Mormon strikebreakers were first hired, but the company soon had to turn to blacks and "aliens"—Japanese and two dozen Greeks, which marked the beginning of an important ethnic shift in Carbon County. As the strike dragged on, support faded, and after one year the UMW gave 250 miners money to leave; the Italians who chose to remain never returned to the mines, their places taken by a rising number of Greek strikebreakers, who in turn would lead a major strike there in 1922.

The broader context for these four 1903 strikes[2] included a major convention that had taken place in San Francisco in which initial hostility toward Chinese immigrants was expanded by a soon renamed Japanese and Korean

Exclusion League, the recent end of the war between Americans and Filipino rebels in the Philippines, and the start of a major economic boom that would be followed by six years out of the next ten in which over a million immigrants would be admitted each year. Between 1901 and 1910 nearly 8.8 million immigrants would enter the country. These four strikes thus all occurred on the eve of events with significant ramifications.

The Spanish-American War (1898) had marked a new level of Americans' assumption of white, Anglo-American superiority. The reaction to the war itself reinforced demeaning attitudes toward peoples of color and etched more deeply negative assumptions about the inferiority of different ("non-white") races. The Japanese and Korean Exclusion League's emergence in 1905, as we shall see, represented that fulcrum on which anti-Chinese hostility was now tipping toward anti-Japanese sentiments and then hostility directed against others from Asia, with profound long-term consequences for all these communities.

Meanwhile, the strikes did dramatize the immigrant workers' central role in various economic sectors, illustrating the increasingly heavy dependency on them across the region. The huge influx of immigrant workers that followed would further fuel the economic expansion underway in the West, but the 1903 episodes had revealed that inter-ethnic friction was quite persistent (especially the hostility of white Americans and northern Europeans toward others), even though the strikes also demonstrated that newer groups were either familiar with unions and militant labor actions or that they learned quickly and would not always remain passive victims or perennial scabs to be exploited by owners and managers. Or both. That inter-ethnic cooperation took place in several of these confrontations was also a significant indicator of more to follow. That the 1903 Mexican-led strike in Clifton-Morenci is considered the most significant in Arizona prior to the First World War reinforces these points still further.[3]

CHAPTER NINE

Foreshadowing
Twentieth-Century Patterns

*T*HERE WAS AT LEAST ONE other event during 1903 that renders it a pivotal year, an appropriate break point between the first era of this work and the opening of the new century. During the month of the Oxnard strike, March 1903, President Theodore Roosevelt signed into law two Acts of March 3, one codifying U.S. immigration law and the other limiting eligibility for citizenship. A year and a half earlier, President William McKinley had been assassinated by anarchist Leon Czolgosz. Now, Congress took another unprecedented step, adding to the list of those immigrants who were inadmissible "anarchists, or persons who believe in or advocate the over throw [of governments or the rule of law] by force or violence." The United States could henceforth bar prospective immigrants on the basis of their political beliefs, a provision with profound consequences ever since. The naturalization law disqualified from citizenship any person "who is opposed to all organized government, or who is a member of or affiliated with any organization entertaining and teaching" such ideas or the propriety of assaulting or killing government officials. In addition, the immigration legislation, besides detailing all the numerous categories of persons now denied admission, provided for the deportation of illegal aliens—up to three years after admission.[1]

Our narrative has begun with the last quarter of the nineteenth century because events during that period foreshadow much that unfolded in the lives of immigrants in the twentieth-century West. It was clearly an era in transition, decades marked by continuity and change—continuities that would not cease in 1900 and changes that would segue into other novel developments shaping the West. Thus, we turned to Scandinavians, Germans, Mexicans, and Chinese as representative of the "old" immigrant groups, yet Scandinavians and Germans would continue to arrive in significant numbers prior to the First World War; the number of Mexicans crossing the border, spurred by the economic pressures and the 1910 Revolution, would jump enormously; and while the number of migrants from China understandably declined, a new category of Chinese soon began entering the country—principally paper sons and daughters of those claiming to be native-born Chinese Americans—along with sizeable numbers of other Asians.

The broad array of occupations held by the nineteenth-century newcomers, whose numbers in the West exceeded 1.1 million by 1900, underscored the theme of their critical contribution to the growth of the region. At the same time, their economic Americanization soon became apparent in their labor actions—joining unions and striking—that recurred from Hawai'i to Colorado. Americans responded differently to the various populations newly arriving. Some were seen from the outset at assets, especially those going into farming and related occupations; others were viewed as inferior, of questionable whiteness, candidates for exploitation and dual wage arrangements; and the Chinese, among the top half-dozen foreign-born groups as late as 1900, were viewed as so alien as to pose an economic and cultural threat. They had to be removed or their numbers dramatically reduced.

That pressure on the federal government to remedy this "problem" coincided with the surfacing of American nationalism, energized by the impressive growth of the post-Reconstruction nation. The convergence of political issues and nationalist sentiments prompted the government to assert the nation's sovereignty by enacting unprecedented legislation that marked the beginning of strong federal controls over admissions and naturalizations and the creation of a bureaucracy to define and implement the watershed laws. They especially targeted a people perceived as a racial threat, the Chinese, and then added to the various classifications of generally objectionable individuals (e.g., those impoverished, diseased, mentally disturbed, likely to engage in immoral behavior) those whose political beliefs (anarchism in particular) were thought to pose a threat to the nation's stability—in a sense a politicized version of the fears regarding the Chinese. They were, of course, markedly different kinds of "threats," but the actions taken against both revealed Americans' racial attitudes and their anxieties about political non-conformists: singling out two species of deviation (racial/cultural and ideological) that enable us to look back and identify the limits of Americans' tolerance. The peoples of the West would grapple with such issues repeatedly during the twentieth century.

The same nationalist fervor that led to assertions of sovereignty at home also fed the passions of imperialist enterprises abroad, which led to the annexation of Hawai'i and the partial incorporation of the Philippines (and other islands). They quickly played significant roles in the western economy as well as in the racial composition of the West, adding further to the racial anxieties that thereafter periodically beset the region.

Briefly put, the opening era well lays out for us the four themes that unite this narrative. We see representative groups arriving who continued to enter and came to be viewed as the forward points of a continuing immigration that doubled the foreign-born population in the West by 1920 (1890–1920), further enriching its diversity. We witness the critically important and very diverse economic roles these newcomers performed as consumers as well as producers. We confront the dramatic watershed of federal regulations and bureaucratic control. And, finally, we recognize that these immigrants went through important stages of adjustment, which deepened the mark they made on American society. For those choosing to remain, their experiences helped them define the ways they might be able to fit into American society. They thereby modeled patterns of acculturation and accommodation—from limited to substantial— that most subsequent immigrants who also planned to settle replicated throughout the twentieth century. The links they forged materially defined their ties with American society and the quality and longevity of the bonds with their homelands.

PART 2.

Opening and Closing Doors, 1903–1923

W. E. B. DuBois wrote soon after 1900 that the central problem of the new century would be "the problem of the color line."[1] From the vantage point of over 100 years later, we now recognize that in the American West the problem of race had split into two aspects: a multiplicity of color lines and the insatiable need for immigrant labor. The latter was heavily responsible for fostering the pluralism of the former; the former, in many cases, profoundly shaped the character and dynamics of the latter. Of course, immigration was not entirely the cause for all color lines. Native Americans, African Americans, and most pre-1900 Mexican descendants remained victims of color lines largely apart from any immigration. On the other hand, not all immigrant groups faced the hurdles and constraints of color lines, but for those who did the results were often tragic; for the others those same walls of prejudice and discrimination frequently worked to their advantage by reducing job competition and facilitating their own advancement.

The successive waves of immigrants and migrants ensured that the history of the twentieth-century American West would be riven with the fissures of color lines. If it is self-deceiving to envision the people of the West today without the evolving rainbow of color lines, it is equally misguided to describe its present racial configuration without reference to the serial in-migrations from around the country and across the globe.

There are two emphases in part 2. First, we examine those whose admissions heavily predate 1903, for example the Chinese, Norwegians, Swedes, and French, who exemplified a range of experiences in the West that suggests the important and varied roles they played. These diverse groups contributed a broad array of skills, but their very diversity at times provoked waves of competitiveness and nativism that became embedded in the nation's legal systems. We also turn to those whose principal migration took place in the early twentieth century, including the Japanese and other Asians, Greeks, Italians, Basques,

Portuguese, Armenians, and especially Mexicans. We approach early-twentieth-century ethnicity by examining these new groups that became more visible along with the continuing impact of the older ones. Doing so allows us to compare experiences and to see how the different populations coped with and contributed to life in the new century. The second emphasis for these two decades is on the major investigations of immigrants, the further trend-setting legislation regarding admissions and naturalizations, and the impact of the First World War on immigrant communities. Federal and state laws became more restrictive and immigrants were compelled to adapt to the expanded controls and restrictions. A significant portion of part 2 is devoted to these momentous developments.

We begin with six immigrant and second-generation stories—by a Greek, Dane, Jew, Japanese, and two Italians; three men and three women—stories that take us to the beginning of the century and illustrate the central themes highlighting both their experiences and the broader framework by which we can better grasp the escalating number and variety of newcomers.

CHAPTER TEN

Immigrant Stories and the West in the 1900s

ARGYRIS KARAHAL WAS 15 when he and a half-dozen other young men from his small village in northern Peloponnesus, Greece, went by horses to Kalávrita, where they caught a train to Athens.[1] His father had borrowed over $100 for his son's ticket to America plus the "show money" needed upon arrival at Ellis Island. He had wanted his son to become a monk, but Argyris had envied his uncles who had been sending money back home and who had now returned from America. "I got jealous . . . and wanted to go and be like them, have a little money in my pocket, and that was the fever in 1905." Still, it was hard to part with his family: "I was afraid and I cry, especially when I kissed my grandmother and my father and mother." It was even more difficult for some of the other boys, who were only 12 years old. Yet, they began the journey, and Argyris estimated that there were about 300 young Greek boys on the ship, many of whom he knew from school. The general plan was "to make money and go back [to Greece] in four or five years." Although he knew no English, Argyris was optimistic that he would succeed by teaching Greek to Americans: "I thought everybody wanted to learn Greek." Quickly he realized that this was not the case. He tried peddling with his uncle Antonios in Chicago, living with 15 to 20 others in one room above a stable. But he was too bashful to go through the streets with his uncle and an old, blind horse, shouting out the fruits and vegetables they had for sale. He did go to the Hull House in the evenings to learn English.

Then Argyris was hired for a construction crew on the Southern Pacific Railroad out in Burbank, California, along with perhaps 60 other youths who had been on the ship and had also gone to Chicago in search of employment. The combination of manual labor and hot weather rapidly proved to be too much for Argyris, who was small and slender. He stayed on as a water boy for the construction crew. About one and a half years passed, by which time the group of young men had begun to split up: "some of them stayed in California, some of them come to Texas, some stay in Chicago, some they went to Utah, and some going up to different places in the United States, [especially Georgia]." Argyris went first to Pasadena and took a job digging ditches, which he soon found unendurable. By that time, his uncle from Chicago had come out to California. He began working as a gardener and employed his nephew. A cousin of Argyris's father (whom he also referred to as his uncle) was similarly self-employed in California but disliked it. He migrated to Temple, Texas, south of Waco, and began selling taffy and other candy from a cart. He prospered enough to open a store and invited Argyris to join him "because he thought I was speaking good English, better English than he did."

After a few years his "uncle" sold the business, and the two went to Houston, where they teamed up with a third Greek to purchase a "picture show" (movie house) offering ten-minute movies for five cents. In 1910 they sold it for a profit of $200 each. His uncle, who was 26–28 years old, next opened a confectionery store and went back to Greece to find a wife, which he did, returning with her six months later. The uncle and the other Greek partner then advanced Argyris credit and supplies to begin a confectionery business in Marshall, Texas, near the Louisiana state border. Argyris in turn wrote to a schoolmate living in California, inviting him to join him in the business. They were the only two Greeks in Marshall, but they prospered, and Argyris soon paid for tickets to bring over two brothers from Greece. In a gesture to gain acceptance in Marshall, the four Greeks kept the shop closed on Sunday mornings and all four would go to church—"any churches, especially Catholic and Baptist and Methodist."

Yet, they felt lonesome. Argyris learned that his uncle had taken over a confectionery in Waco—originally called Karahal's Candy Kitchen and renamed the Palace of Sweets. The uncle offered Argyris a half share. It was 1912. Argyris sold his Marshall business, made a $3,500 profit, and took out a loan for over $10,000 to buy out his uncle's partner. With the Hippodrome Theatre and Baylor University nearby, they were quite successful. Then, World War One began. Although not a citizen, 27-year-old Argyris enlisted. While he was stationed near San Antonio, the Palace of Sweets continued to generate considerable profits. When in 1920 his sister died, Argyris made his first return trip to Greece after an absence of 15 years. A year passed—"I was glad to see my family, but that year I miss the United States. I wanted to come back." He returned to Waco, bringing his 14-year-old sister. The Palace, with seating for 120, remained profitable until the Depression. However, because the business was doing relatively well—the children "didn't have any other place to go then"—

Argyris and his uncle slowly recovered, charging 5 cents for ice cream, 10 cents for an ice cream soda, and 15 cents for a banana split. Argyris recalled that Greeks all over the country were establishing confectionery businesses, even in small places. He estimated there were about 50 in Texas, and all were called Olympia or Palace of Sweets, he claimed. "And one from another they learn something that they thought would be profitable." He was eventually earning about $1,000 per year, "big money at that time," and in 1937, at aged 47, he decided to go to Greece to find a wife and bring her back, which he did.

Argyris completed his account with three comments. First, initially many Greeks worked in mines and on railroads, yet many also apprenticed themselves in shoeshine shops and confectioneries. He believed that many of the latter prospered enough to add on restaurants. Second, "Now [1971] most of the Greeks they are in the restaurant business," whereas the second-generation Greeks became "professionals. Lawyers, doctors—lots of doctors. Prominent doctors." Third, many Greeks attended church, especially Episcopalian churches. In the Greek churches, such as in Houston, "They speak English. The ceremony's in English. Of course some of the rest is in Greek. Some in Greek and some in English. But the ceremony's in English all the time for the new generation."

So well did Andrew Sorenson recall where he and other Danes farmed in Kittitas County, east of Seattle, that he drew a map identifying the location of some 24 farms more than 65 years earlier in the area known then as the Danish Farming District (see map 2).[2] Andrew was born there around 1900 and grew up there. His father had left Denmark at age 18 to avoid military service. Upon arriving in the United States, he made his way westward until he could take the Northern Pacific Railroad bound for Seattle. Although recruited for logging work, his father jumped off the train in Ellensburg, in Kittitas County. He married there in 1895 and bought an 80-acre section in what became the Denmark (or Danish Farming) District. It had opened up after irrigation was extended to the area by a farmer's co-op. Dairy farming was popular, and many Danes there had cows: "I'll swear to this day [my parents] had 150 [cows] and I had to milk them." Perhaps there were not really that many, but the farmers did begin to pool their butter, developing a creamery, establishing a co-operative by the early 1920s, and adopting the brand name Darigold two decades later. Andrew, who eventually took over his father's farm, became a board member in 1934.

Unofficially, the primary school he attended was referred to as "The Denmark School." The Danish parents, who had not had much education, encouraged their children to go on to college, and while there was some antagonism between Danes and the "Yankees" that "would creep up from time to time" and some real social distance among the Danes, by themselves the Danes generally got along. Yet Andrew found that apart from his family "others were pretty

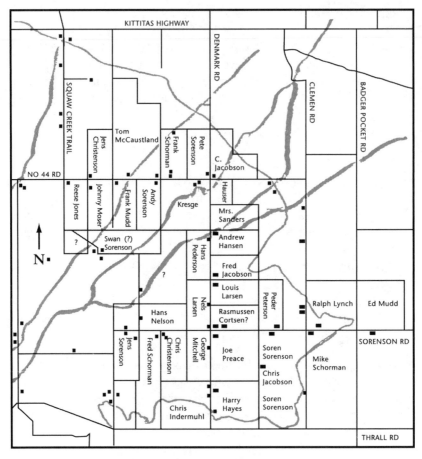

KITTITAS COUNTY, WASHINGTON   **SCALE: 1 inch = ½ mile**
Township 17 N., Range 19 E.W.M.

Map 2. Land ownership in the Denmark farming district of Kittitas County (1905–1910) as remembered by Andrew Sorenson. *From an interview with Andy Sorenson, March 20, 1975, KITTITAS Project, KIT 75-9sa, Washington State Archives.*

much clannish, that is they knew each other from the old country and they were . . . self-satisfied with their own company." They had come from Jylland, the main peninsula of the country, whereas his father had come from Sjaelland (the island on which lies Copenhagen) and his mother from the small island of Bornholm in the Baltic Sea.

Many of the other families had come to America with the attitude that "if they wanted to talk Danish they would have stayed in Denmark. They tried to talk English." Andrew's family felt differently, and "I couldn't speak a word of English until I started school. . . . I don't believe any of those [other] second generation out there could speak a word of Danish." When interviewed in 1975, he said he would speak Danish "if I can find someone to talk to," yet his own children spoke no Danish because "I couldn't get them to sit still long enough" to learn it. Akin to the language division, he noted that the Danes were quite active politically but "were split all over the place." For example, his father was Republican, and all the rest of his family were Democrats. In terms of tradition, his family had continued to eat Danish food because his mother had gone to cooking school before migrating to America, and he had maintained contact with relatives in Denmark. He had visited there twice, for "the biggest part of my family is still in Denmark." He went with his father in 1925; in 1961 he took his wife and two children, spending two months there "to renew acquaintances."

Orphaned at 16, young Nina Kanyer came from a city in eastern Italy that had been Italy's but was transferred to Yugoslavia following World War One. She had worked as a bookbinder before deciding to migrate to America in 1921 to join her brother in the mining community of Roslyn, a small town of about 3,000 persons in the Wenatchee Mountains southeast of Seattle. The following year she married Tony, a Yugoslav immigrant coal miner. Disturbed and disappointed by the conditions in Roslyn, which she regarded as backward even compared with those in Italy, she contemplated returning home. "It was really rough here. It was just the basic mining town, and rough . . . the men was rough. And still when we was talking to the elder people that was here, they say that we had it made, compared to what they went through."

Nevertheless, going back was not a realistic option: "But since that time . . . I did try to adjust. I say, 'no way to go back.' So I tried to learn the way that it's here, and I'm happy. I would be a lot more happier if I had, you know, my family closer, things like that. . . . [Still,] I was one of the lucky ones, I wasn't really ever broke." But life in the 1920s and 1930s was a struggle. In their first home, it was so drafty and cold that when she carried warm water for male lodgers to wash, "it was frozen by the time I took [it] upstairs." They had no refrigerator, and she relied on a vegetable garden, canning, smoking sausages, and home-made beer and wine. In addition, she acknowledged that the mines were dangerous, the strikes costly, the wages sometimes uncertain, and at times workers had to pay the bosses to get hired. The men would emerge from the coal mines so blackened the children would ask, "Who's that man coming?" And, "when he washed clean they didn't recognize him." The fires, explosions, strikes, accidents, and illnesses convinced the mothers to "make sure that the children don't go [to work] in the mine."

On the other hand, Nina did not recall discrimination directed against her because she was Italian; she felt "I'm just as good if not better than the next one" in part because she went to night school: "I did want to improve myself." For the most part, each ethnic group generally kept to itself, and she and her husband frequently went to the Italian lodge for dances, picnics, and simply to have some fun, seeing that "It was a big production to go to Seattle . . . you're almost preparing the whole week." Nonetheless, although the immigrant adults tended to remain socially apart (except "when something was community"), "the children was all together, didn't make any differences what the parents [said or did]."

Nina gave birth to two sons. Both served in World War Two and Korea. Although she had not worked outside the home after her marriage, during that World War she did take a job in a cannery. When asked how she felt about Italy being "on the other side," she replied, "my family is American. I was American the day I got married, because my husband [took out his citizenship] . . . before we got married. So, I always thought that America was my country." When asked about how other Italians felt, she noted that many had come even before World War One, and the fact that "so many came here so young . . . they didn't even have any, how would I say, love for the old country, because they . . ." "Didn't have any ties to it?" asked the interviewer. "Yeah, because they came early."[3]

Camilla Saivetto's sister lived in Seattle and encouraged her to come to America because, "if I would come to this country, the way I always did work, I would be a millionaire in no time!" Unhappy with life in her home and with her father's drinking, she fled at age 15 and, turning 18 during World War One, worked for two and a half years in a foundry. She subsequently started a knitting business with three women employees. At that point, "I decided to drop everything and come to America," which she did in 1920, departing Piedmont, in northern Italy. Steerage conditions on board the ship convinced her that "if I had to go back like that [to Italy] I'd rather be dead . . . I would never go through [it]!" Yet, "It took me a long time to get used to America because America, it was hard to understand; you have to make yourself completely over." With some exceptions, such as her clothing. You see, Camilla was about 20 when she arrived and was accustomed to wearing short dresses several years before the style caught on in the States. "Everybody expect me to look like old country. . . . you know them old people come with long dresses, but I dressed more in style than the people here." Workers in the street would comment on how she showed off her legs, she said. "My dresses are . . . what can I do about it? They [were] all short." She would not change even though she soon married an Italian miner, James (whom most called "Jocko"), who was far more traditional. They also lived in Roslyn, where Camilla became friends with Nina Kanyer.

Camilla's acculturation continued, and she pointed out how she had had to learn about the foods and shopping, although easing the situation were the many Italian stores and Italian-speaking merchants. Moreover, "they used to deliver at home, too. When I used to tell my husband, 'You would want to go back to the old country? Look at the service we get here. . . . Go to the old country, are you nuts?' I said, 'You go yourself.'" Meanwhile, "I'd always try so hard to improve myself, to be an American, that's what I wanted to be. When my kids were born, I couldn't speak English very well and I didn't want them to go to school and talk broken English. . . . [I]t should be learned correctly."

Shifting her focus to a topic dear to her, she continued. "I wanted to be an American citizen and my husband didn't want me to go to school. They had night school in them days, and he wouldn't let me go. I said, 'But, I think you're unreasonable. If you are not ambitious enough, please don't stop me. I got to learn how to read and write.' So, I went to school and I got my papers and then I pestered him and pestered him to get his papers. I said, 'You want to be so many years in this country [without being a citizen].' 'Oh, I don't want to stay here all my life,' he said. 'When we have enough money, we are going to go to old country.' I said, 'You can go by yourself. I'm staying right where I am. I'm not going back to Italy for no money, and you just make up your mind if you want to go, you'll be on your own.' He finally gave up. . . . he could see that I meant what I said." Eventually, he also admitted to her that he must have "had a rock in [his] brain . . . to forbid [her] to go to school when [she] wanted to go so bad." Worried about what might happen if another war broke out, she continually urged him to become a citizen. Finally, he responded to her urging and did so.[4]

While Camilla took in laundry to make money in order to improve their home, such as remodeling the bathroom to include "one of the first bathtubs in Roslyn," Jocko also had to deal with divisions in the miners' unions, strikes, the dependency on the company store—where "the minute the miners would go on strike the credit was cut off"—the murder of union leader Bob Ruff, and especially poor health due to the working conditions: "My husband's lungs are really bad. Doctors . . . said that his lungs are like a sponge, so full of phlegm and everything. [H]is back and both feet were broken in mining accidents and, during the union organizing strike of the late 1930s, he secured a job building highways, but cement dust burned his eyes because he wore no goggles." Enduring it all, he went back to the mines after the strike, continued until he retired in 1953, age 64, and then resumed mining until the early 1960s, when they began closing the mines. By that time, Jocko was drawing Social Security and a United Mine Workers pension.

At the time of her interview in 1976, Jessie Bloom, 89 years old, had been living in Alaska for 54 years. Her parents had migrated from Lithuania to Cork, Ireland, in 1880. Their name had originally been Shapiro, but in Ireland they had it changed to Spiro. They soon moved on to Dublin, where her father, a Talmudic scholar, eked out a living as a sub-agent selling passenger tickets to migrants bound for the Americas. Her mother earned money preparing legal documents for those seeking to remain in Great Britain.[5] Jessie was born there in December 1887 and grew up in Dublin until around 1910, when she got a secretary's position in London. Back in Dublin the following year for a vacation, she met a childhood friend and second cousin, Robert Bloom, who had come back for a family visit from Fairbanks, Alaska, where he owned a general merchandise store. Bob and Jessie agreed to wed, but he had to return promptly to Alaska. He told her to remain in Dublin and that he would send her the wages lost from her London job until he could come for the wedding the following year. She described herself as "a kept woman" until he arrived in May 1912. They wed, sailed for America, and went on to Seattle and then to Fairbanks. Over the next five and a half years they had four daughters.

When they arrived in Fairbanks, Jessie found that Bob had been living behind the store and that the town was still outgrowing its early stage as a mining camp. Bob had the whole building moved next to a carpenter's shop run by a Norwegian and then he attached the two buildings together. The kitchen was a log structure connected to the shop. Soon, Bob had the building lifted and enlarged. Notwithstanding all the challenges, Jessie was prepared, for in Dublin Bob had "told me that I'd. . . . [have] an entirely different type of life to what I had been leading in London. So I was ready for anything." Her husband had also stressed that "he didn't want to do any business with women and he didn't want them in the store." His customers—prospectors, trappers, and woodcutters—"felt more comfortable if there were no women around."

Part of adapting involved working around the demands of extreme seasons. Thus, they would order their whole "outfit" for delivery once the river was navigable—the outfit being one's groceries and all one's staples for an entire year. Jessie supplemented it with a garden and moose or caribou meat kept frozen on the back porch. In one of several long separations, Bob sent Jessie on ahead to Dublin to have her second child while he went east to buy supplies. She arrived in Ireland in September 1914. The First World War had just begun. She remained there through the April 1916 Irish Easter Rebellion in Dublin and the massive British assault crushing it. In June the American consul quickly granted Jessie U.S. citizenship to enable her to depart at once on an American ship bound for the States.

In 1923 she went to Seattle while Bob was going there for merchandise, but because "the navigable season [was] so short" and "because once the winter comes it was difficult to get in or out," she had to remain there for two years. Jessie pointed out, "It's nothing unusual with Alaska unions [marriages] . . . to be separated in those days." Later, when she sent her daughters to school in Dublin in 1928, Jessie remained there with them until 1937. Bob came only in 1932–1933, and Jessie went back to Fairbanks for their 25th anniversary. A year later, in July 1938—having left Jessie to run the store—Bob sailed for Ireland to visit his daughters and returned the following March. Jessie's account ends with one daughter becoming "an American doctor" in London during the war and another becoming an architect who wed an Englishman.

Little was said in Jessie's interview about ethnicity, or about ethnic ties. We know Bob originally bought his building in Fairbanks from Jewish merchants in Seattle and that commercial connections between Seattle and Alaska did involve Jewish merchants.[6] Although this interview was done for a Jewish project, the combination of the Spiro family changes that began in Ireland and the nature of the early community Bob and Jessie found in Fairbanks would suggest that their particular experiences were far more ethnically neutral and their integration quite advanced.

To set forth one contrast, the Blooms' experiences certainly differed, for example, from those of the early Norwegians in Petersburg, in southeast Alaska's Inside Passage. That community centered around the canneries established in the mid-1890s by Peter Buschmann, a Norwegian immigrant from Trøndelag. Predominantly, Norwegians worked in his canneries, and Norwegian fishermen gravitated there and did much of the catching, achieving enormous success with trap fishing rather than nets and seines. By 1940 the community was 98 percent Norwegian, and for years Norwegian was the principal language spoken there. The Sons of Norway Hall, built in 1912, remains a prominent feature of the community, which continues to number around 3,300 persons, not many more than in 1940. The city's Website in 2003 still offered the greeting "Velkommen to Petersburg, Alaska" and proudly noted that "the biggest week of the year" is the "Little Norway Festival" that, for the past forty years, has fallen "around May 17, Norway's Constitution Day"—a celebration of "the homeland of Peterburg's founding families."[7]

Chotoku Toyama's life was quite different from the other accounts profiled here, and so was his account. When he wrote it in 1924, he was a student at the University of Southern California.[8] He was born in a coastal town in northern Hokkaido, Japan, in the mid-1890s. His father was president of the school there. Upon completing high school, Chotoku moved to Tokyo to continue at the Buddhist-run Nichiren University. He lived and studied there for a decade and came to view himself as an "Oriental made man." He added (writing now in California) that that did "not mean the impossibility of Americanization," and therefore assimilation, "if I wish to do so." His assessment was that "All Japanese immigrants also have become Americanized greatly and they are wishing to do so. . . . I would say that the Japanese in California could become Americanized except that they are not given the chance or room to do so."

Chotoku had first learned about America from a teacher in Japan and from Japanese returning from the United States. It was especially admired after the First World War "by all Japan" and "was known as the richest country in the world." In fact, the image among "the average Japanese" was "that all Japanese immigrants in America, especially in California, are supposed to be very rich. . . . *America kaeri* ('come back from America') is used as an expression for 'rich man.'" Indeed, some return and "act like millionaires for the demonstration of marriage, while they are nothing but poor farmers, employees, or gardeners. . . . In general, it was believed. . . . that one could get money easily in America." However, Chotoku had also heard about the Asian exclusion movement in California and "the anti-Japanese atmosphere" there. Despite advice to the contrary, he journeyed to Los Angeles in December 1920, sailing in first-class accommodations. He was obligated by his arrangement to remain in Los Angeles for at least two years under the supervision of the Nichiren Buddhist church (located in Seattle, San Francisco, and Los Angeles).

Some of his acculturation process had begun even before he migrated, for Chotoku had been informed that America was "the 'lady first' country, while Japan is a 'man first' country." This called to his mind the Japanese view that "the man who is too kind or blindly loves his wife is called '*Sainoroji*' (. . . namely, the man who is stupid or too sweet on his wife). In America all men seemed to me as '*Sainoroji*.'" Chotoku also learned that "In America the people have many keys, whereas in Japan few have a key." When his unlocked apartment was robbed, he understood why "America is a 'key' country as well as a country of democracy and money. . . . Of course, 'key' itself means 'distrust for others.'" Part of his acculturation also involved his recognition that he could read and write English, but his "enunciation was not right." That proved to be important, for while silence and courage were virtues of Japanese men, "the American lady and gentleman easily speak to each other socially."

Chotoku discovered other elements of Americanization: "Japanese immigrants had become intolerant," and they had changed. In America "they are neither pure Japanese, nor American; they are hybrid in the mental and physical condition." He attributed that to "the influence of Japanese exclusion atmosphere in California and sex relations (lack of women)." Other things that "shocked" him included the housing discrimination, the "dangers of crossing streets," and the "leg dance or shimmy," the kissing, "the candor with which Americans discuss love affairs and sentimental matters in their daily conversations," "the freedom of young women," and the extent to which the "American-born children [Nisei] are quite American, both in thought and custom." Consequently, "the foreign born parents cannot harmonize with them," sometimes resulting in conflicts "between parents and children." Among the Issei, first-generation immigrants, the antidote was thought to be the Japanese language schools for the Nisei, he observed, in order "to overcome the language handicap between parents and children . . . , but this is not so effective, because the children do not like to speak Japanese. They never speak Japanese except to their parents, therefore they make little progress."

Chotoku also emphasized (and somewhat exaggerated) the impact of the

California Alien Land Law on the stability of Japanese families: "[T]hey are obliged to move from one place to another all the time as employees." The "economic handicaps" made them "nomadic, unsettled, and restless." Some doubted the existence of any justice in America, and others were trying to move to Mexico or South America or to change occupations. Even students seeking housing in Los Angeles (including Chotoku), such as in Hollywood, Rose Hill, and Boyle Heights, encountered notices declaring "Japanese Keep Out," "Swat the Jap," and "No more Japanese wanted here."

Chotoku's concluding observations were that "All Americans are too proud of their racial superiority"; they proclaim democracy but fail to include "the spirit of democracy"; "they are social and efficient in the use of inventions but act as if 'money is everything.'" Economically, America is "a capitalistic autocracy"; and "Americans misunderstand and misjudge foreign peoples" due to their "'America First' point of view." Nevertheless, most Japanese immigrants "cannot live in Japan again, because they are too much Americanized." If they do return, they "come back to America very soon."

Once again we have six brief life stories that outline a host of issues and themes which are repeated among numerous groups during the early twentieth century and thereafter. All four dimensions of change can be found in these accounts. The migrants tended to be quite young, disproportionately male, and most often single, and many had constructed images of American wealth before they departed their homelands. Not uncommonly, it was those same images that prompted their initial decisions to go. What people related about America in letters and articles weighed heavily but could not entirely outweigh the sight of those actually returning. In so far as they could, such individuals literally wore their success (or relative success). They had begun to change styles of clothing and behavior, values, aspirations, and language, while expressing a zest for the pace of American life. It was infectious; it bred a fever, even among modest young Japanese ladies considering marriage proposals from across the sea.

Whereas geographic mobility was a general thread in many narratives, once in America Nina and Camilla married and remained in Rosyln, where their husbands worked, just as Andy remained in Kittitas County, where he was born and raised and later farmed. On the other hand, Argyris's many journeys to Chicago, California, and across central and east Texas could not match Jessie and Bob Bloom's multi-year forays from Fairbanks to Seattle and Ireland. Their attachment to Dublin was singular for the duration of times abroad and the periods apart from one another. However, they never abandoned their niche in Fairbanks, nor did Andy or Nina and Camilla forsake theirs, nor, for example, did the numerous Norwegian cannery workers and fishermen in Petersburg, Alaska. Argyris eventually found his, too, and his travels, business ventures, and return to visit Greece to find a spouse—along with his sponsorship of two brothers and a sister—characterized the experiences of many newcomers.

If Argyris's tireless entrepreneurialism (given his modest roots) typified the attitudes of others we encounter—such as Armenians, Lebanese, Jews, Chinese, and Japanese—the struggles, uncertainties, dangers, and outright exploitation endured by the immigrant miners of Roslyn would confront many thousands of other immigrants in the West. And that was the case not only in copper, coal, and other hard rock mines but also on railroad construction and maintenance crews, in logging operations, on large-scale industrial farms, and from urban construction projects to merchant ships at sea. Meanwhile, Andy's attachment to the Denmark District and the successful co-operative founded there would have parallels in other rural communities where immigrants owned, leased, or rented land (such as the Japanese in the Hood River Valley and Germans in and around Castroville, Texas), along with the critical labor that immigrants provided during harvest times throughout the West. What runs through many of these accounts is the conviction that in America opportunity was a real possibility, especially for the children: they did not need to remain on the farm or ranch, or in tiny hamlets, and certainly not down in the mines.

This belief in the children's future was part of a larger pattern of adaptation and accommodation. Chotoku stresses the extent to which America was changing the newcomer—to the degree that they could not readily go home and remain contented there, just as Argyris could not remain in Greece after one year. Even though more than an estimated 35 percent of those arriving from Europe in the early twentieth century did return home (with some groups, such as the Chinese, Japanese, Greeks, French, and Italians, having return rates between 45 and 50 percent), the impression of displacement from the homeland endured.[9] In reality, many immigrants here did change, often under the gentle but persistent pressures to acculturate that suffused so much of what they encountered or, more forcefully, when they were confronted with the more abrasive and insistent demands of the Americanization programs of the First World War era. The exceptions would be those who were quite isolated in an enclave carved out by choice or developed out of necessity in the face of hostility from the dominant group or other minorities. Over time, in most settings we see evidence of changes in foods, language usage, religion, values and habits, patterns of association, attitudes favoring citizenship, and, especially, gender relations—the extent of independence many women found, nurtured, and expanded, including the choice of marriage partners.

Several individuals referred to the inter-generational language problems that often created a gulf between parents and children or chasms across communities. Andy describes other (some times political) intra-group divisions; Nina refers to the social distance between the newer ethnic groups; and Chotoku, while unsettled by the behavioral differences between Americans and Japanese and the hostilities and legal obstacles facing many Japanese immigrants, nonetheless concludes that the Issei he has observed have become too Americanized to return to Japan.

Finally, behind many of these accounts were concerns about regulations that could affect the newcomers' ability to return to the United States after visits to their homelands. The administration of the laws could be positive or negative. During the 1916 rebellion in Ireland, Jessie was hastily given U.S. citizenship to enable her to depart quickly for America. Camilla benefited from the change in naturalization laws that allowed her to apply independently for citizenship. Chotoku, however, was disturbed by the government-supported Americanization program and specifically by the impact of the Alien Land Acts on the Japanese. Once again, we see that immigration does not take place in a vacuum, and the new legislation regulating admissions, citizenship, and wartime (and post-wartime) programs directed at the foreign born certainly troubled immigrants. At critical times, such events influenced their decisions about their plans in America. The theme concerning government actions, as with the other three overriding themes of change, cuts across our entire time period.

These short accounts demonstrate how reactions to new land versus homeland spanned the spectrum from disengagement to translocalism to transnationalism. Out of a variety of motives, many immigrant men and women determined to settle and remain in America and returned only sporadically to their homeland, preserving shallow ties. Others, who experienced mixed sentiments about remaining permanently, elected to stay and and began to adapt to their new home, gradually (sometimes imperceptibly) distancing themselves from their homeland and maintaining sporadic, limited bonds. Still others, more determined to return to their homeland or to retain strong connections to it, kept it close to their heart, holding on and as firmly attached to it as others were detached. What these stories offer is an insight into how the twentieth-century American West changed these immigrants just as the immigrants changed the West.

CHAPTER ELEVEN

Who Came?

THE FIRST DECADES of the new century proved to be symbolic of the West's dynamism and development for much of the rest of the century, although only one-ninth of the nation's population lived there in 1910. Of great relevance, the media revolution just getting underway was soon heavily concentrated in the West and commanded the nation's attention precisely because much of that revolution—the Hollywood industry and its productions—sharpened in very concrete ways the nation's awareness of the broader western transformation underway. However, the media mavens were not always attentive to the new peoples arriving in the region with the brains, brawn, and determination upon which much of western society and economy would come to depend. The spectacular achievements in many parts of the region frequently masked the darker side of this unfolding history: the considerable discrimination, racism, exploitation, and then deportations, internment, and both institutionalized and informal barriers of various kinds that many minority groups could not evade and that were slow to fall.

Immigrants were crucial (albeit unequal) partners in the region's growth, and they were critical (albeit unequal) targets of victimization. Whether we consider the immigrants' multiple contributions and achievements or the multiple hurdles and barriers they faced, their stories most often remained rather local, or forgotten, invisible to mainstream society, or, in the case of many of those of European descent who were eventually accepted by the mainstream society, long overlooked. Let a somewhat humorous observation published at the end of 1901 underscore the point. Joaquin Miller, a West Coast writer, published an essay on the Chinese and, having worked in mines, felt qualified to comment on the personal habits of miners, in particular about changing clothes and bathing:

I never knew a Chinese miner who did not. I never knew any other foreign miner who did. In fact, I never knew one of the other [non-Chinese] foreigners to take a bath of any kind, except by accident. . . . [Moreover,] I never saw a drunken Chinaman. I never saw a Chinese beggar. I never knew a lazy one. . . .[1]

Miller's lampoon of the anti-Chinese stereotypes would illustrate the ludicrousness of them except that their consequences were so drastic for the Chinese and, subsequently, for many other immigrant groups.

To set the stage, consider that the Chinese population in the West declined by nearly one-third between 1900 and 1910 and by another third during the next decade, due mostly to the Exclusion laws (emigration plus deaths; see chapter 4 in part 1). Decreases were reported in nearly every state. At the same time, Japanese communities soared by well over four-fifths and then by another 11 percent—figures that undoubtedly would have been greater had the Gentlemen's Agreement not been negotiated (1907–1908), shutting out Japanese laborers (see below).[2]

Nearly 9.6 million immigrants entered the United States between 1899 and 1910; however, the net foreign-born population grew by under 3.12 million (23.4 percent). In the West the foreign-born population jumped during this decade by over 56 percent; in the rest of the nation the increase was just over 27 percent. (During that decade the overall percentage growth in the West among the native born was triple that elsewhere in the country.) During the 1910s, in percentage terms, the West grew by twice as much as the remainder of the nation (26 percent versus 13 percent), and despite the war in Europe, even its foreign-born population expanded by one-sixth versus less than one percent elsewhere in the country. Include all foreigners in 1920 and the West's immigrant population had doubled since 1900 versus rising by only one-third outside the West.[3]

Equally dramatic, the second-generation white population in the West rose by far more than twice the percentage elsewhere in the first decade of the 1900s. Between 1900 and 1920, the white foreign stock (immigrants and second generation) came close to doubling in the West (a jump of more than 95 percent), whereas in all other regions that growth was just one-third. As a result, in 1910, nearly one-fifth of the West's *entire* population, was second generation—the children of immigrants. More specifically, 10 of the 12 mainland states had total populations that were one-fifth to one-quarter second generation. These figures were virtually the same in 1920. Taken together, the foreign stock remained at roughly 32 to 33 percent of the West's entire population during these decades. In other words, nearly one-third of the builders of the West at that time were the children of immigrants or immigrants themselves.[4]

It seems reasonable to expect that some of their influences contributed to the region's social and cultural development as well as its economic development. If we consider just music, it becomes quite evident that immigrants brought musical styles that were borrowed and absorbed by mainstream local societies, from Tex-Mex and salsa songs and dance to German and Scandinavian Sanger-fests and large-scale choral festivals (from Texas to Washington), to the Japanese *obon* dance festivals with the *bon odori* costumed dancers in Hawai'i and Los Angeles. Can one doubt the ubiquitousness of Chinese, Mexican, and Italian foods, with styles that vary with the different places of origin in the home countries? People became familiar with Scandinavian foods (perhaps even Norwegians' lutefisk), as they did with the Japanese noodle dishes (with saimin becoming Hawai'i's equivalent of hot dog fast foods). From Cinco de Mayo and September 16 (Mexican Independence Day) to the Chinese New Year to the Norwegians' Syttende Mai (May 17, Independence Day), immigrant festivals became widely accepted and often heavily attended by more and more persons across ethnic lines. Music, foods, festivals, and even cross-borrowing of words all reflect the cultural enrichment that accompanied the immigrants.

A major fourth area of cultural contributions falls under religion, for there is little doubt that the Catholicism of Mexicans, Basques, Irish, Germans, and southern and eastern Europeans (aside from the Eastern Orthodox) was quite pervasive in the West. The Lutheranism of the Scandinavians has left a considerable mark at the very least throughout the Pacific Northwest. Judaism in major centers, especially along the coast, the Mormonism of northern Europeans in Utah, and Japanese Buddhism in Hawai'i and various communities along the coast (along with smaller groups, such as the Sikhs, Armenians, and Germans from Russia) all had an impact on local communities, celebrations, social and mutual aid associations, and other community activities that gradually attracted non-members to observe and recognize these as part of the defining diversity of the region. As the number of inter-marriages rose, the likely exposure to these cultural practices also increased, even if only symbolically observed.

The character of the West that emerges by the time of the Roaring Twenties has been attributed, to a considerable degree, to Americans resettling from the East, Midwest, and South, whereas it was actually the product of the in-migrations of foreigners, their children, and Americans of various native-born generations and races.[5] Moreover, with a significant part of the resettlement patterns including moves by individuals relocating within the West, cultural patterns were most likely carried and shared. The argument here is that these diverse peoples entering as well as moving about the region were a dynamic factor shaping the West's milieu not just economically but also culturally. Old-time Americans did not migrate alone or build the West by themselves. We simply cannot dismiss the other one-third of the population.

These broad patterns obviously varied among the individual states and territories. If the Asian populations came to dominate the Hawaiian portrait, the Mexicans who began pouring into Texas, Arizona, and New Mexico shortly before, during, and after the Revolution would have an enormous impact on those states and territories—and soon from California to the Midwest. Similarly, the heavy Scandinavian and Canadian movements into the Northwest, especially Washington, helped influence the character of those states. The foreign-born populations doubled in Texas (a growth of 103 percent from 1900 to 1920) and California (more than 106 percent), but they were easily surpassed by Washington (more than 138 percent) and Arizona, whose foreign-born population more than tripled (from 24,233 to 80,566).

Other states' ethnic variations reflected fluctuating economic conditions—such as mining in Colorado, Wyoming, and Montana—and return migrations to homelands with the outbreak of the First World War. Utah, on the other hand, despite its mining operations, had experienced its major growth during the nineteenth-century Mormon in-migrations, and now its white foreign stock population limped upward, registering the smallest increase in resident foreigners (10 percent). In contrast, Texas experienced a huge economic transformation from ranching to cotton and fruit and vegetable production, attracting great numbers of aspiring white farmers (and investors) from the East and South. One in four white Texans in 1920 had come from another state, but they included the smallest percentage of second-generation Americans (6.6 percent) compared with the general regional average of about 20 percent.

A few group-specific examples underscore the remarkable diversity and vitality of the West at this time. Utah was now witnessing the passing of a generation with the drop in the number of foreign-born Danes, English, Scots, and Welsh and relatively small increases in Norwegian and Swedes. As a percentage of the total state population, the second generation also experienced a steep fall (from 42 percent to 31 percent, 1900 to 1920). Meanwhile, Arizona's mining communities were now drawing numerous workers from the Austrian Empire (such as Croatians, Montenegrins, and Slovenians), Greece, and Italy. With its prominent mining communities, notably Bisbee, Globe, Jerome, and Clifton-Morenci, and burgeoning agricultural industry, Arizona, as noted, saw its foreign-born population triple, but chiefly due to a doubling of the number of reported Mexicans.

During the first decade, Washington State experienced the largest percentage increase in foreign-born persons (130 percent), the preponderance of them Swedes, Danes, and Norwegians, together with Germans, Greeks, and peoples from the Russian Empire—as well as a near doubling of Canadians. Neighboring Oregon's foreign-born numbers rose by 72 percent by 1910, and, again, the principal groups were Canadians, Danes, Finns, Germans, Greeks, Italians, Norwegians, and Swedes. California's population, on the other hand, reflected the overlapping trends underway among old and new groups in this transition period during the first decade of the 1900s. Its populations of English, Danes, Scots, Germans, Norwegians, and Swedes all increased modestly but were outstripped by the strong gains in the number of Canadians, Mexicans, Greeks, Italians, Portuguese, Slavs, and others from the Austrian and Russian empires.

Hawai'i represented a distinctive case in one respect because its population included 12,500 persons of mixed Asian or Caucasian and Hawaiian ancestry. Its Chinese community dropped negligibly, whereas the number of Japanese rose by 6 percent (to 59,786). Besides Hawai'i, the Japanese were quite spread out on the mainland, with significant increases in Colorado, Oregon, Washington, Utah, Wyoming, and especially California—essentially for much the same reasons Europeans were being drawn to those destinations.

Thus, in the opening decade of the twentieth century several points were clear, with variations among the states adding up to consistent trends for the region. All the states reported significant growth in their foreign-born populations, including Idaho, Montana, Wyoming, and Colorado.[6] In those states mining continued to be a profitable industry in many communities, attracting numerous largely unskilled laborers. Sheepherding was still drawing many Basques, and there were pockets of agricultural activities and continued homesteading in Idaho and Montana. Whereas migration from the traditional sources in northern and western Europe either continued or, as in Texas, at least leveled off, the construction, extractive (mining, fishing, logging), and agricultural economies (especially the rapidly expanding cotton agricultural industry) were attracting southern and eastern Europeans, Asians, and Mexicans, many of whom were not originally intent upon settling. Even among the flood of Mexicans seeking to escape the Revolution and civil war, many did not originally plan to remain. With the influx of Asians and southern and eastern Europeans—and, increasingly, Mexicans—into the lower strata of the local economies, the native born gradually abandoned many of those jobs either because they were moving into higher positions or into other fields, or because those less-skilled positions became associated with the new minorities and therefore were viewed as unsuitable by whites.[7]

By 1910, two other demographic dimensions were shaping the growth of the West. A majority of foreign-born whites were living in urban settings in Washington, Oregon, Colorado, Utah, and California, with the greatest percentage in California (64 percent, which is not surprising given that nearly 62 percent of the entire state population resided in urban centers). However, throughout the region decidedly rural populations were still commonplace, for jobs were readily available in extractive industries. Nevertheless, shifts were underway that would steadily draw more immigrants and their families to the cities, with one dramatic representation of that trend being the movement of the Chinese into Honolulu and San Francisco.

Nor was it surprising to find high ratios of males among the white foreign-born population in states and territories where economies continued to rely heavily on rural or extractive industries. These areas were relatively isolated, and high percentages of laborers were sojourners. In Utah, on the other hand, the ratio of men to women was almost even (1.3:1), as it was in Texas, Washington, Oregon, and California—due to the larger percentages of native-born persons and families. Where group-specific data were available, we can see that the gender imbalance among the Japanese was declining, reflecting both a shift from *dekasegi* (sojourning) to *imin* (settling) and the era of the picture brides (*shashin kekkon*). On the other hand, the formidable legal obstacles stunted the Chinese communities and produced such male to female ratios as about 4:1 in Hawai'i, 10:1 in California, and 22:1 in Oregon.[8]

Several conclusions follow from this brief demographic overview. Generalizations about "Americans" coming to the West and defining its character (particularly in the Pacific Northwest and Southern California) must take into account that many of them were second generation and still close to the immigrant experience. Consequently, given the size of the foreign-stock population, we need to incorporate into any description of the growth and development of the West the factor of multiple generations, both foreign born and native born, together shaping as well as adapting to life in the vast region of the West. Moreover, the fact that many persons were migrating not only from outside the region but also crisscrossing and resettling *within* the West suggests that such persons could well have established bonds that threaded the different parts of the region together, along with the many economic connections that were materializing. Such connections would likely have contributed to the dissemination of attitudes, ideas, and cultural practices. For example, shared concerns regarding immigration issues and ethnic and religious organizational ties transcend state boundaries in the region. Finally, the shifting composition of the immigrant communities was beginning to reflect the new government policies intended to screen out individuals and groups regarded as unacceptable for admission, along with regulations defining eligibility for citizenship and categories of illegal aliens who could be pursued and removed. The nation's quest for order and control of its borders was gradually being pitted against immigrants' ambitions and immigrants' needs.

CHAPTER TWELVE

The Dillingham Commission and the West

*I*N 1907 CONGRESS authorized the creation of a commission to do a thorough examination of immigrants in America. The Immigration Commission was chaired by Senator William P. Dillingham (R-VT). It submitted its 41-volume report to the 61st Congress in December 1910. The conclusions drawn by the commission have long been faulted for their distortions demeaning the new immigration. Indeed, they were "neither impartial nor scientific, taking for granted what it set out to prove regarding the inferiority of the New Immigrants," wrote Oscar Handlin.[1] However, the data gathered that would be used to buttress those conclusions have not been faulted and remain valuable resources, although one needs to separate out the many stereotyped descriptions and comments accompanying that data. Still, those biases in the interpretations of the findings and in the descriptive comments are quite revealing because it appears that they were generally accepted as valid. All of which is particularly relevant because the commission's recommendations framed the immigration-related debates that followed and ultimately found their way into the federal immigration laws of 1917, 1921, and 1924.[2]

A major concern of the commission was to examine the role of immigrants in key industries. Since that is a major aspect of this study, and the commission's three volumes on the West (pt. 25: vols. 23–25) are a leading contemporary source of such information (though based on sample data), a concise overview of those volumes will add to our portrait of immigrants in the western economy in the first decade of the century.[3] Central to what emerges from these studies was how far immigrants were willing to journey for work and how diverse were the jobs they were willing to accept—with some cultural preferences for certain types of work. Given that and the vastness of the region and the multiple migration paths into it, ethnic variations are detailed for similar industries in different parts of the West. Not surprisingly, racial and ethnic hierarchies of preferred employees were quickly established, and stereotypes of various groups of workers were soon evident, serving as rationales for those hierarchies. In the final analysis, the reports make it abundantly clear how critical immigrant labor was for many economic enterprises throughout the region; without them the West would have experienced economic paralysis or stagnation.

Part 25: volume 23 examines the Japanese and East Indians. Mainland Japanese men concentrated in railroad track maintenance work, agriculture, construction, logging and millwork, canneries, and, in urban areas, domestic service and small businesses. Relatively few went into mining and smelting. The Japanese, Italians, and Greeks constituted a majority of railroad maintenance workers in the Pacific Northwest, whereas in the Southwest more Native Americans, Chinese, Mexicans, and whites were hired. In Nevada and Utah, the mix was Chinese, Mexican, Japanese, and Greeks.

Whereas logging opportunities were available to Japanese in Washington and Oregon, the sawmills were usually closed to them. Because cannery operators were more willing (if not eager) to hire minorities, Japanese workers equaled only 6 percent of logging workers but over one-third of cannery workers (3,600)—a majority of whom worked in Alaska (and most of the rest in Washington and Oregon). By way of contrast, in central California three-fifths of the workers in the vegetable and fruit canneries were Greeks, Italians, and Portuguese—perhaps half of whom were women (including second-generation women).

While some Japanese accepted mine work, and large numbers initially labored for the railroads, they rather quickly shifted either to urban self-employment or agriculture, which they much preferred. Also motivating their choices were the harsh working conditions and limited job opportunities in railroad, logging, mining, and cannery employment. One transition was to first obtain summertime agricultural harvesting jobs, as did thousands from Seattle, San Francisco, and Los Angeles. Over 10,000 Japanese, along with Chinese, Koreans, Asian Indians, Mexicans, and (in Colorado) German Russians, worked on such labor-intensive crops as fruits, grapes, vegetables, and, especially, sugar beets. In Colorado the distribution was distinctive for this crossroads of migration. Among the 15,000 sugar beet harvest workers, there were over 2,600 Japanese, more than 2,600 Mexicans, and nearly 6,600 German Russians. The Japanese and German Russians saved their earnings and rapidly transitioned to the ownership or leasing of farmland. The Dillingham Commission estimated that 6,000 Japanese were already involved in farming about 212,000 acres on more than 4,000 farms. The commission also noted emphatically that "white men have never been employed to any great extent in [harvesting] work" (inplying that Greeks and Germans from Russia, who were employed in agriculture, were not white).[4]

Many Japanese were reported moving into the cities, from Seattle to Los Angeles and east to Denver and Salt Lake City. When not leaving the cities for temporary agricultural and railroad work, they entered domestic service and established laundries, tailorshops, barbershops, boardinghouses, hotels, restaurants, pool halls, various crafts, and other businesses directed at fellow Japanese — just as Italians, Greeks, and Germans did. For example, between 1900 and 1909 the number of Japanese-run businesses in Seattle jumped from 50 to 478, in San Francisco from 336 to 500, and in Los Angeles from 106 to 495. Along with them came a community infrastructure with numerous hotels, restaurants, organizations, business associations, temples, and newspapers.

It was rather striking that the Dillingham Commission chose to devote a portion of its Pacific Coast report to one of the newest and smallest groups, East Indians (today usually labeled either Asian Indians or South Asians). Nearly 5,800 were admitted during the first decade of the 1900s, mostly via British Columbia into Washington, Oregon, and California. Most were Sikh farmers from the Punjab, in northern India, and three-fifths of them worked as laborers. Quite likely they were singled out because several hundred had obtained jobs in sawmills in Tacoma and Bellingham, Washington, before being forced out by white workers in 1907 due "partly to race feeling and partly to a dislike of the East Indian dress, religion, [and] manner of living." They were perceived as unadaptable and difficult to employ because of their lack of English language skills and their caste traditions, which barred them from eating food prepared by others. All of this made them less desirable than the Swedes and Norwegians. They had also been used as strikebreakers, replacing Italians in Tacoma. Many moved on to agricultural work in California, where they were used in and around Sacramento to replace or at least to counterbalance the Japanese. They were regarded as prototypical of the new immigrants, because, despite working in labor gangs and their allegedly "low efficiency," they worked for less, migrated for jobs, and boarded themselves at little expense. They also stood out because of the remarkable sums they remitted to their homeland: 31 sent $4,320 in 1908 (retaining an average of merely $31), and in Marysville, California, in eight months between December 1907 and July 1908, Indians sent home over $34,000.

The other revealing component of volume 23 was the stereotypes illustrating the prejudices regarding newcomers: The Japanese were preferred to both Greeks and Mexicans. The Greeks were not seen as industrious as the Japanese "and are intractable and difficult to control," whereas the Japanese were "more industrious, more ambitious, more tractable." They were also viewed as "more alert, more progressive, and more temperate than the Mexicans, who, when of the peon class, are generally deficient in those qualities." However, the Mexicans "are stronger and more obedient than the Japanese" and less likely "to make organized demands for higher wages and better conditions";[5] still, they are "inferior to native white men and North Europeans" and "given to drink and irregularity at work after payday."

Volume 24 (volume 2 of part 25) focused on agriculture. The commission stated rather categorically that agricultural industries in the West had "*developed an immigrant labor economy.*" It was an industry already producing one-quarter billion dollars in crops by 1907 just in California—and observers all agreed that it could not have happened without immigrant workers. It reflected the irregular work conditions and requirements for a "general migratory labor supply" that white Americans would not accept as well as living conditions that Asians tolerated but "which would not be endured by most white men." The fact that intensive agricultural operations existed where few other industries did meant that large numbers of native-born unskilled or semi-skilled workers were not ordinarily available. Consequently, such enterprises required laborers who would be willing to "follow the seasons."

Some Italians, Portuguese, and other whites did do such work, but they lacked the labor gangs that Asians had developed in order to readily provide the large numbers needed. Local residents tended to confine themselves to packinghouses and canneries. For example, in the Sacramento Delta and San Joaquin area one could find Italians and Portuguese working the (often reclaimed) land—along with a scattering of Swedes, Swiss, and Germans—but "the orchardists and growers, the Italians to a certain extent excepted, have long been dependent upon Asiatics for the large amount of hand labor required. In fact, these industries have been largely developed since this dependency became an established fact . . . , [and] the ranchers [also] maintain that laborers of this type are essential to [their] success."[6]

Sugar beets, truck gardens, berry fields, vineyards, hop yards, and other hand-labor-intensive crops all relied on immigrants. Employment on the more mechanized cereal and hay farms, along with dairying and stock raising, were not objectionable to white workers. What whites shunned in various places were the calls for 2,500, to 10,000 laborers for harvests for just a few weeks at a time. "The majority of temporary or seasonal workers [in California] are immigrants, including Japanese, Chinese, Koreans, East Indians, Mexicans, Italians, Portuguese, Armenians, German Russians, and Dalmatians." Of course, the more that Asians were involved, the more "odium" was then attached to that particular work and the more it became disassociated from "white man's work."[7]

Frequently, workers were hired by members of their own ethnic group (Italians by Italians, Portuguese by Portuguese, etc.), which indicated that some mobility was taking place, and men were moving from laboring to tenancy and land ownership, notably among Italians, Portuguese, Japanese, Armenians, and German Russians (and others not mentioned). But few Mexicans did so, because, the report asserted rather superficially, "they are generally lazy and lack ambition to rise to higher industrial positions [ownership]." In Southern California "this race offers a . . . substitute for the Asiatics in the most undesirable occupations." In terms of learning English, the derogatory assessment continued, Mexicans were "notoriously indolent and unprogressive in all matters of education and culture." Even though the views varied, the report concluded that "All employers agree that the Mexicans lack ambition and that they are addicted to the vices of drunkenness and gambling to an unusual degree."[8] This remark, expressed before the great surge of Mexican immigration, suggests that such stereotypes had already become well entrenched, a legacy of late 1800s encounters.

The labor machinations were notorious in agriculture. When an "intemperate" and allegedly unambitious group of Mexicans went out on strike in 1908, German Russians were used to break that effort. However, in northern California, Mexicans and Asian Indians were employed to undermine the Japanese. In Colorado, Mexicans served as a check on the German Russians, while in Idaho, German Russians were hired to break a strike by Japanese. In Orange County, California, Japanese were preferred to Mexicans, and the remaining Chinese to the Japanese, whereas Italians were given the choice for jobs over all three.

The situation was the same in the newly annexed territory of Hawai'i, where, by 1905, almost 184,200 workers had been imported (at a cost of $9 million) to labor on the plantations, including over 111,100 Japanese, nearly 44,500 Chinese, more than 11,400 Portuguese, 6,900 Koreans, 5,000 Puerto Ricans, and 2,350 other Europeans. However, this was an exceedingly fluid situation, especially given that contract labor was no longer permitted. Between June 1900 and June 1910, for example, 77,421 Japanese came to Hawai'i, but 75,186 left, including 5,500 children born on the Hawaiian Islands. Only 3,850 Chinese arrived during that decade, but 13,920 left, among whom were 1,166 Hawaiian-born children. It is possible that this situation in Hawai'i was included in volume 1 of the report (rather than in volume 24) because of concerns that, despite higher wages for Caucasians in Honolulu, Europeans were not being drawn to the Islands in the numbers hoped for. Those who had come were frequently of urban backgrounds unsuitable for plantation employment among the 43,917 working in Hawai'i in 1909. They were being replaced by far greater numbers of Asians, who did not display any "promise to rise to the civic or economic dignity of the communities of farming settlers in the mainland states." And that hasty assessment was asserted even though the report noted that the Japanese were already establishing businesses, co-ops, canneries, rice mills, and even a sake brewery.[9]

The bulk of the volume on agriculture was devoted to the mainland states, concentrating on particular crops, detailing the enormous economic contributions of the immigrants, and commenting on the steps many of them had taken to create communities, churches, and organizations, learn English, and acquire citizenship (where possible). The vast array was most instructive. Among those covered were Scandinavians in the San Luis Obispo area of California and in

Washington and Oregon; Germans in Anaheim; Portuguese in San Leandro; Dalmatians in Pajaro Valley, south of San Jose; Scandinavians, Germans, Italians, and Japanese in the Seattle area; Italians, Portuguese, and Swedes in Santa Clara County (California); Japanese, Chinese, Mexicans, and Italians in California's Imperial Valley; Chinese in the Sacramento River delta; northern Italians in Sonoma, Napa, Fresno, and Madeira Counties of California, plus Portland, Denver, San Francisco, and Seattle; German Russians in Colorado and near Fresno; the Japanese in the San Joaquin Valley; and western European (English, Scottish, Irish, German, French) vintners in California, together with their Spanish, Portuguese, Dalmatian, Slavonian, and Mexican workers. The report explicitly stated that the grape industry has "from the time it assumed importance been dependent upon immigrant labor and principally upon Asiatic labor."[10]

Finally, and so well illustrating the extraordinary diversity and centrality of immigration in agriculture, the report concentrated particularly on the Fresno area, noting the Danish, Swedish, German, Italian, Portuguese, German Russian, Armenian, Chinese, and Japanese farmers (along with native-born Americans) and the extensive number of immigrant women in the packinghouses. Initially, most were northern and western Europeans until the growing number of Armenian, German Russian, and Italian women gradually prompted the others to withdraw.

The third volume of the Dillingham trilogy on the West (volume 25) focused on "Diversified Industries," which included railroads, mines and smelters, logging and shingle mills, cement and powder factories, salmon canneries, and such urban businesses as cigar manufacturing, cotton mills, and the sewing trades. The full array of details is well beyond our scope here, and only key representative points will be cited. We examine the railroad situation because so many examples in the report not only captured the exceptional pluralism among western workers but also the remarkable variety in terms of where particular groups of men worked, what jobs they could obtain, and how much they would be paid. The report noted a shift in the background of workers during the 1890s and the first decade of the 1900s, the increase in non-Europeans, and the finding in 1908 that almost three-fifths of 24,183 railroad workers in the West were foreign born, concentrated in construction and maintenance. An earlier reliance on Irish, Germans, Swedes, and Norwegians was giving way to Greeks, Italians, Mexicans, Japanese, and then Koreans.

By 1910 Mexicans were becoming the principal group employed on railroad construction and maintenance projects in the Southwest, frequently being hired out of El Paso. The further north one went, the more frequently one encountered Asians and northern Europeans and soon more and more Greeks, Italians, and those from the Austro-Hungarian Empire. Multiple wage systems were being employed by the railroads, with Mexicans (lowest) to Japanese to Italians and Greeks to Irish and other northern Europeans and Americans (highest). The railroad shops were largely the preserve of Americans and northern Europeans, and whereas English, Irish, Germans, and Scandinavians made up only 6 percent of maintenance workers, they comprised close to two-fifths of the shop workers. Otherwise, lines were drawn based on those who were "intractable," "adaptable," "sober," "trustworthy," "quarrelsome," "lazy," "progressive," "difficult to satisfy," "suited to the climate," and "crafty." Greeks were considered least desirable. Mexicans were "easily satisfied" because they were "without ambition or much ability," and "drunkenness is the Mexicans' greatest weakness." Nonetheless, between July 1908 and February 1909 five agencies in El Paso sent out 16,471 Mexicans to various railroads in the Southwest. Greek agents were providing from 950 to nearly 2,600 workers per month.

The situation was similar among electric railway workers, where forty-three "races" were represented, especially the 41 percent in their sample from Mexico, Ireland, Italy, England, Germany, Canada, Sweden, Norway, Greece, and Japan. Over four-fifths of construction and maintenance workers were foreign born, while the majority of train operators were native born and second-generation whites. Acculturation and acquisition of English language skills were hampered among Mexicans, Italians, Greeks, and Japanese because they worked in gangs, which isolated them. For example, even among Mexicans present a decade or longer, only 42 percent spoke English, whereas among most northern Europeans the figure was closer to 100 percent.[11]

The Dillingham Commission focused on Colorado, Montana, Arizona, and California mines and smelters and sampled 8,586 mine workers, two-thirds of whom were foreign born, plus nearly one-sixth of second-generation workers (together 79.3 percent). Among the 40 nationalities, the leading ones were the English, Irish, Mexican, and northern Italians, followed by Canadians, Finns, Croatians, Dalmatians, Germans, Herzegovinians, Slovenians, Swedes, and Montenegrins. Again, particular groups were prominent in different states: for example, Mexicans in Arizona; English, Irish, Canadians, Finns, and Croatians in Montana; Swedes and Slovenians in Colorado; and Italians, Herzegovinians, and Montenegrins in California. Mexico was to Arizona what Canada was to Montana—a major source of workers from a contiguous nation. Still, the commission could not resist further disparagement of Mexicans, for, it concluded, their working-class children, "so far as can be seen, are no more progressive than their immigrant fathers."[12]

The 1,406 lumber and shingle mill businesses, concentrated in Washington and Oregon, displayed a number of parallels to other industries and experienced similar changes and comparable stresses. In 1900 only 30 percent of the nearly 17,500 men in logging and related work were foreign born, and a majority of them were Canadian and Scandinavian. But their proportions shifted during the early 1900s as Germans, English, and Irish began moving in and then more Scandinavians, Finns, Russians, Austrians, Greeks, Italians, and finally Japanese and Asian Indians. By 1908, three-fifths of a sample of 3,430 workers were foreign born, most notably 877 Scandinavians and Finns, who were greatly favored because they had adapted, learned English, and were receptive to U.S. citizenship. Whereas Germans, Scandinavians, and Italians frequently obtained jobs but soon moved on, Greeks were not sought because they were seen as "not particularly industrious" or tractable but rather as "clannish." These factors increased the reliance upon the Japanese, primarily in Washington State. By 1909 there were 2,240 Japanese in 67 lumber mills and lumber camps, but scarcely any in the 417 shingle mills.[13]

A brief synopsis of other industries overwhelmingly reinforces the points made at the outset regarding the West's dependency on immigrant and second-generation labor during the early years of the century. In the 42 coal and coke industries sampled in California, Washington, Utah, Wyoming, and New Mexico, four-fifths or more of the workers were foreign born, representing 43 nationalities. In the seven cement plants, 70 percent were foreign-born Italians and Mexicans. In three urban occupations, a sample of San Francisco cigar makers found 69 percent were foreign born—notably Mexican, German, northern Italian, and Spanish, and one-quarter of them were women. (By that time, most Chinese had been forced out.) After the 1906 earthquake more foreign-born women took jobs, especially southern Italians, but, not unexpectedly, native-born women were paid more. In the city's sewing trade, where nearly all the workers were women, over one-third were foreign born (principally northern Italian), and another two-fifths were second generation (largely Irish and German). Across the Bay, in Oakland's cotton mills, where two-thirds of a group of 540 workers were foreign born, three-quarters of them were Portuguese, as were a majority of the second generation.

In the salmon fishing and canning industry, over 56 percent of the fishermen and oystermen were foreign born, and nearly one-third of the first- and second-generation laborers were Scandinavian, especially members of the Fishermen's Protective Union in 1908 (which was also one-quarter Italian).[14] None were Asian. In the canneries, Japanese began to join the dwindling number of Chinese. As both declined, more white girls and women moved in along the Columbia River and on Puget Sound. Native Americans worked in the canneries along Puget Sound as well as in Alaska. However, even there the workforce was predominantly Asian (Chinese, Japanese), plus some Koreans and Asian Indians. (Filipinos began coming in the 1920s.) That Asian mix held true for San Francisco's five canneries, too.

The three volumes of the Dillingham Report make it clear that in 1910 no one argued that white Americans—or even just northern European immigrants—could have operated (or even wished to operate) the West's many different enterprises, urban and rural, without the continued inflows of foreign workers, men and women, and the second-generation children.

CHAPTER THIRTEEN

The Continuing Evolution of Immigration and Naturalization Issues and Policies (Asians)

*H*ISTORIAN MATTHEW FRYE JACOBSON'S observation about American attitudes regarding immigration offers a good point of departure for exploring specific group experiences and the evolution of immigration policies at this time: "The entire period from 1876 to the 1920s was marked by a varying . . . doubt about the desirability of continued immigration."[1] Essentially, the debate that began with the Chinese and the 1882 Exclusion Act, observed Erika Lee, "forever changed America's relationship to immigration in general." Critical to this development was Congress asserting its supremacy in this realm, an assertion endorsed by the Supreme Court in 1889 in *Chae Chan Ping v. United States* (130 U.S. 581). Therein it affirmed "the legislative and constitutional foundation for federal immigration restriction and exclusion based on national sovereignty."[2] Any reluctance on Congress's part sufficiently evaporated with the Scott and Geary legislation so that in the Act of April 27, 1904 (33 Stat. 428; 8 U.S.C.), Congress with impunity amended its April 1902 law (32 Stat.176; 8 U.S.C.) and extended Chinese exclusion indefinitely "until otherwise provided by law." The act declared that exclusion shall now be "continued without modification, limitation, or condition." The United States government was fully embracing its role as a "gatekeeper nation."

The context for this sweeping legislation—seemingly rather minor given the two decades of exclusion—was anything but that to both the Chinese and non-Chinese Californians. The event was symptomatic of some of the dilemmas facing the Chinese and the institutionalized discrimination they endured in San Francisco. For example, in March 1900 the plague broke out there, and officials decided to deny its presence in the city—except in Chinatown, where, they claimed, it was being concealed. In a replay of a smallpox outbreak a generation earlier, officials blamed the Chinese because of their general refusal to use public hospitals. Even though the Six Companies had established the Tung Wa Dispensary, the Chinese feared the public health procedures and kept the sick hidden. In May they were initially barred from leaving California without proof of vaccination. The plague was brought under control, especially with a systematic effort in 1904 to eradicate rats, but the negative image of the Chinese had once more been institutionally reinforced in the first year of the new century.[3]

Nineteen months after the outbreak, the mayor of San Francisco, James D. Phelan, published an essay concerning the coming vote to renew the exclusion provision, "Why the Chinese Should Be Excluded."[4] Viewing the non-assimilative character of the Chinese and their "undesirability as citizens," he claimed that the "evil" has continued and that the Chinese were non-assimilable particularly because they had come under contract, which was untrue on the mainland. On the other hand, trade with China had risen from $28 million in 1882 to $38.1 million in 1900, underscoring Phelan's contention that "commerce is not sentimental." However, resorting to another old argument, he claimed that Chinese laborers in the city were "crowding out" white workers, that their continued presence undermined the goal of settling the United States with "a desirable citizenship," and that they would dissuade free persons from coming to America.

Later that month, November 1901, a "California Chinese Exclusion Convention" took place in San Francisco, with, it was reported, 3,000 persons in attendance representing communities and civil, labor, and patriotic organizations from San Diego to Yreka. Phelan was the major leadoff speaker.[5] He asserted that California needed to educate those on the East Coast about the Chinese problem. Thomas J. Geary, elected chairman of the meeting, then argued (incorrectly) that continued exclusion would come at no great cost because China "offers no market to the white people at all." Befitting that jingoistic era, he declared that "we can conquer all other people who oppose us industrially or otherwise." Then, Andrea Sbarboro, the Italian immigrant entrepreneur and founder of the immigration-based Italian Swiss Colony of Asti, spoke next, urging the removal of San Francisco's Chinatown. D. E. McKinlay, who worked for the U.S. Department of Agriculture, called for the empowering of immigration commissioners to determine those Chinese unlawfully in the country and to deport any convicted of a felony. He pressed the point because of the relatively new phenomenon of paper sons entering under false identities. He asserted that for the claims of births in America to have been true, every Chinese woman would have had to have borne 500 children![6] Resolutions were approved to petition the president and Congress to extend the exclusion as well as one urging the executive board of the Chinese Exclusion League to plan a meeting concerning "Japanese and Asiatic immigration."

The Chinese had not responded passively to exclusion, and the Six Companies sponsored a number of lawsuits challenging various aspects of the exclusion, the severe restrictions on reentry, and the mandatory registration procedures. The Chinese migrants also resorted to various strategies to get smuggled across the Canadian and Mexican borders. Erika Lee estimates that about 17,300 entered illegally between 1882 and 1920, paying in 1890, for example, $23–$60 along the Mexican border and as high as $300 to be brought across the Canadian border. That earned the Chinese Lee's label as "the country's first illegal immigrants." Efforts to tighten the Canadian border created sufficient pressure by 1906 to close off the "Chinese leak" that the Chinese began shifting their operations chiefly to the Mexican border, particularly west of El Paso. The numbers steadily increased there, along with elaborate mechanisms of evasion. And they were not alone, for Syrians, Greeks, Hungarians, Russian Jews, and Italians, along with some women from France, Belgium, and Spain, likewise sought to enter illegally. Officials were less concerned about the Europeans but did report 2,492 apprehensions of Chinese along the southern border just between 1907 and 1909. In 1903, following passage of an act codifying immigration law (see below), the immigration service had begun keeping more complete records along the border but only sporadically applied the inspections to Mexicans. The Chinese were viewed as the threat—to the nation and "to national sovereignty." However, the United States had more success persuading Canada to curtail the illicit transfers than they did with Mexico.[7]

Meanwhile, young Chinese in America were as increasingly frustrated with American policies as they were with the impotence of the Qing government. It failed to resist the efforts of the United States and European powers to carve up China into spheres of influence and to demand broader extra-territoriality (extending diplomatic immunity to their citizens) and trading rights that currently favored all but the Chinese. Japan's defeat of China in the 1894–1895 Sino-Japanese War was also regarded as shameful, and it was soon followed by the short-lived Boxer Rebellion in 1900, a preview of the mounting resentment against foreign nations' humiliation of China.

Kang Youwei had been exiled from China and joined Sun Yat-sen and others in 1899 to organize a revolutionary group, the Baohuanghui (referred to as the Bao)—described by Janet Leung Larson as "the largest and possibly the most influential overseas Chinese organization that has ever existed."[8] It soon had 5 chapters in North America and 50 by 1903. Two years later, it was estimated to have 160 chapters around the world and some 70,000 members, Chinese of all backgrounds. It emphasized the teaching of citizenship and entrepreneurial skill, and it did indeed create a vast network of businesses, schools, and newspapers. When it appeared in May 1905 that China was inclined to accept the indefinite exclusion of laborers and their spouses from the United States, the action fueled a resentment that stemmed from other episodes of discriminatory treatment in the United States. Kang and the Bao planned a massive boycott protest against American goods in China.

Using telegraph technology, the leadership was able to coordinate actions in China and between China and the other countries with Bao chapters in order to launch the united boycott in July 1905. Chinese in America also established the General Society of Chinese Residing in the United States for the Opposing of the Exclusion Treaty. The boycott lasted for nearly a year and resulted in more than a 50 percent drop in American exports to China between 1905 and 1907 (from $57 million to $26 million). The diplomatic policy impact was limited to China's refusal to renew its treaty with the United States, but the effort did politicize merchants, led to cooperation between intellectuals and merchants, and sparked the formation of other voluntary organizations prior to the 1911 revolution in China.

In addition to the collective responses, prominent Chinese challenged the distortions that Americans used to justify exclusion. Ng Poon Chew was a well-educated minister, newspaper editor, and civil rights advocate. In January 1908, he wrote "The Treatment of the Exempt Classes of Chinese to the United States: A Statement from the Chinese in America," denouncing exclusion as contrary to both the original treaties and the original intent of Congress.[9] He quoted U.S. Senator George Hoar's statement that enforcement of exclusion "has almost become an extermination law" and President Theodore Roosevelt's 1905 State of the Union address, which declared that the mode of enforcing exclusion was a "grave injustice and wrong . . . to the people of China and therefore ultimately to this nation itself." He cited Secretary of Commerce and Labor Oscar Straus's report to Roosevelt in 1907 that such discriminatory laws "are alike opposed to the principles of the Republic and to the spirit of its institutions." Ng pointed out how the laws contradicted the treaty and unjustly manipulated the definitions of laborer, teacher, student, and merchant and that, in the execution of the Geary Act, officials violated the provision concerning the treatment of exempt classes and their arrest. He pointed to recent anti-American boycotts, to the decline in visiting students who had previously brought back to China favorable images of the United States, and to the reality that Chinese immigration of exempt classes even at 10,000 per year would equal only 1 percent of European immigration. Finally, he quoted Secretary of War William Howard Taft that Congress and the president should "disregard the unreasonable demand of a portion of the community, deeply prejudiced upon this subject, in the Far West."

Of course, despite dwindling numbers, there were clusters of Chinese outside of San Francisco who were doing their best to cope with the limitations they faced and to fit in to American society as best as possible, such as in Locke, California, and Pocatello and Boise, Idaho. Beyond them, the legal, literary, and protest efforts were largely in vain. However, one of the most successful efforts of defiance came as a result of nature: the San Francisco earthquakes and fires of April 18, 1906. Those fires destroyed municipal and immigration records. Since no one could challenge their veracity, thousands of Chinese were now able to claim birth in the United States and, therefore, the right to visit China, return to the United States, and bring in one's wife and children. The number of Chinese women admitted rose from a mere 88 in 1906 to over 300 in 1913 and 1914 and a peak of 938 in 1924. Approximately 6,863 women entered between 1905 and 1924 out of a total of 44,589 Chinese admitted. Many young men were brought in as "paper sons" of U.S. citizens and were provided with detailed information in "coaching papers" (or crib sheets) on the family of the "fathers" bringing them in. The "parent" usually paid about $100 for each year of the child's age, or the "child" paid that sum to get in. Other Chinese went through elaborate preparations to present themselves as merchants qualified to bring in their spouses and children, or to enter the country as a new merchant. Officials, soon aware of these strategies, detained Chinese arrivals on Angel Island, in San Francisco Bay, sometimes for weeks or months between 1910 and 1940, questioning them repeatedly to discover contradictions that would expose their false identities.

Q. Counting from the same side or right side, in what row was your old house located?
A. Counting from the right, the 2nd row, the last house in that row.
Q. The right side of your village is what point of the compass.
A. West.
Q. When you say West, are you standing in your village looking out towards the front or are you standing in the front looking towards the village?
A. I face the south, on the right.
Q. Is the right hand side of your village the head or the tail?
A. It does not make any difference; in my village we have no head or tail; I cannot tell you which is which. . . .
Q. How old were you when your father died?
A. He died when I was about 6 or 7 years old.
Q. You testified, when you went home to China last that he was with you going to China at the age of 9. What do you have to say to that?
A. My uncle took me back to China.[10]

During the delay, many whiled away the days carving dozens of poems into the walls of the detention barracks:

> Leaving behind my writing brush and removing my sword, I came to
> America.
> Who was to know two streams of tears would flow upon arriving here?
> If there comes a day when I will have attained my ambition and become
> successful,
> I will certainly behead the barbarians and spare not a single blade of
> grass.[11]

Shih-shan Henry Tsai reports a total of 6,327 Chinese were barred from entry between 1892 and 1925.[12] In the mid-1950s, the U.S. government was asked by the Six Companies to establish a Confessions Program in order to allow such paper sons and others who had entered illegally or through fraud to come forward and to regularize their status. Tsai reports that some 10,000 did so in San Francisco alone. Between 1957 and 1965, some 30,440 Chinese nationwide either confessed or were "implicated"—identified as having entered fraudulently by those confessing.[13]

In the early 1940s the Filipino author Carlos Bulosan summed up his experience in America: "I feel like a criminal running away from a crime I did not commit and the crime is that I am a Filipino in America."[14] Many Japanese would have already endorsed that view by the early 1900s, for no sooner had indefinite Chinese exclusion been achieved than those hostile to the Japanese turned on them. By 1910 the only nationality groups explicitly barred from admission to the United States were (along with Asian prostitutes) Chinese laborers and their families and, by diplomatic agreement, Japanese laborers.[15] Aside from the relatively small number of Koreans (7,226 in the years 1903–1905) and Asian Indians (6,400 in the years 1899–1914) who began entering, the Japanese and Chinese were the principal immigrant peoples of color during this period in the American West.[16] It is they who were the first to be explicitly targeted for denial of entry, or more specifically the laborers among them—even though during the five years preceding exclusion (1878–1882) the Chinese constituted only 3.4 percent of all immigrants and in the five years leading up to the 1907–1908 Gentlemen's Agreement between the United States and Japan (1903–1907) (see below), the Japanese represented merely 1.74 percent of all those admitted. In the 13 mainland states and territories the Japanese made up 2.3 percent of the foreign born in 1900 and 4.15 percent in 1910 (7 percent in California).

   In terms of the larger context of immigration into the West, denial of entry was a policy decision of huge significance. In addition to its obvious impact on the Japanese and Chinese, it represented a further assertion of America's sovereign power over who might enter the nation. The policy opened the door to closing the doors. The principle of targeting individuals as members of specific groups was now established (aside from those decisions based on individuals' physical, mental, moral, occupational, or financial characteristics). These were the first steps toward the National Origins System in peacetime and the reloca- tion and incarceration of citizens in wartime.

We saw earlier in the Oxnard strike of 1903 that the Japanese demonstrated a willingness to take all kinds of work, predominantly in agriculture, and a readi- ness to mobilize themselves and even collaborate with others to defend their jobs and wages.[17] They rapidly shifted from agricultural laboring to agricultural entrepreneurialism, buying, leasing, and contracting for farmland.[18] During the 1900s the Japanese were also reported as having over 3,000 businesses in the West, particularly 2,548 in California, marked by a very dramatic leap in San Francisco from 90 to 545 (1900–1909) and in Los Angeles from 6 to 473. Their successes, though quite modest, made their numbers seem so much more omi- nous to white Americans, and their urban concentrations, where Chinese were also conspicuous, began to generate apprehensions. It was relatively easy to transfer the hostility felt toward the Chinese to other Asians and South Asians. Effortlessly, "The Chinese Must Go!" became "The Japanese Must Go!" and the Chinese Exclusion League quickly became the Japanese and Korean Ex- clusion League.

In a 1904 meeting in San Francisco, the American Federation of Labor (AFL) adopted a resolution asking that "the Chinese Exclusion Act . . . be en- larged and extended" to provide for the exclusion of "all classes of Japanese and Koreans" except those specifically exempted in the 1882 legislation. The follow- ing year the Japanese and Korean Exclusion League (JKEL) was established on May 7, 1905, and on that day the first Anti-Japanese Convention was held in San Francisco. Most of those attending were delegates of labor groups.[19] Among the speakers were Mayor Eugene Schmitz, of the Union Labor Party; Andrew Furuseth, Norwegian-born president of the Sailors' Union of the Pacific; Norwegian-born Olaf A. Tveitmore, secretary of the Building Trades Council as well as president of the new Exclusion League; and Scottish-born Walter Macarthur, editor of the Sailors' Union publication *Coast Seamen's Journal*.

In that spring of 1905 the *San Francisco Chronicle* seized upon the issue of Japanese immigration that would soon be promoted by the Exclusion League. Its yellow journalism came through clearly in the increasingly inflammatory headlines: "Crime and Poverty Go Hand in Hand with Asiatic Labor"; "Japanese a Menace to American Women"; and especially "Brown Asiatics Steal Brains of Whites." On April 15 the *Chronicle* tried to justify its attacks by pointing out that it was a San Francisco paper, few undesirable southern Europeans reached the West Coast, and "Japanese immigration for the present is a question for the Pacific Coast . . . and so . . . we are asking for what we think we can get."[20]

As the situation deteriorated and hostile sentiments were more freely ex- pressed, it came as no surprise that they would soon be heard in Washington.

California congressman Everis Anson Hayes, a Republican representing San Jose, spoke before the House on March 13, 1906, drawing members' attention to "the industrial menace that the Japanese are to be in the near future."[21] He was asked to submit legislation for Japanese and Korean exclusion, a bill that represented, he asserted, "the desire of at least 95% of the people in my district [and] . . . the State of California." He argued that exclusion was an issue "of domestic policy" and that hundreds of this "coolly [sic] class of laborers" are coming who are unreliable. He predicted that, without exclusion, if even only 3.5 percent of the Japanese came to America that would represent 1.438 million persons.

Already in his district and in neighboring Santa Cruz County, Hayes continued, "pleasantly and profitably employed" whites working in agriculture have been displaced by some 2,000 Japanese, who were accustomed to (and more willing to accept) far lower wages. Citing a report from San Francisco (compiled by the Japanese and Korean Exclusion League), he illustrated his case by focusing on Chinese competition and low wages and claiming that in Stockton white laundry workers are employed for 10 hours but "Mongolians" for "sixteen to twenty." San Francisco union cooks worked 10 to 13 hours and earned $60–90; Chinese and Japanese labored 14 to 16 hours, and the Japanese received just $35. In each case Hayes presented, Asians worked longer hours for lower wages than did white union men, because they "can live on less than any other human being in the world" and "have no social standard . . . no morals . . . [and] unclean habits." Workers needed to organize against the menace, he insisted. "The very existence of the Republic depends upon it." Furthermore, "the white people of the Pacific Coast have no relations of a social nature with the Japanese now there and it is not desirable that they should have." Children need to be protected from "the oriental environment with its semi-barbaric ideas and its stifling moral atmosphere." The solution, Hayes concluded, was to extend "the Chinese exclusion act to include all Mongolians."

Hayes's inflammatory speech was one component of an on-going campaign for Asian exclusion. In that context the San Francisco School Board had announced a plan in May 1905 to assign Japanese children to an Oriental school. No action was then taken, but five weeks after Hayes's speech the great earthquake struck San Francisco. In the months that followed there were a number of assaults on Japanese men and then a call for a boycott of Japanese-owned businesses. At the same time the JKEL pressured the school board to implement its earlier decision regarding the Japanese. The board, relying upon the provision in state law permitting segregated schools for children of "Mongolian" and Chinese descent, voted on October 11, 1906, to segregate the 93 Japanese students (68 foreign born, 28 American born), along with Korean and Chinese children. That precipitated an international imbroglio.

President Roosevelt described the move as "a wicked absurdity," and in his 1907 State of the Union address asked for "fair treatment for the Japanese as I would ask fair treatment for Germans or Englishmen, Frenchmen, Russians, or Italians." Recognizing the military power that Japan had recently demonstrated in defeating Russia in the Russo-Japanese War, Roosevelt needed a solution that would save face for the Japanese and placate both sides. The president invited Mayor Schmitz and the school board members to Washington, and there they explained that the underlying motive was a termination of Japanese immigration. In exchange for San Francisco withdrawing the segregation order, Roosevelt agreed to seek a halt to the immigration of Japanese laborers. The response in California was largely negative and highly critical of Roosevelt. The *San Francisco Call*, in keen competition with the *Chronicle*, condemned the president's intervention in the local controversy. On December 6, 1906, it editorialized that "the National body politic can assimilate the European of whatever grade, but never the Asiatic. They are aliens always, no matter what their civil status. The proposition to naturalize them is preposterous." Two months later it expanded upon that theme: "Roosevelt's power will not make one white man out of all the Japanese in the Nipponese Empire. California is the white man's country, and not the Caucasian graveyard" (February 11, 1907).[22]

The press, the unions, and the Exclusion League whipped up anti-Japanese hostility. Moreover, a review of 50 newspapers along the coast at that time found 47 critical of the Japanese and the president. In January 1907, in the *Oakland Tribune*, former San Francisco editor Col. John P. Irish challenged this tide of hostile feelings, noting that "no teacher nor school principal ever protested against the Japanese pupils" and "no . . . protest was ever made against the Japanese pupils by the parents of white pupils." He added that the Japanese "did not crowd white children out of the schools" and that the Japanese had behaved and dressed properly. The segregation order was done "without popular demand or suggestion." Herbert Brown, superintendent of Japanese Missions on the Pacific Coast, defended Japanese women, the patriotism of the Japanese, and their willingness to acculturate. He quoted educators, school superintendents, David Starr Jordan, president of Stanford University, Governor George R. Carter of Hawai'i (where nearly 6,400 Japanese and Chinese children were in the public schools), and the Inter-Denominational Missionary Conference. But the defense went beyond morality and assimilability. A Fresno fruit grower stressed to the press the need for the Japanese, "because we are wholly dependent on their labor. If they are excluded, we shall have to give up our farms and go out of business." Orchardists in the Santa Clara Valley also told the *Chronicle* "that to exclude the Japanese would be equivalent to pauperizing ourselves."[23]

On March 11, 1907, President Roosevelt issued Executive Order No. 589, barring Japanese and Korean laborers from migrating from Hawai'i to the mainland. Secretary of State Elihu Root began negotiations with his Japanese counterpart, Takahira Kogoro, involving an exchange of notes since called the

Gentlemen's Agreement (1907–1908). In the notes Japan agreed to halt the migration of Japanese laborers to the United States but was not asked to bar the emigration of Japanese wives to join their husbands. With many Japanese Issei (first generation) beginning to shift their goals from *dekasegimin* (sojourners) to *imin* (settlers), the Issei were able to initiate *shashin kekkon* (picture marriages) and the profound transformation of their groups into ethnic communities. Such actions only inflamed anti-Asian sentiments. Indeed, not only did the opposition to the Japanese not abate following Roosevelt's Order and the Gentlemen's Agreement, but it was also expanded to include Asian Indians. In that same year, 1907, the JKEL changed its name to the Asiatic Exclusion League (AEL) so as to include all Asians in their quest to complete the closure of immigration from Asia.

Meanwhile, representative of the changes taking place in the mindset of the Japanese was the four-month-long strike in 1909 on the Hawaiian island of Oahu by some 7,000 Japanese plantation workers. They were protesting the dual wage system that favored the Portuguese (whose monthly income was one-fourth greater than that of the Japanese). The mammoth effort by this "blood union"—based on common ethnicity—was supported by such Japanese organizations as the Japanese Physicians Association and the Honolulu Retail Merchants Association. But it was the strikers' statement that was so telling: "We have decided to permanently settle here . . . to unite our destiny with that of Hawai'i, sharing the prosperity and adversity of Hawai'i." Consequently, they denounced the conditions on the plantations as "undemocratic and un-American" and emphasized that their objective was to create their own "thriving and contented middle class—the realization of the high ideal of Americanism."[24]

These accounts of the Chinese and Japanese experiences during the early 1900s illustrate the impact of stereotyping and fraudulent attacks in whipping up hostility toward immigrant groups, the limited and uneven effectiveness of minority protests and resistance, their consequent need to develop alternative, even illegal, strategies to enter the country, and the increasingly punitive immigration policies and more elaborate bureaucracy mobilized to implement those policies. As Erika Lee summed it up, the Exclusion Laws wrought five major changes: they provided for the first federal inspectors—begun 1875; established the first attempts to identify and monitor foreign-born persons by requiring specific documents for admission and readmission—the equivalent of a passport; mandated certificates of residence—precursors to the "green card"; defined illegal immigration as a criminal offense; and provided for the first deportation laws.

The changes for the Japanese were equally dramatic, illustrating how government policies could redefine the context of reception and the parameters within which the immigrants could operate. The policy and agreement compelled them to make choices sooner than they might have wished to with respect to departing or remaining. The policy change limited their freedom of movement between the Hawaiian Islands and the mainland, and the restrictions pressured those choosing to remain to find spouses and hasten the development of communities and community organizations in order to cope with the hostility aroused by the controversy.

The two following case studies highlight the new reality that American laws and policies were becoming less and less benign. Signaling the new view of immigration as a labor issue, the responsibility for enforcing immigration policy was transferred in February 1903 from the Treasury to the new Department of Commerce and Labor. The following month, in the Act of March 3, 1903 (32 Stat. 1213; 8 U.S.C.), Congress codified the nation's immigration laws, establishing the benchmark for the government's regulation of immigration. Much of the act covered the administration of the law, the commissioner general of immigration, the inspectors, the Special Boards of Inquiry, and the elaborate list of detailed questions to be asked of each arriving person. Three sections combined previous legislation detailing all the categories of excludable persons for physical, mental, moral, political, and economic reasons, such as epileptics and those with "loathsome" diseases; persons having had "attacks of insanity"; prostitutes, polygamists, and those guilty of moral turpitude; anarchists; and particularly those "Likely to Become a Public Charge [LPC]." The law also explicitly banned contract labor or any prior payments, agreements, or promises of jobs with the exception of skilled workers where such persons are not available in this country, along with specialists and those in the arts and professions. Further, the act barred illegal immigration, penalized those assisting illegal entries, and allowed for deportations of illegal individuals up to three years after their entry. There were no quotas or limits placed on any specific nationalities except, in the other legislation, on the Chinese. The Act of February 20, 1907 (34 Stat. 898; 8 U.S.C.) essentially repeated the 1903 provisions but doubled the head tax to four dollars and somewhat enlarged the list of persons to be denied admission. Of great importance, in that 1907 legislation Congress provided for a commission to "make [a] full inquiry, examination, and investigation . . . of immigration." This became the famous Dillingham Commission Report.

Although there were not yet any serious obstacles to admission other than for the Chinese (and, by executive agreement, for the Japanese), the Act of June 29, 1906, the Basic Naturalization Act (34 Stat. 596), did have a direct significance for immigrants in the West. This codifying legislation provided for a registry whereby all those men arriving could obtain certificates attesting to their legal admission. Provisions for naturalization included: 18 years of age; a Declaration of Intent at least two years prior to petitioning for naturalization; a Petition for Naturalization within two to seven years after filing a Declaration of Intent, and two photographs accompanying the petition; five years residency in the country, including a year in the locale where the petition was filed (subsequently reduced to six months) and two witnesses from each location of residence who could testify as to the applicant's good moral character and attachment to the Constitution; an ability to speak English except if one had applied for a homestead; and the oath that one was not an anarchist or polygamist and that the applicant renounces "absolutely and forever all allegiance and fidelity" to any other government or leader. Section 15 provided for cancellation for fraud or for taking up residence outside the United States within five years of naturalization.

Less than a year later, the Expatriation Act of March 2, 1907 (34 Stat. 1228; U.S.C. 17), focused on five important points: If a naturalized citizen took up residence in one's home country for two years or anywhere else for five years, "it shall be presumed that he ceased to be an American citizen." "[A]ny American citizen" taking "an oath of allegiance to any foreign state" or "naturalized in any foreign state" "shall be deemed to have expatriated himself." In addition, "any American woman who married a foreigner shall take the nationality of her husband." However, the Act of February 10, 1855, granting citizenship to any foreign-born woman marrying a U.S. citizen—and who is otherwise lawfully qualified—was retained, including the woman's right to remain a citizen if thereafter divorced. Finally, children born outside the United States to U.S. citizens were declared citizens if, at the age of 18, they indicated an intention to remain such, while the children of aliens born outside the country automatically become naturalized when their parents became citizens if the children were still minors and, upon reaching maturity, they resided for five years in the United States.

But the battle to draw the lines around the various groups of immigrants centered on determining who among the newest peoples met the criteria of whiteness and therefore the statutory requirements of eligibility for naturalization. The notion that a definition of white was someone who was non-black would not meet the standards, although those standards were rather ambiguous and inconsistently applied. Some relied on "scientific" evidence and others on "common knowledge." Some looked to congressional intent and others to precedents, yet prior to the Ozawa and Thind cases of 1922 and 1923, respectively, the precedents were not clear-cut, and a number of groups in the West found their legal status in limbo because their right to be naturalized had not been resolved. We have noted that whiteness was, in reality, not ascriptive but quite often reflected the extent of a person's Americanization and his or her demonstration of those particular behaviors, values, and principles.

In 12 court cases up to 1909 individuals sought to establish a white racial identity that would enable them to acquire U.S. citizenship. Three cases involved Japanese, 3 were Chinese, 2 were mixed Asian, 1 was Burmese, 2 were Native

American, and 1 was Mexican. Only Robert Rodriguez, of San Antonio, succeeded but less on the grounds of whiteness than of the precedent of the Treaty
of Guadalupe Hidalgo (and subsequent diplomatic agreements; see discussion
of *In re Rodriguez* in part 1). Seventeen other cases came before the federal
courts between 1909 and 1916 wherein the plaintiffs (or main party to the case)
included 6 Syrians, 4 Asian Indians, 3 Filipinos, 1 Armenian, 1 Japanese, and 2
German Japanese. The dilemma was evident in the 6 Syrian cases (only one of
which was in the West), for 3 Syrians were declared to be white and 3 not. Both
"common knowledge" and science were used in the former but only "common
knowledge" in the latter three. All 3 Asian Indians and the Armenian were
defined as white.

The "transparency factor" in the "common knowledge" argument, writes Ian
Henry Lopez, is the "assertion that everyone knows what white is," which, of
course, was untrue. However, it was becoming clear to some that "whiteness"
was "socially fashioned and cannot be measured, or found in nature."[25] As more
and more persons entered the country from the Middle East, South Asia, Japan, and southern Europe, these immigrants did not encounter obstacles to admission based on race, for no such provisions yet existed (aside from the two
exceptions noted above, Chinese and Japanese laborers). Yet, having been admitted, many would face great uncertainties when they applied for the Declaration of Intent to become a citizen or, beyond that, filed the Petition for Naturalization. The courts proved to be formidable arenas of uncertainty for the
newest of the nation's new immigrants. Given the exceptional diversity of the
West's foreign born, this was an acute issue there.

CHAPTER FOURTEEN

Miners, Merchants, and Entrepreneurs
Europeans Compete with Europeans (Greeks and Others)

T HE ODYSSEYS OF GREEKS in the West during the first decades of the new century are remarkably representative, for they ranged from laborer to daring entrepreneur, from itinerant sojourner to dedicated community builder, from Salt Lake City and central Texas to Hilo and Honolulu. Although the examples of the Chinese and Japanese show that race did become a volatile factor, in many respects the Greek life stories demonstrate that many aspects of the immigrant experiences might have been race neutral but not free of "race" issues, for those now grouped among European whites were not always so identified a century ago. Many were frequently marginalized because they were labeled non-whites. Many relied on padrones or other contractors for employment, while others had no such intermediaries and were ambitious risk-taking entrepreneurs. Not a few of the laborers got caught up in anti-strike situations when they were brought in as strikebreakers; more than a few of the entrepreneurs failed in their initial business ventures and resumed wage work or tried their business skills again.

Most men recognized strong financial obligations to their families and even to their communities in the homeland and sought to fulfill them, including contributing to the building of religious institutions and other community-assistance projects in their villages. Nonetheless, many eventually chose to abandon sojourning for settlement and returned home only to find wives whom they could bring back to America. Gradually, numerous Greeks came to recognize the value of U.S. citizenship.

Harry Mantos arrived around 1907. He followed others out West, first getting a job laying railroad tracks near Salt Lake City and then digging trenches for water lines in Twin Falls (Idaho), loading mail in Green River (Wyoming), serving as a mucker in the Bingham Canyon (Utah) copper mines, as a boot-black in Omaha (Nebraska), a trackman back in Green River, and a line worker for a can manufacturer in Deadwood (South Dakota). He then went back to Bingham Canyon until 300 Greeks went on strike for higher wages in the summer of 1909, prompting Mantos's still further travels to Seattle and a job with a boat builder. Apparently, he remained in Seattle until he returned to Greece in 1922; at some point during the prior dozen years he had acquired U.S. citizenship. In 1937, some 30 years after his initial crossing, Mantos returned to Bingham Canyon to work in the open-pit copper mine.[1]

In dramatic contrast, George Likouros emigrated from Vasara, near Sparta, Greece, to New York City in 1877. He held various jobs, including selling lemons from a cart, and worked his way across America to San Francisco to meet up with his older brother, John, who was a Civil War veteran. During the next decade they changed their name to Lycurgus (they thought it would be easier for Americans). John built a business in fruits and vegetables, with links to Hawai'i and Australia. George worked with his brother for a time and then bought the Oyster Grotto restaurant in Sausalito (just north across the Bay from San Francisco). There, he met the sons of Claus Spreckels, the sugar baron. As another adventure, George sold the restaurant and, with savings of $4,000, went with the Spreckels sons to Hawai'i in 1889, hung out with friends of the king, became a fervent supporter of Queen Lili'uokalani, and leased a hotel on Waikiki Beach, the Sans Souci.

George formed a close friendship with Peter Camarinos, who had come from the same region of Greece and had established the California Fruit Market in Honolulu in 1883. The Lycurgus and Camarinos families would become the two principal and intertwined Greek clans in early-twentieth-century Hawai'i. George established himself as a white-suited bon vivant and prominent entrepreneur, eventually leasing the Volcano House in the Hawaiian National Park, on the Big Island, and acquiring the Hilo Hotel, among other ventures. He also gradually became *barba Yorghi* ("uncle George") for sponsoring the migration of some 30 relatives and friends to Hawai'i. Many of them opened a variety of businesses, from the Pahoa Lumber Mill to the Aloha Taxicab Company. Meanwhile, back in Sparta, George met Athena Geracimos, age 19, married her, and brought her back to Hawai'i, where she gave birth in 1904 to the first Greek child born on the Islands. Geracimos family members were also brought over. When Athena died of cancer in 1937, George chose to remain in Hawai'i, dying there in 1960 at the age of 101. He and Athena had successfully launched much of the pre–World War II Greek community in Hawai'i—about 200 persons on the eve of the war.[2]

Much earlier, Peter Camarinos had come over to the United States, as had his brother Demetrios, his cousins, and his nephews from Tsintzina and nearby Vasara, Lycurgus's home village. Before Peter, Christos Tsakonas had arrived in 1873, began peddling in Chicago, and opened his first candy and fruit shop in Milwaukee in 1882. With that success, he gradually initiated a migration stream of young men, mostly Tsintzinians and Spartans, including Peter. He established a franchise chain of candy and fruit stores across the country—the Greek-American Fruit Company. Peter set up his franchise in Honolulu in 1883, and Ioannis and Nikolas Chronis did the same a year later in Los Angeles, hiring Chinese to pick lemons and oranges. Others established a store in San Francisco in 1888. Tsakonas returned to Greece in 1900, having carved a significant and successful migration channel that continued into the twentieth century.[3]

Yoryis Zisimopoulos (which became Zeese), whom we met in the book's introduction, had similar experiences crisscrossing the country and the West, and everywhere he went he found nuclei of Greek communities, especially in and near the Utah mining operations. The one in Salt Lake City was adjacent to the railroad tracks, with Lebanese, Italian, Japanese, and Slavic stores and businesses nearby. It had previously been the residential area of Scandinavian, German, and Dutch Mormon converts. Indeed, Helen Papanikolas recalled, scattered throughout those Utah mining areas when she was growing up, such as Helper and Bingham Canyon, were places known as Woptown, Bohunk Town, Nigger Town, and Greek Town. But the Greek communities there, as well as in similar locations—including Pueblo, Colorado; Pocatello, Idaho; Hartville, Wyoming; and Carbon County, Utah—differed from those in Portland, Tacoma, or even Honolulu. Hundreds of young, single Greek men moved about from railroad camp to mining town to construction site and the like, becoming a floating reserve labor force that made it more difficult to define where the boundaries of their scattered community were.

But one thing that was clear in Utah was that if you were Greek and wanted a job, you had to see—and pay—Leonidas Skliris. Born in 1880, Skliris arrived in the United States at age 17 with no money and few skills. He peddled, learned English, and became a railroad track foreman. By 1902 he was in a position to capitalize on the huge railroad expansion, for Salt Lake City had become a hub for the Union Pacific Railroad and the Denver and Rio Grande Railroad, linking also the coal and copper mining and smelting centers of Utah. With Scandinavians and many other northern Europeans preferring farming and Basques concentrating on shepherding, there was a huge labor shortage. Finns began moving in during the 1890s, followed by Italians, Serbs, Croatians, Slovenians, and then Japanese and Greeks. Like others, Skliris moved up from foreman to contractor for the Denver and Rio Grande. He provided strikebreakers for the railroad and then, in 1903, for the mining companies being struck in Carbon County. With Utah doubling its industrial capacity between 1900 and 1910 and the Utah Copper Mining Company in Bingham Canyon shifting from silver to copper (and, in 1907, to low-grade copper ore mining with one of the first open-pit mines), the demand for low-skilled labor at half the wage of skilled American workers enabled Skliris to expand his services and provide the railroad and mining companies with hundreds of Greek workers. His fee was $20 for the job placement and a dollar a month thereafter. Anytime a Greek got fed up and changed jobs, he would have to pay Skliris again. The 1910 census indicated that 4,039 Greeks were living in Utah.

Skliris's network soon reached all the way back to Greece, Papanikolas wrote, drawing from all over the Peloponnesus: "Their relatives were taken first, from brothers to cousins far removed, then relatives of relatives." When he needed scabs he hired from outside the region, such as from Crete. To bypass the anti-contract labor laws, his agents would instruct recruits to say upon arrival that they had no job but were going to meet relatives, and to provide a fictitious address. By 1911, Greek workers were so angry with Skliris's stranglehold that in February they wrote a letter to Governor William Fry, signed by 500 Greeks, protesting the exploitation. Already in August 1908, some 300 men had walked off the job to protest wage cuts, a remarkable demonstration of unity given that they were not yet unionized. Meanwhile, they soon had to face the challenge of a workforce that was becoming increasingly diverse. In 1911 Bingham had "1210 Greeks, 639 Italians, 564 Croats, 254 Japanese, 217 Finns, 161 Englishmen, 60 Bulgarians, 59 Swedes, 52 Irish, and 23 Germans." The Greeks (and others) began to join the union in greater numbers, and in June 1912 the Western Federation of Miners had its constitution translated into Greek (which it had earlier done into other languages).

Many more joined the union, and on September 12, 1912, against their leaders' advice, more than 1,000 miners voted to strike (including 800 Greeks—many from Crete—plus Italians and Serbs). They were seeking higher wages, union recognition, and the end of the padrone system—intent on ousting Skliris. At that point, 200 Japanese miners asked to join the union. The strike persisted, with Greeks still ignoring their community leaders. Skliris fled his hotel apartment, but the strike continued, although suddenly split by the Greek government's call (September 30) for Greek men to return for military duty due to the outbreak of the Balkan Wars. Two hundred Greeks left, and the company then brought in Italian, Greek, and, especially, Mexican strikebreakers, crushing the strike by mid-November. Despite the fact that the *Deseret Evening News* had proclaimed that "the white element has been forced against its will to strike"—implying the strikers were basically non-whites—

the failed strike had demonstrated an exceptional degree of inter-ethnic and intra-ethnic cooperation.[4]

The pattern of Greek employment in neighboring Wyoming was similar to that in Utah—men drawn to work on railroads and then in the mines. Peter Douvas traveled to Hartville after hearing about jobs and good wages there. Friends and relatives followed, and Douvas and still others went on to Rock Springs (Wyoming) as well as to Cheyenne, while Germans were drawn into ranching or moved into Casper, Cheyenne, Hanna, and Sheridan. Poles, Hungarians, Czechs, and Slovenians also migrated into the latter two mining communities. The Colorado Fuel and Iron Company had bought up the copper-mining area of Hartville, and by the early 1900s recent immigrants there consisted principally of "Italians and Greeks, scores of Swedes, English, Lebanese, Japanese, and others."

The difference in Wyoming was apparently the absence of a padrone and any company town controlling their choices. There was thus an openness that enabled many Greeks (and Italians) to indulge their "premium on personal independence" by establishing restaurants, bars, grocery stores, shoe repair shops, bakeries, barber shops, meat markets, and, of course, coffeehouses (*kaffenion*). The 1910 census reported 1,915 Greeks in Wyoming, and Cheyenne became their center for social action in Wyoming. There they established the Greek Orthodox Church of Sts. Constantine and Helen. A few years later the Greeks took over a Russian Orthodox Church in Rock Springs, and it became the second Greek Orthodox Church in Wyoming. Forty years later they remained the only two. Branches of other Greek organizations were begun in Cheyenne as well, while the Hellenic Society of Socrates was founded in Hartville in 1912. Indeed, Hartville Greeks maintained a sufficient interest in Greek affairs that two dozen returned home when the Balkan Wars began.[5]

Somewhat different kinds of opportunities drew Greeks to other towns and cities. In a number of such communities there proved to be more stability, enabling the Greeks to create viable jobs rather than ones on the move or relying on networks of fictive kin and floating pools of unskilled workers, as was the case, for example, in the mining towns of Utah.[6] For such Greek workers, transiency and home villages had far more reality, for they had no plans to remain. In Salt Lake City, where 658 Greeks were recorded in 1910, a small cadre of Greek businessmen did establish the Greek Community of Utah, an organization for raising funds through dues in order to build Holy Trinity Greek Orthodox Church. In addition to the array of businesses listed above, there were also boardinghouse keepers, doctors, lawyers, and newspaper editors. The populations of these communities usually swelled during the winter months, bolstering the businesses, and yet many ventures failed and those entrepreneurs frequently had to return to wage work.

The Greek population in 1910 ranged from 226 in Denver and 258 in Tacoma to 701 in Portland, 963 in Seattle, and 2,274 in San Francisco. These relatively small clusters of people served as bases drawing in others during off-seasons and enticing some to establish businesses. Young Greek men sought their fortunes by establishing businesses at the same time that they remained preoccupied with *prika*—the dowry that families were obligated to give on behalf of daughters and sisters before the brothers could marry. In a sense the *prika* represented one of the immigrants' strongest transnational bonds to their homeland. "No one expected or planned to become a permanent resident of America," noted Robert Theodoratus. Consequently, relatively few applied for U.S. citizenship.[7]

Lack of land and job opportunities at home and the desire to escape the Turks and army conscription, along with the need to meet the *prika* obligations, proved to be strong incentives to stay and work. Thus, the young Greek men took a broad array of the usual jobs, frequently beginning with unskilled ones, for example, in logging or lumber industries in the Northwest, on railroad crews, in construction and even mining—wherever they could find work during the warmer months. They did so in "an almost continuous movement of men between isolated working sites . . . and larger urban neighborhoods during the winter months," particularly during the first decade of the century when so many first arrived in America. What set Greeks apart from many others engaged in much the same way, such as Italians, Croatians, and then Mexicans, was that an unusual number of Greeks tried to start businesses to escape the grind facing unskilled workers. The pattern was markedly visible in Seattle, where almost one-fourth of Washington's Greeks resided in 1910. There, the full array of Greek-owned businesses could be found, from shoeshine parlors and saloons to meat and fish markets.

The number of Greeks in the state remained nearly the same between 1910 and 1920 (around 4,200), and to meet a variety of needs, they proceeded to establish local self-help or mutual benefit societies, mostly based around common homeland villages. In Seattle, there was the Apollon Lodge (Rhodes); in Tacoma, the Palatea Society (Marmara), Siana Society (Rhodes), Monolithos Society (Rhodes), and the Lerian Society (Leros); and in Price, Utah, the Pan-Cretan Brotherhood. The Pan-Hellenic Union was organized by the Greek Embassy, and in the 1920s, there were the two principal pan-Hellenic groups, AHEPA (American Hellenic Educational Progressive Association) and GAPA (Greek American Progressive Association), along with the St. Nicholas Greek Orthodox Church in Tacoma, Holy Trinity in Portland, and St. Demetrios in Seattle.

Another level of association was the *kaffenion*, the ubiquitous Greek coffeehouses that were centers of the immigrants' social life. They were established by and for persons from the same village—so much so that it was well understood that "one never went to a coffee house of another group," in part, said one Greek man who had arrived in 1905, because "they had very little in common."

After the First World War, the division was not only one separating those, say, from Smyrna from those born in Marmara but also those who took sides in the intense political rivalry that arose during the war between King Constantine I and the followers of Eleutherios Venizelos, head of the Greek Liberal Party. These rivalries created a deep divide over which side to support in the war, with the king favoring Germany or neutrality. For a generation or more, immigrants in America carefully selected their *kaffenion* based on its political preference.[8]

Patterns of adaptation among the Greeks had parallels among numerous immigrant populations in the West. The account of their experiences touches upon themes repeated in many works about workers in western industries, particularly mining, logging, farming and farm laboring, and the laying and maintenance of railroad tracks. The specific occupational choices by individuals and groups were often overlapping but not identical (clearly many Slovenians and Croatians, for example, were relatively more willing to remain with mining than were Greeks and Japanese). As the Greeks and many others quickly discovered, most opportunities for newcomers tended to be for unskilled workers with a high tolerance for low wages. Many jobs were seasonal and frequently quite dangerous, and the living and working conditions were often abysmal. The immigrant laborers, especially after 1900, were in many cases reduced to the status of transient groups of disposable workers. Many immigrants were willing to cope with such uncertainties, hardships, and perils because they had come with few applicable skills, usually spoke little or no English, and aimed to save money and return home. Others coped by organizing unions to challenge the mistreatment, the dual or multiple wage systems, the exploitation, the excessive number of work hours, and not uncommonly the requirements to live in company housing and shop only in the company stores as well as (in a number of cases) to rely upon labor contractors for employment—with fees paid up front. It was therefore not unusual for migrant and seasonal workers to seek relief by retreating to nearby towns and cities during off seasons and winters, seeking out enclaves with familiar foods, religion, spoken languages, shared cultures, friends, and relatives.[9]

In part 1 we discussed a variety of Jewish entrepreneurs, many of whom either brought with them business skills or, with the help of experienced compatriots, learned these skills, while also figuring out how to survive in the West. Many of their enterprises differed dramatically from the types pursued by the Greeks, providing a contrast of immigrant endeavors and a glimpse of the range of businesses they ventured. One more after 1900 stands out from all the rest not just because of the predominance of Jews who were involved in practically the West Coast creation of this new industry but also because it rapidly became an enormous commercial success, one that helped reshape a major segment of American culture and solidify the nation's and the world's image of the American West. Few accomplishments by immigrants could compare with the movie industry in making the case for the immense impact of immigrants on the economy and culture of the American West.

In this realm entrepreneurs helped create and distribute a new world of commerce and entertainment. Many of the men and women who emerge as leaders of this industry in California both behind and in front of the cameras were immigrants, making their contribution all the more remarkable given the industry's impact. Those leaders would not only contribute enormously to the prosperity of Los Angeles but, as the wizards of a whole new media, would also transform parts of the West into enormous cultural symbols. In the process, they fashioned images of the West that immeasurably strengthened the region's attraction and added to its mystique as a world of peoples. Moreover, they were social newcomers, and their newly emerging industry appealed to Jewish immigrants involved in other worlds of entertainment, especially vaudeville. Hollywood was soon attracting an exceptional number of Jewish writers, producers, directors, and performers. Individuals of other backgrounds followed, too, but movies (and later television) seemed to offer creative opportunities unburdened with previously existing, embedded interest groups where antiSemitism, already a significant problem, could present formidable hurdles to their participation.

In 1912 Canadian-born Max Sennett and his Keystone Comedy Company established themselves in Los Angeles (actually nearby Culver City), and early in 1914, Cecil B. DeMille relocated his fledgling film production facilities to Hollywood, still a rural suburb of Los Angeles. Just before that, Jesse Lasky, his brother-in-law Sam Goldfish (soon renamed Goldwyn), and W. W. Hodkinson set up Paramount Studios. Adolf Zukor entered the picture and ousted Hodkinson. Goldfish left Paramount, eventually teaming up with Louis B. Mayer and Marcus Loew to form MGM. Carl Laemmle established what came to be Universal Studios, as Douglas Fairbanks Jr. and Mary Pickford created United Artists. Within a year of DeMille's move, David W. Griffith made the remarkably path-breaking but profoundly racist film *Birth of a Nation*; Zukor initiated the "star system" by transforming Theodosia Goodman into Theda Bara; and soon thereafter English immigrant Charlie Chaplin began receiving one million dollars a year for his silent movie innovations. Besides the many early entrepreneurs who were Jewish immigrants, it turned out that, along with Goodman, many actors and actresses in the 1920s and 1930s were also Jewish (and if not immigrants, then second generation), including Max Aronson (Broncho Billy, "the First Cowboy Movie Star"), Al Jolson, Douglas Fairbanks Jr., Paulette Goddard, Edward G. Robinson, Peter Lorre, George Burns, Jack Benny, and Fanny Brice. As we see during the 1930s (in part 3), Hollywood also attracted many Jewish refugees—writers, producers, and directors fleeing Nazi Germany and areas being overrun by the Germans. Not only did the movie industry become a $1.5 billion per year industry within one decade, but quite rapidly it also began playing a seminal role in fundamentally identifying, shaping, and re-shaping many features of American culture.

Moving beyond that exceptional world of entrepreneurs, three major occupational areas—mining, agriculture/logging/shepherding, and fishing/canneries—show how varied the ethnic distributions were for most immigrant workers and what kinds of experiences such men and women had in representative locations. Two distinct areas of employment during the early 1900s—mining and Hawaii's plantations—well illustrate the challenges confronting immigrant workers, who provided the indispensable labor pools and yet were regularly exploited.

The Cripple Creek, Colorado, mining communities provide a powerful contrast with Butte, Montana, and Bingham Canyon, Utah; Leadville and Ludlow, Colorado; and Bisbee and Clifton-Morenci, Arizona. The men of the Cripple Creek mining towns of Victor, Goldfield, and Cripple Creek, in Telluride County, were hard rock (gold) miners who, in many cases, had worked in such mines in the north central states or came from families of such miners. They "brought with them a heritage of older working class understandings and associations." One central understanding was that the Chinese had been run out of the mines in California and Nevada, and they were "never" to be let in again. And in Cripple Creek they never were. The attitude was summed up in a resolution by the Victor Miners Union in February 1902: "Given 'the higher standard of living of the Caucasian race than that of the Mongolian race,' it was 'an utter impossibility for the white race to compete with the Mongolian race in the labor market.'"[10]

The men whom it was said belonged here had roots in Ireland, England, Wales, Scotland, Germany, or Scandinavia. In 1900 they equaled about 87 percent of all the foreign born and 93 percent of the second generation in Cripple Creek. All together, 51 percent of the Cripple Creek men were foreign stock. However, most of the mine owners were native-born men living in Denver and Colorado Springs who had scarcely any feel for the working-class bonds of these miners. When the Western Federation of Miners (WFM) first went on strike on February 7, 1894, for an eight-hour day, Populist governor Davis H. Waite intervened and facilitated a settlement four months later. During the next decade the WFM and other unions consolidated their hold on the communities, and by 1902 there were 54 union locals covering most areas of employment. Working women were paid more there than elsewhere, although that was more a reflection of the high cost of living than of gender equality, for gender roles were sharply defined.

The prevailing attitude was that Cripple Creek was "a 'white man's camp'" that excluded "Asians, southern and East Europeans, and Mexican Americans—

but not African Americans." And, while Greeks, Japanese, Hungarians, Austrians, Italians, Croatians, Czechs, Poles, Serbs, Slovaks, Slovenians, Mexicans, and Mexican Americans were hired in other mines—copper and coal mainly —"Cripple Creek miners never let them in the District." Elizabeth Jameson emphasizes that whiteness prevailed over other differences among certain Europeans, and it "defined who was barred from the District. Race and ethnicity were both exclusive and inclusive concepts. They defined who was kept out and what linked and separated the diverse peoples who could stay."[11]

Attitudes also crossed class lines. In fact, "the 'white' miners . . . banned [those listed above] and joined with merchants and managers to campaign for Asian exclusion." In addition to the political and occupational aspects, most of those northern Europeans in the district tended to live close to one another so that there were few distinct enclaves. Although there were Irish, Swedish, Scottish, and Welsh societies as well as a Catholic Church, ethnic lines tended to be somewhat fuzzy, for the prejudices shared against the newer groups "eclipsed older ethnic rivalries." If we recall that a cardinal feature of whiteness was the degree of Americanization, then it is understandable that those groups were rejected (language and customs aside) because they were perceived as less acculturated and because they worked for lower wages, lived on less income, and remained overly committed to sending money back home.[12]

In the spring of 1902, as they were consolidating their holdings, mine owners established the Mine Owners Association (MOA) to present labor with a united front and to integrate mining and smelting interests. The confrontation began as a dispute against one smelting firm in March 1903, following several strikes elsewhere and the refusal of the legislature to implement a referendum, passed by a 2–1 majority, in favor of an eight-hour working day. It escalated to a work stoppage against the mines supplying the smelter and spread to other mines by August. The MOA responded by declaring that "a reign of terror existed" and requested that the recently elected—and very pro-business—governor, James H. Peabody, send troops to preserve order. Troops arrived by September 10 and began arresting union leaders on the grounds of "military necessity" even though no violence had occurred. The MOA used this opportunity to replace union miners with non-union Finns, Norwegians, and Germans, who quickly defected. Sabotage and a mine explosion persuaded the governor that Telluride County was in "a state of insurrection and rebellion." He declared martial law on December 4.

A month later, 22 miners were summarily arrested and banished from Colorado. Three weeks later a cage cable in a mine was cut, sending 15 non-union miners to their death. In early February, 83 more striking miners were arrested and deported to New Mexico. In mid-March the Citizens Alliance—an MOA vigilante group—seized 60 union men and supporters and deported them, too, leaving their families behind. When 74 returned, they were banished once more. Meanwhile, in the same month, the MOA instituted a working card system that was, in effect, a permit to work and a means to blacklist union members. In mid-May, 80 striking Italian men were forced to march eighteen miles when they refused to sign up. Ten were eventually dropped at the New Mexico line. Toward the end of the month, with some 900–1,000 on strike, 300 went back to work. Then, early in the morning of June 6, non-union workers who had completed a shift were waiting at the Independence Depot train station when an enormous dynamite explosion killed 13 and wounded 6. The next day 28 more union men were deported. Martial law was again declared by Colorado's adjutant general, Sherman Bell, who immediately moved to banish 73 more strikers, declaring, "It is a military necessity. They are men against whom crimes cannot be specified, but their presence is regarded as dangerous for law and order."[13] A few days later 33 strikers were deported and then 51 more by early July.

Not only had the union been crippled in Cripple Creek, but the whole notion that white manhood could "bridge class differences" also collapsed. However, while the MOA had been seeking replacement miners among Scandinavian, Slavic, and Italian miners, some element of the older attitudes persisted, for no Mexicans or Japanese strikebreakers were hired. Cripple Creek never fully recovered.[14]

The labor situation in the copper mining community of Butte, Montana, was different. It was not dominated by a coalition of miners of various northern European origins but rather by an overwhelming coalition of one: the Irish. Picking up our story from part 1, no European groups in Butte were systematically excluded as in Cripple Creek, and during its peak years thirty languages could be heard in Butte. The community was a powerful magnet for Irish miners, with many having previously worked in mines in Michigan and Pennsylvania as well as in Nevada, Utah, Colorado, and California. The Irish who went there to settle did not wish to be part of (or to remain in) the floating labor pool, and they regarded such transient workers with disdain as the least favored for hiring.[15] By 1910 more than 10,000 men worked in Butte's 300 mines. In contrast to Cripple Creek, the Irish came to dominate much of the economic and political life of the Butte community and the Butte Miners' Union. Nevertheless, while there were in excess of 10,000 Irish in Silver Bow County (Butte) by 1910, there were also nearly 3,000 Austrians (various peoples from the Austrian Empire), more than 2,500 Germans, almost 1,600 Italians, and 1,500 Finns. The Greeks were among the smallest groups at this time. In 1909 thirty-five different national populations could be identified; Silver Bow County was more than one-third foreign born (versus 23 percent in Cripple Creek); the second generation made up nearly two-fifths of the population (compared with 28 percent in Cripple Creek). Not unexpectedly, a number of groups were carving out their own community niches, making Butte quite "fragmented and pluralistic."[16]

The presence of niches did not prevent some ethnic tensions and social distancing. The *Butte Bystander* in 1897 referred to the southern and eastern European miners as "brutish, ignorant men"—"three centuries behind northern Europeans in intelligence." Even 13 years later, in 1910, the *Butte Evening News* headlined "Bohunk Invasion—3,000 Slovaks imported," referring to them as "European Chinamen" who had come to replace "white men." And yet, so invested were the leaders in achieving stability and persistence that there were no work stoppages by the Butte Miners Union (BMU) between 1878 and 1914—a period of 36 years. Eighty percent of the Butte miners belonged to the union, which, like much else we have observed during the first two decades of the new century, was dominated by the Irish; in fact, the Irish Catholic Church was the city's largest. On the other hand, the Irish born continued to be strongly transnational and fiercely committed to their homeland and its goal of independence from England. Ireland was home, not the United States. They "were no less Irish for their emigration," writes David Emmons; when the First World War commenced, they supported Germany. "The American declaration of war broke the heart of Irish Americans."[17]

But changes had been underway for some time. Standard Oil had taken over Anaconda Copper Mining Company in 1899, a year before Marcus Daly's death. It began to streamline the management of crews in the mines, eroding Irish favoritism. The Panic of 1907, declining copper prices, inflation, and increased competition from Arizona mines convinced Standard Oil of the need for a more disposable workforce. Italians, Greeks, Finns, and South Slav miners were hired to replace the Irish and Cornish. Perhaps that was inevitable given the slippage in Irish immigration from its 1905 peak, but it still represented a new company strategy. Then, in March 1907, some 500 Finnish miners were let go, charged with being Socialists. The BMU chose not to strike, even proceeding to renew its contract. In December 1912, the company introduced the "rustling card system"—similar to that introduced in Cripple Creek eight years earlier—requiring the sort of detailed information by which troublesome prospective miners could be screened out.

By 1914, the BMU had lost over 40 percent of its members. Increasing dissatisfaction with the BMU led to an outbreak of violence in June and the formation of the Butte Mine Workers Union. When a fire broke out on June 8, 1917, in the Speculator Mine, killing 165 men, a new group, the Metal Mine Workers Union, called a strike to challenge the rustling card and demand greater safety, six dollars a day in pay, and recognition of the union. The company resisted, for it had less and less difficulty finding replacement workers. The Irish working population had fallen by one-fourth, while the newer miners were a significantly more transient labor force and, therefore, more manipulable. By 1918, 38 countries were represented in that workforce, which now included men from Persia, Egypt, Syria, Armenia, Turkey, Afghanistan, and Bolivia.[18]

Twenty-six miles west of Butte was the smelting center for the Anaconda Copper Mining Company. Anaconda was regarded as "Montana's most consciously working class city." It was a city so overwhelmingly unionized that it represented "a community unionism." That prompted one waitress to declare that if you were a scab, "you might as well went out and killed your mother." Anaconda had the diversity seen in Butte. Half the entire city was foreign born in 1900, and some 25 percent were Irish. But because of its relatively small population (fewer than 20,000) and the fact that the immigration laws later cut off replenishments of that foreign born, a unique situation was already evolving, namely a de-emphasis on ethnicity. On the one hand, that placed a premium on whiteness so that non-whites were viewed as a threat to wages (by 1900 most Asians had been driven out). On the other hand, historian Laurie Mercer points out,

> the Anaconda Company became more important than ethnicity in forging identities; most townspeople worked for wages and were united by economic class. Although ethnic identity may have blurred class differences at times, working class women and men were conscious of the income differences separating families regardless of heritage. Ethnic cooperation, fostered by the Catholic Church, Anaconda neighborhoods, sports teams, and leisure activities laid the ground work for cross-ethnic collaboration.

They lived, worked, prayed, and played together; at the same time they were preserving ethnic associations, celebrations, and kinship ties. Most importantly, for them there was no ambiguity, no gray area, in all this: "they claimed identities as white or non-white workers, men or women, Catholics or non-Catholics."[19]

The fact that Anaconda had ceased to be a company town and retained its small size and relatively homogenous white, working-class social structure enabled it to postpone the kind of conflicts that plagued Cripple Creek and Butte. Nevertheless, in the case studies of those two major mining towns we see both opposite responses to diversity and examples of stages in the labor movement. The evidence on nineteenth-century mining (leaving aside the Chinese placer mines) suggests that many miners were American born and certainly American born of northern Europeans. Even as late as 1910 in Leadville, Colorado, 31 percent of the 7,500 miners were native born (third generation or later).[20] What the Cripple Creek example presents is an interim phase that included the appearance of a larger, overlapping proportion of northern and western Europeans as native-born Americans began moving out of mining or up in the business. In contrast, the Butte study revealed a greater percentage of southern and eastern Europeans. There, corporations were pushing for greater control and making more decisive efforts to increase the percentage of those particular new workers because they were viewed as tractable, disposable, and, at least initially, inclined to tolerate lower wages. In both cases Asians were by and large intentionally absent, but in Bingham Canyon, Utah, in 1912, where Greeks were quite prominent, some 200 Japanese sought to join the union during the strike there.

In the first decades of the century there were numerous parallels in the labor trends in Utah, Wyoming, and Colorado—in fact, from Montana to Arizona and Texas. Many immigrant miners circulated across these neighboring states. Particularly present during the 1903–1904 Carbon County, Utah, strike were the Finnish, Slavic and Italian miners, including leader Charles De Molli, an Italian organizer who spoke Finnish, French, Italian, English, and a Slavic language. De Molli was particularly prominent during the strike because the union identified 356 Italians at one of the four mines, 246 at a second one, 172 at a third, and 74 at the fourth. Given this visibility of Italians, the comment made by Carbon County commissioner James A. Harrison in November 1903 was not unexpected: "The Italians as a class live on about one-third what it costs an American miner, while at the same time they make the same amount of money for the same work. They have money saved to leave the country or remain in idleness for months."

Most of the strikebreakers brought in were Mormons. Then, the Church of the Latter Day Saints feared the negative political repercussions, so the Mormons withdrew. The company next turned to African Americans, Japanese, and Greeks—the first Greeks in the county. The strike fell apart, and many striking miners moved on, except for 250, mostly Italian, holdouts. In November 1904, the United Mine Workers sent them train fare and told them to leave. The next strike action in Carbon County occurred in 1922 and was led by Greeks.[21]

The sequence of in-migrations by miners was especially evident in Bingham Canyon, Utah, where in 1880 only a handful were not native-born Americans or northern Europeans. During the next two decades more Finns and Swedes arrived, along with northern Italians and, after 1900, Slovenians, Croatians, Serbs, Montenegrins, Armenians, Bulgarians, and Greeks. The Bingham-Garfield Railroad imported some Japanese and Korean workers, and that may have been their access to the mines. In 1912, when the major strike took place, among those walking out were 1,210 Greeks (many from Crete), 639 Italians, 564 from the Austrian Empire, 217 Finns, and 254 Japanese, but merely 161 English, 59 Swedes, 52 Irish, and 23 Germans. Many of the strikebreakers were Mexican, a number of whom choose to remain in Bingham Canyon. At the end of the First World War, two-thirds of the Utah Copper Mining Company's 1,800 workers were foreign born, now including 416 Japanese and Koreans, 406 Greeks, 151 Italians, 72 Armenians, 55 Albanians, and 100 more representing another 15 nationalities. In 1922, when Greeks led the strike, the company stopped keeping records of workers by their nationality.[22]

Meanwhile, Poles, Hungarians, Czechs, and South Slavs (Croatians, Slovenians, and Serbs) had learned about Wyoming's coal mines and were drawn to several of them, such as Poles to Sheridan and South Slavs to Rock Springs in Sweetwater County. Because Rock Springs was a company town, miners received the available homes, and no ethnic enclaves were likely to form. As the South Slavs began to remain, marry—nearly always to women of the same nationality—and settle in, they created mutual benefit societies, such as the Slovenska Naroda Podpornan Jednota (Slovenian Mutual Benefit Association). Friendships, marriages, and associations were all part of the network building essential for finding work. In Utah one sees comparable patterns. The South Slavs in particular (perhaps 4,000 by 1924) concentrated in unskilled labor positions on railroads and in mines and smelters, enabling them to form "a significant portion of the industrial working class" in Utah. Serbs and Croats went to Bingham Canyon and Midvale and the Slovenians to Carbon County. Many eventually found that "the fight for daily bread" could best be won in America. They began families and organized fraternal unions and lodges—one by the Croats and another by Serbs, plus the Slovene society and the Jugoslav Socialist Federation. And each soon had its own newspaper. The Croats and Slovenians attended the Greek Orthodox Church, finding that it bridged but did not erase ethnic differences. However, the church did remind them of religious and political differences in the Balkans that had not been left at the border. They had also become familiar with unions while working in Europe as well as in Montana and in the support they gave to the 1903–1904 Carbon County strike. They would continue to be pro-union during the 1920s and 1930s.[23]

Whereas many mines in Colorado, Wyoming, Utah, and Montana had international labor forces, nearly all workers in the coal-mining operations at the Eagle Pass Coalfield near Laredo, in Webb County, Texas (not far from the border), were Mexican or Mexican American. By way of contrast, in north Texas's Thurber County, the mines drew Italians and Poles from Oklahoma as well as Mexicans. The Mexicans were paid less, possibly because the mine operators looked to such rationalizations as that by P. L. Mathews in his 1917 article in *Coal Age*. He asserted that the Mexican expects whites to be superior because "his intellect has dulled," and he would accept a dual wage arrangement because of his "avoidance of responsibility and his lack of loyalty and ambition." Nevertheless, "the region was dependent on Mexican labor."[24]

In Arizona, patterns seemed to have been a blend of Texas, Wyoming, Colorado, and Utah: American presence but with Germans, Scots, Irish, and Cornish immigrants coming in. With the introduction of the pneumatic drill, the need for skilled hard rock miners declined rapidly, and southern and eastern Europeans as well as Mexicans were soon sought out by mine owners in Bisbee, Jerome, and Globe. "The copper towns were miniature models of industrial America," writes Thomas Sheridan, "tiny colonies where the immigrant surge from Europe swirled into the Arizona territory. The rest of Arizona might speak

English, Spanish, or Apache, but in Bisbee or Globe the Babel [that was] . . .
reshaping cities like Cleveland and Chicago could often be heard." In a number of cases mining camps were segregated, and few Mexicans were tolerated,
whereas in Clifton-Morenci Mexicans predominated. In Ray, Jerome, and Bisbee, they were a vocal and active minority. In Jerome, too, the mine workers
included Italians, Irish, Scandinavians, Russians, Canadians, British, Greeks,
Spanish, Germans, Slavs, and Mexicans. In fact, so many were Mexican that on
Cinco de Mayo (May 5) and Mexican Independence Day (September 16) the
mines closed, schools ended early, and the town celebrated.[25]

In Clifton-Morenci (northeast of Tucson, near the New Mexico state line)
and the copper mines in those communities, where most of the unskilled workers were Mexican, the situation was as Sheridan described. Earlier, the presence of Chinese workers elevated the racial status of Mexicans, according to
Linda Gordon. Once the Chinese were forced out, whites turned on the Mexicans. Those who were "secure whites" made the Mexicans "non-whites," lower-
ing their status to justify lower wages. In effect, a Mexican wage was paid for
"Mexican" work, and since Mexicans were also being classified as "not-white,"
there could be no such thing as Mexican Americans. Thus, Mexican Americans and Hispanos were often lumped together with *mexicanos* as foreigners.
Community concern over these various immigrant labor groups in Arizona (in
particular, Mexicans and southern and eastern Europeans) prompted 400 community members and a nativist union local to appeal to the 1910 constitutional
convention for Arizona statehood, urging that it adopt two propositions that
would exclude aliens without first papers (Declaration of Intent) from all public works projects and prohibit anyone from working in mines who did not
speak English, as well as any workforce consisting of more than one-fifth aliens.
(At that time 60 percent of those working the smelters in Arizona were Mexican.) The proposals threatened "the entire foundation of Arizona's extractive
economy," and both were defeated.[26]

Contrary to the stereotypes, it has been persuasively argued that Mexicans
were actively defending their interests at this time. They demonstrated a growing strength and willingness to take action, including striking with or without
union support, beginning with a strike in Ray in 1900. Three years later, in
Clifton-Morenci, Mexicans and Italians collaborated in planning and launching a strike. The Arizona legislature had reduced the workday from ten to eight
hours, and the mine owners used that as an excuse to reduce wages, assuming
that the two principal groups of miners were essentially docile and would not
react in any militant fashion. But the *mutualistas* mobilized the Mexican workers in early June 1903, and the two groups joined forces, comprising most of the
3,500 strikers. Historian Thomas Sheridan argues that this would prove to be
the most significant strike in Arizona before the First World War—and Mexicans were in the forefront of it.

The episode persuaded the WFM to seek the inclusion of the newer immigrants by translating its constitution and procedures into "Italian, Slavish, and Finnish languages" and by reaching out to Mexicans, who again walked out (in vain) in Metcalf in 1907. In mid-1915, virtually all the Latino workers struck the Ray Consolidated Copper Company, demanding the same wage levels set earlier that year in Globe-Miami. Two months later, 5,000 walked out in Clifton-Morenci, with Mexicans again initiating the action together with Italians and Spaniards. This time there was a combined Anglo and Mexican leadership and support from all the Anglo craft locals. Other "strikitos" (little strikes) continued for two more years, with workers squeezing out more gains.

The events at Bisbee in 1917 were the culmination of this wave of strikes by a variety of groups that were coalescing. The outcome was a "counterattack by the corporate and political forces against the potentially, ethnically unified work force which had been created in 1915."[27] Bisbee, just west of Douglas near the Mexican border, had a population in 1908 of more than 20,000 persons, making it the largest town in Arizona. Some half dozen or so years earlier Phelps Dodge had bought the Copper Queen and other mining companies in Bisbee, leading to consolidations. The situation was still in an early phase in terms of the establishment of unions—that is, until workers organized the Bisbee Miners' Union in 1910. Grievances over wage formulas, working conditions, and safety increased, as did discrimination against union members. The Industrial Workers of the World (IWW, the Wobblies) seized the opportunity to step in and present management with a list of demands. Management flatly refused to negotiate, and the strike began in June 1917, with 2,000 of the 4,500 workers walking out (as well as in Jerome).

A month later, company officials seized the telegraph office, and Sheriff Harry Wheeler deputized 1,200 men, mostly company employees. Wheeler and his men took boxcars from the El Paso and Southwestern Railroad and set up a vigilance committee to try strikers and their sympathizers—who included reputable businessmen in town. At 6:30 A.M. on July 12, Wheeler rounded up 1,186 men, mostly strikers, who were then loaded into boxcars and taken to the desert town of Hermanas, New Mexico (along with 67 Mexicans from Jerome). They were left with no food or water and without shelter for two days until they were rescued by the U.S. Army. Of that group of 1,186 from Bisbee, 199 were native-born Americans, and 468 were U.S. citizens. Among the nearly 1,000 foreign born there were 20 nationalities, including British, Germans, Serbs and other eastern Europeans, especially South Slavs. Possibly one-fourth were Mexican. The deportation was akin to the ones earlier in Cripple Creek, and the reasoning given was rather similar. Although some men were arrested for the interstate deportation, none were prosecuted because the judge found justification under the "law of necessity," and nothing in federal law was violated. The U.S. Supreme Court upheld that decision. Labor historian Carlos Schwantes has concluded, "Next to the round up of Japanese Americans in World War Two, this Bisbee deportation [was] the greatest mass violation of civil liberties in the twentieth century West."[28]

Foreigners left Bisbee in droves. Perhaps half the large Slav population, one-fifth of the Italians, and nearly all the Finns were gone by 1920. In fact, within six months of the strike, the Bisbee city directory claimed that "no foreign labor is employed in the mines" there. Almost twelve years later (May 1929), the *Arizona Labor Journal* declared that Bisbee had "rightfully earned the reputation of being the 'last stand of the white miner,'" for over nine-tenths were now American citizens.[29]

Exploitation and mistreatment of workers abounded during these decades in other parts of the West, such as in Nevada, Idaho, and Washington, although the exact ethnic combinations varied slightly in relation to what has been referred to as the "shifting ethnic coalitions."[30] The nadir was reached in the spring of 1914. The events go back to the late 1880s, when four-fifths of Colorado's coal miners were English-speaking. Following the 1903–1904 strike (particularly at Cripple Creek) many miners left, including one-third of the 27,154 members of the WFM. Italians, South Slavs (i.e., Serbs and Montenegrins), Poles, and Greeks moved in. By the 1910s, Leadville, Colorado, was not unusual in having a population that was 29 percent foreign born and 40 percent second generation, with an array of miners that had shifted to a predominance of southern and eastern Europeans. At the time the September 1913 strike in Ludlow was launched by 9,000 miners against John D. Rockefeller's Colorado Fuel and Iron Company, there were 32 nationalities among its 12,000 miners, spanning geographically from Mexico to Great Britain, Italy, the Balkans, and Greece. In October, Governor Elias Ammons called out the National Guard, many of whom were veterans of the 1904 coal strike.

Within the next six months the strikers and their families were evicted from their company homes, and hundreds moved to set up a tent village. On April 20, 1914, the Greek Easter Sunday, the National Guard opened fire on the tents, including a machine gun mounted on an armored car. They then set the tents ablaze. Seven miners, 2 women, and 11 children were killed: foreign-born men and women and mostly American-born children. The women and children, most of them Italians, huddled together in a dug-out area and suffocated during the fire. The nation reacted with outrage, and only then were federal troops brought in to restore order. The strike failed, but by that time a total of 66 persons had been killed, many of them immigrants—and their wives and children. Carlos Schwantes concludes that in terms of the "overall variety, duration, and severity of conflict between labor and management," Colorado had the worst record of any state between 1890 and 1920.[31]

FIGURE 1. "Sami People on reindeer drive, Seattle, 1898." Photograph by Edward Curtis. Courtesy Museum of History & Industry, Seattle.

FIGURE 2. Chinese family, ca. 1892, Southern California. Courtesy Anaheim Public Library.

FIGURE 3. Charles C. C.,
Emil Schuetze's Chinese
laundryman, Corpus Christi,
Texas, 1890s. University
of Texas Institute of Texan
Cultures at San Antonio,
No. 076-0246, courtesy of
Mrs. J. R. Cade.

FIGURE 4. Scandinavian
threshing crew working with
Peter Mattson, possibly Troy,
Idaho, ca. 1891. Courtesy
Museum of History &
Industry, Seattle.

FIGURE 5. Asian construction crew, Pacific National Lumber Company, Washington State, ca. 1910s. University of Washington Libraries, Special Collections, C. Kinsey 2609.

FIGURE 6. Basque men with child, Jordan Valley, Oregon, ca. 1914. Oregon Historical Society, #OrHi38052.

FIGURE 7. German colonists at Keystone, Wyoming, ca. early 1900s. J. E. Stimson Collection, Wyoming State Historical Department Archives, No. 2402.

FIGURE 8. Portuguese men butchering hogs, Hanford, San Joaquin Valley, California. Man in center may be Ignacio Luis Desiderio. Photograph in permanent collection of the Kings County Library, Hanford, California. Also part of the San Joaquin Valley and Sierra Foothills Photo Heritage Project.

FIGURE 9. Filipino, Portuguese, and Japanese sugar workers, Ewa Plantation Co., Oahu, Hawai'i, ca. 1910. Bishop Museum, Honolulu.

FIGURE 10. Finnish man operating drill, Shattuck Mine, Bisbee, Arizona, early 1900s. Immigration History Research Center, University of Minneapolis.

Figure 11. Halibut fishermen, Alaska, ca. 1920s–1930s. Museum of History & Industry, Seattle.

Figure 12. Cannery workers, Apex Fish Co., Seattle, 1913. University of Washington, Special Collections, A. Curtis 27682.

FIGURE 13. Danish carpenters, lunch break, Ballard, Washington, ca. 1900. Museum of History & Industry, Seattle.

FIGURE 14. Chinese clothing shop, Honolulu, ca. 1915. Photograph by On Char. Bishop Museum, Honolulu.

FIGURE 15. Norwegian American Club, wearing traditional *bunad* clothing, Seattle, 1907. Ballard Nordic Heritage Museum.

FIGURE 16. *Norden Sangerforening*, Norwegian Men's Chorus, Seattle, ca. 1910. Ballard Nordic Heritage Museum.

FIGURE 17. Greek immigrant night school class, Salt Lake City, 1915. Photograph by Harry Shipler. Used by permission, Utah State Historical Society, all rights reserved.

FIGURE 18. Meeting of Portuguese members of the Foresters fraternal society, Honolulu, ca. 1900. Photograph by Tai Sing Loo. Bishop Museum, Honolulu.

FIGURE 19. Jewish children in costume for Purim, Temple Beth Israel, Portland, Oregon, 1898. Jacobs Family Photographs Collection, Oregon Historical Society, OrHi25946.

JAPS!

You came to care for lawns--
          We stood for it.
You came to work truck gardens--
          We stood for it.
You started your open markets--
          We stood for it.
You sent your children to our public schools--
          We stood for it.
You moved a few families in our midst--
          We stood for it.
You proposed to build a church in our neighborhood,
- BUT -
We DIDN'T and WE WON'T
stand for it!

You impose on us more each day,
until you have gone your limit.

We Don't Want you with us,
So GET BUSY, and
.. JAPS, MOVE OUT OF ..
HOLLYWOOD!

FIGURE 20. Flyer distributed in spring 1923, Hollywood, California. William Carlson Smith Collection, Special Collections and Archives, University of Oregon Libraries.

FIGURE 21. Filipino agricultural workers, California, early 1930s. Bancroft Library, University of California.

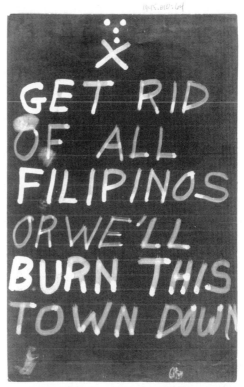

FIGURE 22. Anonymous letter to chief of police, Sunnyvale, California. Bancroft Library, University of California.

FIGURE 23. Colorado National Guard with Gatling gun outside Goldmining Exchange during miners strike, Cripple Creek, Colorado, 1903. Denver Public Library, Western History Collection, No. 23124.

FIGURE 24. Man inspecting underground shelter at United Mine Workers tent camp, Ludlow, Colorado, 1914. Nearly a dozen women and children suffocated in the shelter from a fire set by the Colorado National Guard. Denver Public Library, Western History Collection, X-60482.

FIGURE 25. Striking miners and supporters being loaded onto boxcars, Bisbee, Arizona, 1917. The miners were shipped to Arizona and abandoned in the desert. Immigration History Research Center, University of Minnesota.

CHAPTER FIFTEEN

Land, Labor, and Immigrant Communities
Hawai'i and the Mainland (Asians, Portuguese, Armenians, and Scandinavians)

W E HAVE SEEN THAT, by its sheer size, the mainland economy in the American West held out many opportunities for immigrants but often left them vulnerable to exploitation. If we include Hawai'i, we add another dramatic dimension. In the late 1930s Carey McWilliams emphasized that "the availability of large reserves of cheap labor unquestionably accelerated the pace at which agriculture was industrialized in California." And elsewhere, too. However, he added, the expectation that the opening of the Panama Canal would encourage many European farm workers to migrate to the West failed to materialize, compelling growers to rely upon imported "suppressed racial minority groups." The inherent potential tension in this development was expressed by the secretary of the Anti-Alien League of Hood River Valley, Oregon, in 1919—an organization created by the local American Legion. "We certainly do not intend to permit this essentially American valley to become a Japanese colony as have some sections of California."[1]

In terms of farm labor there were only a few significant exceptions to McWilliams's observation: smaller farms where the farmers relied upon the labor of their wives and children during planting and harvest seasons; the Women's

Land Army during the First World War (and the Women's Land Service in Southern California), where women—along with high school students—were recruited to help with the harvests (and, by doing so, "obscure . . . a growing dependence on foreign born workers"); and, during the 1930s, the Dust Bowl and other mid-America, Depression-era refugees who flocked to the West seeking work—even farm labor—in the process, displacing minority workers.[2] And "even" was the point, because once defense industry jobs began to materialize, whites fled the fields as quickly as they had earlier feverishly invaded them (see part 3).

Prospective Japanese immigrants to America believed that "in America money was hanging from the tree and one could rake up treasure like fallen leaves." In contrast, white persons who were also heading for the West Coast maintained that they "quickly and virtually unanimously came to look on first the Chinese and later the Japanese as the carriers of poverty and social decay . . . hirelings of grasping corporations, bonanza farms, and urban sweatshops that prospered only because Asians could be hired for so little and thus they threatened the whole fabric of economic opportunity and small enterprises for whites." In Hawai'i, however, people thought of themselves not by occupation or as Americans but in terms of ethnicity because, it was observed, "the fears, joys, hopes and needs of the vast majority of Hawaii's peoples . . . were determined mainly by their ethnic identity."[3]

Although the flow of trade and people between the Hawaiian Islands and the mainland steadily tightened the bonds between them even before the overthrow of the queen in January 1893, it is clear that race and ethnicity meant quite different things there than in the mainland states. Whites/Caucasians/haoles were a minority who could not readily impose social norms on the Island populations, and the cultural standards had been shaped earlier by the more open and accepting Hawaiian monarchy. Yet, the defining variable was the calculated decision of those who controlled the Hawaiian Sugar Planters' Association (HSPA) to draw workers (until 1900, by contract) for the more than 50 plantations from a variety of national backgrounds in order to replace the Chinese and then to counterbalance the Japanese. By the time the Oahu Pineapple Growers Association was established in 1913, over 200 Japanese *farmers* were able to join. Between January 1903 and July 1905, when the Japanese pressured Korea to cease its labor emigration, 7,500 Koreans migrated to Hawai'i, of whom 1,386 returned to Korea within a few years, and 1,087 moved to the mainland before the presidential order largely closed off that route. Shortly after that, Filipinos were next invited.[4]

The planters ceased recruiting Japanese in 1906 and turned back to the Portuguese (including those from the islands of Madeira and São Miguel [Azores]). At least 5,300 Portuguese came between 1906 and 1913, together with 8,000 Spaniards. Among others, only 650 Asian Indians entered in 1908–1909, and 2,000 Russians between 1909 and 1912. The limited success in bringing in these groups, who were largely of urban background, can be seen in the census data, where the number of Portuguese peaked at 9,377 in 1884, dropped to 6,512 in 1900, and in 1920 stood at 5,794, notwithstanding the arrival of probably more than 5,300 during the intervening two decades. Thousands had relocated, primarily to California.[5] In fact, Ruben Alcantara recalled in 1982, when the first groups of Filipinos arrived from the Tagalog-Manila area beginning in December 1906, the planters realized that their expectations of a rural, manual-labor population arriving was off the mark. "These people are too citified," he declared, expressing the HSPA reaction. "We want unskilled laborers for the plantations. [The present lot] would be too unhappy to do manual work in the plantations for ten hours a day. So give us rural people."

Between 1909 and 1921, there were 31,418 Filipino men and 6,481 Filipino women and children who migrated to Hawai'i. Over the next dozen years those figures would more than double, although the HSPA ceased paying passage in 1925. Critical assessments put it this way: Hawai'i had a colonial economy dependent on distant markets and low-wage labor as a vital "cheap raw material." Those workers, its "instruments of production," were a "commodity" to be factored in to production costs. So impersonal had plantation relationships become that the HSPA president told the press in 1930, "From a strictly ethical standpoint, I can see little difference between the importation of foreign laborers and the importation of jute bags from India."[6]

The ethnic situation in Hawai'i during the first two decades of the century was marked by several conspicuous patterns. To begin with, few Europeans immigrated; the Europeans who were there were in more responsible or supervisory positions on the plantations, or they most likely migrated to the urban areas. The Chinese were likewise eager to leave the plantations behind them. They either relocated to the mainland until barred from doing so by executive order in 1907 or also shifted to the urban areas (mainly Honolulu and Hilo), where they developed an elaborate business and community infrastructure. Many others did return to China, whereas the Japanese hung on longer on the plantations—along with the increasing number of Filipinos—largely due to a combination of greater numbers that enabled them to create more complete communities there, centered around the plantation store, and because they were able to press the HSPA for improvements in their wages and in the quality of their living conditions. Eventually, they, too, began to depart, but did so over a three-decade period, and they also began to transfer to the mainland until 1907. However, a fair number of Nisei still worked on the plantations in the 1930s; in 1932, the Japanese still made up nearly one-fifth of the plantation labor force. Nevertheless, the exit of most Issei and Nisei prompted the conclusion that "the most far-reaching development in the Japanese community was movement off plantations into independent farms or businesses in Honolulu."

In contrast to the Chinese, many Japanese, having farming backgrounds, demonstrated the same pattern as in the western states: they moved from working on Hawaii's coffee and pineapple plantations to farming those crops on their own lands (both owned and leased). By the end of the 1920s, there were 3,000 Japanese growing pineapples and 1,300 families growing coffee. In fact, already by 1914, four-fifths of Hawai'i's coffee was being grown by Japanese farmers. Others went into fishing, and, paralleling the Chinese, many also moved into the urban areas—establishing businesses or going into skilled trades there—or they returned to Japan.[7] The Koreans also saw no future in remaining on the plantations; no longer bound by contracts after 1900, they were one of the fastest groups either to move to urban areas or to return to their homeland.[8]

But for those Asians who remained, another major development soon began taking place. The Japanese called it *Yobiyose jidai* (the period of summoning kin), the picture brides (*shashin kekkon*). Japanese and Koreans in particular, many of whom came with no families, now sought to begin one. They were now *eijū dochaku*—ready to live there permanently. Between 1907 and July 1924, there were 14,276 Japanese and 951 Korean picture brides who arrived in Hawai'i. As a result, by 1920, 46 percent of the Japanese and 30 percent of the Koreans in Hawai'i were females. The Filipino population was only 20 percent female, and the Chinese population was 31 percent female, although that was mostly female children.[9]

Unquestionably, the expansion—and, I would reemphasize, survival—of the plantations was impossible without immigrant labor. Consequently, dominating the plantation labor scene by the end of the first decade, the Japanese launched a major strike in 1909 to protest living and working conditions as well as wage inequalities.[10] They were objecting at last to a variety of unpalatable living conditions on the plantations, especially as the number of women and children increased (21,000 Japanese women and 14,446 children present in 1908—with 5,000 children attending school). They objected to the fact that "white" field hands (here including Puerto Ricans and Portuguese) averaged about four dollars per month more than did the Japanese (roughly $22 versus $18) and that the price of basic commodities in the plantation stores had gone up 25 percent since 1905. They went out on strike on Oahu on May 9, 1909, and organized the Higher Wage Association, the first such plantation trade union movement. The HSPA retaliated by getting some of the leaders arrested and hiring strikebreakers, Koreans among them, at $1.50 per day compared with the 69 cents the Japanese were earning.

The four-month long strike cost the planters $2,000,000. In the short run it was crushed, but it garnered reforms soon after. Although the Japanese did not win at that time, they did gain much respect for their effort. Although the HSPA moved to increase the number of Filipinos as a counterbalance to the Japanese, three months later it also raised wages, eliminated the nationality-based pay arrangements, instituted a bonus system, and began improvements in medical care and plantation housing. Perhaps the HSPA had grasped the meaning behind the comment by one Japanese strike leader: "We have decided to permanently settle here, to incorporate ourselves with the body politique of Hawaii — to unite our destiny with that of Hawaii."[11]

The wage grievances of the Japanese and the scope of their 1909 strike illustrated how stereotyped were the distorted conclusions of the soon-to-be-released Dillingham Commission Report regarding Hawai'i (1:712–13): "The average Japanese family was *contented* with less than half of the income of the average Caucasian or Hawaiian family" (emphasis added). Nonetheless, it continued, whites were leaving Hawai'i because of the insufficient difference in their standard of living compared with Asians, "which the white man thinks his race dignity demands." The result, it asserted, was that a "most serious problem" existed because certain races are being replaced "by other races and nationalities having a lower standard of living." Indeed, such stereotyping carried over to inter-group relations, for a Japanese grower acknowledged that he had been hiring Filipinos because "there is no need of providing them with decent living houses . . . they are used to living on cheap food" and can be readily dismissed.[12]

Ironically, by the late 1910s dissatisfaction surfaced once more because the cost of living for plantation workers had gone up 41 percent since 1916 for single men, nearly 28 percent for couples, and about 44 percent for families. In December 1919 the Filipinos established the Filipino Federation of Labor (FFL), and the Japanese founded the Japanese Federation of Labor (JFL). They sought wage increases as well as equality in pay for Japanese women, along with changes in the bonus pay system. The Japanese and Filipinos joined forces in a second major strike in 1920 that permanently changed the dynamics of plantation labor in Hawai'i and set a precedent for inter-ethnic cooperation. On January 19, 1920, some 3,000 Filipinos walked off the job; a week later 8,300 Japanese also struck the plantations on Oahu. (Some Spanish, Chinese, and Portuguese joined in the strike.) The HSPA hired a rainbow of strikebreakers, including more Filipinos, and launched a propaganda campaign, charging that the JFL was "an anti-American movement designed to obtain control of the sugar business of the Hawaiian Islands." Three months into the strike the two federations merged into the Hawaiian Laborers' Union, ending the "blood unions" and acknowledging their recognition of the need for a non-racial labor organization.[13]

In June the strike was called off at great cost. It appeared to be another failure for the workers, except that within three months the HSPA increased wages by 50 percent, bonuses were made monthly rather than annually, ethnic wage differentials were eliminated, and housing, water, and sanitation facilities were all improved. Still, the strike had coincided with the Japanese reaching a critical mass in population and focusing more on self-employment, farming or urban work, and the education of their children. Within the next two years 2,500 men left the plantations, and the Filipinos would become the most numerous group of workers remaining. By the end of the decade the number of Japanese men had plummeted 54 percent. Ronald Takaki concluded his study of Hawaiian plantation workers with this assessment of 1920: "While Hawaiians, Chinese, Japanese, Koreans, Portuguese, Filipinos and [others] retained their sense of ethnicity[,] many of them also felt a new class awareness."[14]

Two other interrelated developments were emerging from the mingling of these peoples where there was no socially and culturally dominant white American group, or a large number of whites competing economically with Asians. This mingling of ethnicities, cultures, families, and languages, especially among the Hawaiian born, gradually gave rise to a pidgin English that was shared by "Locals," along with an evolving subculture marked by a greater degree of inter-group tolerance and referred to as "Aloha Kanaka." Writing in the mid-1930s, sociologist William C. Smith concluded that an important ingredient in this emerging culture was that "the mixed bloods are, in considerable measure, responsible for the inter-racial harmony." Not only did a higher comfort level develop on the various levels and types of interaction, but, Smith determined, that comfort level made Asian American youth in Hawai'i less reluctant to preserve elements of the traditional cultures than on the mainland—all of which contributed to the distinctive Hawaiian milieu.[15]

Furthermore, the Chinese, many of whom had moved into Honolulu, were becoming "quintessentially American, conservative in politics, enterprising in business, conspicuous in consumption, and, above all, successful." They were soon fully matched with haoles. Paralleling the Chinese, the Japanese community demonstrated several important patterns that we eventually see among others but that are singularly important here because the Japanese went from 14 percent of the population in 1890 to nearly 43 percent in 1920. However, while two-thirds had come from just three prefectures in Japan—Hiroshima, Kumamoto, and Yamaguchi—the divisions among them did not immediately disappear in terms of the separate marriage and socialization patterns nor in their collective prejudice directed at the 16,536 Okinawans (1924), who were regarded as inferiors. These Uchinanchu did not speak Chūgoku-ben, the principal Japanese dialect among the migrants in Hawai'i, and were ridiculed as hog raisers and hog eaters. The Okinawans would wage a long campaign to eradicate the stereotypes, while developing their own institutions, including an Okinawan Buddhist temple.

In general, the Japanese (still mostly the Issei) created an impressive array of institutions, including Buddhist temples (notably the Honpa Hongwanji in Honolulu), 144 Japanese-language schools, Christian churches, and organizations reflecting their adaptation and accommodation, such as the Honolulu Japanese Women's Association (1916), the Young Men's Buddhist Association (1918), the

United Japanese Society (1932), a Japanese YMCA (1902), and the Japanese Benevolent Society (1892), which raised funds in 1932 for the Home for the Aged. They also established nearly a dozen newspapers by 1924, professional associations (among them the Japanese Physicians Association in 1896 and the Japanese Dentists Association), organizations among coffee and pineapple farmers and fishermen, and, symbolically, in 1914 a joint Japanese-Chinese venture in Honolulu, the Pacific Fishing Company. In addition, in the same manner as language usage would change with the generations, so too would traditional values and ceremonies, especially the summer time Bon Odori Festival, with its elaborate traditional outfits and special large-group dances.[16]

Tomizō Katsunuma, who was born in 1863 in Fukushima, became a college professor in Tokyo, joined his brother in 1889 in Utah, subsequently became a Mormon, was naturalized in Utah in 1895, and served in the Utah National Guard. Besides recruiting other Japanese to migrate to the United States, Katsunuma became an inspector for the Bureau of Immigration in Honolulu for over two decades, until 1924. Several others managed to acquire Hawaiian citizenship and, through that, U.S. citizenship, whereas others had their citizenship revoked. Some 50 Japanese were naturalized in various states until the case of Takao Ozawa reached the U.S. Supreme Court in 1922 (see below). Of course, as the number of Hawaiian Nisei in high school rapidly increased during the 1920s, they would soon be eligible to participate as full-fledged citizens. Perhaps it was the promise of citizenship that prompted 11,000 Issei to volunteer for military service in the U.S. Army on the first day of registration in Hawai'i in April 1917.[17]

Previously, I noted the predominance of Chinese farm labor in the mainland West in the late nineteenth century, particularly in California (in contrast to African Americans and Mexicans in Texas, for example), and then the precipitous shift in the 1890s as Japanese immigrants displaced and replaced Chinese workers, whose numbers were falling. A small percentage of Chinese and white farm laborers would continue to be seen until about 1920 in such places as in the Sacramento Delta and the San Gabriel and San Bernardino Valleys. The 1903 Oxnard Sugar Beet Strike by Japanese and Mexican workers was a significant development calling attention to the growing importance of that crop and to the emergence of Japanese and Mexican workers as significant forces in the agricultural labor market, which continued to be the situation for decades. By 1906 there were an estimated 38,000 Japanese working as field hands, especially during harvests. With another 14,000 working as railroad section hands, there was a good deal of movement in and out and across both areas of employment.[18]

In August 1913, a major confrontation occurred at the Ralph Durst Ranch, in Wheatland, California, one of the largest hops growers. McWilliams reported that of the 2,800 people there, some 1,500 were women and children. Half the workers were foreign born, representing 27 nationalities or more, including Syrians, Italians, Asian Indians, Japanese, Puerto Ricans, and Mexicans. Durst had deliberately over-advertised the number of workers needed in order to acquire a surplus and thereby drive down wages. He then charged for drinking water, blankets, and tents and provided merely nine toilets for 2,800 persons. Conditions were wretched, and during a rally inspired by the IWW (Industrial Workers of the World), a riot erupted. Four people were killed, and Governor Hiram Johnson called in the National Guard. They arrested 100 workers, and 2 labor organizers were convicted of the murders. Nevertheless, the riot did lead to the establishment of the California Commission of Immigration and Housing, which extensively investigated farm worker conditions over the next two decades and recommended reforms.[19]

Beginning in the early 1900s, primarily along the Pacific Coast (but even as far east as Utah), it would also become increasingly evident that small contingents of Filipinos, Asian Indians (mostly Sikhs), and Koreans (as well as white male workers) were entering the agricultural labor force. Only 7,348 Asian Indians are reported to have entered the United States between 1899 and 1910 (many via British Columbia), a limited number because of the rather intense opposition that rapidly rose against these workers. Moreover, the new immigration law in February 1917 (see below), establishing the Asiatic Barred Zone, closed off most of their immigration. Increasing the Sikhs' visibility and marking them as outsiders (and therefore not whites) were their distinctive dress (especially the religiously mandated turbans), largely vegetarian diets, sparse number of English speakers, and a pattern of exclusively relying on work gangs of males who would migrate together. (Though mostly Sikhs, they were erroneously identified as "Hindoos.")

The 1917 strike for higher wages launched by Sikhs and Mexicans in Southern California's Inland Valley (due east from Los Angeles, extending some 20–60 miles) highlighted not only which groups were prominent in those fields but also the reality that these various agricultural labor groups were no more docile than their Hawaiian counterparts. More formal union organizing efforts would mark the 1920s and 1930s. Sporadic strikes did occur before that time, too — and so did the nativist attacks on Koreans, Sikhs, and other Asians. Indeed, the assaults demonstrated that even though the necessity for such immigrant labor was widely acknowledged throughout much of the region (e.g., Texas, Arizona, Colorado, Utah, Idaho, California, Oregon, Washington), that fact did not dissuade those who feared the new diversity from trying to force out those workers.

It is reasonable to conclude that because Southern California's Mexican workers were not seen as a racial threat (through inter-marriage) to "the whiteness of the citrus belt," they rather quickly became the "exploited minority of choice," as one historian put it. At the same time, in California's Inland Valley the multi-ethnic labor force was intentionally kept segregated in order to keep them divided, hampering unionization efforts. When that strategy did not work, more determined efforts were employed. For example, after workers went out on strike in 1919 for higher wages, a group of 400 "white citrus belt residents" rounded up 31 "disturbers" and—reminiscent of Cripple Creek and Bisbee—deported them to Los Angeles. During the 1920s the Ku Klux Klan would also attack workers' colonies.[20]

The situation was, in truth, actually quite dynamic, with men (mostly) moving from railroad work, logging, or even domestic service to agriculture, and from agriculture to canneries and packinghouses or to urban job markets. Quite often they were connected to jobs through labor contractors, such as Saburo Tanaka and Daigoro Hashimoto.[21] Men (and increasingly their families with them) were migrating in ever widening circles from Texas and New Mexico into Arizona and up into Colorado and Utah; throughout California from the Imperial Valley to the San Joaquin and Sacramento Valleys; and up the Willamette Valley into Washington State as well as into and out of eastern Washington and Idaho. Wives and daughters would frequently be the ones to find the jobs in packinghouses.

Another dynamic was the eagerness with which both Japanese and Asian Indians sought to acquire land by sale, lease, or contract and begin their own farming of fruits and vegetables (and some staple crops), just as Italians had been doing in the Bay Area and Chinese in the Sacramento Delta. There, especially, the Chinese had labored to drain the lands and build levees and then embarked on the cultivation of their crops, including such new ones as asparagus. Chin Lung and George Shima both became known as "Potato King" for the vast enterprises they each developed there. Lung, for example, leased more than 1,000 acres in 1904 and had 500 Chinese working for him raising potatoes, beans, onions, and asparagus. (In 1912, shortly before the passage of the California's Alien Land Act, he bought 1,100 acres northwest of Stockton and then 2,000 more near the Oregon border.) Farther south, in Orange County, it was the Chinese farmers who in 1891 had developed the methods for growing celery in marshlands. One immigrant, reported only as K. Ikuta, first grew rice in California, and for years the Chinese in the Delta labored to grow it successfully. By the 1910s they were doing so, from 6,000 acres in 1913 to 32,000 in 1915. In response to wartime demand, they increased the acreage to 142,000 by 1919—before the market seriously contracted.[22]

By 1909 the Japanese in California had been working their own lands for at least a decade, yet even in 1909 they still dominated the agricultural labor workforce—reportedly 70 percent of the asparagus workers, nearly two-thirds of the cantaloupe laborers, nine-tenths of the gardeners, seven-tenths of the deciduous fruit workers, 85 percent of the lettuce harvesters, and most of those working sugar beets. But it was clear from the 16,449 acres already owned and 153,682 leased where their hearts were. Most Japanese farming ventures were individual enterprises, even where co-ops were subsequently established. Abiko Kyutaro, for example, was profoundly committed to getting Japanese back onto farms by buying land and establishing colonies, which he did in the San Joaquin Valley, south of Turlock and near Livingston. There, he began the Yamato colony in 1907, followed by the Cressey colony in 1918 and Cortez the following year (with first occupants in 1924). The initial colonies prospered during the First World War, particularly because those Japanese focused on truck farming of vegetables.

Regrettably, the greater tolerance shown toward the Japanese during those few war years evaporated by 1919, when Senator James Phelan declared, in reference to the Japanese farmers, that "the rats are in the granary . . . and they are breeding with alarming rapidity." "If this is not checked now," he cautioned, "it means the end of the white race in California . . . and the end of our western civilization." The following year, near Yamato, signs appeared, "No more Japanese wanted," and a year later, in July 1921, a group of vigilantes from Turlock attacked nearby Japanese ranches and deported 58 melon workers by truck— revealing that this was the work of white locals, who mostly could afford to have trucks at that time. The police refused to respond.[23]

In Oregon the Japanese encountered severe hostility in the central and eastern parts of the state, and few ever settled there. Initially, through the labor contractor Shinzaburo Ban, many hundreds worked for railroads and then shifted to farm labor and farming. They were already farming by the beginning of the century. Yet by 1905 one-fourth were still with the railroads while 35 percent were farming for themselves, such as in Multnomah County (Portland) and in the Hood River Valley. They first began working in the valley in 1902 and operated their own farms by 1908. In two years 7 had farms, and by 1920 some 70 families owned 1,200 acres, requiring intensive labor to clear the land and harvest the strawberries, then asparagus, and then pear orchards. The arrival of picture brides nearly quadrupled the female Japanese population in Oregon (from 201 to 769), enabling many more men to give up work on railroads and in sawmills for farming, which could not be managed alone. By 1928 there were 208 Issei in the Hood River Valley (mostly from Hiroshima and Okayama) and 265 Nisei children.[24]

A contemporary report indicates that before 1900 students and businessmen were the principal migrants from British India. Between 1899 and 1920, a total of 7,348 Asian Indians arrived in the United States, and at least 1,658 left. The 1910 census found 5,424 on the mainland and another 362 in Hawai'i, for a total of 5,786. Among the many jobs the Asian Indians were willing to take were those on railroads, in street paving, even in hotels and restaurants, but mainly in agriculture. However, a large number also worked in the lumber industry in the Pacific Northwest—which became their "training ground" in America. So much so, it appears, that, as Ronald Takaki put it, they "were especially feared as labor competitors by white workers." One upshot of that occurred in September 1907, when a riot took place in Bellingham, Washington, where some 400 to 500 white men rounded up over 150 Indians working in the mills and shipped them to British Columbia, Seattle, and Oakland. Unnerved, most left. Given their small number and their poverty, they were most likely scapegoats —but also an entirely safe target. At the same time, another consequence of the anti-Asian hostility being directed toward these Punjabi Sikhs was the government's stringent application of the LPC clause in the immigration law—the denial of admission on grounds they were "Likely to Become a Public Charge," and 3,543 were so excluded.[25]

Besides the Bellingham clash, several other similar but less dramatic episodes occurred, including at Everett and St. John, Washington. Asian Indians may not have always been able to evade government scrutiny, but they did agree to avoid those places that were potentially violent. They gradually worked their way southward, finding employment as farm laborers in the orchards of the Sacramento and San Joaquin Valleys as well as in the Inland Valley east of Los Angeles and then in Imperial Valley. It was reported that of the 2,600 Asian Indians in California in 1920, some 2,000 were Sikh, many of whom settled in Marysville, Yuba City, and Stockton, where the first Sikh Gudwara (temple) was established. (The remainder consisted of about 500 Muslim and 100 Hindu.) Generally, the Indians, having come from the Punjab, where many owned land, shunned unions because they wished to be farmers and saw themselves as short-term sojourners, not part of the farm labor class. By the second decade of the century they were leasing lands to grow rice in the Sacramento Valley, vegetables and fruits in the San Joaquin Valley, vineyards and fruit orchards in the Fresno area, and cotton, grain crops, and cantaloupes in the Imperial Valley. Jawala and Bisaka Singh, in the footsteps of Shima and Lung, became known as the "Potato Kings" of Holtville. El Centro, Brawley, and Holtville—at the eastern end of San Bernardino County—became important centers for the Indians in the Imperial Valley, as did Marysville in the Sacramento Valley, where Hakim Khan was soon growing rice on a 1,000-acre farm. While Asian Indians preferred to hire their own, as did the Japanese, other farmers at times preferred the Indians as a wedge to keep Japanese and Mexican workers separated.[26]

In view of the small number of Asian Indians who entered the country before the Asiatic Barred Zone was enacted in 1917, four developments mark this group. Notwithstanding the language and cultural differences, they were regarded as good workers, but they could not avoid the dual wage system and the job competition, especially with Japanese and Mexicans. They strove to acquire land in California about as rapidly as did the Japanese, and they proved to be quite successful in the three major valleys discussed (Sacramento, San Joaquin, and Imperial), even though, beginning in 1910, they started sending considerable amounts of remittances to families in India.

The passage of California's Alien Land Law (Webb-Heney Act) in 1913 and the acts of 1920 and 1923 prompted a unique response by several hundred Punjabi men. Records suggest that, beginning in 1916, a few hundred married Mexican women, with Indian brothers sometimes marrying Mexican sisters. (The more acculturated also ceased wearing the turban.) One ulterior motive was to place land titles in the name of the wives, for they were eligible for citizenship. The Punjabi were not entirely barred from ownership and leasing until 1923, and yet they had begun marrying seven years earlier. Starting in 1934 they found it expedient (after a court case) to transfer titles to their children. A by-product of these 300 marital unions (1913–1949) was the growth of a unique, multi-generational Punjabi-Mexican community in both the Imperial and Sacramento Valleys. Anthropologist Karen Leonard contends, given that the Mexican women were one of the few groups whom the Asian Indians could readily and legally marry, that the marriages actually represented "commitments to permanent residence in the United States."

For community building and protection, the Indians organized such groups as the Khalsa Brotherhood, the Pacific Coast Khalsa Diwan Society, the Sikh-American Education Society, the Muslim Association of America in Sacramento, and the Hindu American Conference in Sacramento to help Indians acculturate and adapt to America (1920), and the Hindustani Association, or Ghadar Party, in 1913 to promote the renewal of India and the ouster of the British. The last one led to the expulsion of its leaders for violating American neutrality laws.[27]

Environmental conditions, market opportunities, available natural resources, adequate capital, and determined personalities all came into play in different locations and with different outcomes. Abiko Kyutaro's colonies succeeded, as we shall see, because of that combination of variables. In Hood River Valley a different format of individual ventures and co-ops was employed to market the produce. The Kona coffee producers on the Big Island (Hawai'i) had ideal conditions and a unique product. For the Chinese in the Sacramento Delta, or the Asian Indians in the Imperial Valley, or the Japanese in Kona, sheer grit and determination (and a measure of cleverness) carried the day—along with Colorado River irrigation into the Imperial Valley, the proximity of Sacramento, Stockton, and San Francisco to the Delta, and the good timing and natural conditions for the Japanese in Kona.

Seito Saibara provides one other kind of illustration. A political activist and lawyer in Japan, he was, at age 37, elected to Japan's House of Representatives in 1898. He converted to Christianity, became president of a Christian college, and decided to study theology in Connecticut. In the United States he met the Japanese consul, Sadatsuchi Uchida, who had toured Louisiana and Texas and had enthusiastically reported the potential there for rice cultivation. He persuaded Saibara to visit Texas with him in 1903. Saibara gave up theology to organize a rice-growing colony of 1,500 persons in Texas—the first Japanese Christian colony in Texas. He purchased 304 acres for $3,750 near Webster (between Houston and Galveston). Two cousins—a journalist and wine merchant— came from Japan and bought an additional 300 acres near Saibara's, as did a tea merchant. The four hoped to constitute the nuclei of this colony. Others came; some prospered, but most failed, sometimes for over-producing. The foreman of one of the larger projects, Yonekichi Kagawa, came in 1907 and set up his own farm with his wife and twelve children, most of whose descendants are still in Texas. However, high wartime prices could not last. The market collapsed; re- trenchments followed, and some of the original planners quit in 1924.

Saibara and his fellow rice farmers at least had the satisfaction of getting Texas's Alien Land bill modified to omit those currently living in Texas, making it far less punitive than in the Pacific Coast states. It was, however, federal legis- lation that was a critical factor in Saibara's decision to quit: the Immigration Act of 1924, which almost closed the door entirely on Japanese immigration, doom- ing plans for replenishments for Saibara's colony. At the age of 63, he and his wife moved to Brazil, farmed rice there, tried to jump-start another colony, aban- doned that, and returned to Texas to live out their remaining days on the farm of their son Kiyoaki. Saibara died in April 1939, and Kiyoaki continued to farm rice until 1964, retiring at the age of 79 and dying eight years later. In still another twist, the man responsible for getting the amendment to Texas's 1921 land legis- lation that exempted current residents was Sabura Arai. He had come to San Francisco in 1884, lived on the East Coast for 20 years, relocated to Wharton County, Texas, in 1906 to farm rice, and became a community leader in Hous- ton and an influential man with the state legislature. When the law was enacted, Arai shifted to the nursery business—a 462-acre operation employing between 70 and 100 employees—and remained in the nursery and then landscaping busi- ness for 40 years. A Texas-size story with a cast of Japanese immigrants. Different context, different leadership, different outcome. These Texas farmers did not have to continually fight off nativist opponents and hostile competitors.[28]

Laurence Oliver was—and yet ultimately was not—your typical Portuguese immigrant. On his 16th birthday, in March 1903, he left for America and went to New England, long the center of Portuguese life in America (especially Mas- sachusetts) and home to more than half of the foreign-born Portuguese. His first jobs disappointed him, and in 1906 he accepted his father's appeal to join him in San Diego. After taking the train to San Francisco and a steamer to San Diego, he began work in the fish market of a relative for one dollar a day. Even- tually, he, like Manuel Medina, who arrived in San Diego in 1919, acquired fishing boats and fished for tuna; both men became quite rich.[29] At about the time all this was taking place, over one-third of all foreign-born Portuguese lived in California, mainly concentrated in Alameda County—Oakland, Haywood, and San Leandro. In fact, in 1911 the *Saturday Evening Post* did a story on San Leandro, describing it as "almost as Portuguese as old Lisbon itself."

The Portuguese presence, while not extremely visible, did extend back to 1850, with over 3,400 present in California in 1870, and this may help to explain historian Leo Pap's assessment of how the Portuguese fit into California life, especially in the San Joaquin Valley: "The Armenians, German-Russians, Italians, Japanese, and Chinese . . . were regarded as 'foreigners' by Fresno natives partly because they had come to the United States more recently than the others and were economically weaker." Those "others" included Danes, Germans, and Portuguese.[30]

Somewhat more than 15 percent of those Portuguese arriving between 1899 and 1921 gave California as their intended destination.[31] Principal migration streams went to New England. However, others would then follow Oliver's path, relocating from New England's crowded communities to California's less urbanized environment, particularly since they were primarily interested in farming (and, secondarily, in fishing). Likewise, just between 1911 and 1914 an estimated 2,000 relocated from Hawai'i to California. Although Portuguese were still going to Hawai'i in the early 1900s for jobs on the sugar plantations, many were from urban backgrounds and quickly disliked both the work and its negative association with non-whiteness. Still, returning home was a less feasible or less desirable option than relocating to California.[32]

By 1920, there were records of 58,997 persons of Portuguese foreign stock in California. A majority of the foreign born were from the Azores and were especially interested in trades, fishing, and dairy farming rather than initially pursuing higher education or even attending parochial school in their churches. Indeed, by 1915 Azoreans already owned half the dairy farm lands in the San Joaquin Valley and, together with those along the Central Coast, were producing half the state's dairy products. In 1923 they established the Association of Milk Producers, and their prominence continued for decades as they shifted from tenant farming to farm ownership. In addition, just as the Chinese and Japanese farmers introduced crops that are now part of America's salads, John Avila, of Merced, first popularized the sweet potato, now an American staple.

The divisions among the Portuguese persisted, possibly because of their preference for a rural lifestyle and their varied origins and communities (mainland Portugal, Azores, Madeira, Cape Verde, and the split between rural and urban concentrations), as well as the lessened pressure on them to assimilate in California. The darker Cape Verdeans were excluded from Portuguese associations for decades. There was limited inter-marriage among the various subgroups and even condescension among them toward those remigrating from Hawai'i, labeling them Kanakas. Still, the Portuguese did establish the Portuguese-American League to promote citizenship, and several individuals emerged to pursue local politics in the early 1900s. Appropriately enough, a Portuguese woman was later elected mayor of San Leandro in 1941, and a Portuguese American man was elected mayor of Sacramento in 1959.

For much of the twentieth century the San Joaquin Valley, especially Fresno and its neighboring communities, was one of the three centers of Armenian life in America together with New York City and Worcester, Massachusetts. The vignette in the book's prelude on the Seropian brothers sheds some light on the roots of that community.

Sam Azhderian was a pharmacist in Fresno who spoke Armenian, Turkish, Arabic, French, and English. This was an impressive feat, but these were the languages spoken by many in the Armenian diaspora. The Armenians have been an important immigrant/ethnic group not because of their great numbers nor because theirs were highly prominent urban enclaves (that is, until 1965 and the shift to Los Angeles and vicinity), nor because of their exceptional personal visibility (although, subsequently, author William Saroyan, California governor George Deukmeijian, and several wealthy philanthropists, among others, changed that group profile). Rather, the Armenians are a distinguished immigrant people in the American West because they were one of the first major refugee groups to flee to America, one of the first non-native peoples in America to have experienced genocide in their homeland in the late nineteenth century (1894–1896) and early twentieth century (1915), and they were one of the first diasporic people of the twentieth century, scattered into at least 17 nations. They are a people for whom migration to America became something of an in-gathering (much as Israel would be for Jews), with California a principal resettlement destination. Yet, characteristic of strong transnational bonds, they remain a people for whom their homeland has remained at the center of their thoughts and organizational activities, especially every April 24th, when Armenians commemorate the 1915 genocide in the Ottoman Empire.[33]

Although American Protestant missionaries played a significant role in educating and converting Armenians in their homeland and familiarizing them with the opportunities in America, and in central California in particular, 90 percent of Armenians remain members of the Armenian Apostolic Church. But the distinctions are pronounced because, adds Berge Bulbullian, "the Apostolic Church deals with its members as Armenians who live in the United States; Protestant churches treat their parishioners as Americans with an Armenian ancestry."[34] Armenians brought with them to Fresno a distinct language, religion, customs, intense national identity, powerful attachment to their homeland, and, arising from their experiences in Asian Turkey, a long experience as an inward-looking, enclave-oriented people. Of necessity, as has been the case with other groups that were minorities in their homelands, the Armenians found that to survive they needed to rely on their wits, a commercially oriented risk-taking approach to their trades, and frequently self-employed,

urban or agricultural endeavors. With that insularity came, as also was the case
with many Jews, a high premium being placed on endogamy—marriage only
among fellow Armenians. Even socializing or dating with *odars* (outsiders, foreigners) was severely discouraged by immigrant parents.

Ironically, circumstances made any prospect of immediate return to their
cherished homeland as improbable as it was for contemporary Jews fleeing the
Russian Empire. Like the Jews, the Armenians, feeling stateless, opted promptly
for American citizenship. Also like the Jews, their combination of values, customs, and mores did not preclude a variety of internal differences due to religion, intermediate homelands, and even political ideology (especially after the
Soviet takeover of the short-lived Republic of Armenia in late 1920). Nonetheless, in the flip side of the traits which Armenians nurtured to survive as an ethnic religious minority (often in less than amicable settings), the perceptions of
non-Armenians in the Fresno area was that the Armenians were clannish, aloof,
aggressive in business, and just very different—in fact, too different and non-
American to be white. Consequently, we have here a people that struggled to
establish their whiteness and their eligibility for citizenship (e.g., *In re Hallad-
jian*, 1909), while coping with an array of discriminatory actions and restrictive
covenants directed at them.

U.S. immigration data suggest that about 71,000 Armenians were admitted
between 1895 and 1917 and between 3,000 and 5,000 before that period. There
were an estimated 78,000 in the country in 1919, but the 1920 census reported
only 36,628 foreign born, of whom 5,689 lived in California (no data on second
generation). Although during the peak reported years (1899–1910) 2,564 newly
arriving Armenians gave California as their intended destination, we find here,
too (as with the Portuguese and Scandinavians), that "the vast majority migrated to Fresno after spending years in Armenian colonies in the Eastern industrial centers." For example, a 1903 study of 67 males in Fresno revealed that
31 had worked in eastern and midwestern cities for an average of 5.7 years before
migrating to California.[35]

At the same time that the Seropians were trying to gain a commercial foothold in Fresno, Melcon Makarian arrived, planted fig trees, and, with his son,
Henry, eventually created the largest fig orchard in the world at that time. Others
introduced the casaba melon and the Armenian cucumber (along with less familiar crops, such as kiwis and pomegranates) and began planting vineyards for
grapes, although many had had no agricultural experience but had the desire to
be self-employed. By 1933 Armenians controlled 70 percent of the wholesale
fruit and vegetable business in the San Joaquin Valley. Several decades earlier,
a Dane, Peter Peters, had "discovered" raisins when he saw the changes in a
drought-affected Muscat grape crop he could not sell. That is relevant here because by 1902 Armenians were growing 15 percent of the raisin crop on 16,000
acres. The California Raisin Growers Association was founded in 1898 and the

California Raisin Company in 1912. Its brand name was Sunmaid. Yet prices and production remained unstable until World War One and then plummeted afterward. Prohibition was the next disaster as vintners shifted their product to raisins, doubled the crop, and collapsed the market, forcing many Armenians beginning in 1923 to sell and move on.[36]

Actually, for years Armenians had been moving into nearby communities, such as Reedley, Parlier, Sanger, Salinas, Kingsburg, Fowler, and the one they founded, Yettem, along with Visalia, Tulare, Bakersfield, and Modesto. In addition to farming in these communities, many Armenians were merchants, grocers, weavers, shoemakers, tailors, other craftsmen, and various professionals. In the decades prior to the Second World War, many women also labored in the fruit and vegetable canneries and packinghouses in central and northern California. Groups would go, with their children, for as long as six weeks to Emeryville, Yuba City, and Stockton. Perhaps as many as one-third of the women in those packinghouses were Armenian, working alongside Italian, Spanish, Portuguese, and Mexican women. Moreover, one of the largest packinghouses for raisins had been built by an Armenian near Fresno, Alfred Lion, and many women worked there, too. Armenians would eventually pool much of their own resources to establish the National Raisin Company and its successful brand name, Champion.[37]

Armenians differed sharply from many other groups we have looked at here, for they did not include large numbers of migrating workers. By and large they traveled to the area they had identified, or had been directed to, and generally remained within it. That resulted in an Armenian community in whose development we can more readily identify a classic example of the past in tension with the present, of tradition versus adaptation. The residential and business enclave in Fresno, south of the railroad tracks, expanded beyond those early boundaries chiefly after the Second World War. There, the community established five churches (two Apostolic, three Protestant). One of the Apostolic Churches, Holy Trinity, was only the second such congregation in America, established in 1900. The Armenians established language parochial schools and started Armenian language newspapers. Also, 600 men among them demonstrated their commitment to their homeland by volunteering to fight against Turkey during the First World War, and California Armenians raised $75,000 for war relief in Armenia.

But at the same time that they were constructing the framework of their community, they were facing continuous obstacles, including exclusion from social groups, sports teams, high school clubs, and country clubs. Farmers, schools, retail stores, and banks would not hire Armenians, and real estate covenants specifically barred the sale of property to blacks, Asians, and those from the Turkish Empire, persons considered non-white. In 1931, shortly after the Mexican Americans had formed the League of United Latin American Citizens and the Nisei had established the Japanese American Citizens League, Armenians organized the Armenian American Citizens League to fight such discrimination, but it would take another generation to make real headway—aided by the Americanization of the second and third generations.[38]

So few studies of the West include the Pacific Northwest that, together with the focus on immigrants of color, the effect has been tantamount to an oversight of many European peoples who unquestionably helped shape the contemporary West. Scandinavians in particular have been written off as "melted." Their response to America was certainly unusual, but they did seek a balance between their ethnicity and their Americanism rather than entirely giving up one for the other. Three women—a Norwegian, a Dane, and a Swede—provide succinct expressions of the reactions of many of their compatriots. Henny Hale came from Norway in 1923 at age 20 when her uncle in Tacoma sent her a ticket. She was irrepressibly eager to come: "We thought America was lined with gold all over the place"; "I didn't know what I let myself in for, but I wanted to go to America, period. . . . I was possessed, I just wanted out." She expected to return home within five years, "But you never do, you never do." Grethe Petersen arrived at age 22, and on her first day in America, at Ellis Island, she was given breakfast—two eggs, toast, and potatoes. "I had never had two eggs, period. So I thought, is this America? What do you know! I could not get over it—two eggs!" Only 10 when she left Sweden, Elsie Odmark recalled her view: "I have never forgotten that hungriness [in Sweden] and I have never been hungry in this country."[39]

Other stories convey the ways those who settled in provided a link between the old and new lives. Inga Marie Humlebekk (1888–1963) was a formidable Norwegian-born woman whose activities earned her the title "Mother Norway of the Pacific Northwest"—after she first raised a family. Born in May 1888 in Kokksund, she emigrated in 1909 to Seattle, becoming a governess. On her first return visit to Norway in 1915, she met the man she would later marry, Frode Frodesen. He became an immensely successful contractor of major construction projects throughout the Northwest. After she raised three children, Inga became increasingly active in the Norwegian American community in true transnational fashion, first by leading tours to Norway in 1937 and 1938 and then, during the Second World War, by traveling the length of the Pacific Coast showing her travel films, giving major speeches, and raising thousands of dollars for Norway war relief. She organized Nordmanns Forbundet (Association of People from Norway) in her home and became the Pacific Coast correspondent for *Aften Posten* in Oslo and for *Nordisk Tidene* in New York. For several years she edited the official publication of the Daughters of Norway, *Døtre av Norge*, and became president of several Norwegian organizations. Not content with all that, she wrote plays and poetry, organized Syttende Mai (17th of

May) celebrations, and was a founder of the Norse Home. Inga's accomplishments were ongoing, demonstrating a strong commitment to her culture and homeland.[40]

Ole Oleson Kittilsby and Mari Klev were married in October 1878 in Norway and migrated to America two years later. After a few years (and three children) in Minnesota, they resettled in Lilliwaup, Washington, and had four more children. They homesteaded there, and Ole also built one of the first fish hatcheries in Alaska, regularly journeying there until they once again moved, this time to Seattle in the 1920s. During the Second World War contact with families in Norway was cut off, but in 1972 a grandson and his wife rediscovered the Klev and Kittilsby families. On August 4, 1994, some 200 descendants, including 25 from America, held a reunion in Haglebu, Eggedal, Norway.[41] So, perhaps these Scandinavians did not completely melt. They did integrate more rapidly than almost any other European peoples, but links survived and traditions were cherished. When hundreds of people in Tacoma came out on May 17, 1914, to celebrate the centennial of the Norwegian Constitution (still the most cherished public holiday for Norwegians), they did so because that heritage was still relevant and their ethnic pride still strong. These vignettes represent those sentiments, for Scandinavians bridged the older and newer waves of immigration. And the connections extended even to those who had arrived before the 1870s. It has been suggested, for example, that "the Danes who went to Zion [1850s to 1860s] took the strangeness out of migrating to America, and their stories expanded the horizons of those who remained in Denmark."

For Danes and Swedes the 1880s were the peak years of their migration to the United States (88,132 Danes and 391,733 Swedes) and almost so for Norwegians (176,586). The Norwegians' foremost decade was the 1900s (190,505), which was also very strong for Danes (65,285) and Swedes (249,534). If we add in the 242,516 who arrived in the 1870s, these three peoples had strong migration patterns extending over nearly a half century of changing immigration groups. Finnish immigration, on the other hand, was sparse prior to the 1890s (1872–1892: 29,385; 1893–1900: 35,527) but accelerated during the early 1900s, reaching to more than twice the number of Danes (133,065).[42]

Between 1899 and 1910, almost 10 percent of these Scandinavian groups (70,083) indicated their intention to reside in the West, especially Washington and California. As described earlier, there was also a significant secondary migration, mostly from the Upper Midwest to the Far West. Reviewing their motives suggests that they migrated from the Midwest to the Far West both on a quest and in protest—seeking economic opportunities and (for many) the chance to escape the constrictive environments in many small, especially rural, midwestern communities. The "protest" part of that statement in the West could be seen in the splintering of church communities, the low attendance at many of them, the absence of ethnic churches in other places, the rather

short-lived struggle in many churches to preserve native languages before suc-
cumbing to the changes and shifting to English language usage, and in due
time the merger of several synods. Most Scandinavian resettlers did not invest
themselves as emotionally in a specific church (or for so long a period) as did,
for example, French Canadian and Polish Catholics.[43]

The "quest" of many, especially young, single women, was a search for jobs
out of necessity or because their skills (or command of the English language)
were limited. But for a large percentage—by all accounts well over a majority—
of the men in all four groups (and later among Icelanders, too) their quest was
for opportunities in fields they knew best: fishing, logging, milling, mining, agriculture (which included dairy and poultry farms and other livestock), and as
merchant seamen. As one scholar put it, "The occupational structure offered
positions . . . with which Nordic immigrants were traditionally familiar—and
hence a relationship [could exist] between the occupational structure of the
place of settlement and that of the place of emigration." Those Scandinavians
who headed for the rapidly expanding towns and cities—from Spokane and
Yakima to Tacoma and Seattle, Portland and Silverton, Fresno and San
Francisco—often brought a knowledge of skilled trades, such as tailors, carpenters, bakers, newspaper editors, and shipbuilders (who drew in many other
craftsmen and seamen).[44]

What is noteworthy are all those who found opportunities beyond their expectations, building canneries, establishing whole shipyards, expanding trade
skills into major engineering or construction firms, transforming farms into
sizeable orchards as irrigation became more available (such as in Yakima), and
even building upon successful businesses to establish banks. However, many
of those who were more recent arrivals or who had come with fewer skills or insufficient capital—or who encountered fewer opportunities or less luck, or
who were sojourners planning to return (or some combination of all these
factors[45])—remained to find employment as laborers, sailors, cannery and
packinghouse workers, miners, loggers, sawmill operators, railroad trackmen,
carpenters, construction crews, hotel and restaurant staffs, and modest farmers
and dairymen.[46]

Where they were not raising families or working on the family farm, or in such
urban family businesses as grocery stores, delis, dry cleaners, or boardinghouses,
the women sought employment as laundresses, domestics, servants, packinghouse workers, and, later, in various clerical positions.[47] Grethe Petersen, born
in Denmark in 1900, came to America in 1922, wed two years later, operated a
dairy with her husband, and later opened a deli in Seattle. It succeeded in great
measure because of the popularity of her homemade Danish foods. In fact, she
went back to Denmark to learn how to prepare such foods as *rullepølse* (cold
cuts) and *leverposte* (pâté).[48]

Men not only concentrated in farming, fishing, and forestry (as the Census

Bureau today labels this trio) but also either dominated those occupations in the Northwest (or, in California, the poultry/egg business in Petaluma and the dairy industry in and around Fresno) or were so numerous as to play a critical role. The Dillingham Commission estimated that 10,000 workers in Washington's wood-related industries were Scandinavian—equaling one-fourth of the workers in a laboring population representing 40 nationalities and consisting of three-fifths foreign born. In the case of the Swedes, in Washington at one point near the beginning of the century, they accounted for so many of the loggers that "Scandinavian" was the working language among them, and they so dominated the shipping of lumber to the mills that it was said to be run by the "Scandinavian navy." After three failures in the logging business Simon Benson established the Benson Timber Company in 1895, floating lumber all the way to San Diego. He then built major hotels (the Benson and Columbia Gorge Hotels) and established the Portland Polytechnic School. And such a Scandinavian presence was not alone along the coast, for in Montana by the 1920s three-fourths of the contractors in the logging industry were Scandinavian.

Other areas with a strong Scandinavian presence were coastal shipping and the salmon and halibut fishing industries, especially after 1900. They came to have leading roles in the Association of Pacific Fisheries (as fish brokers, boatbuilders, marine architects, and inventors of fishing gear and cannery equipment). In fact, so visible did their presence become that, at times, people referred to the herring fleet as the "Norwegian Navy," and by 1920, some 95 percent of the halibut fisherman and many of the halibut boat owners were Norwegian. In 1908, Scandinavians still constituted a near majority in the Fishermen's Protective Union, with 3,000 of the 6,775 members. When Peter Buschmann developed his salmon trapping method (and subsequently founded Petersburg, Alaska), it was said that in one season he caught 200,000 to 300,000 more salmon than did all the fishermen in Norway.[49]

For the farmers, growing new crops also required learning new farming skills. As mentioned, Danes in the Fresno area only serendipitously "discovered" raisins, while other Danish farmers expanded into dairy production and formed the Danish Creamery co-op. Dairying and ranching by Danes also contributed to the early development of Solvang, California (along with its renowned Danish Folk School, established in 1911; tourism followed later), while others who went to northern California, particularly Humboldt (nearly two-thirds of whom were from Jutland and Schleswig), substantially contributed to the lumber and shipbuilding industries there. Danes were quite widely dispersed in California, from Humboldt to Mendocino (north of San Francisco) to Los Angeles and San Diego. At the same time, besides those in Washington and Oregon, thousands of Norwegians—first and second generation—were farmers in Montana or lived and worked in Great Falls, Butte, Anaconda, Missoula, Billings, and Helena (25,000 by 1940).[50]

There were many ways that Scandinavians moved up the occupational ladder, contributing to their own success and enriching the local economies. Ole Nissen demonstrated that it was who you knew, not just your skills. He was a Danish tailor in San Francisco in 1907, then in Selma in the San Joaquin Valley. Later he went on to Eureka; Vancouver, Washington; and finally to Seattle. He operated a highly successful tailor shop there from 1925 to 1967, benefiting from the fact that he belonged to the Danish Brotherhood in America and played cards regularly with men who were bankers and other prominent businessmen. Nissen began to accumulate a lot of steady business from their wives.[51]

In so many instances the impact of the various Scandinavian groups was related to their eagerness to adapt to the American environment and products. For example, many Scandinavians took logging or mill jobs to save money to buy farms, and, historian Jorgen Dahlie adds, "it was as farmers and in the rural environment that the majority of immigrants worked out their destinies and gained full acceptance in society."[52] They took advantage of new opportunities for mobility or for potentially greater successes—as they believed were being held out to them by the American model. Thus, Norwegians, who were so familiar with cod fishing, learned salmon fishing "from scratch" and did so from Oregon to Alaska. Once Peter Buschmann mastered this type of fishing, he started his own canneries and attracted many fishermen, such that by 1920 nearly 18 percent of the foreign born in Alaska were Norwegians.[53]

Those who became eminent leaders included representatives of Norway's technical college training, such as Ramm Hansen, an architect who converted to Mormonism, established the firm of Young and Hansen, and obtained the contracts to design the Mormon Church office building and the Federal Reserve Bank in Salt Lake City as well as temples in Mesa, Arizona, Idaho Falls, and Westwood (Los Angeles). His partner was a descendant of Brigham Young. Meanwhile, far to the north, Gudbrand Loman, who was born in Iowa but whose family came from Valders, Norway, partook of the gold rush into Alaska and became the first mayor of Nome, a U.S. district attorney, and a federal judge. He also ran the only photo studio, pharmacy, and steamship company there and then in 1914 established a reindeer business. His son became the "reindeer king of Alaska"—operating the largest such business in the world, with one-quarter million reindeer by 1940. Of a more modest magnitude but an example of clever adaptation and business sense were Edward Frederick (a German immigrant) and his partner Nels Nelson, who built up a second-hand furniture business in Seattle and advertised in all the newspapers. But only in the Norwegian press was the ad in a Scandinavian language.[54]

The latter anecdote suggests why Scandinavians integrated so well. They "deliberately adapted to the American way of life, selecting and incorporating into that 'system' whatever they held to be valuable in their Scandinavian heritage."

They did not perceive themselves as newcomers; like so many immigrants and Americans coming from elsewhere in America to the West, there was an "immediate past" (prior residence in the Midwest) that significantly contributed to their rapid Americanization.[55] And, Scandinavians had an "Americanization virus," the determination to become Americans quickly. They "considered the integration of the best of their tradition with that of the Northwest culture to be a positive step toward assimilation that most Americans applauded," making every effort to portray themselves as "good Americans," in fact, as "almost American" from the start. Moreover, the immigrant press "was one of the significant agencies working from *within* the immigrant community to advance rather than impede assimilation." Not surprisingly, they were regarded as "unusually assimilable," with shared political ideals of individualism, democracy, and liberty, and a readiness to adopt American practices, organizational styles, and customs. They could not be more "white."

However, there was, at the beginning of the century, a negative aspect to that rush to assimilation, but the evidence does not indicate how long it might have persisted. Some Scandinavians adopted American prejudices and expressed an intolerance of Catholics, Asians, Slavs, and Jews, even going so far as to suggest that Greeks, Turks, and Armenians would be better off in the Philippines. Quite early on (1897) they saw Japanese as a threat to the jobs of Scandinavians. Likening them to grasshoppers, one writer in June 1900 declared that the Japanese had come "to take the bread from the mouths of the white men." Perhaps this comment was an exception, an expression reflecting a not uncommon situation that writer Hans Bergmann observed in the mid-1920s, namely that Scandinavians saw themselves as Americans but were really still immigrants. Nevertheless, he concluded, at least there was little of the usual inter-generational strife found in other ethnic groups.[56]

These situations were not without some rough edges, for some did express concern about how they would fit in. Andrew Johnson went with his family to Tacoma. He was harassed in school for his accent and continually called "a dumb Swede." Even in church Swedish Americans would call him a greenhorn. That was not so unusual. In 1930, when she was 24, Astrid Lovestrand migrated with family members to Yakima. She wed a Swede the following year and subsequently had eight children. She recalls, "I was so afraid to name my children because I was afraid people was not going to be able to pronounce them and [would] laugh at their names. Those days, you wouldn't want to [be] recognized that you were Swedish." Her husband, Emil, who grew up in America around the turn of the century, was opposed to her teaching the children Swedish because that was all he knew when starting school and he was also laughed at by the other children.

Such teasing became a far more serious matter during World War One, when even these acculturated persons felt the need to reduce any manifestations of foreignness in the face of nativism and war fears. Danes responded by volunteering for military service (30,000 by July 1918) and purchasing a large number of war bonds to deflect any negative sentiments. Norwegian fraternal groups, such as the Sons of Norway and the *bygdelags* (social organizations based on district of origin), protested the efforts to curb foreign language usage. They issued loyalty declarations but still experienced shame over their foreign heritage. The Norwegian Lutheran Church tried to shed its rural orientation and rapidly shift to English language services, from no services in 1900 to 22 percent in 1915 to 38 percent by 1918. With the rising number of foreign born passing away in the 1920s, the figure for English services reached 50 percent in 1925. Even in Tacoma, Norwegians began to introduce English into their May 17th celebrations.[57]

The quest for acceptance, the wartime climate of hostility to foreign-appearing or foreign-behaving persons, and even the occasional negative responses before and after the war did not prevent or discourage Scandinavians from creating an elaborate network of organizations to bring them together to cherish and enjoy traditions and ethnic fellowship, in many cases beyond the first generation. The most well known included the Sons of Norway, the Danish Brotherhood in America, Svenska Bröderne (Swedish Brotherhood) and Vasa (Swedish fraternal society), the Finnish Kaleva Brothers (Finnish Brotherhood), the Daughters of Norway, Valhalla (Swedish mutual aid society), Freya (Danish mutual aid society), the Norwegian *bygdelags*, the Swedish Odd Fellows, the Finn-Swedish Temperance Society, the Finnish Socialist Club, Dalarna Society (Swedish group comparable to the Norwegian *bygdelag*), and the Scandinavian Pioneers Club of Tacoma and Pierce County, plus the more informal drama, singing, and literary clubs. There were also many newspapers, along with those from the Midwest, such as the *Oregon Posten*, the *California Posten*, the *Western Viking, Dannevirke, Bien, Den Danske Pioneer, Bikuben*, and the Swedish California *Veckoblad*.[58]

Although not much evidence in this regard is available, the $75,000 raised for the Swedish famine, the funds collected for Ålesund (Norway) after its 1903 fire, a 1902 statement that $1 million in remittances were sent by Norwegians, and the $3 million to Scandinavia the following year may be far more modest sums than the many millions attributed to other immigrants.[59] They do suggest, however, that along with the persistence of key homeland celebrations, more ties to the homeland existed than may have been readily documented—an indication that the assimilation process was not complete and that important bonds remained, perhaps not transnational but certainly translocal.

There were two other spheres where changes were taking place, moving the immigrants and their children to the middle of the spectrum (which ran from transnationalism to translocalism to disengagement) and farther from the homelands. One had to do with marriage and women's roles, not unlike what we discover in many groups as part of their Americanization process. Women started migrating to America without families and making their own marriage decisions. Many communities contained a disproportionate number of males and provided women with ample opportunities to choose their own partners. Nevertheless, given language and cultural affinity, endogamy remained quite strong within the first generation. Where women of the same nationality were not readily available, men either returned home to secure a spouse or found a match with a Scandinavian of another nationality. Except among Danes, more women now continued working after marriage, which may indicate other changes in family dynamics, for the employment gave them more independence, self-reliance, and prospects for more active roles within the marriage. Although women were marrying at much the same age as their peers in Europe, marriage in America was "no longer intertwined with familial expectations of property ownership and social standing."[60]

The second sphere of dramatic change involved a core institution of immigrant society, the religious establishment. The central challenge facing Scandinavian churches in the West during the early twentieth century was the "protest" part of our earlier statement—migration from the Midwest in protest and quest. Migrating to the West released many Scandinavians from the "network of forces—language, habits, social approval, subtle coercions"—that arose from being a member of a relatively tight-knit immigrant community. Without that "many would almost certainly [have left] the church" sooner. Therefore, Scandinavians in the West were "less churched," the churches split into new, though often short-lived, variations, and they became "even more American in their external forms than their counterparts in the Midwest." For example, Swedish Baptists, Swedish Methodists, Swedish Mission Covenant, and Swedish-Finnish Baptists were undoubtedly symptomatic of the fissures within the Scandinavian church communities.

The signs of change crept in slowly as Sunday schools introduced classes in English; then more and more services were in English, and denominations changed their names, deleting "Scandinavian," "Danish," "Swedish," or "Norwegian"—especially during the First World War—or when re-forming the denominational combinations in an effort to remain viable if not relevant. Within a dozen years of its founding in Oregon, Silverton's Scandinavian Evangelical Lutheran Church first had to deal with the 1905 request of its Young People's Society for scriptural studies in English, then the hymn books in English, and then the first service in English on July 19, 1910. Meanwhile, it faced a split off by 1906 with the new Silverton Evangelical Lutheran Free Church, whose Norwegian immigrant members held firm to tradition and deferred English language services until 1931. During the Second World War the Scandinavian Evangelical Lutheran Church also became more ecumenical, if not responsive to wartime pressures, and renamed itself Trinity Lutheran Church.[61]

Other pockets of tradition endured for a time, besides in Selah, Washington, or Silverton, namely in Danevang, Texas, where the trustees of the public school would not even hire a non-Danish teacher for its rural school until 1938. But the forces of Americanization almost always prevailed, and invariably community leaders came to the point when their younger generation viewed their parents' native tongue as a foreign language to be studied in school. By the 1920s the Danish Lutheran Church, which had played a rather limited role in the lives of the widely dispersed Danish immigrants, shifted to English classes and services and eventually dropped Danish from its name.[62]

Some who have studied Scandinavians have omitted Finns because the language and customs were so different. Nordic studies tend to be more inclusive, especially because of the Swedish-Finnish overlap in populations. Certainly, the regional histories were different (and Finland was still under Russian rule in the early 1900s), and the political fervor was distinct (a strong Socialist vein developed among Finns as well as strong temperance and consumer co-op movements). Homeland conditions were especially dire, and scant food, minimal incomes, the many American letters and photos, and the reports on wages drew Finns to America. The country's modernization also started later, as did its major migration streams to America. One estimate concludes that 380,000 went to America, of whom about one-third returned home. The occupations they pursued were rather narrower in scope than among the three Scandinavian peoples, in part because of the Finns' non-Germanic language (it is related to Hungarian) and strongly rural background, and undoubtedly because of political conditions.

Their networks did lead them to concentrate in mining, logging, fishing, and the merchant marine. In a study of Seattle in 1900, for example, 36 percent of the Finns gave their occupation as miners and 36 percent as seamen, far greater percentages than among the Danes, Norwegians, and Swedes in that study. In addition to the mining communities in Colorado and Utah, where hundreds of Finns could be found, or in Alaska, where they were surpassed in numbers only by Norwegians, they were—as pointed out in part 1—quite numerous along California's coast north of San Francisco, from Mendocino and Fort Bragg to Eureka, in Humboldt County. There, they particularly sought out work in the logging operations, sometimes buying land after it had been logged, too.[63]

Still, Astoria, Oregon, remained the focal point of much Finnish interest, with the Columbia River attracting loggers, fishermen, and even farmers to Astoria and nearby communities, such as Ilwaco, across the Columbia, where B. S. Seaborg (originally Sjöberg) built the Aberdeen Packing Company cannery, and Deep River, which was on a tributary in Washington's Wahkiakum County. It became a Finnish community, well illustrating just how far immigrants were willing to go in distance and circumstance in order to locate economic opportunities.

Located in wetlands, the town of Deep River was almost entirely built on pil-
ings to elevate buildings and the plank streets well above high tide. It thrived as
a depot for nearby logging operations that began in the 1870s and remained a
viable Finnish community for about six decades. By 1917 the Finns had built a
number of public structures, including schools, a sauna, a pool hall, and the
Deep River Holy Trinity Evangelical Lutheran Church (1898). While some
men developed farm lands (using dikes)—and later dairying and truck farming—here, too, logging and salmon fishing offered the major opportunities in
the region, along with the sawmills and canneries. Connections to "the outside" were almost entirely by boat, and between 1909 and the 1930s a riverboat
made daily roundtrip runs to Astoria. As with Ilwaco, another measure of the
isolation here was that the children spoke only Finnish until they began
school.[64]

A rural version of Ilwaco and Deep Water was created in nearby Lewis River
County in 1902 by Finnish miners from Wyoming and Montana who decided
that a diversified agricultural economy was preferable to dealing with the Western Federation of Miners. They, too, established Lutheran churches, socialist
halls, and, of course, saunas.[65]

Astoria was the largest Finnish community west of the Mississippi, with 2,000
foreign-born Finns out of 11,000 people in 1905, and with its canneries and
fishing operations, it continued to be the major draw. At the west end, near the
Union Cannery, known as Uniontown, was the Finnish District. There were
Finnish businesses, a Finnish church, and various Finnish cultural institutions
there. The Suomi Synod relied on Astoria as its western base, established a
branch of its Book Concern publishing operation there, and in 1922 began publication of *Lännen Suometar* (The Western Finn). Finnish lodges were
launched there, with women's auxiliaries. The Finnish Kaleva Brothers (Finnish Brotherhood), which had begun in San Francisco in 1882, established its
second lodge in Astoria. In many businesses, Hilma Salvon remembered, you
had to speak Finnish. Not surprisingly, she met her Finnish husband there. Astoria held its attraction until its canneries closed and ships more easily reached
Portland.

Finns could also be found in San Francisco and Seattle, and in Colorado
and Utah mining communities, but not even Butte's Finntown equaled Astoria's, whose appeal for Finns probably outlasted most of the canneries there.
However, a major fire in 1922 was a setback for the community. Prior to that,
19-year-old Esther Rinne recalled, she had come to Eureka, California, and
obtained a job nearby but with no other Finns. Once a month she would go
into Eureka to speak Finnish with her sister and others. After two years, on a
vacation she visited a sister near Astoria, found a job, met a Finn whom she
married, and settled there.

This later start to heavier Finnish immigration placed the Finns squarely in

the newer wave of immigration and, as indicated, in a rather limited occupational range. Yet, even here the unusual could occur, demonstrating that the
influence of the new land and ties to the homeland could be found surviving, if
not flourishing, in unexpected places and in unexpected persons.

Oskari Tokoi came to the United States in 1891, at age 18, worked in the Wyoming coal fields, and then moved to South Dakota, Vancouver, Seattle (winter
1894) and coal mines nearby, possibly in Roslyn. Then it was back to coal fields in
Wyoming, Leadville, and Ogden, and on to Rocklin, California, where he wed a
Finnish woman. Deciding a miner's life back in Leadville was too dangerous, the
couple returned to Finland in 1900, where he bought a farm and became a store-
keeper. He was now 27. But, it appears the American experience had a deep impact on Tokoi, for he became a member of the Social Democratic Party and was
elected in 1907 to the Finnish parliament (called the Senate). In 1916 his party
won a majority and he became vice-chairman (the equivalent of prime minister)
as well as president of the Finnish Federation of Labor. When the Russian Revolution began, he felt compelled to support the Bolsheviks, who appointed him
Finland's minister of foodstuffs. However, the Soviet effort failed, and the Finns
won their independence, forcing Tokoi to flee the country. He made his way to
Canada and then in 1921 to Fitchburg, Massachusetts. There, until 1959, he was
a member of the editorial staff of the Finnish newspaper *Raivaaja*. During the
Second World War he toured the United States raising funds for Finnish relief,
and in 1944 Finland pardoned him for his Soviet role. In 1949, he addressed a full
session of the Finnish Parliament and died 14 years later, at the age of 90.[66] A remarkable story for an unskilled migrant Finnish miner from the American West.

The impact of America on the homelands can be seen through such extraordinary men as Tokoi. The impact of immigrants on America and vice versa can
be judged by the lives and contributions of numerous men and women, such as
Anna Guttormsen Hought, who captured key qualities in the efforts put forth
by Scandinavian immigrants, particularly in the Pacific Northwest.[67] Tokoi
took his American experiences back to Finland. Anna took her American experiences to heart, and her exceptional life story displays much of the essence of
the Scandinavian encounter with America.

Twenty-year old Anna first came to America in 1907 and settled in Wisconsin. She struggled there for five years and returned to Norway to care for her
mother for five years. Her brother lived in Montana and wrote to her about the
new Homestead Act that reduced the waiting time and the period of time each
year one had to live on the land (seven months per year). She went to join him
in September 1916, and he walked 35 miles to meet her. Unfortunately, she had
delayed her arrival by a week but could not inform him. After they were finally
reunited, he filed land claims for her and acquired a 12- by 14-foot shack for her
"home" (which she appropriately mispronounced as "shock," for she thought it

was for the chickens). Three years and many ordeals later, 32-year-old Anna and her brother, John, owned 320 acres of Montana land.

She recalled, "I don't think that my homesteading experience was unique. At that time there were many single women homesteading in Montana, many of them young widows . . . out there burning sagebrush and cow chips for quick heat." The nearest community, named Content, was miles from her farm. The nearest town, Malta, was 35 miles away. On February 28, 1920, Anna wed Ed Hought—in a Methodist Church in Great Falls, that being their only option. Despite the isolation, people came to the home for the wedding celebration and brought food. "As for the loneliness, we got used to our neighbors being a distance away. Anyone living within fifteen miles we called neighbors." Some were Norwegian, others were Swedes, Scots, and Germans, and "so Content became something of a melting pot." When Anna gave birth to her daughter, Nora, Ed was gone and returned three days later. They faced such challenges remarkably well, even when they were confronted with one of Montana's 20-year drought cycles that began in 1918. Half of Montana's farmers lost their land between 1921 and 1925, and then half the commercial banks failed. By the time Ed and Anna had their first good crop, in 1932, prices had plummeted.

To compound their problems, Anna had heart problems and suffered from anemia, requiring fresh liver every day. But the town was 35 miles away, and there was no refrigeration. Her problem would persist for years until liver extract became available. However, when Nora went to school in 1935, they sold the farm and moved to Malta. Ed died in 1954, and Anna relocated to Seattle in 1969 to live with Nora, her husband, and the three grandchildren. Finally, in her 90s, Anna made two trips to Norway. At the age of 93 she was still teaching Hardanger-style embroidery in West Seattle. Her determination to make the land work, her commitment to ensure Nora's education, her desire to visit Norway after a lapse of over six decades, and her involvement in Seattle teaching and encouraging Norwegian crafts in her 90s were all representative of the Scandinavian story in the West.

Factions, fissures, and fusions were all part of the immigrant-to-ethnic processes and were repeated over and over. Could they have played a role in Ralph Strom's decision as to when to visit to his homeland? He waited 36 years before returning to Sweden (1948). Magnhild Johnsen put it off a mere 9 years; Grethe Petersen waited 12 years; and Henny Hale finally returned to Norway after a lapse of 54 years. Anna Hought waited even longer. Rather than elements in the larger Scandinavian American community (with which she had had limited contact), it would seem that—besides whatever personal sentiments were involved—Anna's own hardships, struggles, and lack of close family members left behind were responsible for the passage of more than six decades before she, too, visited Norway.

Anna was a rather more extreme example of how ethnic connections with the homeland could become diluted over time and across generations. At the same time, fissures and fusions taking place among Scandinavians and their ethnic associations could underscore tensions between cultural retention and acculturation, between traditional national identities and new ethnic or American loyalties. Such dilemmas about holding onto culture and traditions on the individual level gradually became widespread enough to cumulatively surface at the community level, for, as we saw, many organizations underwent significant changes as they edged toward ever more Americanization. Nevertheless, the list of those institutions that survived beyond the immigrant generation, along with family ties nurtured across great distances and decades—and the accounts of families rediscovered by second- and third-generation relatives—remind us that during those early decades so many really were still newcomers. Indeed, many elements of Scandinavian ethnicity persisted—sometimes aided by the flows of new immigrants but in many instances through the efforts of the children, the same children whose own Americanization brought about so many of the changes their parents had to grudgingly concede.

What we observe, then, is a mixture of processes, retention and modification, and then fairly rapid adaptation and accommodation, a combination that may have been somewhat easier for the Scandinavians than for many other groups because, as white northern Europeans, they generally "blended rather easily into the mainstream of American culture." That ease of incorporation reduced the usual stresses connected with making homeland-related and ethnic-related choices—especially as they observed their children carrying forward the dynamic (and changing) amalgam of transformations and preservations which they themselves had initiated.[68]

CHAPTER SIXTEEN

Newcomers, Old and New (Italians, Basques, French, and Mexicans)

*I*N 1914 A STUDY OF Italians in Utah reported that "the Greeks and Italians are perhaps the most careless and shiftless people found. . . . Comfort to them is unknown unless it is in the form of a smoke by the fire or a drink. . . . The standard of living among them [Italians] is lower than of any other nationality." Lucile Richens, writing in the 1930s about her community of Sunnyside, Utah, noted that "I was raised with a wholehearted contempt for Greeks and Italians and other southern Europeans who lived there. . . . Intermarriage with foreigners was considered almost as bad as death." However, she added, "If they became Americanized it was not so bad." Protestant northern Italians had been migrating to Utah since the 1870s, with most finding employment in mines and on railroads. By 1893 anti-Italian stereotypes were already evident, but it was the participation of over 400 in the 1903 Carbon County, Utah, mining strike that brought down on them accusations of being "bloodthirsty, nonwhite, stiletto-in-hand" anarchists. Still, they held on to their culture and Italianness (Italianità), established some businesses, truck farms, and fraternal and mutual aid societies; had Italian newspapers sent from San Francisco and New York (but did not establish language schools); got to see Columbus Day made a state holiday in October 1919; and, during the 1920s, celebrated that day and marched with floats in Pioneer Day parades.[1]

In neighboring Wyoming the Italians experienced little discrimination, perhaps because they numbered only a few hundred, mostly northern Italians.

They adjusted relatively well because many had experienced step migration—living and working in other locations—before reaching the West. They summoned others via chain migration but did not rely on padrones to secure mining and railroad jobs. They lived alongside other peoples in several mining communities where company towns precluded ethnic enclaves (as in Hartville), operated a variety of small businesses, such as in Cheyenne—where the only Italian enclave developed—and larger enterprises, too, including Henry Bertagnolli's Union Mercantile and Supply Company in Rock Springs (open for over nine decades). They established only some rather short-lived Italian associations, for Wyoming would become a melting pot for Italians.[2]

Italians had been migrating to the West throughout the second half of the nineteenth century, with the volume of that migration steadily rising and with primarily northern Italians at first and then more and more both northern and southern Italians. In California their number quadrupled between 1900 and 1920 (tripling in the West overall). By 1910 Italians were the leading group among the foreign born in Nevada, second in California, Colorado, and New Mexico, and fifth in Oregon, Washington, and Montana.[3] Although a majority of Italians were in various rural and extractive occupations, large numbers of them settled in (not just near) urban centers across the West, including Denver, Phoenix, Reno, Los Angeles, Portland, and Seattle. But their most pronounced presence was in San Francisco, the magnetic center for the Italian western experience—their "western capital," as Walter Nugent put it.[4] Nearly 24,000 Italian immigrants resided there in 1920, along with 21,700 second-generation children.

The first two decades of the twentieth century reveal that Italians were seeking jobs in widely scattered parts of the West and, in the main, occupations in mining, agriculture, and logging and lumber mills (and, in the Northwest, with railroads and marble quarrying, too). A significant number soon shifted from agricultural wage labor to truck farming near many expanding urban centers; others opened fresh fruit and vegetable markets in those communities; and a key number of them expanded what became such valuable enterprises as the grape and wine industries and the fruit and vegetable packing and canning operations. By 1905 half the Italians in California were engaged in agricultural pursuits. Italians also soon dominated the fishing industry in California (especially Genoese and Sicilians), from San Diego to San Francisco, particularly displacing the Chinese. Along with those non-urban pursuits, a growing number began a variety of businesses, trades, and professions in the cities, such as restaurants, saloons, grocery stores, hotels, construction firms, tailor shops, and craft trades as well as law offices and medical practices—and, singularly, branch banking. The result was considerable visibility for the Italians in many parts of the West.[5]

Not only was San Francisco the only North American city with a substantial number of both northern and southern Italians, but also between 1899 and 1914

some 70 percent of Italian immigrants arriving in California were from northern Italy, and over nine-tenths had come directly from their homeland. As the
population of Italians increased and the percentage of southern Italians rose,
attitudes toward the Italians began to change. Already starting in the 1890s they
were being associated with criminal groups in Italy (e.g., the Black Hand) and
were being perceived as an economic threat (especially by unions), even
though the presence of Asians and Mexicans would eventually deflect some of
that prejudice away from the Italians.[6]

Many northern Italians physically and culturally blended in more readily
with Americans and northern Europeans than did southern Italians and Sicilians. The latter were southern Europeans, commonly with darker features,
nearly all Catholic, and culturally perceived as apart from Americans and
northern Europeans, marking them as not-white persons. They were often initially employed as strikebreakers; not unexpectedly, they frequently clustered
together with other Italians, such as in San Francisco's North Beach district,
despite the early gulf between northerners and southerners. They were widely
perceived as sojourners temporarily present in America and bent on returning
to Italy (which was actually somewhat less true for Italians in the West). The
Italian population comprised only 4 percent of the foreign born in the West in
1900, increasing by 80,000 to 7 percent in 1910 (124,677). That made them the
fifth largest immigrant group in that year, behind the Germans, Mexicans,
English, and Canadians. Despite the war, by 1920 their numbers had risen (to
140,552), yet they continued to trail the Mexicans, Germans, Canadians, and
English.[7]

As part of the swelling number of southern and eastern European workers during this time, the Italians were caught up in the economic growth of the West
and the boom times after 1900, including the various labor movements. The fact
that 13 of the 18 miners killed in the deep-shaft explosion on July 11, 1910, in the
Lawson mine (Black Diamond, Washington) were Italian and that a number of
those killed in the Ludlow (Colorado) Massacre three and a half years later
(April 20, 1914) were Italian attests to their unmistakable presence in the occupation of mining. From Carbon County and Bingham Canyon, Utah, and Cripple
Creek, Colorado, to Ely, Nevada, and Roslyn, Washington (as well as Idaho,
Montana, and Texas), Italians could be found in various kinds of mining opera-
tions. In addition, passing up on the greater capital requirements for large-scale
farming and orchards (one exception being around Bryan, Texas, about 80 miles
northeast of Austin), many preferred to move into truck farming. They then provided fruits and vegetables to those living in cities across the West, including
Billings, Anaconda, Great Falls, Salt Lake City, Denver, Galveston, Cheyenne,
Laramie, Reno, Portland, Seattle, Monterey, Santa Barbara, and San Francisco.
In the process they also either introduced or popularized lima beans, artichokes,
green bell peppers, eggplants, broccoli, and vine-grown tomatoes. Others went

in for dairy farming, especially along the California coast from Santa Barbara to San Simeon, while, as noted, many others engaged in fishing. In 1911 it was reported that Italian fishermen brought in 35 million pounds of fish worth nearly $9 million, and Italian farmers just in California sold $65 million in produce.[8]

Meanwhile, in 1881 Andrea Sbarboro had launched what became a major vineyard in northern California, Asti, recruiting Italian-Swiss workers and creating a thoroughly Italian environment in that "Italian-Swiss Colony." The Gallo, Rossi, Martini, Petri, Guasti, and Mondavi families also initiated major wine-producing operations, while the DiGiorgios in the San Joaquin Valley gradually created what became the largest fresh fruit growing and shipping operation in the world. Marco Fontana crafted "the largest fruit and vegetable canning organization in the world," using the Del Monte label. And, in October 1904, Amadeo P. Giannini started the Bank of Italy, initiating branch banking after the San Francisco earthquake. There were 24 branches in 18 cities by 1918 and 62 branches by 1922. Eight years later, he renamed it the Bank of America. It would become the largest in the world by 1945.[9]

The Italians in California provide interesting contrasts in the variety of community formations. The one in San Francisco was never an enclave isolating Italians, even with 14,000 there by 1900. So, too, Los Angeles, with the smaller cluster of some 2,000, was even less of an enclave. Their numbers rose but as they moved, for example into Lincoln Heights, they encountered Irish, Canadians, English, and Germans. Although on North Broadway a number of businesses did develop, along with a newspaper and by 1904 St. Peter's Church, no Italian enclave emerged. What did distinguish the Los Angeles "colony" was the fact that most men had been in the United States before resettling there; many had their first papers for citizenship; married men and their families outnumbered others; half the men were self-employed; and half the men planned to remain in that city.[10]

In contrast, the village of Occidental, on the coast north of San Francisco, contained many northern Italians who had sought work in the nearby lumber mills and dairy farms. Many became self-employed charcoal burners. Such networks as that launched by Ermengildo Gonnella served to draw family members from Lombardy and Tuscany. Although a church was built in 1903, it did not play a central role in the community. Rather, the isolation enabled them to retain their language and traditions and for several decades initially to confine their marriages almost entirely to other Italians. Farther south, Italians began migrating to San Diego in the 1870s to fish. After the San Francisco earthquake, Genoese and others moved to San Diego, too, learned from the Japanese how to catch tuna, and established a number of fishing companies that became quite prominent. In the 1910s, some shifted to retailing through restaurants along the harbor, much as was being done in San Francisco. No major community developed there, but the Italians remained prominent in the fishing industry until the Second World War.[11]

The Italian experiences, particularly in California in the first decades of the century, were undoubtedly a mirror for other groups entering the West in considerable numbers at the same time. Many individual Italians were extremely successful, and many more contributed through a variety of enterprises that were substantial but not as stellar. But, Paola Sensi-Isolani and Phylis Martinelli point out, their regional impact, besides their businesses and farms, was certainly their low-wage labor contributions to agriculture, lumber milling, mining, construction, and other industries. Perhaps it could have been somewhat different, except, notes historian Dino Cinel, "the general desire of virtually all Italians [was] to go back to Italy." It would take time and several round-trip journeys to the old homeland "before Italians started to see emigration not as an extension of their lives in Italy, but as an end in itself." Moreover, not only did they tend to live in mixed communities far more commonly than did Italians concentrated in Eastern cities, but they were also initially very divided by regional attachments and the friction between northern and southern Italians.[12]

Although they certainly had a sufficiently critical mass from Denver to San Francisco to establish organizations, mutual aid societies (including the Sons of Italy), newspapers (17 in San Francisco), a hospital (San Francisco, too), and even a pro-Republican Party group in Portland, such organizations were largely based on Italian places of origin. Loggia Mazzini (1880, San Francisco), established for all Italian veterans, was the first such organization to rise above such divisions. After the earthquake, banker Giannini reached out to Italians of all origins to open bank accounts. By 1910, two newspapers there were offering broader coverage than that of just an individual region or society. Yet, it was the concern of the California Progressives about the possible influence of the IWW (Wobblies) that prompted the state to establish the California Commission of Immigration and Housing, which, among other projects, sought to better coordinate Italian efforts to help their own needy. That prompted community leaders to meet in mid-October 1916 to establish the Italian Board of Relief of San Francisco, led by Marco Fontana and Domenico Ghirardelli. Notwithstanding such actions, historian Andrew Rolle contends that in the West "the Italian generally expended less effort to retain his folkways than did other nationalities." As a result, the immigrant colonies "simply failed to preserve their identity" and in most places would amount to little more than "temporary congregations of immigrant workers."[13]

We have been exploring the experiences of major immigrant groups in the West, but many others in the region have been entirely or substantially invisible in most historical accounts. Their stories, however, do add to our understanding of both their economic roles and their social and cultural contributions to the diversity, which many now acknowledge but few have examined in depth. For example, in 1910 there were 27,227 French-born persons in the

West, of whom 17,390 (63.9%) lived in California. There were also 9,465 persons from Spain, among whom 4,218 (44.6%) likewise resided in California. One authority reports that in the four key states of California, Nevada, Idaho, and Wyoming there were 8,398 Basque persons. That population is divided between those with roots in the French Pyrenees—one of the three "principales régions" from which French migrated in the late nineteenth and early twentieth centuries, according to Annick Foucrier—and those Basques whose origins lay in Spain's main northern provinces of Navarro and Viscaya.[14] The Basque split was particularly evident in Wyoming, where a Basque community developed in Buffalo, but the 1910 census reported no Spanish immigrants in that state—because it was French Basques who had migrated there (and 341 French-born persons were recorded there). The Spanish Basques more frequently established chain migrations to Idaho, with Boise becoming the leading Basque urban center. In 1910 there were three times more Spanish than French in that state (1045 versus 333).

Still, the experiences of the Basques and non-Basque French overlapped, especially in San Francisco and Los Angeles. They left their mark on the West— and contemporaries were quite aware of their presence. Pedro and Bernardo Altube and Juan Bautista Achabal illustrate this point with regard to the Basques. The Altube brothers had been working for their brother in Argentina when they learned about the California gold rush. Seeing a golden opportunity to feed the miners, they hastened to California, bringing with them skills in handling cattle and sheep, which they had learned in Argentina. They were the pioneers for other Basque young men who soon followed, learning shepherding from those who had been in South America and eventually getting paid in livestock so they could begin their own flocks. The two brothers developed a hugely successful cattle and sheep ranch in Independence Valley, along the eastern state line of California. Pedro, who was 6 feet 8 inches tall and nicknamed *palo alto* (tall pole), bought up land and water rights in the valley. He took advantage of the free lands to drive cattle into Nevada as well as bring Basques to tend the flocks across several states, paying them in sheep until the turn of the century, when he shifted to wages. He set up slaughterhouses in San Francisco and a dairy operation south of San Francisco in an area known since as Palo Alto. Pedro, referred to as the "Father of the Basques in the American West," died in 1905, leaving a vast estate to his wife and brother.

Meanwhile, Juan Achabal, who was born in the Basque region of Spain, came to San Francisco in 1893, moved up to Boise, learned herding, and within about a decade had 8,000 sheep (later the flocks would range as high as 80,000–100,000). Fifty-nine men worked for him. He wed a Basque woman, received U.S. citizenship—changing his name to John Archabal (thinking it would be easier for Americans to pronounce)—and continued to prosper into the 1940s. He became a wealthy and prominent community leader in Boise, was responsible for promoting what became the annual Sheepherders' Ball in 1929, and helped establish the Independent Order of Spanish-Basque Speaking People of Idaho in 1940. But his own children insisted on speaking English.[15]

Despite the Basques' contribution to Idaho's economy, the *Caldwell Tribune* declared in July 1909, in a clearly contradictory voice, that it disliked the itinerant sheepherders because they "have some undesirable characteristics that the Chinese are free from. They are filthy, treacherous and meddlesome." Then it added, "However, they work hard and save their money. [Yet?] they are clannish and . . . have a foothold and unless something is done [they] will make life impossible for the white man." Four years later, U.S. Senator Key Pittman (D-NV) described Basque sheepherders as "lacking in intelligence, independence, or anything else. They are just about as near a slave as anybody could be," living "in the lowest possible way for a human being to live." Moreover, they "do not know what a home is and do not recognize the authority of government . . . [and] rarely seek to become citizens of the country to which they are imported."[16]

The Basques' experiences demonstrated not only that even those from western Europe could at times encounter hostility but that many rural French persons also went into the cities and found employment there. Most Basque immigrants at this time were rural and remained rural, although like so many others, they relied upon the cities as the places for meeting, marrying, and resting. Juan Miguel and Martina Aguirre left Montevideo, Paraguay, for San Francisco in 1849 and in 1866 opened "the first Basque hotel in North America," the Aguirre Hotel. What the *kaffenion* were for the Greeks, the *ostatuak* were for the Basques, and more: temporary boardinghouses; social centers; clearinghouses for jobs, travel aids, and translations; and ideal places for matchmaking— from Los Angeles to Boise and even in New York City, but with a large cluster of them for years in downtown Los Angeles. *Euskaldunak* (Basque women) migrated to find work in such places, knowing that they could most readily find spouses there as well. (In one study of 150 Basque men, 85 percent had met their wives in an *ostatauk*.[17])

For a generation or more, shepherding remained preeminent among the newcomers. Although the Basques had not initiated open range "tramp" herding, they readily exploited the opportunities, moving to high country in the summers and down to desert lands for winter grazing (transhumance). Many at first concentrated in the San Joaquin Valley, where, for example, in 1880 there were reported to be in four counties 885,600 sheep. But severe droughts and then the disastrous winter of 1887–1888 convinced Jose Navarro and Antone Azcuenaga to move their sheep north to Oregon's Jordan Valley, a desert trek that nearly killed them. However, they persevered, and that valley in eastern Oregon would become one of the major centers of Basque shepherding. Azcuenaga would make enough money to acquire a 3,000-acre ranch and open the Jordan Valley Hotel.

   With the 1890s–1920s the principal era of Basque migration, chain migration determined where many went. The Viscayan went north, whereas the French Basques and Navarrese mostly remained more to the south, in California, Nevada, Arizona, New Mexico, Colorado, and Wyoming. For example, in 1902 Jean Esponda, a French Basque, found work in Wyoming, remained, and subsequently drew many family members to the town of Buffalo. Gaston Erramouspe, another French Basque, went from Nevada to Green River, Wyoming, in 1912 to help his injured brother. He, too, remained, and other family members followed. Gaston eventually became a wealthy rancher. A small community of Basques also settled in Carbon County, Utah, and took up mining or shepherding, while about 100 others lived in Salt Lake City, setting up their social center in the Hogar Hotel. Meanwhile, two-thirds of those who had entered the country between 1897 and 1902 were Spanish Basques, with large majorities being single men between age 18 and 30, and mostly they headed farther west and to the Pacific Northwest.[18]

   Although by 1910 the census reported 2.95 million sheep in Idaho, 5.2 million in Montana, 5 million in Wyoming, 3.1 million in New Mexico, 2 million in Utah, and 1.4 million in both Nevada and Arizona, not all were owned or herded by Basques, who were concentrated in California, Nevada, Oregon, Idaho, and Wyoming. In Montana, for example, no Basques herded. Nonetheless, the use of the open ranges of public land by Basques and others had begun to encounter resistance. In 1900 sheepherding was barred in forest reservations except in Oregon and Washington. In March 1909, Gifford Pinchot, President Theodore Roosevelt's new chief of the U.S. Forest Service, declared that transients could no longer get allotments to graze. Only those who owned land near national forests or who were U.S. citizens could get access. Newly arrived Basques found few "traditional" jobs and had to take mining work; others who were more experienced shifted to dairy farming, as had Altube, or settled on ranches, as did Archabal, or, like Domingo Bastanchury, moved into agriculture. By 1905 he had 3,000 acres of orange trees, reputedly the largest such grove in the world. Other herders who wed (almost always Basque women) or who had weathered long enough the extended periods of isolation would gradually shift to agriculture.

   The combination of more restrictive policies in the early 1900s and then the post–World War One economic downturn, followed by measures in the 1920s further limiting access to grazing lands, pushed Basques into other endeavors. Consequently, even in Boise, "the nation's leading Basque center," where most of the 2,500–3,000 Idaho Basques lived in 1922, Basques sought jobs other than herding, and fewer than 5 percent of the second generation herded sheep. Nonetheless, Boise remained the only "concentrated urban experience of Basques in America."[19]

   The non-Basque French influence in the West was quite different and concentrated along the Pacific Coast, where more than three-quarters resided in

1910. Half of those in California were in San Francisco and Los Angeles Counties. Annick Foucrier draws an interesting distinction for this little-studied population.[20] Those who migrated to California prior to the last decade of the nineteenth century, though relatively few in number, "lent to San Francisco a certain sense of refinement through the arts, Parisian fashions, cuisine, and the hand-finished work of the French laundries." During that time, the French created a complete community, so much so that "Jusque dans les années 1890, on peut vivre à Los Angeles sans parler l'anglais. L'espagnol et le français suffisent" (Until the 1890s one could live in Los Angeles without speaking English. Spanish and French sufficed.).

The French established mutual aid societies, regional associations (notably La Lige Henri IV), clubs (such as L'Harmonie la Gauloise and Le Cercle Français), and newspapers (especially *Le Franco-Californien*). It was said that in San Francisco in 1898 the French were very prominent in, among other businesses, restaurants, wholesale and retail wine shops, laundries, dairies, bakeries, hairdressing salons, hotels, printing firms, libraries, and vineyards (notably Paul Mason), and north of Montgomery Street, one could find a French cultural enclave. They also shared North Beach with Italians, Germans, Russians, and other groups, but on certain streets of "Butcher Town" (just south of the city center) French was reported to be quite a common language. At the same time, transnational ties to France were maintained by letters, accounts in the French press, chain migration, return trips (it took only two weeks by the last decades of the nineteenth century), fund-raisers to help with disasters in the homeland (including 20,000 francs in 1906 for the miners in Courrières and over 120,000 francs for victims of floods in Paris in 1910), and earlier the willingness of hundreds of young men to return to fight for France in 1870 in the Franco-Prussian War.[21]

Despite the gains, two sets of developments that would bring about important changes began in the 1890s and early 1900s: the French immigrants were now more and more of rural origin, and many planned to return home (and many were Basque, too). They held onto local traditions and established new, more regionally focused organizations (e.g., La Société Alsace-Lorraine de San Francisco). In addition, many families, with an increasing number of second-generation children, began to disperse, and as these French families were beginning to integrate into the mainstream, they were not teaching their children French. The shifting perspective was also apparent in the trend of attributing distinctions or achievements by Franco-Americans to the individuals involved rather than to the collective French community.

Nevertheless, several important signs of ethnic continuity were still evident. The French organized to help those left homeless by the 1906 earthquake in San Francisco, and Raphaël Weill contributed his own resources to provide shelter for 5,000 women and children. Many French persons were soon spreading out to Oakland, other parts of the Bay area, and Los Angeles, and yet a year after the First World War began, they organized a French Relief Fund Club. To mobilize voters the following year they reestablished the Lafayette Political Club (but, in the San Francisco branch, they steadfastly refused any participation by women until 1953). When the United States entered the war on April 6, 1917, the French community in San Francisco resumed participating in July 4th celebrations, which they had ceased doing in 1896. After the war (June 1919), they organized the Mutual Aid Society for Veterans of the Great War, and in 1932 French women created the French War Brides Club.

During the height of the Roaring Twenties, French immigrants of various backgrounds, ever eager to preserve some of their culture, once again established a variety of new clubs. Nonetheless, nativism during the war and the One Hundred Percent movement afterward did convince even more of the French to abandon the use of their native language. And if that and the continued dispersal and assimilation were not weakening the French community quickly enough (except during the war), Prohibition was a major blow to their vineyards and distributors, important French enterprises. "Sacramental" wines and raisins could not entirely substitute, and even when Prohibition ended, it was not until 1950 before the industry fully recovered. Moreover, the French could not hold back the impact of federal laws, for the imposition of the quota laws in the 1920s intensified the decline in French migration, with the 10,500 per year average (1899–1910) falling to a quota ceiling of 3,100 in 1929.

The Basque experienced many of these developments, too, with numerous hotels, which had been so important to them, closing in Los Angeles and San Francisco. Pockets of Basque settlements would endure, but legislation virtually ending the tramp herds and access to free range lands by 1934 (the Taylor Act) would substantially dry up the flow of young Basque men to America even without the low quota of merely 131 set for Spaniards in 1924.[22] Though there were not great numbers of French and Basques, they were both sufficiently numerous to have made well-noted contributions to western society during the century following the gold rush. They serve as reminders that immigrant peoples in small groups also contributed to the western economy as well as to its social and cultural development.

There remain many other groups whose migration experiences in the West during the early twentieth century enrich our understanding of the era and their impact upon it. We cannot here do justice to all of their stories, but it would be no exaggeration to state that the history of major areas of the region during the entire century begins to undergo radical changes with the commencement of the Mexican Revolution in 1910. Of course, there had been considerable cross-border movement prior to this time, accelerating with the completion of the Mexican railroads north to the border, the expanding mining and agricultural enterprises in the Southwest, and the recession and rising

economic discontent in Mexico in the years just prior to 1910. Historian Rodolfo Acuña reports a 6 percent decline in Mexico's population between 1910
and 1921, or between 1.9 and 3.5 million persons, due to the many upheavals
that accompanied the Mexican Revolution, including large-scale migrations
in unprecedented numbers north to the United States. And although many
considered the move as temporary until peace returned, when it did return,
many thousands did not, at least not before the Great Depression set in.[23]

So mammoth was the impact of Mexican immigration that a number of
points are important for setting the stage for the discussion that follows. Central
to Mexican immigration has been the proximity of homeland, which profoundly shapes the ebb and flow of (literally) millions of Mexicans—legal and
undocumented—into the United States. This pattern of circular migration is
governed by the push and pull of political and economic forces and networks of
cross-border chain migrations. Immigration and census data provide only an
approximation of this dynamic phenomenon. The former cannot capture all
the illegal and informal migrations, and the latter can record only some of the
movements between the decennial and annual reports. The rivers of migration
("streams" cannot do it justice) would prove to be crucial not just for the immigrant communities but also for the railroads, farms, orchards, and mines in the
Southwest and then for the rapidly expanding urban centers and their multiplying array of job openings for unskilled and semi-skilled workers.

This immigration (already underway during the years shortly before the
Mexican Revolution) played a role in some of the principal transformations of
the economic West, as "isolated resource regions" were gradually organized
around "provincial trading centers" (e.g., Tucson, Casper, Spokane).[24] Those
areas evolved into sub-regions dominated by major metropolitan cores, which
increasingly drew on the rapidly growing number of Mexicans seeking jobs.
That in turn accelerated metropolitan growth and expanded the job market.
The metropolitan cores eventually linked grand-scale agricultural enterprises
sustained by federal irrigation projects, other extractive industries, and urban
manufacturing, service, and distribution facilities (likewise vastly expanded by
federal spending during the two world wars). Through these western cores all
three (agricultural, extractive, and urban-centered enterprises) were steadily
woven into the fabric of national and global markets.[25]

While some have argued that the nineteenth century's destructive treatment
of Latinos had faded by the early 1900s, to be replaced by the class conflict and
exploitation of incipient capitalism, enough events transpired to support the
view that prior patterns of social inequality, economic exploitation, and political disenfranchisement did influence the reception of migrants during the first
half of the new century. The demands of globalizing capitalism undoubtedly
created additional pressures or incentives to exploit a relatively weak, hardly
united labor force, but the earlier negative perceptions and treatment of Lati-

nos did become part of the historical memory that was revivified by the large-scale entry of *mexicanos*.[26]

Whether deep rooted or of recent origin, the institutional racism that Mexicans and Mexican Americans encountered in the 1800s thereafter emerged as the flipside of the claims by Americans that many parts of the western economy would have suffered huge losses, or could not have developed to the extent that they did, were Mexicans not available to satisfy the mushrooming labor demands. The urgent appeals for workers escalated with both the economic growth and the major declines in European and Asian immigration that were solidified by the war and the federal quota legislation of the 1920s.[27]

In reality, Mexican immigration served as a double safety valve: a release of serious socio-economic tensions in Mexico—because so many were able to migrate (rather than remain a potential festering political sore)—and a release of hindrances to western economic growth that would have resulted from a shortage of unskilled, migratory, and rather "tractable" labor.

Although abuses of Mexicans and Mexican Americans would climax during the 1930s with one of the worst episodes of civil rights violations—the coerced repatriation of Mexicans and their American-born children—many Mexican Americans were already striving for social, economic, and political acceptance, equal civil rights, and opportunities to integrate into mainstream American society as members of an ethnic, not racial, population. For years Mexican Americans would campaign for those goals by distancing themselves from the conditions affecting Mexican migrant workers. At the same time, patriotic attachment to their homeland and negative responses to both institutional and the public's mistreatment of them would dampen many Mexicans' interest in acquiring U.S. citizenship, yielding one of lowest naturalization rates among all groups of newcomers. Not until the 1990s do we witness Mexicans, the largest immigrant population, applying for American citizenship in unprecedented numbers, and that was largely due to the amnesty program launched in 1986.

Expansion of the local economy in Southern California during the last decades of the nineteenth century and the shrinking number of Chinese workers increased the demand for Mexican laborers, starting with Southern Pacific Railroad's use of section gangs in 1893. Drawn in ever-greater numbers from the states of Michoacán, Guanajuato, and Zacatecas, they would become "indispensable in building the region's economic prosperity." To a considerable extent, Mexican migration patterns in the early 1900s echoed those of other groups, such as Scandinavians, even though they were migrating from a homeland just across the border. Data on Mexicans in Los Angeles prior to the Second World War reveal that a majority did not migrate directly from their home village but had engaged in step migration—as did many Scandinavians from the Midwest. The percentage migrating directly to Los Angeles after entering the United States declined dramatically from 40 percent prior to 1910 to nearly 14 percent during the 1920s. Before 1910, 23 percent had been presumably working elsewhere in the country before reaching Los Angeles—a figure that rose to 36 percent in the 1920s, and the percentage who had lived in Texas before making their way to Los Angeles jumped from 30 percent to over 54 percent. Another one-fifth had been in Arizona. Other data corroborate this step migration.[28]

In Southern California the shift to walnut and fruit cultivation (lemons in particular) provided opportunities for "Chicano family labor." In the growing cities they began to find jobs, for example, in construction and street paving and for the railroads, urban electric railways, and utility companies. With the commercial and merchant classes dominated by Americans and German, English, and Irish immigrants, it has been argued that Mexican workers found their position in the blue-collar labor market had been "determined" by patterns of proletarianization already set in motion before 1900.[29] The Southwest had the lowest percentage of workers in manufacturing (9.1 percent), and even though many jobs were available, steady factory employment was scarce, so that it was difficult to avoid a heavy reliance upon various extractive occupations (mining, agriculture, lumbering, fishing). The First World War certainly created more employment opportunities, more job diversity and specialization. The postwar in-migration contributed to a significant growth in San Diego, El Paso, San Antonio, and Houston as well as Los Angeles and San Francisco. In Los Angeles, for example, where the Mexican population jumped from 29,757 to 97,116 during the 1920s, Mexicans soon dominated public works, transportation, building supply, and service industries and, following the war, moved into rubber and steel manufacturing, meatpacking, food canning, automobile production, textiles, retail trade, laundries, and domestic service.[30]

Many also continued to leave the city during the summer harvest season. Thus, by 1910, north of Los Angeles (around Santa Barbara) Mexicans were already picking over 2.2 million pounds of walnuts, making possible what would soon become a million-dollar-per-year industry. Similar occupational patterns were emerging in and around other urban centers. It was clear to manufacturers, transportation firms, and the directors of corporate agricultural businesses—citrus, in particular—that by the 1910s and 1920s many were relying predominantly on Mexicans for the manual, unskilled, and semi-skilled jobs, and in many cases specifically seasonal, migratory Mexicans.[31]

It is now equally clear that opportunities for mobility among Mexicans were intentionally limited to preserve that type of labor supply. Mexicans were disproportionately held at or near the bottom of the job ladder, their positions largely static. In California's major cities 64 to 81 percent of the jobs were blue collar, with white-collar positions "virtually closed" to the men. And those Mexican workers were often paid 20 percent to 50 percent less than others, providing little economic security even in the 1920s. Some 15 percent to 30 percent of the women were gradually able to get low-end white-collar employment, often in shops catering to Latino consumers. However, Anglo community leaders began to realize that their goal of a non-union, migratory, expendable manual labor force was not to be realized, for Mexicans were frequently arriving as families, and those families were remaining. Employers and those community leaders had to confront the problems of housing, schooling, health care, and Americanization.[32] Dr. George Clement, of the Los Angeles Chamber of Commerce, caught the irony here of what was an essential truth by the 1920s: "The Mexican laborer, if he only realized it, has California agriculture and industry in the hollow of his hand. *We cannot get along without the Mexican laborer.*" But that economic reality inflamed the sentiments of those who recognized their dependency on a people they regarded as socially, culturally, and religiously inferior and whose socialization they now had to address.[33]

In the Inland Valley to the east of Los Angeles, the number of Mexican workers in the orchards and packinghouses had risen between 1914 and 1919 from 2,317 to 7,004 (a number that would top 10,000 pickers by 1926). By that time they were being viewed as "the exploited minority of choice," increasingly required to work year-round, perhaps because there were growers who viewed the Mexicans as half-civilized and no threat to "the whiteness of the citrus belt." Still, growers had to acknowledge that with white workers leaving the ranches during the war, the trend was toward the establishment of permanent settlements by Mexican workers and their families—along with smaller numbers of Chinese, Filipinos, Sikhs, and some Koreans.[34] As a result, hubs, *colonias*, began to take shape, such as in El Monte (Hicks Camp) and Claremont (Arbol Verde), and social, cultural, and economic issues emerged where employers and residents had hoped they would not.

Enforcing Prohibition was one expression of that concern during the 1920s, which sparked the formation of a Ku Klux Klan chapter in Pomona, one-quarter of whose members were the ranchers. The Inland Valley chapter was determined to ensure "sobriety and social control" through the use of intimidation, night riding, and public rituals. Rev. Bob Shuler, a prominent Methodist minister and spiritual leader of the Klan, described Mexicans as "diseased of body, subnormal intellectually, and moral morons of the most hopeless type." Nor was the situation helped when Archbishop Edward J. Hanna wrote (in 1926) about the Mexicans' "low mentality" and their capacity for only limited assimilation. In "too great numbers" they posed a threat to "our civilization," and he urged the exclusion of Mexicans "of low mentality."[35] Given this climate of opinion, it was no surprise when Carey McWilliams referred to the *colonias* as "jim-towns" —places where Jim Crow–like conditions prevailed.[36]

This period was extraordinarily dynamic, with increasing numbers of Mexicans moving north in search of refuge and work, and many relocating in a step migration. The reported foreign-born Mexican population jumped from

103,393 in 1900 to 221,915 a decade later, to 486,418 in 1920. When the Depression began the number of Mexican foreign born was more than six times that of 1900, and the total Mexican-descent population topped 1.44 million. Along with the massive population jump was the beginning of a major redistribution. When the century began, 68 percent of Mexicans lived in Texas, and that steadily declined to 52 percent (1920) and to 41 percent by 1930. In 1920, 89 percent still resided in the Southwest.[37]

The great influx certainly affected the physical expansion of existing communities, such as in Los Angeles, where the move outward by Latinos (and other immigrants) to Lincoln Heights, Boyle Heights, and Belvedere was marked by a rejuvenation of Mexican culture. However, relations between Mexicans and Mexican Americans were tense at first, marked by distrust and mutually derogatory stereotypes. As one migrant who had come in 1916 put it, they simply "didn't like each other." Anastacio Torres told an interviewer, "I don't have anything against the *pochos* [slang for Mexican Americans]. But the truth is that although they are Mexicans . . . they pretend that they are Americans. They only want to talk in English and they speak Spanish very poorly." Another migrant, Tomás Mares, also noted that "the so-called *pochos* here don't like us. They think that because I come from Mexico I am going to take the country away from them. But our worst enemies are the Mexicans who have lived here for a great many years and have . . . become American citizens." In yet another twist, when *nuevo mexicanos* were faced with the rising number of Mexican immigrants, whom they viewed as inferior, they began to refer to themselves not as Mexican Americans but as Spanish Americans (and also as Hispanos).[38]

The Mexican Revolution—and the social revolution it ignited—affected many places along the 2,000-mile border; events often blurred the boundary line. For virtually no other group in the West, including Canadians, did homeland events have such immediacy or prolonged consequences. The U.S.-Mexican border has been referred to as "one of the world's great cultural borderlands," where residents have lived and worked within a sphere that has tended to be somewhat isolated from the mainstream, or heartland, of both societies. However, individuals living there have still been caught up in the dynamics of a world that combines their national culture, border conditions, and often the local idiosyncrasies of their ethnic group. The on-going connections remained as much political, social, and cultural as economic, overlaying all the political and military events that periodically swept back and forth across the border.[39] For example, in 1910, from his offices in San Antonio, Francisco Madero issued a call to arms against President Porfirio Díaz. His agents set up their headquarters in El Paso, supported by Mexicans in the city. On May 8, 1911, they launched an attack across the Rio Grande from El Paso against Ciudad Juarez and captured it. Shortly thereafter, Díaz resigned.[40] Celebrations followed in Ciudad Juarez and El Paso. After 1920, that American border center would cease to be a staging area for armed movements and cross-border clashes.[41]

For a long time El Paso was the Mexicans' principal gateway to the United States. The city was the "regional market place of cheap labor." It was also a leading example of the blend of "cultural continuity and cultural change" that was shaped by influences from both home countries as well as by the almost four-fold increase in population between 1900 and 1920 (and over five-fold by 1930). At the same time, the racial stratification in wages persistently limited occupational opportunities for Mexicans and Mexican Americans. Typical was the El Paso Smelter, which in 1914 paid Mexicans $1.50 per day but white skilled workers $6. Few Mexicans were placed in the skilled positions. A major business in the city, Popular Dry Goods, placed Mexican women employees in the basement and paid them $10–20 per week, while white American women on the main floor earned $37.50–$40. In the 1920s American carpenters earned $8 per day and their Mexican co-workers only $3.50–$4.50. A key role in the city was played by the *renganchistas*, the labor contractors, notably Ramon Gonzalez. Between July 1908 and February 1909, there were 16,171 Mexicans who were farmed out to several railroads, and in 1911 requests for 9,000 workers came in. By 1919 the five major sugar refiners had also set up labor agents in El Paso.[42] Throughout the Southwest and Midwest, whether the product was copper, cotton, coal, sugar beets, or railroad maintenance, El Paso was (besides a political haven) the principal conduit for Mexican labor at this time.

The economic exploitation, ethnic strains, and sharply defined segregation of El Paso were equally pronounced far to the east, in the Lower Rio Grande Valley and its Winter Garden District. There, Anglos snapped up the ranch lands, sometimes for pennies an acre. Northerners and southerners moved into the state, each with different economic motives and a different racial ethos. Irrigated and dry farming and refrigerated rail cars now increased the potential for distribution of more vulnerable fruit and vegetable crops, and ranch lands were converted to commercial agriculture—cotton production and vegetables, in particular. By the first decade of the century, the paternalistic culture of the ranches was gradually giving way to a more detached, impersonal, capitalistic wage labor system.[43] Farmers there declared that "We have to have the Mexicans as cheap labor," because, said a tenant farmer, "the white labor won't do this work. The Negro would not do it. He is getting $4 or $5 a day in town. We are dependent on Mexicans." Of course, conceded another tenant, "If we didn't have so much cheap labor, we wouldn't plant such big acreage of onions." And yet, Mexicans were still viewed as "a decadent race," "outside the social order but a necessary part of it," confined to "separate and subordinate institutions that rigidly defined their position as farm laborers."[44] Mexicans were willing to endure such inequalities and discrimination because, they insisted, they were only "temporarily in a foreign land." Most planned to return home. As the migrant Tomás Mares put it, "more than anything else . . . I want [my chil-dren] to go to a Mexican school so that they will be educated in their own coun-try and learn to love and respect it."[45]

Given similar conditions in the Jim Crow South, violence against Mexicans in South Texas intensified at this time. The prevailing social order was becom-ing more bifurcated with the collapse of the prior political alliances between the Anglo machine and local Latino leaders. A plot known as El Plan de San Diego, to kill all white males over age 16 and return the Southwest to Mexico, was set to begin February 20, 1915. The destruction of Anglo property, attacks on livestock, railroads, farms, and post offices, which resulted in the deaths of 33 Anglos, ignited retaliatory violence and a large-scale killing of Mexicans that continued into mid-1916. With civil war raging on across the border, violence had already preceded the *tejano-mexicano* attacks, and El Plan has been viewed historically as "an excuse" for counter-violence by Texans. It has been esti-mated that the number of Latinos killed was in the "low thousands." In many cases Texas Rangers, together with vigilantes, were in the forefront of the "counter insurgency" and murders. "No person of Latino heritage was fully as-sured of safety" in the Lower Rio Grande Valley. By June 1916, there were 50,000 U.S. troops along the border area there.[46] To prevent any repetitions of such extreme unrest, Anglos responded by hastening the imposition of political restrictions on the *tejanos* and cementing Jim Crow–style segregation across South Texas.

The tumultuous decade of the 1910s was marked by political struggles be-tween new farmers and older political machines. Where the former were more numerous, *tejanos* were effectively neutralized; where the latter held on and more Mexican American ranchers were present, the conditions were less ex-treme. Nevertheless, "The segregated society was a new order." Capturing the sentiment of the time was a remark by a ranch manager's wife regarding the schools: Let the Mexican have a good education, "but still let him know he is not as good as the white man. God did not intend them to be; He would have made them white if He had." The comment is not surprising given historian Neil Foley's observation that "Mexicans, including Mexican Americans, had become like the Chinese, [to be perceived as] a culturally and biologically infe-rior alien race."[47]

In the short run *tejanos* suffered dearly, but their irate reaction to the failure of the Mexican government to intervene on their behalf would lead a number of them in the late 1920s to embrace Americanization. Their aim would be to proclaim their whiteness in order to ameliorate the racial system that had been put in place. The League of United Latin American Citizens was one important outcome of this effort in 1929.

We thus come full circle regarding "whiteness." Clearly and repeatedly the term refers to cultural and not physical attributes. Witness Neil Foley's observation that "manly courage was constitutive of whiteness." He points out that in Texas white identity represented an imagined homogeneity, so that Czechs and Germans, though differing in language, culture, and religious and educational institutions, "still thought of themselves as whites when they were in the company of Mexicans and blacks." Poor whites, destined to remain poor tenants, were regarded as lacking "certain qualities of whiteness." Although Mexicans were generally segregated in the South Texas and the Rio Grande Valley region, the tri-racial dynamics in Central Texas gradually prompted whites—those particularly from the South—to develop an alliance with Mexican sharecroppers and tenants.[48] The accompanying cultural fusion forged a "cultural borderlands cross-roads between the South and the West"—underscoring the reality of Texas as a bridge to the Southwest. With those developments came a double phenomenon of "Mechanization and Mexicanization," accelerating the cultivation of cotton in Central Texas, land consolidations that displaced farmers, and the rise of a farm labor population consisting of a Mexican majority but including blacks and "whites."

Across the Southwest, Mexicans became a key variable in the rise of corporate agriculture,[49] including in Colorado, where the sugar beet industry became heavily dependent on Mexicans as well as Spanish Americans (*Hispanos*) from New Mexico.[50] By the 1920s in various locations across the region, the accompanying systems of economic exploitation and discrimination, extensive social controls, and widespread political disenfranchisement reflected a fusion of economic necessity, historical precedents, political emasculation, a gaping cultural divide, and calculated opportunism.

CHAPTER SEVENTEEN

The First World War
and Americanization

*P*RIOR TO 1914, the federal legislative and executive actions relating to immigration had placed restrictions on Asians (principally Chinese and Japanese
laborers and the spouses of Chinese workers) and on several more-or-less generic groups of people (mainly, those with physical or mental disabilities or diseases, those likely to become a public charge, possible prostitutes, and those
subscribing to anarchist political views). The head tax stood at four dollars per
person. By and large the gateway to the United States was still open—and certainly that was the case along the U.S.-Mexican border. The First World War
had a profound impact on American immigration and on many immigrant
populations. The West, though physically far removed from Europe, was not
immune to the international developments building toward war. Certainly,
European immigrants followed events affecting their homelands. The impact
on immigration lay less in the severity of the laws and policies enacted or implemented during that time than in the precedents they set and the forces for
change they unleashed.

The war and its aftermath accelerated the movement toward the restriction
of immigration, just as it set in motion programs that were intended to pressure
immigrant communities to quicken their progress toward Americanization.
By the 1920s, major modifications in naturalization laws and the eligibility for
citizenship by Congress and the courts would parallel the adoption of immigration quotas and, in fact, become inter-connected in the 1924 legislation. The
policy changes represented a determination to exercise a greater control over
who would be admitted into the country and then into its civic polity. This

amounted to a further assertion of national sovereignty over the nation's borders. The overhaul in 1924 (including the implementation of the National Origins program in 1929) and the creation of the Border Patrol in that same year completed the transformation—the substantial closure of the American gateway beyond Asians—which had been put in motion during the Great War to end all wars.

Roiling the waters and also perceived as radically inspired were a number of labor actions in the West from shortly before the war until a year and a half after it ended, most often involving immigrant workers, and some of which have been noted already: the Ludlow strike of 1913–1914; the shingle weavers strike in Everett, Washington (led by the Wobblies) in 1916; and six months later, again in Everett—a city on whose streets "one could hear Norwegian, Swedish, and German and sometimes Italian and Greek"—a violent confrontation between "invading" Wobblies and deputized residents, which left 12 persons dead.[1] In 1917, there were three confrontations—the major strike in Butte (following the Speculator Mine blast and marked by the lynching of labor organizer Frank Little), the multi-ethnic strike in Bisbee, Arizona, and the lumbermen's strike in Oregon. Then came another strike in 1918 in Butte; in January 1919, two months after the war ended, the orange pickers' labor action in the Inland Valley (east of Los Angeles); a month later, one of the most spectacular general strikes in American history, involving 60,000 workers and paralyzing Seattle; and, in early 1920, the Oahu plantation strike.[2]

Against this backdrop of labor unrest, the war triggered "a free floating anxiety" and a growing need for a sense of national unity and social stability—more specifically, what was often expressed as a yearning for conformity to preserve the social order: One Hundred Percentism. When the Germans declared a policy of unrestricted submarine warfare against the British on January 30, 1915, followed by the sinking of the *Lusitania* in early May, it sparked what John Higham called a "spectacular" reversal in American nativism against what had been a sacrosanct German American population. That prompted Germany to impose a temporary halt on the new policy. With the prospect of war approaching, a major immigration law was enacted over the president's veto. The new law represented a reassessment of the place of immigration in American society and established immigration restriction as part of the national defense.[3]

Although the United States remained neutral for the first thirty-three months of the war, it did gear up production for its own arsenal and sales to the combatants. The Irish applauded the neutrality, as did Germans and Scandinavians. In Butte, for example, the Irish explicitly expressed their support for the Germans, while many German youth headed to the Fatherland to serve their country.[4] Elsewhere, Americans began to worry about the loyalties of the one-in-seven persons in the country who were foreign born, especially given the arrival of

13.69 million Europeans in the 14 years prior to the outbreak of the war—1.09 million of whom indicated their intention to live in the West (8 percent). Well before the U.S. entry into the war in April 1917, various agencies had begun to devise programs to ensure the newcomers' loyalty, to discourage overt support for embattled homelands, and to inculcate American language, values, and practices. At the same time, nativism became more evident—that intensive, defensive nationalism that would persist for years and ultimately find its foremost expression in the revival of the Ku Klux Klan between 1915 and the early 1920s. Historians Michael Malone and F. Ross Peterson labeled it "an extension of the immediate postwar super patriotism," but John Higham also described it as a "fusion of primitive race feelings" and a manifestation of insecurities in the face of extensive and rapid changes in American society. Its goal was a "coercive conformity."[5]

The outcome of the Selective Service Act represented another set of responses to the war. In the final tally, about one in five men drafted was foreign born: one-half million men—including many thousands who waived their right to exemption in order to serve—along with thousands of second-generation Americans. However, so many of the foreign born had no knowledge of any English that the initial situation was a disaster for military morale until the Camp Gordon Plan was implemented. The plan called for such troops to be divided up by language, with native-speaking officers and with instruction in the native languages in order to teach the soldiers English and American culture. It also provided for ethnic-specific celebrations and religious observances, thus conveying the sentiment that their traditions were still legitimate in American society. The plan was initiated in many camps. In one documented instance where it was set up out West, at Camp Cody, in New Mexico, some 600 Mexican soldiers were involved. The result was a huge boost in morale, contributing to the naturalization of 155,246 soldiers in the United States and more overseas, along with the 32,510 who applied even before the draft and the plan were put in place.[6]

The declaration of war on April 6, 1917, precipitated several exceptional developments in addition to the internment of about 6,000 enemy aliens. The calculation that one-third of the nation's foreign born came from enemy nations now meant that they were more likely to be viewed as suspect outsiders. With a focus on radicalism as a chief threat to the country, state legislatures began outlawing "criminal syndicalism," advocacy of violence against the state. The U.S. Congress (October 1918) authorized the deportation of radicals who were accused of advocating sabotage or violence. The creation of an America First campaign by the U.S. Bureau of Education (actually begun in September 1915) was an outreach program that paralleled the Bureau of Naturalization's plans for citizenship education begun in 1917. With that, state councils of defense were established throughout the West to organize courses offering

American history, values, and language and to prepare immigrants for American citizenship. But this national Americanization effort has been assessed as a "comprehensive process of social engineering and regimentation." Expressing its underlying sentiment, Grace Raymond Hebard, of the Wyoming Council of Defense, explained the program's rationale this way in March 1918 regarding the loyalty of Germans: There was no such thing as a German American—"Either they are for us or against, and they cannot be both American and German."

Many of those policies and programs were largely implemented beginning in 1918, and well before then foreigners and overt foreign behavior had already become the targets of American fears concerning the huge population of newcomers, most of whom were not citizens.[7] (Approximately 45 percent of males in 1910 were citizens, but another 4.13 million had come after the census, and most were not yet eligible.) The roughly 6,000 German and Austro-Hungarian enemy aliens interned during the war were in "War Prison Barracks," one of which was at Fort Douglas, Utah. Meanwhile, "Greeks, Dutch, French, Belgians, Ukrainians, Poles, Serbs, Italians, and others were arrested because U.S. Marshals could not tell who was and who was not an 'enemy alien.'" The latter individuals were soon released, but those actually interned were held until well after the war. One-third of them chose repatriation to Europe.

Although negative, anti-German responses may have been less numerous or less concerted in the West, a number of hostile episodes did take place. Besides discouraging the public use of foreign languages and prohibiting the instruction of them in public schools (as in Washington State; Oregon; and Helena, Butte, and Lewiston, Montana), Governor Will Hobby vetoed funding for the University of Texas German language department. Silesians in Texas—who had long used their native language in their churches and, until the war began, had maintained language schools to keep their children away from any non-Polish cultures—now faced strong pressures to switch to English. Such wartime nativism did take some bizarre turns. German-born Paul Isenberg and Capt. Heinrich Hackfield had become partners in one of Hawai'i's five companies controlling the sugar plantations, shipping, and department stores. When the war broke out, they lost control of the company because of their ties to Germany. Carl Haberlach, a Swiss immigrant who managed a co-op dairy in the coastal Oregon town of Tillamook, was tarred and feathered, as was Guido Poenisch in Richmond (California), T. Smith in Amarillo (Texas), and an unnamed man in Tacoma (Washington). A shoe shop owner in Yakima (Washington) was arrested as an espionage suspect because, it was said, "he spent much time hunting and killing rattlesnakes for some mysterious purpose." "Suspicious" individuals in Port Angeles (Washington), Billings, Napa (California), and Globe (Arizona) were forced to kiss the American flag. Others were beaten or threatened with lynching, with the most outrageous episode involving Fritz Seitz in Denver, who was saved from a lynch mob and taken to the hospital in critical condition, only to be jailed for inciting the riot. In a combination of actions shortly after the United States declared war on Germany, a German in a Wyoming restaurant gave a toast, "Hoch der Kaiser" (Long live the kaiser). He was promptly hung from a beam but was cut down before dying. He was then forced to kiss the American flag and ordered to leave town.

While such events were taking place in many western locations, the state demonstrating one of the most intense pursuits of loyalism was Montana. It enacted one of the harshest sedition laws in the country in February 1918, and its format was copied by Congress a few months later. Of the more than 200 arrested there, 79 were convicted of sedition and not pardoned until May 2006. They included a variety of blue-collar and rural workers, among them butchers, carpenters, cooks, teamsters, bartenders, farmers, miners, lumberjacks, and one housewife. More than half were foreign born, and many were German or Austrian. Forty-one served time in state prison. Most of their violations were utterances considered disloyal—pro-German or anti-American—that were frequently exclaimed in saloons and usually accompanied by "strong or vulgar language." Fred Rodewald declared that Americans would have difficult times if the kaiser "didn't get over here and rule this country." Adam Steck went to prison for calling the American flag a "dirty rag" and America "bankrupt already" and incapable of licking Germany. "No, they never did and they never will." Martin Wehinger was sent to the state penitentiary for 18 months for telling a group of Teamsters that "we had no business sticking our nose in there [Europe], and we should get licked for doing so."

Germans and others tried to persist in using their native languages in various ethnic contexts and called for a more even-handed view of the war, but once the United States entered the combat, such efforts were in vain. The Irish and Germans in particular were then more concerned about purchasing Liberty Bonds and demonstrating their loyalty to the United States. In fact, in Billings, Pocatello, Richmond, and San Diego, individuals were coerced and intimidated into buying bonds. Moreover, in the spring of 1918 four German-language newspapers closed down—the *Galveston Herold*, *Colorado Herold* (Denver), *Germania* (Los Angeles), and *Washingtoner Staatszeitung* (Seattle). And Germans were not the only ones targeted. While Mexicans were among those groups signing up for military service in large numbers (which Rodolfo Acuña sees as the beginning of the emergence of a truly Mexican American population that established the postwar organizations), the far more ugly expression of nativism toward Mexicans in Texas surfaced in a generalized wartime response to the "Brown Scare"—the large numbers of entering Mexicans—and allegations of Mexican collaboration with the Germans that were stirred up by the Zimmerman Note in early 1917. Such fears had already been heightened in Texas in the reaction to the violence surrounding El Plan de San Diego in 1915.[8]

In fact, many westerners seemed to have concluded from recent events that the real danger was not only from European enemies but also from unassimilated Asians and inferior Mexicans. U.S. Senator James Phelan (D-CA) had put it this way in 1916: "We on the Pacific Coast have been holding back . . . a real, silent, but overwhelming invasion." Because race was at the forefront of western concerns, different notions of assimilation and incorporation had to be considered, besides the fears raised about Mexicans in response to news regarding alleged plots. Asians could not be naturalized and, hence, could not experience full Americanization even if desired. Americanization programs directed at such foreigners were implemented throughout the West during and after the war, yet the racial preoccupations were not limited to uncertainties surrounding non-Europeans. Ellwood P. Cubberley, dean of Stanford University's School of Education, claimed that the newer Europeans were "largely illiterate, docile, lacking in initiative, and almost wholly without the Anglo-Saxon conceptions of righteousness, liberty, law, order, public decency, and government." In his view, they represented a "serious case of racial indigestion" for the nation—another way of saying they were surely not white.[9]

Even though some programs did have a semblance of planning and realistic objectives (e.g., in Montana, Arizona, and New Mexico), others did not, and after the war many states moved to cut funding for these programs. In fact, the California Commission of Immigration and Housing (CCIH) had one of the best programs, but by 1920 funds were being reduced as sentiment shifted to disillusionment and restriction. Although CCIH's role was doomed following Republican victories in the 1922 state elections, its 1923 report expressed the optimism behind its original objectives: Americanization "was more than teaching English to foreigners. Americanization . . . is the encouragement to decent living, and making possible the attainment of decent standards. It involves the development of national ideals and standards." Nevertheless, Frank Van Nuys points out, "the commission's tolerance had virtually no effect on California's on-going campaign against Asian immigrants." In the end, the state-run programs, which peaked in 1919–1920, were of limited success because immigrant bashing, talk of race suicide, and the Mexicanization of the Southwest undermined support for them. Moreover, the necessary centralization and federal coordination of state programs never materialized. Even innovative ideas, such as Colorado's America First Societies, which had enrolled 5,000 immigrants by 1919, promoting loyalty and American ideals, could not be sustained. In addition, "Immigrants themselves set individual or group agendas frequently contrary to what either industry, organized labor, or Americanization experts thought was best for them."

In the final analysis, the programs "did not alter the calculus of racial privilege and power in the New West," for white Americans retained that power, privilege, and leadership. Throughout the 1920s Asians and Mexicans (and probably some European peoples, too) felt that they had little to gain from "education for citizenship."[10]

CHAPTER EIGHTEEN

State and Federal Laws and Decisions, 1917–1920

*L*EGISLATION ENACTED DURING this period and decisions by the U.S. Supreme Court confirmed many immigrants' assessment that the hegemony of white Americans made the pursuit of citizenship a pointless endeavor. The Alien Land Laws were a major expression of the fears and hostility elicited in Americans by Asian ambitiousness and entrepreneurialism, beginning with California's land laws in 1913. As we have seen, what began with a transfer of opposition to the Chinese into demands that the Japanese (and then Koreans and Asian Indians) must also leave the country escalated with the effort of San Francisco to segregate Japanese schoolchildren, followed by the Gentlemen's Agreement in 1907–1908. The trend then took a more ominous and burdensome turn in 1913 with California's passage of the Webb-Heney Alien Land Act. The state law was expanded in 1920 and 1923 (making it more punitive) and replicated by nine other western states (Oregon, Washington, Arizona, New Mexico, Idaho, Montana, Texas, Utah, and Wyoming) and at least seven other states (Louisiana, Kansas, Missouri, Arkansas, Minnesota, Nebraska, and Florida).[1]

Meanwhile, federal immigration law in 1917 created an Asiatic Barred Zone and in 1924 the general exclusion of most Asians. By that time the U.S. Supreme Court had embraced the concept of "aliens ineligible for citizenship," which was incorporated into the 1924 immigration law. In fact, the concept had already been adopted by Congress two years earlier when it enacted a law that said an American-born woman of Asian origin who weds an Asian—a man ineligible for citizenship—automatically loses her citizenship. Nor was there provision for reclaiming it since, by her marriage, she had become an ineligible alien, too (see below). The climax of this long train of abuses would be internment and incarceration during the Second World War. The legislative and judicial trail over the course of the dozen years ending in 1923 was a crucial prelude to the immigration law enacted in 1924—a display of racism, nativist anxieties, gender bias, and a determination to exercise U.S. sovereignty by imposing ever greater controls and restrictions on America's immigration and naturalization policies. Once more, by examining the prior decades we see the unfolding precedents that set the stage for dramatic legal changes that directly impacted immigrants in the West and those seeking to migrate there.

Underlying the Japanese response to discrimination and hostile organizations was *gaman*—Japanese for sticking things out, enduring difficult circumstances. Japanese immigrants certainly displayed *gaman* in the face of repeated acts of hostility and discriminatory treatment beginning in the first decade of the century. By 1909 Japanese farmers in California owned 16,449 acres and were leasing another 137,233 acres, enough to be perceived with alarm by the Asiatic Exclusion League (AEL) as a threat it was determined to halt. Still, the campaign took four more years, for many businesses benefited from the Japanese concentration on fruits and vegetables, as did others from the trade with Japan. By 1911, the AEL was in decline, and the businessmen behind the Pan-Pacific International Exposition were opposed to anti-Japanese legislation. Then, in April 1912, Senator James Phelan described to Democratic presidential candidate Woodrow Wilson how "the Japanese are a blight on our civilization, destructive of the home life of the people, [and] driving the natives to the city for employment." Wilson replied with a campaign statement that year announcing, with regard to the Chinese and Japanese, that "I stand for a national policy of exclusion. We cannot make a homogeneous population out of a people who do not blend with the Caucasian race. Their lower standard of living as laborers will crowd out the white agriculturalist and is, in other fields, a most serious industrial menace."

A year later, Wilson, now president, told the Japanese ambassador that the U.S. government could not intervene in the pending alien land legislation because it was a state matter. In Japan there were crowds demanding a confrontation with the United States, but Governor Hiram Johnson pressed for action, and, on April 22, 1913, Wilson declared that if Johnson and the California legislature determined that it was necessary "to exclude all aliens who have not declared their intention to become citizens from the privilege of land ownership," he would not object. On May 19, the governor signed the Webb-Heney Alien Land Act. It provided that neither "aliens not eligible to citizenship" nor corporations with a majority of its stock held by such individuals could purchase land or lease land for longer than three years. There were loopholes, however, notably the short-term leasing provision, corporations in the names of Nisei, and purchases by these American-born Japanese. Over the next seven years Japanese and Japanese Americans acquired 48,062 acres and leased 313,150 more acres. In 1920, they owned or leased 387,919 acres.[2]

The Native Sons (and Daughters) of the Golden West, the American Legion, the California AFL, and the California Grange launched a state-wide initiative in 1920 that passed by a 3-1 vote. This Alien Land Act of 1920 banned rentals of land, all leases by corporations with stock held by aliens ineligible for citizenship, and the guardianship of land for American-born minor children by such aliens. All but the latter provision (including a ban on sharecropping) were upheld by the Supreme Court between 1921 and 1923. California further tightened the guardianship provisions in 1923.[3] As noted, over the next two decades nine other western states followed California's precedent. Ownership there plummeted by 1925 from 74,769 acres to 41,898 and leased lands fell from 313,150 acres to 76,397. Masao Suzuki argues that the 1920 legislative changes, not the post–First World War agricultural depression of 1920–1921, was responsible for this steep decline in Japanese farm operations, because the fruit and vegetable industries had not been very adversely affected by that short depression.[4] Some strategies to get around the new obstacles emerged (including the Punjabi-Mexican marriages), but the net effect over the next 18 years, combined with other legislative and judicial actions by the federal government, was increased antagonism in Japan and frustration experienced by Issei and Nisei, who continued to seek ways to access economic opportunities otherwise closed to them in many parts of the West.[5]

On February 5, 1917, four days after Germany announced the resumption of unrestricted submarine warfare, Congress overrode a presidential veto and enacted the Immigration Act of 1917 (39 Stat. 874; 8 U.S.C.).

The law codified previous laws in terms of admissible aliens, registration, illegal aliens, and the many classes of exempt individuals as well as adding some important provisions. It enumerated approximately 33 categories of persons to be denied admission (most previously proscribed, such as polygamists, prostitutes, anarchists, contract laborers, those avoiding military service, and those likely to become a public charge). To them, it added natives of what was called the Asiatic Barred Zone, which included the area from Indochina westward beyond the Subcontinent to the Persian Gulf and south to Indonesia, along with prior limitations on laborers from China and Japan. However, the zone was so configured as to specifically omit Japan and Korea. Furthermore, the act now required a literacy test of all those 16 and older (with some exceptions[6]) in English or a newcomer's native language. In addition, the new law banned all forms of solicitation of immigrant workers outside the United States and provided for the deportation up to five years after entering of certain classes of persons violating the enumerated classes of those to be denied admission. One other provision bearing on the West authorized the establishment of rules for inspecting aliens entering from Canada and Mexico.

The Act of October 16, 1918 (40 Stat. 1012; 8 U.S.C. 137), underscored the determination to exclude "any alien who, at any time shall be or shall have been a member" of a lengthy list of anarchist, syndicalist, or radical type of organizations. The act provided for both exclusion and expulsion of such individuals. The Immigration Act of May 10, 1920 (41 Stat. 593; 8 U.S.C. 157), spelled out the criteria for the deportation of various classes of aliens.

The particular impact of the 1917 law—doubling the head tax to $8, forbidding recruitment of laborers and any form of contract work, and providing for inspection at the border—immediately depressed the number of Mexicans crossing the Texas border (still their principal place of entry at the time). The enactment three months later of the U.S. military draft also prompted thousands of Mexicans to return home. Those developments quickly elicited protests from farmers and railroad directors across the Southwest that there would be serious labor shortages (obviously harmful to the war effort) unless these provisions were suspended. Agricultural groups pressured Secretary of Labor William Wilson to suspend provisions of the new immigration law. On May 23, 1917, Wilson invoked the "Ninth Proviso" of that act, enabling him to permit the emergency admission of temporary workers by setting aside the new head tax, literacy requirement, and ban on contract labor. The order limited Mexicans to six months in agricultural work, thus establishing a unique category of persons temporarily admitted.

After the war ended, continued complaints of labor shortages persuaded Wilson to extend the program until March 1921. Close to 72,900 Mexicans entered with documents under this program. It has been said that many thousands of others entered "without documents." A June 1921 report evaluating the program indicated that 21,400 Mexicans who had been recruited "deserted . . . and disappeared." The poor treatment and low wages, especially in Texas, would influence Mexico's demands when negotiating the Bracero program during the Second World War.[7] Meanwhile, this temporary labor strategy established the precedent for that wartime Bracero program. It also etched deeper the migration streambeds that would be followed by many hundreds of thousands of Mexicans during the 1920s—those with documents, refugees fleeing the war and civil war of the Cristero Revolt, and those crossing, as many had, informally: *sin papeles* (without papers).

At the same time that Congress enacted war-related immigration laws, it also passed the Act of May 9, 1918 (40 Stat. 542; 8 U.S.C. 324), enumerating a lengthy list of individuals who, if they met certain conditions (during the period of the war), could have their naturalization expedited, or waiting time reduced to three years. The act specifically declared that "any alien serving in the military or naval service" could apply "without making the preliminary declaration of intention and without proof of the required five years residence within the United States." That phrase — "any alien" — would eventually (1935) enable several hundred Asians (persons otherwise ineligible for U.S. citizenship) to acquire it. Also, Section 1 in particular noted that "any native-born Filipino," 21 and older, who had filed first papers and had honorably served for three years in the Navy or Marine Corps could, without proof of five years residence within the United States, apply for citizenship.[8]

CHAPTER NINETEEN

The Early 1920s
Threshold of Momentous
Changes

*T*HE FIRST WORLD WAR, the events leading to it, and those that followed certainly affected the composition of the West's population as well as its
economy. Eight states or territories experienced a decline in their foreign-born
communities between 1910 and 1920 (Wyoming, Oregon, Utah, Nevada,
Idaho, Hawai'i, Colorado, Alaska), but they contained less than 23 percent of
foreign-born persons in the region. Their combined drop was only 8.8 percent
of their 1910 total, which was more than offset by the 27 percent increase in the
other six states (Washington, Texas, New Mexico, Montana, California, and
Arizona). The principal growth factor was the profound impact of the Mexican
Revolution in the Southwest and beyond, for the Mexican-born population experienced a 119 percent leap (nine-tenths of them in the West), making that the
singular demographic event of the decade in the West. The 296,268 more foreigners in the West represented nearly a 17 percent change compared with the
minor ripple of less than 1 percent in the rest of the country (net 93,862). Similarly, second-generation whites advanced by three-tenths in the West versus less
than one-fifth elsewhere. (Nevada was the only western state to report a drop.)
Quite significantly, this second-generation growth included one-quarter million persons who had migrated from other states. (See tables 3.1 and 3.6 in the
appendix.)

Other changes suggested important trends in no small measure due to the
war. The foreign-born population of Germans fell by almost one-fifth across the

region (in California, Oregon, Washington, and Texas) and by nearly 18 percent among the Irish (likewise across the region but notably in California and Montana). Although no great changes occurred among the English, Hungarians, and Greeks, the other main groups experienced modest increases, such as the French, Italians, Norwegians, Swedes, Portuguese, and Canadians. At the same time, including Hawai'i, the Japanese foreign born rose by 11 percent, while that of the Chinese shrank by just over one-third.

In the long run these developments in the West would be precursors of further major changes outstripping those in other regions. In the short run, however, they fed the anxieties behind the nation's fears about its homogeneity. After the war, for example, many immigrants quickly demonstrated their persisting attachment to their homeland by campaigning for those countries' independence. Even as advocates of Americanization strove to continue these programs, declining appropriations and a rising disillusionment about the extent of the immigrants' attachment to America seemed to signal their end. There were tales of immigrants' defiance of Prohibition; a series of postwar strikes that often involved an expanded ethnic array of immigrant workers; the shift of many big businesses toward greater mechanization, softening their need for the renewed immigration of unskilled and semi-skilled workers; the influx of Mexicans who more and more replaced southern and eastern European and Asian workers in the West (and, to a degree, in the Midwest, too); the increasing popularity of the Ku Klux Klan (especially in the West), representing a convergence of southern and western racism; and the reception that had been given such works as Madison Grant's 1916 diatribe, *The Passing of the Great Race.* Along with those factors were the combined pseudo-scientific racism and alarmist assessments by eugenicists; the apprehensions aroused by the combination of postwar race riots, the Red Scare, the Palmer Raids against suspected Communists and Socialists, and the fear of infiltration by foreign-born Communists; and, finally, the escalating number of immigrants seeking admission in 1920–1921.

All these factors evoked a sense of alarm that too much was changing and that not enough had changed that needed changing. Likewise disappointing was the failure to realize the wartime hope for the achievement of homogeneity — the millennial expectations of a "purified, regenerate society," as John Higham put it. What remained of the nation's homogeneity seemed on the verge of dissolution from a renewed assault by the rapidly rising number of newcomers. Nativists charged that the literacy test had failed to filter out enough immigrants, and even the AFL called for a two-year immigration moratorium—a time out for the processes of adaptation and assimilation to take greater effect. The nation had not been unified, nor had it been purified.[1]

With such nativists as Congressman Albert Johnson (R-WA) moving into strategic positions in Congress (in his case, as chair of the House Committee on

Immigration) and Senator William Dillingham proposing legislation for immigrant quotas based on his commission's report a decade earlier, the tide was rapidly turning. His bill, as negotiated with the House, imposed a temporary one-year ceiling of 357,800 immigrants, based on 3 percent of the foreign-born population in 1910. In this Emergency Quota Act of May 19, 1921 (42 Stat. 5; 8 U.S.C. 229) about 55 percent of the quotas were allocated to northern and western Europeans and most of the balance to southern and eastern Europeans; 1 percent went to non-Europeans. The colonies of the European powers were given separate quotas, severely limiting what might be available to them. Moreover, most Asians were excluded, based on earlier laws, whereas migrants from the Western Hemisphere were exempt. By proposing a system "based on the pre-existing composition of the American population," this temporary measure, concluded Higham, "proved in the long run the most important turning point in American immigration policy."[2] Although that conclusion, written during the 1950s and before the immigrant revolution of the 1960s, may be overshadowed by our appreciation of the consequences of the Chinese Exclusion legislation, Higham's assessment still carries considerable weight.

One cannot minimize what else this 1921 legislation initiated. Setting a tone for most future immigration legislation, it held that "preference shall be given so far as possible to the wives, parents, brothers, sisters, children under 18 years of age, and fiancées (1) of citizens of the United States, (2) of aliens now in the United States who have applied for citizenship . . . , or (3) of persons eligible to U.S. citizenship who served in the military or naval forces" between April 1917 and November 1918. Furthermore, in the decade 1901–1910 northern and western Europeans had accounted for almost 22 percent of the 8.8 million persons admitted; between 1921 and 1924 that percentage rose to nearly one-fourth, while that for southern and eastern Europeans fell from 71 percent to 41 percent. At the same time that the objective of shifting immigration sources back to northern and western Europe was being set in motion, immigration from Canada jumped from 2 percent to over 18 percent of the total and that from Mexico from less than 1 percent to 8.7 percent. As would occur repeatedly, the intended consequences were achieved—along with the unintended.[3]

The stepping-stones to a new era of immigration could not be set down without several key ones in between, for the novel legislative order of the day concerning immigration required resolution of outstanding issues regarding citizenship. The link between the two has often been overlooked. One new law and two U.S. Supreme Court decisions were pivotal.

One of the first targets of newly empowered women's groups after acquiring the right to vote with the Nineteenth Amendment was the inequitable treatment of women's legal rights. In the Acts of June 29, 1906, and March 2, 1907, discussed earlier, their citizenship had been tied to the decisions of their spouses—if an alien women wed a citizen, she became a citizen; if the husband were alien, the American-born woman took the man's nationality, and if the wife were also foreign, she remained an alien. If the husband then became naturalized, the foreign-born wife automatically acquired citizenship, while the American-born wife could then apply to have hers restored. The Married Woman's Act of September 22, 1922 (the Cable Act, 42 Stat. 1021; 8 U.S.C. 367) largely separated the two genders. It declared that women would no longer acquire citizenship by virtue of either the spouse's status or his actions (or inaction in terms of applying for citizenship). Women would now have to apply and qualify on their own, but in lieu of having to file a declaration of intent and reside in the country for five years, only one year would be mandatory for wives of U.S. citizens (amended to three years in 1934).

This reform, which now provided that American-born women would no longer cease to be citizens as a result of marriage to a non-citizen, had one fatal exception: "any woman citizen who married an alien ineligible to citizenship shall cease to be a citizen of the United States" (sec. 3), with no provision for such a woman to regain her citizenship *during* her marriage. Moreover, if a native-born woman lived for two years in her husband's homeland or five years with him elsewhere outside the United States, she was presumed to have expatriated herself—as would happen to a naturalized female citizen. She would have to reapply for citizenship even though she was American born. The fatal exception, we have pointed out, was that a U.S.-born Asian American woman, having lost her citizenship through marriage to a non-citizen Asian man, could not reapply for citizenship because she had become an Asian ineligible for citizenship. Whether she was divorced or widowed made no difference. She could *not* reacquire her birthright citizenship. This persisting bias did not apply to American-born men, and it would take a dozen years of struggles by women before they achieved the full deletion of these blatantly sexist provisions.

Meanwhile, less than two months after the Cable Act became law, the U.S. Supreme Court handed down its historic decision in *Takao Ozawa v. United States* (260 U.S. 178 [November 13, 1922]). Ozawa had come to the United States in 1894, graduated from Berkeley High School, went to University of California–Berkeley for three years, moved to Honolulu where he raised a family, and then applied for citizenship in 1914. In March 1916, his request was denied. Prior to the Naturalization Act of June 29, 1906, "several hundred Japanese immigrants" (Ichioka indicates 420) had been able to acquire citizenship in lower courts, and President Theodore Roosevelt even recommended that Japanese be permitted to be naturalized. No action was taken. Ozawa's case was appealed after the first denial and was followed avidly within the Japanese community—where ineligibility for citizenship was viewed as a national insult. The U.S. government was concerned about the international repercussions of Ozawa's appeal and asked the court to defer action until the war ended. Ozawa submitted his petition with a lengthy description of his background and his belief that he was certainly a better candidate for citizenship than Benedict Arnold: "In name, I am not an American, but at heart I am a true American." His attorney argued that the original 1790 law did not intend "free white person" to be an exclusive category or a racial category but only one referring to those who were not black or slaves or Indians.

Justice George Sutherland's opinion pointed out that the law limiting citizenship to white persons and those of African ancestry had not been altered by the Act of June 29, 1906. The intent of the law was not to define who was *excluded* but, affirmatively, who was *included*: free white persons, whether the Founding Fathers knew of other groups or not. Crucially, he concluded that estimating "the mere color of the skin of each individual is impracticable" due to gradations within groups. Rather than defining a scientific category, the measure of eligibility is only "what is popularly known as the Caucasian race." "The determination that the words 'white person' are synonymous with the words 'a person of the Caucasian race' simplifies the problem." Ozawa, not being Caucasian, was therefore not a white person and, consequently, remained ineligible for American citizenship. *Rafu Shimpō*, the Japanese newspaper in Los Angeles, published a cheeky response, expressing Japanese pride (*yamato-damashii*). Since it did "not believe whites are the superior race," it was "delighted" that the Court "did not find the Japanese to be free white persons."[4]

Two months later, the court was again faced with the issue of Asians and citizenship, this time involving an Asian Indian, Bhagat Singh Thind. Two court decisions had concluded such individuals were white and qualified for citizenship (*United States v. Balsara*, July 1, 1910; 180 F. 694, 2nd Court of Appeals, New York, and *In re Ajkoy Kumar Mazumbar*, May 3, 1913; 207 F. 115, North Dakota). Thind, a veteran of the First World War, had been naturalized in Oregon. The U.S. examiner challenged the judge's decision and appealed it.

On February 19, 1923, Justice George Sutherland again delivered the decision regarding this highly educated, high-caste Brahmin Hindu. Ozawa had been rejected because he was not Caucasian, for that term was popularly equated with white persons. But Thind's claim to be Caucasian and therefore white because of his Aryan roots compelled the Court to recognize the scientific ambiguities and the "irreconcilable disagreement as to what constitutes a proper racial decision." Furthermore, Aryan was a language, not a physical characteristic, and the one could not be taken as representative of the other when much mixing had occurred in India. Although Caucasian as equivalent to white is used in common speech, it was hardly likely to have been familiar to the authors of the 1790 Naturalization Act. Therefore, any substitution of terms would be confusing. Instead, "the words of the statute are to be interpreted in accordance with the understanding of the common man," and that understanding was that "white person" was meant "to include the only type of man whom [the Founding Fathers] knew as white"—northern and western Europeans. Hence, the words "free white persons" are "synonymous with the word 'Caucasian' only as that word is popularly understood." Finally, not only was Aryan not to be taken as equivalent of white person, but the Asiatic Barred Zone of the Immigration Act of February 5, 1917, also explicitly excluded immigration from India. That represented Congress's opposition to Asian immigration, which could be taken as "persuasive of a similar attitude toward Asiatic naturalization as well, since it is not likely that Congress would be willing to accept as citizens a class of persons whom it rejects as immigrants."

No cheeky remark followed this decision. The government, in fact, moved to denaturalize Asian Indians, and, in despair, Vaisho Das Bagai committed suicide five years later. In addition, California officials used the decision to apply anti-miscegenation and Alien Land Laws to Asian Indians. Between 1920 and 1940, about 3,000 Asian Indians—nearly half of those in the country—returned home.[5]

The debates were already underway about making the quotas permanent. Inevitably, those debates and the resulting legislation became the framework within which we must analyze many of the changes at that time affecting ethnic groups in the West and their impact on it. Most, if not all, non–Western Hemisphere ethnic groups would be affected by the momentous legislation passed between 1917 and 1923 and subsequent measures that would follow in the next half-dozen years. Western states were jumping on board to enact their own Alien Land Laws (8 of 14 states or territories passed such legislation, with Utah and Wyoming doing so during the Second World War) and to expand anti-miscegenation statutes, while Asian immigrants and their children were strategizing on how best to evade the destructive effects of these legislative and judicial assaults. At the same time, tens of thousands of Mexicans were pouring into the Southwest (as did thousands of Filipinos) and spreading into the Midwest, too.

Concurrently, tens of thousands of midwesterners were flowing into the Southwest—from Texas to Los Angeles. Although the environment they entered was frequently stained by racism, segregation, economic exploitation, and complex dual wage systems, opportunities would open for many of these newcomers because the new laws and court decisions were curbing opportunities for others. In addition, parallel with this influx of diverse peoples and momentous legal changes, we also see unions suffering the setbacks of failed strikes, numerous episodes of violence, and pressures for open-shop work places. During the 1920s the West's economy—especially that of the extractive industries—was undergoing changes, with declining prices, mechanization, greater corporate controls, and vanishing support for unions. Hawai'i's great plantation strike of 1920 proved to be the exception, altering labor relations in that territory.

As a consequence of the numerous shifts and changes, the many European ethnic populations had to determine how they would respond to the labor situation on the mainland and to the prospect of legislative restrictions on future immigration and their ability to return home and then re-emigrate, perhaps with new families. Migrants and immigrants also had to confront the remarkable expanding urbanization, increasing industrialization, dramatic corporate agriculture and factory farms, and major technological innovations in many parts of the West. At one end of the spectrum, ethnic group members in certain locations had to figure out how to cope with the renewed nativism and the resurrected Ku Klux Klan. At the other end, they all would need to determine what balance they could strike between the preservation of their traditions and the continued pressures to adapt to America's society and its institutions as well as to the pervasive appeal of the consumer and cultural revolutions taking place all around them. For many peoples, ties to their homelands would be severely strained, gradually loosening with the passage of time and the new lives and families they were building in America. Even those from nearby homelands would not be entirely immune to the attractions and opportunities of American life.

Virtually no part of the West was untouched by these developments, but they would now be taking place within the harsher context of immigrant quotas; communities of people dealing with the vulnerability that came with disqualification for citizenship; and newcomers being viewed as inferior, as threats to the social order, as not quite white and perhaps not even assimilable. Within a few years would come new threats to a number of these ethnic populations. The years between 1900 and 1923 had posed considerable challenges to the region's many peoples, both those long present and the new populations still converging on the West, and they set the stage for still more novel conditions and challenges.

In this second of the four periods covered in this work, dramatic and historic events uniquely defined it as it grew out of the precedents of the prior ones. The two decades leading up to 1923 were marked by huge influxes of ever more diverse immigrant populations, a blend of on-going old ones and accelerating new ones. The judicial and legislative framework was defined more explicitly during these years, while expanding the restrictions first laid out in the previous quarter century. As the western economy became more enmeshed in national and global capitalism, western leaders and entrepreneurs relied increasingly on the contributions of newcomers and their children, even where those leaders and entrepreneurs were themselves foreigners. Those who chose to settle and remain had to do so within the context of more restrictions and borders erected by a more nationalistic government that was responding not only to optimistic predictions but to admonitions and fears as well.

Our process of addressing these points is based on the four interrelated themes of this narrative—changing populations; changing economic conditions; changing federal and state laws targeting immigrant populations; and changing ethnic cultures in response to American society (and vice versa)—measuring how far to pursue the accommodation and estimating how open mainstream society would be. We now turn to the next 18 years, from 1924 to 1941: years of trauma, years of hardship, years of anguish, and years of unparalleled unconstitutional public policies. And then Pearl Harbor. The immigration of the first two decades of the new century had certainly made the American West more than ever a world of peoples. What happened next was very much shaped by the prior half century.

PART 3.

"Give Me a Bug, Please"

RESTRICTION AND REPATRIATION, ACCOMMODATION AND AMERICANIZATION, 1923–1941

Countless immigrants have come to America and struggled to learn English. The proverbial story—here serving as the title to part 3—where a newcomer asks for a commonplace item (in this case seeking a *bag* from a store clerk), but what comes out is quite different (a *bug*), reminds us of the challenges of fitting into a new society, as so many have eventually done. And they do so, we so readily forget, by giving the invaluable assets of their labor and creativity.[1]

In 1931 Herman Feldman, a Dartmouth professor of industrial relations, concluded that "Without immigration the vast growth of American industry in the last century probably could not have been achieved." Moreover, "[t]he history of American racial relations in industry may be read as a succession of attempted substitutions of one racial group for another. Thus, we find that the hardest, dirtiest and poorest-paying work has been passed over to the 'freshmen' who have been so insistent upon entering the American institution." Eight years later, Carey McWilliams added another angle to that analysis when he referred to the "tidal wave" of newcomers to the West after 1900. The economic value of those immigrants had become "apparent with the influx of Mexicans, Japanese, Filipinos, Yugoslavians, Russians, and other groups." He recognized that "[t]he availability of [such] large reserves of cheap labor unquestionably accelerated the pace at which agriculture was industrialized in California." Congressman Emanuel Celler, a champion of immigration, had put the issue in layman's terms during the debates over what thereafter became the Johnson-Reed Immigration Act of 1924. If all the foreign born were gone, he asserted, "there would, perhaps, be no rolls for breakfast, no sugar for the coffee, and no meat for dinner . . . no butchers, no bakers, or candlestick makers."[2]

It was undoubtedly true that this tidal wave was part of the overall problems California carried into the twentieth century, problems, observed Kevin Starr, that "did not differ from [those] faced by America as a whole . . . after 1915: population growth, the rise of an urban industrial society, race relations, labor-management relations, questions of conservation and ecology, questions of health, and questions of education and welfare."[3] However, for Starr what set the West apart after the First World War was, first, an expanding urbanization conjoined with extensive agricultural and other large-scale extractive industries (even as the relative proportion of most rural populations shrank) and, second, a reshaping of the profile of the West due to the increasing (and shifting) diversity of both its native and foreign-born populations. Thousands of Americans and European immigrants (as well as Canadians), many of them step migrating to the West, struggled to define the region's society principally as a homogeneous white one.[4] They labored to secure that in the face of a racially pluralistic reality which became ever more colorful, despite the substantial curtailment of Asian immigration. Few other areas in the country during this period experienced such a convergence of European, Asian, Latino, Native American, and African American peoples—and certainly not within an environmental context comparable to that in the 14 states and territories of the American West.

There was, for good and for ill, a definite awareness of this multicultural reality, resting to a considerable degree on the central economic roles played by immigrants and the children of immigrants. These workers were welcomed in many locales, suspect in others, and inevitably exploited by countless individuals and institutions across the West. In the broader socio-cultural realms, however, the newer groups remained for a time less visible, although that would change with shifts in the political climate, economic conditions, the sources and numbers of the immigrants, and the pace of their acculturation and that of their children. Visible or not, steadily etched into the region during and after the First World War were additional signs of the formation of more ethnic communities. They were part of the urbanization and commercial expansion along the coast, out in Hawai'i, and from the region's hinterlands to its trading centers. Many parts of the West were at this time becoming more knitted together in such sub-regional networks, with both immigrant and second-generation persons major threads in this western fabric, notwithstanding the restrictions on immigration erected between 1917 and 1929 and the reactionary policies of the 1930s. The upheavals of the Great Depression at home, the emergence of Fascist governments abroad, and the outbreak of wars in several parts of the world then precipitated new chapters in the West's immigrant/ethnic history.

The accounts of these men and women again reveal many aspects of the lives of these new generations, their places in the evolving society and economy of the West, the extent of their transnational bonds with their homelands, and the consequences of the new immigration and naturalization regulations. Though conditions were changing dramatically between the Roaring '20s, the not-so-roaring '30s, and the spreading war in the early '40s, the four dimensions of change can still be consistently identified. The patterns of change we now trace involve not just who came but who left; not just economic growth but economic collapse; not only a monumental recasting of immigration legislation but also policies that exclude a new category of persons seeking refuge; and not only changes in terms of modes of adaptation but, as well, conflicting strategies for negotiating ethnic accommodation in the face of the fears, hostility, and hysteria of Depression and wartime America. In the final analysis, we will see that these are decades scarred by widespread violations of the constitutional rights of immigrants and their children, primarily in the West.

CHAPTER TWENTY

A World of Peoples
The 1920s and 1930s

M ARIA ABASTILLA BELTRAN was born in September 1903 in Nega-lian (La Union), the Philippines, and raised in Baguio City.[1] Her mother was a teacher; her father operated a business. Maria graduated from a nursing pro-gram, worked for four years in Philippines General Hospital, and journeyed to the United States to complete a degree in public health nursing. After spending time in Philadelphia, Cleveland, and Chicago, she was told in October 1929 to report to school in Seattle, where she completed her studies in two years. Dur-ing that period she also participated in the establishment of a Filipino Women's Club (since renamed Filipino-American Women's Club), which became part of the nascent Filipino American community. She married a Filipino from Ilocos Norte in November 1931 and obtained a job in a hospital for 15 years. She "didn't find very much discrimination in nursing," or at least "they pay us all the same." Eight years after their marriage, and following a general lawsuit challenging restricted covenants against house sales to Filipinos, Maria and her husband bought a home. Both earned good incomes and often shared their meals with many other Filipinos hurt by the Depression.

Maria and her husband raised three children, and when asked how they identify themselves, she replied, "I make them understand that they are Filipi-nos": Some Filipino families "try to raise their children like Americans and they don't like the Filipinos" because "some of the Filipino people prefer to be white than Filipino. But I think that's wrong"; "I'm very proud of my back-ground." Although nearly 2,200 Filipinos took advantage of the 1935 Repatria-tion Law to return home, those remaining "paved the way" for the next generation of newcomers to obtain jobs more easily.[2] In Maria's case, "I was just plain lucky" finding employment, she commented. Others would apply for different jobs, and employers "would look at you and if they know you are not white they will say [the job is] already taken." Perhaps overlooking the fact that Filipinos were ineligible for U.S. citizenship until July 1946, she mentions that she did not obtain her U.S. citizenship until 1947, when Kings County (Washington State) required it for employment: "So it was more convenient . . . than anything else," although "I was always wanting to go home." After all, "[w]e don't want to forget the Philippines. . . . We love the Philippines but we love this country, too." By the time of her interview in 1975, after more than 40 years in America, her life was "more American than Filipino," "but in my ways I am [still] Filipino." She traveled four times to the Philippines on vacation, yet she would not consider returning there: "I'd love to . . . but when I am there I remember my [12] grandchildren over here. I am homesick and I have friends here, you know, and I am homesick [for the Philippines,] too. You get used to things like that. . . . [I'm here] for over forty years and you can't forget it."

Zacarias Manangan was born in San Nicholas, Pangasinan, the Philippines, two years after Maria Beltran, but his experiences differed considerably.[3] He got married at age 18 to Honorata; his parents, who were farmers, arranged the marriage. He completed two years of high school and then worked on their farm for about six years. He migrated to America in 1929, leaving his wife and three children and promising to return in three years. A neighbor had worked in Hawai'i, and he and others had been sending money home. "I believe," Zacarias conceded, that "was the very core" influencing his decision to migrate. Soon, 700 persons were on the ship, 100 from his community, and they sailed directly to Seattle. Having no friends or relatives in Seattle, Zacarias's network for job information became those men who had been on that same ship. At the outset, they sought employment on a railroad through a Japanese contractor, pledging to join no union. This job took Zacarias to Montana, North Dakota, and Minnesota. After returning to Seattle, several pooled their money, bought a car, and journeyed to California in search of employment. They found jobs picking grapes, tomatoes, carrots, and, all the way down in Imperial Valley, lettuce, peas, watermelons, and cantaloupes. Although they were hired only for seasonal work, "we didn't have any recreation at all."

Afterward they went back up to the Auburn, Washington, area, where riots broke out in several communities because the people "didn't like the Filipinos out there" and would insult them, provoking fights. Meanwhile, Zacarias participated in the attempt to organize workers as part of the Filipino Cannery Workers and Farm Laborers Union. They staged strikes in several communities east of Tacoma to raise wages and improve workers' living conditions. Around 1935, he and two or three others rented land to farm—which they did for six

arduous and not-too-profitable years. Given such conditions and meager earnings, the men determined that "it would be better for us to be alone [without
families] and if we have some money left . . . what we have to do is send [it]
back home." Zacarias also helped organize "the Filipino Brotherhood of Auburn and Vicinity." "One of the main reason [sic], I believe [was] to try and convince these people [in the community] that we have some sort of intelligence,
we are civilized people." About 1,000 Filipinos were in the area, mostly single
men but some married to whites, even though "I believe the Filipinos were not
supposed to, you know, marry white people, Caucasians, at that time."

Although not a citizen—and he never became one—during the Second
World War Zacarias worked in a shipyard in Bremerton and afterward became a
gardener. In 1936 he joined and was then active in the San Nicholas Pangasinan
Brotherhood Association (after the war "we accepted people from . . . different
towns"—"with some restrictions"). By the time of the 1975 interview he had
risen to the presidency of the Filipino Gardeners Association. With all that organizational involvement, his roots were clearly replanted in America, but not
until his first trip back to the Philippines in 1962 (for "a little vacation back
home")—33 years after migrating—did he apply to bring his wife to the United
States. It took five more years to secure her a visa. Seven years later the couple
was still discussing the merits of acquiring U.S. citizenship but had not filed papers for it. However, given the martial law under Ferdinand Marcos then in
force in their homeland, Zacarias dismissed the idea of retiring there. Besides,
"this is great country, there's lots of opportunities over here . . . as long as you are
willing to struggle for it."

Asked how she felt about Zacarias remaining away 30 years more than he had
promised, Honorata simply replied, "In time I forgot him."

Andrew Kan was born in Guangdong Province, China, in about 1855. His
father was a merchant and farmer.[4] At age 14, Andrew had to leave school to
work, and the following year he sailed to San Francisco "on account of the gold,
lots of money in this country." At that time in San Francisco "Chinese treated
worse than dog," with young "hoodlums" pulling queues, slapping men, and
throwing rotten vegetables and eggs and even stones at them. "Nobody would
ever try to stop them." After working for an uncle for a short time he began a
decade of doing domestic work for whites—"the only place I learn
English. . . . The daughter of the lady I work for help me with few lessons. I
study very hard." Toward the end of that phase he converted to Christianity but
at a considerable personal price: "I lose lots of friends. . . . My relations outcast
me. They afraid I bring disgrace and curse upon the families." In 1880 he
moved to Portland and began his own business, the Japanese Bazaar, because
people were interested in Japanese goods and "Chinese goods not amount to
much." Some five years later the Chinese were driven out of Portland, but be-

cause his store was "in the white district . . . they no touch me, they forget all about" me. He also bounced back from severe losses during the Panic of 1893. By the time he went bankrupt in 1916–1917, he had amassed—and lost—a fortune of several hundred thousand dollars—"due to family trouble." He admitted that he had been swindled by relatives working for him, who had in the process also wrecked his credit. He relocated to Seattle, began anew in the same line of business, and once again prospered, making some $145,000 in seven years.

Andrew had also married in 1893. "I think my wife born here—I don't know." But she was a Christian, a "mission girl." He had not known much about Chinese women or about American customs and American women, for "young Chinese boy not allowed to look at women on street. I very bashful. . . . very seldom see women with men." Moreover, he did not wish to pay thousands of dollars for a traditional Chinese woman and, in his words, thereby reinforce Chinese customs. They had four children. He sent his son to a university until his business failed. "My boy he go Chinese school, too. He should have learned a lot, but my old woman no good, too much indulgence, not make them work hard enough." His son would continue to be a problem, in part, Andrew claimed, because of the bad influence of Andrew's wife on their son.

It was the mid-1920s when he was interviewed. He criticized Americans for not working as hard as the Chinese, but he also censured the Chinese because "they do not live among the better class of white people. They live among the low class of white people," people with "no morality, no Christian spirit. . . . I thank the Lord I am a Christian." He hoped "to make a larger fortune next few years, so I can soon stop and help the people of China . . . and the poor people of this country." With more family members having converted to Christianity and "because I have made money in this country," Kan was now welcomed back. In fact, he had become active in the Presbyterian and Episcopalian churches and helped fund the building of a Methodist mission in Portland.

Years earlier, Kan observed, because of the hostility toward the Chinese, he would not have wanted to become a U.S. citizen—"It would not have been right." More recently, he "would have been delighted," and given his years and successes in America, "I should be able to become American citizen." This attitude did not represent a complete break with his homeland. After a lapse of 46 years he went back to China twice in 1916 and twice again in 1923. Then, in 1924, nearly 70 and in weak health, he took note of the reality that in China there was "no authority, no protection, climate poor, no sanitation, but on account of my age I think I must go back to China to live among my family"— among those who would treat him properly. He claimed that his wife was spoiled and had "all the vices . . . of the American people with none of the virtues. I wish she had never been born. . . . [I]t not right for Chinese man born in China to marry Chinese woman born in America. They will not be happy."

Moses Fadal, his wife, Mary Lalo, and their two infant children arrived in Waco, Texas, in 1898. They had migrated from Beirut, at that time considered a part of Syrian territory under Turkish rule.[5] All the families who migrated from there to Waco continued to identify as Syrian long after the creation of Lebanon. His paternal uncle had preceded them and encouraged them to migrate. Eight years later, George Fadal was born in Waco, as were six other siblings. The family had not fled *from* their homeland but rather *to* America in search of opportunity. Why Waco? For no particular reason, said George. "Nothing that I know of at all other than the one [person] that came first is the reason they came here." For his father, who had been a brick mason, "[i]t was just a matter of trying to make a living." His father began as a peddler in the Waco area, selling "goods, clothes, you know . . . socks and underwear and overalls and things like that." George's maternal aunts and his father's brothers likewise migrated to Waco, as did one brother-in-law. So few families from his parents' homeland migrated to Waco that in 1977 George could provide nearly all the family names: Fadal, Bashara, Macdessey, Mackosher, Khoury, Ezar, and Ammouri. When his parents arrived, both were illiterate in Arabic and spoke no English. And yet, George would learn "very little" Arabic "because every one at home was speaking English except mother, and she—she finally got . . . pretty good in English." George's wife, however, did speak Arabic. Having resided in the same neighborhood in Beirut, her family knew his from there and had migrated to Waco around 1900.

By the time George was in high school his father owned two "confectionaries," selling fruits and groceries. Between 1923 and 1925 two of his brothers opened drugstores, all father and son enterprises. Neither brother had gone through a pharmacology program but had passed the state exam by having had on-the-job training, which was permitted in Texas at that time. George had hoped to become an engineer. His father's ill health, however, compelled George to leave school and work in the stores.

The families were all Christian—"Episcopal faith or Greek Orthodox, whichever"; they had been Greek Orthodox in Beirut. In the late 1920s, with close to 40 Syrian families in Waco, they had informally organized the Syrian Association "for more of a religious and charity thing, club like." In 1931 they raised funds to erect a building for social, cultural, and religious purposes. It was completed in 1935, and each month a Greek Orthodox preacher would come and conduct services there. Nevertheless, George pointed out, Greeks were not members of the Syrian Association; "it was strictly for the Syrians." It served to keep alive memories of their culture and homeland, and "we tried to instill in the youngsters coming up the purpose of the whole thing." It was also for "keeping the group together here in Waco." It soon became part of the Southern Federation of Syrian and Lebanese-American Clubs, located in Houston, and contributed to various local civic projects. By the late 1970s the Syrian community had grown to about 65 families but not from additional in-migration. Most were now Episcopalian.

Given that few immigrants had come to Waco since the 1920s, only a few families were of recent origin. George reiterated that even in 1977, decades after its founding, "You can't belong to the Syrian Club unless you are married to a Syrian girl or you're a Syrian, one of the two." He did concede that Arabic speakers from elsewhere would be eligible, although none were members at that time. And, not surprisingly, none of George's children spoke Arabic. "They understood a few words and that's about it." George also confirmed that few persons still maintained contact with those in Beirut, and there was little involvement in the rise of Arab nationalism since 1945. If such involvement had been present at all in their community, it would have been among those born abroad who still had feelings for the region, rather "than the ones that were born here." Finally, when asked about Zionism, the "threat from Israeli expansion," and Middle East politics, George responded, "I just never have paid too much attention to it because I felt like whatever they were going to do, they were going to do it . . . I just never did take any sides."

Florence Silverstone Flaks was born a year after George Fadal (1907).[6] Her uncle, Abe Weinburg, had heard about a gold strike in Alaska in 1880, migrated to what became Juneau, and urged his 15-year-old sister to follow. She did, leaving her father and stepmother in their shtetl (small village) on the Lithuanian-German border and traveling directly to Juneau. She soon moved on to Seattle and met and married a Russian Jew in 1889. Florence was one of the sister's eight children. Although Florence's mother raised them as agnostics, she sent Florence to temple school when she expressed an interest in Catholicism. While majoring in music and education in college during the late 1920s, Florence began volunteering at the Settlement House, offering classes in Americanization and English for foreigners. "It was just the sort of thing that was customary in the early 1930s and late 1920s."

Shortly after she married in 1932, Florence heard about the efforts of the Council of Jewish Women (CJW) in Seattle to assist Jews trying to leave Germany (Hitler became chancellor in January 1933), and she got involved in the program. The CJW persuaded President Roosevelt to approve a "blank affidavit" allowing children to enter the country if adequate homes were provided. The Jewish Joint Distribution Committee (JDC) in Europe selected the children, and "all we needed for them was homes, and we couldn't get them." Florence and the CJW struggled to find potential housing accommodations and located merely two in Seattle: Florence's and that of one of her relatives. Florence took in 12-year-old Gerda, who would remain thereafter a part of Florence's family. Gerda married a Jew and raised three children in a Jewish environment, children Florence viewed as virtually her own grandchildren.

Meanwhile, Florence moved up in the CJW and became president of the Seattle chapter between 1939 and 1941. Under her leadership they adopted the
Port and Dock Project, which on some days processed 100–200 refugees who
had fled via Russia, Siberia, Manchuria, and China. They would meet each
boat, put the refugees up in the Frye Hotel or members' homes, and then send
out inquiries to Jewish communities, seeking family members across the country. While many were reunited, Florence added that "we could have done so
much more" for the children, but other communities would not take them. "It
was such a disheartening thing." The most common excuse was that it involved
too much responsibility. There were no federal programs, such as would later
be enacted for Cubans and Southeast Asians. Moreover, the JDC had had considerable difficulty getting access to potentially eligible children even before the
war began.

Ironically, in 1947 Florence met a newly arrived Czech refugee, a baker
named Ernest Hanis. She and her husband opened a bakery with Hanis. At that
point, "I quit all organizations," and the three of them operated the bakery until
1971, when she and her husband sold their part of the ownership to Hanis.

Mr. K. Torikai was an embittered man whose brother and parents had died and
his three sisters remained in Japan.[7] He claimed not to know how old he was
when he arrived or even how long he had been in America (perhaps 25 years).
"If you do not count [the years] and do not think [about] it you do not get old."
After graduating from high school, and over his father's objections, Torikai
sailed to America. He went to San Francisco until the April 1906 earthquake
and then moved to Seattle, where he operated a series of unsuccessful businesses. In one instance, after being beaten, he failed to get any police assistance. Overlooking his negative attitudes with customers, he claimed that
Americans would not patronize his store because he was Japanese, and with
business so poor, he could not even sell it. He and his father subsequently rec-
onciled upon his return visit in 1915, yet Torikai still "felt that he did not fit in."
When he had first arrived, "he made up his mind to be a real American, so he
would not speak Japanese at all or eat Japanese food, or wear Japanese clothing,
or do anything Japanese." "I did it because I thought that to be successful in
America I must be American but . . . I got no success here, all time trouble.
Americans do not treat us right. We try hard to be American but Americans say
you always Japanese. Irish become American and all the time talk about Ireland; Italians become American even if do all time like in Italy, but Japanese
can never be anything but Jap. That is what they say." Americans also called all
Japanese Charley, which he saw as an insult, just like "Jap."

Compounding Torikai's problems was his marriage to a young white
woman, Mina Minthorn. They divorced in 1912, embittering him further and
prompting the observation that "the best type of Americans do not inter-

marry." A woman who weds a Japanese must "find all her happiness at home [because] she is considered outcast among most Americans." Their one child, Lucille, born in 1909, was removed from her parents' custody about two years following the divorce and permanently placed with another family. When she was interviewed by a court-appointed official in 1920, the official reported that she was "ashamed of her Jap father."

During the 1920s, Mexican researcher Manuel Gamio interviewed Mexicans who had migrated to the United States.[8] While most of Gamio's interviews were not as extensive as those thus far presented here, as a group they provide insights into the kinds of experiences these men and women had *al norte* and their perceptions of American society and culture. Given the fact that Mexicans had become the dominant labor force in the Southwest and for nearly half a century have remained America's largest immigrant population (legal and undocumented), these sentiments and recollections proved to be prescient.

  Distilled from interviews in Gamio's collection are four themes that stand out: first, the great variety of jobs Mexicans were willing to accept were jobs often obtained via local networks that quickly developed; second, the prejudice among Anglos that *mexicanos* frequently encountered engendered a reciprocal hostility toward both Americans and American culture; third, the deep attachment of *mexicanos* to their homeland fostered intense resistance to American naturalization; and fourth, a longing to return to Mexico and to do so with one's children inclined migrants to insulate themselves from American influences. The beginning of the large-scale repatriation of Mexicans and Mexican Americans during the year Gamio's volume was originally published (1931) would reinforce Mexicans' fears and distrust.

  Carlos Almazán left his family's tenant farm in Michoacán to work in Mexico City. After 15 successful years in a meat shop, he was forced by the Mexican Revolution to find other employment. When the currency collapsed, the situation compelled him to leave. Over the next five years his brother and friends directed him to jobs in Mexico and across the border to a streetcar line construction project, then a meat packaging plant, a brickyard, and finally a rented farm. He also organized a Comisíon Honorifica (which coordinated celebrations of Mexican holidays) and planned a colony for returnees in Mexico, "for I have always wanted to go back to Mexico as soon as it might be possible." In fact, "I have always been with one foot in the stirrup, ready to go back." "I don't believe that I will ever return to this country, for I have here spent the hardest days of my life . . . and earned the least." Besides, he added, "the people here don't like us, for even the Japanese treat the Mexicans without considerations of any kind . . . and as we are submissive they do whatever they want with our labor."

  At the age of 20, Jesús Garza surreptitiously left his father's home in Aguascalientes with some of his father's money. He found jobs on railroads in San

Antonio and outside Dallas that were beyond his physical ability. Laying pipes and digging a well in Dallas also proved to be too strenuous. Eventually, he obtained work peeling vegetables in a restaurant and then as a dishwasher, after which he trained to be a cook. At that point he decided to visit his family. "But I found everything different, very dull, and very changed. I no longer wished to stay there but to return to Dallas." He re-crossed the border, heard about Los Angeles, changed his plans, and headed west. Falling ill, he stopped in Phoenix, found a job in a sanatorium for a time, and then made his way to Los Angeles, quickly finding a job as a cook in a hotel alongside Americans and Greeks. Generally, he was treated well, and in each prior job he was promised employment should he wish to return.

Juan Bergunzolo was not so fortunate, beginning with acreage he share-cropped in Abasolo, Guanajuato. The owner took over the farm, said "only a very small part belonged to me," and "kept everything," leaving him nearly broke. In 1913, pressed by the Revolution, he migrated to Los Angeles, worked in the same brickyard as did Carlos Almazán, and toiled harvesting sugar beets, oranges in San Bernardino, and alfalfa in Chino. Twice he was given bad checks for shipments of alfalfa, one time by a "chapo" (Japanese) with whom he had been doing business for some time. Another "chapo" left Juan's brother holding a $450 bad check. "I don't like the customs of this country anyway . . . I don't want my [children's] children to be *pochos* [Mexican Americans]. That is why we are all going so that their children will be born over there and they will be brought up good Mexicans." "For my part, all the time that I have been in this country I have thought of going back to my country."

Two accounts of Mexican women are atypical in their specifics but important in illustrating the struggles of women crossing the border. Elisa Silva was married at age 17 but soon divorced her abusive spouse. After her father died, 20-year-old Elisa, her mother, and two sisters migrated *al norte*. Unable to sew or speak English, Elisa took a job in a dance hall, earning $20–$30 per week, while her older sister found employment sewing and her mother sent the younger girl to school. Three years later, that younger sister was attending business college. Now 23, Elisa reflected that, "Of the customs of this country, I only like the ones about work. The others aren't anything compared to those of Mexico. There, the people are kinder than they are here, less ambitious about money. . . . I [also] don't think of remarrying because I am disillusioned about men, but . . . if I do marry some day it would be with a Mexican. The Americans are very dull and very stupid. They let the women boss them. [However,] I would rather marry an American man than a *pocho*."

Seventy-two year old Doña Clarita Galván, a native of Guaymas, Sonora, had already resided in the United States for 52 years at the time of the interview in the late 1920s. She was married at 15, widowed at 18, and married again at 19 to Felipe Galván, shortly after entering the United States. They had been married about 46 years when he was, she believed, poisoned by his partner in a mining venture in Arizona. Earlier, she had operated a restaurant in Florence, Arizona, and, following Felipe's death, she did so again in Tucson. She also rented rooms to Mexicans fleeing the Revolution and did well until she was robbed. Afterward, recalling her mother's curative and midwife skills, Clarita, who was also a devout Catholic and admirer of Pancho Villa, became a *curandera* (folk healer), focusing in particular on tuberculosis and venereal diseases. After more than a half century, "she has not learned to speak English nor has she felt a need for it, for all her relations are with Mexicans."

Jesús Mendizábal, a native of Zacatecas, had been in the United States almost as long as Clarita—48 years, most of it in Phoenix. Right off, he declared, "Although I haven't any complaints against the Americans, I haven't made myself a citizen of this country nor will I ever change my citizenship." For most of the first 38 years he worked in mines in Arizona, interspersed with occasional jobs in Phoenix. His experiences were generally quite positive, even after having suffered a disabling injury to his hand a decade earlier, precluding him from doing more mine work. He was now principally selling Spanish-language newspapers, yet he remained optimistic. "I believe that the Mexican is well treated in this country. . . . I like everything that there is in this country a lot." His three children were all in school, and he was intent on their finishing even though he realized that "they are being Americanized here in the American school. They are speaking almost more English than Spanish"; "since they were born here, [they] don't know anything about Mexico." Although they are U.S. citizens, for Mendizábal "one has to be patriotic and that is why I haven't changed my nationality and I want to go back to Mexico in order [that] my children . . . also may be Mexican citizens."[9]

Twelve persons: four women, eight men, six nationalities, careers ranging from unskilled migrant worker to entrepreneur to *curandera* to a nurse with an advanced degree. Several had one foot outside America's door, ever ready to go back to their homelands (Andrew, Carlos, Jesús M., and Juan), especially where that homeland was in close proximity—a short journey across the border. Some were particularly concerned about shielding their offspring from Americans and American culture, wishing to return home with them. Others waited decades to emigrate to their homeland, or they did so and found the gap between their new lives and their old home village too great to bridge (as did Torikai after about 15 years). Some found contentment with America; some traveled extensively in search of employment. Some were ambivalent about acquiring U.S. citizenship, and a number of them flat out refused ever to consider naturalization—even after being in the United States over 50 years (Clarita). Yet, Marie acquired citizenship for pragmatic job-related reasons.

The two second-generation persons (George and Florence) had different experiences. George knew no Arabic; Florence had picked up some German and Yiddish. George was part of a small, well-knit community that had created a local organization and which, 40 years later, still nourished an ethnic identity but not ties to their homeland; in fact—and perhaps intentionally—most of them avoided any involvement with Middle East issues. Florence was not reared in a Jewish environment but rediscovered her Jewishness. She became for a time very involved in Jewish community and refugee affairs, although she was also quite willing to abandon all that activity after the war in order to co-own a bakery.

Immigration did not take place without a price. It affected communities, family members in the homeland and in the new land, and, of course, the migrants themselves. Most journeys crisscrossed the American West, and only George's family essentially remained in one location. Events of the interwar era involved, or affected, most of those included here. Their lives were shaped by their cultures and their times: the expanding economic opportunities, the rapidly increasing urbanization, the persistent demands for migrant and settled laborers, and the revival of collective bargaining campaigns. For those entrepreneurially inclined, the opportunities for small business ventures in the urban centers enabled them to provide both general and ethnic goods and services. The array of ethnic businesses was an important part of on-going communities. Meanwhile, shaping the broader context of reception for these newcomers were the new federal and state immigration- and labor-related policies, along with the era of scarcity triggered by the Depression. Finally, the West's populations, foreign born and native born, could not be indifferent to world events and, though living in the West, even along the Pacific Coast, they, too, would be caught up in the unfolding holocaust in Europe. On different levels and to different degrees, these 12 individuals represent the immigrants and their children who were participants in western life during the interwar period.

Their experiences illustrate the continuing and still-changing diversity of groups, the changing variety of economic roles, the complexity of the changing government policies, the persistent struggles to determine how far to extend their accommodation to American society in the midst of inevitable cultural changes, and the mounting challenges posed by the inescapable changes taking place between the immigrant parents and the rapidly expanding second generation. These themes still defined the immigrant experience in the West, but there were signs of dramatic departures from the past that distinguish the interwar years and set the stage for the Cold War era.

The immigration laws of 1917 and 1921 were stepping stones to the landmark Johnson-Reed Immigration Act of 1924 that imposed more severe restrictions on European immigration, called for an overarching National Origins System of quotas, and nearly closed the door completely on Japanese immigration—

and on that by other immigrants ineligible for citizenship. While the 1917 law has been labeled "the first significant general restriction of immigration ever passed," the 1924 act "marked the greatest triumph of nativism," with an importance that "is hard to overemphasize."[10] It set the stage for many subsequent immigration laws (e.g., the system of family and occupational preferences). The precedent-setting Supreme Court decisions regarding citizenship, along with the Cable Act, allowing most U.S. females to retain their citizenship when marrying immigrants, likewise affected numerous immigrant communities in the West, just as did the Immigration Act itself. The legislation and court decisions impacted current residents and the migration streams of others—perhaps without intention—especially those from the Americas. The effect of these developments on the West was nothing less than tectonic—fundamental, profound in their consequences, affecting all else and thus reshaping the demographic history of the West.

Nonetheless, as historian Walter Nugent notes, the presence of new immigrant groups from Asia and the Pacific regions "further established the West as the America of the twentieth century before the rest of the nation realized what that was": "the west was richly multicultural." On the one hand, that may account for why some held that, by the early twentieth century, "the West was already resistant to generalization."[11] And yet, that multi-culturalism did not fade even among the very numerous second generation. Perhaps paradoxically, a homogeneous aspect of the West lay precisely in its numerous areas of continuing heterogeneity: significant centers and clusters of diversity that could be found throughout much of the West even though the specific groups might vary. Thus, if that multi-culturalism were less the case in Idaho, then it was more so in neighboring Washington and especially in distant Hawai'i. If it were only somewhat so in Oregon and Wyoming, then it was much more the situation in neighboring California and Colorado. But no state or territory in the West was without its complement of diverse—mostly immigrant—peoples.

Although economic forces and demographic realities frequently cast peoples together, the variations among the larger patterns remind us that, within the multi-ethnic skeletal framework, there were fractures—the enclaves that "remained the rule," creating fissures among populations based on immigration status, race, religion, gender imbalance, and social class. If the newly begun highway systems would gradually come to symbolize the interlocking of the region's subsections during these years (Route 66, for example, was completed in 1932[12]), then immigrant-saturated Boyle Heights in Los Angeles would, for more than a generation, symbolize the urban potential for multi-cultural neighborhoods and cities.[13] Possibly, it was for cosmetic purposes that Seattle renamed its Chinatown the International District, but it would take on that character thanks to immigration (and restricted convenants elsewhere); by the 1930s most Asians and Asian Americans in Seattle lived there.[14] Segregation and the barrioization of both whites and nonwhites would become evident in many communities across the West during the interwar period—an unenviable similarity reinforcing the counter-pressures of homogeneity and heterogeneity.

Meanwhile, the Newlands Reclamation Act of 1902 had marked the commencement of significant federal spending for aqueducts and irrigation projects that vastly increased the available agricultural lands (beginning with Arizona's Salt River Valley). That spurred agricultural industries and factory farms that were soon heavily dependent on both large-scale capital investments and—in the absence of extensive mechanization—sizeable contingents of foreign-born migrant laborers. We have seen, however, that many small farmers (not infrequently immigrant and second-generation farmers), unable to compete with the emerging agribusinesses, concentrated on truck farming and on smaller tracts the cultivation of labor-intensive fruit and vegetable crops that produced sizeable yields.[15]

Although on the eve of the First World War merely 5 percent of the nation's manufactured products came from the West, the early interwar years witnessed increases in the production and growth of other industries, especially in the Los Angeles area.[16] Nevertheless, it was the Second World War that provided the West with its industrial turning point. Until then, agriculture, mining, logging, fishing, and other extractive enterprises (including the newer ones of gas and oil) remained the preeminent bulwark of the western economy. Paralleling these on-going extractive businesses in many areas of the West for some time had been the equally remarkable urbanization. The signs were now quite visible of an emerging metropolitan West that would create hubs—financial and commercial enterprises that linked the productivity of the new industries and the older, extractive ones. Each hub gradually encompassed greater and greater adjacent areas of the region.[17] Acting as catalysts for the accelerated integration of the West into the national and global economies were metropolitanization, the network of railroads, the Panama Canal, the development of more extensive port facilities and coastal shipping operations from Seattle to San Diego (and Honolulu), the beginning of ribbons of paved highways, and the expansion of both the newer industries and many of the extractive ones—culminating with the massive economic growth during the Second World War.[18]

Rural or urban, the West was never far removed from the federal government. Its pervasive presence in the West was especially evident through its mushrooming array of policies concerning the vast stretches of government-owned public lands; the Taylor Grazing Act enacted during this time (1934), which prohibited non-landholding, non-citizen herders from the further grazing of their massive flocks of sheep on those lands; the various immigrant restrictions and quotas; the establishment of the Border Patrol;[19] and, across the 1930s, the fallout from the harsh, constricted refugee admission policies. All had a direct impact on the West. So, too, would the increasing federal expenditures in the region (in addition to the irrigation projects), including a railroad line in Alaska, dams, hydroelectric plants, rural electrification, highway construction, and then such labor-oriented New Deal programs as the Works Progress Administration (WPA), the Public Works Administration (PWA), the National Youth Administration (NYA), and the Civil Conservation Corps (CCC). All four funneled a disproportionate amount of federal dollars into the West during the 1930s, breaking down the isolation of many rural communities and providing employment for, along with white Americans, thousands of immigrants and their children as well as for African Americans, Native Americans, and New Mexican Latinos.[20]

Unquestionably, a major contribution from the West to the nation during these years was the Hollywood film industry, an industry initially dominated by many immigrant producers, directors, and performers. Their films would capture essences of American culture, and the new companies at first distributed them in the universal language of the silent movies, which by 1926–1927 were transitioning to talkies. Not only were those both behind and in front of the cameras during these early years frequently foreign born, but so, too, were the audiences that turned to the new art form to learn about American society and values. In addition, with so many films set in California locations, the images of the West added to its mystique and magnetism, and during the Depression, movies provided unmatched escapism.[21]

It has been suggested that the First World War had no lasting impact on the West because it was a European war, and, in fact, studies of wartime recruitments do focus on the Northeast and Midwest.[22] However, its more general, sweeping effect undoubtedly did not leave the West untouched. The Progressive Era optimism among social scientists — "that acquisition of the appropriate knowledge, the proper facts, would allow them to make the right decisions and promote social justice" — was "redirected" by the war and postwar events and, it would appear, was "hijacked" by nativists. Yet, that social justice actually included controlling the admission of "[t]hose who did not fit traditional white, Anglo-Saxon American norms." Not surprisingly, the wartime era did prove to be too powerful to neutralize, for it generated anti-German (and anti-foreign) sentiment in the West that would be directed both at many individuals whose loyalties seemed suspect and at publications and educational programs that were perceived as a threat to wartime unity.

The wartime mindset meant that being "part American was no longer enough," which translated into the belief that being "from western Europe was not enough; one had to be a *Protestant* from western Europe." With that conviction, it came as no surprise, as we saw earlier, that the war spurred American nationalism — a strong patriotism that was expressed in the "One Hundred Percentism" and Americanization movements, with the latter continuing in the

West during the early 1920s. The actions of certain groups in speaking out about, or even taking action on behalf of, their homelands during the war and while the peace treaties were being negotiated at Versailles cast doubt on their patriotism toward their adopted land. That, in turn, was interpreted as weakening the case for pluralism—and continued large-scale immigration.[23]

The wartime political climate, even prior to the formal U.S. declaration of war, amounted to a "crusade against 'hyphenated Americans,'" as Bill Ong Hing puts it, a time soon marked by a "fear of the proliferation of anarchy and violence." An emphasis on those three traits—100 percent American, western European, and Protestant—undoubtedly shifted the long-standing "debate between narrow and broad visions of who could become an American" to the narrow one. It therefore followed that the war might go beyond nationalism and bring on a convergence of those nativist anxieties and fears that had periodically surfaced regarding the nation's immigrants. It contributed to the revival of the Ku Klux Klan, which spread into the West; hastened the end of Progressivism; and set the stage for the widespread, postwar repudiation of labor radicalism and labor organizing, which, like the violence arising during Prohibition, were associated with immigrants. All these developments would profoundly influence the contours of immigration legislation during the "Tribal Twenties."[24]

Finally, the temporary Mexican labor program begun in 1917 had not fully expired by June 1921 and contributed to the greater influx of Mexicans—legal and undocumented—during and after the war. The curtailment of European immigration with the Acts 1921 and 1924 and the National Origins System in 1929 did not apply to most Western Hemisphere migrants or to U.S. nationals. Consequently, the new legislation actually spurred Canadian and Mexican immigration and most likely contributed to the escalation of Filipino migration to the mainland in response to calls for workers to replace Europeans laborers. The Mexican and Filipino migrations sparked very dramatic reactions during the 1930s.

The two decades 1920–1940 were, in retrospect, interwar years, yet for many immigrants then living in the West they held a significance starkly transcending the notion of those years as just an interlude between other momentous events. Those years witnessed the ending of an era of relatively open immigration for many peoples; the accelerated shift to the Western Hemisphere as a key source of newcomers and workers for the American West; the modification of the criteria for U.S. citizenship; the onset of one of the worst economic crises in the nation's history; and the implementation of policies resulting in some of the worst travesties in American ethnic history as the Depression enveloped the nation and war followed.

CHAPTER TWENTY-ONE

Demographic Trends
A Changing West and
Changing Westerners

BY 1920, ON THE EVE of extensive immigration restrictions and after several decades of intense immigration and inter-regional and intra-regional migrations, who were now the foreign born and the children of the foreign born in the West?[1] More than one in seven of the nation's immigrants lived there in 1920 (2.06 million) and, in turn, they made up over one-seventh of the West's total population (15 percent).

Immigrants and the children of immigrants together accounted for over one-third of the West's total white population.[2] Between 1900 and 1920 the percentage growth of the foreign-born population in the West was twice the national average and almost that much greater for the second generation. Combined, the West's white foreign-stock population had nearly doubled (95 percent); the increase elsewhere in America was just one-third.

Consider first the foreign born and three sets of variables in 1920: population size, shifts among the leading groups, and demographic profiles (gender, urbanization, recency of arrival, and citizenship). We then look at changes among the second generation.

Population Size and Location
Between 1900 and 1920, in five states (Arizona, California, New Mexico, Texas, and Washington), the number of foreigners doubled, and in Arizona the number more than tripled. Over twice the percentage of immigrants in the West

arrived between 1914 and 1919 compared with elsewhere in the country (17.7 percent versus 7.5 percent). Nevertheless, a far smaller proportion were now going to the six Interior Western states (Colorado, Idaho, Montana, Nevada, Utah, and Wyoming) than were migrating to the Primary Western states and territories (Alaska, Hawai'i, California, Oregon, Washington, Texas, New Mexico, and Arizona). By 1920 more than four out of five foreigners residing in the West lived in that Primary West.

Leading Groups
There was considerable continuity as well as some changes among the ten largest foreign-born populations. Groups associated with the "old" immigration continued to be among the prominent ones in the West—alongside newer ones. Among the top ten, there were declining numbers among Germans and Irish and the appearance of two new populations, Japanese and Russians (plus the Filipinos; see note in the appendix, table 3.1). The West's top ten peoples equaled three-fourths of the foreign born in 1920. Their distribution across the West (table 3.2) suggests something of their potential significance, although not necessarily their specific visibility. For example, although their numbers fell by one-tenth, Germans were still among the top five groups in every mainland western state except Nevada, where they were sixth. Canadians—physically, culturally, and organizationally nearly invisible—were among the five leading immigrant populations in eight states (and the most numerous group in Washington, Oregon, and Montana). Italians were also among the top five in eight states, equally divided between the Interior West and Primary West. Mexicans, on the other hand, now overwhelmed the Southwest tier of Texas, New Mexico, Arizona, and California. Finally, sharing the spotlight of near anonymity with Canadians, the English were still among the most prominent foreign-born populations in ten states: California, Idaho, Montana, Oregon, Washington, Arizona, Nevada, Texas, Utah, and Wyoming—and the top group in the last two states.

Demographic Variables
Of the many characteristics that have a bearing on the demographic profile of the foreign born, a half dozen warrant brief mention. They have a connection with how recently foreigners were admitted (the men in particular), how well they were adapting to American society, how they were perceived as newcomers, and how they envisioned their future—returning home or making America home.

- Gender Balance. Nationwide, between 1900 and 1920 there was an increase in the proportion of males. Although in every western state but Utah there was a modest trend toward gender parity, overall the West remained decid-

edly more male than the rest of the country—both for the total population
and the foreign born, especially in Alaska, Nevada, and Wyoming (and probably Hawai'i) (table 3.3). Only in New Mexico and Utah did foreigners edge
close to the national figure. With the enactment of restrictions, many more
of those who were settling permanently began bringing in spouses (most
often wives) and children. With females generally making up a majority of
immigrants beginning in 1930, the shift in the gender ratio among immigrants would dramatically quicken.

- Urban/Rural Shifts. The move to urban living was pronounced and well
  underway, although in the West, understandably, significant differences remained between it and the rest of the nation. That reflected the continued
  prominence of rural livelihoods and extractive industries. The percentage of
  foreigners in urban areas of the West did rise sharply after 1900 (from 45 percent to 56 percent), nearly doubling in Arizona and climbing by 10 to 15 percentage points in California, Oregon, Utah, and Washington. Four states remained significantly below the national figure for urban populations: Idaho,
  Montana, Nevada, and New Mexico. In fact, except in California, Oregon,
  and Washington, foreigners in the West were significantly less urban in 1920
  than those elsewhere (see table 3.4).
- Recency of Arrival. Nearly 18 percent of foreigners living in the West in 1920
  had been admitted between 1914 and 1919 (including nearly 35 percent in
  Texas, Arizona, and New Mexico combined). That had a bearing on the percentage naturalized by 1920 and on the number who had taken out their first
  papers for citizenship. In other words, in political and cultural terms, almost
  347,000 immigrants in the West in 1920 were truly newcomers. John Gavit's
  1922 classic study of naturalization in the early 1900s and in fiscal year 1914
  came to a number of important conclusions regarding the correlation between recency of arrival and naturalization rates, several of which are particularly relevant here: "It would appear that every year of residence *added to
  ten* increases the probability of efforts toward citizenship"; "length of residence, rather than native language, is the dominant factor in determining interest in citizenship"; and "in addition to length of residence, the economic
  status—of the individual and family—is a most important factor in determining the interest of the foreign born in acquiring citizenship." Finally, Gavit
  found the average waiting time for men age 21 and older upon arrival was 10.6
  years, with those representing the "old" immigration actually waiting longer
  than those of the "new" immigration.[3] This analysis certainly held true for
  much of the West.
- Citizenship. The variables regarding citizenship become clearer when we
  compare Mexicans with others. The combination includes (a) racial eligibility; (b) recency of arrival and age upon arrival; (c) ethnic, gender, and marital
  status; (d) educational levels and rates of literacy; (e) attitudes regarding the
  United States and responses to treatment by the host society (socially and economically); (f) social class and the extent of one's economic achievements;
  and (g) loyalty to homeland along with long-term personal or family goals

(including expectations of returning). All factored into accounting for why only 3.3 percent of Mexican adult males in the West were naturalized and, therefore, why only 15 to 21 percent of all foreigners in Texas, Arizona, and New Mexico had been naturalized. In contrast, in Montana, 63 percent had been naturalized, largely due to the fact that just about three-quarters of the English, Irish, Norwegian, Swedish, German, and Canadian men and women there were citizens and that less than 8 percent of the state's foreign born had been recently admitted. Among those more recently arrived groups, the picture was rather different, for only 44 percent of the Yugoslav, Russian, Finnish, Greek, and Italian men and women were naturalized (table 3.5).

- Male Citizens. The percentage of males, 21 and older, with citizenship in the United States did not much change between 1910 and 1920 (from 45.6 percent to 47.8 percent), for the number of additional new male citizens (280,793) was nearly equaled by the increase in total foreign-born males 21 and older (281,635).[4] However, there was a near doubling of those men with first papers, up from 8.6 percent to 16.1 percent.[5] In the West the percentages of both new male citizens and those with first papers edged up (to 45 percent and nearly 13 percent, respectively). These somewhat lower percentages most likely reflected the larger proportion of recent immigrants, especially Mexicans, as well as the other variables outlined above.

- Female Citizens. Female citizenship responses were tabulated for the first time in 1920 (table 3.5), and the higher percentage of naturalized women in the West (almost 56 percent) may well represent the fact that a greater percentage of male citizens brought wives over to America, who in turn benefited from automatic derivative citizenship until the passage of the 1922 Cable Act. That appears to be the case because merely 1.4 percent of the women age 21 and older had themselves taken out first papers to initiate their own application.[6]

Parenthetically, prior to the Ozawa and Thind decisions of 1922–1923, and despite laws and earlier cases to the contrary, 1,199 Chinese and 390 Japanese in the United States had received U.S. citizenship by 1920, of whom 102 Chinese and 127 Japanese were in Hawai'i.[7] The considerable variations (and irregularities) outlined here are reminders of the complex blend of factors affecting the ease or difficulty of completing the screening process. The new laws and administrative policies on immigration and naturalization compelled many white and non-white immigrants to re-examine their choices and plans in America.

Second Generation
Another consideration regarding the long-term impact of the foreign born involves the greater prominence of the rising number of second-generation children. (Only data for white persons are available.) Their proportion in the West was reported at more than one-fifth of the total white population during the century's first two decades, even with the near doubling of their number (table

3.6). We have already discussed the number who resettled from both outside and inside the West. The relevance of all this is that more than one million children of immigrants living in the West in 1920 had relocated (or had been taken by their parents) from their state of birth, with over 207,000 of them having moved from one western state to another. In six states the number of such persons doubled by 1920, foremost in Washington. Besides constituting one-fifth or more of all white persons in 12 western states, the second generation comprised a majority of Hawaii's population. Indeed, with foreign stock representing nearly 88 percent of *all* persons in that territory, it is no wonder that a distinctive culture evolved there.

These findings highlight a major point regarding the mainland: the cultural influences carried to the West were not all borne by Americans with deep roots in the nation's past. Along with the more than two million immigrants of all origins were those one million children of immigrants (out of 2.64 million) who had been born in other states and who were part of that westward migration. They comprised a significant segment of the people leaving their imprint on western society during these years. To virtually every western state they brought elements of their ethnic American cultures and merged them with the cultures of the immigrants and with those of other native-born Americans.

Consider two contrasting examples: Nearly 49 percent (almost 1.59 million people) of California's *entire* white population in 1920 (3.26 million) were immigrants or second-generation persons. Of the latter, close to 375,000 were born in another state. On the other hand, in Texas, only one-fifth of the state's approximately 3.92 million white population (about 0.81 million persons) were white foreign stock, with fewer than 75,000 children of immigrants having resettled from other states. Thus, over nine-tenths of whites who went to Texas and who would significantly shape the character of that state were third- and later-generation native-born Americans (including African Americans)—men and women further removed from the immigrant experience. In California that "old" native-born population made up less than three-fourths of those resettling. While variations on those themes illustrated by California and Texas took place throughout the West, the overriding fact was that 35 percent of all westerners in 1920 were immigrants or the children of immigrants. *The West was not built just by old-stock, white Americans.*

CHAPTER TWENTY-TWO

Institutionalizing the Quota System
1924

*F*OR THREE DECADES opponents of the nation's open doors theorized, propagandized, and campaigned for immigration restrictions. The Dillingham Commission's 1911 report focused on the alleged flaws of the "new" immigrants compared with the "old" ones (referring to Europeans only) and recommended overall limits on admissions, including a literacy test. A proposal to allocate admissions by national quotas "formalized" that old-new division, however imperfect it was, and thereby "framed the debate" that followed. "Among the commission's legacies," historian Robert Zeidel points out, "were the literacy requirement and the quota system." Its report and recommendations actually "rejuvenated the stagnant restrictionist movement." The 1917 immigration law, with its Asiatic Barred Zone and literacy test—which proved to be too little too late—"signaled a massive change in the way people thought about immigration restriction," concludes Cheryl Shanks.[1] By identifying and setting apart regions for purposes of immigration control, the act added to the precedents in law for curbing other group-specific immigration besides that of the Chinese. It reaffirmed the principle of immigration regulation as a legitimate feature of national policy.

The context for further changes came with the postwar climate outlined earlier: the Bolshevik Revolution; the contrived Red Scare; concerns about foreign sources of radicalism; the racial and labor unrest; Prohibition and portrayals of immigrant criminals flagrantly violating it; and the revival of immigration in

1920–1921. Opponents viewed the latter as a flood, an invasion, a threat to the nation's homogeneity. The transition in the Pacific Northwest from "wartime super-patriotism" to targeting radicalism as a foreign menace captures the mental shift that made Americans more receptive to immigration restrictions. "Between 1918 and 1919," writes Kristofer Allerfeldt, "nativist prejudice smoothly repositioned itself, moving from the condemnation of the wartime fifth columnist to the hunting of the Red terrorist." The "small-town intolerance" that would, for example, shortly feed the Ku Klux Klan phenomenon, particularly in Oregon, nourished the deepening public perceptions that "radicalism was an alien import and the obvious way to halt it was to stem the tide of aliens."[2]

In the absence of organized and effective counter-arguments by business, political, and ethnic group leaders, the long-festering racial notions regarding immigrants from southern and eastern Europe and from Asia surfaced and revealed increasingly sympathetic audiences for restrictions in various regions across the nation. The talk was now more about the need for homogeneity rather than promoting a melting pot or addressing employment needs. With increasing dismay about "hyphenism" came a wish for a "smelting" process (instead of a melting one) that would remove "harmful" alien elements among the newcomers and thereby restore a broader uniformity closer to the nation's origins. Emphasizing fanciful claims by eugenicists, the restrictionists' call for homogeneity for the nation's sake in effect fused racism with nationalism. For example, Gino Speranza, an Italian American lawyer, authored a series of articles in 1923–1924 asserting that the colonial stock of racially and culturally similar groups (obviously denying any place for Native Americans and African Americans) was responsible for making America and American democracy what they became.

Such arguments reinforced the general postwar disillusionment and strengthened the beliefs concerning the need for immigration controls. The shifts were akin to a catharsis: having supported, tolerated, sometimes applauded the newcomers, Americans now appeared to be spent. In terms of immigration it was time for a timeout. Controlling this immigration seemed essential because, as Speranza put it, the prevailing conviction was that the ethnicities underlying the nation's white core homogeneity were "vital" for the nation's unity and the preservation of its democracy. These essential qualities could not be acquired by some simple transformation. However unsubstantiated, that appeal on behalf of inherited cultural traits, tradition, and patriotism further cemented the notion of a racial nationalism. Immigration had ceased to be just an economic issue, concludes historian Robert Divine; it had become a cultural and ethnic one.[3]

In a climate also marked by the unparalleled popularity of the revived Ku Klux Klan, the restrictionists found receptive audiences and insubstantial resistance. The Johnson-Reed Immigration Act was approved 323–71 in the House and 62–6 in the Senate and was signed by President Calvin Coolidge on May

26, 1924. Virtually every western representative and senator voted for the bill.
The May 1921 Emergency Quota Act had set the maximum at 355,000, based
on 3 percent of the 1910 foreign-born population—with 55 percent allotted to
northern Europe and 45 percent to southern and eastern Europe. The May
1924 law provided for a ceiling of 164,666 and a three-year formula based on just
2 percent of the foreign born in 1890. After that, a National Origins System derived from analysis of the 1920 census was to be inaugurated, with a maximum
of 153,714 quota immigrants. A Quota Board was created to determine the distribution. Late by two years and battered by fierce debates for and against the national origins approach, its formula was accepted by President Herbert Hoover
and Congress and implemented as of July 1, 1929. With that, Mae Ngai concludes, the National Origin hierarchies "assumed the prestige of law and the
mantle of fact."[4] The starkly lower quotas became the mark of the southern and
eastern Europeans' inferiority, an inferiority now accepted as a given.

The Chinese Exclusion Law had introduced the novel idea of rejecting individuals because of their ethnic (racial or national) group identity rather than on
account of their individual characteristics (e.g., disabilities, illnesses, criminal
actions, prostitution). The quota laws extended the concept of racial and ethnic criteria to all Europeans (the 1917 act had already established the Asiatic
Barred Zone). The 1924 law, taking its cue from the recent Ozawa and Thind
decisions and the wording of the California and Washington Alien Land Laws
(upheld by the Supreme Court in November 1923[5]), prohibited the admission
of most aliens ineligible for citizenship. The motive behind the insertion of
that provision, aimed directly at the Japanese, was fixed on an injudicious remark by Japanese ambassador Masanao Hanihara that was interpreted as a
"veiled threat" to the United States.[6] The law "codified the principle of racial
exclusion," embittered Japanese leaders, and reinforced the sense of "powerlessness" among the Issei in America, whose exclusion from the body politic
now seemed permanent and irreversible.

This major piece of legislation, whose provisions would prevail for four decades, "comprised a constellation of reconstructed racial categories in which
race and nationality . . . [were] disaggregated and realigned in new and uneven
ways." Indeed, the very premise of the National Origins System was based on
the fallacy that national origins and identities were unchangeable over time,
with intermarriage having only a modest effect. Nevertheless, the formula that
was developed ranked Europeans "in a hierarchy of desirability." It attributed
to them both a modifiable *nationality-based* identity (they could enter and become U.S. citizens) and an ascriptive, unmodifiable *racial-based* identity resting on their degree of shared whiteness (not all were regarded as equally white).
In other words, the implication *in the law* was that in general Europeans would
be accepted as white persons eligible for citizenship, but because they were still
differentiated (and differently valued) on many levels by nationality or place of

birth and cultural background, they could, on that basis, be allotted quotas that favored western Europeans, who were principally credited with settling the nation prior to the late 1800s.[7]

The 1924 law did reinforce the link between race and ethnicity for most non-Europeans, racializing those particular national origins. Asians (and Pacific Islanders) were now unalterably and perpetually foreign, that is, being inherently unassimilable and thus ineligible for citizenship, they were on that basis inadmissible.[8] The profound implication of the National Origins System for the nation's self-identity was that the allocations, concentrated nearly all with western Europeans, by and large diminished the status of southern and eastern Europeans and degraded Asians and Pacific Islanders. Then, by omitting Americans of color from the calculations of America's national origins, both immigrants and their American-born children (beginning with African Americans, the nation's involuntary immigrants as well as various peoples from the Americas) the Quota Board in effect "eras[ed] them from the American nationality."[9]

Because for decades the immigration laws of 1921 and 1924 so profoundly affected the flows of immigration to the American West, we need to have an explicit grasp of their key provisions. In the Act of May 19, 1921 (45 Stat. 5; 8 U.S.C. 239), Section 2 enumerated those excluded from the quota allocations, including principally those from the Asiatic Barred Zone (who were now mostly denied admission) and persons who had resided for at least one year in another Western Hemisphere country (altered to five years in 1922), for such persons faced no numerical limits. Even though no formal categories or classifications of designated persons were yet defined specifically allotting any fixed percentages of slots within the quotas, Section 2 did state that "preference shall be given" to immediate family members (wives, parents, siblings, minor children, fiancées) of U.S. citizens and of aliens who had either applied for citizenship or had served in the military during the First World War.

In terms of the allocations of national quotas and special categories within them, the Act of May 26, 1924 (43 Stat. 153; 8 U.S.C. 201) included several major changes that set the direction of immigration on new courses. Section 2 required that U.S. consuls abroad would henceforth issue visas prior to the applicants' departure for the United States, effectively ending most of the elaborate screening that had been done at Ellis Island and other ports of entry.

Section 4 defined those not subject to any quotas ("Non-quota immigrants"), beginning with both the wives and unmarried children under age 21 of U.S. citizens. (In 1928 husbands married to citizens prior to June 1928 were added; that cutoff would be periodically updated.) It now exempted from any limited quotas those persons *born* in Western Hemisphere countries rather than those resident five years or more (closing a loophole for secondary migration). American-born women who had lost their citizenship by marriage and who were seeking admission (having divorced or been widowed) were also classed as non-quota.

Carrying the 1921 legislation a step further, the law now established specific percentages for the preferences *within quotas*: Half were set aside for parents of adult citizens and, where the country's quota was 300 or more, those skilled in agriculture (plus family members). The remaining 50 percent would go to wives and minor children (under 21) of resident aliens.

Section 11 provided that a more restrictive temporary ceiling of 2 percent of the foreign-born population present in 1890 was to be replaced by a National Origins System. That "system" provided that a group's annual quota allocation for admission would be a proportion of the 150,000 overall total permitted to enter equal to the group's percentage of the "inhabitants" of the "continental United States" in 1920 (resulting in an actual total, 153,714). As noted, those omitted from the calculations—and therefore allocated no quotas—included (in addition to persons born in or native to Western Hemisphere countries) Pacific Islanders and descendants of slaves (essentially Africans) and individuals ineligible for citizenship (principally Asians). Section 13 further specified "persons not to be admitted" even if they fell under eligible categories (e.g., non-quota spouses) unless they were "otherwise admissible." To make that point more explicit, Section 13(c) included what has sometimes been labeled the Asian or Japanese "Exclusion Act." It declared that, with few exceptions, "No alien ineligible to citizenship shall be admitted to the United States." For over two decades that restriction would bar Asian spouses of U.S. citizens, in effect placing greater weight on race than on family reunification.[10] Race—that is, being Asian or Pacific Islander—took precedent over being the spouse of a U.S. citizen.

Congress made the National Origins System effective as of July 1, 1929. The 22 leading nations in terms of quotas allocated can be found in table 3.7. Most of the allotments were distributed among the most prominent groups entering the West. Thirty-eight others were given the minimum of 100, including India, China, and Japan, although 8 of those 38 denied admission to all persons born in those countries except individuals otherwise admissible, in other words, those of European origin—white persons.[11]

The 1924 law quickly had both intended and unintended consequences. Intended were cuts that favored immigration from "traditional" sending countries. As planned, overall immigration plummeted 45 percent between the early and late 1920s, though in the West the drop was closer to 37 percent (1925–1929 versus 1920–1924). Likewise, compared with the peak years just before the First World War (1910–1914), the United States admitted during the late 1920s three-fourths fewer persons among those intending to reside outside the West compared with about one-fourth fewer among those who intended to live in the West. Central to those declines were the restrictions placed on southern and eastern European and Asian admissions, which fell by about three-quarters, while newcomers from northern and western Europe rose by more than one-fifth. All of these were intended consequences.

The unintended results are apparent in the 12 percent rise in Canadians admitted and a near 29 percent jump among Mexicans.[12] American insensitivity—perhaps indifference—to the Asian response to Section 13(c) created another unintended result, its impact on the Japanese. As historian Wayne Patterson succinctly put it, the provision was "a terrible shock to Japan." Such a blow to Japanese pride, with its implicit loss of face, was not easily forgotten. In contrast, various factors yielded a more considered decision by Congress not to curtail Mexican immigration, despite impassioned speeches calling for such legislation (see below). Thus, greater political calculations were made concerning the importance of neighboring Mexico's response. That largely validated Emory Bogardus's 1934 assessment that "up to 1928 the United States treated immigration entirely as a domestic affair"—subject to pressures from interest groups within the United States that favored such unrestricted admissions. Thereafter, it was "no longer to be viewed as a purely national affair."[13]

Several trends stand out. The number of arriving immigrants going to the West edged *upward* 8 percent during the 1920s but *dropped* elsewhere by one-third (1921–1930 versus 1911–1920). One-third of all western newcomers were Canadians and Mexicans, and well over one-half million persons were admitted through the Texas cross-border ports of entry during the 1920s. The continuing lure of the West was juxtaposed with the uncertainties surrounding the new laws and the region's rather volatile economy during that decade—with highs and lows in different parts of it even before the Depression set in (e.g., in Texas agriculture, Montana copper mining, and the Los Angeles real estate boom). More persons went to the West, yet emigration from it declined by one-fourth. That drop in the number emigrating may indicate that, despite the economic fluctuations, many immigrants were doing reasonably well and were holding firm, planting roots, or simply giving up on frequent circular migrations.[14]

On the other hand, it is also true that many newcomers either did not go where they had told officials they were going, or they subsequently relocated, or they left the country before the 1930s, especially from Texas and Arizona. It is true that relocation was especially evident among Mexicans, who often headed to the Midwest and to California.[15] Every western state except California and Oregon suffered foreign-born population losses, but for specific nationalities the picture is more complex. Not surprisingly, there were significant increases by 1930 in the total numbers of most northern and western Europeans in the West (British, Scandinavians, Dutch, and Swiss)—plus the large increases among Canadians and Mexicans (combined, over 197,000). Modest changes were reported among many other Europeans, such as among the Germans, Italians, Poles, Czechoslovaks, Yugoslavians, and Russians, whereas declines could be seen among Austrians, Finns, Greeks, Portuguese, Chinese, and Japanese. In the latter cases emigration was frequently the factor involved in the drops rather than movement to other states.

Notwithstanding the many variations by group, sex ratios among both the general population and the foreign born continued moving toward more gender balance. For the immigrant population, this may have been helped, as suggested earlier, by a dramatic shift that becomes noticeable during the 1920s. The number of white foreign-born males in the West decreased by 72,889, whereas the number of females rose sharply by 131,845. Apparently, more women were arriving, many men were departing, and other men were bringing in families that included wives and daughters. Nevertheless, while the overall ratio in the West was 109 males per 100 females (109:100) in 1930, among the white foreign born it stood at about 133:100 (including Mexicans)—compared with 144:100 in 1920.[16] Foreign-born males were conspicuously more numerous in the heavily non-urban Alaska Territory (468:100), Nevada (233), Wyoming (172), and Idaho (165)—with New Mexico and Arizona (also among the least urban) right behind. (See tables 3.3 and 3.4.)

In fact, the most urban western state, California (73.3 percent), had the second lowest sex ratio among its immigrants (128), following Utah (111). There, Mormon family migrations during the second half of the nineteenth century and a sizable second generation had produced a nearly gender-balanced population (statewide 105). Similar early group migrations to Texas—along with considerable in-migration of native-born Americans—resulted in the closest statewide balance in the West in 1930 (104).

These trends, distinguishing areas of greater or lesser gender balances, point not only to increased migration of women but especially toward patterns of more stable settlement and either the establishment or the reunification of families. While most evident where there were increasingly urban communities, the shift to urban living did not preclude a labor strategy among, for example, Mexicans, where families set up households in cities but still followed the harvests before returning to their urban homes. Nonetheless, many of the occupations in the more rural areas (i.e., those more migratory, extractive, and isolated) continued to draw heavily on male populations except where families acquired farmlands, particularly among Scandinavians, Germans, Czechs, Portuguese, and Japanese.

The persistence of rural lifestyles in the region (and the many immigrants who still farmed) was starkly underscored by the fact that in the rest of the country well over four-fifths of all immigrants were urban dwellers (84 percent), whereas by 1930 the West topped 50 percent urban, with only three-fifths of foreign-born whites living in those urban areas. In California, Utah, Oregon, Washington, Texas, and Colorado, half or more of the immigrants were urban folk (ranging from 73 percent to 50 percent), whereas in New Mexico about one-fourth and in Idaho and Nevada one-third or fewer lived in towns. The continuing increases in urbanization directly affected foreigners, for they quickly sought more economic opportunities in those growing western cities.

In other words, the rising urban ratio among the foreign born suggests a trend toward more urban communities and corresponding changes toward more urban occupations. At the same time, the 25-point gap for urban white immigrants in the West (versus the higher figure for the rest of the nation) clearly reflects the continuing importance of the rural, extractive jobs for many western immigrants (with fishing and related occupations, such as canneries and shipbuilding, being among the main extractive but largely urban-based exceptions). Lifestyles and occupations among newcomers and their children would continue to be affected by the particular divide at this time between urban and rural occupations and the accompanying divisions of urban and rural communities. Over the next dozen years, this would have important consequences for Mexicans, Filipinos, and the Japanese, in particular.[17]

Given the trends, California and Texas display remarkably contrasting patterns during the 1920s that highlight the complex demographics during these decades. Nearly three-quarters of western newcomers were going to California or Texas (72 percent) and two-thirds of those departing left from those two states (68 percent). Their differences are reminders that regional portraits can still possess unusual state variations. In the 1920s, California's foreign-born population grew by over 316,300, of whom 268,500 (85 percent) had been admitted in the 1920s. Regarding Texas, more than one-third million newcomers said they were headed there, but in 1930 only 90,000 immigrants (27 percent) reported having entered in the 1920s. That supports studies that have pointed to significant out-migration from Texas during those years, particularly among Mexicans migrating to jobs in the Midwest and California. Other Mexicans were compelled to depart (usually back across the border) when the bottom fell out of the Texas agricultural economy in the late 1920s.[18]

These two brief examples touch upon the continuing immigration to the West during this period, the sizeable inter-state migration into the region, the varied and changing economic fortunes of the immigrants, and the considerable fluidity of the foreign-born population as many departed the country, some died, and others either achieved their objectives and left or moved elsewhere in search of them. Thus, on the one hand, there continued to be significant economic growth and population expansion for many parts of the region during the early and mid-1920s, especially among second-generation persons. On the other hand, the legislative changes and economic fluctuations by the late 1920s also made for volatile situations and uncertainties that would worsen for some groups as opportunities dried up and then Depression-stimulated conditions took hold, striking so heavily the unskilled and semi-skilled workers. In the West, many of these workers were immigrants.

CHAPTER TWENTY-THREE

Divided Yet Interlinked
The Rural West

WENTY-FOUR-YEAR-OLD Inder Singh, a Sikh, migrated from India to America in 1905. For several years he worked on ranches near Los Angeles, and in 1919 he began farming near El Centro, in California's Imperial Valley. Three years later he wed a Mexican woman and, he recounted in mid-1924, "through her I am able to secure land for farming. Your land law can't get rid of me now; I am going to stay." Marriage to a Negro woman "would" prompt his fellow Sikhs to kill him, he claimed (erroneously), whereas wedding "an American woman" would provide "no advantage" since she would lose her citizenship.[1] He complained about the freedom women enjoyed and the mistreatment he received by American immigration officials. While he kept up with conditions in India, he gave up some of the Sikh customs regarding his hair and beard, and, consequently, "I . . . have lost my religion." While he was on good terms with his Japanese and American neighbors, as well as with his Mexican in-laws ("They are better than most Mexicans."), he wanted to quit farming because it was "entirely too hard."

Willard A. Schnurr took an interest in the Asian Indians, although there were relatively few in Los Angeles. In 1919, about 2,600 lived in California in clusters from Imperial Valley to the San Joaquin Valley and Fresno, Sacramento, and north of Yuba City in the Sacramento Valley. Schnurr suggested that 2,000 were Sikhs, 500 Muslims, and just 100 Hindus.[2] Most had been driven out of British Columbia, migrating further south with expectations of traveling in the United States, getting an education, and then returning home—and, indeed, some 500 did so in 1919. But circumstances changed, and many sought jobs in various mills, or on railroad construction or maintenance crews, especially in Washington State, until confronted with violent demands that they leave. Migrating further, they concentrated primarily in agriculture, first as laborers and then some as farmers. By the early 1920s they owned about 2,100 acres and farmed in California's three great valleys: Imperial, San Joaquin, and Sacramento. Together with rented lands, those in the Imperial Valley who moved beyond labor employment worked 32,380 acres. Most, however, did not achieve such a transition and remained itinerant laborers, harvesting grapes, tending fruit trees, planting rice, and picking cotton. Many had first worked in the asparagus fields, "stooping over all day long . . . from four thirty in the morning until seven at night." Subsequently, they went to the celery fields and on to fruit orchards, and, after that, to picking hops. (In one place the Muslims were offered 15 cents more per day if they would pray only three times daily instead of five, since each call to prayer took 15 minutes.)

At about this same time, R. Chand had been in the country 18 years, 9 of them working on ranches or as a laborer in Imperial Valley. He wanted American citizenship, although he resented American prejudices and challenged them. He had come to study agriculture in order to bring modern techniques back to India, but he was forced to seek work. Still, he maintained that sojourners had spurred trade with India, influenced agricultural methods there, and made "contributions to the nationalist schools in India."[3]

The Chinese had been brought into Orange County, California, to cultivate celery and chili peppers.[4] Although most were not inclined to own and operate farms, they still found themselves victims of violence and persecution by whites. They gradually retreated, abandoning their labor camps. In Santa Ana, a rumor began that a case of leprosy had been discovered in the Chinese quarter, and whites burned down the entire district. Japanese soon began replacing the Chinese in Orange County and were welcomed because their labor-intensive techniques were ideal for celery cultivation. It did not take long before they began leasing land until the soil was depleted, and beans and sugar beets replaced celery. The Issei moved on to growing red and green peppers in a unique corridor of some 300 acres between Anaheim and Huntington Beach. They soon monopolized production (including the drying houses)—until the Alien Land Laws were enacted. As they moved west from Garden Grove (where citrus orchards were being planted), the Issei began transferring land titles under the names of their Nisei children.

By the 1920s it appeared that "just as many Japanese . . . were still farming but under a different form." While one observer noted that "they want to farm, and a good many of the Americans want them to farm," a bank officer concluded that, despite the business that the Japanese contribute, "in the long run it will be the best thing for the country to have the Japanese out." Despite pressures to move on, some 20 families in Garden Grove were sending their children to a

Japanese school. Two Christian churches had Japanese ministers, and three Japanese mutual aid associations had been established in the county, along with Young Men's and Young Women's Clubs. At the end of 1923, the Japanese Association of Southern California reported that 1,051 Issei and Nisei resided in Orange County and belonged to four associations.

The experiences of the Japanese farmers highlight the inevitable interdependency of urban and rural communities and the critical juncture of the interwar years in these patterns. Urbanization, even metropolitanization, was overtaking rural areas and offering new and expanded employment options luring workers from the farms. At the same time those very same expanding cities remained as reliant as ever on the fruits, vegetables, and staple crops produced by the farming communities. Immigration quota laws forced political leaders, together with producers and managers in many economic sectors, to consider replacement sources of farm labor.

Meanwhile, the unremitting economic and political instability in their homelands was compelling several different peoples—in particular groups exempt from the new quotas—to look to the American West as a place where they might improve their lot in life. Such diplomatic and domestic realities created uncertainties in the market place and complicated migration and employment options. Compounding the problems were federal labor-related reforms during the 1930s recognizing the right of collective bargaining, which was not extended to farm workers. Government agencies at most levels also tolerated harshly oppressive and vigorously anti-union agricultural and packinghouse owners' associations. State officials endorsed programs for the removal of immigrant workers and their families who were unemployed and regarded as a burden on the local welfare relief agencies. Federal officials likewise condoned measures involving the repatriation (often under duress) of Mexican families that included tens of thousands of U.S.-born children, citizens who were thus deprived of their civil rights. Congress would even respond to western political pressures by agreeing to grant independence to the Philippines in 1934 in order to terminate Filipinos' right to unlimited entry into the United States as nationals.

Farmers and farm workers remained largely invisible to most Americans, although paradoxically the invisibility fed the nativist penchant for destructive stereotyping. Nonetheless, the employment fluctuations, the deplorable living and working conditions, and dual wage systems in many parts of the West neither persuaded desperate immigrants to shun such jobs nor convinced growers to ameliorate those conditions. In the case of Hawaiian sugar plantations, such improvements came too late in the 1920s to entice many Nisei men to return to the plantations, and mostly Filipinos (who had been brought in since about 1909 to work on the plantations) had taken the place of many Japanese field workers. In his study of Asian immigration, sociologist William Carlson Smith ventured the assessment in the mid-1930s "that the traditional plantation system in Hawai'i could not be maintained on the basis of citizen labor with an American standard of living." But, following the strike of 1937 (see below), further improvements were made. That strike marked the last by an ethnic union there, and, in fact, many Filipino laborers were leaving the islands, frequently heading for the mainland rather than returning to the Philippines.[5]

Earlier, historian David Montgomery indicates, white Americans moving west had "quickly and virtually unanimously come to look on first the Chinese and later the Japanese as the carriers of poverty and social decay . . . hirelings of grasping corporations, bonanza farms, and urban sweatshops that prospered only because Asians could be hired for so little," thereby threatening opportunities for whites. On the other hand, in 1920, Frank Davey provided a dose of racial balancing. He had prepared a report for the Oregon legislature on a controversy over the hiring of Japanese farm workers in eastern Deschutes County. He pointed out that "if men who are prepared to have the development [in that county] accomplished by the aid of white labor are unable to obtain such help—[that is,] if white men refuse to do the work—then they are ready to do the next best thing and permit the work to be done by anybody who is willing to do it."[6]

The Scandinavian contrast in neighboring Washington State was direct and to the point. Far fewer of them were pushed into migratory jobs by a desperation comparable to that of the Mexicans, or by the racial animosities directed at the Japanese or Hindus, or by the sparse skills of the Croats, Greeks, and Italians. More often, lack of heritable land, or a desire to evade military service, escape religious conflict, or a quest for opportunity or adventure motivated Scandinavians to migrate. The broad compatibility between Scandinavian and American cultural, religious, and even physical characteristics eased these newcomers' acceptance and accommodation to life in the Pacific Northwest. It helped that so many of these Nordic newcomers had first lived in the Midwest and that many were continuing in agricultural pursuits. Even in 1930 nearly one-fifth of western Scandinavians (including Finns) still lived on farms, and well over three-fifths of those families were in the Pacific Northwest (Montana, Idaho, Washington, and Oregon).

Martin Rasmussen, a Dane who came to America in 1923, is representative of those who followed this path. He recollected, "to go to America, I didn't think there was much to it." By his account, notes historian George Nielsen, "In nearly every way, including their values and desire for economic success, the Danes fit the American system." Gordon Dodds summed it up, expressing the optimism felt by many, although more asserted than the actual reality: "[B]y 1920 the Nordics were either assimilated or on the path to assimilation."[7]

Based on agricultural traditions brought from Japan, Issei farmers chose to concentrate on labor-intensive specialty crops, often using reclaimed lands. Rather quickly they came to play an exceptionally prominent role in western agriculture, especially in truck farming of fruits and vegetables, just as many Chinese had done earlier. Numerous Italians were similarly engaged. The agricultural achievements of the Issei were considerable, particularly in Washington, Oregon, Hawai'i, and California. They grew, among other items, lettuce, beans, berries, cauliflower, peas, cabbage, celery, carrots, and radishes, and they established a commanding presence in several urban produce markets, notably Seattle, Portland, and Los Angeles. By 1914 they already managed 70 percent of the stalls in Seattle's famed Pike Place Market. Within another decade they supplied three-quarters of the region's vegetables and, for a number of years, even half of the milk supply there. At the same time, they quickly dominated Hawaiian coffee production, and by the 1920s, writes Kevin Starr, George Shima, California's "Potato King," "controlled the dairy, potato, floral, and truck garden markets in much of California."

Even though the top 10 percent of growers harvested 55 percent of the staple crops, eventually developing "industrialized plantations" (also labeled "industrial agriculture"), the Japanese retained their prominent place in truck farming (along with the Italians), as they did in parts of Oregon near Portland and near Seattle, among other locations. While Roy Fukuda developed what became the standard variety of celery, K. Ikuta successfully cultivated the first rice harvests in California and by 1918 had 25,000 acres planted with rice. Within about a dozen more years, he was producing crops worth some $20,000,000 per year. In southeast Texas, as noted earlier, Japanese—led by Seito Saibara— bought up large tracts in hope of establishing colonies specializing in rice production using imported Shinriki seed—a superior, high-yield strain of Japanese rice. In 1921 Kumazo Tanamachi established a truck farm near San Benito, just north of Brownsville. Kichimatsu and Fuji Kishi developed a 10,000-acre farm where they also tried cultivating rice until prices collapsed after the war. Then they turned to cabbage, vegetables, and fruit. (It did not hurt that they also discovered oil on their land.) Such Japanese in particular were the beneficiaries of the urbanization of the 1920s, for growing cities represented expanding markets for their various crops.[8]

Market potential was important, but it soon became clear to the Issei men that they could not realistically engage in farming without the help of women. Heizo Yoshino described his wife's contributions during the Depression-ridden early 1930s:

> I was never a great success, and I owe my wife, Kazue, a lot that I can live decently today. She was born in Tokyo and raised in Kizarazu, Chiba Prefecture. She married me in Japan in 1915 and two years later came to the States to join me. . . . [She] had had no experience with farm life. But she did well. In the strawberry harvest time she paid more than a 100 pickers every day, put things in order in the packing house, and supervised 20 hands. . . . [and, at that time,] we had three boys and one girl, and I am very thankful to her.

Komaji and Shiego Takano recalled that "the farm wife got up at 4:30 or 5:00 in the morning and after preparing the breakfast she awakened the pickers. She also had to fix their lunches by noon. Dinner was after 7 PM, and before that she had to prepare the bath, too. Of course, she had to clean up after each meal. After finishing the day's work, by the time she got to bed it was already after midnight. Finding time between jobs during the daytime she [also] went out to the field and helped pick [strawberries]."[9]

The California Alien Land Laws of 1913, 1920, and 1923, Washington's 1921 law, and Oregon's 1923 legislation compelled many Japanese and other Asians to farm by subterfuge, as Kazuo Ito put it, entrusting the ownership to whites or placing lands under their Nisei children's names. (There eventually were more than a dozen states with such statutes.) The Japanese remained politically powerless to effect any changes in the racist legislation. (One exception, due to lobbying by prominent Issei community leaders, was Texas, where current residents were exempted from the new law.) The Japanese continued to farm, but the adverse consequences of the land laws could be seen in California. There, having peaked in 1920 at 5,152 farmers working over 458,000 acres that they owned (16 percent), leased (68 percent), or held under contract (15 percent), the Japanese saw their share plummet to just under 308,000 acres five years later, never returning to the 1920 level. Others were pushed into the very cities that had enabled them to prosper agriculturally. Many who had remained farm laborers were succeeded during the 1920s by Mexicans and Filipinos.[10] Still, in the 1930 census we find that close to half of all Japanese on the mainland lived in rural areas, and one-third were on farms. In Hawai'i just about three-fifths still lived in rural areas.

Of course, as the Alien Land Laws made patently clear, the efforts of Japanese immigrants to demonstrate their embrace of Americans' aspirations for property, mobility, and entrepreneurialism did not sit well with their American role models. For example, Japanese melon farmers encountered hostility by white farmers near Turlock, California (southeast of Stockton), who drove off the Japanese farmers' workers in July 1921. Around the same time, in Hood River Valley, Oregon, those who established the Anti-Asiatic Association (AAA) included a pledge for new members wherein they attested to the belief that

the rapidly increasing Japanese ownership of land in the Hood River Valley meanaces [sic] our welfare and threatens the ultimate domination of our Home Land by Asiatics . . . [;] that no child born in this country should become a citizen unless his parents belong to a race eligible to citizenship; that no one but a natural born or fully naturalized citizen should be allowed to own or lease land; [and] that the immigration of Asiatics to the United States should be prohibited.[11]

Inductees pledged not to sell or lease land to Asians. Moreover, in 1919, the AAA's predecessor, the Anti-Alien League, had declared, "We certainly do not

intend to permit this essentially American valley to become a Japanese colony
as have some sections of California." A few years later, V. S. McClatchy, publisher of the *Sacramento Bee*, used similar language before a U.S. Senate hearing. He described the Japanese as dangerous and unassimilable: "they come
here specifically, professedly for the purpose of colonizing and establishing
permanently the proud Yamato race. They never cease being Japanese."[12]

When Princeton biologist Edward Grant Conklin referred to Mexicans with
his question—"Do we want to bring about the mongrelization of America?" or
when Rev. Bob Shuler (a Methodist minister in Los Angeles and reportedly a
spiritual leader of the Klan) described Mexicans as "diseased of body, subnormal
intellectually and moral morons of the most hopeless type," they were not just
adapting stereotypes from works on Mexico but were transferring stereotypes
they associated with Asians as well as resurrecting other post-1848 depictions of
the Mexicans.[13]

One small but significant indicator of the cultural differences among the diverse workers was revealed in June 1924 by L. C. Lee, the local manager in the
Imperial Valley for the American Fruit Growers Corporation:

> I cannot go to the field and give orders to any individual Filipino, but must
> issue all orders or complaints to the spokesman [boss]. In making a contract
> for Filipino melon pickers, I have my dealings with the spokesman, but
> every man in the group signs the contract; if there are 75 pickers they must
> all sign. In the case of a Japanese group, all will discuss the contract and only
> one man will sign it. The Hindus will also make contracts when one man
> signs up for the entire group. Mexicans generally hire out as individuals.
> Among the Negro workers it is every fellow for himself. . . . This also holds
> true of the white laborers.[14]

Earlier, sociologist Robert E. Park had interviewed W. S. Fawcett in El Centro, who was the only white man growing cantaloupes when he began in 1908.
The rest "were all Japanese or Greeks." "I used to employ Japs to pick grapes,"
said Fawcett, but the "Japs are foxy" and were worse at picking grapes than cantaloupes. And, thus, the farmers shifted "from Japs to Mexicans. They stand the
heat. We use Americans for teamsters. Greeks come in every year. They travel
about; they come from as far north as Fresno. They pick grapes and melons and
then go north. . . . In the lettuce we use Mexicans. The same men who work in
the lettuce work in the cantaloupes. . . . [But,] we do not consider the Filipino
as good a worker as the Jap. He is not as reliable."[15]

Throughout western agriculture the conclusion made about California's situation was considered to be generally applicable: Farm workers were "at once
indispensable and despised. They were the essential reason for the prosperity of
California's industrialized agriculture but were the state's least prosperous
workers."[16] The reality was that farm owners felt driven to hire the cheapest

farm labor, for it was the one variable whereby they could strive to control costs. Carey McWilliams's remark in the late 1930s regarding sugar beet workers held for many other circumstances where year-round agricultural activities were not required, as they were on Hawaii's plantations and the citrus orchards in the San Gabriel and San Bernardino Valleys east of Los Angeles: "The difficulty involved was [being able] to recruit large numbers of workers, on short notice and for a brief season, in the fields . . . cheaply and effectively."

A white man interviewed by Paul Taylor in the mid-1920s in Dimmit County, south Texas, remarked that "the more ignorant they are the better [agricultural] laborers they are." The literacy test, mandated by the 1917 Immigration Act, "keeps out the best laborers and lets in the worst."[17] Of course, the less education such men had, the more likely they were presumed to be "docile" and "unambitious" and unthreatening to the established order. There was also a saying, Taylor added, that "if a Mexican wears guaraches [sandals] he is all right. If he wears shoes, he is tolerable, but if he wears boots and talks English, he is no good." Nonetheless, with European and Asian immigration curtailed, growers were compelled to rely upon Mexicans and then Filipinos, who were only too willing to step in.[18]

Imperial Valley farmers in the late 1920s opposed restrictions on the admission of Mexicans, wrote Emory Bogardus in 1934, because with quotas "the Valley as an agricultural region will revert to a desert." A Texan similarly commented that south Texas "would be blowed up without the Mexicans, or if they stopped immigrating." At first it was claimed that both Mexican and Asian workers were crucial to the local economies, but by the First World War the emphasis was just on Mexicans. When America entered the war, agricultural interest groups successfully petitioned for waivers regarding admission requirements ("Ninth Proviso," 1917 Immigration Act), whereby more than 72,000 Mexican laborers were specially admitted between 1917 and 1921.

The shift to a principal reliance on Mexicans was well underway—by means fair or foul. During the 1920s anti-vagrancy laws were utilized in Texas to arrest Mexicans and force them to work for two weeks during the cotton harvest. They were seen as a ready supply of workers, and Mexican towns were depicted as "labor camps" for U.S. agriculture. Many growers of large-scale specialty crops were "almost entirely dependent upon Mexican labor," observed Bogardus. Meanwhile, in Arizona, cotton cultivation followed earlier enterprises in mines, railroads, and other types of agriculture. It was soon acknowledged that Mexican labor had become "the foundation of Arizona's economic growth." In a sweeping assessment during the 1920s, Charles Teague, president of the California Fruit Growers Exchange and head of Limoneira Company (Ventura), explicitly conceded that "the great industries of the Southwest—agricultural, horticultural, viticultural, mining, stockraising and so on—are to a very [sic: great?] extent dependent upon the Mexican labor."[19]

Nevertheless, even more than previously with Asians, the reliance upon Mexicans (and then on Filipinos) posed several dilemmas for white Americans. It was assumed that these people were sojourners who would be returning to their homeland after the harvests. By 1921 it was observed that many Mexican men and their families among the mounting number of newcomers were beginning to settle down and take up residence in cities. Although they followed the harvests, they set up homes, for example, in a *colonia* near Tucson or in one of those established east of Los Angeles, such as Hicks Camp and Medina Court in El Monte and Arbol Verde and La Colonia in Claremont. They acquired automobiles for migrating just several months each year between farming areas and were even being labeled "gasoline gypsies." Others found steady employment for much of the year (in, for example, citrus groves) and ceased following the harvests. In 1930, nearly 55 percent of *mexicanos* in the West resided in urban areas, as did half of the Mexican American population.

The difficulty was that growers needed these workers, but their presence conflicted with the broader objective among whites "of creating racially homogeneous communities." As a Texas school official put it, Mexicans "do not have the ground work of religious ideals. . . . [T]he Mexicans are Catholics. . . . But that doesn't correspond to the other types of religion as a foundation" for education. Moreover, Mexicans and the many Italian newcomers (among other Catholics) also tended to oppose Prohibition. True, the Mexican was preferred to the Filipino, said George Clement, manager of the Agricultural Department of the Los Angeles Chamber of Commerce, because of the latter's "susceptibility to disease" and because "the Mexican is never a biological problem. He rarely marries out of his own people. A Mexican man never marries a white woman. . . . The Filipino is complicating matters here."

Thus, despite a mixed European ancestry, romance language, Catholic religion, and familiar political institutions, the Mexicans had still been racialized "as second-class, non-white citizens." Furthermore, they were depicted as "villagers accustomed to a primitive life." It was said that when they crossed the Rio Grande they "jump[ed] three centuries." In fact, in 1931, Herman Feldman quoted Constantine Panunzio's 1927 depiction of the Mexicans' living conditions in the United States, highlighting the gap between them and white Americans but actually revealing the tenacity of stereotypes, often borrowed from descriptions drawn from within Mexico:

> A typical Mexican town in any of the Southwestern states consists of two rows of adobe houses, usually without windows and floors. The entire town is dirty, mothers, fathers, children. The latter play around half-dressed . . . until they're fat and mother throws them out and they are forced to shift for themselves. The reason for the poverty is not hard to find. Every time a Mexican receives his pay he goes on a "toot."[20]

Call it racial tugs-of-war—or, racial preferences versus racial realities. Quite commonly across the West during this period, growers found themselves unable to hire—or to afford to hire—white American workers for harvesting and other limited-skill jobs (except as supervisors, or where machinery was involved, or as teamsters). The only time when this was less true was during the darkest period of the 1930s Depression, when white migrants were desperate enough to stoop to wage levels usually reserved for minority workers. At that time, for example, 6,000 (mostly white) persons per month—especially farmers and their families—were entering California, many—but certainly not all—of them fleeing Dust Bowl conditions. Between July 1935 and January 1940, one estimate claims that 352,000 came to California, half of them from Oklahoma, Texas, Arkansas, Missouri, and Kansas.[21] Otherwise, white men from Hawai'i to Texas tended to decline jobs already associated with groups regarded as inferior.

However, we should remember that these communities included more than these key groups. In the Livingston, California, area (south of Turlock), for example, the 1940 census reported 1,000 persons in the town and 2,500 in the area around it. They included English, Irish, Scots, and Germans (45 percent), Portuguese (10 percent), Mexicans (8 percent), Japanese (6 percent), Russian Mennonites and Belgians (5 percent each), and Swedes and Italians (4 percent each), along with smaller numbers of Armenians, Greeks, Filipinos, Slavs, African Americans, and Native Americans.

In 1925 journalist Konrad Bercovic reported on the exceptional multi-ethnic make up of California's agricultural workers, including Sikhs in the Sacramento Delta, Armenian vineyard workers near Fresno, Dalmatian fruit growers in Santa Clara, Italian artichoke farmers in Santa Rosa, and Basque sheepherders in Bakersfield, along with 5,000 Albanian Italians, 2,500 Swedes and Danes, many thousands of Volga Germans and Portuguese, and smaller numbers of Greeks, Norwegians, and Yugoslavians, all concentrated in Fresno County.[22]

Indeed, to cast this western diversity in an even broader perspective, in 1930 (before the Depression made its full impact) 1.15 million white foreign-born and second-generation persons in the West lived in rural farm settings—nearly 364,000 foreign-born persons, along with almost 787,000 children of immigrants.[23] For example, in 1940, almost one-half of all immigrant Czechs and well over one-third of the Swiss lived on farms, along with approximately one-quarter of the largest European group, Germans (42,590). Scandinavian rural farm populations ranged from nearly 18 percent (Swedes) to over 22 percent (Danes), with more than one-fifth of all Scandinavians still farming—and, among those, three-fifths were in the Northwest (Norwegians, Danes, Swedes, and Finns). Thus, in the West, Texas Czechs and Germans; Washington and California Scandinavians; and California Swiss, Italians, and Portuguese represented especially prominent clusters of immigrant farming communities.

And yet, 31 percent of all western immigrants living and working on farms in 1930 were Mexican—nine-tenths of them in Texas, Arizona, and California.

Mexicans and Filipinos did indeed become the leading agricultural labor groups during the 1920s and 1930s, with Filipinos already constituting 18 percent of California's workforce by 1930, traveling from harvest to harvest in groups of 20 to 70 men. Most of the 45,208 *manongs* ("old brother" or "old timer," the first generation) reported on the mainland in 1930 were single men in search of work (many having originally come for an education but lacking resources). Although they held diverse jobs, they were predominantly at the bottom of the employment ladder: one-fourth were service workers, close to one-tenth worked in the Alaskan canneries (and were referred to as *alaskeros*), and three-fifths were agricultural workers, who were rapidly replacing the dwindling numbers of Asians along the coast (whereas the Mexicans were the dominant labor force across the Southwest). It was perhaps not unexpected that about three years earlier, in late September 1927, the California State Federation of Labor passed resolutions urging restrictions on Filipino migration and in support of independence for the Philippines as the solution for curbing their unrestricted admissions.

It is unlikely that the Hawaiian Sugar Planters' Association (HSPA) would have endorsed that, having imported 118,556 *sakadas* (Filipino contract workers) into Hawai'i between 1909 and 1934 (of whom 15,043 were women and children). In 1922, following the major strike of 1920 that accelerated the departure of Japanese workers from the plantations, the Filipinos constituted two-fifths of the sugar plantation workers and seven-tenths in 1932. By then, the HSPA had ceased recruiting them.[24]

That policy change, combined with the poor wages and working conditions and the passage of the Tydings-McDuffie Act (March 24, 1934)—providing independence for the Philippines in a decade—was largely responsible for the emigration of nearly 58,300 Filipinos from Hawai'i by 1935. An estimated one-fourth of them moved to the mainland.[25] From Fresno to Yakima, in addition to their roles in the pre-harvest tasks of pruning, thinning, weeding, and transferring of seedlings, Filipinos constituted vital labor contingents in the harvesting of potatoes, beets, apples, hops, and asparagus, among other crops. And yet, like their predecessors and the Mexicans, they continued to be criticized, denounced, and attacked.

Under these conditions, minorities were not above stereotyping themselves or other minorities. Writing in the late 1940s, Manuel Buaken argued, "In harvesting of asparagus, Filipinos are exclusively used. The reason is simple. The agile, medium and low built Filipino can move faster than the clumsy, stocky built Mexican, the lank Hindu, or the indolent Negro." He claimed that the real competition facing Filipinos was not with whites but with "Orientals"—

many of whom were displaced by Filipinos. "This is only natural. The stamina of the Filipino as a worker is much greater than the Chinese, the Japanese, the Mexicans, and other minor nationalities."[26] The Filipinos also generated considerable tension because many proved to be less docile and more militant workers than Americans had expected. The young men also invested considerable sums in dressing well and frequenting taxi dance halls in order to dance with the young white women employed there. The interest they demonstrated in socializing with white women (few Filipinas were present) exceeded the tolerance levels of local white men.

Even more of a concern to growers and their allies than these manifestations of social and cultural chasms was the unexpected labor militancy of both Filipinos and Mexicans, as earlier had been the case with the Japanese. Recall the 1903 Mexican-Japanese Oxnard sugar beet strike and the 1920 Hawaiian strike by a coalition of Japanese and Filipinos that resulted in the formation of the multi-ethnic Hawaiian Laborers' Association. A key difference in Kona, (Hawai'i), Santa Rosa (California), Kings County (Washington), or the Imperial Valley (California) was that many Japanese and Asian Indians wanted to own or lease land, but only a comparatively small number of Mexicans and Filipinos were so inclined. The 1920 census did report that 12,142 Mexicans operated farms, nine-tenths of them in Texas, and a small contingent of Filipinos struggled to acquire the right to farm on lands leased from Native Americans in Washington. Furthermore, Mexicans did not initially evoke nativist labor responses because they did not at first appear to be activists as were Filipinos and because "relatively few . . . ventured from the fields and railroad tracks into more competitive employment."[27] Nor did Mexicans provoke encounters through social activities wherein they were overtly seeking white women.

But they soon did spark opposition by their labor actions. Before the contemporary era of Chicano historical scholarship, the impression was that Mexicans had been rather docile, non-militant, weakly organized workers. We now recognize, at least beginning with the 1903 Oxnard strike, that for about 45 years Mexican farmworkers, at times in alliance with others, did frequently strike (or were organized by others and did so) even in the depths of the Great Depression. And they achieved some successes, although in the final analysis they were overwhelmed by coalitions of growers and packers and the collaborative support of police, courts, and other government agencies. The growers' associations were willing to endorse vigilante action and supported political lobbying to prevent the extension of collective bargaining rights to agricultural and associated employees (notably in the packinghouses and canneries) in the 1935 National Labor Relations Act. After the Second World War, they would continue to successfully squash any further support by Congress for these workers.[28]

A few illustrations will suffice. By 1927, of the 54,000 workers in the Imperial Valley, 20,000 were Mexican, and the resident Mexicans were, as Paul Taylor put it then, "becoming a permanent part of the culture of the valley." In April 1928 Filemon Gonzalez, president of the Benito Juarez Mutual Benefit Society of El Centro, proposed the establishment of an Imperial Valley Workers Union—an idea suggested by the Mexican consul. The Miguel Hidalgo Mutual Benefit Society of Brawley joined them, and the group eventually became known not as a union but as the Mexican Mutual Aid Society of Imperial Valley (MMASIV), with over 2,740 members. Filipinos were excluded from the organization because they had previously undercut the wages of Mexican lettuce workers. Their principal adversaries were the huge grower-shipper-absentee "farming industrialists," such as the Times Mirror Company, which held 8,000 acres, and the Southern Pacific Railroad, owner of 42,000 acres. Many of these farms were operated by Issei tenant farmers.[29]

In May 1928, with the cantaloupe and melon harvest beginning, MMASIV sought from the growers higher wages, better working conditions—including ice for their water—and "lumber and brush enough to build sheds." Although no formal strike was called, the sheriff shut the union office, arrested Mexicans without warrants as vagrants and disturbers of the peace, and arranged to have them held in jail on $1,000 bail each. Right across the border, a Mexicali newspaper, *El Nuevo Mundo*, declared that if the workers would return to Mexico— "the apparent desire of the sheriff"—there would be "an agricultural catastrophe" in the valley, in effect driving home the point about the Mexicans' critical role in the American Southwest. Gonzalez emphasized to the consul that they were seeking improvements by legal means and were not driven by "ANY COMMUNISTIC IDEA." The workers soon retreated but did receive wage increases and other concessions, including ice.[30]

In January 1930, MMASIV and the Communist-led Trade Union Unity League (TUUL) launched a strike during the lettuce harvest on issues similar to those in 1928. Approximately 10,000 workers walked off the fields, including 7,000 Mexicans, 1,000 Japanese, several hundred Filipinos, and over 1,000 others. TUUL had organized the Agricultural Workers Industrial League (AWIL) to mobilize workers, but when growers used the 1919 Criminal Syndicalism Act to arrest AWIL members, the strike failed. The AWIL was reorganized as the Cannery & Agricultural Workers Industrial Union (C&AWIU; still Communist influenced).[31] It launched a strike during that summer (1930) in Santa Clara Valley, an area specializing in canned fruits. Many women were employed in the canneries, with rivalries between the American, Portuguese, Italian, and Mexican women. A 20 percent wage cut prompted 2,000 to strike, and their numbers quickly swelled to 16,000. Soon, strikes followed in Lodi, Walnut Grove, Fresno, Visalia, Bakersfield, and the San Gabriel Valley.[32]

The C&AWIU organized numerous strikes over the next four years, especially during 1933 (24 of the 37 total strikes occurred that year, involving 48,000 workers). The climax came with "the largest and most successful" agricultural strike in American history until that time. On October 4, 1933, an ethnic mix of workers (about 95 percent Mexican, plus Filipinos and Okies) launched a strike against cotton growers in the San Joaquin Valley. It was one of the state's most lucrative crops ($12.4 million), and workers sought a pay raise from the current 60 cents to 90 cents per 100 pounds of picked cotton. By mid-October about 12,000 workers in five counties, stretching along a 114-mile line, were on strike. Growers may have been counting on the presence in the area of approximately 180 workers for every 100 jobs in the valley, but in reality most of the Mexicans were residents, not migrants, which enabled them to organize and mobilize support more effectively. Mutual aid societies and other industrial groups (many with relatives among the strikers), as well as Mexican merchants, supported them. While ideas and strategies were borrowed from the labor movement in Mexico, it was the various efforts of the women to sustain the strike (including walking the picket lines and keeping the families fed) that enabled this multi-ethnic labor force to win a pay raise. After 24 days they accepted 75 cents per 100 pounds.[33]

Shortly thereafter, Mexicans in Imperial Valley tried negotiating with growers; then they called a strike in January 1934 and sought help from the C&AWIU. The reaction of growers and law enforcement was violent, and two workers were killed. By February 19, the strike had been crushed. As of mid-1939 the C&AWIU had played a role in 170 strikes involving 90,000 harvest, packinghouse, and cannery workers. In 1937 the Congress of Industrial Organizations (CIO) sponsored the formation of the United Cannery, Agricultural, Packinghouse, and Allied Workers of America (UCAPAWA), which came to exert a dominant organizing role in the late 1930s. In that same year (1937), as mentioned, the last ethnic-based plantation strike in Hawai'i occurred, on Maui, and several hundred Filipinos walked out, their numbers eventually reaching 3,000. However, a strike leader, Manuel Fagel, who had organized a secret Filipino nationalistic labor group operating behind the scenes of the strike (Vibora Luviminda) refused to strengthen the labor action by expanding it with a multi-ethnic membership.[34]

The process of suppressing immigrant worker organizations occurred in two steps. First, in order to cope with rapidly transforming national and international market conditions, growers and shippers formed numerous co-ops— such as the California Wine Makers Corporation in 1899, the California Walnut Growers Association, the California Almond Growers Exchange (under the brand name Diamond), California Raisin Exchange (Sunmaid), and California Fruit Growers Exchange (Sunkist)—for sugar beets, asparagus, and other produce. Second, farmers, growers, packers, and shippers, among others, having taken the first steps toward collaboration and led by the Chamber of Commerce, met in Fresno on March 28, 1934, and established the Associated Farmers of California (AF). They were determined to tolerate no repetition of

1933. The AF declared that its policy was no "unionization of farm labor on any basis." It even opposed housing programs that might stabilize the workforce and facilitate unionization.

The AF endorsed any tactics to break strikes and sabotage unions, including deputizing American Legionnaires, sanctioning vigilante groups, employing strikebreakers and spies, and enlisting the aid of local law enforcement agencies and courts—as well as arranging for welfare agencies to withdraw relief from the families of striking members.[35] Ultimately, the combined forces enlisted by the AF, the accusations of subversiveness against labor leaders, the deportation of foreign-born union leaders, and the outbreak of the Second World War proved to be too much for most agricultural unionizing efforts. Tragically, post-war strategies of deception would still outmaneuver the workers; the effective organization of farm workers would have to wait two more decades.

CHAPTER TWENTY-FOUR

Filipinos
The Newer Immigrant Wave
Bridging the Rural and
Urban West

HISTORIAN JOHN WHITEHEAD concluded that by 1910 "the Pacific Slope from San Diego to Puget Sound had been transformed into an urban-industrial society tied to national markets and transportation systems."[1] It was actually both more and less than that. Agriculture and other extractive enterprises remained critically important components of the western economy along the coast as well as in the Interior West. Up to the Second World War there continued to be a certain seamlessness between the urban and rural Wests, with each relying upon the other for sustenance and prosperity. As we noted, many immigrant workers lived in cities and seasonally moved about the various harvests or railroad construction and maintenance jobs, or shifted to urban employment as they heard of opportunities, followed networks of friends and co-workers (often traveling in groups), and signed up for work to support their education.

The coastal areas were not yet a fully emerged industrial corridor; that would become reality during the Second World War, with its colossal Pacific theatre and military buildup from San Diego to Seattle. Until then, various manufacturing concentrations would appear in the narrow urban subsections along the coast and in some interior sections, such as in Texas. Together they represented the developing modern West, with commercial links extending along the coast, out to Hawai'i, up to Alaska, northeast to Montana and Idaho, east to Colorado and Utah, southeast to Arizona and Texas, as well as out from Texas. After the First World War and the enactment of the new federal laws dramatically shrinking many streams of European migrants, we saw how the changes in immigration flows immediately deepened the demands for new sources of cheap, docile, and generally unskilled workers beyond the available numbers of Asians, Mexicans, and African Americans. Between 1906 and 1926, approximately 150,000 Filipinos (as U.S. nationals) are reported to have left the Philippines, with 52,800 going to work in Hawai'i and over 45,200 journeying to the mainland. At the same time, during the 1910s and 1920s, many non-Asian immigrants and Filipinos moved from Hawai'i to the mainland.[2]

During the interwar decades a growing population of Mexicans and Hispanos from the villages of northern New Mexico, as well as many German-Russian families, provided a crucial labor force for the sugar beet industry centered in northern Colorado, while many other Mexicans moved out of Texas to the Midwest, westward into Arizona, Imperial Valley, on to Los Angeles, and up the coast. The more complex and diverse the western economy became, the more immigrants etched migration stream beds crisscrossing the region, providing indispensable labor resources, developing new community clusters (*colonias*—actually of many ethnicities), initiating urban enterprises, and significantly enlarging the consumer base for both rural and urban businesses. Particularly noteworthy were the large numbers of Filipinos, along with smaller groups of Mexicans, Chinese, and Japanese, who regularly journeyed up to the Alaskan salmon canneries, joining (when not competing with) Alaskan Natives and the wives of (predominantly Norwegian) fishermen. In 1930, a peak year for the *alaskeros*, 30 percent of the 14,135 "shoremen" (non-fishermen working in the canneries) were Filipino.[3]

What Carlos Bulosan, the renowned Filipino immigrant writer (1913–1956) related may have actually represented his own peregrinations—or he fused his wanderings with those of his fellow Pinoys, or Filipinos, to more fully convey their tribulations during the Depression and war. Whatever the case, his account powerfully conveys what one of the principal migrant labor forces endured at this time—a dizzying series of stopping places and types of employment. It unfolded in this manner. He arrived in Seattle in July 1920 and went to Alaska to work in the canneries.

> One afternoon a cutter above me, working in poor light, slashed off his right
> arm with the cutting machine. It happened so swiftly he did not cry out. I
> saw his arm floating down the water among the fish heads.

He moved then to Washington's Yakima Valley for the fruit harvests, down to Stockton—a major center of the West Coast Filipino community "because they had no other place to go" except for the nearby vegetable harvests—and on to Los Angeles, San Diego, and Imperial Valley.

Manuel Buaken relates the story of Filipinos who worked in dreadful conditions in Imperial Valley—including shacks with earthen floors and no sanitary or bathing facilities. After four months, the labor "boss divided $50 between 15 men, or a total of $3.33 for each of them—the sum total of their pay for four months of hard labor. The catch was in the contract, which . . . had allowed the boss to take out unlimited sums for their keep," which usually meant food, clothing, gambling, and sexual services.

From Imperial Valley (where El Centro was a gathering place for Filipino workers seeking work in the fruit and vegetable harvests), Bulosan and companions traveled up to Bakersfield and Idaho (more harvests), Billings (sugar beets), and back to Portland. They soon were on the road to Klamath, Santa Maria, Nipomo, Lompoc (various harvests), to San Luis Obispo, briefly to New Mexico, returning to Santa Barbara, Los Angeles, Seattle, San Diego (seeking all manner of employment in hotels, restaurants, and domestic service in the cities), and Coronado Island. "I walked back to town [San Diego, from Coronado] and tried to get a room but all the hotels refused me." Bulosan's cycle then resumed: to Stockton, San Luis Obispo, Lompoc, Oxnard, Los Angeles, San Jose, and again to Seattle before he was hospitalized for two years in Los Angeles for tuberculosis (1936–1938). A female social services worker told the bedridden young man, "You Filipinos ought to be shipped back to your jungle homes."[4]

In many places they were callously exploited or cheated of their wages (even by Filipino contractors). In 1928 a contract was offered by Goon Dip and Company for work at the Pacific American Fisheries in Port Muller, Alaska. Dorothy Rony recounts what followed:

> "[T]he length of the season would be determined by the contractor. . . . Workers were expected to labor eleven hours per day, from 6:00 a.m. to 6:00 p.m. The worker would be paid $240 for the season . . . , with twenty cents per hour overtime. A sum of $2.20 would be paid for labor on Sunday during the fish run. If the employee did not want to work overtime or on Sundays, the worker would be fined fifty cents per hour not worked." If there were any work stoppages requiring replacements, the "employee would lose pay to these workers, and have money deducted to pay for their food and board. . . . [I]f the worker did not stay the whole season, the worker could not get return transport to Seattle, and round-trip transportation costs would be deducted from the worker's wages."[5]

Filipinos were violently attacked by Americans—especially when viewed as competitors.[6] They witnessed detectives, unprovoked, capriciously shoot a Pinoy in a pool room, and they were beaten, driven out of town by police, and abandoned at the state border. When seeking employment, an apartment, even a hotel room, they faced repeated discrimination up and down the coast in both rural and urban locations. They attempted to form Filipino unions in the face of the beatings and even the murder of Filipino union leaders.

Perhaps Bulosan was not entirely aware of the extent to which Filipinos were victims of a half-century legacy of anti-Asianism, or, perhaps, he recognized that these young fellow Filipinos had neither a homeland government to defend them—which even Mexicans sometimes had through their consuls—nor a strong tradition of mutual aid organizations to intervene on their behalf. Whatever the underlying thinking, he "understood it to be a racial issue, because everywhere I went I saw white men attacking Filipinos. It was but natural for me to hate and fear white men." This race hatred was all the more incomprehensible, because although "western people are brought up to regard Orientals or colored people as inferior, . . . Filipinos are taught to regard Americans as our equals. Adhering to American ideals, living American lives, these are contributory to our feeling of equality."

As a result of his encounters, Bulosan became deeply embittered—for a time "almost dying within" and transformed into someone "as ruthless as the worst of them," descending to violent crime and cheating fellow Filipino gamblers. He eventually found himself and became a survivor, undoubtedly due to his discovery of a love for writing. With his brother, Macario, Carlos Bulosan emerged with an immigrant's newfound appreciation for America, notwithstanding their many trials and setbacks.[7]

Between his arrival in the mid-1920s and his role in helping to organize the Cannery Workers and Farm Laborers Union (CWFLU) in Seattle in the spring of 1933 (Local 18257), Antonio Rodrigo also migrated in search of stable employment, beginning with the Alaskan canneries around 1927. For six years he traveled and worked, often alongside other ethnic groups, until 1933, when he was laid off. At that point, his role in the formation of the CWFLU found him focusing on wages, workers' lack of controls over hiring (particularly the stranglehold of Chinese, Japanese, and Filipino contractors), harsh working conditions, and the arbitrary supervisors. Although within two years the union moved from an exclusively Filipino membership to one with a broadened base that included Chinese, Japanese, some African Americans, and some whites, it retained characteristics of a Filipino mutual aid society. (For example, it collected money to pay for shipping home the bodies of union president Virgil Duyungan and his treasurer Arelio Simon, who were assassinated in a restaurant in December 1936. A nephew of a contractor was blamed, but Rodrigo maintained that it was a professional hit.[8])

The case has been well made that "the working lives of Asian immigrants and their children in the canneries industry are at the center of the history of the Pacific Northwest and the West" and that, as an extractive industry, these fish canneries were "almost as significant to the West's development as timber, minerals, or agriculture." The industry began in the 1860s along the Columbia River, and within two decades canneries had been established on Puget Sound and in Alaska. "Cannery towns" developed around the factories, with the Chinese and then the Japanese ever more prominent among the "shoremen." That gave a clear edge to Chinese and Japanese contractors, compelling even the later arriving Filipinos to obtain jobs through them. In the early 1930s, Pio de Cano maneuvered into position as the leading Filipino contractor. Still, and regardless of ethnicity, contractors became a major target of cannery workers, particularly because of their exploitation and manipulation of wages, living expenses, and other "services."

Throughout the interwar years white Americans and Europeans (and, in Alaska, Native peoples, too) controlled the fishing, with all others equaling less than half of one percent of the fishermen. In Alaska, whites and Alaskan Natives —notably wives of fishermen—generally comprised a majority of the shoremen, too. Chinese, their numbers falling in the 1930s, made up 6.5 percent of that workforce, and the Japanese, whose numbers were likewise declining in the late 1930s, equaled 8.3 percent. Beginning in 1921, more than 950 Filipinos, many of them students seeking seasonal employment, first journeyed up to Alaska's canneries; by 1929 one-quarter of the shoremen were Filipino.[9] Even though a majority of the Filipinos during the early 1920s had migrated from Hawai'i to California (and thence up to the Pacific Northwest), a shift was underway. Just between 1923 and 1928, the percentage entering via Hawai'i sank from 85 percent to 35 percent as more and more Filipinos, seeking to fill the opportunity gaps created by the new American immigration laws, sailed directly from the Philippines to Los Angeles, San Francisco, and Seattle (as did Bulosan) and then often sought work in Alaska.[10]

Writing passionately in the mid-1940s about these workers, Buaken noted, "the Filipinos in Alaska invested only their youth, their honest labor, and their lives against the unhealthy conditions, exhausting drudgery, and the nearly intolerable working conditions of the cannery industry." Nevertheless, in 1930 the number of *alaskeros* reached its highest count of 4,200, working along with whites, Native Alaskans, Asians, and Mexicans.[11] After that, the number drifted downward, although between 1936 and 1939 they remained second in number only to whites. Contributing to this visible role of Filipinos was the onset of the Depression and the previous tightening of admission requirements, especially along the nation's southern border. The number of Mexicans legally admitted in 1930 and thereafter dropped by 69 percent. In retrospect, Filipinos "remained as the central work figures in Alaskan salmon canneries for more than sixty canning seasons," with some staying on to work with such other seafood products as crab and shrimp. A number of Filipinos began to plant roots in Alaska, marrying Alaskan Native women and establishing the Filipino Community of Juneau in 1935, the first Filipino organization in Alaska.[12]

In the Lower 48 in 1930 there were 45,200 Filipinos (compared with 63,052 in Hawai'i)—over four-fifths of whom lived in the West and among whom there were only 2,940 females (a more than 14:1 ratio). If they did not make it straight away to Alaska, Filipinos sought out such men as Marto Orlanes, who opened an employment agency in Los Angeles in 1922 for Filipinos. There, jobseekers found work "as porters, dishwashers, busboys, janitors, and housemen—the only types of work open to them"—unless they joined the harvest-cannery circuit. However, in the late 1920s Orlanes actually got 500 Filipinos jobs as extras in mob scenes for fast-rising Hollywood filmmakers. Buaken lamented the fact that Filipinos were not given more opportunities in filmmaking, for had they been, "there would be at present [mid-1940s] several Filipino movie stars."[13]

Herman Feldman correctly understood in 1931 that because Filipinos were American nationals who had mixed "freely with American whites" in their homeland, they objected to being treated as an alien race when in the United States proper. Most were single; few of those with wives had brought them, and the women who did migrate usually did so for educational or training purposes. Given the steep gender imbalance—and the fierce opposition of white American men to Filipinos dating and marrying white women—the Filipino men showed a great interest in going to the taxi dance halls and spending freely on the dime-a-dances, quite often with young white girls.

With so many of the young men in their 20s and single, Manuel Buaken suggested that they spent their earnings liberally, had a reputation for smart dressing, and sent little money home. In contrast, the Chinese and Japanese supported their ethnic businesses, such as by purchasing goods imported from the homeland. Even "[t]he Mexicans patronize their Mexican stores more than they do the American market and stores."

A San Francisco judge, Sylvain Lazarus, demeaned these Filipinos as "a race scarcely more than savages" and ordered police to arrest those seen with white girls. Early in January 1930 the Chamber of Commerce in northern Monterey County, California, denounced Filipino workers on moral and sanitary grounds as a threat to white workers. During that month, further attacks were reported in the press, and at about the same time a vigilante group was angered by the establishment in nearby Watsonville of a Filipino dance hall that hired white women. The convergence sparked a riot in that community on January 21. A Filipino worker was killed, and 60 others were injured. Eight days later a Filipino clubhouse in Stockton was bombed.[14]

Given the somewhat volatile mixture of their attitudes and the reactions to them, it is not surprising that while many young *manongs* still married white women, numerous other Filipinos were inclined to seek spouses among other ethnic groups. Allison Varzally reports that in Los Angeles County between 1924 and 1933, 701 out of 1,000 Filipino marriages were exogamous, and nearly half of those 700 were with non-whites.

Mexican and Mexican American women were frequently preferred, although even that was not without its complications, as Gavino Visco found when he applied for a license to marry Ruth Salas. The judge ruled that she was white and, therefore, that Visco could not marry her. The couple argued that she was—as most Mexican Americans were—part Indian and, hence, nonwhite, despite Mexicans being officially classified as whites. The marriage was then approved. That such racial feelings complicated the interaction of Filipinos and Americans was also made quite clear when the anti-miscegenation law was invoked by the Los Angeles county clerk to bar Salvador Roldan from marrying a white woman. Roldan likewise fought this, and the local court overturned the county clerk's decision. The county appealed, and in early 1933 the California Court of Appeals upheld Roldan's right to marry on the grounds that he was a Malay, not a Mongolian, which was not on the list of groups prohibited by the state's 1880 law from marrying whites. The legislature promptly amended the law, as did 12 other states. The following January (1934), the U.S. Supreme Court, in *Morrison et al. v. California* (291 U.S. 82; 54 S.Ct. 28), reinforced the racial divide by reaffirming that the right to citizenship "excludes Chinese, Japanese, Hindus, American Indians, and Filipinos, though they be not of the full blood."[15]

What the laws could not readily correct, nor Filipinos easily remedy, was the derogatory public reference to them as "monkeys" (or "little brown monkeys") who lowered "the morale and dignity" wherever they lived. Justice of the Peace D. W. Rohrback, of Pajaro, California, was said to have described them as "little brown men about ten years removed from a bolo and breach cloth." The secretary of the California State Federation of Labor leveled the erroneous accusation that "large numbers of them suffer from venereal disease, tuberculosis, and brain tumors." And the bias was not among whites alone. A Japanese father in February 1930 had taken steps to annul the marriage in Stockton of Felisberto Suarez Tapia to his daughter, Alice Chiyoko Saiki, and to prevent Tapia from ever seeing her again. With this embarrassment coming only weeks after the Watsonville riot (with its attacks on Filipinos) and the bomb blast at the Stockton headquarters of the Filipino Federation of America, Tapia reacted by urging his fellow Filipinos to boycott Japanese businesses in protest. The Japanese retaliated by refusing to hire Filipinos. Although Filipinos wished to present themselves as equals of Americans—western in "customs, ideals, family life, religious [sic], government, and civilization"—and thus entitled to date and marry Americans, they were aware of the pitfalls of pursuing this. Dr. Daniel Bonecilli Begonina, of Livermore, California, observed that "The Filipinos are not permitted to date an American. You are scared. You don't know what is going to happen. You were scared in public, scared of losing our jobs. We were looked down upon, just like . . . animals."[16]

It got even worse. The secretary of the Central California Chamber of

Commerce made the rather shocking statement that "the Filipino is just the same to us as the manure that we put on the land." They are not our brothers, he went on, "not our social equal." "We have got to have the Filipino to do that work. . . . [T]hat's his place in *this* society." Meanwhile, organizations on both sides of the Tapia-Saiki controversy mobilized—the Filipino Workers' and Businessmen's Protective Association, the Filipino Safety Committee, and the Filipino Federation of America (headquartered in Stockton) versus the Japanese Association. Charges and counter-charges went beyond the immediate issue, bringing to the surface differences over work habits, wages, and labor practices. In the end, Tapia lost his lawsuit against Alice's father, who prevented Tapia from seeing his daughter again.[17]

The Tapia-Saiki episode, with the hostilities that surfaced and the Filipinos' nascent efforts at community mobilization, had occurred within the first decade of large-scale Filipino migration to the mainland. It revealed that this group of young men, among whom were a significant number of comparatively well-educated individuals (and a small but growing number of educated women, too), would not embrace docility as a coping strategy either at work or away from it. Moreover, the "Hawaiianos," though including far fewer educated young men, proved to be as capable of organizing and striking as were their mainland Pinoy brothers. But whereas we have seen that the Hawaiian Sugar Planters' Association (HSPA) encouraged family migration as a means of dampening the men's enthusiasm for strikes, for mainland growers the "most sought after workers [were those who were] unmarried, younger men in the prime of their lives and unencumbered by families." They believed that unattached Filipinos would more readily depart following the harvests, could be paid less and provided more primitive housing, and would be more controllable —more readily hired and fired. Yet, they, too, proved capable of organizing, and as Carey McWilliams concluded at the end of the 1930s, "once the Filipino began attempting to organize, he ceased to be a desirable worker."[18]

Beyond the individual efforts, collective ethnic needs persisted, especially in view of the fact that Filipinos came from a number of islands and had not yet secured a national identity that fully transcended regional homeland differences. On the personal level, Filipinos established extended families by sharing living expenses and adopting "uncles" as fictive kin and women as surrogate mothers, sisters, and aunts. On a community level, the "[p]ioneering first-generation immigrant Pinoys organized communities, founded associations, initiated community traditions, and published newspapers." Seattle and Stockton were the primary centers of Filipino activities, although additional clusters could be found from El Centro to Alaska. A Rizal Day celebration was held in Bremerton, Washington, as early as 1920 (when there were only 5,600 on the entire mainland). Six years later, Filipinos were copying Americans by organizing in Seattle a Miss Philippines contest for Rizal Day as a money-raising venture among community groups. The Filipino Federation of America had been established in Los Angeles a year earlier, and a chapter was founded the following year in Stockton. In Seattle, where there were only 1,614 Filipinos in 1930, businessmen and other community leaders had already organized the Philippines Commerce and Labor Union two years earlier.[19]

Caballeros de Dimas Alang, a nationalistic fraternal group founded in the Philippines, had established chapters in Hawai'i and Seattle. Filipinos also responded to the discrimination and violence that targeted them by organizing the Filipino Community of Stockton and Vicinity in 1930 and subsequently the Committee for the Protection of Filipinos Rights, with branches in many major cities. A Filipino Women's Club was created in Seattle in 1932 and a Daughters of the Philippines in Stockton around 1936–1937 (which targeted second-generation women). There were others tied to the homeland, such as the Balagtas Society for Tagalog speakers, the Sinukuan Lodge of the Gran Oriente Filipino (San Francisco, 1929), the newspaper *Philippines Mail* (1931), and, akin to the Filipino Laborers' Union (1933), a number of unionizing efforts.

Local organizations were also founded to help those who were left unemployed by the Depression but who were determined not to return home as jobless failures. A small number of Filipinos began to establish businesses, notably restaurants, pool halls, food stores, even a pharmacy, and, especially, as with Pedro Ponce (whose story is told in part 4), barbershops. As their visibility increased, they not only challenged (sometimes forcefully) discrimination and stereotyping, particularly against such derogatory labels as "Little Brown Monkey," but they also insisted on their right to date white women—publicly. In addition, they apparently felt accepted enough by 1937 to hold a Filipino carnival in Stockton. Still, many believed that they "were all trapped here in a pit of economic slavery. We are only allowed to do unskilled work, and in this we must compete against Mexicans, Chinese, Japanese, and Negroes."[20]

Filipinos did encounter strong opposition from whites when they sought to operate farms or to seek skilled jobs in various mills and factories—and especially when they combined those labor efforts with attempts to date or marry white women. This prompted Buaken to insist that Filipinos had not taken jobs away from whites, especially during the Depression years, because Filipinos largely confined themselves to menial service positions. "An American laborer took such work only as a last resort, but the Filipino knows he must take these for keeps because this is the only type of work open to him in the United States." This was true even in the U.S. Navy during the 1920s, where an annual average of over 4,000 Filipinos were largely confined to the roles of ship stewards, cooks, and valets. In addition, over 7,000 joined the merchant marine, and almost 8,000 others worked in vessels engaged in coastal shipping. That is, until the 1936 Merchant Marine Act imposed a requirement that 90 percent of a ship's crew operating out of U.S. ports had to be U.S. citizens, which crippled the role of Filipinos on such ships.[21]

On land, Filipinos organized to demonstrate their resistance to discriminatory work conditions. Indeed, Filipinos came prepared, for they had seen strikes
being employed in the Philippines as early as 1872 and the first trade union, the
Union Obrera Democratica, organized in February 1902. Within a year there
were an estimated 20,000 union members in 150 such organizations in Manila—
only a few years before migration to Hawai'i began. A familiarity with unions
was carried by many to America. Only five years after arriving in Hawai'i (1911),
the Filipino Federation of Labor was founded. The Filipino Higher Wage
Movement helped trigger the famous 165-day strike in 1920. Four years later, in
April 1924, some 1,600 Filipinos on Kaua'i began a protracted strike, but one
that split Visayans and Ilocanos. The latter were urged by an Ilocano labor commissioner from the Philippines not to strike. Six hundred, mostly Visayans, remained out. In early September a clash at a strike camp in Hanapepe between
Filipinos and police resulted in the deaths of 16 workers and 4 policemen. The
strike failed, and 13 years passed before the Filipinos again walked out. That
time, in April 1937, about 1,500 persons on Maui launched the last major strike
by an ethnic-based union, the revived Filipino Federation of Labor. Leaders
were arrested; the premature labor action failed; and Filipinos turned to the
more broadly based, emerging labor movement on the Islands.[22]

In view of the power of many growers' associations, cannery firms, and labor
contractors, and their willingness to use violence to suppress unions, the efforts
by the agricultural and cannery workers to unionize along the Pacific Coast
had to surmount intimidating obstacles. In 1930, near Seattle, Filipino farm
workers organized the Filipino Labor Association, which had some successes
but was overshadowed three years later by the Cannery Workers and Farm Laborers Union (CWFLU). Unlike its predecessor, the Cannery and Agricultural
Workers Industrial Union (CAWIU), the CWFLU aimed to include salmon
cannery workers, exclude foremen and contractors, and unify the Filipino subgroups of Ilocanos, Tagalogs, Visayans, and Pangasinans. It also gradually
opened its membership to Chinese, Japanese, African Americans, and whites
and soon affiliated with the American Federation of Labor.[23]

As briefly mentioned earlier, one of CWFLU's major objectives was to end
the hiring power of the Chinese, Japanese, and Filipino contractors. The contractors launched competing organizations, which ended up merging with the
CWFLU. That the confrontation had its dangers was brought home by the killing of the union president and treasurer in December 1936. However, that only
tightened the organization's unity, broadened its outreach, and strengthened
the resolve to neutralize the power of cannery foremen and labor contractors.
Meanwhile, the Alaskan Cannery Workers Union (ACWU) had also been established, and in 1937–1938 both the ACWU and the CWFLU voted to join the
new Congress of Industrial Organizations (CIO) because of its more inclusive
vision and outreach to both skilled and unskilled workers. The two unions

eventually affiliated with the major new umbrella organization within the CIO, the United Cannery, Agricultural, Packinghouse, and Allied Workers of America (UCAPAWA)—which was in 1944 renamed Food, Tobacco, Agricultural, and Allied Workers (FTA). Finally, beginning in the late 1930s and resuming toward the end of the war, the CIO and AFL competed with the Alaskan Native Brotherhood and Alaskan Native Sisterhood groups for the right to organize Alaska's salmon cannery workers.[24]

By that time, the combination of racism and resentment over the Filipinos' activism had taken its toll. Already in 1928 a bill had been introduced in Congress to reclassify Filipinos as aliens in order to bar their admission. Neither it nor a similar bill introduced by California's U.S. Senator Hiram Johnson the following year passed. In January 1933 the Hare-Hawes-Cutting Bill was enacted providing for Philippine independence, but the Philippines legislature rejected it over issues related to tariffs and naval bases. Congress subsequently approved the Tydings-McDuffie Bill (March 24, 1934) without the objectionable clauses, and the Philippines legislature accepted that version. This act provided for Philippines independence in a decade, placed a limit of 50 persons to be admitted annually, and classified Filipinos as aliens ineligible for citizenship. Congress then followed that with the Filipino Repatriation Act of July 10, 1935 (49 Stat. 478–79), offering Filipinos free passage home from the mainland until January 31, 1937 (extended to December 31, 1938). The stipulation (Sec. 4) was that those going home this way could only return as quota immigrants. Fewer than 2,200 took advantage of the offer—and most of those who did apparently were students completing their education. For those who had not completed their schooling, returning home was a sign of failure. In fact, as Emory Bogardus suggested at that time, "It is hard enough [for a Filipino] to return to his home community without having achieved wealth in the United States, but it is unbearable to return at public expense." Moreover, added Robert Vallangca, in his study of Pinoys, many never wished to go back because they had not graduated or had not saved much money, or they had grown "accustomed to a life without roots or responsibilities." Zacarias Manangan, who migrated in 1929 as we related earlier, did not go back for 33 years. Nevertheless, between 1933 and 1935 some 10,000 did return on their own, and another 7,400 did so between 1935 and 1937—without federal assistance. Given the shame and return limitations tied to the government's offer, the free passage was not seen as really free.[25]

The Filipino experiences between the wars touch upon themes and issues valuable for understanding many other groups' trials and tribulations as well. Filipinos experienced considerable racism and many forms of discrimination, even violence, in both urban and rural locations—especially when they began their own efforts to unionize and improve their wages and working conditions. The *manong*—young, inexperienced, migratory—were vulnerable to exploitation, deception, and dual wage arrangements. Still, they were a critical labor force. If, by the late 1920s, they and Mexicans had not been present, many businesses and growers would have been unable to meet their production goals or would have simply found their enterprises largely paralyzed. Consequently, in Hawai'i, Alaska, and along the Pacific Coast, Filipinos unquestionably filled major labor needs created by the combination of the nation's various new immigration laws and quota system and by the vast expansion of industrial agriculture, truck farming, packinghouses, and canneries, as well as a host of urban enterprises.

Like other peoples of color, Filipinos in a number of western states faced significant legal hurdles to land use, inter-marriage, and citizenship, notwithstanding that they were more than clusters of uneducated young men and varied considerably in their levels of education and background.[26] Finally, despite their regular migrations, Filipinos did foster bonds between fellow islanders that linked many rural and urban centers, with key communities in Seattle, Stockton, and El Centro whose outreach extended well beyond city limits. In the process, they established networks crisscrossing much of the West—from Hawai'i to the mainland and from Alaska to San Diego. They created a "regional community," much as that described by Sarah Deutsch for New Mexican "Hispanos" in villages near the Colorado state border, where, of necessity, the wives assumed new and quite expanded family roles. The extent of the *manongs'* commitment to family and community back home varied so much that it is difficult to make the case that they also maintained an extensive transnationalism. Rather, the uneven, intermittent, sporadic ties and sparse involvement in homeland affairs, along with the quite varied remittance and visiting patterns, all point, at best, to a translocal version of homeland bonds. Most likely, more than a few were like Zacarias Manangan, leaving a wife who would have to contribute to the support the family, manage the home, and raise children for husbands and fathers who might or might not ever return.

CHAPTER TWENTY-FIVE

Divided Yet Interlinked
The Urban West in the Interwar Years

T HE WEST EXPERIENCED remarkable social changes during the 1920s. In fact, over the three decades prior to the onset of the Depression, the West experienced extraordinary growth, its total population jumping 147 percent compared to 52 percent for the rest of the nation. And that expansion included a significantly diverse population of natives, newcomers just arriving, and immigrants from other regions of the country—together with westerners following migration channels transecting the "lower 12" and extending out to Hawai'i and up to Alaska. Old stock and foreign stock did migrate to rural areas undergoing economic transformations, but far more flocked to the cities in unprecedented numbers. The three states reporting the most exceptional growth from 1900 to 1930 were Washington (202 percent), Arizona (254 percent), and California (282 percent).

Even in the 1920s, with new quotas and shifting sources of immigrants, the region's percentage growth was still twice that of the rest of the nation (31 percent versus 14 percent). The data specifically bear out the descriptions of the heady days in California during the 1920s, for the population of that state grew by two-thirds during that decade—well more than twice that of any other mainland western state (the population of Hawai'i expanded by 44 percent). And California surpassed all western states and territories except Hawai'i in the size of its total foreign-stock population. In 1930 immigrants and the children of immigrants amounted to an astonishing 45 percent of California's entire state population. Montana and Washington were just behind (44 percent and 43 percent, respectively, but with smaller populations).[1]

Although no state approached Hawaii's nearly 82 percent foreign stock, no other states in 1930 held as low a percentage of foreign stock as did Texas (under 17 percent) and New Mexico (approximately 21 percent). And it was not for lack of growth, because the overall Texas population rose 91 percent (1900–1930), and its foreign born, fueled by Mexicans flooding across the border since 1908, had doubled (103 percent). It was the in-migration of American-born persons that continued to vastly outnumber arriving immigrants. Meanwhile, New Mexico's general population more than doubled, yet with its economy much more rural, ranching, and village based, it drew fewer immigrants. Across these three decades New Mexico's foreign-born population had risen to nearly 29,800 in 1920, only to fall by 5,800 with an exodus that included some 3,900 Mexicans and 1,100 Italians, Germans, Austrians, and Brits. In 1930 only Nevada had a smaller immigrant population.

Much of California's vast economic growth during the 1920s was in and near its urban areas (fruit and vegetable canning and packaging, petroleum and refineries, manufacturing, automobiles, construction, filmmaking, etc.), and it carried much of the West's expansion. California's foreign-born population jumped by nearly 47 percent during this decade, while that of all the other western states and territories (except Oregon) fell. Thus, the West's nearly 204,000 overall increase in immigrant population took place largely in California.[2] Nonetheless, the continued fluidity of immigrants coming and going in the West was still apparent in the late 1920s, during which time the number of immigrants who were admitted and who gave an intended destination in the West steadily declined, and the number departing rose after 1927. Yet, in fiscal year 1930 (ending June 30), with the economy already in disarray and 11,500 more persons emigrating from the region, 31,800 other newcomers designated western states as their destinations. More dramatic changes in this migration equation become evident by the early 1930s.[3]

With the continuing migration in the West, the transformation to metropolitan society was underway, representing "the major change in [twentieth-century] American history," concludes Walter Nugent. And city fathers (and mothers) were well aware of the population leaps after 1900, leaps that would only pause during the Depression before being swept forward by military spending and military preparations even before Pearl Harbor. The cities had been quick to celebrate the onset of the new age, to announce in no uncertain terms that they would be leaders of change. Portland had initiated the celebrations with its Lewis and Clark Exposition in 1905 (population growth: 234 percent, 1900–1930). Seattle followed with the Alaska-Yukon Pacific Exposition four years later (growth: 353 percent). San Francisco proclaimed its recovery from the shattering earthquake of April 1906 with the Pan Pacific International Exposition in 1915 (growth: 85 percent). And in 1915–1916 San Diego entranced visitors at the California Pacific Exposition (growth: 736 percent). Of course, there was Los Angeles, which soared 1,108 percent—with no exposition but with many oil wells, industries, Hollywood, an alluring environment and climate, and newly absorbed communities.

A dozen developments shaped the context and components accelerating urbanization during the interwar years. We could detail the many urban industries during the 1920s—from garment manufacturers, canneries, and packinghouses to automobiles, oil wells and refineries, smelters, and new assembly-line factories. We could observe how, on the one hand, the Depression did slow some of the hectic growth from the prior decade and, on the other, how certain enterprises provided even more employment during that decade, such as the expanding aircraft industries and New Deal construction programs. The period before 1940 was a prelude to the take-off period of the metropolitan West that Carl Abbott sees commencing in 1940.

In terms of the region's larger context, agriculture, logging, and many packinghouse operations continued to be rural-based enterprises, as was truck farming, on which all the cities depended for fresh fruits and vegetables in their markets. As we have noted, immigrant rural populations by no means vanished during this period—homesteading, for example, was still being pursued by Scandinavians in Montana in the 1920s. Consider the German, Polish, Mexican, Czech, and Japanese farmers in Texas, the Japanese coffee farmers in Kona, Hawai'i, the Russian German farmers and sugar beet workers in Colorado and Wyoming, the Filipinos working their lands on the Yakima Indian reservation in Washington State, Basque sheepherders still tending their great flocks of sheep in California, Nevada, Oregon, and Idaho (until the 1934 Taylor Act curtailed much of their use of public lands), and native-born Americans and American corporations operating the major grain and cotton staple factory farms together with the multitude of small communities providing for the needs of the numerous laborers and farmers. (And in between, in various sizes, were the mining communities.)

Rural life continued to be a vital part of the western economy. Japanese and Italian truck farmers as well as Japanese orchardists and nurserymen could be found near many cities all along the coast, and they would continue to play major economic roles there until 1942. In other words, "ruralness" by no means died out simply because urban populations were increasing. In fact, Nugent writes about "rurbia"—the areas just outside cities where one could find small industries, seasonal agriculture, and, in places, logging and milling communities. (As that receded with expanding suburbias after World War Two, the term "exurbia" would come to be used for that transitional setting beyond the suburbs, which earlier had fit the rurbia label.)[4] Meanwhile, the expectation long present in Panna Maria, Texas, at this time was that "the rural Polish communities will remain islands of Slavic culture in a sea of American, Hispanic, and Germanic culture in the foreseeable future." Others also remained attached to that lifestyle.[5]

Because many agricultural-related operations were not far from the cities and towns (even 30–40 miles), we find that immigrants continued to journey out from El Paso, Los Angeles, Stockton, San Jose, Spokane, and elsewhere to follow the crops and then return to their urban enclaves during the winter months, just as Filipinos would seasonally migrate from San Francisco, or Stockton, or Seattle to the Alaskan salmon canneries. Moreover, urban-based farm and packinghouse workers would also continue to be active in labor organizing activities, some in enterprises adjacent to the cities. Perhaps they were even more so inclined due to their exposure to urban life and living standards.[6] Generally illustrative of this is Vicki Ruiz's discussion of Mexican women who worked in canneries and fruit-packing plants at this time and who helped their families move from a "family wage economy" to a "family consumer economy." The latter, above subsistence level, enabled them to buy "extras," such as radios, records, and additional clothing. (In 1930, one-fourth of these working women in the Southwest were classified as industrial workers, and 50–70 percent were single.)[7]

The key to the multiplying urban centers was that they became the principal places that newcomers from abroad encountered newcomers frequently from middle America. The cities of the West were "collections of urban communities," co-existing in good times due to their interdependence and the expanding links between them—the networks of transportation and communication that secured the West as a region. Much of that urban growth was taking place just as the relatively new urban electric rail systems faced the escalating competition of automobiles and the construction of highways and bridges beginning in the early 1920s.[8] Local economies grappled for greater shares of the growing foreign trade. While some agricultural enterprises—truck farming and citrus crops, for example—continued in close proximities and with vital connections to the cities, other rural endeavors seemed more removed from the nearby modernizing city life. In 1919 Oregon became the first state to use a gasoline tax to fund highway construction and maintenance, and such roads not only enabled truck farmers to reach urban markets more readily but also, as Kristofer Allerfeldt pointed out, made it "increasingly possible for those working in isolated regions to return home to their families more or less when and where they liked." Obviously, migrant workers would more easily move between harvests as more roads were constructed. Further illustrating this transitional phase, Los Angeles County in 1929 still had many agricultural enterprises, and many businessmen remained reluctant to let go of their rural past. They held on to lands with specialty crops and, recalled one, farmed them from their city office by hiring "Japanese and Mexicans to do [the actual farming] for them."[9] Urbanization was feverishly underway, but the borders between the cities and towns and the rural hinterland remained at this time blurred and permeable.

Not surprisingly, migration patterns begun well before and during the First World War persisted afterward. If many people continued to relocate to Los Angeles and its nearby towns for retirement and health cures—especially persons from Illinois, Missouri, Ohio, and Iowa—more Mexicans were now beginning to head for California rather than Texas (as others headed for the Midwest). During the 1920s the net foreign-born Mexican population increased by about 116,700 in the West—particularly in such urban centers as Los Angeles, Oakland, San Diego, Denver, Dallas, El Paso, Houston, and San Antonio. By 1930 the Los Angeles Mexican population had exceeded that of El Paso.

More and more farmworkers were relying upon automobiles for their sojourns in an effort to free themselves from a reliance on labor contractors. So extensive did this rural-to-urban-to-rural migration become that in 1928 Los Angeles was described in the *Saturday Evening Post* as "the great Mexican peon capital of the United States." In a related scenario, those Japanese who were not responding to the Alien Land Laws—by putting land titles in their Nisei children's names or by working out some complementary relationship with white Americans (which Asian Indians were doing, too)—were abandoning agriculture for city life in, for example, Honolulu, Los Angeles, and Seattle. They sought employment operating hotels, restaurants, pool halls, dry goods shops or other trades, or entered different types of domestic and personal service, or turned to fishing, floral nurseries, landscaping, and gardening. In Hawai'i during the years following the 1920 plantation strike, many Japanese adopted the Chinese pattern, moving to Honolulu and starting businesses there, as did smaller numbers of Koreans, Filipinos, Portuguese, and other haoles (Caucasians). Then, the HSPA tried, with limited success, to attract urban Nisei back to work on the sugar plantations, although in more skilled and supervisory roles.

The Canadian-born population in the West jumped by 40,000, with most newcomers in this decade heading for Seattle, Tacoma, Portland, San Francisco, Oakland, San Diego, and, especially, Los Angeles.[10] And yet, although they were flowing into the cities, Canadians did not create enclaves. In San Francisco many other immigrant groups did carve out their own areas, frequently with a mix of residential and business establishments. The Irish were concentrated in the Mission District, while North Beach was more Italian, the Downtown heavily German, the Western Addition more Jewish, and Grant Avenue and Stockton Street predominantly Chinese. After the First World War Russians (many being Jews and others White Russians) settled farther west of the Western Addition, north of Golden Gate Park, while to the southwest, in the Outer Mission District, one soon found Irish, Italian, and German Catholic entrepreneurs and professionals.[11]

Automobile and garment industries, trades, construction, fishing, and any number of service occupations drew clusters of immigrants to the new and expanding urban enclaves, many from rural and small-town communities and many directly from their homelands. Urban jobs were often more plentiful as the 1920s progressed due to mandated reductions in the admission of many new arrivals. In addition, the sharply negative responses to unions by the early 1920s often guaranteed open shops for the newcomers. Nevertheless, very unstable, if not dire, economic conditions during the mid-1930s in San Francisco—as in Seattle immediately following the First World War—ignited nearly unprecedented general strikes. The West—urban and rural—proved to be anything but immune to labor's struggles.[12]

As expected, many urban settlers shifted occupations. Italians (originally Genoese and then Sicilian) already dominated fishing out of San Francisco and then commercialized the tourist appeal of Fisherman's Wharf (and likewise in Monterey and San Diego), while still others controlled San Francisco's refuse collection for decades. Elsewhere, as in Salt Lake City or "Little Italy" in Cheyenne, Italians opened shoe and boot shops, tailor shops, groceries, and taverns, just as the Greeks in Tacoma, Portland, and even in Rock Springs, Wyoming, started bakeries, barbershops, groceries, confectionaries, meat markets, and coffeehouses. Japanese in Seattle and Los Angeles were securing a broad array of enterprises—most servicing the needs of fellow Japanese (hotels, restaurants, barbershops, clothing stores, and pool halls were particularly favored) but, especially in Seattle, often concentrating a whole array of enterprises on the non-Japanese trade, too. These patterns included a heavy reliance on wives in domestic services as well as in retail work, often as non-paid labor in the family business.

As the Nikkei (Japanese emigrants and descendants) community stabilized and families grew in Seattle, there was an increased demand for female Japanese language teachers and midwives.[13] Similar trends were evident in Honolulu, too (and to a lesser extent in Hilo, on the Big Island), where many groups large and small (Chinese, Japanese, Korean, and Portuguese) were launching an array of businesses that soon extended beyond the respective ethnic groups. They were also concerned about providing more substantial educational options for their children, particularly among the Asians. Even the small population of Greeks in Honolulu saw its young men moving into professions and skilled labor jobs or establishing businesses. The women would follow traditional family paths, some having been brought over from Greece. The scene represented that combination of enduring homeland patterns with increasing integration into American society.[14]

Depression-era changes also shaped Los Angeles and several other communities. The repatriation movements that were largely carried out in the early 1930s against Mexicans and afterward against Filipinos (see below) did little to etch the city's image as an equitable place, although too few recognized that at the time. However, late in the 1930s and early 1940s defense industries began to draw many men and women from rural and urban areas, which opened opportunities for those eager to leave their current, and often desperate, situations. Many of them were migrants who had come West, usually leaving behind even worse situations. That in turn renewed opportunities for those, especially in rural locations, who remained behind but now (once again) faced less competition.[15] Many Mexicans who had left the United States—or had been repatriated to Mexico—managed to return, and for a short time the improving job prospects helped smooth over some of the anxieties and uncertainties created by the city's injustices a few years earlier. This series of developments, set off by the Depression, did not affect just Los Angeles. However, the magnitude of events there were not only greater than in many other cities, but what followed during the war years would be both singularly dramatic and traumatic.

Boyle Heights, in East Los Angeles, offered a preview of where major parts of the urban West were heading in the twentieth century—and what other groups were determined to prevent. It was well known since the 1900s for its progressively more polyglot population that came to include Jews, Japanese, Blacks, Mexicans, and Russian Molokans, as well as smaller numbers of Armenians, Chinese, and Italians. It would undergo a remarkable transformation not so much with the Depression as with the outbreak of the Second World War and new employment opportunities elsewhere in the city. East Los Angeles represented one part of rapidly expanding Los Angeles. Central Avenue became the heart of the African American community. Aimee Semple McPherson's remarkably popular Foursquare Gospel services in her 5,000-seat Angelus Church served as a social and cultural magnet within the city for recently transplanted midwesterners and southerners. And Carey McWilliams suggested one more feature of this city's metropolitization, one that included multiple working-class and rising middle-class neighborhoods. In the absence of both the city's "first families" (the *californios*) and deep-rooted social traditions, many Angelenos adopted the emerging motion picture elite as their "arbiters of taste and style." At the same time, many people were so readily relocating their residences that they tended to weaken the very Midwest-style neighborhood ties they had eagerly sought.

Not surprisingly, because the relatively new economic and entrepreneurial elites of Los Angeles had primarily concentrated on capitalizing on the influx of so many newcomers, they themselves offered little in the way of a coherent social and cultural vision for the city, especially after having subordinated or ignored most minority groups. That left to the various quite recent migrant populations the task of defining the city.[16] The result would be a largely decentralized, sprawling, ill-defined urban complex with compartmentalized communities, some bounded by restricted covenants and clear social class lines and others hemmed in, even isolated, by poverty, class, and race. The long-term cost of such polarization and marginalization would become apparent as groups arrived or expanded their neighborhoods (thereby encroaching on others), and still others resettled further westward (to the more affluent Los Feliz area or to the newly established Beverly Hills, for example), or over into the San Fernando Valley. All these patterns fostered a social and physical environment that ensured members of many ethnic groups would rarely encounter one another except in (frequently unequal) job settings.

The interwar years, the 1930s in particular, saw the emergence of young adult second-generation men and women in many urban communities that had taken root by the First World War. This would be particularly apparent among Mexicans, Chinese, Japanese, Italians, Norwegians, Swedes, Danes, Portuguese, Greeks, and Armenians. This generation would bridge American culture, values, consumerism, and their ethnic traditions. These young adults articulated more substantive, more independent roles for women and sought employment outside the ethnic community where possible—and in ethnic niches when need be. Alternatively, they created new opportunities where feasible and formed their own associations in schools, in religious institutions, and within the broader ethnic community. Some groups would share Rev. Shimmon's experiences (see below) and struggles against the status of perpetual outsider (or even a "non-white" status); others would be as fortunate as Paul Bergsaune, encountering few (or less formidable) hurdles between them and mainstream society. Many would come to share Philip Hitti's mid-1920s doubts about the infallibility of Americanization as advocated by many organizations because they failed to convey that "Americanization is a spiritual process" of which learning English is but one step. "America . . . is a set of ideas, institutions, ideals" that take more than one generation to absorb, for assimilation is not a melting pot but "more of a weaving process of old and new."[17]

And this was exactly what immigrants saw as luring their children away from tradition, sometimes even driving a wedge between the generations. Symbolically, what Issei recalled about their Nisei offspring living in Seattle's Nihonmachi (Japanese community) was just what frustrated many parents in other groups: "Japanese food was plentiful but the boys often preferred hot dogs and baloney." Many youths, like Fresno's Armenian children and the Polish children of Panna Maria, Texas, were urged to hold onto their traditions, religion, and their parents' language and to socialize and marry within the ethnic group. Yet the teenage Chinese, Japanese, Italians, Scandinavians, Germans, Jews, Greeks, and Mexicans were being drawn ever more strongly to American culture by the public schools, peer groups, new musical styles, radio programs, and the irresistible appeal of the cinema (especially with the talkies beginning in August 1926) and its emerging star system. Attractive and sometimes daring new dress, hair, and cosmetics styles along with the latest dance crazes formed a combination that mixed consumerism and overt sexuality. Parallels to the cultural struggle that George Sánchez described as the competition between Mexicanization (*lo mexicano*, that which is of the Mexican culture) and Americanization (*lo americano*) could be found among numerous peoples, especially as the children acquired an education beyond their parents' levels and were exposed to a culture and individuals far different from their parents' community. And they were also hoping for careers their parents could only have dreamed for them.[18]

Inevitably, the cultural struggles carried over into the delicate issues of dating and marriage. With them came the matter of relationships among the interwar generation that brought to the forefront the challenges of whiteness versus "non-whiteness," "multiple and hybrid identities," and the emotional fallout from such "ethnic crossings." Given the legal obstacles of the anti-miscegenation laws and the strong cultural aversions to intermarriage held by parents in most new groups, the teens and young adults initiating relationships across ethnic boundaries—for example, Filipinos, Mexicans, Chinese, Japanese, and Armenians—had to overcome formidable cultural, social, and sometimes religious obstacles. Although there is no way to quantify how extensive these ties were, the anecdotal evidence is considerable. The marriage records for non-whites— for example, in Los Angeles County during the 1920s and 1930s—do suggest a heightened frequency of inter-group unions rather than inter-racial marriages with whites. Between 1924 and 1933, half of the Filipino intermarriages, three-quarters of those of the Japanese, and nearly all of those by the Chinese involved other non-whites.[19] In Honolulu this was more and more commonplace.

Despite the strains, conflicts, and inter-generational friction, life in urban ethnic communities did provide opportunities for ethnic persistence concurrently with the attractions of American society; it offered challenges and temptations of all sorts but also afforded avenues for ethnic group members to strengthen their identities. They built temples, churches, synagogues, youth centers, and mutual aid societies and lodges, such as the Greeks' AHEPA (American Hellenic Educational Progressive Association) and GAPA (Greek American Progressive Association), the Italians' Sons of Italy, the Norwegians' Sons of Norway, and the Jews' B'nai B'rith. However, if American society could compel Italian viniculturists to follow Prohibition laws by shifting to the production of "sacramental wine" or for a time moving into other occupations, so, too, did its pressures and appeal prompt other changes by the immigrant parents—some as the fallout from the First World War and others in response to the urgings for change from their predominantly English-speaking, American-born second generation.

The immigrant generation still retained the leadership of their communities, yet they were increasingly concerned about how to preserve the children's participation. Such issues were conspicuous among Germans, who did not initially abandon teaching German—as in Oregon. So, too, would the situation be among Texas Poles and Norwegians and Swedes in Washington State. Ethnic churches and ethnic newspapers gradually conceded the need to shift to English to maintain the children's interest, involvement, and readership. Mergers often hastened the process. Although the Germans tried to maintain their native tongue, the consequences of the war could not be indefinitely ignored, and by 1930 German-language parochial schools were largely gone.[20] Soon second-generation organizations began to require U.S. citizenship for membership and English as the language of their proceedings. Such was the case with AHEPA, the Japanese American Citizens League (JACL), the League of United Latin American Citizens (LULAC), and then the Mexican American Movement (MAM). Valerie Matsumoto reports that there were some 400 Nisei clubs in Los Angeles by the late 1930s.[21]

The urban centers appealed to those fired by ambition, especially men and women who moved west in quest of success in America. Many pursued it. Some secured it, but others it eluded. American-born Amadeo P. Giannini stands out among the array of successful ethnic group leaders. Giannini built his Bank of Italy into the largest banking institution in California. By 1922 the bank had 62 branches in the state, and by 1927 it held the savings of one-fifth of all Californians. However, success appeared to favor Europeans disproportionately. The exceptionally large presence of non-whites—or those so perceived—undoubtedly "whitened" more rapidly those of European and Canadian origin. Although the achievements of George Shima, K. Ikuta, the Kishi family, Chin Lung, and Jawala and Bisaka Singh, all described previously, demonstrated that exceptional success was not limited to white persons, nor—as John Archabal showed—was it confined to white Protestants. The Alien Land Laws, restricted residential covenants, persistent dual wage practices, inferior and segregated schools, blatant job discrimination, and the harsh exploitation of agricultural workers all closed doors of opportunity for many ambitious second-generation men and women, especially those newly graduated from college—and particularly those of color.

That was the case for many Chinese and Japanese Americans who were compelled to take jobs within their enclaves—for example, selling insurance, working in fruit stands and various markets, or, for women, taking jobs in language schools and as secretaries, nurses, seamstresses, and beauticians. In rural areas many Nisei continued farming the family lands, while in Hawai'i some went to work on plantations, frequently taking over more skilled jobs previously held by Portuguese.[22] About 10,000 Nisei were sent to Japan for part of their education, returning imbued with Japanese nationalism and labeled Kibei by their Nisei compatriots. Others, like John Aiso (see below), took jobs in Asia, where they could profit from their language skills. Even though over three-fifths of Nisei would renounce their Japanese dual citizenship, they would not be seen by fellow Americans as simply Americans. Strongly Americanized though they were, they were still regarded with suspicion and as irremediably foreign.

Success, of course, took many forms, and politics was another realm for its pursuit. A brief example illustrates the point. The election of Jewish governors, senators, and congressmen (and one congresswoman: Florence Prag Kahn) was followed in the limelight with the election of Angelo Rossi as San Francisco mayor (1931–1944) and Dennis Chavez as congressman and U.S. senator from New Mexico (1931–1965). Other members of ethnic groups would soon enter politics, too.

At the same time that the second generation was emerging and seeking to identify its place in their ethnic communities, the interwar years had marked an important era of transition for the immigrant generation. Many of those who had arrived prior to the First World War and had not yet determined whether or not to settle now had to face more restrictive admission laws. In the 1920s if they decided to visit their homeland, they were compelled to choose whether to return or remain in America but without spouses from the villages or region of their origin; or to arrange (by return visit or proxy) for a marriage and the migration of their new partners (often entailing a lapse of several years and a renegotiation of dowry expectations); or to bring over the families they had left behind; or to seek mates among those already present or from a different generation or ethnic group (especially if their group were small or lived in an isolated area); or, perhaps, to adopt a less conventional strategy, such as the Chinese employed, namely sponsoring paper sons, a wife, or (more rarely) paper daughters. Many immigrants had already begun families in America, and we witness during this time the significant expansion of the American-born or American-raised second generation and the very apparent strains in the links which the immigrants had preserved with their homelands, their families, and communities of origin.

However those homeland ties may have been strained, they did not entirely break down, especially if individuals encountered negative experiences in America or more promising circumstances in their homelands, or if events cast native lands in a new light. Thus, some Issei looked upon Japanese expansion in Asia during the 1930s with pride and closely followed events there. Many Italians admired Mussolini and viewed his successes as enhancing their own status in America. For others, the onset of the Depression prompted significant numbers of immigrants to return home so that for 1932–1935 the United States had a negative outflow of emigrants (table 3.8). Nonetheless, many did respond to the narrowing of the American gateway by planting roots, creating families, and acquiring U.S. citizenship—whether their homeland bonds faded and the remittances they sent dwindled, or whether they never lost the emotional ties with the land of their origins.[23]

For many, those ties could be very strong, as we see from an episode in Texas in 1936. In the depths of the Depression, a Polish Boy Scout delegation visited Texas to participate in its centennial celebration in Dallas. During the Polish

Day program, an elderly man approached the Polish scout leader. In a low voice, in Polish, he asked, "Are they from Katowice?" pointing to the Silesian scouts. "I wanted my son to see them. He was born here. He has never seen anyone from Poland." He paused. "How is it in Poland? I will probably never see our country. I'm too old. Eighty-three. Surely I will not see it." After a moment, the elderly man put his arm around the scout leader's shoulders and implored, "When you come back to Poland, kiss the blessed soil and greet all my beloved Silesia." He could not finish, for the tears were streaming down his face, and he turned away. His son, about 40 years of age, stood by, unable to say anything. His father then turned back to the scout leader and said again, "And you won't forget to say hello to Silesia for me, will you?"[24]

CHAPTER TWENTY-SIX

Urban Landscapes and Ethnic Encounters

*L*ITTLE IF ANYTHING in the West was simple, and the hurdles of hate, fear, and discrimination were challenges many immigrant groups had to face. Some have been described in previous chapters. For a few years in the early 1920s the Ku Klux Klan was especially active in Colorado, Washington, and Oregon, where a pro-Klan governor was elected, and even in Utah and Texas (along with the American Legion in several locations). The western Klan was variously described as a revolt against modernism and for solidarity among WASPs (White Anglo-Saxon Protestants), or a "hooded progressivism" made up of "traveling salesmen of hate" who believed "that the state must be kept free of alien influences whether papal or Bolshevik." They portrayed themselves as "self-appointed guardians of Americanism, [launching crusades] against diversity and dissent" and particularly hostile to blacks, Catholics, Jews, radicals, alien land ownership, foreign language church services, and private parochial schools. But not all groups succumbed to their pressure. When the Klan marched in Salt Lake City and drove through Greek Town, young Greek men followed them and pulled off their hoods, revealing that some of the agitators were prominent citizens. Greek, Italian, Slavic, and Irish Catholic railroad workers in Utah developed an elaborate system to report the identities of Klan members. The organization soon disbanded in that state.[1]

By comparison with other groups in other urban communities during the 1920s, the presence of about 75–100 Assyrians in Turlock, California, less than 50 miles south of Stockton in the San Joaquin Valley, would appear to be just one more instance of a group clustering in one more community through chain migration. However, even this small group of Assyrians was by no means homogenous, for about half were Baptists, and the other half were divided between Presbyterians and Methodists. An episode involving them that took place early in 1924 illustrates the confrontations that were occurring in the urban centers of the West. Relatively new communities of native born and foreign born met and clashed because—with only a few exceptions—the newcomers, often no matter their country of origin, were not yet seen as American enough to be regarded as fully "white." Rev. Shimmon, an Assyrian Presbyterian minister who was fluent in English, had been welcomed into the local church and even named an elder. Assyrians had been church members for over a dozen years, and all went well until Shimmon's 24-year-old son won the heart of a young woman of Scottish origins, whose father was church treasurer. The Shimmons and the young woman's mother supported the relationship, but two financial pillars of the congregation, one of them the city attorney, pushed through a church resolution on February 12, 1924, declaring that "it will be for the best future advancement of the Christian life of the Assyrian people . . . to form their own organization . . . and commence their own separate services."[2]

The minister, a Rev. McCulloch, summoned Shimmon and the two instigators—William Graybiel and R. F. Wells—and explained to Shimmon that he "had all the rights and privileges of membership. . . . but this was a race problem; the *white* families do not want you here!" And, Wells added, "We don't seem to have room enough for your children and ours." McCulloch later told an interviewer that he opposed intermarriage, adding, "Ask [Professor W. C.] Smith what he would do if his daughter were engaged to a black Assyrian." He ventured that to Assyrians Americanization meant inter-marriage and that they would have their children "marry far beneath them if the person whom they marry is white. This is also the idea of the Armenians and arises also to a limited extent with Italians." However, no Armenian had been received into the Presbyterian Church in Fresno.

During the same period as the Shimmon affair a number of racially tainted episodes were taking place down in Los Angeles, revealing some of the urban community tensions emerging as large numbers of new groups found themselves colliding in their quest for space and autonomy.

By 1907 Japanese families were already living in the Hollywood area of Los Angeles, near Sunset Boulevard and Bronson Avenue. They owned homes, maintained truck gardens, operated food markets, and worked as gardeners and at other enterprises that drew limited attention to them. Some converted to Christianity, and the more recently formed groups gathered for services in different homes. In this neighborhood Rev. T. Horikoshi began Bible classes in 1912; a Japanese Young Men's Christian Association center was started; and, eventually, despite strong opposition by Buddhists, a separate Japanese Presbyterian Church was established. Relations with their white neighbors on Tamarind and Bronson Avenues, near Le Conte Junior High School, were said to have been amicable. The Japanese were relatively few in number—for example, there were 1,300 students at Le Conte, only 12 of whom were Nisei—and they were not viewed as posing a threat. But in the fall of 1922, a 12-year-old Nisei boy, John Fujio (or Fugue) Aiso, was chosen student body president by a 600-vote majority. His Issei parents had converted to Christianity and moved to that neighborhood to give John more diverse experiences. Instead, anti-Asian sentiments surfaced, stirring students and their parents.

Aiso was faced with a number of fellow ninth graders (supported by their parents) who filed a complaint that "we stand for America and want no one but an American as our student body president." Another student put it this way in a petition meant to rouse other classmates: "I believe in the United States of America. . . . It has taken root in my heart and soul and I protest against any Oriental taking the place of president of our student body. Give us an American boy." He *was* born in America, replied Aiso, affirming his Americanness, and he stated that he had no intention of returning to Japan. The principal, M. W. Chandler, confirmed the fairness of the election, and in November the faculty agreed. The local press reported the episode, and yet a month later, Chandler quietly voided the election. A revised student government was set up, and Aiso was elected one of 12 "commissioners," that for student welfare. He later recalled that it was "some of the rough boys" who initiated the move against him and that he had gotten along well with most other students.

John Aiso went on to Hollywood High School, where he was eventually slated to be valedictorian. He had also been chosen winner of an oratorical contest that qualified him to represent the school in the city-wide contest. The winner there would compete nationally in Washington, D.C. But Aiso was told by his principal that his participation "'would upset the peace of the different schools in the city'" and that it would not look good for him to hold both positions. He would have to choose. He opted to be valedictorian. The runner-up did win the city-wide oratory contest, and fellow students then raised enough money so Aiso could accompany him to Washington as his "manager." Aiso met the president of Brown University there, who offered him financial support to attend Brown. Ironically, on the current Hollywood High School list of distinguished alumni, Aiso's name is the first listed. Yet, his accomplishments did not stop there. A distinguished student at Brown, he graduated in 1931 and became the first mainland Nisei to attend Harvard Law School, receiving his degree three years later. What followed graduation is a remarkable account of a Nisei, undeterred by racism in the schools, who continued overcoming trials and hurdles during the interwar and postwar years.

A brief leap forward completes his exceptional story. Aiso had taken a year off during college to learn Japanese in Japan, but, he recalled, "they didn't want me. . . . I am the offspring of immigrants, get the hell back to America, you don't belong here." Even when he returned after law school and became director of a British company in Manchukuo for several years, he heard it whispered, "but he is only the son of an immigrant." Drafted into the U.S. Army in 1940, he was soon brought into what became the Military Intelligence Service Language School. He was quickly promoted to chief instructor and then director of the school for the duration of the war. For the 16 months following Japan's defeat, Aiso worked in General Douglas MacArthur's headquarters in Tokyo. Yet, this extraordinary story does not end there. He returned to Los Angeles and, beginning in 1952, was appointed to the municipal court, was promoted to the superior court and the state Court of Appeals, and, finally, was selected as justice pro tem of the California Supreme Court. He retired in 1972 and in November 1984 was honored by the Japanese government.[3]

But we must return to that winter of 1922–1923, for shortly after the Le Conte matter appeared settled, news spread in the neighborhood that a Mrs. Horikoshi, a white woman and wife of the Presbyterian pastor, had arranged to buy a property, almost across from the school, on which the congregation planned to build a Japanese Presbyterian Church. On April 23, 1923, around 200 persons (and possibly several hundred more) met in the American Legion club room to protest the church construction plans. As one of the flyers put it, people in the area had "stood for" [tolerated] Japanese families, children, and businessmen, "But we DIDN'T—and WE WON'T stand for" a Japanese church "in our neighborhood." "We Don't Want you with us, So Get Busy, and . . . Japs, MOVE OUT OF . . . Hollywood." The church was viewed as representing "a Japanese colony," "a wholesale invasion." In highly melodramatic terms, the *Hollywood News* reported the following day that "Americanism flamed high, burned with the white heat of patriotism and burst into a hissing, roaring conflagration of wartime passion." When a Dr. E. S. Bickford went forward to speak on behalf of the Japanese, he was shouted down with epithets, "White Jap, white Jap," and allegedly a cry to "Lynch him," forcing Bickford to retreat. George Burns, who was reported to be a former U.S. senator from Massachusetts (except that there had been no senator with that name) and now a resident of Los Angeles, urged that action be taken to halt the church. "You people here on the Pacific Coast are facing the greatest battle that has ever threatened the white man," exclaimed Burns. "It is to be the fight against the yellow man." Representatives of other areas that had fought to bar Japanese (or were in the midst of doing so)—such as in Pico Heights, Rose Hill, and Belvedere—voiced their support. Rose Hill's G. L. Loyd described how they had succeeded by posting signs all over declaring, "Japs, Don't Let the Sun Set on You Here. Keep On Moving. This is Rose Hill."

A small group organized the Hollywood Protective Association (HPA), and Mrs. B. G. Miller, whose home was a few doors away from the proposed church lot, hung a large banner across the front of her home, the photo of which has ever since symbolized the tempest that beset a number of western communities between the wars. Standing in front of her house, Miller defiantly pointed up to the banner: "Japs Keep Moving. This is A White Man's Neighborhood." Emulating "The Belvedere Plan"—which involved plastering that community with signs declaring "The Japs Must Go"—Mrs. J. O. Poole, secretary of the new HPA, had a sign painted on her sidewalk: "Japs. You Are Not Wanted." R. Bowles, president of the HPA, described how they would pressure those considering the sale of their property to Japanese, or to "un-American" "white scum" who "will purchase property for" them. Other methods employed included pretending to be a city attorney and going with a policeman (often unaware of the ruse) to intimidate Japanese businessmen; making anonymous, untruthful calls to the police to report that whiskey was being manufactured in a house being used as a church (this being the era of Prohibition) or that prostitution was going on there; initiating condemnation proceedings to get the city to purchase the lots for parks; serving false papers to get contractors to stop construction on Japanese properties; mobilizing boycotts of Japanese businesses; and persuading local banks not to lend to Asians and local realtors to limit home or property sales "to people of white extraction." A lawyer who had defended some Japanese, J. Marion Wright, reported being stopped on the street by women who told him that "he ought to be ashamed of himself for defending a Jap. A Jap isn't human."

The Church Extension Board of the Los Angeles Presbytery expressed its "sympathy and support" to the fledgling Japanese congregation, and Rev. Horikoshi was grateful, but by mid-May 1923 the HPA was claiming 500 members, with support from "80%" of the Hollywood community—and even from the Ku Klux Klan. The following January 1924, the HPA renewed its efforts. A large crowd gathered on the 14th to discuss claims that the Japanese or their "white allies" were trying to buy lots on nearby streets. The members feared that "Soon, instead of Hollywood the Beautiful, it will be Hollywood, Home of the Japanese." Some of those objecting to the proposed church were themselves Presbyterians, but, in the end, the support from the regional church administration for the Japanese church proved tepid. Even the Hollywood Congregational Church made a greater effort to mobilize support for the Japanese church. By springtime Horikoshi gave up the effort to build his church on Tamarind Avenue.[4]

In October 1924, several months after the Tamarind Avenue confrontation subsided with the decision to abandon the plan for a Japanese Presbyterian Church there, Mr. and Mrs. Sessions, residents on adjacent Bronson Avenue, were interviewed. They had been living there since 1910 and indicated that "we have never seen anything to object to in the Japanese. They have been here about the same [length of] time." More recent neighbors "didn't use to object to them," but now "those people will believe anything they hear about the Japanese, no matter how unreasonable it is. They have heard someplace that every Japanese has leprosy and they believe it." Moreover, "the Japanese keep their places up well; they are among the best looking houses along the street." They recalled speaking with "Mrs. S." a few years earlier. Asked then about her Japanese neighbors, Mrs. S. had replied, "'they don't bother me. They are quiet and I never see anything of them.'" Now, "that same woman is one of the bitterest against them."

The interviewer went to Mrs. S., who exclaimed that "the Japanese are a wild people. They never could be Christianized in a 100 years. Haven't you noticed what a wave of Buddhism has been sweeping over the country the last few years?" She went on. "The Japanese are greedy; all they care about is money. . . . The Japanese said they should have California because it bordered their ocean and really belonged to them. And if it had not been for the earthquake we should have had war with Japan. They were prepared to come over here and wipe us out."[5] Moreover, she continued, "Do you know that some of our highest officials are under the influence of Japan, congressmen and senators controlled by Japanese money?" And, "They are a filthy, dirty people"; their "women have no virtue nor modesty. . . . A woman told me there was [sic] no virtuous women in Japan over 13 years old." In fact, in the nearby Presbyterian Church, "they had a Jap living there with an American woman. Fine example to set before these boys and girls. . . . And they are all bootleggers."

Later, Mrs. S. reported how her mother had been unable to sell her property because, the realtor said to her, Japanese lived nearby. She then added, "I have no racial hatred; the Japanese are all right when they stay where they belong, just like the Negroes. But they should be segregated." Nevertheless, she then went further. "The Japanese ruin every piece of land they are on [and "have ruined our berries and vegetables"]. . . . I do not believe the Japanese should be allowed to come here at all; they have nothing in common with Americans. . . . I would much rather live next door to a Chinaman, because the Chinese have no designs upon our country." She concluded that "either [the Japanese] have to stay where they belong, and do as we say, or else there is going to be war. And it won't be the pleasantest war in the world either."[6]

Mrs. S. and the other residents on Tamarind and Bronson—many of whom had arrived within the previous half-dozen years—were not alone in their alarm over the presence of the Japanese. The Japanese were the target of much conflict in this rapidly expanding metropolitan region. Several community leaders in Pasadena—two pastors and a member of the City Commission—wrote to the Japanese Association in that city in January 1923, expressing concern over—and opposition to—the news that the association was giving adjacent land to the Buddhist Association to build a temple. On their minds was the "great question" of "whether or not the Japanese can really be Americanized and assimilated," because that "can only be accomplished through Christian Americanization." Raising funds to build a Buddhist temple "would seem to indicate to the American people that the Japanese people did not want to be Americanized or assimilated" and that "would have a very detrimental effect on future legislation regarding the treatment of Japanese in this country." It also appeared, they suggested, that the purpose of the temple "was not so much for the sincere study of Buddhism as it was an opposition movement against the growing Christian church. The effect of such an anti-Christian movement would be to estrange the very people who are the Japanese['s] best friends." Denying any sectarian motive, they acknowledged that for Japanese planning to return to their homeland, "the study of Buddhism is perfectly legitimate in this country" but not "from the practical standpoint of both Americanization" and friendly relations between Americans and Japanese. The building plan was abandoned.[7]

The timing of these events indeed coincided with the postwar, rapid growth of the Los Angeles region and the convergence of native-born white Americans—many from the Midwest's middle America—with Mexicans, African Americans, Japanese, Jews, Italians, and other European immigrants. The three-to-one statewide vote for Proposition One on the 1920 ballot, tightening restrictions on direct and indirect land ownership by aliens ineligible for citizenship (e.g., affecting Japanese and South Asians in particular), captured the climate of opinion at that time—opinions, reinforced by the 1920–1921 recession, that recently arrived Americans were quick to adopt. A man named Duffy had relocated in 1920 from Chicago to the city's Pico Heights area.[8] He soon become president of the Pico Heights Protective Association (PHPA), which was dedicated to pressuring Japanese homeowners to move and white neighbors not to sell to them. Perhaps indicative of how such actions can escalate with little substance behind them, Duffy acknowledged that "I did not know anything about the Japanese—[and] had probably never seen one." But other whites "explained to me . . . how the Japanese were coming in and driving the white man out," such as by offering to work for lower wages and then taking over the jobs (like landscaping), only to raise the prices of their services soon after.

Churches appeared to pose an even greater threat because they portended large numbers of Japanese being drawn to them, which would stymie the ongoing campaign to drive Japanese residents away. When in 1923 the Methodist Missionary Board proposed to build a church for the Japanese on nearby 12th Street, amid several other churches and small businesses, the opposition quickly escalated (notably by the PHPA), as it did simultaneously in Hollywood, Pasadena, and Long Beach (where a protest was also raised against a Japanese Presbyterian church). Although shown the church plans, opponents claimed that the church would include a dormitory and school as well. The Japanese insisted that was not at all the case. The Committee of the City Council deliberated for

weeks. Undoubtedly swayed by a petition signed by 2,600 residents who were
said to have been "born the world over" (as the *Los Angeles Ledger* put it), the
committee denied the building permit—notwithstanding that a Japanese
Christian church and Buddhist temple were then being constructed downtown.

Byron Wilson, district superintendent for the Methodist Church, later
claimed that the opposition was rooted in "commercialized race prejudice."
However, months later, when three members of a nearby church were interviewed, they simply said that the Japanese were objectionable, although they
could not explain why. One woman replied to the female interviewer with
"extreme disgust," "I can't imagine any white woman would be asking such a
question as that." The three women did concede that they personally knew no
Japanese and had had no dealings with them. At that point they walked away,
refusing to discuss the issue further. Mr. Duffy was less reluctant about describing the Japanese, employing the usual litany—they were "dirty," "tricky,"
deceitful," "can't be assimilated," "can't be Americanized," and the church
was intended to be "a gathering place for all the Japanese Methodists in Los
Angeles." Besides, "their religion is a religion of the Mikado; their Mikado
isn't just a human being to them; he is Christ on earth . . . and that is always
their religion at heart. . . . A Jap is always a Jap at heart."

When T. M. McClellan, editor of the *Ledger,* criticized the petition in late
September 1923, he asked why send missionaries to Japan and then restrict the
departure of the Japanese converts? Would they, he rhetorically pondered, "be
subjected to this same restriction in case they decided to go to hell?" Mrs. J. G.
Fitzpatrick, who lived three blocks from the proposed church site, replied to the
editor that "The Creator intended the different races of this earth should live
apart. . . . God commanded Christians to go unto every land and preach the
Gospel . . . [but] that does not mean that we must bring or invite . . . Japs, Chinese, Hindus, Africans, and Eskimos . . . to our land." She accused the Methodist leaders of being outsiders who were segregating the Japanese in their own
churches and "planting" them in Pico Heights. She then posed the question, "Is
it fair that a Jap church be located in a white neighborhood?" She noted that
there had been about 200 Japanese families in Pico Heights, but at least a year
before the community had begun urging them to relocate. Their number had
shrunk to 70, "and the work is going on."

McClellan later remarked, "I can't for the life of me see why people object
so to the Japanese. . . . I don't want the country overrun with them, but . . . we
have plenty of room and could make use of a lot more. We need them the
same as we need horses and tractors. We need them to work on our farms and
do our gardening. Here a few years ago the Irish ditch diggers were making a
big fuss because all the Italians were coming into this country. But what did
the Italians do? They only lifted the Irishmen out of the ditches and onto the
police force. All these Irishmen, and some other folks that have come from the

four corners of the earth, have a lot to say about their country and who should be here, just as though they had never lived any place else themselves."[9]

All inter-ethnic situations were not the same, and such inter-group conflicts were not universal, as the brief story of Paul Bergsaune's experience brings out. It provides a stunning contrast to those just detailed. Born in 1910 in Rissa, Norway, he decided at age 18 to join his four brothers and two uncles in America. Arriving in Seattle via Nova Scotia and Vancouver, he lived with one brother while "learning carpentry, cabinet making, and English. He soon became proficient at all three," recalled his wife. While his uncles attended the Norwegian Lutheran Evangelical Church, the brothers joined the Norwegian Methodist Church, where Paul met and married Marion Jenseth. They settled in Ballard, the center of Norwegian-American life in the Pacific Northwest. Not only did the Bergs (they shortened their name to a more "American" one) become active in the church, but Paul also joined the Leif Erikson Lodge No. 1 of the Sons of Norway. He campaigned for years to establish the Norse Home, a retirement facility, and then served on its board for 30 years and was its president from 1955 to 1965. In addition, he was active in several associations, including Nordmanns-Forbundet, Trøndelag, Nordlandslaget, and Romsdalaget—four organizations of Norwegians from central and northern Norway. A carpenter and builder, he contributed his skills to constructing a lodge hall in Seattle and elsewhere. A high point of recognition came in 1962, at the Seattle World's Fair, where his daughter was "Miss Norway," and Paul was awarded the St. Olav's Medal by Norway's King Olav V.

Rural or urban, ethnic groups experienced contexts of reception that ranged from amicable and accepting to hostile and rejecting. Urban areas frequently intensified the experiences by their greater number, variety, and proximity of peoples and by the stresses created in the more concentrated environments. As we have seen, there was a considerable array of variables at work. Let us look more closely at several urban settings and the experiences of a few specific ethnic groups.

"Los Angeles seemed to defy all laws of municipal gravity and growth," writes Earl Pomeroy. Its leaders labored to construct a railroad terminus, acquire San Pedro, and annex the 20-mile-long Alameda corridor so that the city could claim San Pedro as "Los Angeles Harbor." Simultaneously, between 1915 and 1930 the city incorporated enough land to quadruple its size from 108 to 440 square miles, thanks to the exploding ownership of cars there. Its expansion was freeform. It was like an "enormous village," commented writer Louis Adamic in 1925. Between 1900 and 1930, as noted, the population of Los Angeles grew an astonishing elevenfold, and its neighbor, Long Beach, jumped 703 percent. San Franciscans might taunt Los Angeles as "a one-lung tourist

town," but it had its growing industries and trade, new port facilities, and expanding movie industry, the tenth largest America industry in 1929. Then
there were the numerous businesses directly and indirectly linked to that new
industry. All prepared the city for its economic leadership role in the state and
region and, thereby, its extraordinary appeal to dozens of immigrant and ethnic groups.

Even before Los Angeles mushroomed, Seattle had aggressively reached out
to the future after the disastrous fire there in 1889. City leaders lowered steep
streets, carved a canal to open Lake Washington to the sea, and filled in enough
tidal flats to build a new central city waterfront. When gold was discovered in
the Klondike, precipitating a great gold rush through Seattle, the city was ready.
Port complexes from San Diego to Seattle were becoming the principal centers
of the urban West, just as Honolulu was for the Islands, while El Paso, San Antonio, Phoenix, Denver, and Salt Lake City, among others, would be the anchors
for economic growth in the Interior West—largely thanks to the railroads and,
later, networks of highways. However, while the railroads helped drive the central demographic, commercial, and employment force behind much of the development of the late-nineteenth- and early-twentieth-century West, the on-
rush of further changes prompted the somber conclusion that by the 1920s railroads, which had peaked nationally at 254,000 miles of track during the war, "no
longer led the way West."[10]

Much of what happened in the West during the interwar years was linked to
this accelerating urbanization, particularly during the 1920s and the settling of
immigrant families in the cities. Across the country during that decade over
19.4 million persons migrated from countryside to city, including significant
numbers who migrated from western rural areas to urban centers.[11] We have
also seen that Germans, Italians, Irish, Chinese, and German Jews were long
present in San Francisco, as for decades were Norwegians and Canadians in
Seattle and Ballard; Swedes and Canadians in Tacoma; Germans, German
Jews, Swedes, and Chinese in Portland; Italians in Denver and Los Angeles;
Chinese, Portuguese, and Japanese in Honolulu; Greeks in Salt Lake City;
Basques in Boise; Mexicans and Germans in San Antonio; Mexicans in El
Paso; and Mexicans, Chinese, Japanese, Italians, and Jews in Los Angeles.

Many who were putting down roots had been migrant or plantation workers,
or had worked on railroads throughout the West, in mines from Butte to Clifton-
Morenci, or in Alaska's canneries, or had operated farms now made legally
more difficult to retain. In a number of cases the moves were a response to prejudice and discrimination that were at times "intense and sometimes violent,"
driving Armenians from Fresno to Los Angeles, for example, as Chinese earlier
had been forced to flee many sites across the West in the late nineteenth century
and to retreat in an ever greater concentration in San Francisco. There were
even those who resettled following the failure of Jewish utopian agricultural

experiments, such as in Clarion, Utah, and as had happened before from
Painted Woods (North Dakota) to New Odessa (Oregon).[12]

An overview of the cities reveals that many of the demographic changes that
were now associated with the West were taking place in its urban areas. An
analysis of 25 principal cities across the West during the 1920s reveals that only
in Butte, Montana, did the total population decline during the decade. For example, Forth Worth and Houston both grew by 111 percent, El Paso by 53 percent, and San Antonio by 43 percent, while Texas as a whole gained only 25
percent. Seattle and Salt Lake City solidly kept pace with their respective states,
rising 16 percent and 19 percent, respectively. On the other hand, Portland
grew merely 17 percent, whereas Oregon increased by 22 percent. California,
with a statewide increase of 66 percent, best illustrates that the urban explosions of the 1920s were substantially among its "newer" metropolitan centers.
Long Beach expanded by 157 percent, Los Angeles by 115 percent, and San
Diego by 99 percent, compared with San Francisco at 25 percent and Oakland
with 31 percent. And the shift from rural to urban was equally apparent in Hawai'i, where Honolulu's growth exceeded the territory's between 1910 and 1930
(164 percent versus 139 percent).[13]

The foreign-born populations acted upon changes in perceived opportunities, as did the newly arriving immigrants. During the 1920s the number of foreign born doubled in Long Beach and Los Angeles and rose by more than half
in San Diego. San Francisco and Oakland's numbers were more modest, but
these five California urban centers also reported in 1930 one other measure of
the state's vitality and appeal: from 19 to 29 percent of all the foreign born in
those cities arrived during that decade—with the high of 29 percent in Los Angeles. Elsewhere, the census suggested, there was actually considerable movement of foreign newcomers (entering and departing) even where the total
growth was either moderate or in the negative. Portland's total foreign-born
population inched up by merely one-tenth of a percent, yet more than one-
sixth of those 50,228 present in 1930 had been admitted only in the last decade.
Nearby, Seattle's immigrant numbers dropped by 3 percent, but over one-fifth
of its 78,342 foreigners in 1930 were newcomers. El Paso had an 8 percent increase and Dallas 7 percent; still, one-third were newly arrived in El Paso and
almost one-fifth in Dallas. In Salt Lake City the foreign-born figure decreased
by 9 percent and in Fort Worth by 34 percent, although in both cities nearly
one-fifth of those present in 1930 had entered the country during the 1920s.
These figures certainly suggest significant percentages of population turnover,
with moderate persistence rates, on-going migration patterns, and a not incon-
sequential degree of continued uprootedness among many of the urban foreign
born.[14]

Los Angeles may be taken as the benchmark for the 1920s when it comes to
assessing the array of immigrant groups arriving and departing, given that its

foreign-born population doubled during the decade. Fifteen specific immigrant groups were examined in the various urban centers across the West, and only in Los Angeles did all but the Chinese increase in number. In Houston the 9 percent growth among foreigners was spread across 11 groups, with little or no decline among the others.[15] Denver can be viewed as the opposing benchmark. Its immigrant population fell by one-seventh, with declines registered in 13 groups and a small increase reported only for Mexicans. In cities as widely set apart as San Antonio, El Paso, Dallas, Oakland, Portland, Seattle, Spokane, and Tacoma, the Canadians, Italians, British, Scandinavians, and Russians (many being Russian Jews) all rose in number, whereas in many locations the German, Austrian, French, Greek, and even Japanese populations shrank (see table 3.18).[16]

Finally, one last but quite distinct index of the changes can be seen in the rapidly growing city of Honolulu, which had expanded in two decades (1910–1930) by 164 percent and where Asians comprised 58 percent of the city's population in 1930. The Japanese had become the most numerous group in the city, their number having almost doubled to nearly 47,500. The Chinese and Koreans both increased, and Filipinos went from 87 persons to almost 4,800. At the same time, the Portuguese (the largest European group) saw their numbers rise 38 percent (to 12,100). Nonetheless, the whole Caucasian population still made up only 28 percent of the city's population.[17]

It is clear that the western states were as diverse as Hawai'i was different from Idaho, and the urban experiences were likely to be replete with similar variations. Few cities lent themselves to the ambiance of San Francisco, or the well-recognized locales of Seattle, or the widely scattered communities of Los Angeles, whose inhabitants infrequently crossed paths outside of workplaces. Two brief references illustrate what urban-bound immigrants might encounter, one on occasion, the other all too often.

marie rose wong (as she preferred to write her name) studied the Chinese community in Portland, where a combination of anti-Chinese sentiment, Chinese ambivalence about planting roots, city license fees for vendors, and then an Alien Land Law resulted in the presence of Chinese but no Chinatown. Owners of properties used by the Chinese preferred to rent rather than sell buildings. A downtown section of associations, gambling and prostitution houses, and other businesses evolved anyway. However, by the early 1900s, with Portland expanding, building prices skyrocketed, and the Chinese district split in two. Leases in the old area south of Burnside Street expired, and that area was then redeveloped. The other section, to the north, remained but was hardly set apart from its surroundings. By 1910, notwithstanding the family associations and tongs, there was no defined, recognizable Chinatown to which Chinese could readily gravitate; rather than an enclave, wong suggests, there was a "nonclave." In general, what we have here, as with other successive waves of newcomers in various cities (notably Poles and Italians in mid-century Los Angeles), is a not uncommon situation where neighborhoods dissolve, ethnic groups disperse, and then remnants of those groups struggle to preserve an identity and sense of community without the physical concentration of businesses and other ethnic institutions in a particular location.[18]

In 1950 Harry T. Getty described pre–Second World War Tucson's Mexican community.[19] It had all the earmarks of a brown Jim Crow set of conditions, akin to what could be found in other smaller communities, except that between 1910 and 1930 Tucson's population grew from 13,200 to 32,500, of which about one-third were Latino. Nearly all Mexican residences were confined to an area south of the Southern Pacific Railroad tracks. Restricted covenants and outright discrimination kept them there. Nearly all laborers were Mexican, and only a handful of sales clerks were hired "'for the benefit of the Spanish speaking people.'" Elsewhere they were excluded because of their "accent" and the opposition of such key unions as those of the railroad firemen and brakemen. Only 3 percent of the teachers were of Mexican origin, and although segregation was not formally imposed, there were in reality "Mexican" schools. Moreover, after Mexican children reached the tenth grade, dropout rates jumped. As one young man said, "What's the use of getting a good education? The Americans get the jobs."

In addition, if Anglo and Mexican students in junior high school were seen going steady, the principal acknowledged that "we always let the parents know. We have no objection at all but we think the parents ought to know it." Not surprisingly, few marriages took place between Anglos and Mexicans (that is, Mexican Americans) and those that did mostly involved Anglo men in the military who had been born outside Arizona. In the strange permutations of interracial contact, the law barred inter-marriage, yet Mexicans were defined for this purpose as Caucasians and, as a result, could not wed blacks, Hindus, Mongolians, Malays, or Indians. Even the Anglo-Catholic priest of an all-Mexican parish expressed his opposition to inter-marriage: "We advise against such marriages, pointing out the difficulties of such marriages in getting along with one group or the other."

A few token Mexican Americans belonged to the country club and the chamber of commerce but not to the professionals' social clubs, although they owned 199 businesses. Politically, the Latinos were usually discounted unless some were paid to organize voters. The Latinos responded to these conditions by establishing their own newspapers and organizing fraternal, social, and religious associations. In particular, in early 1894 the Latino elite formed the mutual aid and political activist organization Alianza Hispano-Americana. By 1910 it had over 3,000 members throughout the Southwest; three years later women were admitted. Other organizations were more closely affiliated with the Catholic Church.

As segregated and as discouraged as they might have been, the Mexicans and
Mexican Americans not only created networks binding their community together, but they also demonstrated that they could, on occasion, unite and mobilize, reminiscent of earlier, successful strikes and perhaps foreshadowing future civil rights efforts. In 1936 a new manager of a local department store fired
the Mexican sales staff in order to hire Anglos. The Mexicans boycotted the
store and forced the manager to rehire the original staff.

Given the exceptional ethnic and racial diversity taking root in the West, we
would certainly agree with Carl Abbott's observation that the "cities were arenas
that concentrated conflicts among groups and cultures," particularly in the
West. The variations of western urban life were considerable. They ranged from
the almost stereotypical situation of groups divided by railroad tracks in Fresno
and Tucson, or by isolation in barrios as in Santa Barbara and El Paso, to the
somewhat overlapping yet still generally distinct subdivisions in Seattle or the
shifting and successive ones in Denver, Salt Lake City, and Los Angeles. San
Francisco, with its white foreign stock at 57 percent of the population in 1930,
was about one-sixth each Irish, Italian, British/Canadian, and German, and 8.5
percent Scandinavian—many with corresponding ethnic areas. There were similar concentrations of Asians in Seattle, Marysville, Yuba City, Stockton, Sacramento, San Francisco, Oakland, El Centro, Los Angeles, and, of course, Honolulu. Rapidly expanding Mexican barrios were in Houston, Dallas, San Antonio,
El Paso, Denver, San Diego, Oakland, and, especially, Los Angeles. There was
also a steady influx of African Americans into, for example, California cities
where their choice of residential areas was similarly restricted. It becomes
readily clear that the dynamic impact of immigrants and ethnic groups across
the western urban landscapes was quite pronounced.

We can better understand the impact of these urban ethnic communities by
looking at two examples, the Jews and Italians in Los Angeles and the exceptional racial situation in Honolulu. Its unique setting and unique combination of peoples provides a valuable contrast to mainland conditions. Together
these illustrations highlight the spectrum of urban ethnic realities in the West.

The early interwar years began as an interlude for Jews in the West, for the
recent waves of Sephardic and eastern European Jews had dried up by the
1920s. The Los Angeles economic bubble temporarily burst in 1927, weakening
the immediate attraction of the city, and the influx of refugees from Europe's
Fascist regimes would not begin for another half-dozen years.[20] The pioneer
generations had generally retired or died, and many in the second generation
(and third in places) were moving into different occupational endeavors. Those
of eastern European origin in particular were seeking out college educations
and white-collar or professional positions rather than continuing in family businesses, as were many of the German Jews. In either case, such occupational

choices enabled many to survive the Depression with fewer disruptions. None-theless, until the 1940s "a substantial Jewish working class made a living in Los Angeles." Moreover, although congregations on the East Coast had frequently been based on shared hometown origins, such was not the case in Los Angeles. Immigrants who did make their way there "had made too many stops en route to organize upon a *landsleit* [hometown] basis." Elsewhere, in Seattle, Port-land, and San Francisco, eastern European, German, and Sephardic Jews had established separate newspapers, synagogues, and social organizations. In Den-ver there were even two competing consumptive relief hospitals for Jews.

In view of the fact that merely 2,500 Jews resided in Los Angeles at the begin-ning of the century, San Francisco, whose Jewish community dated back to the gold rush, was viewed as "the New York and Jerusalem of the Far West," as Har-riet and Fred Rochlin put it. However, a major transformation had by now be-gun. The Jewish population in Los Angeles grew to nearly 20,000 during the First World War, then more than doubled by 1923, surpassing San Francisco's. It jumped by half again during the next few prosperous years to about 65–67,000 in 1927. By 1941 there were an estimated 130,000 Jews in Los Angeles—a fiftyfold increase in four decades, creating a Jewish population three times the size of San Francisco's. (While some communities thrived, others struggled. The Jewish community in Tucson pretty much went into a hiatus until the 1940s, and such smaller ones as those in Casper and Cheyenne, Wyoming, struggled to stay viable—discovering during these years that the automobile had become "the medium for Judaism" by effectively linking far-flung groups and communities as never before.[21])

In Los Angeles congregations tended to be based on neighborhoods rather than place of origins even though, for a time, eastern European and German Jews "neither worshipped nor kept company together and did not always flatter each other." The Hungarian American Club, the Roumanian Aid Society, the American Jewish Committee, and the American Jewish Congress reflected the earlier, deeper divisions between central European and eastern European Jews. From 2 Los Angeles synagogues at the beginning of the century, the number increased to 30 in the 1920s. The 1936 U.S. Census of Religious Bodies reported 42 in 1936, with about 82,000 "members," although a 1941 survey located only 32 synagogues.

Although in the first decade of the new century there were only those few syna-gogues, we do find a Hebrew Benevolent Society (HBS), a B'nai B'rith lodge, a Ladies HBS, one Jewish newspaper, and soon chapters of the Industrial Re-moval Office (IRO), which sponsored the relocation of immigrant Jews from eastern cities. By the 1930s, there were dozens of organizations. Even by 1917 the women's Friday Morning Club already had 1,500 members and by 1924 the B'nai B'rith—"the representative Jewish organization in Los Angeles"—had 2,000 members. During the Depression, groups began to explore joint associations and federations, such as the Councils of Jewish Women. In August 1937 the Los Angeles Jewish Community Council, United Jewish Welfare Fund, and the Los Angeles Jewish Council merged and were collectively renamed the United Jewish Council. Ninety-two organizations affiliated with it.

At the same time as the movie industry was finding its base, eastern European Jews who had migrated from the East Coast and Europe began settling outside the downtown and wholesale business district of Los Angeles, while other (more affluent) Jews moved further west—to Hollywood and the Central Wilshire and the Wilshire-Pico districts. For quite some time Temple Street and the downtown had been the center of the Jewish community, but here, too, changes were underway.[22] Overwhelmingly, the interwar years belonged to the communities in Boyle Heights and nearby City Terrace. The area had actually been developed for residential purposes by several Jewish investors: Charles Jacoby, Louis Levin, and Herman Silver. In 1908 merely two Jewish families resided in Boyle Heights, but within the next few years downtown residents relocated the Workman's Circle (a Yiddish cultural and political organization) to the Heights. They then transferred the Congregation Talmud Torah there in 1912, which would eventually build the famous Breed Street Shul (synagogue). Two years later the Jewish Home for the Aged opened. Families soon followed these institutional relocations.

During the 1920s many Jews from the Midwest and the East Coast settled in the Heights. The working class found more affordable housing opportunities there, for no restrictive covenants were employed. However, more acculturated immigrants and second-generation children seeking new opportunities, along with investors, other entrepreneurs, and members of the movie industry, now began resettling further west. And yet, by 1929 more than 10,000 Jewish households could be found in the Heights, and over 14,000 by 1938 (about 35,900 Jews in 1941), making Boyle Heights "Los Angeles' first authentic Jewish neighborhood" and the largest Jewish community in the West. On the eve of the Second World War about one-third of the city's Jewish population lived in the Heights, making up 40 percent of that area's population. The absence of restrictive covenants also enabled somewhat more affluent Jews to purchase homes in adjacent City Terrace (about 6,200 households by 1938). By this time there was such a wide variety of peoples in the Heights that the Federal Housing Administration concluded in 1939 that the neighborhood was "hopelessly heterogeneous" and that its "diverse and subversive racial elements" posed too much of a risk to warrant more than its lowest rating for home loans.[23] The people of the Heights were penalized for being integrated.

During the 1920s, "on the main streets [of the Heights] . . . were stores where Jews bought and sold, Yiddish was freely used, and Saturday and Jewish holidays were marked by festive appearances and many closed businesses." Even during the 1930s "the Jewish quality of Boyle Heights was still on display in its streets."

Leo Frumkin fondly recalled the neighborhood: "To this day I'll run across people I haven't seen in thirty or forty years. It's just a certain bond . . . [and] that bond just never existed, doesn't exist among anybody except the kids from the heights. It was a large family. . . . It was a fellowship." Added James A. Tolmasov, "When you see a white person, what nationality are they? Are they Irish or just Germans, or Armenians, or what? We never paid much attention to that. You went to school with kids that were walking on the sidewalk with you. You made friends with them. . . . We weren't picky . . . and we respected each other."[24] And for some contact, sidestepping ethnic boundaries would lead to relationships and even marriages that bridged races and religions.

While antisemitism was generally not virulent in the West, "social prejudice against Jews penetrated all social strata," and they were barred from law firms, fraternities, and major social clubs in Los Angeles and San Francisco. That prompted them to establish their own, notably the Hillcrest Country Club and the Concordia Club. The Klan was a problem for Jews in a few places as well, particularly in Portland. At the same time, the Jewish role in western politics also declined as other groups and leaders emerged, and second-generation Jews preferred other professions. On the other hand, the "first professed Jewish governor," Moses Alexander, had been elected in Idaho in 1915, followed by businessman Simon Bamburger in Utah two years later, and in 1930 both Arthur Seligman in New Mexico and business leader Julius Meier in Oregon were also elected governor (notwithstanding that Oregon had been a hotbed of the Klan a few years earlier). In fact, Julius Kahn represented Oregon in Congress for 12 terms between 1898 and his death in 1924, and his wife, Mary Prag Kahn, completed his term and won reelection six times before being defeated. She was the first Jewish congresswoman.

Part of the ways Jews coped with changing conditions and the challenges of antisemitism has been described as "instrumental acculturation." Here, Jews focused their patterns of adaptation on language, business or occupational skills, and the "general ways" of American society, while defending Jewish values and maintaining communal solidarity. It was a "collective survival strategy." That adjustment pattern also entailed resistance to dispersal and a reliance on a host of mutual aid and other ethnic organizations. Certainly, this pattern held in most urban centers across the West, although by the time of the interwar years probably the most famous exception had emerged in Hollywood. Jewish pioneers in the movie industry left behind their old occupations and much of their Jewishness (and some Jewish spouses). They remained relatively detached from the Jewish community but not indifferent to it, while proceeding to fashion new identities as remarkable risk takers and innovators.[25] But they still had a profound impact in terms of their concerns about antisemitic activists targeting their new enterprises. Moving into the vacuum of a new, cutting-edge industry, they were concerned not to stir up prejudices against it. They created a media magnet that would draw many Jewish performers, producers, and hope-fuls (as would radio). Paradoxically, however, they did take the precaution of changing actors' Jewish-sounding names to reduce their ethnic visibility and make the industry less of a target for antisemites. For example, Douglas Ullman became Douglas Fairbanks Jr., Asa Yoelson appeared as Al Jolson, Fanny Borach as Fanny Brice, Emanuel Goldberg as Edward G. Robinson, Laslo Lowenstein as Peter Lorre, and Nathan Birnbaum as George Burns.

What does all this amount to? Jews have often been described as one of the foremost urban peoples in America. They carved deep migration paths and de-veloped extensive communities and elaborate organizational structures to assist and protect them from mainstream rejection and antisemitism. In the process, many pursued occupations that placed a premium on economic independence, professional careers, and entrepreneurialism. They were drawn to new kinds of enterprises where established groups and institutions either did not yet exist or were minimally present. They would also take risks and novel paths, but they would not forget to shield themselves from prejudice. Many of their strategies (especially various self-defense and anti-discriminatory ones) and patterns of community mobilization would become models for other minorities. In the process, Jews made contributions to the growth of the West out of all proportion to their numbers.

Central to the Italian urban experience was the challenge of overcoming local and regional loyalties rooted in the homeland. Of course, they were not alone in facing that hurdle, but it was complicated by the presence of many north-ern as well as southern Italians among those arriving in California. By and large the process of coming together in Italian—as opposed to Tuscan, Pied-mont, or Lombard—organizations crystallizes around such events as the es-tablishment of the Italian Welfare Agency in San Francisco in 1916, the found-ing of the Italian Catholic Federation in 1924, the expansion of Sons of Italy lodges by 1925, and the more active efforts by the Catholic Church to play a role in Italian immigrant communities (to which the second generation proved more responsive).

An Italian nationalism was now rising among numerous Italian immigrants during the interwar years, especially among postwar immigrants, who fre-quently were veterans and *fuorusciti* (émigrés who had fled Italy). It was prod-ded by a combination of pride in Mussolini, bitterness over Italy's humiliation at the peace negotiations at Versailles, and frustration with the difficulty of se-curing respectability due to the on-going discrimination by Americans, who viewed the group through a lens of criminal and violence-prone stereotypes. But anti-Fascism was a pronounced reality, too, notably by activists who were among those who had more recently fled Italy, and that also represented a more collective identity. The fact that young Italian Americans who were reaching adulthood during those years frequently spoke little or no Italian and identified less and less with their parents' homeland troubled the older generation. The trend toward a more Italian American identity and community could also be gauged by the declining subscriptions to Italian newspapers. Perhaps another major symbol of the transition underway from Italian regional to Italian American came in the fall of 1930 when (partly for strategic banking reasons and out of pique with Mussolini's policies) Amadeo P. Giannini merged his Bank of Italy (40 percent of whose stockholders were Italian) with his Bank of America of California under the name Bank of America. In 1932, he mobilized the bank's influence behind Roosevelt's presidential campaign.

Still, many of the communal activities were taking place in the San Francisco Bay Area, where Italians were most concentrated, with at least one-third of the state's Italian-born residing there in 1930. Significantly, the city of Los Angeles lay between San Francisco and the small but prosperous Italian community in San Diego that focused on fishing, canning, and, by the 1920s, retail trade along the waterfront. In fact, by the late 1930s more than one in seven tuna boat owners in San Diego was Italian. The Los Angeles Italian-born population, consisting predominantly of northern Italians, rose steadily from under 2,000 in 1900 to 3,800 in 1910 and to nearly 12,700 in 1930, although this was still less than half the figure for San Francisco. There was no Italian neighborhood as such in Los Angeles, but there was an Italian "ethnic density" along North Broadway (the center of today's Chinatown), and the Italo-American community did come to be called "La Colonia."

Italians began moving eastward into the Lincoln Heights neighborhood of Los Angeles in the 1920s and 1930s. Estimates of the Italian population there ranged from 4,200 to 8,000 in 1930. The Catholic Church was "not a unifying force" for these Italians, nor did Saint Peter's Church there become a nationality parish until the 1950s. Rather than being a center for reinforcing ethnicity, the church promoted Americanization through the Italian Catholic Federation. Basically, it was not until the 1920s that Italian cultural, religious, and social organizations appeared in Los Angeles, far later than in San Francisco's community, which did number 16,200 in 1910. Besides the fact that the Los Angeles Italians were less concentrated residentially, this slower and more limited community development perhaps occurred because Italian immigrants, in prior step migration moves by those heading for Los Angeles, had lived elsewhere in America, adapting along the way to their new American environment. Alternatively, it has been suggested that the Los Angeles pattern took form because Italian immigrants had more diverse origins and weaker organizational traditions, or because they returned less frequently to Italy and retained weaker homeland ties. Or that they had settled in with families and were acculturating more rapidly. Whatever the combination of factors, the upshot was that scarcely any regional, homeland associations (except the Garibaldina Society) had been established earlier that could have become the predecessors to the national organizations, as occurred in San Francisco.

Nevertheless, despite the shallow organizational roots, during these interwar years some social groups did begin to appear in Los Angeles, including a branch of the Sons of Italy and Italian lodges of the Elks, Foresters, and American Legion, the Sicilian Club, the Organization Giorgio Kastriota, the Italian veterans group Associzone Italiana ExCombattenti, and Italian Pioneers of California (1929), as well as the Dante Alighieri Society, the Italian women's Club Eleonora Duse, the Italian-American Club, and the Italian Cultural Institute of Los Angeles (late 1930s). They represent a mix of first- and second-generation associations. The Los Angeles Italian Chamber of Commerce was established in 1925, indicative of the number of successful businesses that had been started in the region, notably Secondo Guasti's vineyards in Ranch Cucamonga and Pietro Pozzo's construction company. However, the 1936 strike by Italian cannery workers in San Pedro and the clashes between the Italian Fisherman's Protective Association and the larger Hook and Line Fisherman's Union signaled the Italians' greater acceptance of, and movement into, the labor movements.[26]

The presence of a critical mass of a group often triggers community developments. Thus, in the early 1930s, finding sufficient numbers present, the Italian government established a *dopo scuole* program (after-school language and culture instruction), with 47 schools in California, 5 of them in the Los Angeles area. In 1935 it appointed a consular representative for the city, Duke Roberto Caracciolo di San Vito. This move followed Mussolini's 1929 Conciliation Treaties with the Vatican, which had won him support from the Italian Catholic Federation. It was all part of Mussolini's plan to establish "emigrant enclaves as fugitive outposts of the once far-flung 'Roman imperium.'" Nevertheless, a few years after the establishment of the Dopo Scuole program, criticism of the political overtones of the materials used led to the abrupt closure of the program in Los Angeles. That sentiment was an expression of the growing disenchantment in the city with Fascism that became part of the response to Mussolini's invasion of Ethiopia in 1935 and to his efforts to recruit volunteers and raise funds for the military effort.

The transitional nature of these years for Italians and Italian Americans can be seen in the parallel stages of community development. One stage was the steady dilution of regional ties that were replaced by a considerable number of Italian immigrants who admired Mussolini and enjoyed the heightened status of Italians that came with his early successes. A second stage was the shift from a stew of local identities to a classically fused ethnic national identity—Italian and American, especially among the second and third generations. As disenchantment with Mussolini increased, that first line of thinking shrank, and even more weight was concentrated on the Italian-American identity, organizations, and communal image. Nonetheless, in reality, by the eve of the Second

World War neither had all the regional identities dissipated, nor all the pride in Mussolini, nor all the negative stereotypes that had been stoked by the violence and lawbreaking during Prohibition and which were associated with Italians.

Those particulars aside, many of the themes and issues involving immigrants and their children in the urban West can be seen in the Italian example— combinations of step migration and direct migration; many individuals already familiar with elements of American culture; the formation of a wide variety of associations that bespoke both of the acculturation and integration underway during this period and the still-enduring homeland ties and involvement in homeland affairs; the gradual residential dispersal as newcomers arrived with more occupational skills; the steady improvements among the second genera- tion that better positioned them for more mobility and, with that, relocation into better residential areas; and the in-migration of other immigrant groups, creating pressures from below that frequently worked to the advantage of those already present.

Hawai'i represents a distinctive but important example of both the rural and urban West, and we conclude this chapter by exploring developments taking place there. The uniqueness of the territory, and Honolulu in particular, lies in the plantation economy, the majority Asian population, the inter-racial dy- namics, the economic ties of the Hawaiian Islands to the mainland, and the fact that so many workers moved from Hawai'i to the mainland. In conformity with the 1885 Foran Act, the Hawaiian Organic Act of April 30, 1900, ended contract labor in the islands, freeing those who chose to do so to remain and complete their agreement, or leave.[27] Many Japanese took up farming on their own, but few Chinese would have anything to do with that. Instead, since the 1900 law also barred Chinese from relocating to the mainland, they could emi- grate, return home, or, as so many did, set a principal pattern of relocating to Honolulu. Among other reasons, most immigrants who moved to that city did so to escape the rigors of plantation life, the harsh living and working condi- tions, and the abuses at the hands (and whips) of the *lunas*, the white (usually Portuguese) supervisors. What the Chinese began many others would emu- late, in the process creating a multicultural urban environment that dramati- cally surpassed any other city in the West.

The interactions of mingling, exchanging foods, participating in each other's holiday celebrations, developing a "local" identity and unique patois, and even- tually dating and inter-marrying across ethnic and racial lines contributed to the growth of a society that would be dominated by the Asian presence. As indi- cated, Honolulu's population grew by 164 percent between 1910 and 1930 (52,183 to 137,582), but the foreign-born figure rose only by roughly one-third during that time, to almost one-fifth of the total. All told, Asians and Asian Ha- waiians made up at least 58 percent of the total number of persons in 1930, thereby defining the character of the city. Political scientist Lawrence Fuchs recognized early on that the people "thought of themselves" not by occupation or as Americans "but as haoles, Hawaiians, Portuguese, Chinese, Japanese and Filipinos." Ethnicity was the driving force in their "ways of life" and goals: "For the kamaaina haoles [locally born whites], the goal was to control; for the Hawaiians, to recapture the past; for the Portuguese, to be considered haole; for the Chinese, to win economic independence; for the Japanese, to be accepted; for the Filipinos, to return to their home in the Philippines."[28]

The ethnic groups were differentiated partly by length of residence in Hawai'i and largely by just those cultural preferences and traditions that set groups apart. In 1930, almost three-fourths of the haoles lived in Honolulu, as did 71 percent of the Hawaiian Chinese, one-third of the Japanese, two-fifths of the Koreans and Portuguese, but less than 8 percent of the Filipinos. As soon as their contracts were completed, the Chinese began gathering in Honolulu, making up one-quarter of its population in 1900. They operated laundries and worked as tailors, dressmakers, cooks, bakers, waiters, servants, storekeepers and café owners, even as peddlers. Their "overriding goal," wrote Fuchs, was success "based on economic independence and occupational prestige." Parents made great sacrifices for their children, insisted they remain in school, and urged them to avoid the discrimination of haole-run firms. They established manufacturing businesses and banks, and many children then operated them, while other second-generation Chinese—English-speakers, educated, usually Christian, and, of course, citizens—went into professions (teaching, medicine, dentistry, and law), business, skilled crafts, white-collar and even service jobs but rarely into organized labor or back into agriculture. Their attitude was one that stressed achieving and demonstrating their Americanization and their mobility. Thus, a McKinley High School graduate responded to HSPA efforts to attract Asian youth with the observation that "there is a limit in making agricultural work attractive. To send a young man through high school and then ask him to labor in the fields is, under the present social system, another absurdity."[29]

The 1890s assessment, that "A Chinaman . . . remains a Chinaman as long as he lives and wherever he lives," was not borne out, for by the 1930s the Chinese "represented the most successful adjustment of an immigrant group to life in Hawaii." In fact, they became "quintessentially American, conservative in politics, enterprising in business, conspicuous in consumption, and, above all, successful." While the establishment of a republic in China in 1911 stimulated both a renewed interest in that homeland and the establishment of 13 Chinese language schools (attended by 40 percent of Chinese students in 1929), the Chinese had early on established the Chinese Students' Alliance and a variety of clubs stressing business, cultural, and political interests as well as some based on village and class origins. Whereas the older generation looked to events in China, the children looked to those in Hawai'i, establishing the Hawaiian Chinese Civic Association by 1925. In 1930 Chinese Americans represented over 8 percent of registered voters. Already in 1917 William H. Heen had been appointed circuit court judge and eventually was elected attorney for the city and county of Honolulu before being elected to the territorial senate in 1929. In 1927, other Chinese were elected to the Honolulu Board of Supervisors and the Territorial House of Representatives. Hiram Fong, who graduated from Harvard Law School, also became attorney for the city and county in the mid-1930s and, in 1938, was elected to the lower house of the legislature. In 1959 he became Hawaii's first U.S. senator and served three terms.[30]

Although Japanese made up nearly one-sixth of Honolulu's population as early as 1900 and 30 percent two decades later, the most significant development for them was the shift from plantation work to farming or a business in Honolulu or Hilo. Indeed, by the time of the First World War, four-fifths of Hawaiʻi's coffee was grown by Japanese in Kona, and by 1930–1931 some 1,300 families labored on this crop, while 8,000 others grew pineapples. Although conditions on the plantations played a key role inducing Japanese to relocate to the cities or to strike out on their own as farmers (paralleling the mainland trend), after the 1920 labor action Japanese strikers were blacklisted, compelling those so identified to leave the sugar plantations. Many headed for Honolulu. Consequently, whereas 19,000 worked the plantations in 1919, 13,000 Japanese were so employed five years later. Their share of the plantation labor force plummeted from nearly three-fourths early in the century to 54 percent during the First World War and, by the time of the Depression, to just 19 percent. Filipino plantation workers filled the void, rising to 70 percent of all workers by 1932. Those percentages would shift around until the war because some Nisei did turn to the plantations during the job-scarce Depression at the same time that thousands of Filipinos were leaving the islands. At the outbreak of the Second World War, 31 percent of plantation employees were Japanese and 53 percent Filipino.[31]

Nonetheless, the trend was clear: Japanese were migrating to Honolulu, and not only were they encountering other groups, often for the first time, but they were also meeting fellow Japanese from other prefectures and islands for the first time—and not without "open hostility." The Issei had come principally from Hiroshima, Kumamoto, and Yamaguchi as well as from Fukuoka, Wakayama, and Okinawa. With 45 percent just from Hiroshima and Yamaguchi, their dialect, Chūgoku-ben, became the prevailing one on the Islands among the Naichi (those from the principal Japanese islands). That was to the disparagement of others, particularly Okinawans, whose original dialect (hōgen) differed appreciably from mainstream Japanese.

In response to many of the same pressures of land scarcity and taxes that had compelled other Japanese to migrate, an estimated 26,500 Okinawans, who referred to themselves as Uchinanchu, had emigrated from the Ryukyu Islands by

1927, with some 10,100 going to Hawai'i. The Uchinanchu possessed cultural and linguistic differences from other Japanese and were shorter in stature and darker in complexion. The men were frequently hairier than other Japanese, and many of the families engaged in raising pigs before the Second World War, although pork was rarely eaten by the Naichi prior to the war. The Uchinanchu were regularly discriminated against, taunted, teased, and seen as "second-class Japanese" unsuitable for marriage. They responded by maintaining their social distance from the Naichi and establishing their own associations and churches. The war began to soften the hostility between the two, but that pattern of inter-action well illustrated—as did the gulf between northern and southern Italians, German and eastern European Jews, and Visayan and Ilocano Filipinos—how members of ethnic groups lumped together by outsiders frequently had to sur-mount significant internal cultural and social class differences in order to achieve some ethnic unity.[32]

As with so many others, the urban setting eventually brought together those migrants from the various "ken" as members in, for example, the Hiroshima-Yamaguchi Prefectural Association. Older differences were gradually submerged in the process of establishing language schools, Buddhist temples, business and professional associations, and women's and youth groups. Hastening this fusion was Japan's December 1924 law withdrawing automatic citizenship for Hawaiian-born Nisei and requiring Issei parents to register their newborn with the consul within 14 days of the child's birth. By 1933, some 5,500 Nisei had expatriated themselves, and some 32,000 Nisei had not acquired Japanese citizenship be-cause their parents had not registered them. Moreover, the Nisei simply "did not share the memories of the prefectures or the needs that brought the immi-grants together in the kenjinkai."[33]

The processes of adaptation did continue—especially in Honolulu—and some Japanese organizations were created early on, such as the Japanese Physi-cians' Association, the Japanese Dentists' Association, the Japanese Benevolent Society (JBS), the Japanese YMCA, and the Honolulu Japanese Chamber of Commerce. By the time that the United Japanese Society was established in August 1932, some 40 organizations existed and joined in the merger. During that year, too, the JBS raised funds for a nursing home. Other organizations, created shortly before the interwar years, continued to be effective, including the Honolulu Japanese Women's Association (1916), the Young Men's Bud-dhist Association (YMBA, 1918), several newspapers (such as *Hawaii Hōchi*), and by 1916 at least 144 Japanese language schools with some 14,000 children (the first school having opened in 1896).

A 1920 federal commission report on 163 Japanese schools, with an enroll-ment of some 20,000 students, viewed the schools as detrimental to the stu-dents, retarding their progress and confusing their sense of loyalties. It proposed abolishing the schools. Those favoring Americanization programs endorsed the recommendation, maintaining that students should be "fully immersed in American institutions," with "one language under one flag." The Japanese saw the schools as providing cultural links and inter-generational ties and promoting morality, not dual loyalties. The report prompted the territorial legislature in 1922–1923 to impose controls on the schools and then levy a tax with the aim of closing them down. At that point a major split opened within the Japanese community between those favoring conciliation and those wanting confrontation. Led by editor Fred Kinzaburo Makino, 87 schools joined a class action lawsuit in 1923, despite the opposition to that strategy by the Japanese consul. In February 1927, the U.S. Supreme Court upheld a lower court ruling that the legislation was an unjustified interference in the Japanese community. As a result, by 1940 there were over 200 schools, with 40,000 students. Meanwhile, Dennis Ogawa argued, if the 1909 plantation strike represented "resistance" and the strike of 1920 "change," then the judicial action of 1927 and the subsequent quest by many Japanese for conciliation signaled "accommodation" and growing American loyalty.

Takie and Umetaro Okumura, who led the conciliators, urged parents to "Think and act from the point of view of the American people" and build the children "into good and loyal American citizens." Representative of the changing attitudes and especially the cultural pressures of Americanization, the Okumuras' Honpa Hongwanji Buddhist temple adopted some radical modifications. They established a YMBA, athletic events and clubs, and an English department within the temple. They made Sunday the worship day along with the day for Sunday school, altered hymns to sound more Christian-like, and added religious elements to the traditionally civil Japanese marriage ceremony. Although a 1923 study of 6,550 Nisei found 4,000 of them had no involvement with religion, as a result of the events related to the schools issue and the temple, "Hawaii would never be the same." Ethnicity on the Islands had received considerably greater legitimacy.[34]

The pace of integration could also be seen in public institutions and in politics. In 1911 Steere Noda was the first Nisei to graduate from McKinley High School, Honolulu's only high school. In time, so many Nisei were attending McKinley that it was referred to as Tokyo High. Haoles began demanding a second school, and Theodore Roosevelt High School opened in 1932. Noda went on to become a lawyer. He hoped for political office, but the war thwarted that ambition. Another Nisei lawyer, Wilfred Tsukiyama, became deputy district attorney for Honolulu city and county from 1929 to 1933, district attorney from 1933 to 1940, and, eventually, the first Nisei Chief Justice of the Supreme Court of Hawai'i.

In 1920, Japanese represented less than 3 percent of registered voters; by 1930 there were 7,000 Chinese and almost 13,100 Nisei of voting age. By 1936 the latter comprised one-fourth of registered voters. They began to seek local offices on the different islands (particularly the boards of supervisors) and seats in the territorial legislature. Whites were soon trying to thwart Nisei voting, frequently challenging individuals' eligibility. The Japanese for the most part voted Republican, but that did not affect the opposition to them and their exclusion from most federal and territorial jobs, including in the schools.[35]

Filipinos in Honolulu offered a strong contrast to the Chinese and Japanese because not only did they bring fewer skills with them but what they did bring was a goal to "work hard, save money, and return as quickly as possible to their families in the homeland." The HSPA recruitment of Filipinos had all along emphasized a preference for those with low skills and limited education. Therefore, those coming to Hawai'i were scattered, isolated, basically rural, and possessed little business experience or skills. Filipino students principally went to the mainland; the *sakadas* (as the temporary migrants referred to themselves) went to the islands, and 85 to 90 percent of them were unskilled. Although some did migrate to Honolulu after the strikes in 1920 and 1924, and 4,800 were reported there in 1930, only 13 percent of Filipinos were urban in 1940. They held the poorest and least skilled jobs in the city. They had the fewest persons in professional, managerial, or clerical occupations, even allowing for the fact that they were relative newcomers. In fact, in Honolulu in 1930 there were just two Filipino lawyers and three teachers. Given the millions of dollars they were sending home or saving to take home, there was little capital accumulation in Honolulu during these decades. In 1931 Filipinos operated only 9 businesses and just 36 by the end of the decade. The larger reality was that while close to 118,600 Filipinos migrated to the Islands between 1909 and 1934 (87.3 percent males), during that period close to 58,300 "Hawaiianos" returned home, and almost 18,600 went on to the mainland. Thus, their impact was principally on the plantations during the 1920s and 1930s, where the Filipinos were most accurately described as an "agricultural industrial proletariat."[36]

In light of events involving Asian immigrants and their children during these interwar years and the advances by the second generation, sociologist William Carlson Smith concluded in the mid-1930s that there existed "so little feeling of prejudice against the Orientals in Hawaii doubtless due, in considerable measure, to the absence of a class of poor whites in direct competition with the Orientals." Compared to the experiences Asians were having on the mainland and what shortly unfolded there for Japanese Americans, Smith's observation would prove to be quite prescient.[37]

CHAPTER TWENTY-SEVEN

From "Reoccupation" to Repatriation
Mexicans in the Southwest between the Wars

*I*N JULY 2003 EMILIA CASTANEDA related her "nightmarish" experience as an eight-year-old girl in Boyle Heights. It was 1935, and her mother had just died of tuberculosis. Her father was too impoverished to buy flowers for the grave. Then he was pressured into "repatriating," along with Emilia and her older brother. The two children, both U.S. born and, hence, U.S. citizens, had never been to Mexico and were now migrating to their father's home state of Durango. Nine years later, Emilia's godmother secured the girl's U.S. birth certificate, and with that Emilia was able to reenter the United States, find a job in Los Angeles, and get married in 1949. Fifty-four years later she joined a class action suit by Mexican Americans seeking damages for the violation of their constitutional rights in one of the most egregious such episodes in American history. How and why it happened speaks volumes about the mercurial context of reception for immigrants in the West, especially during the interwar years.[1]

"All borderlands share the border experience," observed Oscar J. Martinez, a scholar of the U.S.-Mexican border history, but he concluded that this one is unique in its "physical distance from central areas and constant exposure to transnational processes." With the exception of its border with Quebec, nowhere else does the United States share a border with a culturally distinctive population (aside from Native Americans). The difference in the Southwest is that there the groups are deeply racialized, and the socio-economic and cultural gulf has been wide enough to prompt a reference to this border as "one of the world's great cultural borderlands."[2] During the late nineteenth and early twentieth centuries, El Paso continued to be a major gateway for Mexicans entering the United States, their Ellis Island. It had also been, as described earlier, "a staging area" for armed movements participating in Mexico's revolution and civil war. The border had been nearly invisible during the 1870s and partially monitored in the early 1900s, principally against illegal Chinese immigrants. Only with the creation of the Border Patrol in 1924 did the southern border become more strictly maintained. It is not surprising, then, that the geographical, cultural, and certainly economic borders between the United States and Mexico were exceedingly blurred—before and since. As a prominent western historian put it, "It is one thing to draw an arbitrary geographical line between two spheres of sovereignty; it is another to persuade people to respect it." And, I might add, to get governments to enforce it, especially when this particular border region is "an ecological whole," extending north and south well beyond the line.[3]

As a consequence of this reality, parts of Texas were in many ways an extension of Mexico in religion, folklore, architecture, medium of communication, cuisine, folk beliefs, and elements of language and music. Mexican and Mexican American children's exposure to Americanization during these years resulted in a combination of "cultural continuity and cultural change" within those Mexican and Mexican American communities. Out of that dynamic came "a distinct Mexican border culture," extending north well beyond El Paso and Laredo and amounting to a complex set of cultural images found along much of the 2,000-mile border from Brownsville to San Ysidro.[4]

This confluence of cultures creates "the unique almost non-Anglo character of the Southwest" and, some maintain, a "magical realism" that shapes, in a transnational fashion, the character of the American Southwest. Viewing the borderlands, one can see that the observation by the former U.S. ambassador to Mexico John Gavin makes sense—that the history of the United States and Mexico has resulted in "a marriage without the possibility of divorce." One could therefore view the First World War era as the courtship, the Second World War years as the engagement, and the period of the Korean War as the wedding. With the "in-laws" so close by, metaphorically speaking, it has been easier for Mexicans to make the choice to retain the language and culture even if the home villages are far from the border. Already in the middle of the twentieth century, Carey McWilliams surmised, "the Mexicans of the Southwest will never 'assimilate' in quite the same sense that other immigrant groups have assimilated. They are not really immigrants; they belong to the Southwest." It is still asserted today that, even at the coast, the proximity of Mexico has contributed to a "southern California regional consciousness [that] is in large part forged by" identities that transcend the border.[5]

The fact is, of course, that by the 1910s and 1920s Mexican influences north of the border existed in tension with the forces and influences of Americanization. On the one hand, facing considerable discrimination, segregation, and isolation, Mexicans were understandably inclined to stick close to their barrio, fellow Mexican workers, and their traditional culture, especially if they planned to return to their homeland. On the other hand, it became exceedingly apparent by the First World War that there was emerging a powerful symbiotic relationship. The presence of the United States served as both a safety valve for a Mexico going through a revolution and then the Cristero Revolt and as an escape route of immense importance for Mexicans desperate for employment or just safety.

During the war and following the enactment of the quota laws, Mexicans were in a position to provide a considerable amount of labor in the form of thousands of mostly unskilled and semi-skilled men and women. Between 1911 and 1920, some 219,000 Mexicans were admitted to the United States; between 1921 and 1930 almost 459,300 were reported legally entering—at a time when federal immigration laws aimed at reducing or closing the portals for further European, Asian, and even much of Caribbean immigration. In other words, as essential as the United States was to Mexico during these decades, so Mexico was to the United States. However, compared with Americans, Mexicans were racialized, based predominantly on their color, religion, physical features, language, low levels of education, limited job skills, and cultural disparities. They were regarded as "sometimes white." Legally, for the most part, they were regarded as white, but in reality they were not white enough to save them from both a Jim Crow–style of segregation and disparities in employment and wages that left them chronically at or near the bottom of the employment scale throughout these years.

The historical context was clear. Mexicans' general contact with Anglos "was minimal." "Segregation, working class status, and the geographical mobility of Mexican men and women reinforced their identity as Mexicans." Social isolation did tighten cultural and familial ties and traditional identities, but it also fueled the Anglos' negative, "racialized national identity" image of Mexicans, which in turn encouraged Anglos to reaffirm an American identity that was "for all whites as [only] *white.*" White or not, Mexicans were also perceived as posing no threat to American citizenship because they were viewed as sojourners uninterested in naturalization. Yet, the dilemma was more acute for Mexican Americans and those of Mexican descent who were already U.S. citizens and who were, in many instances, struggling to define an ethnic rather than racial identity. That dilemma was brought home right at the onset of the Depression, when a Texas sociologist expressed the prevailing attitudes toward Mexicans and Mexican Americans. He declared that America had no place for "partly colored races." A Texas labor historian asserted a year later (1931) that Texas had blacks, but now "a second group alien in background and language and not readily assimilable" was present—the Mexicans—and she feared that both Blacks and Mexicans might seek vengeance against whites in Texas.[6]

In 1921 James Slayden, a Texas congressman, had written that "In Texas the word Mexican is used to indicate the race, not the citizenship or subject of the country." While one-quarter of Mexicans in Texas were born in the state, "they are 'Mexican' just as all blacks are Negroes though they may have five generations of American ancestry." Seven years later, Texas congressman Claude Hudspeth was asked at a hearing if he viewed Mexicans as being just as good as white men. He angrily shot back, "No, I have never said that and you know it. You know I don't believe that, so why do you ask me the question? No Texan has ever said that that I ever heard." In the same year Charles McKenny, commissioner of labor for Texas, told a hearing on Western Hemisphere immigration that "a nation cannot survive when the necessities of life are produced by an inferior and servile race"—namely, Mexicans. In fact, University of California professor Sam Haines denounced Mexicans as also being a "menace to democracy" and the source of "another race problem" for America. One option was given by those who viewed Mexicans as neither black nor white; they were simply "non-white." Historian Robert Forster, writing in 1926, claimed that Mexicans were actually "Asiatics" or even Africans and, therefore, unfit for self-government. Mexicans were lumped together with Mexican Americans, and both were seen as a threat to American whiteness. Indeed, among white Americans' greatest fears was that their daughters would marry Mexicans, just as southern whites deeply feared such unions between their daughters and blacks.[7]

During the interwar years the prominent sociologist Emory Bogardus was regarded as a savvy and knowledgeable scholar, but his 1934 book, *The Mexican in the United States*, expressed elements of the Mexican stereotypes as forcefully as one might have heard anywhere at that time. He quoted an article indicating that a Mexican's "highest expression" lay not in success or acquiring material wealth but in "music and songs and dances, in pottery making . . . not in owning." He asserted that Mexicans had "little social control" in their community; "many are inherently lazy and shiftless" and had a "reputation for financial irresponsibility." As peons, "with little training in the meaning of private property concepts," they were prone to steal—inclined simply "to pick up anything that interests" them. When working, such unskilled Mexicans were "likely to take time off freely. They live so largely in the present that time has no particular meaning to them." They were also challenged when it came to morality, for these peons were "victims of uninhibited emotions" and possessed "a simple, childlike faith" with respect to religion. In the final analysis, eugenicists were concerned about the "dangers [from] a large infiltration of Mexican blood into the racial stock of the United States."[8]

Mexican Americans resisted portrayals that melded them with *mexicanos*, but they were less united on counter strategies. A Latino in Arizona may have felt that "we are all Mexicans anyway because the *gueros* [blondes] always treat all of us alike." Another, who had come in 1916, recalled that "we didn't like each other" (a not unusual occurrence among newcomers), with Mexican Americans ridiculing immigrants as cholos (low-class persons), and the immigrants in turn referring to the Mexican Americans as *pochos* (those with no clear identity, diluted Mexicans speaking Spanglish). Sarah Deutsch contends that the Ku Klux Klan in New Mexico during the 1920s was responsible for the shift in perspective there that portrayed Latinos as a racial group and not as an ethnic one. Those of Mexican origin—going back from one to ten generations—rejected that assertion and insisted they were white Europeans. Improbable, but so were most of the race-based discussions at the time.[9]

For years most Mexican American leaders (and perhaps ordinary citizens who joined the new organizations) spurned the idea of perceiving the two populations in the same pot, sharing a common fate. In fact, one major objective of the League of United Latin American Citizens, established in Texas in 1929 by Mexican American veterans, was to specify both American citizenship and English language usage as prerequisites for membership. That was part of their personal effort to demonstrate "the assimilable character of people of Mexican descent." Their "American Dream" was akin to that of other immigrants and children of immigrants: rising expectations and the quest for respectability—legitimacy in American society—and, with that, genuine economic opportunities, security, political rights, and a stable family life. In fact, LULAC's goals were typical of other second-generation ethnic group members: Americanization through cultural pluralism. Members wanted to join the mainstream and dismissed the view that theirs was merely a minority organization. They moved in 1932 to permit women to establish LULAC auxiliaries, and two years later, with such leaders as "Mrs. J. C. Machuca" of El Paso, the women established Ladies' Councils, which further reflected the middle-class orientation of the organization. Clearly, LULAC's objectives resonated among Mexican Americans, for by the early 1940s there were 80 chapters in Texas, New Mexico, Arizona, California, and Kansas.

The persistent dilemma for LULAC revolved around how best to combat the racism and segregation that targeted them without being swept up into the debates regarding Mexican immigration and Mexican workers. They campaigned for exemptions and exceptions to segregationist practices, especially those involving public accommodations and facilities, such as in theaters, hospitals, pools, and restaurants, which were seen as places where discrimination was a particular affront to their middle-class aspirations. In response they would use boycotts and other strategies, including supporting Mexican American professionals and businesspersons. For example, in San Antonio in the early 1930s they established the Association of Independent Voters as well as the San Antonio School Improvement League (SIL) in 1935, which was led by Eleuterio Escobar. He was the owner of a furniture company and also headed LULAC's committee on education. Emphasizing the critical role of education in helping children escape poverty, the SIL gathered the support of 73 organizations in its campaign for new schools. They obtained three.[10]

Beginning in 1941, several Mexican American leaders of civil rights efforts in Texas, notably M. C. Gonzales, Alonzo Perales, and (later) George I. Sánchez—supported by Mexican officials and the Spanish-language press on both sides of the border—campaigned for a Racial Equality Bill in 1941 and 1943, calling for "full and equal [access to public] accommodations" for "all persons of the Caucasian race"—meaning Mexicans and Mexican Americans, too.[11] Only a non-binding (unenforceable) "Caucasian Race—Equal Privileges" Resolution was approved in 1943. The effort suggests a continuity of struggles from the 1930s that went on during the war and continued afterward, when indeed they would begin to be more successful.

Nonetheless, although they campaigned against school segregation and discrimination in public venues and urged Mexican Americans to register, pay their poll tax, and vote, LULAC's leaders did not directly challenge the overall Jim Crow system and its racial hierarchy. In Texas they "walked the color line" between whites and blacks and were caught between cultural loyalties to Mexico and the defense of their own legal status as U.S. citizens. That is why their 1941 and 1943 legislative attempts concentrated on obtaining equal rights on the basis of their whiteness, not equal rights for all Texans. Moreover, in South Texas, where there was a higher percentage of Mexican American landowners and ranchers, there was comparatively little official discrimination and segregation. Mexican Americans there were more likely to be enumerated as whites (for the census) and were able to participate in local politics. Where there were few Mexican American landowners, formal segregation prevailed, and Mexican Americans were usually disenfranchised. That contrast suggests "that being Mexican derived its meaning within the social and political context provided by the local class structure" and not by any inherent, fixed set of racial definitions.[12]

By attributing their problems to white Americans' negative reaction to Mexican immigrants rather than placing responsibility on the long record of American racism, members of LULAC distanced themselves from *mexicanos* and, consequently, for years endorsed restrictions on immigration and even supported repatriation. Still, it is well to remember that during the 1930s LULAC, like the Japanese American Citizens League, was a fledgling organization. The more profound social and economic realities were in the fields and cities where working-class Mexican Americans and *mexicanos* were most often cast together. For example, in El Paso's barrio, Chihuahuita, with its "almost total racial separation," Mexicans "remained economically underdeveloped, politically manipulated, and socially segregated."[13]

To the west, in Arizona, where roots were less deeply set than in El Paso, Clifton-Morenci displayed elements of a "colonial economy," writes Linda Gordon, yet the system of segregation there (especially in Clifton) was first "under construction" in the early 1900s and would be fully implemented only in the 1920s. Further westward, Mexicans were arriving in Los Angeles in huge numbers during that decade. In fact, *mexicanos* there outnumbered Mexican Americans by 2–1 in 1920 and—with the 150 percent increase during that decade (to 53,650)—by 5–1 in 1930. Given those numbers and the industrial conversion of the downtown that was beginning to take place, there was considerable eastward dispersal of the Mexican and Mexican American populations from downtown to Boyle Heights and into Belvedere. George Sánchez points out that there was no "Little Mexico" at this time, in part because there were class divisions influencing the dispersion and also because in Boyle Heights there was a plurality of Jews along with other newcomers. The Heights would become, as part of East Los Angeles, "the greatest of American barrios"—but not until the residential transformations during and after the Second World War and the exodus of the Jews and other non-Mexicans (including the government's forced removal of the Japanese).[14]

By the 1920s, Los Angeles surpassed such Mexican and Mexican American centers as El Paso (a hub for refineries and construction), San Antonio (a hub for agriculture and cattle trade), and Denver, a city with 7,000 Latinos, principally Hispanos from New Mexico (drawn by Colorado's sugar beet industry). The technological makeover of Los Angeles at this time provided many opportunities for Mexicans and Mexican Americans, although mostly in unskilled and semi-skilled jobs. That exploding opportunity structure in the Los Angeles region owed much to the harbor, the Panama Canal, the Owens Valley aqueduct, oil deposits and refineries, the railroad network, and the inter-urban electric rail, plus the opening of some 4,000 new factories between 1900 and 1930 that added to the vast array of manufacturing and service jobs.[15] And, of course, there was still the citrus empire extending eastward across the valley of the Inland Empire, along with other agricultural enterprises throughout Los Angeles and surrounding counties. Those employment markets, from Santa Barbara down to Ventura and east through Los Angeles County and Orange County to San Bernardino, attracted great numbers of Mexicans. And it appears that substantial numbers of those workers were relocating from elsewhere in the Southwest after having labored there for as many as 15 or more years. Along the way it is quite likely that they acquired some familiarity with American society, economy, and culture.[16]

Notwithstanding the prevailing agricultural labor image of the Mexicans "as

fluid reservoirs of agricultural laborers"—just as Paul Taylor reported at that
time for Dimmit County—a shift was underway. Mexican men and women
were now more commonly urban, unskilled blue-collar workers, filling the rapidly expanding number of bottom-tier jobs. Urban or urban/rural (with jobs in
both locales), most were paid a "Mexican wage," which usually meant a dual
wage system with lower sums for Mexicans, also referred to as the "Mexican
wage differential."[17] During "the first third of the twentieth century," Albert
Camarillo determined, "[w]age differentials often ranged from 20 to 50 percent
less per day for Mexican workers performing the same jobs as other workers."
Prior to the June 1933 El Monte Berry Strike (and many of those farmers were
Japanese immigrants), some of the 1,500 workers received as little as 9 cents per
hour. A month later, with the strike settled, wages were set at $1.50 for nine
hours, or 20 cents per hour when not working a full day.[18]

Undoubtedly, some of the worst working conditions for Mexican women
(who comprised one-seventh of Mexican workers in 1930) existed in San Antonio during the 1930s. "By 1926 . . . the large number of Mexican immigrants in
the city had depressed the wages of unskilled labor to the point that hand labor
was cheaper than machine shelling" of pecans. Individuals and families working at home were paid 6 to 8 cents per pound. By 1934 the pay was reported to
be a mere 2 to 3 cents per pound and by the late 1930s just 4 cents. "Whole families working together could not earn enough for the barest subsistence," noted
a contemporary observer. Adults were earning "an average of $2.50" weekly.
Women doing hand sewing there faced similar conditions. "One worker reported that she was paid forty-two cents for twelve hours' work on a single dress
that sold for eight dollars in an eastern store." Of 100 such "homeworkers" interviewed, 53 earned less than 5 cents per hour. Managers in the pecan-shelling
factories lamely tried to justify the pitiful pay scale by contending that workers
could eat all the pecans they wanted; besides, they would only spend higher
wages on "tequila and worthless trinkets."

These were the lowest industrial wages reported during the 1930s. Consequently, a reduction in 1934 from 6 cents to 4.5 cents per pound of pecan
halves and from 4 to 3.5 cents for pieces provoked a strike by 8,000 workers. It
soon collapsed, however, and a year later a similar fate befell another strike attempt. Then, in February 1938, Texas Pecan Shelling Workers Union members once more walked off their jobs. Soon, the 6,000 strikers had the leadership of Emma Tenayuca—La Pasionaria—a fiery 23-year-old CIO labor
organizer. They also gained the support of UCAPAWA (United Cannery, Agricultural, Packinghouse, and Allied Workers of America), although to deflect
hostile attacks (such as red-baiting), it actually forced Tenayuca out because
of her Communist sympathies. Mexican businesses aided the strikers, and city
leaders threatened to shut them down if they continued to do so. After six
weeks the strikers won by arbitration a 25 cents per hour minimum, but at that

point owners reverted to mechanization. Their labor needs plummeted to 2,000–3,000 workers—and by 1950 to a scant 350.[19]

LABOR STRUGGLES AND THE
ANTI-MEXICAN CAMPAIGN

In 1930, the U.S. Chamber of Commerce had acknowledged that Mexicans picked "more than 80% of the perishable commodities produced in the Southwest." Before the full impact of the Depression was felt, one found in many southwestern urban as well as rural locations a recognition that Mexican workers had rapidly become a key factor in the region's economic growth. All too willing to migrate or relocate, willing to accept lower wages than others did, willing initially to work where others had walked out, willing to remain in dead-end, largely unskilled jobs, willing to endure segregation and substandard living conditions—all this made them a desirable labor force. By sheer numbers they would continue to be desirable even after some began to challenge existing conditions, including by striking. As Neil Foley cleverly described their role in the growth of the Texas cotton industry, it had been due to "Mechanization and Mexicanization." The assessment of the situation in Texas during these years may well have been as true and as widely accepted throughout much of the Southwest: Mexicans were "outside the social order but a necessary part of it."

But that view was especially held while the economy remained firm. Not surprisingly, many unions excluded them, and employers routinely exploited them. In some locations fellow workers of other ethnic groups were segregated from them to forestall collaboration, much as the Hawaiian plantation authorities did with their workers. Anglos routinely stereotyped them while admitting their indispensability, applauding the fact that Mexicans infrequently sought land ownership or leases and rarely applied for citizenship. The Texas Anglos valued them to the extent of guarding them against "labor theft."[20]

Even prior to the 1920s, having seen strikers summarily shipped out of Colorado and Arizona, Mexicans had good reasons to fear that changing conditions could prompt Americans to expel them. The fear resurfaced periodically, along with a sense of vulnerability and an anxiety heightened by illegal Mexican migration. Apparent since the First World War, it had begun to rise in earnest by the mid-1920s, as visa fees, head taxes, and other costs and requirements for entering had increased. The situation finally prompted the government to fund a Border Patrol in May 1924. Soon thereafter, the agricultural economy began to sag, and it did not take long before Anglos were endorsing a sentiment expressed by Dr. Roy Garis in his various public and published attacks on Mexicans: They had become "foreign usurpers of American jobs." Beginning in Texas in 1927, with officials targeting illegal aliens for deportation, the "usurpers of jobs" were being labeled usurpers of unemployment relief, and many were compelled to return to Mexico.[21] When the stock market crashed, and the economy began to falter, Mexicans were portrayed as pariahs, responsible for the Depression conditions. More of them started returning home voluntarily (and less voluntarily in Texas). By 1930, some 8,438 had been formally deported, and at least 13,000 had emigrated more or less on their own in the late 1920s and early 1930s. With the Act of March 4, 1929, making the illegal return of deported persons now a felony, along with the existing provision whereby those seeking admission could be rejected if viewed as "Likely to become a Public Charge" (LPC), the machinery and precedents for large-scale repatriation and deportation were falling into place.[22]

In this tragic twist of fate Mexican workers were rapidly redefined from essential to expendable. Paradoxically, they had been essential workers of expedience, vital in both city and countryside in meeting "the difficulty in getting other labor than Europeans and Asians." Yet, in times of economic distress, they remained vulnerable, subject to immediate dismissal, or worse.

Under pressure from restrictionists eager to impose a ceiling on Mexican admissions, the Hoover administration in 1929–1930 urged border personnel to reject Mexicans who could not meet the LPC criteria. Instructions to consulates were tightened and generally taken as prompts for demanding from visa applicants more thorough proof of resources and assets. President Hoover reported at the end of 1930 that visas to Mexicans had dropped from about 4,000 per month to 250. In fact, between 1929 and 1932, annual Mexican immigration fell from 40,154 to merely 2,171, while officially recorded annual emigration of Mexicans jumped from 7,195 to 36,992. For just those four years Mexican emigration was 111 percent of immigration (64,889 versus 58,361), whereas for the rest of the nation emigration was only 37 percent of the number admitted. Even so, official emigration data clearly did not reflect the high volume of voluntary departures and other repatriation efforts that escalated beginning in 1931. By 1932 the repatriation and deportation of Mexicans was well underway, with a reported 138,500 having been "forced or persuaded" to leave in 1931, including, for example, 6,400 from Phoenix and over 5,000 from San Bernardino. These measure were the logical, if not inevitable, consequence of the social, political, and economic treatment of them during the previous decades. Moreover, having racialized Mexican Americans as one with Mexicans, white Americans lumped them together and treated them the same. Many would be the swept up, sometimes indiscriminately, for repatriation and deportation to Mexico—aliens and U.S. citizens, old people and children, families and parents separated from their children, the infirmed and those determined to depart with their dignity intact.[23]

Francisco Balderrama and Raymond Rodriguez reported that "labor unions, veterans' organizations, taxpayers' associations, and patriotic groups joined the chorus of protest against spending funds to assist aliens"—including the National Club of Americans for America. Officials "were incessantly bombarded with letters and petitions." Shortly, various federal programs (usually for jobs) were being locally implemented by limiting benefits to citizens and to those with first papers. With many public work projects then being operated with such prerequisites, including such a requirement enacted by California in August 1931, more pressures were added to the woes of Mexicans who were resisting deportation but who had previously declined to pursue American citizenship. Financial assistance varied widely, if and when they could get relief. For example, Texas would provide only $7.08 per family per month compared with $31.35 in California.[24]

Rodolfo Acuña describes two aspects of the repatriation movement, with one in Texas, where half the Mexican laborers worked in agriculture. Both they and displaced cotton tenant farmers were targeted for repatriation, beginning in 1927 and continuing for about seven years. The second scenario was an urban one, chiefly in the Far West and the Midwest. The Hoover administration tried to place the blame for the Depression on the alleged presence of 400,000 illegal aliens, as claimed by Secretary of Labor William Doak. Reports that federal agents were pursuing these individuals prompted local governments to target them for deportation or to pressure them to depart voluntarily, such as Los Angeles coordinator for relief C. P. Visel did in early 1931.

Those being deported principally came from Los Angeles, San Diego, San Francisco, Portland, Seattle, Fairbanks, El Paso, Phoenix, Denver, Kansas City, Chicago, Detroit, Pittsburgh, New York, and New Orleans. Nine of the 15 cities, not surprisingly, were in the West. Carey McWilliams recalled how Los Angeles County justified its actions by calculating the savings in public assistance—$77,249.20 per trainload of Mexicans to the border—for a cumulative savings of $270,219.12. The county was regarded as "the hotbed of the repatriation movement." Between 1931 and 1934 the county shipped out 12,668 Mexicans and their Mexican American children, with the support of Mexican consul Rafael de la Colina and such luminaries as the famed painter Diego Rivera initially urging voluntary departure.

Dropped at the border, many had been primed to expect aid from the Mexican government and relocation to farmlands in the interior or to their own villages. Instead the *repatriados* quickly discovered that little assistance was forthcoming. The situation at the border rapidly deteriorated, and even American groups and individuals got involved in providing aid to these abandoned souls. Official and unofficial supporters ceased encouraging people to depart, especially families that included American-born children. Between 1935 and 1938 only 3,560 were transported from Los Angeles to the border.[25]

This "repatriation nightmare" compelled Baldarrama and Rodriguez to pose the inevitable question: "How many people were actually repatriated? Hundreds, thousands, tens of thousands, hundreds of thousands, a million, two

million? In all honesty it is virtually impossible to cite a specific number. . . .
There are . . . 'guesstimates.'" Weighing the various figures released at the
time, they venture as a "reasonable" estimate that "approximately one million"
were removed or pressured into leaving, or about one-third of all Mexicans in
the United States. Another estimate suggests that, in the Southwest, half left
from Texas and one-fourth more left from just four counties in California—Los
Angeles, San Bernardino, Riverside, and San Diego. That certainly made the
repatriation "the most significant and crucial event to befall *Mexico de afuera*
residents during the twentieth century."

From a broader, more ideological perspective, the argument has been made
that the repatriation movement arose from Americans' refusal to see Mexicans
as permanent members of U.S. society, for the movement actually targeted resident aliens more so than temporary workers or illegal aliens (as Operation Wetback would do two decades later). Furthermore, the contention goes, by including Mexican Americans among those urged to leave, officials "underlined
the widely held belief that Mexican Americans had no legitimate claim to the
United States as their home country." A major study focusing on the Mexican
and Mexican American community in Los Angeles finds a void created by the
departures despite the increased number of Mexican applications for first and
final citizenship papers. Repatriation accelerated the movement of the second
generation into leadership positions within the community, although the resid-
ual impact of the upheaval was that they felt like "ambivalent Americans."[26]

By and large politically powerless at this time, most Mexican Americans
lacked the resources and experience (except for some in New Mexico) to adequately protect themselves against repatriation. As a result, many communities
both in the Southwest and Midwest would be deeply affected by the repatriation and deportation measures, especially as community leaders began to recognize that those forced to leave were not just workers but also "consumers of
goods and services who contributed to the economic well-being of the community."[27] The lesson, unfortunately, was not well learned; far too few mainstream
American individuals or groups came to their defense.

Nevertheless, there were some inspiring, climactic moments during the interwar years—events whose long-term political significance went beyond the
strikes, beyond the formation of LULAC and the various *mutualistas*, and beyond the emergence of cultural institutions revolving around music, theater,
the press, and radio. Of great significance was the April 1939 gathering in Los
Angeles of nearly 1,000 delegates, representing 73 organizations. Called El
Congreso de Pueblas de Habla Española (the Congress of Spanish-Speaking
Communities), this conference marked a "watershed in Mexican American
political history." It was symbolic of the many union-organizing efforts and
the rural-to-city-to-rural migration that helped forge region-wide lines of communication that broke down isolation and increased political acculturation.

There were also the efforts of Emma Tenayuca, Luisa Moreno, Josephina Fierro de Bright, along with Bert Corona, George Sánchez, and Edward Quevedo, to convince Mexicans and Mexican Americans of their shared fate and their need to work together in order to persuade Anglos to recognize their own role in polarizing American society. "By explicitly linking the plight of Mexican immigrants (and other Spanish-speaking workers) to Mexican Americans' own on-going struggle to gain equal rights as American citizens, [El Congreso] broke important new ground" in the struggle to incorporate immigrants and ethnic minorities into the American mainstream. The alternative outcome to incorporation was a contrary policy of continued exclusion that would with certainty convince immigrants to preserve their cultural traditions. In 1940, labor-activist Luisa Moreno, speaking about Mexican immigrants before the Los Angeles American Committee for the Protection of the Foreign Born, declared, "These people are not aliens. They have contributed their endurance, sacrifice, youth, and labor to the Southwest. Indirectly, they have paid more in taxes than all the stockholders of California's industrialized agriculture, the sugar companies and the large cotton interests that operate or have operated with the labor of Mexican workers."

With that meeting and the formation of the student organization Mexican American Movement, Mexican Americans stood on the threshold of activism, a political counterpart to the numerous strikes launched by Mexican and Mexican American workers across the West during the depths of the Depression and symbolized by their participation in UCAPAWA and the labor action against CalSan (California Sanitary Canning Company) four months after the Los Angeles meeting. The convening of El Congreso had clearly highlighted the reality that Mexican Americans were still in the process of exploring how to explode the myth of their political docility. Unfortunately, the almost vigilante-style hostility by the Associated Farmers (AF), the exclusion of agricultural and related workers from federal guarantees of the right to collective bargaining, the outbreak of the Second World War, and the extensive use of braceros (contract laborers) starting in 1942 stymied their efforts. Together, these developments put on hold both the labor-focused and the politically focused struggles that had begun to take shape by the end of the interwar era. During the war Mexican Americans in Texas and California continued the battles to secure equal rights. They had limited success, but the precedents for continued activism were evident. Anticipating the trend a few years after the war, Carey McWilliams recognized that, by 1940, "the myth of the docility of Mexican labor had been thoroughly exploded"—even if later historians were slow to recognize the accuracy of McWilliams's observation.[28]

Thus, by the end of the 1930s, the Mexican and Filipino repatriation movements had run their course, and the 1939 Congreso had demonstrated that

Mexicans and Mexican Americans were keenly aware of the continuing discrimination they faced. Many understood that they were not yet regarded as
"white enough" to be fully accepted. Some may have believed that they would
never achieve that acceptance, whereas many who gathered in Los Angeles in
April 1939 were determined to overcome the inequalities and, in the process,
secure a higher status, better jobs outside their enclaves, and a reduction in
the discrimination directed against them.

Education, they already understood, was one key arena for this struggle. Indeed, eight years earlier, one Mexican community took a stand against segregation efforts by the Lemon Grove School District, near San Diego. And they
won. In January 1931, the all-white school board voted to segregate all 75 Mexican American children at the elementary school. The parents refused to accept
this decision, and the children boycotted classes. With the aid of the Mexican
consulate, the parents—immigrants from Mexico's Baja California—sued. On
March 11, San Diego Superior Court judge Claude Chambers ruled that the
board could not take such action because Mexicans were considered white,
and by segregating them, the board denied "the Mexican children the presence
of the American children, which is so necessary to learn the English language."
Faced with the loss of state school funds, the board chose not to appeal, and the
matter was dropped.[29]

Few recalled such positive actions from the 1930s by parents, workers, and
community activists, but many of those who then went off to war returned with
a determination to resume those movements for equal rights for immigrants,
workers, students, and women—indeed, all *mexicanos* and Mexican Americans. The struggles would be momentous, the results historic.

Darker Turns during the Interwar Years
Workers and Refugees

P EDRO PONCE WAS BORN in Cebu, in the Philippines, in 1900. He was Visayan, and when he was 22, he and 39 other young men sailed to Hawai'i. "If I'm alive, I'll be back in three years," he told his mother. He went to the Mana-maulu Plantation in Kaua'i. "The work was very heavy and we were always being made to go faster by the *luna*. Workers were only being paid ten cents an hour; one dollar per day." Two years later, labor organizer Pablo Manlapit came to the island and urged Filipinos to strike for two dollars a day. The strike was, labor historian Edward Beechert concluded, "haphazardly planned and conducted," but Ponce and other Visayans still walked out on April 1, 1924. He then joined some in a strike camp in Kapa'a, while the rest kept the strike going to the south, at Hanapepe.

Tragedy struck on September 9, when "special deputies" lined up, with machine guns, on both sides of the road in to Hanapepe. They fired on the strikers, killing 16. Four policemen were also killed. A mass arrest of strikers followed. In Kapa'a, the strikers—lacking resources, unprepared for a drawn-out work stoppage, and unable to pay any rent—were forced to build shacks on the beach and scramble for ways to keep the strike going. Meanwhile, in December, a young woman named Cresencia (no maiden name given), also Visayan, arrived with her aunt and uncle in Kaua'i. Working at first as a laundress on a plantation, she met Abe, a Tagalog-speaking *sakada*. "We couldn't understand one another's language. This man was from . . . the northern part of the Philippines. . . . I said

to him, 'You know, it doesn't make any difference if you speak to me even
slower. I still don't understand what you are talking about.' . . . [A]nd, besides
that, I didn't know the customs or character of this man." Moving up to Kapaʻa,
Cresencia began preparing food for the strikers and there met Pedro, who offered to serve as a translator between Cresencia and Abe. He persuaded the man
to give up his efforts to wed Cresencia. On May 21, 1925, police invaded the
Kapaʻa beach camp and arrested the men, ending the strike. "When they got out
of jail," Pedro recalled, "some of my companions went back to work in the sugar
plantations. Some went to work in pineapple. Others even went to America, to
the Mainland, to work there. And some went home by themselves to the Philippines." Pedro, however, married Crecensia, resumed an old skill, and opened a
barbershop in Kapaʻa that he operated for the next 50 years. Cresencia gave birth
to six children and also proved to be an effective *hilot*, or folk healer.[1]

The 1924 strike, infrequently mentioned compared to the strike of 1920, revealed the workers' deep discontent with the sugar industry, the continuing
exodus of workers as management tried to shift away from a reliance on mostly
unskilled Filipino day workers, and the general collapse of unions, whose position had weakened similarly to those on the mainland during the 1920s.

The strike coincided with the passage of the Johnson-Reed Immigration Act
and discussions in Congress about cutting off Filipino immigration. On the
one hand, that debate spurred the HSPA to launch a "massive campaign" to
recruit Hawaiian-born youth to work on the plantations, claiming schools were
"over-educating" children. On the other, the strike and the congressional warning signals led to a 1926 HSPA-funded report that stressed the need for the
HSPA to address issues of housing, medical care, the quality of *lunas*, the
length of working days in the mills, and community conditions — problems that
were still not fully resolved when Filipinos went on strike one final time, again
prematurely, in April 1937, this time on Maui. The HSPA had ceased recruiting
Filipinos in 1927, but they continued to come until the Philippine government
halted the migration of workers in 1931. By then the HSPA was trying to send
some 7,200 Filipinos back to their homeland as part of that shift to Hawaiian-
born workers.

However, the story does not end on that note, for the account of the Ponces
was not just related to one of the most deadly U.S. strikes of the century — one
that is little known when compared, for example, to the Ludlow Massacre. It
highlighted the persisting labor issues during the 1920s versus the use of repatriation by business and government as an anti-union weapon to reduce the
number of unwanted workers. Those issues were still present during the 1937
strike, along with the Filipinos' continuing struggles with divisions within the
group, the responses by newcomers trying to avoid being hired as scabs, and
subsequently the Filipinos' efforts to organize, strike, and hang on at great personal cost (even when weakly organized and vulnerable to criminal syndicalist

and trespass laws and deportation—in this episode that of Pablo Manlapit). All this was part of the Filipinos' quest for higher wages, better working and living conditions, and "respect." In retrospect, the plantation strikes would have been unnecessary had the hugely rich HSPA not been blinded by its own success. "Wages were only the most immediate and direct cause of the labor unrest. Dignity and opportunity ranked equally high in the minds of workers."

The 1937 strike was the last in Hawai'i initiated by an ethnic-based union and actually took place along with the revival and expansion there of large-scale organized labor. In that year the Hawaiian Islands Federation of Labor was established, open to all races, skills, men and women, and workers in either agriculture or industry. It drew in all 29 existing Hawaiian unions. Eventually, thanks to federal legislation recognizing the right to collective bargaining, the International Longshoremen's and Warehousemen's Union (ILWU) would become the dominant umbrella labor organization in Hawai'i.[2] Consequently, while the HSPA's campaign to focus on hiring citizens over foreign workers had represented a major shift in policy after eight decades of reliance on immigrant workers, the ILWU's mid-summer Hawai'i strike in 1938 and again in 1940 likewise signified a new phase in the territory's labor history, for many Japanese, Portuguese, and Filipinos participated.

Concurrent with the period of the 1937 strike were others on the mainland—for example, the Santa Clara Valley packinghouse workers against the California Processors and Growers (CPG) in Stockton in 1937, sparking "the worst riot" in that city's history; the San Antonio pecan shellers in 1938; and the UCAPAWA employees of the California Sanitary Canning Company (Cal-San), who commenced their labor action at the end of August 1939, with Latinas playing more prominent leadership roles. All the strikes had to cope with the frustration of agriculture and related businesses being omitted from the New Deal's collective bargaining legislation together with the combined efforts of growers' and packers' associations to sabotage all unionization and collective bargaining.[3]

Two other developments coursing through the decade are worth noting here because they had long-term consequences for the West. First, intense anti-Semitism and anti-immigration sentiment hampered efforts to bring to America the exodus of European refugees trying to flee the Nazis once Hitler became chancellor of Germany in January 1933. In the end, too few refugees were admitted. Second, relations with Japan steadily deteriorated, and war preparations were already under way in Hawai'i by 1939. In fact, at least two years earlier, sociologist William Carlson Smith reported that in Hawai'i "the military men talk much about an inevitable war with Japan and discrimination against the Japanese, be they alien or citizen."[4] However, no Japanese spies were uncovered apart from those attached to the consulate. These two groups would pay dearly for the fears of the American public, the paranoia among military and political leaders, the manipulative campaigns for action by special-interest groups and various newspapers in the West, and a president whose prejudices and failure of will fostered an exceedingly calculated leadership at the expense (at the very least) of Jews and Japanese. We cover the dilemma of the Jewish refugees in this chapter and take up the issue of the Japanese in chapter 29.

The repatriation of Mexicans was traumatic principally across the Southwest and in parts of the Midwest, but it may not have elicited much of a reaction outside their communities, for the Mexicans were still an unfamiliar people to most others. So, too, moves to pressure Filipinos to leave occurred along the Pacific Coast (and in a few other locations, particularly Chicago), but here, also, the small size of that population meant that the deportations drew sparse attention from most others. Congressional proposals to impose further sweeping curbs on immigration—which might have called attention to the nation's increasing fears of "foreigners"—had nearly succeeded in March 1931.[5] Events kept that issue alive, because if the combination of deportations and repatriation was one strategy for closing the golden door, refusing to modify the laws to save refugees in the face of impending international disaster was certainly another. Although the American tradition of asylum was acknowledged, the Act of 1924 and the National Origin System contained no distinct provisions for such persons. In fact, Roger Daniels points out, "In American immigration law there [had been] no distinction between refugees and other immigrants, and the word *refugee* does not appear on the statute books until 1934."[6]

Within four months of Adolf Hitler coming to power in January 1933, massive book burnings took place in Germany, and the assault on free expression and what came to be labeled "degenerate art"—especially by Jews—alarmed German artists and intellectuals. An exodus was underway by springtime. Within two years an estimated 80,000 Germans had left the country, four-fifths of them Jews. By 1937 approximately 135,000 Germans had emigrated, and about 10,000 scientists had fled by 1939. Ordinary citizens and businessmen, along with professors, artists, musicians, writers, and others—from Germany, then Austria, and then Czechoslovakia and elsewhere—were moving to what they believed would be safe havens elsewhere in Europe. And they eagerly sought American visas. President Roosevelt scarcely responded to appeals urging a more rapid processing by consuls to ensure that the full annual German quota of 25,957 would be filled. The president "simply did not want to interfere or even to know what was really going on."

In the fiscal years from July 1, 1932, to June 30, 1942, there were 121,574 Germans (and Austrians beginning in 1937) admitted as quota immigrants, the majority of them Jews (see Country of Birth, table 3.9). That number amounted to less than 46 percent of the available quota slots during a period when the

United States experienced four years with emigration exceeding admissions (table 3.8).[7] Legislation to ease the admission of refugees never left congressional committees, and when Roosevelt called for an international conference in 1938 at Evian, France, no policy changes were envisioned. Nor were any made when the Nazis burned the synagogues four months later (November 1938). Three months passed, and Senator Robert Wagner and eventually Congresswoman Edith Nourse Rogers introduced bills to admit 20,000 German children over a two-year period. Roosevelt told his wife that she could speak to the measure, "but it is best for me to say nothing." In hearings, Secretary of State Cordell Hull based his opposition to the bill on the grounds that it would require more personnel and "additional office space."[8]

A *Fortune* magazine public opinion poll in March 1938 reported that 41 percent of respondents believed Jews had too much power; four months later another of its polls found 67 percent opposed to admitting additional refugees. In April 1939, 83 percent felt that way and merely 8.7 percent supported the idea. Tennessee congressman James Taylor dismissed "this refugee bunk," arguing that it was "just another scheme to bring additional thousands here who are not wanted in Europe." It was in that climate that Roosevelt allowed the Wagner-Rogers bill to die and also refused to intervene in May 1939 as the world watched the SS *St. Louis* steam up the East Coast with over 900 persons. Predominantly Jews, they were desperate for a haven, and most held valid but not yet eligible U.S. visas. Persistent anxiety due to the sluggish economy together with anti-Semitism—which was particularly evident in State Department and consular services and publicly in major radio programs—proved far too potent a mixture for the president to risk his political capital. Still, six months earlier, in late 1938, Roosevelt had, in fact, ordered that six-month visitors' visas be reissued semi-annually to some 15,000 political refugees currently in the country. In the summer of 1940 he would order that the processing of visas be expedited for individuals of "superior intellectual attainment [and] of indomitable spirit," who had been able to escape to Portugal, North Africa, and Shanghai. A list of 3,268 persons was drawn up, yet only 1,236 visas were used by January 1941.[9]

Based on available data, 69,123 German and Austrian Jews were admitted into the United States between 1937 and 1940; these Jews represented 46.6 percent of all Jews accepted during those years. They made up 78 percent of all those allowed in who had been born in Germany and Austria (table 3.9). Historian David Brody has offered a trenchant analysis of why American Jews did not press for changes in policies or exemptions, even the mortgaging of future quotas which had been suggested. For most of the 1930s leaders of Jewish organizations shared the widespread conviction that the quota system was satisfactory and should not be changed and that Jews should be given visas within the quota limits—even after the German takeover of Austria (Anschluss) in March 1938 and the destruction of the German synagogues eight months later. In view of the hostile public opinion polls and increasingly anti-Semitic radio programs, the leaders feared that lobbying for changes would inflame anti-Semitism and only result in further restrictions.

Brody argues that Jews focused on helping the needy *at home* more than on the rescue of refugees abroad. Others feared job competition, preferring anti-German boycotts and demonstrations. It was also assumed (rather erroneously at this point) that many German Jews would bring Yiddish culture with them and that American Jews would be identified with such Jewish "aliens," undermining their own efforts to achieve Americanization and acceptance. Jewish leaders urged refugees to go to Palestine.

Thus, a hostile climate, combined with economic and political anxieties and misgivings, silenced Jewish efforts to obtain policy modifications and hobbled their assistance to refugees until the unfolding catastrophe became widely known and could no longer be ignored. Jewish attitudes began shifting to a more global perspective and a sense of a shared fate among Jews. Such would be the case in the West, too, although the arrival there of predominantly secular Jewish refugees made the task of resettlement in the short run much easier.[10]

It is not certain from immigration records just how many of those who fled the Nazis in Germany, Austria, and elsewhere in Europe and were admitted to the United States then moved on to the western states and territories. Several factors came into play. One calculation is that of all those who did migrate (about 100,000), "between January 1933 and December 1941 almost eight thousand were academics and probably another fifteen hundred or so were artists, cultural journalists, or free floating intellectuals." Although Los Angeles did not present a great attraction for many refugees, the region's climate, job opportunities (especially the draw for so many artistic and literary refugees of the prominently Jewish/European leadership in Hollywood), the critical number of émigrés and immigrants already present, and a Jewish community approaching 100,000 by the end of the 1930s held some appeal. Most of the prominent Jewish refugees were secular Jews—and so were many of those American Jews who had earlier relocated to the West. Newcomers settled where Jews were establishing community footholds. Max Vorspan and Lloyd Gartner indicate that 94,700 Jews resided in three newer clusters: Beverly Hills, Hollywood, and the neighborhood of Beverly–Wilshire–West Central Los Angeles. Together, these newer communities made for a powerful magnet, and among those refugees who did come, it was said that they had been "exiled in paradise." Kevin Starr suggests that as many as 10,000 émigrés relocated to Los Angeles and that half of them were Jews. Vorspan and Gartner report 2,500 in 1939, with 1,500–2,000 refugee families by 1942.[11]

And yet, while many leading European figures settled in the Los Angeles area, others went to places as diverse as Seattle, Portland, San Francisco, and Salt Lake City, where there were a host of Jewish organizations. For example, in addition to the Jewish defense associations, such as the American Jewish Committee and American Jewish Congress, which monitored pro-Nazi groups, there were assistance agencies, including the Jewish Welfare Fund, B'nai B'rith, Jewish Social Services Bureau, the Portland Committee on Émigrés, and the Washington Émigré Bureau. The latter raised funds and sought sponsors for refugee families. (Recall the story of Florence Flaks and her efforts to assist Jews trying to leave Germany recounted in chapter 20.) The Portland local committee processed 344 émigré cases and settled 66 persons in or near the city by March 1939 and 81 more during the first nine months of 1940. Many of these refugees had exceptional skills but no extended family to sponsor them.[12]

The émigré "community" in Los Angeles—concentrated particularly along the hillside enclaves west of Griffith Park and out to Beverly Hills, Bel Air, Brentwood, and Santa Monica—contained some of the most brilliant men and women to have fled Europe at this time. Specifically, Lawrence Weschler declared that his essay on this community—this "Weimar-on-the-Pacific"—was dedicated to "[Arnold] Schoenberg and Igor Stravinsky, Bertold Brecht and Charles Laughton, Thomas Mann and Heinrich Mann, Lion Feuchtwanger and Franz Werfel, Alma Mahler-Werfel [widow of Gustav Mahler] and Salka Viertel, and for Richard Neutra and Rudolf Schindler, Theodor Adorno and Max Horkheimer, Ernst Toch and Erich Korngold, Hanns Eisler and Mario Castelnuevo-Tedesco, Bruno Walter and Otto Klemperer, Fritz Lang and Jean Renoir, Christopher Isherwood and Aldous Huxley[, and] . . . for the scores of émigrés who, fleeing the upsurge of European fascism, . . . briefly transformed Los Angeles into one of the capitals of world culture."[13]

Composers, authors, actors, playwrights, poets, writers, architects, philosophers, directors, and others joined those who would come to be regarded as giants of cinema, such as Ernst Lubitsch, Billy Wilder, William Wyler, and Otto Preminger and stage director Max Reinhardt. Of course, many clung to each other and failed to integrate into Los Angeles society. Others could not wait to return to Europe and its perceived superior cultural environment, which they regarded as rich both in ideas and in the "continuous context of anticipation of ideas and culture." By returning to Europe, they believed they would escape what conductor Henri Temianka described as Los Angeles's "unlimited indifference and passive benevolence toward anything and anybody"—or what composer Ernest Krenek called "the echolessness of the vast American expanses." Still others found themselves unable to adapt vocationally or cope with the downward mobility, a phenomenon described by some of them as producing the "dachshund effect": Two dachshunds meet in Santa Monica, and one assures the other, "Here, it's true, I'm a dachshund, but in the old country I was a Saint Bernard!"[14]

Adjustments involved musicians required to join unions, medical and dental professionals needing more training, lawyers facing extensive reorientation to a largely different legal system, writers adapting to a new cultural milieu, and various artistic individuals having to accommodate to the rather unique scriptwriting and musical composition demands of Hollywood—what one composer referred to as the American preference for "mindless" "tunes." While the adjustment of many to Los Angeles was marred by anxiety about family members left behind, there was also the struggle to find Americans willing to sponsor newcomers by posting bonds, often for persons they did not know. That compelled the émigrés to move out of what was often an insular lifestyle. By the late 1930s, the efforts by Jewish community groups to raise funds met with complications: anti-Semitism remained widespread, remnants of the Ku Klux Klan and even some pro-Nazi groups were known, and organizational and ideological divisions split Jewish communities. The latter problem revolved around such matters as the degree of concern that should be directed toward local versus international affairs; pro- and anti-Zionism; socialists opposed to conservatives; traditionalists versus the more Reformed Jews or even secular Jews; men's B'nai B'rith lodges and emerging women's groups; Sephardics apart from Ashkenazis; civic activism as opposed to the quest for internal unity; and, finally, the continuing uncertainty about how assertive to be—how best to lobby for policy changes in a climate tainted by hostile public opinion and reticent political leaders.[15]

Nevertheless, there were many refugees who did obtain employment in Hollywood, or who acquired teaching jobs at local universities or positions with the Los Angeles Philharmonic, or who were able to resume their professions, as did architect Richard Neutra, playwrights Bertolt Brecht and Lion Feuchtwanger (also a poet), and author Frederick Kohner. (Kohner's 1957 novel, based on his daughter's experiences growing up, embodied the "quintessential California girl" in print and film: Gidget.) And, suggests Weschler (perhaps wryly), in terms of one other aspect of their impact, we still have "one of the very emblems of the Southern California lifestyle," psychiatry, "which originally arrived on the scene on the couches of fleeing émigrés."

The "so-called Weimar colony" did fade by the 1950s, due to aging, deaths, emigration, and the harassment of McCarthy-era investigations, but its significance remains. The human crisis created by the rise of Nazism reached across America to the West, and the impact of this immigrant population would be felt in a number of western communities, leaving elements of an enduring cultural legacy.[16]

CHAPTER TWENTY-NINE

Aliens and Race Issues on the Eve of the Second World War

AMERICANS MAY HAVE BEEN isolationist during the 1930s, but there also existed the long-expressed fear that a war with Japan was inevitable. Japan's invasion of Manchuria and its rejection of the 1922 naval arms limitation agreement, both in 1934, and its rejection again in early 1936 set President Roosevelt's course toward anticipation of a possible war with Japan. Germany's invasion of Poland in September 1939 and the fall of France the following June compelled Roosevelt to take precautionary steps that included enacting the first peacetime draft in U.S. history, obtaining additional defense appropriations (which had been raised in 1936 and which enormously impacted the western economy),[1] instituting the Lend Lease program with England, curbing the sale of iron, steel, and other strategic materials to Japan, and signing alien registration legislation to thwart possible fifth-column activities and monitor non-citizen residents.

The Alien Registration Act of June 28, 1940, also known as the Smith Act (54 Stat. 670), had three principal parts. First, it explicitly prohibited "any persons" from influencing "the loyalty, morale, or discipline of the military or naval forces," counseling disloyalty among military personnel by any means, or advocating the overthrow of the government or organizing any group with that goal. Second, within five years of entering the United States, any aliens involved in such activities, or caught assisting the entry of illegal aliens, or violating restrictions regarding arms possession, would be deportable. Also, if foreigners were convicted more than once "at any time after entry" of violating the above provisions, they would be deportable. Third, Title III of the act required all foreigners to register and be fingerprinted in order to obtain a visa, and it mandated that all aliens, "now or hereafter," 14 and older and in the country 30 days or longer, be registered and fingerprinted. Adults would register for younger children, who would be fingerprinted upon reaching the age of 14. All aliens had to go to a post office for the registration form, and address changes had to be reported within five days.

The outcome of this registration process in 1940 by nationality is not readily available, but the report by state totals reveals that whereas 65 percent of the foreign born in the West lived in California and Texas in 1940, 76 percent of registered aliens resided there, suggesting a greater number of non-naturalized foreign born could be found in those two states than elsewhere in the West. Three years later the percentage of aliens in those two states had fallen to 69 percent, principally due to the drop in California, which was likely the consequence of the removal of most Japanese from the state and the 81,243 naturalizations during the intervening years. However, as the Immigration and Naturalization Service's June 1943 report indicates, the total number of aliens in the West had gone up by over 53,700 since 1940, raising the West's share of resident aliens to over 22 percent (see Tables 3.10 and 3.11).

Usaburo Katamoto was born in Japan in 1896, the son of a boatbuilder. In 1910, at age 13, he migrated to Hawai'i and eventually began working in his father's boat shop in Honolulu. In 1922 he acquired his own shop and two years later was hired to build and repair boats for the Hawaiian Tuna Packers. During the 1920s Usaburo also married, had five children, and joined the Kakaako Japanese Community Association in his immediate neighborhood, later becoming its vice-president. That neighborhood, near Punchbowl Street, "was like a Japanese camp," he recalled, and most men there were fishermen, often specializing in particular catches. "And, the boat builders those days, you can say all Japanese because other nationality can't stand that hard work." He acquired a second boat shop next door; business was going well, and even "the inspectors were very easy on us." When the work on a boat was completed, the new owners celebrated, and the builders were commonly thrown into the water. That, explained Usaburo, was why he never bothered to buy a good watch!

"It was Sunday, December 7. Morning time. We [Japanese] were supposed to get first aid graduation at that Kokusai Theatre. . . . [T]hen the graduation ceremony don't start because, you know, plenty fires on; they say that enemy plane. We felt that the Japanese attack but we didn't want to say, you know.

"Somebody says, 'No, that's the U.S. Army taking target practice.' Well, it didn't look like that. It's more real stuff, you know. Then a plane came from Diamond Head [east] side of town and went over the city.

"Some say, 'Eh, that plane don't look like U.S.'s plane 'cause the body is shorter. . . . A different shape.' We can see that Japanese flag mark on the body.

So you know it's got to be real attack." The police told them to remain until they were escorted home. He was then questioned about where he had been the night before. He had attended a wedding party, which he left early. "Any way, my story true; they didn't bother me for a while after that."

He resumed working at his dry dock and was even given a submarine to repair. "Then weeks passed and everything was calm down." That's when two FBI agents came to his work place and took him to their office. His wife was already there, but they sent her home. "They showed me what they holding me for. Had all that papers. And I just glanced at it, you know. My brother was in the Japanese navy and just pre-war, you see, Japanese tanker used to come in quite a bit . . . his friends come and visit us . . . and congregate at the Japanese consul. That sort of records were held by FBI office . . . typed all out, you know. They say, 'We are holding you for this.' Well, there's nothing we can say about it. Just about everybody else been getting pulled in, . . . so I wasn't any excited. Was kinda expecting it. . . . As soon as December 7 attack, that afternoon, they start pulling people in already. From then on, every day, you know, mostly every week, they got so many pulled in. So when they got to me, an FBI says, 'Where you been hiding?' I say, 'No, I wasn't hiding. I just been working.'"

Usaburo was not permitted to see his family and was held for several days. The FBI agents were expecting to release him. "I thought so, too," but instead they transferred him to Sand Island, in the harbor, and then to the mainland, Angel Island. From there he and other Japanese were shipped to Fort Sam Houston, Texas, and from there to an army prisoner camp in southern Texas, and finally to Santa Fe, where he remained until the war ended. Only then was he placed on a troop ship bound for Hawai'i.

"When I get home, it was good to see the family. [A] few of my friends and my kids and wife was waiting at the pier. We shake hand and it was good. But was just—nothing special. We expected all those things. The only thing I felt was that we lost a good three years. In fact, three years and ten months. . . . [W]hen I come back I see all my friends made big money and sitting pretty. . . . They made easy money and sure made good fortune. You know, before the war, I was intend to go back Japan. See, my first son was there already. But after the war, the idea of going back Japan is out already."[2]

Shikata ga nai—"it can't be helped." Loosely put: that's the way the ball bounces.

In one part of the conclusion to his account of Franklin D. Roosevelt's handling of the Japanese and Japanese American issue, historian Greg Robinson notes that "Roosevelt failed to transcend the prejudice around him in his direction of public policy." Robinson had opened his work with a key assessment, namely that "Franklin Roosevelt's view of Japanese Americans as immutably foreign and dangerous was a crucial factor in his approval of the internment." The formation of Roosevelt's thinking began early in the century, following Japan's defeat of Russia and Roosevelt's mounting concern over Japan's naval power. After that came the writings of Homer Lea (1909, 1914) predicting war with Japan because of the presence of Japanese immigrants and their "social and legal exclusion." In fact, Navy strategists feared that the 1913 California Alien Land Act might actually be used as a pretext by Japan to declare war. Lea's second book further fed Assistant Secretary of the Navy Roosevelt's "perception that Japanese immigrants were the source of U.S. conflict with Japan."

Lothrop Stoddard's 1920 book, *The Rising Tide of Color against White World Supremacy*, focused on "the racial difference of Japanese Americans as an innate source of danger." In an interview shortly before Stoddard's book appeared, Roosevelt had expressed support for the dispersal of newcomers to rural areas and their rapid Americanization in order to discourage their self-segregation in urban colonies. Roosevelt said in a 1923 article that Japanese should be excluded, "on racial grounds, from equal citizenship." He asserted that Americans "do not want non-assimilable immigrants as citizens, nor do they desire any extensive proprietorship of land without citizenship." Roosevelt reiterated these ideas in 1925, believing that a racially based explanation would be more acceptable to the Japanese because "they would feel the same repugnance and objection to having thousands of Americans settle in Japan and intermarry with the Japanese as I would feel in having large numbers of Japanese come over here and intermarry with the American population." He regarded it as a matter of "the undesirability of mixing the blood of the two people" and a threat to the social and cultural cohesion of a nation.[3]

During his first year as president, Roosevelt had the State Department investigate possible espionage along the West Coast. In January 1934, he had been informed by the California and Oregon congressional delegations that any easing up of immigration policy regarding the Japanese would have significant political consequences. By spring 1936, Roosevelt was concerned about possible fifth columnists in the Japanese community.

Army planners had long feared the loyalty of Japanese in Hawai'i should there be an invasion. A 1933 report by the military concluded that Issei and Nisei displayed such Japanese racial traits as "moral inferiority" and, summarizes Robinson, "fanaticism, duplicity, and arrogance." The report declared that they posed a threat to the American character of Hawai'i, that a majority would be disloyal to the United States, and that many would sabotage the defense of Oahu. A Navy report in May 1936 focused on security issues, given the contacts in Hawai'i between crews on Japanese commercial vessels and Japanese residents. Such staff personnel had relatives on the islands, delivered mail, and visited Japanese businesses, temples, and schools. "In fact," the report claimed, "every effort . . . appears to be deliberately calculated to advance Japanese nationalism." Roosevelt's momentous response was that anyone in Hawai'i meeting with such individuals "should be secretly but definitely identified and his or her name placed on a special list of those who would be the first to be placed in a concentration camp in the event of trouble." Roosevelt appeared to accept the military's position "that the Japanese-American community in Hawai'i constituted an inherent and undifferentiated threat to national security" and "that Japanese Americans ["as appendages of Japan,"] whether alien or U.S.-born, were potentially disloyal." In order to ensure the security of Hawai'i, he condoned extraordinary measures.

The president then learned that military intelligence had long been gathering a list of Japanese American "suspects," a list that included teachers, merchants, and others simply because they were prominent in the Japanese community.[4] And yet, in November 1940, the FBI issued its own assessment of the Hawaiian situation and utterly rejected the previous military intelligence reports. They found few who were suspect—mostly recent arrivals—and concluded that the Issei were decidedly "American in ideals and principles" and their Nisei children had little sympathy for Japan and were clearly loyal to the United States. Nonetheless, by early 1941 a master list had been assembled with information on about 2,000 Japanese in Hawai'i and on the mainland who were to be arrested in the event of war. Expanded by information gathered from a raid on the Japanese consulate in Los Angeles, the final "ABC list" of enemy aliens was divided into those viewed as (a) "immediately dangerous," (b) "potentially dangerous," and (c) just suspect.

Not satisfied, in the fall of 1941, Roosevelt secretly hired John Carter to establish a network of agents among several alien populations. Carter selected Curtis B. Munson to investigate the Japanese. Munson's October 1941 report stated that Japanese Americans "will be quiet, very quiet," except for some paid agents "and the odd fanatical Jap." In Hawai'i, he added, they were "98% loyal to the US," and he stressed his greater concern about violence *against* the Japanese. Overall, the Issei, having settled in America, have only a weakened loyalty to Japan and the Nisei (leaving out the Kibei) even less. The Nisei "are pathetically eager to show their loyalty," and the Issei appeared intensely determined to avoid "concentration camps or irresponsible mobs."[5]

At that time Roosevelt requested that the Census Bureau provide the residential location of Japanese based on the 1940 census. (It eventually provided information, but one level removed from specific house addresses.) The president's suspicions extended "to the entire Japanese American community" despite the FBI and Munson reports that there was no "Japanese problem." By late November 1941, Roosevelt's concerns about sabotage and the immediate apprehension of "suspects" were tied to his long-held beliefs that Japanese Americans were simply dangerous.[6]

While these developments do reveal Roosevelt's biases, they must be set against the views of those who shaped his policy options, including Secretaries Henry Stimson and Frank Knox and his military leaders, for they were pressing for action. Few, however, initially advocated something as drastic as removal, relocation, and incarceration because it was unprecedented to take such actions against U.S. citizens where no charges had been brought. Roger Daniels, the foremost authority on this history, maintains that Roosevelt's pre-1942 attitudes did not pre-determine what followed, given developments in California and the political and military pressures Roosevelt faced once war actually began. Other pre-conditions included decades of racism against Asians, resentment of Japanese mobility, the feasibility of action because of their concentrated communities, and the external threat posed by Japan itself, which had convinced military leaders that a corresponding internal threat existed.

Daniels stresses, "Only if we understand that the racist image of the Oriental in the American mind was so strong that many otherwise sensible people could literally believe *anything* about him will we begin to understand why Americans reacted to the Japanese as they did." Once Pearl Harbor was attacked, in fact by December 11, officials high up in the administration were already voicing demands for a mass incarceration. Finally, the media were rampant with utterly false, derogatory, misleading, and inflammatory stories, many of which had been allegedly spread by military officers. They share responsibility for re-aligning the thinking of a great many Americans along the Pacific Coast to the effect that Japanese Americans posed a dire threat. President Roosevelt may not have disseminated those ideas, but he also did nothing to temper them and nothing to protect their victims.[7]

Ironically, the *Honolulu Advertiser* ran a headline on November 7, 1941, "Japanese May Strike over the Weekend." They had it all correct; they were just off by exactly one month.[8]

FIGURE 1. The "melting pot" in Hawai'i: children in native dress. From left, British, Filipino, Korean, Hawaiian, "Uncle Sam," Japanese, and Portuguese. Photograph by Tai Sing Loo. Bishop Museum, Honolulu.

FIGURE 2. "Anastacio Gayten, 101 years old, still laying bricks. Born in 1846, he came to the U.S. in 1860 and was still working in San Antonio in September 1947. Credited hard work and lots of sleep for his longevity." *San Antonio Light* Collection, University of Texas Institute of Texan Cultures at San Antonio, No. L-3742-A.

FIGURE 16. Mexican American women working at sawmill during World War II. NAU.PH.97.33.7.3, David Rodriquez Estrella, Los Recuerdos del Barrio en Flagstaff Collection, Cline Library, Northern Arizona University.

FIGURE 17. Contraband seized in raids on German American homes, San Antonio, February 1942. *San Antonio Light* Collection, University of Texas Institute of Texan Cultures at San Antonio, No. L-2910-A.

FIGURE 16. Mexican American women working at sawmill during World War II. NAU.PH.97.33.7.3, David Rodriquez Estrella, Los Recuerdos del Barrio en Flagstaff Collection, Cline Library, Northern Arizona University.

FIGURE 17. Contraband seized in raids on German American homes, San Antonio, February 1942. *San Antonio Light* Collection, University of Texas Institute of Texan Cultures at San Antonio, No. L-2910-A.

FIGURE 14. Members of the League of United Latin American Citizens, Phoenix(?), Arizona, June 1949. NAU.PH.85.3.51.236, Fronske Collection, Cline Library, Northern Arizona University.

FIGURE 15. Orange packers, Orange Belt Fruit Distributors, including Chonita Veyna and Marcella Gomez, Orange County, California, ca. 1940. Anaheim Public Library.

FIGURE 11. Lloyd Frank and Julius Meyer built their storefront business in the 1870s into this 13-story department store, the fourth largest in America, 1932. Walter Boychuk Collection, Oregon Historical Society, OrHi43189.

FIGURE 12. Tuulikki Paananen, Finnish entertainer, at Finn Hall, Mullan, Idaho, 1920s. Leona Lampi Hassen Photographs, Immigration History Research Center, University of Minnesota.

FIGURE 13. Italian American members of the San Antonio Missions baseball team sharing a spaghetti lunch, June 1939. *San Antonio Light* Collection, University of Texas Institute of Texan Cultures at San Antonio, No. L-2189-B.

FIGURE 9. Arthur Gorian, Armenian immigrant and proprietor of the Magnolia Market, San Bernardino, California, 1940s. Courtesy of the California Room, San Bernardino Public Library, San Bernardino, California.

FIGURE 10. "Charles Ruffo holds handmade boots in his San Antonio shop, a trade he learned from his Italian father," March 1941. *San Antonio Light* Collection, University of Texas Institute of Texan Cultures at San Antonio, No. L-2684-B.

FIGURE 7. Henry Thiele, German-born chef, caterer, and restaurateur, Portland, ca. 1930. Henry Thiele Photographs Collection, Oregon Historical Society, OrHi105640.

FIGURE 8. Julius Strzelczyk moving bale of cotton grown on farm of Mike Pieniazek, Atkins, Texas, 1939. *San Antonio Light* Collection, University of Texas Institute of Texan Cultures at San Antonio, No. L-2198-A.

FIGURE 5. Leandro Avila, president of the International Pecan Shellers Union, under arrest, San Antonio, January 1938. *San Antonio Light* Collection, University of Texas Institute of Texan Cultures at San Antonio, L-1662-C.

FIGURE 6. Pecan crackers E. Gonzales (*second from left*) and Pete Torres (*right*), San Antonio, January 1938. *San Antonio Light* Collection, University of Texas Institute of Texan Cultures at San Antonio, No. L-1739-E.

FIGURE 3. Mexican fieldworker's home, Imperial Valley, California, 1937. Bancroft Library, University of California.

FIGURE 4. Choke setters, Weyerhauser Timber Co., Washington State. So many lumber workers were Scandinavian in the 1910s and 1920s that "Scandinavian" was said to be the language of lumbering there. University of Washington Libraries, Special Collections, C. Kinsey 4812.

FIGURE 1. The "melting pot" in Hawai'i: children in native dress. From left, British, Filipino, Korean, Hawaiian, "Uncle Sam," Japanese, and Portuguese. Photograph by Tai Sing Loo. Bishop Museum, Honolulu.

FIGURE 2. "Anastacio Gayten, 101 years old, still laying bricks. Born in 1846, he came to the U.S. in 1860 and was still working in San Antonio in September 1947. Credited hard work and lots of sleep for his longevity." *San Antonio Light* Collection, University of Texas Institute of Texan Cultures at San Antonio, No. L-3742-A.

FIGURE 22. Four Nisei women from Heart Mountain relocation camp meet with New York City women to plan resettlement through Temple Young People's Fellowships, July 1946. Bancroft Library, University of California.

FIGURE 23. "Our Fond Memories." 1944 Manzanar Relocation Center High School Yearbook. Author's collection.

FIGURE 24. Uncaptioned photograph, inside back cover of 1944 Manzanar Relocation Center High School Yearbook. Author's collection.

FIGURE 25. Thanksgiving dinner for displaced persons family, International Institute, San Francisco, 1952. Immigration History Research Center, University of Minnesota.

CHAPTER THIRTY

Interwar or Interlude?
Twilight and Dawn in the West

*T*HE INTERWAR YEARS were a time of opportunity and challenge for foreign-born residents in the West. Although the 1920s seemed to hold out great promise, especially in California, the economy was actually undergoing important changes, particularly in terms of mechanization and strong fluctuations in agricultural markets. Together with the weakening (and uneven successes) of unions, the economic trends presented foreigners with some difficult choices about relocating to urban centers. Yet, the imposition of immigrant quotas also forced many to decide whether to return to their homelands or settle down in America. Of course, those born in the Western Hemisphere were exempt from the quota restrictions, and the proportion of newcomers admitted from the Americas rose sharply. Still, it was more than the Depression and the evaporation of many economic opportunities that drove numerous immigrants to leave during the 1930s. For example, while tens of thousands were seeking to escape from Germany, nearly 22,100 Germans and Austrians expressed their intent to return to their native land just between 1934 and 1940 (table 3.9).

Stricter enforcement of immigration regulations, especially the LPC provision ("Likely to become a Public Charge"), local policies limiting welfare assistance and public works jobs to citizens and naturalized foreigners (or, in some cases, to those holding first papers, too), and the campaigns to repatriate Mexicans, their American-born children, and Filipinos all had a strong chilling effect—persuading many other individuals to depart voluntarily without further pressures. While many estimates place the exodus of Mexicans and Mexican

Americans at about 500,000–600,000 — and even as high as one million — just the five southwestern states (Texas, Colorado, New Mexico, Arizona, California) lost over 182,000 Mexican immigrant residents between 1920 and 1940, a figure that does not include those entering and departing between census counts, those emigrating informally, and those who entered illegally and departed, which became a significant new issue during the 1920s.

The resulting portrait of immigrants in the West during these years is therefore a mixed one. The entire population of the West rose by 50 percent, but the foreign-born population dropped by 13 percent (to 1.79 million). In addition, the impact of laws, depression, repatriation, and a more rapid influx of native-born Americans was evident in the shrinking proportion of foreign born: from just over one-seventh (14.9 percent) in 1920 to one-twelfth (8.6 percent) two decades later.[1] However, the decreases in most states in the number of foreign born averaged a huge 36 percent but were largely offset by the 22 percent increase in California. (California's nearly 924,900 foreign born amounted to more than half of *all* immigrants residing in the West.) (See table 3.12.)

At the same time, the percentage of naturalized white persons rose in every state by an average of almost 12 points. Overall, the percentage of naturalized individuals in the West went from about 41 percent to nearly 54 percent. This increase was not simply the result of aliens leaving and citizens remaining, or of those remaining and seeking citizenship or even first papers in greater numbers. Together with the drops in the general foreign-born populations in every state except California, the *number* of naturalized persons actually declined along with the number holding first papers.[2] How to explain this? California offset what was happening in the rest of the region, for its number of new citizens rose by a spectacular 169,340, while falling elsewhere by more than 10,900. Those holding first papers rose by over 32,400 in California and everywhere else declined by nearly that same amount. Although the expectation would have been that immigrants would wish to provide such evidence of their Americanizing status in order to secure welfare assistance or jobs, the overall figures outside of California do not corroborate that. Instead, the answer lies in the fact that the number of people naturalized and present in 1940 fell but not as much as did the total number of foreign born. As a result, the percentage of naturalized persons increased. Only in California and Hawai'i (and slightly in Arizona) did the actual number of new citizens increase over that of 1920. Aliens and naturalized persons left during the Depression. (See table 3.13.)

Tracking 25 specific immigrant groups across the West from Europe, the Americas, and Asia reveals, not surprisingly, that 21 groups experienced a loss of population (by an average of more than one-fifth), with increases reported only among those born in the Netherlands, Poland, Russia (USSR), and Canada (the latter up 16.5 percent).[3] (See table 3.14.)

On the eve of the Second World War several points were clear: First, Mexican immigrants now vastly outnumbered all other immigrant groups in the West. Indeed, it was the changing circumstances of Mexicans that most affected the foreign-born profile of the West. During the 1920s their numbers in the West rose by more than one-quarter (to 557,000—with the most dramatic growth being the 124 percent jump in California), before the Depression years witnessed a 39 percent collapse in the number of Mexicans. Reflecting the movement by Mexicans (voluntary and repatriation), the steepest drops in the foreign born took place in three southwestern states (Texas, Arizona, New Mexico), together with the lowest persisting rates of naturalization. In fact, 46 percent of the entire drop in foreign born in the West during the 1930s was a consequence of the Mexican exodus (tables 3.12, 3.13, 3.15, 3.18).

Second, several traditional foreign-born groups continued to be numerically prominent besides Canadians and Mexicans: the British, Scandinavians, Germans and Austrians, and Italians (tables 3.14, 3.18).

Third, the contradictory trends of the two decades emerge with the second generation. Nationally, they rose by one-seventh during the 1920s and then fell during the 1930s (22.7 million to 25.9 million to 23.2 million). In the West, they increased by nearly one-fifth during the 1920s (19 percent) and by almost nine points more during the 1930s (combined, 29 percent for 1920–1940). In reality, all the mainland states experienced decreases in the 1930s that were once more offset by California's increase (see table 3.16). Only California experienced growth in both decades—an astounding 631,000 persons (in addition to the 167,240 increase in foreign born).[4] Nevertheless, because the drops during the 1930s were less than the increases during the 1920s, the fact remained that in 1940 in eight western states the second generation was still more numerous than in 1920—by 853,314 persons.[5] Only Colorado, Idaho, Montana, and Utah—all interior states—showed a net loss between 1920 and 1940 of both immigrants and the second generation, the result of attrition and immigrant emigration. The inescapable reality is that California was the engine driving much of the West's foreign-stock population increases during these interwar decades.

Finally, three additional items fill in the picture. Three-quarters of the foreign born in California resided in urban places, an indicator of the trend in every state and territory where the percentage in urban locations rose. Washington, Oregon, Texas, and Utah led with three-fifths, while at just over one-third urban, Idaho trailed (see table 3.17). Ironically, the total percentage of urban people increased (but only slightly), yet by 1940 the population of the two dozen immigrant groups examined here declined in urban areas (except among the Greeks). This held most notably for the Canadians, British, Germans, Irish, Italians, and especially Mexicans—the latter disproportionately due to the repatriations and voluntary departures. Among the net populations numbers fell, but more of those remaining were in urban locations, hence the higher percentages (table 3.18).

In terms of the gender distribution, California fell in the middle. Even as numbers declined, the trend was clearly toward more equal gender distributions. It was still close to 4:1 in Alaska, 2:1 in Nevada, and more than 1.7:1 in Hawai'i, but the drop in California from 1.53:1 to 1.2:1, though higher than the national figure, was indicative of the shift in the West (table 3.17).

And, in one final observation, and contrary to how mainlanders had perceived it, Hawai'i was soon to become indisputably linked to the mainland by circumstances of the coming war. In its unique multi-racial society we find in 1940 a 58 percent Asian majority (246,099), nearly equal to all those Asians scattered on the vast American mainland (about 254,130). Hawai'i offers an unusual anomaly because, on the one hand, it too witnessed a two-fifths decrease in its foreign-born population along with a small increase in those naturalized during the 1930s (5.6 percent), but on the other hand, the astonishing fact is that 89–90 percent of all the foreign born had taken no steps to acquire citizenship. That had been true in 1930, as it obviously had been earlier and would continue to be a decade later. The reason, of course, is that about 85 percent or more of the foreign born were not Caucasian or African; hence, virtually all were ineligible to apply. That one demographic reality created some dramatically different wartime issues for Hawai'i's Asians compared to their co-ethnics along the Pacific Coast, especially for the Japanese, who constituted 71 percent of Hawai'i's foreign born and 37 percent of its entire population in 1940.

The two decades or so between the wars were no mere interlude for immigrants and their children in the West. Their numbers and composition underwent significant changes as a result of new federal and state legislation; the onset of the Great Depression; extensive in-migrations from elsewhere in the nation; the rapid expansion of urban communities; the development and growth of numerous non-extractive industries offering a host of new employment opportunities as well as many new arenas in which immigrants and their children would play important roles; the traumatic impact of campaigns to repatriate Mexican and Filipino populations, which disproportionately impacted the West; and unfolding events across the globe that soon enveloped many nations in war, channeling new groups to the West and then, fatefully, drawing particular ones already there into the web of those international events—with consequences beyond their ability to control. I reiterate the comment made in the mid-1930s by sociologist Emory Bogardus, who observed that "up to 1928 the United States treated immigration entirely as a domestic affair." Given Japan's response to the 1924 legislation and concerns in Washington about America's Western Hemisphere neighbors, immigration was "no longer to be viewed as a purely national [that is, internal] affair."[6] World War Two would certainly make that quite evident to the American people. December 7, 1941, marked the beginning of America's war; it also represented the beginning of a new era in the history of the American West and its immigrant populations.

The evidence from between the great wars was clearly highlighted by the continued relevance of our thematic threads. In-migration remained a vital force during the 1920s, providing important human resources for much of the West, both in the region's cities and hinterlands. And it was not only a matter of immigrants but also of significant numbers of second-generation men and women (growing up or moving in) who remained closer to the immigrant experience than many older-stock Americans filtering into the West. Increased urbanization was accompanied by an increasing number and proportion of women, further evening out gender ratios. What is more, who came and where they went to were questions profoundly shaped by the critical fluctuations of the western economy, urban and rural, and just as certainly by legislation that represented turning points in U.S. history. The impact of immigration could be seen in the newcomers' continued economic visibility, in the communities they continued to nurture, and in their on-going struggles to negotiate moderate blends of Americanization and cultural preservation. Some responded to Americanization in the wake of First World War pressures, while other newcomers held onto their native cultures in the face of various uncertainties. Meanwhile, the rapidly increasing second generation was pushing headlong toward greater accommodation with American society.

Beyond the immigration-related laws and decisions of the 1920s, government policies during the 1930s—ranging from New Deal recovery schemes and collective bargaining rights to programs coercing and pressuring groups to depart for their homelands—impacted many first- and second-generation persons. Undoubtedly, the thematic threads did intersect, and *who came, to where,* and *in what* economic and political environment affected *who left* and *who remained.* Moreover, changes in policies now implicitly included an international dimension, as it became ever more evident that national immigration policies were less and less detachable from foreign policy. Immigrants soon discovered how their homeland ties could get enmeshed in that new complexity. One dimension of this turn of events was America's confrontation with the phenomenon of refugees urgently seeking havens. The efforts of many to gain admission frequently proved to be in vain, dramatic evidence that the conflicted policies of the 1930s had taken the nation well beyond exclusion of Asian laborers. Policies and attitudes had become rigid and tinged with fear, hate, and self-absorption. These dimensions of overlapping and intersecting developments, together with the dramatically shifting contexts of reception, would continue to profoundly influence the course of western history, for immigration did not cease to be a vital part of the West's development. The Second World War would make that abundantly clear.

PART 4.

America's Dilemma

RACES, REFUGEES, AND REFORMS IN AN
AGE OF WORLD WAR AND COLD WAR, 1942–1952

The late nineteenth century witnessed the dramatic opening of the West, accompanied by the shadows of the closing of America to Chinese laborers and their wives and the seizure of the Kingdom of Hawai'i by an American cabal, who then secured that nation's annexation by the United States. The century closed with an American victory and further annexations following the Spanish American War. The United States handily wrested control of the Philippines from Spain and, following the bloody suppression of Filipino resistance, gained access to a labor population there that proved to be especially valuable in Hawai'i and along the nation's Pacific Coast. At the same time, the new century was marked by remarkable expansion in both the rural and urban West as hundreds of thousands of immigrants and children of immigrants flooded the region. They were newcomers from across the borders, from distant homelands, and often in step migrations from other parts of the nation. The latter included older-stock, foreign-born, and second-generation men and women, American adventurers, entrepreneurs, farmers, and a cross-section of workers—the same as among the new arrivals.

But if for many the West during these years represented expanding horizons and novel opportunities, especially with new technologies and new media, those years likewise cast more shadows as federal and state governments enacted immigration laws, developed additional enforcement machinery, and handed down court decisions that defined a more explicit sovereignty, etched boundaries more deeply, and signaled a renewed search for some comforting homogeneity. Western states were actively involved in the efforts to control immigration, and yet we saw that such regulation led to redirection as more individuals now attempted illegal entry, particularly into the West, along with growing numbers legally admitted from Western Hemisphere countries. The quest for homogeneity appeared to be far from realization. These altered migration and settlement patterns steadily revealed an ever more diverse world in the West that was becoming part of a more urban/rural mix. In many locations were new towns, new industries, factory farms, and even countless oil wells—augurs of a new age.

The seamless webs across the western states, across economic enterprises, across varied living spaces, across a remarkable multitude of peoples and communities continued to define the West as a distinctive region—in times of prosperity and times of depression, times of peace and times of war, times of refuge and times of rejection, times of struggle for human rights and times of limits on those rights—challenging the boundaries of toleration and constitutional protections. Through all these, the new migrants did not so much make the West more different than it might have become had it been settled just by generations of native Americans. Instead, they made it more of what it had long been becoming: a world of peoples from all points across the globe.

We pick up our story here at December 7, move through the war and its impact on various Asian and European groups as well as Mexicans, and then explore the variety of changes following the war that affected immigrants and the native born in the West. We conclude with legal and policy changes in the early 1950s, building up to the 1952 omnibus Immigration and Nationality Act (I&NA), and the story of Dora Sanchez Treviño. The latter leads us to multiple issues related to immigration and ethnicity in the West, and these topics move closer to center stage over the next five decades. As with the earlier periods, these 11 years (1942–1952) saw further changes in who came, what roles they played, and how they adapted to a wartime and postwar society and to changing federal policies. Again, these changes overlap, remaining the core thematic threads of this narrative. Treviño's interesting story suggests that they will persist across the second half of the century, years that will be etched once again by the presence of an important array of both new and old groups.

CHAPTER THIRTY-ONE

Voices from America on the Eve of War

W E BEGIN ONCE MORE with the voices of immigrants and Americans in Hawai'i and in the mainland West. While a number of other personal accounts appear throughout part 4, these nine brief stories dramatically illustrate three important issues for the years from late 1941 on. They take us from Hawai'i, with Japanese and non-Japanese recollections of the Pearl Harbor attack, to the mainland and the experiences of an Issei in Washington State (Yoshitaka) and a Nisei in Oregon (Suma) before and after the attack. Yoshitaka's story speaks to the place of an immigrant's strong ties to his homeland and traditions and the consequences of those choices. Suma, a Nisei/Sansei (second- or third-generation Japanese American) woman, had the common experiences of being on the margin between cultures, compounded by the strains of war. She describes how, as a young woman caught between tradition and accommodation, she emphatically reaffirmed her American loyalty. Yet, she, too, is incarcerated. A second-generation Basque American in Oregon, Antonio offers a significant story of his rise well above his family's modest beginnings to achieve a law degree and a successful practice. He integrates into the mainstream, employs his many skills during the Second World War, and afterward resumes his practice and wins political office. He embodies one kind of the mobility that has long been part of the American Dream. Finally, we look at Angel, a Mexican American, and his recollections from post-war Texas that sharply underscore the persistent racism and discrimination against Mexicans. He struggles against practices and attitudes that long confined most Mexicans and Mexican Americans to the bottom of Southwest society, and he succeeds. His achievement in overcoming some of these hurdles represents the important post-war changes that eventually lead to the Chicano Movement of the 1960s and the fall of many old impediments to Mexican American mobility. Angel's mid-century tale takes us to the point when many minority persons (immigrant and native born) began their journeys in the second half of the twentieth century. These stories represent different generations struggling to find their place in the American West.

Samuel Lindley came to Honolulu from Indiana in 1935 to study at the university. Walking downtown at the beginning of December 1941, "I saw on the front of the railroad station . . . they had set up machine guns. And instead of facing out to the ocean . . . they were facing the street, where they figured Japanese in Hawai'i might attack the railroad station. And also there were machine guns set up in the tower of Kawaiaha'o Church . . . facing along King Street, in case of some kind of local insurrection, I suppose . . . , and my own inference [was] . . . that they were expecting some kind of local Japanese uprising . . . the Japanese were suspect."[1]

In fact, on December 7, Etsuo Sayama nearly had such an encounter. A Nisei born in Honolulu and a university graduate, he was employed at Fort Shafter (Oahu). He recalled "the hysteria and suspiciousness aimed at those of Japanese ancestry" following the attack. When he arrived at the gate to the fort later that day, "I was sent home. And the reason being that when I got to that gate, I showed my pass, but [the sentry] said, 'If I were you, go home.' 'For what?' 'Change clothes.'" Etsuo had blue clothes on, and the sentry "said, 'they got rumors that Japanese parachuters in blue were coming down . . . and they didn't know where, but that was the rumor. So you have the face of a Japanese (chuckles), and you [are] in blue.' Said, 'you know, our soldiers might get trigger happy, you walk around Fort Shafter.' So I went home, changed clothes and went back to work."[2]

Sayama was among 82,000 civilian wartime workers—one-fourth of all those employed in Hawai'i—including, for the first time, a large number of haoles (Caucasians) recruited for manual labor. That was "a unique departure from the upper class Haoles of island society."[3]

Kimiko Watanabe's experience was more tragic. Of Okinawan descent, Kimiko had been born on Maui. In 1938 she married Kiho Uyehara, a commercial fisherman, and at the time of Pear Harbor they had an infant son, Dickie. They lived in Honolulu, although Kiho was frequently out to sea, usually for about ten days at a time. A few days before the December 7, he left once more—telling Kimiko that after this catch, he would give up fishing and seek a job on land in order to be near her and the baby. On Sunday afternoon, after the attack on the harbor ended, American planes on patrol mistook Kiho's fishing boat for a Japanese vessel and strafed it, killing Kiho and two crewmen.

Kimiko learned about it the next day when the bodies were brought in. Fifty years later, remarried and with more children, she still declined to attend ceremonies at the USS *Arizona*. "No. I didn't want to go. . . . And I told Dickie, 'The United States didn't apologize to us. After they killed my husband over here, our government—they didn't apologize to us.' I didn't feel good so I didn't go."[4]

Joe Pacific's life was affected quite differently. He was born in Rome, Italy, in 1904 and, at age 17, came by himself to the United States, sponsored by a cousin in Utica, New York.[5] He began learning the shoe repair trade from his uncle and then moved to New York City and opened his own store in 1928. Like many businesses, it failed during the Great Depression. He married a German immigrant, Dora Emig, and tried his trade once more, earning $27 per week. In 1936 he saw a newsreel on Hawai'i, decided to settle there, and went by train to San Francisco. At the ticket agency, he told the agent—a guy "with a big hat and a big cigar"—that he only had $60 for a steamship ticket to Honolulu. The agent offered him steerage but added, "Don't say that you're Italian, say that you're Portuguese," because those cheap tickets were reserved "for the Hindus, Portuguese, and Colored people."

Joe arrived in Hawai'i in June 1936 and quickly explored the shoe repair scene in Honolulu. "The prices were so high. In New York we used to get nine, ten cents to fix a lady's shoe. To [repair] heels, nine, ten cents. . . . And over here they were getting fifty cents. A man's rubber heel, seventy-five cents. In New York, hey, twenty-five, twenty-six cents." He sought a loan to start his own business but could provide no security or guarantor. Following several rebuffs, he went into the National Mortgage and Finance Company. There, he met Masayuki Tokioka and Clifton Yamamoto. Joe related that a Portuguese shoemaker wanted to sell out and return to Madeira, so he needed $500 to buy out the shoemaker. Tokioka asked, "What do you got for security?" "I showed him my hands. I says, 'These are my security and I pay you back sooner than you want me to pay you back.'" Tokioka and Yamamoto laughed heartily and gave him the loan. And so began what ultimately became a chain of Joe Pacific shoe repair shops in Oahu.

By December 7, 1941, Joe's wife had come over; a daughter had been born; he owned a home and a new car; and he was already well known. Martial law was declared that same day, and the FBI took him downtown the next day to "check your papers"—one of 10,000 who had been earlier investigated. Of the 1,569 enemy aliens actually apprehended, 1,466 were Japanese. Joe was one of 25 German and Italian men held at the Sand Island Detention Center in Pearl Harbor. Many of the Japanese, Germans, and Italians who had been picked up were placed there until they were released or transferred after the facility was closed 15 months later.[6] It would be over 3 months before Joe returned home—

one of the first to be released. At first, Joe recounted, he was asked "a lot of fool-ish questions," to which he replied, "Listen, if I had any use for the government in Italy, I would have gone back. But you see, I'm here. I built a home here." He was informed that he had been detained because his German brother-in-law had written to the German consulate in San Francisco asking if he could join the German army and because Joe's wife "was talking with other German people here [in Honolulu] before the war. And she used to praise Hitler all the time. And I used to tell the woman, I says, 'Shut your mouth, because these people, [if] they find out you like this, we going to have trouble." Added the intelligence officer, "that's why we had to take you in, because [your] brother-in-law was a German, German army, [and] your wife talking like this. We figure maybe you was the same way."

Pacific said he had no idea the government had been tapping phones and opening mail. "I mind my business. I don't think about those things." But a local reporter did come by several times prior to December 7 to talk with Joe's brother-in-law. "And they used to talk so much about Hitler . . . thought for sure that Germany was beating everybody." Joe told them to go elsewhere. While he was put on Sand Island, his wife was transferred to the mainland, and he concluded that the government "had a reason" to do so. "Because if you praise somebody . . . it means that you like that party." Indeed, she also "was mixed up with" a German woman who had come to Honolulu to raise money for Germany. The Germans would gather in a bar in Waikiki. In response to Joe's urging that she get U.S. citizenship, his wife declined, replying, "Me, I'm a good German. I'm a good German."

On Sand Island, Joe had met Otto Kuehn, the only person convicted of espi-onage in Hawai'i, but Joe believed that, other than some members of the Japa-nese consulate, there were no spies living in Hawai'i. I mean, he added: "how the hell you going to spy, go against the country that give you something? If the old country give you something you wouldn't be here." "[I] emphasized to the officer, 'that's why I come over here, to better myself. And I'm bettering myself. I'm making money, and you know it.' Where are you going to find another place like this? I don't mean Hawai'i. I mean the United States in general. You're free to do what you want to do." He would eventually build a chain of seven repair shops on Oahu—and divorce his German wife.

In contrast to the challenges Joe had to overcome is the account of Toso Hase-yama. The oldest of five children, he was born in Hiroshima in 1907. Initially left with his grandparents, he joined his family in Maui in 1921 and later moved on to Honolulu, where he became a tailor. By 1937 he had located his business in downtown Honolulu. When the war began, most Issei could not profit from the wartime spending but instead suffered lost business, assets, and property, including land marked and seized for security or military purposes. Toso was among the 1,466 Japanese on the Islands who were interned, "because he was an alien, a business owner, and a leader in the local Japanese community." "In short," he recalled, "I was anti-American." He had handled the accounting for a club, the Ogata Sonjinkai, which collected donations for Japan and which he was to speedily forward to their homeland. How much? "Quite a bit in fact." "In the end, since I was a *teikokujin* [Japanese citizen] they asked me whether [I wanted] Japan to win or lose. . . . Since I had relatives in Japan and grew up in Japan . . . I said I didn't want Japan to lose. That was the end." Haseyama was sent to Honouliuli, a camp in the mountains south of Schofield Barracks on Oahu, where he was interned until February 1943. In the interim "a huge number of Filipino tailors started up [businesses]." Filipinos, Koreans, and Chinese would violate price control regulations, he claimed, "but the Japanese all were scared and wouldn't do anything" illegal.[7]

On the day Japan surrendered, August 15, 1945, "I was so sad," Haseyama said. "After all, I grew up in Japan, so my Japanese origin remains in my mind." While Americans were celebrating on that summer day, "I just cried and cried. . . . I was devastated."

Yoshitaka Watanabe would later be addressed as *jiichan* (grandfather) by his 21 grandchildren, but in 1908, 18-year-old Watanabe sailed to America to accomplish what so many other Issei planned to achieve: earn enough money to pay the taxes due on the family's lands near Japan's Mt Fuji.[8] Arriving in Seattle, he obtained work in lime quarries and restaurants, earning eight dollars per week. He never acquired the sums he had hoped for, and he returned to Japan one time only—to find a bride to share his life in America. He wed Shizue, and they returned to Seattle. They raised five children and operated a fruit and vegetable produce stand in Pike Place Market, in the heart of the city.

Yoshitaka retained a great pride in his culture, painted watercolors of Japanese scenes, practiced his Japanese calligraphy for hours, and occasionally wrote poetry. He also expressed his traditionalism through a stubborn, authoritative determination to see that his Nisei children learned about their Japanese heritage. After the public school day ended, most of his children went to Japanese language school. His three sons belonged to a judo club. His eldest, Shigeo, was showered with privilege and groomed for college. Yoshitaka forbade his children to associate with Chinese classmates during the 1930s because China and Japan were at war. Not surprisingly, he belonged to Japanese organizations—including one said to be mysterious in its purpose and called Sokokukai. He was active in the Chamber of Commerce, a farmer's group, a poetry club, and a hometown association. While war raged in China, he repeatedly contributed to a homeland war fund. Along with all that, he had converted to Christianity.

Three months after the attack on Pearl Harbor, on March 7, 1942, Yoshitaka was picked up by the FBI as an enemy alien who belonged to Sokokukai and subscribed to its magazine, *Sokoku*. Although no FBI agent at the time could read or speak Japanese, they assumed that any organization with a name that meant "Motherland" was certain to be subversive.[9] Interrogated a month later, Yoshitaka was asked which nation he wanted to see win the war; if he was required to obey the emperor; and if he believed that, upon death, the emperor became *kami* (a god), whom he was to worship. His replies were apparently not convincing, even though he denied any loyalty to Japan because America was home for his family. Six weeks later, the Alien Enemy Hearing Board determined that Watanabe "would offer no definite or convincing assurance of loyalty to the United States." On July 21, 1942, he was declared "potentially dangerous to the peace and safety of the United States" and was transferred from the INS (Immigration and Naturalization Service) facility in Montana to a U.S. Army center for enemy aliens in Louisiana.

In the meantime, the rest of his family was incarcerated in the Minidoka relocation camp in Idaho, along with 7,300 other Japanese and Japanese Americans. It was an internment camp to some, a concentration camp to others.[10] Rev. Emery E. Andrews, of Seattle's Japanese Baptist Church, moved his family to Idaho to assist his Japanese congregants there. He launched a campaign for Watanabe's freedom, vouching for his character and his loyalty to America. At last granted a rehearing in November 1943, Yoshitaka persuaded the three-member Alien Enemy Hearing Board that he wanted to see the United States win and that he had joined Sokokukai only to assist a friend. In December, after a 21-month separation, he rejoined his family in Minidoka. They were released on September 18, 1945, shortly after Japan's formal surrender.

Three days after Hiroka Maeda was born in The Dalles, Oregon, on November 5, 1918, her mother, Masano, succumbed to influenza, which had reached pandemic proportions.[11] Hiroka's father, "Tony," also fell ill but survived. He had two older children and put Hiroka in the care of Horukichi ("Harry") and Motoe Tsuboi. After a few years they adopted the child, whom Harry had earlier renamed Suma. Some time later, Tony Maeda married the sister of Suma's mother, had four more children, relocated to Japan, and then joined the exodus of Japanese to South America, settling in Brazil. His brother migrated to Canada. As a result, Suma recalled, she would eventually have 50 relatives in both South America and Canada. Also, Suma's deceased mother was actually a Nisei, for Suma's maternal grandparents had migrated to Oregon around 1890, traveling up the Columbia River, past the Cascade Mountain range, to The Dalles, where they found employment in the Hotel Dalles. Masano was born there in 1892.

The Tsuboi family had a small truck farm, raising vegetables for market and for a cannery and participating in The Dalles Japanese Produce Association, a co-op. The Tsubois were traditional Issei. Suma's adoptive father "was a very,

very stern man" who "very seldom talked to me." Her mother "was the one that taught me to be subservient more or less . . . not to create waves, not to upset someone. . . . Rather you be hurt than hurting them. . . . But I [also] learned that in this country you speak your piece sometime or you're going to be stepped upon mightily."

They raised Suma as a Buddhist and traveled once a month to services in Portland. She attended the local public school together with a few other Nisei. Whereas other children scarcely discriminated against them, the teachers frequently did, usually by ignoring her. When Suma was beginning high school in the early 1930s, she recounted how an older Nisei boy was elected student body president.[12] As had happened to John Aiso in Hollywood a decade earlier, "Most of the students [liked him, yet] . . . some of the organizations were very unhappy, like the Alumni Association. . . . He served out his term, but there was so much static about it that it was apparently not forgotten." Subsequently, Suma learned that a fierce discussion had taken place among the teachers because she had been nominated for her school's coveted Citizenship Award. "They finally had to give it to another person, because they were so afraid of the comments that the high school would get."

Suma attended a nearby junior college and one in Portland, majoring in journalism. She then went to Japan in 1938 to study Japanese, which she already spoke. Instead of school, she obtained a job at the *Japan Times* doing interviews with visiting European and American dignitaries. She was encouraged to assume Japanese citizenship, but she was certain she held no dual citizenship: "So I knew I was a complete American citizen. There should be no doubt that they could ever make me change any way. I said, 'No, I'm a full-blooded American citizen.'"

By the summer and fall of 1939 her father was ill, relations with the United States were deteriorating, and, she learned, the Germans were helping the Japanese build fighter planes. She also met and became engaged to Ulf, a Norwegian pilot. He had been among a group of young men fleeing the Nazis who had made their way to Japan via Russia. In mid-October she sailed back to America and traveled on to Chicago, where she learned the FBI were investigating her. Shortly after Pearl Harbor they contacted her again: "I think they were talking about [hiring] spies or anybody that was investigating things." She declined to help them.

Later on, while taking a bath on the first Sunday morning in December 1941, she heard the news about the attack and called the FBI men she knew. "They answered the phone, and I said, 'What are you doing down there?' They replied, 'Reading the funny paper.' 'Then you'd better turn your teletype on. Pearl Harbor was just bombed by the Japanese.'" She then called Min Yasui, of Hood River, Oregon, who was in Chicago for a meeting and who later figured prominently in a court case regarding the curfew imposed on enemy aliens and all Japanese along the West Coast. Suma went on to add that "I had been out the night before [December 6] with some of the Japanese consulate people, and there had been no hint of such an outbreak of war."

Suma returned to The Dalles. A few months later the Japanese there were ordered to board a special train to a former mill site converted into the Pinedale Assembly Center, near Fresno.[13] Asked about her parents' reaction, Suma replied, "There was no emotion, no nothing. It was just something they had to do . . . [even though] the strawberries were just ripening." The FBI soon raided their residence because, she concluded, she had received a postcard from a friend who had visited Grand Coulee Dam and had penned the comment, "Wish you were there." The FBI, who had obviously been reading her mail, regarded that as "suspicious."

Suma sold her truck and stored some things with a friend; "other things we just gave away or we had to leave. We didn't have much choice. . . . [I]f somebody didn't buy it or take it over, you left it." On departure day "a lot of townspeople showed [up]. . . . Most of us knew each other. It was a small town." Regarding the train ride, "All I know was that the whole thing was unpleasant. . . . I was a very angry person, but I don't think I ever showed it." And in response to the oft-stated comment that they were incarcerated for their own protection, she asked quite simply: if that was so, "why were the guns pointed at us?"

Following Pinedale, they were transferred to the Tule Lake camp, where "most of the families were more or less kept together. [But] these barracks all looked alike," and some would drink a little too much wine (made from dried prunes) and the next morning "they'd wake up in somebody else's cot. That happened quite frequently." There was certainly no privacy, and she doubts the veracity of movies that later showed refrigerators in the barracks. "I have never seen a refrigerator in one of those barracks—ever." Soon, a group of Nisei evacuees obtained "work release furloughs" for jobs harvesting sugar beets in North Dakota, not far from Sidney, Montana. There they worked, topping tons of beets—which she had never done before. They resided with a German family, who provided them with living quarters in a chicken coop that had a stove, an outdoor toilet, and firewood for them to chop. Suma managed to extend her stay for six months in order to postpone returning to the camp. Even North Dakota's weather was preferable to confinement at Tule Lake.

Soon released in order to relocate to Chicago, she found employment, but not before learning that Ulf had been shot down over England. In the spring of 1944 she met and wed Hugh Bullock and had two children before divorcing him in 1952. What post-incarceration bitterness remained was sharpened by her return to The Dalles, where she encountered a white woman who, like so many Americans, apparently did not bother to distinguish Japanese from Japanese Americans. She "really bawled me out. And she said, 'After all we've done for you! We educated you. We did this—' as if I [had] started the war."

One of the early trails frequently used by early Basque sheepherders out west to drive their flocks northward ran through the Jordan Valley, set along the eastern border of Oregon. Some herders at first barely survived the arduous trek.[14] Eventually, communities were begun there. Basque boardinghouses appeared, and some Basques settled in and near the valley. Anthony Yturri's father had migrated from northern Spain as a teenager and worked for a time in silver mines and stamping mills near Silver City, Idaho, before settling in Jordan Valley with his Basque wife. He had risen to mill foreman, and they used his earnings to buy a boardinghouse in the valley. It appears they operated it for years prior to her death in 1918 during the influenza epidemic.[15]

In October 1914—before the doctor could arrive—Anthony was born in the boardinghouse, the youngest of four children. Two years after the death of his mother, his father married a 22-year-old Basque immigrant, and in that same year his father became a partner in a general merchandise store in the valley for what turned out to be a half-century. The business actually served "almost as a bank in extending credit [and providing supplies] to Basques and non-Basques alike, [and] all the ranchers and farmers and sheepmen in the area."

About a decade later Anthony and his brother Lou were enrolled in Gonzaga University, in Spokane, a Catholic school. But observing the decided lack of young women, Lou persuaded Anthony to transfer with him to the University of Oregon, in Eugene. Nonetheless, as his father had hoped and planned for him, Anthony went on to obtain a law degree, settled in Ontario, Oregon, north of Jordan Valley, and was hired by a law firm there in September 1937. He would maintain his practice there for many decades. At the same time, his political views were being shaped by his father's Catholic, Republican conservatism and vast array of business friends stretching from Boise to Jordan Valley, as well as by his law partner, a conservative Baptist Democrat.

Anthony expanded his horizons beyond the valley, learning about the key role various crops played in the local economy and joining the Lions Club, the Kiwanis Club, and the Ontario Chamber of Commerce. Anthony gradually acquired an ever-broader array of clients. Soon, he was receiving encouragement to go into politics. He became city attorney for Ontario for two decades, and someone in his firm would continue to hold that position thereafter. Through all this, he learned, "there is seldom much of a conflict between the important interests of the agricultural community and the interests of the city. The city is dependent for its economic life, as were the businesses, upon the agricultural community on the outside." And the same was true for the sheep-raising and stock-raising people. Eventually, the mayor of Ontario, Elmo Smith, urged Yturri to run for state office, but the outbreak of the Second World War postponed such a move.

Anthony also noted that a small number of Japanese Americans had lived in the area before 1942 and a much larger number moved in after the war. "[A]nd they fitted into the community quite nicely. Here there didn't seem to be the bigotry . . . that existed in a lot of places because most of them were farmers and they fit right in." They were admired, too, "because they were excellent farmers, very, very good. But they [also] intermingled and they became friends." For years he worked with, and for, them.

After Pearl Harbor was attacked, Anthony anticipated being drafted. He decided to marry his longtime girlfriend, Remedios "Reme" BidegaPneta, a Basque American from Boise, and he then enlisted. Having a law degree and being multi-lingual, he spent the next four years in counter-intelligence. By the early 1950s, Elmo Smith had become governor and again urged Yturri to run for state office. In 1956 he was elected to the state House of Representatives—as a Republican—and served for a dozen years as both representative and state senator. He was also encouraged to run for governor, but he declined to do so, apparently for health reasons.

Anthony and Reme were fluent in Basque and strongly committed to Basque culture and traditions as well as to their Catholic faith. They also remained actively involved in the Basque community.[16] Anthony died in 1989.

Angel Noe Gonzalez was born in November 1929, and he had to discover his heritage, for, he quite forthrightly declared, "it took me 38 years . . . to find out that I was Mexican and I better understand it, that I was going to reach my ceiling as a Mexican and that's as far as the system was going to let me go."[17] Moreover, "the gringos knew they could divide us and they tried." How Mexican Americans in Texas overcame the long-standing Anglo resistance to full participation by Mexican Americans is a story with roots in the 1930s, as we have seen, and more efforts emerging following the Second World War. Yet significant successes, those with an enduring impact, would be realized only in the 1960s.

Gonzalez grew up in Hidalgo County, virtually at the southern tip of Texas, bordering the Rio Grande River. He was one of nine children, and his family's situation became desperate during the Depression when his father died. They turned to the welfare office in Edinburgh, "picking up the flour and beans and . . . fruit once a month"—along with what they might "pick up" in the nearby orchards and packing sheds. "But most of the time we [he and his two young brothers]—well, we grew up in the streets." What saved them was the oldest sister's insistence that they all get an education, the role model of their hardworking brother-in-law, and their own participation in the Catholic Church. Indeed, six of the nine siblings would go on to earn masters or doctorates.

The odds of getting ahead for a Mexican American (especially in Texas) were daunting in the late 1940s and 1950s even with the GI Bill. Angel recalled visiting schools in West Texas that still kept Mexicans segregated. "And any time I went to a small community or any of these places, I'd go downtown and try to visit a Mexican American restaurant, try to find out a little bit about the community, and the thing I was finding is that the Chicanos out in those West Texas areas, the only professional that was considered a professional was a barber. That was as high as they had. They would never see a teacher, maybe one." Moreover, in those "old segregated Mexican schools" there were high dropout rates, "and yet nobody seemed to care about what happened to [the children], if they got an education or not." Angel chose to become a coach and teacher, believing "that if I would go through the white system, and that if I did everything that I was supposed to and if I worked real hard, that I would move up and would have the same opportunity that everybody [had]. And this [was] so false."

Although Gonzalez had participated in various high school sports in Mercedes (a town near the border)—at that time "all of us who were athletes were very well accepted"—when he later sought employment there he was "stopped by those people who accepted me as an athlete." Graduating in 1952 from the University of Texas as a certified teacher, he had great difficulty finding a position—and there were no Mexican American administrators as role models. He would eventually move up to school superintendent of Crystal City, thanks to student protest movements, community mobilization, and the emergence of politically more astute Chicano leaders a decade later.

Japanese, Basque, Mexican American, Italian. Once again the voices of immigrants and their children highlight the dramatic events unfolding during these years. They remind us of the remarkable hurdles newcomers have had to overcome, particularly the stereotyping, discrimination, and exploitation. In some of these cases we see the impact of war and government power and the dangers immigrants faced when those factors of stereotyping, discrimination, war, and the power of the government converged, as they did during the Second World War. We can also observe how so many first- and second-generation persons displayed the resilience and the determination to overcome the obstacles confronting them. In so doing they not only achieved economic or political success but also greater self-esteem and the admiration of fellow Americans. With varying degrees of salience and intensity, the factors of race, religion, gender, cultural differences, educational level, social class, and prevailing attitudes and policies frequently affect the outcomes but always shape the processes of getting there.

The achievements of Suma, Etsuo, Anthony, and Angel certainly illustrate their mobility and the significant contributions they made in the West. Yoshitaka and Joe remind us that the immigrants most certainly added valuable components to the western economy, whether their enterprises were substantial or humble. And, while Yoshitaka was ambivalent and therefore unconvincing about his feelings regarding Japan, Toso, Dora (Joe's wife), and Dora's brother were forthright about their homeland loyalties. They all well represented those with differing degrees of homeland attachment that could either ease their adjustment or, in a crisis, convey the immigrants' reservations about their loyalty to America. Such potential uncertainties haunted Americans who feared the nation's diverse peoples.

CHAPTER THIRTY-TWO

War
Against All Those of
Japanese Descent

*T*HE GULLIBLE, PANICKED RESPONSE to Orson Welles's radio depiction of *War of the Worlds* by H. G. Wells on October 30, 1938, was a foreshadowing of how Americans might respond to a real crisis, such as the attack on Pearl Harbor. Although that took place thousands of miles from the American mainland, the immediate fear was that the West Coast was suddenly and entirely vulnerable, that in a day it had become the nation's frontline of defense. Not only was that shocking because the attack was perpetrated by "slant-eyed people" whom Americans believed were inferior to themselves, but the very deceitfulness perceived behind the surprise attack reinforced the images of Asians as scheming and untrustworthy.[1] Those traits, it was argued, were transmitted across the generations of Japanese and made all the more tenacious by an enduring loyalty to the emperor. Such notions fed into, and were in turn inflamed by, over eight decades of sweeping, all-inclusive, anti-Asian racism.

The preparations, well underway prior to December 1941, for the rapid apprehension of potentially dangerous enemy aliens in the event of war were implemented against Mat Iseri and Eizuchi Tsujikawa in White River Valley, Washington. The police came at night, woke up the men, and took them away with only the clothes they had quickly thrown on. Such dramatic actions, along with the rapid seizure of other leaders and the warrantless searches for contraband items (very broadly defined) shocked friends, family, and communities. That first strategy was a form of "community decapitation" (to leave the community "virtually rudderless"), while the searches prompted many to destroy prized family and personal items from Japan and precious heirlooms that might be viewed as manifesting an excessive attachment to Japan.[2] On December 7, officials detained 736 Japanese aliens; by the following day they apprehended 1,212, plus 559 others; by the 11th they held 1,370 Japanese; and by February 16, 1942, they had picked up 2,192, along with 879 more in Hawai'i. Over 4,000 aliens were in custody by March 9. By July 1 the following were in INS custody: 4,092 Japanese, 2,384 Germans, 794 Italians, and 199 others, for a total of 7,469 persons, most of them men (see the appendix, table 4.1).[3]

During those first five weeks following December 7, there occurred an unprecedented transformation in the mindset of politicians, opinion makers, and the public. The cacophony of accusations of disloyalty in the West—distorted, fabricated, without merit, but arising from a stew of fear, racism, revenge, hate mongering, and economic opportunism—focused not principally or equally on the more numerous Germans and Italians, with whom the United States was also quickly at war. Rather, it was centered on the far fewer Japanese—and not simply on Japanese aliens, now "enemy aliens," but on *all* persons of Japanese ancestry. In the 1940 census 285,115 such individuals were identified by race, 70 percent of them American born and therefore American citizens.[4] Hostility and distrust that had been directed at enemy *aliens* was now transmuted into an anger targeting an enemy *race*. Historian Robert C. Sims suggests that the whole issue of how enemies were viewed may have contributed to this key development. A 1942 Gallup poll showed that Americans focused their hatred of Germany and Italy on specific leaders, such as Hitler, Goebbels, Himmler, and Mussolini, but "Japanese war leaders [had] not been clearly identified in the public mind." Consequently, in terms of Germany and Italy, "Americans tended to think of evil leaders; for Japan they thought in terms of a hated race." Thus, an Idaho newspaper, referring to the need to conserve electricity during Christmas declared, "When Hitler, Mussolini, and the Japs have been blacked out," the holiday lights would be restored.[5]

The editor of the *Anchorage Daily Times* expressed this perception in a December 30, 1941, editorial, "Our Enemy Aliens." True, he said, a roundup of all Japanese "would necessitate large concentration camps," but, even though many were loyal to the United States, "races are involved in this war and special attention must be given any Japanese." The government had no choice, the editorial continued, except "to regard the Japanese population as a potential 'fifth column.'"[6]

The reactions among Japanese and Japanese Americans was a combination of shock, fear, and disbelief that would shortly be compounded by threats of violence against them and the rapid removal of Issei heads of families and community leaders. One example of the potential threat occurred in Clovis, New Mexico, where there were members of Japanese families who had been working for the Santa Fe Railway for over 20 years. With over 200 local soldiers from the Clovis area fighting in Bataan, in the Philippines, people began threatening the Japanese. As the situation deteriorated (Bataan fell to the Japanese on April 9), "there was a fear among officials that the Japanese there might be in danger of a violent attack." With the cooperation of the railroad, Border Patrol officers removed the Japanese at night to El Paso.[7]

Regarding the apprehension of heads of households, even in Alaska responses by police and FBI were rapid, and some Japanese tried to take preemptive action by publicly affirming their loyalty. W. H. Fukuyama, who had been operating a laundry in Juneau and was a 36-year resident of the community, emphasized in the local press on December 8 that "I have lived here a long time and sometimes I feel more American than my children, who were born here.... Japan has made a very bad mistake." The Kimura family immediately placed a statement in the Anchorage newspaper affirming their loyalty "to the country of our adoption and of our birth." They had come there in 1916 after Frank Kimura had served in the U.S. Navy. Although he could not be naturalized, he said, all his American-born children were "proud to be ... citizens," and his son was currently in the U.S. Army.[8]

Although such individuals along the coast and in Hawai'i sought ways to proclaim their loyalty to the United States, the Japanese American Citizens League (JACL), founded by Nisei in 1930, made a determined effort to take over community leadership by declaring that loyalty. As of December 1941, the JACL had 50 chapters and 5,600 dues-paying members. Its leaders tended to be older, and more of them were college educated, bilingual, and in business compared to other Nisei, a majority of whom were in their late teens. Many who did not belong were among those still living in rural areas. The leaders expressed great "faith in the capacity of American institutions to promote economic and racial progress," writes historian Arthur Hansen. Although at first they attempted to be a bridge between Japan and the United States, as war seemed more inevitable, they had focused more exclusively on their American identities and "the attitudes, values, practices, and goals of the American culture." That led them to advocate a position of "deliberate and calculated compliance"—or, as JACL spokesman Mike Masaoka put it, "constructive cooperation."

The JACL created an "anti-Axis" committee that provided information to U.S. intelligence officials identifying "hundreds of Issei" whom they saw as potentially dangerous. Lon Kurashige points out that "The FBI used this information to incarcerate most of Little Tokyo's leadership [in Los Angeles], including officials of ethnic and business associations, journalists and newspaper publishers, Japanese-language teachers, ... Buddhist priests[,]" and activists in such pro-Japanese organizations as the Heimusha-Kai (Overseas Ex-Servicemen's Association), which began in 1937 and had 82 branches with 8,000 members by 1940. Within a few months the JACL was appointed by the War Relocation

Authority (WRA) "the official censor of the Japanese American press." In the long run they believed they would gain more from such strategies. In the short run they had few options but eventually benefited from working with the WRA in terms of jobs and perks in the camps—at the same time that they antagonized most non-"JACLers." Such actions would generate enormous hostilities after the Japanese were transferred to the camps, triggering attacks on some JACL leaders.[9]

The father of Shuji Kimura (no relation to Frank), of White River Valley, Washington, responded quite soberly to the radio news reports on December 7, while his wife turned white. "I guess Japan has become desperate and struck," he said. He told Shuji, "when war comes, we do not know what will happen, but as long as we have food, we can get along for some time. I think that you had better go buy another sack of rice, right now." Food also figured in Tom Hikida's immediate experience. He was a recent university graduate working in a grocery store owned by the Jensens, a German American family. Mrs. Jensen came in that Sunday morning with two large bags of groceries and told Tom, "Here's some groceries because you're not going to be able to buy groceries in town." She explained that Pearl Harbor had been attacked, and Tom thought, "that didn't mean anything to me. I didn't even know what Pearl Harbor was or where it was. . . . 'She must be nuts. This is the United States, you know.'" She recounted being a child during the First World War in North Dakota, and "people would not sell Germans anything. 'That's what's going to happen here,'" she told him. Chinese merchants in San Francisco were quick to make sure Americans knew their identity, posting window signs saying "Chinese store." Filipinos in Alaska soon wore red, white, and blue identification buttons with the word "Philippines" on them. With Korea an unwilling possession of Japan, such Koreans as Mary Paik Lee went to great lengths to make sure people knew she was Korean and not Japanese.[10] Even non-Asians took precautions.

Whatever the combination of historical and situational factors, in that shift from enemy alien to enemy race the constitutional inhibitions against depriving American citizens of their rights and liberties without due process gave way before the greater hysteria. The stronger impulse prevailed to identify a definable, recognizable enemy population, one that had long been the target of jealousy and suspicion and whose guilt by association with the distant enemy was "confirmed" by alleged (but unsubstantiated) subversive actions as much as by the absence of such actions. Indeed, no evidence was taken as evidence that the Japanese were simply lying in wait for the possible invasion. In the end, writes Roger Daniels, "For most practical purposes the government eventually ignored the legal differences between citizen and alien."[11]

The barriers to more extreme, wholesale measures against an entire population were eroded by this fusion of racism, jealousies, attributions of disloyalty, reckless and irresponsible media stories, the desire for revenge and a scapegoat, and the perceptions of Japanese as an Asian/Asian American group in terms of "race" rather than nationality. During the initial months of anxieties and hysteria, the profound failure of political leaders to quiet those public hysterics and to protect fellow Americans further blurred the legal distinctions between foreign-born alien and native-born citizen.

As early as a meeting of government officials in Washington, D.C., on December 11, 1941, Secretary of the Treasury Henry Morganthau Jr. made reference to the idea of massive removals of citizens and aliens. Eight days later, Lt. General John De Witt, head of the Western Defense Command, recommended that all enemy aliens, age 14 and older, be removed to the interior, although for some time he opposed any broad, mass removal that would include U.S. citizens. Then, at a meeting of the Census Advisory Committee in early January 1942, Census Bureau "Director [J. C.] Capt and his senior staff indicated that by January 10 . . . they were already providing tract level data on the Japanese Americans to the military." In other words, they had agreed to do a data run not by Japanese nationality but by Japanese as a race—hence all generations. And, it turned out, not just at the tract level, for they were also providing block-level data, one step removed from individual names and addresses. Calvert Dedrick, chief of the Census Bureau's Statistical Research Division, was sent by the bureau to San Francisco to assist the Western Defense Command and Col. Karl R. Bendetsen—one of the principal architects of the Japanese relocation. Through Dedrick's cooperation, the Census Bureau released "confidential microdata [specific individuals and addresses] on a selective basis in response to stated 'military needs.'" In fact, in the year 2000, the bureau formally and publicly apologized for violating "our principles" by providing that information in 1942.[12]

Secretary of the Navy Frank Knox had already concluded that the Japanese in Hawai'i had been a highly "effective fifth column," "traitors." Opinion polls soon revealed that the public endorsed the notion that mainland Issei/Nisei were no different—and that the Nisei, though American born, were no more reliably trustworthy. On January 14, 1942, Presidential Proclamation No. 2537 ordered all enemy aliens to register for mandatory Certificates of Identification to be carried at all times. California governor Culbert Olson fired hundreds of Nisei civil servants without cause, and in late January the California State Personnel Board barred descendants of those with whom the country was at war from "all civil service positions." Earlier, on January 16, California congressman Leland Ford had urged Secretary of War Henry L. Stimson to relocate "all Japanese, whether citizens or not," to "inland concentration camps." By that same time local leaders and the media were also beginning to demand some actions against the Japanese. As such matters historically tend to do, they fed upon themselves, as anxieties about enemy aliens led to fears of invasion or sabotage and then to hatred of all Japanese.[13]

All this took time to emerge with clarity, both the sentiments and a proposed resolution of the crises. Six weeks passed with no indications of an imminent invasion, yet public pressure continued to mount, and officials moved ahead, formulating a concrete proposal that could be presented to the president.

On January 19, Los Angeles radio commentator John B. Hughes warned listeners that 90 percent or more of American-born Japanese were primarily loyal to Japan. The following day Hearst columnist Henry McLemore (*San Francisco Examiner*) called for "the immediate removal of every Japanese on the West Coast to a place deep in the interior." As he put it, "Herd 'em up, pack 'em off, and give 'em the inside room in the badlands. . . . Personally, I hate the Japanese. And that goes for all of them." On the 21st, General De Witt formally proposed to Stimson the establishment of military zones ("A" and "B") in California from which to exclude enemy aliens, and he subsequently proposed the same for Washington, Oregon, and Arizona. Stimson approved, and Attorney General Francis Biddle agreed to go along with the plan on the 29th. During the next week, Biddle followed that up by detailing what were initially 135 "prohibited areas" along the Pacific Coast and in Arizona "from which all German, Italian, and Japanese alien enemies are to be completely excluded," along with "restricted" or "curfew areas" extending inland (in some places by as much as 150 miles) where the curfew for such persons would be 9 P.M. to 6 A.M.[14]

Sharply ratcheting up public anxieties four days after De Witt submitted his plan to Stimson (January 25) was Supreme Court Justice Owen Roberts's report on Pearl Harbor. He concluded—or was so led to believe by the military there—that "Japanese spies and saboteurs" unconnected with the Japanese consulate had directly contributed to the effectiveness of the attack. A modest number of less than 1,500 Japanese had been transferred to the mainland, for even before Christmas General Delos Emmons, military commander in Hawai'i, found no spies or saboteurs. He determined that the Japanese would be given fair treatment (even though he did not fully trust them), for he fully understood how central they were (at 37 percent of the population) to the economic recovery of the Hawaiian Islands. He would continue to resist calls from Washington for a large-scale round up of Japanese comparable to what soon took place on the mainland—a response endorsed by his mentor, Chief of Staff George C. Marshall.[15]

Meanwhile, on the mainland the Roberts Report galvanized public opinion and crystallized the conclusion that Californians were "living in the midst of a lot of enemies." Four days after its release (January 29) came Biddle's concession to the military's request that enemy aliens be required by February 24 to leave the Military "A" zones. Where would such persons go? There was no plan, historian Stephen Fox concluded. "Where the aliens would go was entirely up to them."[16]

Yet, the outcome in January was still by no means certain, despite the lapse of time and the growing number of more shrill calls for action, particularly from

American Legion chapters, the Native Sons of the Golden West, and the California Farm Bureau Federation. More and more state and local elected officials from Los Angeles to Seattle began clamoring for evacuation and some even for the permanent exclusion of the Japanese. Still, no clear federal strategy had been developed. However, Provost Marshal General Allen Gullion, his chief of the Aliens Division, Karl Bendetsen, and then John McCloy, assistant to the aging Secretary of War Henry L. Stimson, began exploring constitutional limits regarding citizens and the feasibility of a blanket suspension of civil rights for a specified group based on "military necessity." Could it be grounded in the possibility of a Japanese invasion and the likelihood that the Nisei would succumb to "the ties of race and affinity" with their parents' homeland?

DeWitt had already concluded by the end of December that there was no realistic danger of invasion, but the widespread fears persisted, and even before the dangers seemed more immediate and real, the ball—the demand for action—began rolling faster. On January 30, California's congressional representatives issued a resolution calling for the removal of enemy aliens from the West Coast. Two days later, a proposed statement representing the Departments of War and Justice set forth that removal was "not at this time" required by the situation—thus offering an excuse to defer action based upon expediency rather than constitutional principles. But Gullion disliked that draft press release and asked Biddle if he would back removals based on military necessity. Biddle restated his opposition to a mass evacuation of citizens. McCloy argued that the nation's safety came first, compared with which "the Constitution is just a scrap of paper to me." Wavering once more under the pressure from Gullion, Bendetsen, and McCloy to buy into the military necessity argument, De Witt telephoned both Bendetsen and Gullion, expressing his support for mass evacuation—notwithstanding his assessment in late December.

Further betraying his indecision, De Witt met with California governor Culbert Olson the following day (February 2) and was attracted to the idea of voluntary evacuation within the state as part of a "California Plan." Japanese would move to the interior and be employed as agricultural labor gangs. That would address coastal security issues and concerns that such an exodus could draw in large numbers of Mexican and African American laborers, creating (it was suggested) new problems.[17] That same day a *Los Angeles Times* editorial labeled all Japanese potential enemies, and Olson declared in a radio address two days afterward that it was easier to determine the loyalty of Germans and Italians. In a talk to Japanese American editors the governor carried that point even farther, highlighting the racism which the Nikkei were facing at that time:

> You know, when I look out at a group of Americans of German or Italian descent, I can tell whether they are loyal or not. I can tell how they think . . . but it is impossible for me to do this with the inscrutable Orien-

tals, and particularly the Japanese. . . . Promise to give up your freedom, if necessary, in order to prove your loyalty.

Amid this growing hostility to Japanese aliens and their children, Gullion authorized Bendetsen to draft a plan for a mass evacuation, and the Pacific Coast members of Congress renewed their demand that Roosevelt take action. At that point, February 7, McCloy fully accepted Gullion's proposal for a mass evacuation and, Daniels states, "It was McCloy, accepting the recommendation of the Provost Marshal General, who initiated the final push for mass evacuation." The ball was now rolling faster and quickened its speed on the 9th when Congressman Martin Dies Jr. (D-TX), chair of the House Un-American Activities Committee, publicly criticized Roosevelt's administration for being too lax in its protection of the West Coast and too "soft toward the Japanese who have violated American hospitality." Three days later, the foremost liberal American journalist, Walter Lippmann, responding to De Witt's assertion about fifth-column activity in the West (chiefly by Japanese), declared that the Pacific Coast was a combat zone, and "nobody ought to be on a battlefield who had no good reason for being there"—an oblique call for removal. Shortly afterward, moving closer to the Gullion-Bendetsen-McCloy perspective, De Witt told Stimson, "racial affinities are not severed by migration. The Japanese race is an enemy race"—a sentiment he would soon sum up in words ever to be recalled: "A Jap is a Jap and that's all there is to it."[18] The racism and accompanying paranoia were intensifying.

Gullion, Bendetsen, and McCloy now prevailed over Biddle's strong reservations about evacuating citizens. They persuaded Stimson and the president that military necessity justified giving his top commanding officers, through what went forth as Executive Order 9066 on February 19, 1942, the authority to establish military areas "from which any or all persons may be excluded as deemed necessary or desirable." With Executive Order 9066 in hand, Stimson delegated that authority to De Witt but advised him not to remove Italians. California attorney general Earl Warren (soon to be California's governor and later Chief Justice of the U.S. Supreme Court) supported both the negative views of the Japanese and the plans for evacuation: in wartime, "every citizen must give up some of his rights"; evacuation was "absolutely constitutional." The following month (March) a national opinion poll reported that 93 percent of respondents supported the relocation of Japanese enemy aliens, and three-fifths backed the relocation of American-born Japanese.[19]

Approximately 500 families of Japanese ancestry resided on Terminal Island, in Los Angeles Harbor. Roosevelt had transferred the island to the U.S. Navy on February 17, which then ordered all those families to evacuate. Originally given 30 days, all were summarily ordered on February 26, 1942, to depart within 48 hours, with no instructions as to where they should move. Four days later, General De Witt issued his first Public Proclamation, designating "Military Areas" from Arizona to Washington and detailing which classes of individuals might be excluded from them—specifically, enemy aliens and "any person of Japanese ancestry." Congress subsequently passed the Act of March 21, 1942, in support of Executive Order 9066 and the military policies instituted to execute it. Violations were made a misdemeanor, giving the process congressional sanction. On March 24, Public Proclamation No. 3 decreed that in all Military Areas (which now included Idaho, Montana, Nevada, and Utah) enemy aliens and those of Japanese ancestry were to comply with an 8 PM to 6 AM curfew, limits on travel beyond five miles from home, and prohibitions on possessing, among other items, firearms, shortwave radios, and cameras. Meanwhile, Executive Order 9102 (March 18) had established the War Relocation Authority (WRA) as the civilian agency to implement any evacuation, which had yet to be decided or arranged.[20]

The government had been receiving additional expressions of opinion favoring the expulsion of the Japanese primarily because of the persisting anxiety that Japanese invasions remained a strong possibility, a fear stoked by media and public officials. For example, in late February the Los Angeles Times reported "raids" on "secret . . . espionage centers" that resulted in the capture of "scores of alien reserve officers, particularly Japanese." Seattle Mayor Earl Millikin fantasized that 7,900 of the 8,000 Japanese there were loyal, "but the other one hundred would burn this town down and let the Japanese planes come in and bring on something that would dwarf Pearl Harbor." Other fabrications soon appeared, warning of potential subversive plots and raising fear levels even higher. John Curry, representing the California Cattlemen's Association (March 25, 1942), wrote to the president and quoted the Tulare County Cattlemen's Association resolution, asking "that all Japanese aliens and citizens alike be placed in concentration camps under federal guard [and] that such camps be located at strategic points in agricultural sections so that said Japanese may be used, if necessary, in the harvesting of crops."[21]

The Japanese had been urged in Public Proclamation No. 1 (March 2) to go voluntarily to Military Area Two and interior states, and 4,889 persons did just that between March and October. Two out of five headed for Colorado, including between 1,500 and 2,000 who settled in Denver; 30 percent went to Utah. However, many others were met by police at state borders, and most were turned back. Meanwhile, the University of Washington was helping hundreds of Japanese American students, faculty, and staff to transfer to eastern colleges.[22]

These early actions were followed by three turning points that set the fate of West Coast Japanese Americans. First, on March 24, the 54 Japanese families on Bainbridge Island, a short ferry ride from Seattle, were commanded (Civilian Exclusion Order No. 1) to evacuate within six days; they could go anywhere beyond Military Area One. They were the guinea pigs, the first and only group instructed to depart under a C.E.O. but permitted to go voluntarily to "any approved place of their choosing beyond" Military Area One and the prohibited zones. Just three days later, March 27, Public Proclamation 4 ended voluntary evacuation, effective March 29. Santa Anita racetrack, east of Los Angeles, became the first of 17 assembly centers to be opened to receive Japanese who were about to be ordered to evacuate Military Area One. Curiously, even before voluntary departures were dropped, Bendetsen had met with Rex Nicholson, western regional director of the Works Projects Administration (WPA), and arranged for the WPA to assist in the construction and then management of assembly centers, which it did until the end of November 1942.[23]

Second, on April 7, Milton Eisenhower, the director of the WRA, met with the governors of all the western mainland states except California and Texas to discuss their refusal to permit more Japanese Americans to relocate to their states. It quickly became obvious that evacuation followed by voluntary relocation was not acceptable to them. Several governors, notably Nels Smith (Wyoming) and Chase Clark (Idaho), were concerned that Japanese would come and remain in their states. Only Colorado's Ralph Carr offered to cooperate. The conclusion was inescapable: the Japanese would have to be placed in "close confinement" in facilities that would need to be rapidly built on available lands. In other words, unoccupied federal properties were soon identified in California, Colorado, Arizona, Idaho, Wyoming, Utah, and Arkansas—areas that had remained largely unused for reasons that the Japanese would readily come to know. Thus, concludes Roger Daniels, "If the active racism of the West Coast was the initial catalyst for evacuation and the more passive racist climate of the nation as a whole the precondition for its acceptance, the racism of the interior western states was the final determinant of WRA policy."[24]

It is important to emphasize, as the handling of the Japanese on Terminal and Bainbridge Islands revealed, that even *in mid-March 1942 evacuation had not precluded voluntary departure and that such voluntary departure had not precluded voluntary resettlement outside the military areas and prohibited zones.* However, by the beginning of April, the whole process had ceased to be voluntary, and the military established the Wartime Civilian Control Agency, headed by Bendetsen, to coordinate the actual evacuation to the assembly centers and camps, at which point the WRA was to take over. On June 7, De Witt announced that 100,000 persons of Japanese ancestry had been removed from Military Area One.[25]

Third, the tragic irony is that by that very same day, June 7, the United States had completed a major naval victory at the Battle of Midway (June 4–7, 1942), sinking four Japanese aircraft carriers and ending any realistic possibility of an invasion of the West Coast or even Hawai'i. Even though, simultaneously, the Japanese had succeeded in occupying the three outermost Aleutian Islands (which they would hold for about one year), they were too remote to plausibly represent a potential invasion route. That was not the intention of the Japanese action, and any gain from the mini-invasion was far outweighed by their huge losses at Midway. Weighing public anxieties about a Japanese threat against the military's knowledge of the significance of the naval victory, it is evident that that victory at Midway plus the absence of disloyal activities removed any justification for evacuation, much less incarceration, based on military necessity. Notwithstanding the fears and desires for a scapegoat, the failure of political leaders to intervene and protect American citizens of Japanese descent, as noted above, was most glaring and grievous.[26]

The entire camp experience has been labeled a "lawless" episode because a whole people's constitutional rights were set aside. The lawlessness, destructive racism, and bankrupt political leadership are even more blatant in light of this third development. The hysteria had waned; the evidence of disloyalty remained nothing more than unfounded suppositions; a rationale for the eviction and incarceration, which had been fabricated on the unproven basis of military necessity and the suppositions of disloyalty, had ceased to have any merit but was maintained anyway; and the management of the assembly centers (by the civilian-run WRA and WPA) and then the detention and controlled release of all those (by definition, American-born) Nisei under the continued direction of that same civilian agency (WRA) further undermined the military justification of the whole operation.

Nonetheless, the voices of protest were too few, the ethnic group too small; the hostility too deep, the desire for revenge (or a scapegoat) too strong; officials too committed to the policy they had devised, and the U.S. Supreme court soon too willing to defer to various (now spurious) claims by the executive branch and the military to support the evacuation and incarceration. And so the trauma and upheaval continued for nearly four more years.

And though most bitter memories were set aside after the war, they were never forgotten, not ever after President Gerald Ford's apology to Japanese Americans (February 19, 1976) and Present Ronald Reagan's signing the Civil Liberties Act into law (August 10, 1988), which provided for redress and significantly legitimized hidden hurts and shame. Even if the $20,000 per survivor could not entirely make up for the actual financial losses calculated in 1983 at $3.4 to 4.2 billion,[27] many Nisei now felt they could put aside the mask of *shikata ga nai* ("it can't be helped") that had often prevented them from even describing their wartime experiences to their own children. Satsuki Ina, a psychologist, related that elderly persons for years had told people "that camp was a blessing in disguise. But now they admit that that was just a disguise to cover up their shame."[28]

Sally Sudo and her sister revisited Minidoka in June 2003 for the first time since 1944. They had been shipped out from Seattle. Sally was only six. They went to Puyallup Assembly Center and then to Minidoka. Told their camp was ready, they boarded the train, as did thousands of others. It was, she recalled, a frightening trip, with armed guards and shuttered windows. They had no idea of their destination. Her father had come to America in 1899 and was a restaurant worker. "For my father [the relocation] was devastating. He was 64 or 65 when he left the camp and he had lost everything. He lived until he was 88, but he didn't really live, he just existed." In a similar vein but from a different perspective was Celeste Theodor's recollection. She was among a group of orphans sent to Manzanar. She was five. She thought Manzanar "was a wonderful, loving place. Everybody was so sad to leave. We had grown so close." Only years later did she understand the camp's purpose and observed, "It was the adults who suffered terribly. The government tried to tell us it was for the protection of the Japanese American, which was not true."[29]

And, hidden for so long, there remained the pain, the losses, the sense of powerlessness, the ruination of decades of labor, the alienation from one's birthplace and government, the renunciation of one's American citizenship and removal to Japan, and even imprisonment away from the prison for insisting on one's constitutional rights by refusing to sign the "loyalty oath" and pledge to serve in the military while family members were still incarcerated. "Incarcerated" in the camps distinguishes that stage from the "relocation" to assembly centers and "internment" in INS-run camps, a legal term referring to the formal treatment of enemy aliens. (These INS camps were in New Mexico, Montana, Louisiana, North Dakota, and Texas.)[30]

As interned enemy aliens, the Issei were relying on the 1929 Geneva Convention to ensure that they were properly treated. Each was to be interviewed by a three-person Alien Enemy Hearing Board. Matahichi (Mat) Iseri's experience illustrates the pitfalls of these hearings if one wanted to be transferred to a camp with one's family. Mat was born in 1884 and in 1900 joined his brother in North America. He worked at various jobs for six years and determinedly set out to become fluent in English, which he accomplished. In 1906 he sent for a bride, marrying Kisa Okuna. They settled in White River Valley, between Seattle and Tacoma—a district the Japanese called Shirakawa—where Mat and Kisa had 12 children and operated a farm nearby and then a dairy. Mat eventually shifted to operating a grocery store in the mid-1920s, which was quite successful until the growing number of Nisei displayed more interest in shopping at the Safeway supermarket than in his traditional store. Although his business was declining during the troubled 1930s, he was involved with several different community organizations and continued to be regarded as the Japanese community's patriarch, spokesman for the Issei in particular, and liaison with the surrounding American society.

Not surprisingly, Matahichi Iseri was the logical target of the FBI and was among the first wave of Issei taken in the day after the Japanese attack. At 7:30 P.M. an agent and the local police chief, who had been a "good friend" of Mat's for many years, came for him, awakened him, and took him into custody. Iseri was first held in Seattle for nearly three weeks and then was sent to Fort Missoula, Montana, where a hearing was set for January 26, 1942. Drudgery, boredom, and petty humiliations filled the days.

At his hearing, Mat was questioned about his involvement in various groups, particularly the local Japanese Association, the extent of his ongoing ties with Japan, and his loyalty to the emperor. The FBI agent assumed that because Issei, who constituted the association's membership, were not citizens and consequently "owe their allegiance to Japan, they are naturally strongly pro-Japanese in their tendencies." Presumptions and stereotypes shaped the questions, and so the hearing continued, with Mat trying to wend his way between his American loyalties and his regard for his homeland. After indicating that he wanted his sons to serve in the U.S. Army, he was asked, "You don't want your boys to kill other Japanese [those from Japan] do you?" He replied, "That is not likely, but when you find your own house on fire I don't see why I couldn't protect my own home before I do anybody else's house." Asked if the attachment of Issei to Japan was strong, he ventured, "No. Very few think about the old country and they have an awful time to get along in this country with their families and heavy duties." And, "Their grave is here in this country." Haven't there been divisions between Issei and Nisei over conduct and values? Mat replied, "The difference in feeling is the Nisei is always trying to play. They don't want to work . . . they are more for the automobile and too well Americanized. . . ." If Japan invaded and took over, wouldn't your sons be better off and you would then be able to get them to do more? Mat shot back, "I don't know. They are spoiled now. . . . Asking me about Japan it is something like that I have never known anything about. I . . . left there when I was 16 [he was then close to 58]. . . . and never known anything about it since."

Four months later, while he was still at Fort Missoula, and his family was about to be sent to Pinedale Assembly Center (near Fresno)—after which they were scheduled to go either to Heart Mountain or Minidoka—Mat wrote to his family about the imminent departure of the community and sadly concluded, "Of course this is away beyond our control that no one can help it."[31]

As we saw with Watanabe and here with Iseri, the internment of Issei—as enemy aliens—most often involved the forced separation of such men from their families, not uncommonly for years. Among the Japanese from Alaska, every male Issei but four was taken away and kept apart for the duration of the war, mostly in Lordsburg, New Mexico.[32] Nearly all other family members were held in one of the ten WRA-run concentration camps. They were called "concentration camps" because the term had been used for such facilities since the turn-of-the-century Boer War in South Africa; because President Roosevelt had used the term; because American citizens held there were confined without habeas corpus, without charges being brought, without hearings, without the law,

The Matsushita Story of Internment and Incarceration

Iwao and Hanaye Matsushita's story is so poignant, and their correspondence so powerfully conveys the price exacted for internment and incarceration that it is well worth a more extended retelling. Iwao was born in Japan in January 1892. Although persecuted for his Protestant religion, he earned a certificate to teach English in high school. In January 1919, he wed Hanaye Tamura, who was born in March 1898, and they migrated to Seattle in September 1919. At that time there was a thriving Nihonmachi (Japanese community) there, with almost 7,500 persons and nearly 1,500 businesses. In 1920, Iwao obtained a well-paying, white-collar position with Mitsui and Company, a Japanese trading firm. He remained with them for two decades, and the couple accumulated $23,000 in savings. However, when the company offered him a promotion to a position in Tokyo, he resigned, foregoing a pension because he wished to remain in America.

Nevertheless, on December 7 he was taken into custody because his bilingualism, reputation as a teacher, and membership in various organizations marked him as a community leader, a "potentially dangerous" person. He was one of over 1,200 Issei picked up in the first days of the war. He was sent to Fort Missoula and appeared before the Alien Enemy Hearing Board in early February. The board recommended parole, but no decision came from Attorney General Francis Biddle. Iwao was forced to languish in Missoula for more than nine months, while at the end of April, Hanaye, in frail health, was sent off to Puyallup Assembly Center and then Minidoka camp. Meanwhile, Iwao used his time to teach English and U.S. history to other internees and to write to Hanaye.

In mid-July 1942 she told him, "I don't know where we're moving. At the same time I feel uneasy about your future. Be at ease about me. I am somewhat nervous, but my health is well." A month later 6,100 Nikkei from Seattle were shipped to Minidoka, which she found to be "a dreary, forbidden, flat expanse of arid wilderness." As she got more depressed, she wrote, "I am resigned to whatever may happen." At that point Iwao learned his application had been

lawlessly; because there were guard towers and machine guns facing in, not out; because sometimes troubled, sometimes desperate men, such as James Hatsuki Wakasa, were shot for approaching or climbing the barbed-wire fences; and because angry Nisei, fed up with perceived corruption involving the camp administration and collaboration by JACL leaders, triggered a riot in Manzanar in early December 1942 (referred to by the press as a "Jap uprising"), during which soldiers killed two demonstrators. For nearly all of these "prisoners without trial," as Roger Daniels wrote, their only crime was their identity.[33]

Personal accounts abound, capturing the whole array of responses to the evacuation, detention, and incarceration, beginning with the initial shock that war had really come. Community leaders were hastily taken away; family assets and turned down because Biddle was suspicious about his long employment with a Japanese firm until shortly before the attack. For health reasons, Hanaye was reluctant to apply for volunteer internment in an INS facility with Iwao, and he appealed directly to Biddle in January 1943, explaining his Christian upbringing, his two decades in Seattle, the absence of any return trips to Japan, the fact that "I have never broken any Federal, State, Municipal, or even traffic laws, and paid taxes regularly." He added, "I believe myself one of the most upright persons. I have never been, am not, and will never be potentially dangerous to the safety of the United States." Moreover, "[m]y wife . . . is living helplessly and sorrowfully" in Minidoka. Biddle advised Iwao to reapply, and Hanaye sought letters of affidavit for him as well as one noting her deteriorating mental condition.

Ten more months passed, and in late December 1943, Iwao petitioned once more to be reunited with his wife. "Many friends of mine who were here with me in 1942 . . . are now enjoying reunion with their families. My wife, who is ill and under a doctor's care . . . has been patiently waiting for my return for two long years. . . . I don't like her to be tortured like this on account of my being detained here. . . . As we never lived apart in our married life for 23 years before my apprehension, it is simply unbearable to have to live like this for so long. . . . I can assure you that there is not an iota of danger to the safety of the American public when I am allowed to live with my wife."

Actually, on December 18, Biddle had approved the earlier petition from April, and Iwao was notified January 2, 1944. After 25 months in captivity apart from Hanaye, Iwao sent his 148th and final communication to her, a telegram, dated January 6, 1944, which read simply, "Leaving here 10th, Monday afternoon, arriving Twin Falls, Tuesday noon or afternoon."

A few months later, Iwao and Hanaye declined an offer to return to the Pacific Northwest but not to Seattle. Another 14 months passed, and he was offered a job by the WRA in Seattle, beginning August 7, 1945, to assist evacuees returning there. After an absence of 44 months, and with the war not yet ended, he had been given a job by the very government that had incarcerated him as a potentially dangerous enemy alien.[35]

bank accounts in Japanese banks were suddenly frozen; individuals and families were given merely a few days to arrange all their affairs, dispose of (or make arrangements for) businesses, inventories, equipment, property and personal (often cherished) possessions, and then prepare to depart — in most cases with only two suitcases per person.[34] The rushed uprooting was followed by the shock and discomfort of being temporarily housed at fairgrounds and in recently cleaned-out stables and the still greater shock of being transported to desolate camps, half-finished tar paper–covered barracks providing little privacy. Finally, they experienced the assaults of camp conditions on families, their unity, and their discipline. All of this took place in sparse areas, outlined by unpaved walkways and subject to extremes of weather and wind.

Few Japanese in the West could escape the process of interrogation or simply the curfews followed by removal. In Alaska, for example, General Simon Bolivar Buckner, head of the Alaska Defense Command, declared the territory a military area and ordered the evacuation of all Japanese Americans, effective April 25. From around that vast territory 230 persons were taken in, including several who were individually the only person of Japanese descent in their village and many who were part-Nisei and part-Alaskan Native. They were taken by transport to Seattle and on to Puyallup and then to Minidoka. The one variation here was that each person was permitted to take up to 1,000 pounds, not just two suitcases, but that was little compensation for Henry Hope, a Japanese Eskimo of 17 who had been adopted by an Eskimo-Athabaskan couple when he was a baby. He now helped support them, yet he was forced to leave, too. Farewell parties in a number of locations, such as by the workers of the Alaska Glacier Sea Food Company, in Petersburg, could not soften the pain of such uprooting.[36]

From the standpoint of WRA officials, the camps were an exercise in social engineering and Americanization, based on the presumption that the Nisei were not already Americanized. In general, the Nikkei avoided the measures intended to promote a "benevolent assimilation." In fact, aside from the WRA-operated schools, which the younger Nisei did attend, the Nikkei were quick to establish activities in all the camps that enabled them to adjust, to associate, to distract, to learn, to create as well as recreate. They also sought to provide the children with as much normalcy as possible, to ease the pain of disruption and disorientation among the Issei as much as possible, and to reestablish some of the favorite past times—such as baseball, basketball, judo, and sumo-style wrestling. Access to mail-order services proved crucial in helping evacuees make their living conditions more bearable. Among the many more formal activities were libraries, newspapers (English and Japanese), book clubs, gardening clubs, theatrical groups, dances, religious services, even flag and camouflage sewing circles, many school-based activities, and farming enterprises to raise vegetables to supplement the WRA menu (Japanese cooks were recruited to provide traditional or familiar foods, often at substantial savings to the WRA). Also established were Issei- and Kibei-run nationalistic organizations, such as the Kenkyuka (Study or Investigative Group), the Kibei Club in the Gila River Relocation Center, the Sokuji Kikoku Hoshi-dan (the Organization to Return Immediately to the Homeland), and the Hokoku Seinen-dan (the Young Men's Organization to Serve Our Mother Country) in the Tule Lake Relocation Camp and then the Santa Fe Internment Camp.[37]

However, it must be emphasized that this broad array of activities could not really eradicate the ubiquitous presence of "the barbed wire [electrified] fences and the sentry tower[s] with floodlights" as well as the severely unhealthy conditions in many camps (especially Manzanar, Minidoka, Heart Mountain, and

Gila River) due to the arid soil, blowing winds, and harsh environment. Conditions ranged from extreme winter cold to suffocating heat in barracks that were scarcely insulated and hardly sealed against winds and weather. And all of that was compounded by unpaved pathways that became lakes of mud following rains and snow.[38]

> "We were disgusted enough," wrote "Mike" after arriving at Minidoka, "just looking at the place, scorching under a 110-degree sun, so you can imagine how we felt when we were told that our rooms were not yet completed. Some people just broke down and bawled. . . . There are many rattlesnakes and scorpions and besides these there are black widows, bull snakes, beetles, horned toads and of course the very persistent mosquito—we're all just one happy family."

Nor could the efforts to compensate for disrupted communities substitute for missing family members (apprehended by the FBI or INS), disrupted family routines (e.g., eating together was a particular casualty), the "degrading" absence of privacy (in some locations hanging sheets separated living quarters), and strained family relations. There were also new (or freer) ways of socializing between young men and women and other activities that accelerated the generation gap. At the same time, the Issei, whose lifetime efforts had been abruptly taken from them, were psychologically devastated, while relations were strained between various groups, such as among the Nisei between those pro- and anti-JACL, between Kibei and other Nisei, between Issei and Nisei, and between those who supported the 1943 "loyalty oath" and those who opposed that and the draft in 1944. These clashes often became public and sometimes quite violent, with opponents beaten up and some placed on "death lists," as occurred at Manzanar in late 1942.

On the other hand, beginning in 1942, at least in Oregon, Colorado, Utah, Idaho, Wyoming, Montana, North Dakota, and Arkansas, thousands of Nisei obtained work furloughs to assist in harvesting crops. Without their help, farmers would have suffered huge losses, especially the sugar beet growers. Of course, those departures, often for months at a time, further disrupted already distended families. Sucheng Chan indicates that 9,000 left the camps for varying periods to earn money during the harvest times. Thus, in economic terms, Issei and Nisei contributed in many capacities to the western economy not only in the years prior to the war but throughout the war as well.[39] In 1942, some 1,048,000 acres of sugar beets were planted, beginning earliest in Montana, and already by mid-March farmers were eager to obtain Japanese workers, especially since more than half had farm experience. By May 20, General De Witt was authorizing 400 to leave the Portland Assembly Center to assist beet farmers in eastern Oregon. Once Nisei in the centers and then in the camps received reports that it was safe to venture forth, greater numbers did so. Approximately

2,000 internees left Minidoka to work in Idaho, Wyoming, and Utah, in effect "saving" the 1942 sugar beet crop and making farmers and sugar company executives more favorably disposed to the Nisei. It was an opportunity for the Nisei to earn more than the $12, $16, or $19 per month they would earn inside the centers and camps. The Kibei, however, having been imbued with Japanese nationalism during their schooling in Japan, were prohibited from participating.

Some Americans did look kindly on the Nisei workers and endorsed the sentiment expressed by an Idaho farmer opposed to using them. His reasoning was on his sign: "Remember Pearl Harbor." In the final accounting, 9,867 workers were contracted in 1942, 14,062 in 1943, and 9,467 in 1944, in some cases even replacing Mexicans drawn off to better-paying construction jobs. The program was terminated after the 1944 season, for by that time the number of Nisei so employed had declined, in part because many were securing leaves from the camps to work at non-farm jobs in the Midwest and East or to attend schools outside the Exclusion and Restricted Zones. Nor was this move limited to Nisei men, for job opportunities (and college enrollment) enabled many young women to obtain work outside the camps. They were sought after for secretarial, clerical, and factory work, and as beauticians, domestics, and the like. Moreover, although classified as enemy aliens, some Issei were able to work harvesting crops, along with the Nisei young men. A small number of Issei railroad workers were also cleared and permitted leave clearance as early as September 1942 in order to return to jobs in eastern Oregon. Meanwhile, to offset the shrinking numbers of Nikkei farm workers, in May 1943 growers began turning to POWs to do agricultural work, and by June 1944 23 POW camps were participating in sugar beet states: 102,000 workers in 1944 and 122,000 in 1945.

Overall, some 33,000 Nikkei had been permitted "to trade imprisonment for meaningful paid labor experiences." In fact, just as some American farmers had predicted, over 5,000 Nikkei subsequently settled in the sugar beet-growing counties where they had earlier found employment, notably in eastern Oregon, Montana, and Idaho.[40]

In its public statements, the WRA spoke about "evacuation," "relocation centers," "residents," and then "military volunteers," but not about Issei and Kibei resisters or the label "concentration camps." The Nikkei were not all passive and submissive. At various times there was unrest and resistance at Poston, Manzanar, Topaz, and Tule Lake. In Manzanar, by early December 1942, there was considerable animosity developing toward JACL leaders (and others sympathetic to the JACL, referred to as "JACLers") for their opposition to any dissent, their cooperation with WRA authorities, and in reaction to complaints about corruption and the theft of food supplies. The anti-JACLers drew up an actual "death list." Fred Tayama, a JACL district leader before the war, was assaulted, and Harry Ueno, a popular union leader in the camp, was jailed for the attack. A demonstration demanding his release escalated from 200 to some 2,000 persons.

Soldiers used tear gas and then fired on the crowd, killing two and wounding nine others.

Two months later, resisters protesting the loyalty questionnaire declared at a meeting at Heart Mountain that "We are really fighting for the perpetuation of democracy, especially when our fathers, mothers, and families are in concentration camps even though they are not charged with any crime." John J. McCloy, Milton Eisenhower, and Dillon Myer (Eisenhower's successor as the head of the WRA) were "accessories to the incarceration," an incarceration "based on a presidential fiat" that was eventually endorsed by the U.S. Supreme Court. Even in early 1945, some 1,400 men in Tule Lake were considered so difficult and unmanageable that they were transferred to an INS facility for enemy aliens.[41]

Roger Daniels reports that at one time or another 120,313 persons were under WRA control, including 52,800 (nearly all Nisei) who were eventually relocated to the nation's interior; 2,355 who were released to the military, most often either to the Military Intelligence Service Language School (MISLS), headed by John Aiso, or to what became the famed 442nd Regimental Combat Team and the 100th Infantry Battalion; 3,121 transferred to INS internment camps; and 4,724 who requested repatriation to Japan—a combination mostly of Issei, their family members, and Kibei.[42] Although Daniels indicates that 54,127 did "return to the West" (45 percent) when the camps were closed, many others did so subsequently, especially during the 1950s. They made up part of the 82 percent jump in Japanese persons in the coastal states and Arizona between 1950 and 1960. In fact, as Sandra Taylor points out, initially "most of the inmates did not wish to leave the camps," and those who did wanted to be free to come and go "if conditions on the outside proved to be too difficult"—in other words, if they encountered too much hostility. That fear eased more quickly for those heading east than for those venturing to return to the West in 1945. Not unique was the experience of Daniel Inouye, later to become a U.S. senator from Hawai'i. He entered a San Francisco barbershop in an American uniform, clearly missing an arm, which he had lost in combat not long before. He was denied service because, said the barber, "We don't serve Japs here"—the type of encounter with white hostility that made many Issei and Nisei very apprehensive.[43]

Until faced with such circumstances, most Japanese Americans displayed remarkable adaptability to their evacuation, detention, and incarceration. The psychological and emotional toll was certainly greatest among the Issei, who struggled to preserve their family and leadership status in the camps. The impact on the Nisei was more complex. Age, education, and skill levels were especially important variables in determining how well they coped in the camps and how resilient they proved to be afterward. The sense of shame was indeed widespread and persistent, and the reluctance to talk about the camp experience would remain pervasive for a quarter of a century or more.[44]

During the 1970s I invited a Nisei man to speak to my class about his experiences in the Poston Concentration Camp. He described it as somewhat of a lark, for he and his buddies were teenagers at the time and enjoyed themselves. His presentation did not come across as one about an oppressive experience. Less than a decade later, following the often painful, even anguished and frequently bitter personal descriptions presented at the Commission on Wartime Relocation and Internment of Civilians hearings in 1981, the public now saw the truer face of the wartime experience. When my Nisei friend once again visited my class, his tale was now more somber, more disturbed by losses and divided families. He described the years of internment as less a lark than a period where lives were put on hold until drafted or permitted to go east to attend college or take a job. There were undoubtedly "good" times during the camp periods, but now a darker side was unquestionably being revealed that many had experienced but managed to suppress.

The camp experience forced to the surface three legal and constitutional issues of such enduring significance that no account of this episode should conclude without addressing them: (1) the controversy over the loyalty oath questionnaire and the dilemmas confronting those who had been unable to acquire U.S. citizenship; (2) the refusal of several hundred men in the camps to report for the draft (together with the military record of those who did volunteer or respond to the draft); and, (3) perhaps paramount, four court cases that reached the U.S. Supreme Court in 1943–1944 and raised fundamental constitutional questions about military necessity and the conditions under which American rights are — or are not — protected.

Early in 1943 the government administered a questionnaire to those in the camps to determine who might be willing to serve in the military and who were "troublemakers" requiring segregation and tighter control. Questions 27 and 28 of this inappropriately labeled "Application for Leave Clearance" (which is not what it really was) presented a conundrum for Issei and Nisei in part because the same questions should not have been put to Issei, who could not become citizens, nor to the Nisei, who were American-born citizens. Question 27 asked if the respondent was willing to serve in the military or the women's equivalent service. Question 28 asked if the respondent would swear "unqualified allegiance to the United States and foreswear any allegiance to the emperor." If an Issei answered affirmatively to question 28, he or she would be left stateless since U.S. citizenship was unavailable. For a Nisei to answer it affirmatively implied that double loyalties had been present. Many feared being drafted, notwithstanding their response to question 27, unless they said "no" to question 28. The result was that many answered both in the negative (7,600, or 11 percent, said no to the second question), in effect declaring themselves to be "No, No Boys." Approximately 78,000 Nisei were expected to register, but 4,000 Nisei refused to reply to the two questions or gave qualified answers. Thus, perhaps as many as 12,000 Nikkei expressed some form of "disloyalty" either by their answer or refusal to answer. As a result, 6,000 Nikkei were moved out of the Tule Lake camp, and 12,000 "disloyals" were moved in alongside the 6,000 who remained, loading over 18,000 persons into a facility built for 12,000.

When the government next sought 4,000 volunteers from among those in the camps in the beginning of 1944, fewer than 1,200 came forward, prompting the government to reinstate the draft for the Nisei. At that point, 2,800 Nisei did respond to the draft, but many others objected to answering the call while their families were still in the camps. Resistance was particularly intense at Heart Mountain, where Kiyoshi Okamoto and Frank Emi launched the Heart Mountain Fair Play Committee (FPC). They remained firm in their opposition even when denounced by the Japanese American Citizens League as un-American. The JACL urged that they be tried for sedition. In July 1944, there were 63 resisters at Heart Mountain—out of 315 in all the camps—who were found guilty of draft evasion for their refusal to show up for their pre-induction physical. About 200 of the others would later be convicted; the rest were released or volunteered. Those convicted were sentenced to three years in a federal penitentiary, with some being sent to the maximum-security prison at Leavenworth, Kansas, until all were pardoned by President Truman on Christmas Eve, 1947.[45]

Jack Tono, one of the 63 defendants, recalled the pardon and considered it a victory for their cause. "When I testified later at the trial I said all we wanted was our prior livelihoods. . . . Then, we said, we'd go. We weren't completely against defending the country but we first wanted what we had before and then we'd go and fight. . . . I think our group respected citizenship more than anybody in this country because we were actively trying to preserve our citizenship rights, instead of just saying that we're citizens of this country. If you're treated the way we were, there is no such thing as real citizenship. You have to fight and pay your dues. . . . I don't have one regret. If I had to do it over, I'd do the same thing. . . . I did it with a clear conscience." It would take 56 years before the JACL—amid great controversy—backed off of its original condemnation of the FPC. The JACL acknowledged that the FPC members had taken a principled stand in order to wage a legitimate constitutional battle and that they had been political victims. In the year 2000 the JACL national council voted 2 to 1 to recognize what the resisters had done and to apologize for not having acknowledged the value of their efforts at that time. In May 2002 it held a National JACL Resister Ceremony to honor those men as part of its public apology.[46]

During that tumultuous wartime era, some 23,000 Nisei were in the military, and most served in the combined 442 Regimental Combat Team and 100th Infantry Battalion. At first, many were reluctant to be part of an all-Nisei unit, referring to it as a case of "Jap Crow." But it did enable them to excel together most visibly, and over 15,500 awards were given to these men, who largely fought in Europe and North Africa.[47] They were one of the most decorated units in American military history, receiving nearly 9,500 purple hearts—equal to three times the number of men—along with 600 killed, adding considerable legitimacy to the Japanese American community. Such had also been the price paid by other ethnic groups seeking integration into American society.

And yet, of the 15,513 awards, only one was the highest, a Medal of Honor, posthumously awarded to Sadao Munemori, who threw himself on a grenade to protect his buddies. Forty years later Congress directed the U.S. Army to review its records on Asians to see if they had been denied the highest awards and given lesser ones. In 2000 President Bill Clinton bestowed that top honor on 22 more Asian veterans, 20 of whom were in the 442/100. Among them were Ted Tanouye, who used his body to shield his comrades from an exploding land mine, and Yukio Okutsu, who single-handedly wiped out three German machine-gun positions and captured eight German soldiers. It was accounts such as those and the remarkable sacrifices to save the Lost Texas Battalion in the Vosges Mountains of France in late October 1944 that won the Nisei grudging admiration. To save 211 men, the 442/100 sustained 800 casualties and lost 140 men.[48]

The curfews, evacuation, and the concentration camps, along with the Act of March 21, 1942, wherein Congress gave authority to the military to mandate curfews and evacuations in specific military zones, did not go unchallenged during the war years. Four court cases were filed and appealed arguing the unconstitutionality of the three measures involving all persons of Japanese descent in the western military region—or, as Justice William O. Douglas's law clerk put it, their "evacuation, detention, and confinement."[49] These four cases warrant detailed treatment here because they reveal the mindset of the time and the profound legal ramifications for future national security crises. In fact, the four address fundamental issues surrounding the extent of power the government may legitimately exercise in times of emergency. They have reemerged periodically since the Second World War, most recently following the events of 9/11 and the enactment of the USA PATRIOT Act (Uniting and Strengthening America by Providing Appropriate Tools Required to Intercept and Obstruct Terrorism Act).

Because the Supreme Court determined to take a confidential position on key aspects sure to rise in cases challenging the treatment of Japanese Americans, we need to understand the consequences of that decision. The cases involved federal power to establish curfews, to order evacuations, and to incarcerate and detain aliens and U.S. citizens of a single ancestry based on the assertion of military necessity but with no martial law declared and with a civilian agency established to execute the authority given specifically to the military.

At the outset, the majority of the high court justices agreed to keep the curfew separate from evacuation and both apart from incarceration and confinement. In advance, they agreed on three points: (1) curfew and evacuation were justified as protection "against espionage and sabotage"; (2) "The military judgment cannot be rejected by the justices of the Supreme Court"—in effect, agreeing in advance to defer to the claims of military necessity; and (3) the argument about targeting a whole group of citizens in such an emergency was likewise accepted by the high court as reasonable because disloyal persons could not be readily or rapidly distinguished from loyal ones. Justice Douglas, however, was deeply troubled by the absence of mechanisms for rapidly making that determination between loyal and potentially disloyal persons so that the loyal ones could promptly leave the centers and camps.

Justice Douglas's law clerk pointed out to him that at the time the law was enacted on March 21, 1942, most officials "contemplated little or no control over the Japanese once they had left the prohibited area." Circumstances radically changed after the western governors' meeting on April 7. Douglas would later write, "by May, 1942, evacuation, detention in an Assembly Center and [then] detention in a Relocation center [viz. camp] were but steps in a program which had acquired a unitary character." But that was not the original intent of De Witt's policies.

Gordon Hirabayashi, a University of Washington student in Seattle, and Min Yasui, a lawyer in Portland, decided separately to challenge the curfew and the authorization given for it in the Act of March 21, 1942. Hirabayashi denied the military had the authority, and Yasui claimed it was invalid against citizens. Both cases were appealed to the U.S. Supreme Court, which rendered its unanimous decisions for both on June 21, 1943 (*Hirabayashi v. the United States*, 320 U.S. 81; *Yasui v. the United States*, 320 U.S. 115). The decision of the former was applied to the latter. General De Witt had established military areas "as a matter of military necessity," and "such . . . classes of persons as the situation may require" could be excluded from them. The 1942 Act in advance authorized precautionary actions, including a curfew, and made violations of such orders a misdemeanor. De Witt then proceeded on March 24 to establish a curfew "pertaining to all enemy aliens and all persons of Japanese ancestry." On that same day, De Witt also began issuing Civilian Exclusion Orders, directing all Japanese to evacuate. Those in Seattle were required to leave by noon, May 16, 1942.

Hirabayashi claimed that it was unconstitutional for the president to delegate that authority and, further, that the Fifth Amendment prohibited discrimination between Japanese and those of other ancestries. The Supreme Court held that the Act was valid and quoted the chairman of the Senate Military Affairs Committee that "reasons for suspected widespread fifth-column action among the Japanese" lay in the system of their dual citizenship and in the propaganda disseminated by Japanese consuls, Buddhist priests, and other leaders. Those factors justified the evacuation of all persons of Japanese ancestry. Congress and the executive branch possessed the appropriate authority to establish a curfew for "protection against espionage and against sabotage." Consequently, "it is not for any court to sit in review of the wisdom of their action or substitute its judgment for theirs," especially if they "have reasonable ground for believing that the threat is real." The court then focused on circumstances regarding the Japanese that have "prevented their assimilation as an integral part of the white population," emphasizing claims regarding suspect loyalties, "allegiance to Japan," the Kibei who studied there, and the dual citizenship remaining among many Nisei.

"Congress and the Executive could reasonably have concluded that these conditions have encouraged the continued attachment of members of this group to Japan and Japanese institutions." The court also accepted the charge, though unsubstantiated, that Japanese espionage had been an important factor in the attack on Pearl Harbor. "We cannot reject as unfounded the judgment of the military authorities and of Congress that there were disloyal members of that population, whose number and strength could not be precisely and quickly ascertained . . . [and that] such persons could not readily be isolated — and separately dealt with." The court upheld both convictions, which were used subsequently as precedents to sustain the lower court decision in the third case, that of Fred Korematsu.

Korematsu, a welder in San Leandro, California, evaded evacuation orders in order to remain with his Italian American girlfriend. Plastic surgery to alter the shape of his eyes in order to disguise his Japanese ancestry did not prove sufficient, for the FBI arrested him on May 30, 1942. Found guilty of violating a Military Exclusion Order, he was given five years' probation but still taken to Tanforan Assembly Center. With the assistance of the American Civil Liberties Union, he then challenged the congressional authorization allowing the military to incarcerate civilians and citizens without a trial (there being no martial law declared). Pending the outcome, he was still sent to the camp in Topaz, Utah.[50]

However, in *Korematsu v. the United States* (323 U.S. 214; December 18, 1944), the 6-3 Supreme Court decision upholding his conviction was limited to Korematsu's violation of the May 1942 Civilian Exclusion Order, ordering all persons of Japanese origin out of the San Leandro area by May 9. The curfew had been upheld as part of the "protection against espionage and against sabotage," and, consequently, it was not "beyond the war power of Congress and the Executive to exclude those of Japanese ancestry from the West Coast war area." Because the curfew was not found to be a sufficient measure in the event of a Japanese invasion, evacuation was seen as having "a definite and close relationship to the prevention of espionage and sabotage." That exclusion "was deemed necessary because of the presence of an unascertained number of disloyal members of the group, most of whom we have no doubt were loyal to this country." The court again accepted the "military imperative" that authorities could not expeditiously segregate "the disloyal from the loyal," and, therefore, exclusion of all persons of Japanese descent was justified. Further evidence was that approximately 5,000 refused "to swear unqualified allegiance to the United States," and several thousand requested repatriation to Japan.

The court asserted (rather disingenuously) that defining the issue in this case as one of race prejudice "without reference to the real military dangers which were presented merely confuses the issues." Military urgency, not race, was the Court's central assertion:

> He *was* excluded because we are at war with the Japanese Empire, because the properly constituted military authorities feared an invasion of our West Coast and felt constrained to take proper security measures, because they decided that the military urgency of the situation demanded that all citizens of Japanese ancestry be segregated from the West Coast temporarily. . . . The need for action was great, and time was short. We cannot—by availing ourselves of the calm perspective of hindsight—now say that these actions were unjustified.

The Supreme Court thus affirmed the decision regarding evacuation as it had done the earlier decisions regarding curfew violations. Those three cases, as mentioned, deliberately did not address incarceration, and, therefore, the issue would remain how the rationales provided in those three cases might fare when the Court had to confront the incarceration of a U.S. citizen without charges having been filed, the imprisonment of a citizen and his or her detention by a civilian agency that had not been given such powers by Congress, and the execution of military powers in an area where martial law had not been declared. Those precedents would not stand.

Mitsuye Endo, 21 years old, had been employed by the California State Highway Commission in Sacramento until the evacuation. In July 1942 she was asked if she would be a plaintiff in a test case of the constitutionality of her detention on the grounds that she was a loyal American citizen, a Christian, spoke no Japanese, had never been to Japan, and had a brother in the U.S. Amy but had still been incarcerated in the Tule Lake camp. A writ of habeas corpus was filed on July 13, 1942, that she be released or just cause be shown why she was being held in custody. Her request for a permit to leave the camp was granted 13 months later. However, it contained the WRA-imposed condition that the applicant technically "will remain in the *constructive custody* of the military commander," and "Any such permit may be revoked at any time" if "necessary in the public interest." Not cleared to return to Sacramento, she declined the permit. The Ninth Circuit Court of Appeals asked the high court if the WRA in fact had the power to detain people without due process; if the WRA could continue to hold someone whose loyalty had been established; and if the WRA was permitted to grant such a loyal individual a limited, conditional leave that could conceivably be revoked.

In *Ex Parte Endo* (323 U.S. 283) Justice William O. Douglas wrote the decision for a unanimous court, but for over one month Chief Justice Harlan Fiske Stone withheld it, along with the Korematsu decision, until December 18, 1944. Douglas noted that General De Witt had been authorized to establish military areas, and that Executive Order 9102 provided for a civilian War Relocation Authority to oversee the removal of designated persons. All Japanese were ordered to evacuate Sacramento beginning on May 16. Crucially, on August 11, 1942, De Witt gave the WRA, a civilian agency, the authority to issue permits to leave the camps, thus relinquishing "control over the ingress and egress of evacuees from the Relocation Centers."[51]

The writ of habeas corpus held that "no charge has been made against [Endo], that she is being unlawfully detained, and that she is confined . . . under armed guard and . . . against her will." There was no charge nor suspicion of disloyalty. The Court conceded "that it is beyond the power of the WRA to detain citizens against whom no charges of disloyalty or subversiveness have been made for a period longer than that necessary to separate the loyal from disloyal and to provide the necessary guidance for relocation." Moreover, De Witt's report indicated that "Essentially, military necessity required only that the Japanese population be removed from the coastal area and dispersed in the interior." The evacuation program "ultimately developed into one of complete Federal supervision . . . due primarily to the fact that the interior states would not accept an uncontrolled Japanese migration." Endo's detention, therefore, was "not directly connected with the prevention of espionage and sabotage"—the precise rationale for the establishment of the military areas. Douglas concluded that Endo was "detained by a civilian agency," not by the military, and that the WRA "has no authority to subject citizens who are concededly loyal to its leave procedures."

In effect, Congress had approved "civil penalties" for the failure to obey the WRA. "Accordingly, no questions of military law are involved"—nor any defense based on military necessity. Finally, given that opposition by interior state governors to voluntary resettlement by the Japanese, Douglas declared, "detention in Relocation Centers was no part of the original program of evacuation but developed later." Douglas concluded, "Loyalty is a matter of the heart and mind, not of race, creed, or color. . . . When the power to detain is derived from the power to protect the war effort against espionage and sabotage, [any such] detention which has no relationship to that objective is unauthorized." Detaining a citizen as protection against espionage and sabotage was impermissible once the individual's loyalty was conceded.

Anticipating the Endo decision, a day earlier the military had declared that the camps were to be closed, and all those being held were free to leave (other than those at Tule Lake who were regarded as of doubtful loyalty and those who, with family members, had requested repatriation to Japan).

Nothing more was done at the time about the cases and the arguments sustained therein, although, at the height of the Cold War in the 1950s, many Chinese feared that such camps were being readied for their incarceration. The cases were as muted as the Nisei were about the whole experience in the camps—that is, until in the early 1980s, when a team of legal scholars, led by Professor Peter Irons, found documents that government lawyers had withheld from the courts during the trials and appeals of those cases. The information in them would have dissolved the assertions used to justify the claims of military necessity. In effect, the administration and the military had lied before the federal courts. While the three principal decisions regarding curfews and evacuations were set aside, the precedents were not entirely undone. The lengthy detention of alleged suspects following 9/11 reawakened many dormant concerns about the unrestrained use of federal powers, especially against U.S. citizens, as had happened to Japanese Americans.

Some 79,700 were still in the camps in July 1944. Departures began in earnest early in 1945, with various complications, fears, and uncertainties among those who had been detained for so long. Thousands did not initially return to the West; others never did.[52] On September 4, 1945, two days after Japan's unconditional surrender, all restrictions against the Japanese and Japanese Americans in the West were terminated. All but the Tule Lake camp were closed in October and November of 1945; Tule Lake was finally shut as a WRA facility on March 20, 1946. To the very end there were Issei who simply could not believe that Japan would lose. Said one disbeliever at the end of 1944, "Fundamentally, . . . I would go out [of the camp] if I thought that Japan were going to be defeated in this war, but it's evident that Japan is winning the war."[53]

But the incarceration affair did not end there, for there remained one less visible but no less powerful expression of the "pain, outrage, and alienation" and of the "the decline of evacuees' faith in the United States." It concerned "one of the saddest testaments to the injustice of exclusion and detention." During the war, some 20,000 Issei and Nisei filed applications requesting repatriation or expatriation to Japan. As America's victory seemed more certain and fervor waned, thousands of the 5,766 Nisei who had so declared sought to reverse their renunciation of citizenship. That initiated a process which, for many, dragged on for years beyond the war. Lawyer Wayne Collins labored in these multiple cases to persuade the courts that such renunciations, made in the camps under duress, were invalid. The status of some would remain unresolved for over two decades. In the end, 4,724 actually left from the camps for Japan—1,659 Issei, 1,949 Nisei (mostly children of those Issei), and 1,116 adult Nisei and Kibei—as did approximately 2,300 from elsewhere in the country. The final report of the CWRIC adds that such "cold statistics fail . . . to convey the scars of mind and soul that many carried with them from the camps." Not until May 20, 1959, did the federal government complete the restoration of citizenship to 4,978 Nisei who had been left in the purgatory status of "native American aliens" since their renunciations during the war.[54]

This lack of resolution was also true for the thousands who did not leave the country but who lost property, farms, businesses, government jobs, civil service credits, farm equipment of all kinds, and an immense amount of income that could have been earned from wartime contracts and general wartime demand. While the Japanese had lost their livelihoods, many white American farmers, businessmen, and ordinary workers had doubly profited—from the war and from the vacuum created by the removal of Japanese competitors. "In Los Angeles County $16 million of the annual $25 million flower market business was in Nikkei hands." Evacuation occurred "near one of the richest days in the flower business—Mother's Day, which accounts for one-fifth of the annual sale of flowers." Japanese nursery owners had to abandon it all or, in one case, simply turn over $100,000 in itemized, undisposable nursery stock to a U.S. government veterans hospital. George Aratani "ran his family's Central Valley farm, farm equipment, shipping and packing businesses. He estimated that he lost . . . $20 million when he was forced into a camp and left the business to non-Japanese associates." Similar stories abounded outside of agriculture. A fisherman in Monterey, having struggled through the Depression, recalled that "Every cent I owned was invested in my fishing equipment, and I had to store it in the family garage knowing it would deteriorate and be worthless within a few years." A Seattle man sold a 450-room hotel for $2,500. On the very individual level, many people came to Japanese families offering sickeningly low amounts for possessions the Japanese had to unload, such as refrigerators for $5 and new trucks for $25.

In 1948 Congress enacted the Japanese-American Evacuation Claims Act, and nearly 26,600 claims were filed for $148 million in loses. The negotiations wore on, and the government eventually paid out $37 million. While a long-standing figure of losses as amounting to $400 million turns out to have been the estimate of a JACL leader, with no foundation in data, closer analyses for the CWRIC in the early 1980s developed a breakdown of approximate losses in income and property, including inflation and interest, that placed the total between $3.4 and $4.2 billion. The human capital losses and psychological costs could not be calculated at all.[55]

Implicit in the policies developed during the war was the assumption of collective guilt—"guilty by reason of race."[56] The U.S. Supreme Court accepted the contention that persons of Japanese ancestry were non-assimilable and could not be trusted, nor the loyal among them distinguished from the disloyal. Consequently, excluding that whole population rested on "a military imperative." Nearly a quarter-century later, Justice Hugo Black could still remark that people were rightfully fearful of Japanese Americans in Los Angeles, for many were loyal but "many undoubtedly [were] not. . . . They all look alike to a person not a Jap."[57] And yet, once it was conceded that the vast majority of Nisei were, in fact, loyal Americans, the whole claim of a power to detain such persons was without justification or authorization, military or otherwise. To that assessment one adds Justice Frank Murphy's critical voice in the Endo decision: the detention of all Americans of Japanese ancestry was "another example of the unconstitutional resort to racism inherent in the entire evacuation program."

The jockeying behind the high court façade as outlined above and the texts of the decisions themselves make it powerfully clear why the political, moral, and constitutional implications of those decisions and their timing were, and remain, so profound, especially in light of the many controversies surrounding recent claims of abuses of power, power that was said to be based upon the USA PATRIOT Act and even outside of it.

In terms of *political* consequences, the Endo decision was intentionally withheld until after the 1944 presidential election, thus manipulating the impact of the decision.[58] It was not released until after the War Department could first announce that there was no longer any danger of invasion, sabotage, or espionage, and, therefore, the Japanese and Japanese Americans could, on January 2, 1945, begin returning to their homes along the coast.

In so far as the *moral* consequences are concerned, the conclusion of the Commission on the Wartime Relocation and Internment of Civilians emphatically states that "Executive Order 9066 was not justified by military necessity," and that decisions related to detention "were not driven by analysis of military conditions." Rather, they were shaped by "race prejudice, war hysteria and a failure of political leadership. Widespread ignorance of Japanese Americans contributed to a policy conceived in haste and executed in an atmosphere of fear and anger at Japan. A grave injustice was done to American citizens and resident nationals of Japanese ancestry."

Finally, the *constitutional* consequences have not been set aside nor entirely disavowed. Howard Ball argues that the preventive detention involved in the use of the assembly centers and relocation/concentration camps violated the Fourth and Fifth Amendments even though that "evidently did not concern most of the justices." Furthermore, Ball adds, the decisions upholding the evacuation and exclusion of all persons of Japanese descent demonstrate that, under certain circumstances, "some groups' constitutional rights are a dead letter, and individuals may be deprived of due process even if they are loyal, law-abiding citizens."[59]

Six decades after those events, two decades after Ball wrote those conclusions, events following 9/11 involving persons of Arab descent and Muslim faith show that a democratic system can prescribe all kinds of rules and protections, but if there is a dubious collaboration between the branches of government (as Alexander Hamilton warned in *The Federalist* in 1788) even the best checks and balances will not be sufficient. In such situations, ethnic and racial minority groups in particular could be at great risk. These events confirm Mae Ngai's reference to Asian Americans as "alien citizens": persons "born in the United States with formal U.S. citizenship but who remained alien in the eyes of the nation"—even, I would stress, in the eyes and minds of our U.S. Supreme Court justices.[60]

CHAPTER THIRTY-THREE

The Second World War's Other Enemy Aliens
Italians and Germans

W E HAVE COME A LONG WAY since the 1960s, when a major U.S. history textbook included only one sentence about Japanese Americans during the Second World War. But there were other ethnic groups whose histories during the war years were a long time coming. Some stories have moved into the spotlight, particularly those surrounding Mexican Americans as both essential workers and unprovoked victims. Still others were long denied the coverage they deserved. Stephen Fox began his 1990 oral history of Italians during this war with a brief account of four immigrant men who committed suicide when faced with the self-perceived shame of being classified as enemy aliens. They had to leave homes and businesses after years spent carving out new lives in America. The men ranged in age from 57 to 65 and tragically ended their lives in front of a moving train, with a knife, at the end of a noose, and by leaping from a building. None had become citizens. If they had, none of these extreme measures would likely have occurred. In fact, Milano Ripoli, of the Italian Welfare Agency, also learned of three others in San Francisco who, fearing they would be put in concentration camps, also committed suicide.[1]

The wives of many immigrant men learned before mid-December 1941 that they, too, were classified as enemy aliens and, seven weeks later, that, as noncitizens, they would have to leave their homes and businesses in the Prohibited Zone along the coast. They now more fully understood the price of having failed to apply for citizenship. Steve Antongiovanni (of Eureka, California) recalled that "In 1930 [shortly after his mother arrived] there was no immediate need for my mother to become a citizen." "Learning English was not a priority," for "she was in the house all the time and there were Italians all around." She did, however, acquire citizenship in 1942. Also in Eureka, Gino Casagrande indicated that his mother received her citizenship after the war. Why not sooner, he was asked. He replied, "Here's an immigrant that can't speak the language. She's a housewife. She worked in [their] bakery . . . ; she took care of three children. . . . The only thing she was worried about was taking care of her family." In Monterey, Vitina Spadaro described how his mother "All of a sudden . . . realized that she was considered an alien, so she wanted to be part of this country, she wanted to be an American like my father and me." She studied English and the U.S. Constitution and did become naturalized.[2]

While the mother of Anita Pera (who resided in Eureka) "still had this basic love for Italy and [like] a lot of these people hated to give up Italian citizenship," John Molinari, a lawyer in San Francisco, emphasized that "so many of [the Italians] never got around to getting citizenship—had been here for thirty, forty, fifty years. Joe DiMaggio's father, for example, he never applied for citizenship; he was a fisherman. He eventually passed, but it took him a long time." Many fishermen there "were busy or they were afraid of the examination. . . . I had clients that couldn't read or write, even in Italian, let alone English." Thus, in Ugo Giutini's home (in Arcata), his father did not become a citizen, but his mother worked hard to get her citizenship and succeeded.

As with the Japanese, so with German and Italian aliens. The FBI and local police began immediately to round up prominent community members, especially those on the FBI's "ABC" list. Somewhat overeager agents arrested German and Italian aliens *before* the president issued Proclamations 2526 and 2527 (December 8, 1941), declaring that Germans and Italians were now enemy aliens. This initial group of detainees included those in the "German-American People's League" (the Bund) or in such allegedly pro-Fascist organizations as the National Protective Order of Gentiles, the Federation of Italian World War Veterans in the United States, and the Dante Alighieri Society. The detainees also included those who had spoken, written, or taken action in support of Mussolini or Hitler, as did Spartaco Bonomi, former president of the Italian Catholic Federation. Indeed, the Italian government had been urging Italians to celebrate their "Italianità."

Alfonso Zirpoli, a federal attorney in San Francisco at that time and later a judge, acknowledged that "during this period the people in San Francisco thought that Il Duce was pretty good, that he was doing a lot of good work. . . ." Albert Mangiapane, a Sicilian who arrived in 1925, recalled that "Most people thought he was a pretty good guy." Some may have feared him, but women sent their wedding rings to support his war effort, and, said Peter Cutino, "most [Sicilians in Monterey] thought Mussolini was a hero." Joseph Maniscalco, who lived in San Francisco, remembered how his "father had great admiration for Mussolini. He idolized him and that was one of the reasons why he became so irate when there was a war with Italy. . . . And yet, as much as he respected Mussolini and Italy, he *never* wanted to go back to Italy, and he never did. . . . [Eventually] he began to realize that Mussolini did make a big mistake [allying with Hitler and declaring war on the United States] and felt very pro-American. . . . He loved America . . . ; he loved the area. To him, Italy was North Beach." On the other hand, sometimes questionable actions took place, as when the FBI called on Mario Valdastri, a naturalized citizen living in Honolulu. After a short hearing he was ordered interned and shipped to the mainland wearing only his Hawaiian clothes. He recalled having to stuff newspapers inside his clothing to stay warm.[3]

George E. Pozzetta concluded that "No real precision about the number of internees will ever be possible since no government agency had the sole responsibility of keeping records and receiving the often contradictory (and incomplete) figures available." Before Pearl Harbor, 995 Italians and 667 Germans (merchant seamen and workers at the New York World's Fair) had been picked up. Discrepancies in the numbers may be attributable to the fact that many were arrested or taken into custody (one set of figures), subsequently questioned by authorities and then by the Alien Enemy Hearing Boards, at which point they could be freed or be interned in an INS facility (second set of figures). During the first 18 months the terminology was no more consistent than the figures were certain. That 9,405 had been "apprehended," "arrested," "detained," or "taken into custody" did not mean they all continued to be *interned* by the INS. Most of those who had been living in the country were reviewed, paroled, or released without condition. Thus, within 24 hours of the attack, the FBI picked up 1,717 persons (about 77 were Italian; table 4.1). The numbers steadily grew, with reports of a total of 9,405 "suspects" having been detained by the end of June 1942, of whom 7,469 were still being held. Among them were 4,092 Japanese, 2,384 Germans, 794 Italians, and 199 others. The Italian figure for internees fell by the end of the year to 210.

It was fluctuations such as these that prompted Pozzetta to conclude that "approximately 4,000 Italians suffered arrest and/or detention" but that "approximately 200" were actually interned "for the entire war," even though only 86 were under INS control in June 1944. In other words, wrote Pozzetta, relatively few Italians "actually confronted the reality of detention, internment, or evacuation." While the precise figure for Germans was undoubtedly greater, a similar conclusion was true for them, too. The FBI's Final Report in 1945 indicates a cumulative total of 16,062 persons taken into custody by the INS for various periods of time—which included over 7,000 Germans and nearly 3,600 Italians.[4]

These various numbers, however, do not convey just how disrupted the lives of Italians were (and those of Germans and Japanese, too, of course), especially in the tight-knit California communities from Monterey to Arcata. General De Witt's measures affected them profoundly, but the outcome differed dramatically from that unfolding among the Japanese. De Witt's original December 19 proposal to remove all enemy aliens and bar their return to sensitive coastal areas was rejected because there were more than one million European enemy aliens in the country (0.7 million Italians, 0.3 million Germans) and 52,000 of those Italians were in California, concentrated close to the coast and coastal cities. Indeed, there were 7,200 more foreign-born Italians in California than the entire Japanese American population. There were also more than twice the number of German foreign born than Issei (roughly 71,700 versus 33,600). Large numbers of Germans and Italians could also be found in states along the Atlantic Coast, where the logistical problems or removal would be far greater.

In fact, Secretary of War Stimson drew the parallel between economic conditions on the mainland and those in Hawai'i: "The Japanese population is so interwoven into the economic fabric of the Islands that if we attempt to evacuate all Japanese aliens and citizens, all businesses, including that concerned with the building up of our defenses, would practically stop."[5] Thus, to a considerable extent, as we saw with the Nikkei in Hawai'i, demographics—as well as economic realities (too many essential workers) and political realities (too many German and Italian American voters to ignore)—trumped wartime policy decisions concerning these enemy aliens and any possible fifth-column activity among them.[6]

Nonetheless, before that assessment was made, the FBI and police had conducted searches for all manner of potential contraband—guns, radios, shortwave components, cameras, and anything else that could be construed as expressing or representing support for the Axis nations—none of which the Italians ever were able to recover. Perhaps the most outrageous abuse was committed by Alameda County officials, who had previously purchased cars for $35,000 from an Italian car dealer in Oakland. On December 11, they bought five more for $5,309 and then refused to pay, basing their refusal on the 1917 prohibition in the Trading with the Enemy Act.[7]

Meanwhile, more than 10,000 Italians were faced with having to evacuate, which was complicated by the curfew and the prohibition on traveling more than five miles from one's home. Families split up; in Arcata some actually set up homes across from one another on Highway 101, the dividing line between the prohibited and restricted areas. Such was the case with Nida Vanni, whose Italian mother was born in France and therefore was technically not an enemy alien. She remained on the west side of the street, while Nida's father and her own spouse, Angelo, had to move across to the east side. Both men, noncitizens, on the east side, with their jobs on the west side, found themselves, like many others, suddenly jobless. Catherine Sulpizzo remembered that her husband, a non-citizen, "became very, very depressed. He couldn't get a job."

When asked his status, he would have to tell potential employers he was an Italian citizen. "Maybe they would hire him for a day but that was it."

Numerous fishermen in Monterey had to relocate their families to Salinas; many in the small community of Pittsburg, adjacent to the Sacramento Delta, moved to nearby Oakley. About 1,400 were idled in San Francisco, as were hundreds in Monterey; in fact, the estimate given was 600 who were required to move and some 800 family members who joined them. Adding to the Italians' woes, in late February the U.S. Coast Guard barred enemy aliens from fishing in coastal waters and requisitioned perhaps as many as 500 fishing vessels for patrolling the coast. On February 11, the *Monterey Peninsula Herald* reported that "2,234 of the 8,750 licensed fishermen" were enemy aliens "no longer allowed to put out to sea," but the Department of Justice lists only 315 Italian aliens who were barred from fishing in coastal waters. It noted, "Often speaking little English and unable to read or write, many [Italians] avoided naturalization out of fear or embarrassment. Their failure to obtain citizenship prior to the war was to become, for some, a substantial regret."[8]

As a population that included large numbers of citizens and voters concentrated in politically strategic locations in the state and nation, Italians did not accept the new policy with Japanese resignation, or *shikata ga nai*. They organized a Committee to Aid Italians Loyal to the United States to make the case that moving large numbers of Italians (and Germans) would be logistically very difficult. The Sons of Italy was likewise active on behalf of those interned. McCloy warned De Witt that "the social and economic disturbances would be so great" arising from any massive exclusion of European aliens that he urged the general to proceed slowly. Simultaneously, the House Select Commission Investigating National Defense Migration, chaired by John Tolan (D-CA) held hearings in California February 21–March 12. During the hearings, Tolan urged calm and sympathy for the uprooted groups, for he was greatly concerned about the national impact of the evacuation of so many Italians and Germans, especially along the eastern seaboard, where most Italians resided. Indeed, what seemed to sum up the situation were the notes of a presidential cabinet meeting on February 27: "confusion reigned . . . because nobody realized how big the exclusion job would be." De Witt deferred the mass evacuation part of his plan but not the continued apprehension and investigation of individual enemy aliens.[9]

Among the many efforts and gestures expressing the Italians' loyalty (along with the military enlistment of several hundred thousand) was one that expressed particularly strong sentiments. San Francisco's garbage collectors—an Italian union—not only raised $10,000 for war bonds but also displayed a photo with an Italian worker standing next to a sign that read: "Italian blood is in our veins but America is in our heart. . . . Scavengers' Protective Association."[10] A group of 60 prominent Sicilian boat owners in Monterey made a $50,000 contribution to the U.S. Navy in the form of six 80-foot diesel fishing boats. A letter to the president announcing the contribution was signed by A. N. Lucido, president of the Monterey Sardine Industries Association of cannery owners. Not only was Lucido one of the wealthiest Sicilians in Monterey, but one of his sons was already in the army.

Ultimately, fewer obstacles stood between the Italians and a policy reversal of their status than faced the Japanese or the Germans. Clearly, neither Italians nor Germans were targets of the kind of racism that plagued the Japanese. In fact, in Congress and out, voices were continually heard questioning the evacuation of the Italians, and Roosevelt issued Executive Order 9106, March 20, 1942, exempting Italians and Germans from certain restrictions so they could apply for citizenship. By the end of that month popular worries concerning both foreign-born populations were already fading. On May 5, assessing the public's morale and the economic costs of such a massive evacuation, Roosevelt advised Stimson to take no action along the East Coast without his approval.

Two and a half weeks later Stimson gave DeWitt the directive to take no action regarding the mass evacuation of German and Italian aliens in the West. Then, on June 27, with the Japanese removed, De Witt declared an end to the exclusion and restricted zones on the West Coast, although curfews and some travel limitations remained. However, after Roosevelt told Francis Biddle, "I don't care so much about Italians. They are a lot of opera singers. But the Germans are different; they may be dangerous," the attorney general chose Columbus Day 1942 to announce the removal of Italians from the list of enemy aliens. Most restrictions against German resident aliens were removed in January 1943.[11] It is reasonable to conclude that an estimated 3,500–4,000 Italians were apprehended and that 228 may have been the maximum number interned at any one time (October 1942)—or for some period of time—and that cumulatively at least 418 were interned at some point during the war.

Roosevelt's calculated reversal regarding Italians did not close off DeWitt's insistence on his authority to investigate individuals, either aliens or citizens. Apart from the evacuation of enemy aliens in the spring and the curfew and other restrictions affecting more than 50,000 Italian aliens, a separate procedure was launched on September 1, 1942, the Individual Exclusion Program, which could be applied to aliens or citizens. They would be called before hearing boards, such as in Seattle, Portland, San Francisco, Los Angeles, and San Diego. While some five dozen Italians were ordered to appear, only about two dozen were formally ordered to leave the restricted areas (among the 174 persons so ordered). But the consequences could go far beyond just leaving the California coast.

Nino de Guttadauro reported for such a hearing in San Francisco on September 8, 1942. He was an accountant who had worked for the Italian consulate, and he was also a World War One veteran of the Italian Army and president of the San Francisco branch of the Federation of Italian World War Veterans, or Ex-Combattenti. The FBI had carefully investigated him, and on September 29 he was ordered to leave and not enter many of the military areas in the country, covering 29 states from the West Coast to Texas to Alabama and up to Connecticut. He was to report immediately to the FBI when he reached his destination. Over the next 18 months he and his wife and two children had to change residences frequently because he was unable to find work once it was made known that he had been formally expelled from the West Coast. He ended up working as a grocery clerk in Salt Lake City. As his son, Angelo, recalled, "We had become, by military fiat, a family of involuntary gypsies." Finally, on March 13, 1944, his exclusion was rescinded.

In contrast, Sylvester Andriano had been a prominent attorney in San Francisco, head of the draft board, member of the board of supervisors and the police commission, and also active in the Italian-American community as director of a North Beach Italian language school and as a board member of the Italian Chamber of Commerce. The latter drew the attention of the FBI, and though Andriano was a distinguished citizen, he was excluded from Military Area One the day before de Guttadauro was. For one and a half years he worked in Chicago until he returned to see his ailing mother. DeWitt's office wanted to prosecute, but Biddle refused to do so, arguing once more that the program was unconstitutional, in part because citizens were not permitted to confront witnesses.[12]

Germans, despite their large numbers in the West in 1940 (137,600), did not experience the ordeals of the Italians—especially anything akin to those of the First World War Germans. Indeed, Kevin Starr noted, "despite evidence of German sabotage on the East Coast, it never even crossed the minds of Californians—not once if one is to judge by the public record—to contemplate the wholesale roundup and deportation of the thousands of non-citizen German residents" or those of German ancestry.[13] The number of Germans taken in topped 7,000, and somewhat under 3,000 were actually interned at any one time (June 30, 1944). At the time the European war ended in April 1945, the 900 Germans who remained interned were the most ardent pro-Nazis. In September, 500 were deported to Germany. The situation might have been much worse in terms of the pursuit of suspicious enemy aliens, but Biddle had opposed any resurrection of the American Protective League, with its one-quarter million volunteers during the First World War serving as domestic spies on fellow Americans and contributing to the domestic hysteria.[14]

No such actions took place against German foreign born because between 1930 and 1940 their number had dropped by 18,000 in the three most western states (a nearly one-sixth decline), relatively few of those remaining were not naturalized citizens, and among those German aliens there were no reports of subversive actions involving them (or Italians) in the West.[15] Beyond those basic considerations, Germans were also less concentrated along the Far West's coastal prohibited zones; they were also not heavily populating urban places where they might have been seen as posing a security problem; rather, many continued to live and work in central or eastern parts of the Pacific Coast states or were even farther from the coast (e.g., 18,000 in Texas and 7,000 in Colorado). Moreover, many of them were clearly set apart by religion and distinctive cultural practices, including the Germans from Russia in Colorado and Nebraska and German Mormons in Utah, and such groups would not have been viewed as any kind of pro-Nazi threat. Finally, many successfully deflected potential hostility with their financial contributions to war bond drives and their military enlistments.

Having gone through their enemy alien experience during the First World War, not only did the Germans have another American-born generation grow up since that time, but a number of the more German-oriented organizations had also either faded or, along with the churches, shifted to English language in services and meetings, reducing their visibility as foreign entities. In a specific case, the German Latter Day Saints Organization (Mormons) was considered a "political liability" by church leaders in Utah, so it was disbanded when the United States entered the Second World War. Furthermore, the Bund apparently had a far weaker presence in the West, and, added to that, thousands of the Germans (and Austrians) were recent refugees. Many, particularly among those in Los Angeles, were prominent individuals in their fields of endeavor who had had to flee Europe and were unhesitatingly anti-Nazi.

Thus, although an April 1942 national poll reported that 46 percent of those interviewed felt that Germans were the "most dangerous" (compared with 35 percent regarding the Japanese and merely 2 percent for the Italians), that did not translate into much anti-German hostility in the West, possibly because there was no widespread tradition there of anti-Germanness that could be exploited, as was the case during the First World War or with the anti-Asian sentiments at this time. Children did taunt German American children, but that did not equate with the widespread harassment or internment of Germans as the main target for hostility a generation earlier; the Japanese were the pariahs of the present war.

Still, foreigners of various other nationalities were challenged if their loyalties were suspect, and in most reports those singled out frequently had Germanic names. Nonetheless, the German POWs from the North Africa campaign held at Camp Ogden in Utah and in more than a half dozen other locations did not experience harsh treatment. In 1944 and 1945 over 100,000 of them received jobs with nearby farmers or work with the railroads. Some maintained contact with Americans after the war, and still others actually returned to America to settle in the late 1940s, as happened in Utah and Washington State.[16] As noted, on September 4, 1945, two days after Japan's formal surrender, all exclusion and restriction orders against enemy aliens and Japanese Americans were rescinded.

These changes, exceptions, and the seeming contradictions of POWs being recruited to work outside their POW camps must have felt like a roller coaster of events to both the POWs and Americans who hired them or lived near those camps. Alfredo Cipolato's experience captures some of the very mixed circumstances that swept up POWs and other enemy aliens besides most of the Issei.[17] He had been working at the World's Fair when he was arrested; he spoke almost no English. He was sent with a group of Germans first to Ellis Island and then to Fort Missoula. Seventeen months later, a group of detainees was released to harvest sugar beets. The Western Montana Beet Growers' Association had requested 1,850 Italians and Japanese at Missoula to work in the fields for $30 per month (in scrip). After the season many worked as hospital orderlies. Alfredo and a few others even sang with a local church choir. There, he met a young Italian American woman whose parents had immigrated in 1908 and who operated a grocery store. She spoke enough Italian to start a relationship with Alfredo, and they were married in October 1943. They raised five children. The government still ordered his deportation in 1945, and his wife contacted Montana congressman Mike Mansfield. Mansfield got the order rescinded and then urged Alfredo to apply for citizenship as soon as possible as a spouse of a U.S. citizen. He became a citizen in 1948. "Every year I celebrate my 'American' birthday on April 25, the day I arrived in New York. My family will come home then for a big dinner and a birthday cake topped with the American flag. Then, I have my real birthday party, my 'Italian' birthday on October 5, which is another big family celebration."

In light of these events it should come as no surprise that naturalizations surged during the war among those designated enemy aliens, those in the military, and others caught up in the wartime fervor or responding for pragmatic reasons. The number of new citizens peaked in 1944, a total not surpassed for 50 years. Consider the critical importance of citizenship during the war for enemy aliens and the decisive handicaps suffered by Asian immigrants until the law was changed beginning with the Chinese in 1943. Serious disabilities had been imposed on Asians in more than a dozen states, such as prohibiting aliens ineligible for citizenship from owning or leasing land.[18]

As detailed in part 3, beginning in 1940 some five million non-citizens of all nationalities were required to face an extensive registration process, and then in February 1942 there was a second registration specifically for the 938,000 enemy aliens. Non-citizens were confronted with the onerousness of being labeled not just an alien but an enemy alien, and because of that enemy alien status they risked being singled out for scrutiny by government agents, scrutiny that could result in being taken into custody and even interned, or incarcerated, possibly for the duration of the war. As we saw, some experienced the additional burden of being compelled to move their residences out of restricted zones or to strictly observe curfews and travel limitations that fellow ethnic group members with citizenship could ignore. Welfare assistance and defense-related jobs were frequently denied to non-citizens or those without first papers. Of course, non-citizens also did not have the option of sponsoring the admission of family members as non-quota immigrants.

The dramatic development in December 1943, when Chinese became the first Asian immigrant group to become eligible for naturalization, rightly stands forth as a watershed moment. When that privilege had been extended three years earlier to natives of the Western Hemisphere, it was, by comparison, a non-controversial matter. In July 1946, the precedent would be extended to two other ethnic groups, Asian Indians and Filipinos, whose homelands had been America's allies during the war. The positive and strategic political and foreign policy consequences were considerable, for these measures represented major steps toward a color-blind standard for citizenship. They constituted a critical dimension of inclusiveness that would become part of the pluralistic norms of American society emerging from the war (and that were used for propaganda purposes, too). As Evelyn Nakano Glenn put it, "Citizenship is not just a matter of formal legal status; it is a matter of belonging, including recognition by other members of the community."[19] By expanding the boundaries of membership-through-citizenship with these reforms, Americans were moving Asians from the periphery of American society into its mainstream. The Second World War brought home to many Europeans (enemy aliens in particular) what Asians had long known—that *not* possessing American citizenship could have dire, and costly, consequences for oneself and one's family.[20]

The number of naturalizations jumped by 42 percent during the war years (1941–1945), compared with the prior five years: 1.54 million persons now became citizens versus 892,400 between 1936 and 1940. Nearly 110,700 received citizenship in the military (at least 11,600 of whom were Asian, including almost 8,400 persons from the Philippines, 2,100 from China, and 50 from Japan).[21] Of all these new citizens, 207,358 lived in the West, 13.5 percent of the five-year total. Increases were also high among a number of specific populations: Germans (+37 percent), British subjects (+39 percent), Scandinavians (+41 percent), Poles (+42 percent), former residents of the USSR (+48 percent), Italians (+47 percent) and Mexicans (+75 percent).

Finally, two central questions have been raised concerning Germans and citizenship, especially during war time: Does citizenship in and of itself "define national loyalty in times of war?" and "Was citizenship the ultimate proof of [a] . . . finished process of assimilation and hence loyalty?"[22] Certainly, Germans had good reason to be concerned about such issues, but they found the situation in the West during the Second World War far less troublesome than during the First World War. They and other Europeans realized that, given the nation's heterogeneity, Americans actually regarded citizenship as an important measure of loyalty, as a key wartime basis for legitimation and (in most instances) protection. Indeed, the awareness of the advantages was evident when the war ended and there was a 35 percent drop in new citizens in fiscal year 1946 (to 150,062)—two-thirds below the peak figure in 1944. On the other hand, the Nikkei also learned firsthand that being ineligible could prove most costly— and yet they also discovered to their deep chagrin that being native born and possessing citizenship by birth, as was the status of the Nisei, did not always ensure that their constitutional rights would be protected. Such was the lesson they learned from the decisions by the U.S. Supreme Court: in times of crises even the rights accorded U.S. citizens may prove inadequate to stop officials bent on violating those rights.

CHAPTER THIRTY-FOUR

The Homefront in Wartime
Preface to an Era of Change

As TRAUMATIC AS WERE the events of the early 1940s concerning the Japanese and Italians, both aliens and citizens, the extraordinary impact of the war on the West's industries and other populations had enormous, enduring consequences. The war has been described as having produced "probably the most drastic changes in the Far West since 1849." In fact, in April 1943, the *San Francisco Chronicle* described the period as the region's "second gold rush." Historian Carl Abbott, in several exceptional studies, referred to the war years as the "reopening of the West," its "take off" era, the decade that "shifted the American center of gravity westward." "The West ended six years of mobilization and war with a vastly expanded regional market, a new industrial infrastructure, and a new base of workers and wealth." While this time it was predominantly a gold rush to the cities—the connection points and pacesetters for the region—the need for the agricultural labor of Japanese American evacuees, German and Italian POWs, Filipinos, and Mexican braceros certainly reminds us that the rural west of railroads, mines, and industrial farms had not ceased to be vital to the region's economy. The labor of the native and the foreign born proved to be indispensable to those enterprises, especially as many midwestern and southern migrants of the 1930s quickly left the fields for city jobs in the burgeoning defense industries.[1]

Even before December 1941, those regional changes that would enhance labor needs at many levels were visible because of the efforts of many states and local communities to attract federal New Deal dollars. Funds were requested, among many projects, for highway construction in Nevada, Montana, Wyoming, Arizona, and California; for bridges and hydroelectric dams in Washington and California; for aqueducts carving channels down California's Central Valley; and soon for military bases near San Francisco, San Antonio, and San Diego (the latter due to the relocation of about half the Pacific fleet to its new home base there). The principal factor in these developments, especially once war production accelerated, was the federal government's "ubiquitous" "monetary presence in the urban West," which amounted to $35 billion just to California and $5.6 billion to Seattle. That infusion led to skyrocketing employment figures. Between 1938 and December 1941, the Los Angeles aircraft industry grew from 15,930 to 120,000 employees and then to 243,000 in 1943; its shipyards, which had averaged merely 1,000 workers in 1939, jumped to 22,000 by October 1941 and 280,000 in the Los Angeles area by war's end. Between 1940 and mid-1943, 550,000 new jobs were created in the Los Angeles area alone, 65,000 of which were for women in aircraft plants.

The government invested $4.7 billion in shipyards, and Washington State's 88 yards had 150,000 employees, while Henry Kaiser had a quarter-million workers in his various shipyards. Boeing had between 50,000 and 55,000 workers. Over $4.3 billion was used for military bases around the West (aside from Hawai'i), along with $4.1 billion on military production facilities. The needs were so great that they could not be met just by *man*power. In many parts of the West, women quickly flooded the labor markets as men were drafted. In fact, among the 12 western mainland states, only Montana received no funding for a military base or major military industrial site. Aside from that, wartime demand lifted the West from its reputation as America's Third World and revitalized Arizona's copper, zinc, and lead mines as well as those in New Mexico, Utah, and Idaho. The agricultural needs of a nation at war generated demands so great that they could be met only by looking for workers in the nation's POW camps, in Japanese American concentration camps, and beyond the nation's borders to braceros.

Nevertheless, the West, mecca of the outdoor idealists so often captured in Hollywood's films, was on track to become one of the most urban regions of the nation. From the Pacific Northwest's Seattle, Bremerton, Tacoma, Spokane, Vancouver (WA), Bellingham, Everett, Aberdeen, Portland, and even Eugene, to California's Oakland, Vallejo, Richmond, San Francisco, Los Angeles and vicinity, and San Diego. From Honolulu in the west to Phoenix, Tucson, Denver, and Albuquerque, and eastward to El Paso, Houston, Dallas, and San Antonio. Across the region, urban areas were becoming urban centers; cities were becoming metropolitan hubs. Virtually all were benefiting from the war economy. What continued to make these years "nothing short of a social and industrial revolution" was, in addition to the extraordinary infusion of federal money and the acute labor shortage, President Roosevelt's Executive Order 8802 on June 25, 1941, which prohibited government contractors from employment discrimination based on "race, creed, color, or national origin." The Fair Employment Practices Committee (later Commission) was to oversee complaints even though it thus far had no enforcement mechanisms. Still, this was the first such federal declaration, and it may well have provided some additional incentive to that expressed by a Boeing official, who admitted that "We hired anybody who had a warm body and could walk inside the gate."[2]

With the onset of war, the rapidly expanding urban infrastructure, especially in California (which went from 68 percent to 81 percent urban during the 1940s), generated an insatiable demand for workers. The more that native-born Americans were being hired by war-related industries, the greater was the call for immigrants and native minorities (e.g., Native Americans and African Americans)—men and women—to fill the many non-union, semi-skilled and unskilled jobs. Since African Americans migrating out of the South were likewise drawn to the shipyards and other businesses that would hire them, despite on-going discrimination, there still remained an employment vacuum they could not (or would not) fill. Immigrant labor again played a critical role in those particular job sectors—a role it retained after the war.

For example, Trinidad Annunciacion later recalled: "When the war broke out, the competition for Filipinos was keen. Everybody wished there were one or two million Filipinos here. The asparagus industry of California, the salmon industry of Alaska, the shipyards, the aircraft factories, and the construction companies on the Alaska highway scrambled for Filipino workers and did their best to restrain the Army from drafting them." In fact, the HSPA sugar planters made one last effort to recruit Filipinos in 1946 and brought in 7,361 just prior to the Philippines receiving its independence.[3]

By 1944, between 25 and 40 percent of the populations in the Bay Area, San Diego, and Los Angeles had arrived since 1940—and that included, among others, 279,000 African Americans, 800,000 southern whites, and 1,000,000 midwesterners, as well as one-fourth of all new immigrants (1941–1945: 44,044).[4] More than 8,200,000 persons moved west of the Mississippi River during the 1940s. California's net increase by 1950 was 3.679 million (+53 percent), 642,800 in Washington (+37 percent), and 431,700 in Oregon (+40 percent). As noted, most immigrants concentrated in urban settings. A 1947 study of an Oakland shipyard described the workers thusly: "In a not untypical Oakland shipyard one could find Slavs, Russians, Portuguese, Germans, Irish, Chinese, Greeks, Italians, and large numbers of Okies among the milling throng of workers." Even more so than during the 1930s, the influx of hundreds of thousands of white and black Americans from the South and Upper South now "southernized" the southwest region. For example, while Kaiser's shipyard workers in Richmond, California, hailed from Memphis, St. Louis, and Chattanooga, plus Okies and Arkies and others from Missouri and Texas, Bakersfield, in the San Joaquin Valley, came to be known as the Second Nashville, with Okies,

Mexicans, and blacks tying "California more closely to the culture of southern North America."[5]

The huge influx of so many peoples then and now prompted writer David Reiff to point out in 1991 that, "If today, Los Angeles would stop functioning were the immigrants from south of the border not to be on hand to do the dirty work, the reality is that the same was true in 1919 and 1946 as well." The postwar calls for such workers continued even as defense industries quickly scaled back production. Drawing on many populations throughout the West, around the nation, and from across the borders, wartime production demands accelerated demographic changes already underway during the interwar years. Notwithstanding the demobilization, the post-1945 period sustained them, not least of all because of the onset of the Cold War and the outbreak of the Korean conflict.[6] Building airplanes and ships, manufacturing garments, constructing roads and transportation facilities, and harvesting most crops remained quite labor intensive.[7]

Shortly after the war ended, Carey McWilliams quoted a major sociologist's observation that Southern California had become "an archipelago of ethnic, cultural, racial, and socio-economic islands." McWilliams's take on the situation was that "In the population of Los Angeles today are represented important elements of every racial strain that has gone into the making of the American people. This city has become, therefore, one of the most interesting racial melting pots in the nation."[8] Islands or melting pots? In many ways these descriptions apply to many parts of the West, from Hawai'i to Texas. And yet, for several reasons, the image of Los Angeles as a melting pot would turn out to be more wishful thinking than reality. The reality was islands hardly touching at their respective shorelines. A superficial image of melting obscured the underlying tensions, which would eventually boil over without "melting" the city's peoples into a truly larger community.

In the broader picture, the war years did witness elements of a greater ethnic diversity accompanied by heightened expectations regarding jobs, education, housing, and political influence.[9] The combination fueled the tensions, and consequently, those years became "a crucible for civil rights movements in the western cities" that yielded successes in later years. Furthermore, if the war did indeed foster opportunities for some minorities to improve their status, it also cast groups together in new settings that triggered conflicts. Those rising expectations and unresolved clashes (especially among the newer groups) added to the wartime and early postwar pressures, generating among some a greater civic activism. The seeds of the Civil Rights Movement that burst forth in the 1960s in many parts of the West were here and now taking root. But they came with struggles and with a price, for these years, the early 1940s, quickly became marked ones. In one respect, there were at that time glimmers of hope that changes were beginning with the new, more Americanized second generation.

In another respect, they were scarred by the continuing exploitation, subordination, victimization, and, not surprisingly, alienation among other young Mexican Americans whose Americanization had moved along a divergent path, one on which they responded to perceived rejection with defiance and resistance.

SLEEPY LAGOON AND THE ZOOT SUIT–NAVY RIOTS

The summers of 1942 and 1943 in Los Angeles certainly brought this victimization home most forcefully. The Japanese population had been evacuated, African Americans were swiftly moving in to those vacated neighborhoods, and Mexican Americans were caught between the heightened passions and anxieties of war, the deeply entrenched prejudices directed at the young Latino population, and their own feelings of powerlessness in the aftermath of the Depression and repatriation. Although there was much in the 1930s to rebel against, one retrospective view concludes that for Latinos in the West the wartime "changes were no less profound than the Mexican War of 1848."[10] Perhaps that would prove to be the case, but it surely did not seem so in the months following the arrests of 24 young pachucos, who belonged to the 38th Street "gang" (as such youth groups were automatically labeled). They were accused of murdering Mexican-born José Diaz (who was 22 years old and possibly a member of the Downey Boys "gang") during a fight following a birthday party on the night of August 1, 1942. The fight, which lasted less than ten minutes, occurred outside Amelia Delgadillo's home, in an area of East Los Angeles known as Williams' Ranch. Near the murder site was a gravel pit (or a small reservoir) used as a swimming hole and lovers' lane. Its name, Sleepy Lagoon, was taken from a popular song by that title.

Eduardo Obregón Pagán contends that the reaction to the Díaz murder was not simply a manifestation of "anti-Mexican hysteria" but a reaction to working-class youths whose behaviors during these war years were seen as challenging "written and unwritten codes of segregation," conformity, and social propriety. The fact that among those arrested were an Anglo youth, Victor "Bobby" Thompson, and a Hungarian American, John Matuz, suggests that the issues underlying the subsequent events of 1942 and 1943—the trial and the Zoot Suit–Navy Riots—involved much more than Mexican ethnicity. From an Anglo perspective, Mexican Americans were generally invisible during the early 1940s, and therefore the Sleepy Lagoon murder precipitated a media frenzy that fed on the long-standing racism toward those of Mexican origin. But the nature of the media attacks and the fact that the defendants were American born and not all of Mexican origin raised broader issues illustrative of the debates over whiteness that have been discussed throughout this book.[11]

Playing on the name Sleepy Lagoon, the defendants were soon referred to as "goons" and "goonies." Exploiting the negative images of Mexicans in an alleg-edly authoritative report, Sheriff Capt. Edward Duran Ayres described the typi-cal pachuco—due to their supposed Oriental and therefore Mongolian roots—as having an inbred "desire to use a knife or some lethal weapon. In other words his desire is to kill or at least let blood." The high profile, three-month trial was a vehicle to demonstrate the city's recent commitment to cracking down on gangs that seemed more visible and troublesome since the war began and a Naval Reserve Training School was built in Chavez Ravine, in East Los Ange-les. Perhaps the case was also meant to be a useful distraction from the massive incarceration of coastal residents of Japanese descent at that time (especially from the Los Angeles area), the continuing fears of invasion, and anxieties about the war in the South Pacific not yet going very well. The hype regarding this otherwise minor episode and the subsequent trial (with either an inept or indifferent legal defense team) undoubtedly contributed, just five months after the trial concluded (January 1943), to the equally sensational coverage of the misnamed Zoot Suit Riots. The two episodes wholly obscured the various ef-forts of other Mexican Americans that would eventually have positive and en-during social, political, and legal consequences.

The distorted and inflammatory news coverage of the trial focused on the pa-chucos as dramatically representing behaviors and appearances that expressed alienation, marginality, and defiance. Journalists inferred the emergence of a new "enemy within"—juvenile delinquents and gangs of "avenging Mexi-cans." The pachucas (teen girls), with their tight-fitting skirts, transparent blouses, and elaborate makeup and hairdos, were not seen as similar to the white teenage "V" girls but as non-conformists presenting, as author Kevin Starr repeated several times, an "explosive sexuality." The Sleepy Lagoon mur-der case seemed to have no hard evidence that linked the crime to the accused young men. Circumstances quickly showed that this meant little for their fate, because more was at issue than the murder itself.[12]

In the Sleepy Lagoon trial the prosecution proceeded against 22 of the 24 ar-rested. Pagán has reconstructed a reasonable sequence of events based on the testimonies and finds that Díaz had left the party with two guys who, in the pro-cess of trying to mug him, fought with him and then stabbed him twice with an ice pick. He was already on the ground and unresponsive when the accused 38th Street boys and girls arrived. Nonetheless, those 22 boys were tried to-gether for the murder of this one victim (*People versus Zammora et al.*).[13]

Presiding Judge Charles W. Fricke not only publicly demeaned the defense attorneys but, during the trial that ran from October 13, 1942, to January 12, 1943, also prevented the accused from getting haircuts or, for some time, wearing other than the clothing they had on when arrested. He kept them separated as a group, denied them their right to discuss the case with their attorneys, and ignored the absence of anything more than circumstantial evidence connecting the young men (aged 14–22) to the alleged killing of Díaz. Jurors were also permitted to go home each day and read about the trial in the inflammatory press.

The accused were second-generation, high school dropouts, members of one of dozens of "gangs." Many already possessed police records (especially 19-year old Enrique "Henry" Leyvas), and, as noted, not all of them were Mexican American. Yet, all were collectively described in court as "inherently criminal and biologically prone to violence." In fact, many in the group were employed, and two were married and had children. But that, too, meant little, because, recalled Alice Greenfield McGrath, who attended the trial and would come to play a prominent role in the boys' legal appeal, "It was much worse when you saw the expression of Judge Fricke. He despised the defendants. He insulted [defense attorney George] Shibley. If the prosecution made an incorrect motion, Fricke would rephrase the motion and grant it." "This case wasn't about justice," she added. "It was about punishing these kids for being Mexican and for dressing the way they did." Though 5 were acquitted, 17 were found guilty. Three were sentenced to life in prison for first-degree murder (including Leyvas), 9 were convicted of second-degree murder, and 5 were found guilty of assault. In addition, 4 girls who had been with the defendants but had not been cooperative witnesses were convicted of "rioting" and sent to a School for Girls for about 16 months.[14]

One of those convicted, 17-year-old Hank Ynostroza, later recounted that the warden and guards "knew we weren't guilty. The warden told us 'I know you guys are going to go home, you're going to beat that case. So just don't get into any trouble while you're here." While they languished in prison, the Sleepy Lagoon Defense Committee (SLDC) was organized, chaired by Carey McWilliams, with Alice McGrath as executive secretary. It was supported by Anthony Quinn, Rita Hayworth, Orson Welles, and other Hollywood notables, as well as by the Los Angeles Citizens Committee for Latin American Youth (LACC), established a year earlier by the Los Angeles County Board of Supervisors. Activists Josephina Fierro de Bright and Bert Corona, both of whom had been involved with the Congress of Spanish Speaking Peoples a few years earlier, were also working with the SLDC. It focused attention on the fact that the defendants were American, not Mexican, youth and that Mexican Americans should not be depicted as disloyal for seeking their civil rights.[15] Despite efforts to label the SLDC as Communist-linked, the SLDC and the LACC convinced the unanimous Second District Court of Appeals on October 14, 1944, to overturn the conviction, citing insufficient evidence, denial of the right to counsel, and Fricke's overt bias in the courtroom.[16] The defendants were freed, but the news was far less prominently covered, for by the time of this decision the even more inflammatory events of the Zoot Suit–Navy Riots had long since passed, the war was going well, and many passions had subsided.

Equally as important as that miscarriage of justice were the Zoot Suit–Navy Riots of June 1943 between Mexican American pachuco, zoot suit–wearing youth, and gangs of sailors, soldiers, and then civilians. The spark for these clashes arose from the consequences of bringing together many thousands of young men in a setting that mingled races to an extent unfamiliar to most of them. Their differences compounded the stress, fears, and lingering concerns about invasion, the anxieties of men going off to war and disturbed by the sight of other youths so defiant of the norms, and apprehensions about the loyalty of pachucos that had been triggered by news of a government campaign a month earlier (May 1943) which had resulted in the arrest by the FBI of 638 draft dodgers.

One perspective of these events finds "the most violent outbreaks of zoot suit rioting" took place in the "overcrowded military towns" and "industrial conurbations."[17] The existence of marginalized groups of African American and Mexican American zoot suiters—flouting regulations and seemingly avoiding military service—was taken as a challenge by "the predominantly white servicemen stationed along the Pacific Coast" who were about to go off to war. Another perspective relates the riots to a young generation of Mexican Americans emerging from the Depression and repatriation, feeling "disinherited" and "alienated from the aspirations of their parents and the dominant assumptions of the society in which they lived" and, during the year preceding the riot, resentful of the intrusion of young whites at the training school in their own neighborhood—their turf.

The local youths' response to their feelings of being marginalized was an expression combining the styles and mannerisms that were adopted and adapted—notably from the jazz scene—and what they called their "drapes," but which the press referred to as "gangster garb." The young men flaunted their zoot suits, defying the wartime bans on clothing with so much fabric. Likewise challenging community norms were the "female pachucas," with their distinctive, non-conformist dress, hair, and behavior. These joint "countercultural expressions" did not just confront mainstream society but appeared to assume a whole persona of defiance that blended music, dance, clothing, language, and mannerisms.

By contrast were the young military men—many stationed at the nearby training facility but up to 50,000 of them in the city on weekend leave—required to dress according to rigid military standards. Many were away from distant homes for the first time and primed by their boot camp training. They were resentful of the zoot suit–wearing, rebellious pachucos and envious of their flamboyant pachucas. It has also been suggested that many of the soldiers and sailors perceived the locals as defying "dominant expectations of decorum and deference," the "code of cultural behavior and propriety"—defiance of which marked them as non-whites clearly outside the mainstream. Furthermore, it has been argued, for them, as for the Mexican Americans, the "violence was [viewed as] an appropriate response for their gender," a means of preserving "boundaries of race and class"—boundaries of "racialized norms."

That the press focused on the pachucos and suppressed details of the excesses by soldiers and sailors provoked participants on both sides. It would be difficult to find two more disparate populations cast so close together that the fears, anxieties, and resentments of one inevitably clashed with rebellious, sometimes delinquent, non-conforming attitudes of the other.

The clashes between sailors on leave and Mexican Americans may have triggered the first rioters on June 3, 1943, but on subsequent evenings marauding taxi convoys of sailors (and then large groups of soldiers, airmen, and civilians) moved through East Los Angeles, invading movie theaters, bars, and streetcars, dragging out and beating the young pachucos as well as "chasing, stripping, and occasionally beating zoot suit- and non-zoot suit-wearing Mexican Americans and Blacks."[18]

Several other key developments set the stage for the duration and intensity of these encounters. Prior news "accounts" depicted an impending zoot suiter menace. Several initial forays by marines and sailors had occurred in April and May that resulted in violence. Now, for days after the riots began the military police were largely ineffectual. Local police declined to intervene at first, describing events as "sport" and "festive." Ultimately, five nights of rioting took place, with servicemen ignoring orders to cease, until Admiral David Bagley gave up the argument that the sailors were acting in self-defense and cancelled all shore leaves. Even that order was issued only after Major General Maxwell Murray, of the Southern Command Sector, Western Defense Command, had condemned the violence as acts that would not be tolerated. Mexican American youths fought back, but only they were arrested (600 by one estimate). Meanwhile, the local press, especially the *Los Angeles Times*, aggravated events with its distorted headlines and news stories that compared zoot suiters to Hitler Youth, employed military language to describe the actions of rioting soldiers (e.g., "landing parties" and "mopping up operations"), and included instructions on how to "de zoot" a boy.

The report of Governor Earl Warren's investigating committee in March 1945 absolved the Mexican Americans of starting the riots, acknowledged that the riots were a manifestation of race prejudice, and urged that actions be taken to reduce delinquency. The Los Angeles City Council had already acted on an almost farcical solution to the prevailing problems, which it implemented right after the riots: it banned zoot suits.

But too much time had elapsed, and even the 1945 recommendations met largely with public indifference. Nonetheless, other efforts had been taking place within various Mexican American communities to challenge the status quo. They were built less on the discontents and dislocations of the 1930s, which had contributed to the zoot suit phenomenon, than on the efforts of the emerging young adult Mexican American generation to achieve rights, recognition, and respect: civil equality.

Although one could concentrate on the enormous, long-term economic fallout from the war and its profound impact on many peoples in the West, the Sleepy Lagoon trial, the Zoot Suit–Navy Riots, and the protests and wartime riots involving African Americans indicate that there were other serious issues involving inter-group relations that remained unresolved and would carry over into the postwar years. Many men and women returned from the war unwilling to accept a *status quo ante bellum*—relations between minorities and the majority that remained unchanged as if no war, no sacrifices, and no momentous contributions had occurred.

LEAD-UP TO THE COLD WAR YEARS

The backdrop to the new movements included a number of developments affecting many groups, for the war focused attention upon a number of developments: the entry of many more women into the labor force and the impact that had on family life, culture, consumption patterns, and employment opportunities for new immigrant women (most American women, especially white women, afterward relinquished their wartime employment); the renewal of immigration; the arrival of refugees; the liberalization of the naturalization laws; the continued reliance on temporary workers—principally Mexican braceros; and the explosion of illegal immigration.

And then there were the broader and, in some respects, more sweeping contextual changes that mostly followed the war and took off in the years after 1950: the political upheavals from the onset of the Cold War; the changing economic opportunity structure with the emergence of the Sunbelt and the efforts of minority group members to benefit from the educational opportunities of the GI Bill; the on-going, hardly challenged, influx of federal moneys into the West for military, technological, environmental, transportation, and other purposes;[19] the transfer of older industries to other (lower wage, non-union) countries, especially at first the *maquiladoras* across the Mexican border; the ever growing presence of more technologically driven businesses and such new (or over-hauled) industries as petrochemicals, electronics, aerospace, and telecommunications; the vast expansion of transpacific commerce; the construction of suburban industrial parks along with urban renewal projects, both of which compound inner-city employment problems; and America's expanding military presence around the Pacific Basin.

Hard upon the heels of the first of these two sets of developments came renewed political and social challenges, the revival of organizations oriented toward civil rights and politics, the greater presence of minority candidates for public office and ethnic community action groups, and in particular the campaigns to secure the repeal of discriminatory laws and institutional practices concerning employment, land and home ownership, inter-racial marriage, voting rights, and segregated schools. The provocations were longstanding and well known. In the same way that the incarceration of the Japanese was both a culmination and prelude to their American experiences, so the whole way in which the Sleepy Lagoon trial and the Zoot Suit–Navy Riots were handled was a culmination of the negativity toward Mexican Americans, a mainstream reaction to what were perceived as repudiations of the racial status quo. These events turned out to be a prelude to the campaigns for reform that were about to begin, confrontations with the existing racial/ethnic hierarchy that went beyond the efforts of the 1930s and early 1940s.

In the fall of 1943 George I. Sanchez, writing in *Common Ground*, had sought to explain the roots of *pachuquismo*—the beliefs and mindset of the pachucos associated with the zoot suit style.[20] The genesis was an open book in the Southwest, he said. "In some communities . . . 'Mexican' is a term of opprobrium applied to anyone with a Spanish name—citizens and alien alike. . . . In many places these people are denied service in restaurants, barber shops, and stores. Public parks and swimming pools, some of which were built with federal funds, are often closed to them. Some churches, court houses, and public hospitals have been known to segregate them from 'whites.' Separate and usually shockingly inferior, segregated 'Mexican' schools have been set up for their children. Discriminating employment practices and wage scales, even in war industries . . . are still used to 'keep the "Mexican" in his place.'" Furthermore, the pseudo-pedagogical reasons for "these 'Mexican schools' . . . call for short school terms, ramshackle school buildings, poorly paid and untrained teachers, and all varieties of prejudicial discrimination. . . . The establishment of segregated schools for 'Mexicans' lays the foundation for most of the prejudice and discrimination." All this was well described by Harry Getty in his 1950 study of Tucson, and Angel Noe Gonzalez alluded to these conditions in his oral history recounted at the outset of part 4.[21] Be it schools, juries, voting, or employment, Sanchez concluded, "The Spanish-speaking people of the United States need to be incorporated into, and made fully participant members of, the American way of life."

Years later, historian Mario Garcia etched a scene in El Paso in the 1930s and 1940s that emphasized the underlying forces controlling the lives of Mexicans and Mexican Americans at this time and the obstacles they faced in overcoming them. His observations are relevant not only for El Paso but also for Los Angeles and in other urban centers in the Southwest. Important changes were beginning to take place, "a politics of status," although they had not yet confronted the root cause of Mexican American economic underdevelopment in the Southwest: the generalized exploitation of many of these people, "the need by capital to expand by maintaining most Mexicans as pools of cheap and surplus labor." Garcia determined that the political movement emerging then was the work of Mexican Americans (and supporters) who were "more acculturated, more educated and slightly more occupationally mobile than their parents, young Mexican American adults [who] aspired for full integration into the civic life of" their communities.[22]

Begun as a YMCA student group in San Pedro, California, in 1934, the Mexican American Movement (MAM) devoted itself to promoting education and citizenship. Integration was the objective of these second-generation Mexican Americans: "Our future is here" was their slogan. They consisted of educated, upwardly mobile individuals—high school and then college students and, subsequently, such professionals as teachers and social workers. Their goal was to get students to remain in school, especially given the dropout rates of 44–54 percent, and to promote leadership in their professions through conferences for boys and girls. They formed links with comparable organizations in Texas and Arizona and sponsored others, including the Mexican American Teachers Association. They also regarded Mexicans' opposition to citizenship "as a great disservice" and, as George Sánchez put it, "vehemently opposed any resumption of immigration from Mexico," which they viewed as the source of their problems and the obstacle to their mobility and higher status. MAM, a Protestant-based group, separated from the YMCA in 1944 and continued on until 1950. Like the early LULAC, which began in 1929, MAM can be seen as a transitional group, connecting the leadership and organizational efforts of the 1930s with the new round of activism following the war.[23]

In February 1946, Ignacio Lopez, editor of the San Bernardino *El Espectador* from 1933 to 1961, met Candelorio ("Cande") Mendoza, a veteran who had returned from the war and found himself unable to secure a teaching position. Based on Lopez's community-organizing experience in Washington during the war, they established the Pomona Unity League to fight discrimination and segregation and to promote civic and political rights and voter registration. They would use get-out-the-vote drives and support minority candidates. Members included Mexican businessmen, college students, veterans, community leaders, and non-Mexican supporters. With the help of Professor Ruth Tuck and Fred Ross, an expert organizer affiliated with Saul Alinsky's renowned Industrial Areas Foundation (IAF), Lopez recruited some 50 young men and women and established eight other Unity League chapters (ULs) in San Bernardino, Riverside, Chino, Redlands, and San Diego.

They sought allies among blacks and Asians, as well as with the Intercultural Council of Claremont, targeting racism, residential segregation, discrimination in public facilities use, inadequate busing for school children, and such business practices as displaying job signs declaring "White Trade Only" (which they did persuade the Riverside City Council to ban). The UL helped secure the election of Andre Morales to the Chino City Council—the first Mexican American elected to a California city council since the 19th century. The UL also played a role in Edward Roybal's victory three years later for a seat on the Los Angeles City Council. By concentrating on grassroots political organizing, the UL helped force the transformation of race relations in the Inland Valley citrus belt and continued into the 1950s and the emergence of other activist groups.[24]

In September 1947, about one and a half years after the founding of the UL, another group formed that also followed IAF strategies and also benefited from Fred Ross's involvement. The Community Service Organization (CSO) neither claimed allegiance to Mexico nor assigned a leadership role to the Mexican consul. The CSO was created to mobilize and organize voters, to encourage Mexicans to become citizens on the assumption that, as historian David Gutierrez put it, "resident Mexican aliens were not merely sojourners . . . but . . . had become integral members of the Mexican American community." Real protection could only come with citizenship. The CSO first supported Roybal's 1947 run for Los Angeles City Council. Unsuccessful that time, the group devoted itself to a non-partisan voter registration project. Its membership jumped to 800 in two years, and its efforts yielded between 12,000 and 15,000 new voters. In the 1949 election, 82 percent of the registered voters in the district cast ballots, compared with only 39 percent in 1945, and they gave Roybal 8,500 votes more than the incumbent. The following year 112 registrars signed up some 32,000 new Latino voters within a three-month period. As a community advocacy group, the CSO encouraged Mexicans to become citizens, stressing that they need not give up their native culture to do so. Then, they registered the new citizens to vote and mobilized the community around an array of local health, education, and civil rights issues. Within a decade there were 34 CSO chapters with 10,000 members, including such future leaders as the United Farm Workers' César Chavez and Delores Huerta.[25]

Returning veterans carried with them not only memories of earlier negative experiences growing up in the Southwest but also the awareness borne of battles survived that they ought not to go home and fall into old traps, old mindsets, old patterns of behavior. Expectations had risen. Fred Castro, for example, was raised in La Verne, California, near Pomona, and he had fought in Europe. When he and four other Mexican Americans returned and went into a restaurant in Texas and were denied service, they wrecked the place. The military police arrived and defended the soldiers, telling the owner, "As long as these fellas have the uniform on, they are white." The challenge, of course, was to sustain the insistence on the right to equality whether in uniform or not.[26]

Private Felix Longoria, age 25 and the father of one daughter, came from Three Rivers, Texas, situated between San Antonio and Corpus Christi. He had been in the Army for only seven months when he was killed in the Philippines in 1945. Four years later his body was shipped home. Beatrice, his wife, went to the Rice Funeral Home, the only one in that community, to ask for the use of its chapel for a wake. Owner Tom Kennedy refused on the grounds that Mexicans got too rowdy and "the whites won't like it." Her family contacted Dr. Hector Pérez Garcia, who had recently established the American G.I. Forum in Corpus Christi because the Veterans of Foreign Wars and the American Legion in that city had refused to admit Mexican Americans. The American G.I. Forum was to become a civil rights organization devoted to fighting discrimination (see below). Garcia called for a protest meeting in Three Rivers, and 1,000 people showed up. U.S. Senator Lyndon Baines Johnson intervened with an offer to have Longoria buried in Arlington National Cemetery. At that point Kennedy backed down from his earlier refusal, but Longoria's widow accepted Johnson's offer. Fifty-five years after the initial Longoria episode a move to name the local post office after him evoked many of the original divisions and bitter feelings. Texas historian Patrick Carroll reflected that Anglos "believe what their fathers and grandfathers told them: that there was no discrimination" there at that earlier time.[27]

The 1949 event gave a huge boost to what came to be called the GI Forum. Its success would come by fusing American identity with Chicano roots and by focusing on the social and civil rights of citizens, even to the extent of a participating role in significant civil rights cases. Possessing a new sense of entitlement as U.S. citizens, Mexican Americans mobilized themselves across the Southwest, determined not to accept the old status with its flagrant violations of civil rights. By following up the earlier Lemon Grove decision with other legal challenges, and supported by MAM, LULAC, and the GI Forum, among others, Mexican Americans demonstrated that they had acculturated well enough to understand and demand their legal rights and, in the process, contributed to the foundations of the watershed 1954 *Brown v. the Board of Education of Topeka* decision.

That momentous step was taken in Westminster, California, on March 2, 1945, even before the war had ended. Gonzalo Mendez, Thomas Estrada, William Guzman, Frank Palomino, and Lorenzo Ramirez decided, on behalf of 5,000 children of "Mexican and Latin descent or extraction," to challenge their four school districts in Orange County, California—Westminster, Garden Grove, Santa Ana, and El Modeno. Their principal contention was that the districts in effect conspired and, as stated in the lawsuit, by "regulation, custom, and usage," had "segregated said children in schools attended solely by children of Mexican and Latin descent." The administrators denied them access to the other schools "used exclusively by and for . . . White or Anglo-Saxon children"—despite their demands for that access. The result had been that "injury to petitioners is continuous, great and irreparable . . . and does affect their health, rights and privileges as citizens of the United States." Precisely that line of argument would figure at the core of the plaintiffs' claims in the Brown case nine years later.

In February 1946, federal judge Patrick McCormick ruled that the segregation violated federal and state law, was socially unhealthy, fostered antagonism, and denied students the benefit of interaction with students of other cultures. Even if the schools had equal facilities, they would not meet the standard of equal protection of the laws. On April 14, 1947, in *Westminster School District v. Mendez et al.* (161 F. 2d 774; 1947 U.S. App.), the Ninth Circuit U.S. Court of Appeals ruled that the school district officials had overstepped their authority without legislative support and, in fact, were in direct conflict with state law. "Nowhere in any California law is there a suggestion that any segregation can be made of children within one of the great races." School officials therefore acted "entirely without authority of California law," had segregated the children "against their will," and had violated the Fourteenth Amendment "by depriving them of liberty without due process law—by denying them the equal protection of the laws."[28]

A short time later, in four Texas communities, Minerva Delgado and 20 other parents brought suit on behalf of their children for violations of the latter's rights and the absence of any justifying state laws. LULAC and GI Forum filed the class action suit and—employing a strategy based on the recent Mendez decision—contended that the arbitrary and discriminatory actions were contrary to the U.S. Constitution, Texas law, and the Texas attorney general's position. Just 14 months after the Mendez decision, June 15, 1948, Judge Ben H. Rise Jr., U.S. District Court for the Western District of Texas, declared in *Delgado v. Bastrop Independent School District* that segregation for the first grade only might be justified for language adjustment purposes, but otherwise the rights of the Mexican American children had been violated contrary to the Fourteenth Amendment.[29]

De facto segregation persisted for at least two more decades, but these two vital legal precedents were achieved by Mexican Americans six to seven years before the Brown decision, which is identified as having launched the nation's Civil Rights Movement. Mexican Americans, we find, had been demonstrating their political acculturation and their new sense of entitlement since 1945.

CHAPTER THIRTY-FIVE

Wartime and Postwar Agricultural Issues—Land, Labor, Growers, and Unions

T HE SITUATION WAS FAR more complex where Mexicans were involved and the issues revolved around the rights and needs of agricultural laborers. On April 19, 1952, four young Mexican American men killed 22-year-old Ricardo Mancilla Gómez, a bracero working in the Cucamonga area, east of Los Angeles. The Mexican consul responded by withdrawing over 500 contract workers from the Southern California Farmers Association, which distributed the braceros across the Pomona Valley. Supporting Consul Salvador Duhart's decision were 123 braceros, who petitioned for their contracts to be terminated. Four months later, however, Duhart relented and allowed the workers to return. The episode revealed several salient points about the bracero program. It was controversial virtually from the start because Mexican Americans viewed braceros as competition that would displace them for lower wages. Many resented the program and fought it for years. The actions by Duhart demonstrated that Mexican officials were sometimes able to resist American entreaties, just as they had done for about four years (1943–1947) by refusing to permit braceros to work in Texas because of the racism, discrimination, and violence against the Mexican workers. The episode also showed that notwithstanding the many adverse encounters, the braceros were not entirely defenseless. Many times they came together to strike for higher wages and better conditions.

The outbreak of the Second World War created instant demands for available workers, primarily for agriculture but also for railroad maintenance work, lumberjacking, milling, and other jobs. Suspension of immigration law restrictions for such workers was permitted under what was called the Ninth Proviso, Sec. 3, of the Immigration Act of 1917.[1] In late May 1942, the War Manpower Commission reported an urgent need for 6,000 Mexican agricultural workers, and a few weeks later, Governor Culbert Olson telephoned the U.S. Secretary of Agriculture, Claude Wickard, and indicated that "without substantial numbers of Mexicans the situation is certain to be disastrous to the entire victory program." That request and appeal on behalf of the agricultural industry's "consumers of labor" evidently worked.

A month later, the United States and Mexico negotiated an Emergency Labor Program (July 23, signed August 4) that was supposed to provide, via six-month contracts, more protection for both Mexican and American workers (the latter predominantly Mexican Americans) as well as provisions regarding the guest workers' transportation, living expenses, housing, and exemption from military service. Oversight by the U.S. government, which had not been the case a quarter century earlier, now made it "an employer of braceros" — a player in the Southwest's regional racial dynamics. Also, 10 percent of earnings were to be withheld and deposited in special accounts in Mexico's Agricultural Credit Bank. A half century later former braceros were still asking what happened to those many millions taken from their paychecks — but exactly how much is disputed.[2]

In the remaining four months of 1942, nearly 4,200 workers came to work in sugar beet fields near Stockton, but rather quickly one-quarter of them shifted to citrus harvests in fields from Ventura to Redlands. Through Public Law 45 (April 1943) Congress endorsed the temporary worker program, and by the summer of 1945, over 290,000 Mexican laborers had been brought in (58 percent of them for agricultural work). Besides the Mexicans, additional agreements provided for Newfoundlanders, British Hondurans, Jamaicans, Bahamians, Barbadians, and others from the British West Indies. As of July 1945, at almost the war's end, approximately 360,000 workers of various nationalities had come into the country under contract. Even though they worked in 24 states, 57 percent of the Mexicans labored in California. Eventually, some three-fifths of those harvesting citrus crops were braceros and that soon rose to four-fifths. Indeed, as the end of the war approached, around 68,000 (and possibly as many as 76,000) foreign workers were still employed on railroads, and close to 100,000 remained in agricultural jobs.[3]

A significant stimulus to the labor demand arose from the fact that between 260,000 and 300,000 workers left agriculture during the war years seeking better jobs in the cities. Indeed, the cities were viewed as the escape from a rural caste system. With only 100,000 in the labor pool, the need for braceros rapidly became acute. Nevertheless, other Mexican Americans found themselves pushed out by the bracero competition, such as the citrus workers in Orange

County or in California's Inland Valley, where Mexican men by war's end constituted 70–80 percent of field workers, and Mexican women were replacing Anglo women in the packinghouses, in some cases making up two-thirds of the employees. That enabled processing firms to keep wages down, while these women developed their own work culture. Mexican Americans increasingly transferred to factory or construction-type jobs, while many others left Texas and, for example, headed north and west—even into the Pacific Northwest (as did Dora Treviño's father in our closing narrative).

Braceros migrating to jobs in the Northwest made their way to Washington State, Oregon, and even Idaho, which "had the most notorious reputation for discrimination." Whereas "Yakima Valley farms were literally saved from ruin during the war by the arrival of Mexican braceros"—some 1,200 in 1943 and almost 4,400 by 1945—in the final analysis, the Pacific Northwest experiences of the braceros frequently involved "wretched living and working conditions, prejudice, ill treatment, and poor wages." Nonetheless, between 1943 and 1945, over 33,600 braceros worked in Idaho, Washington, and Oregon, and 46,900 by the end of the agreements in 1947. As Erasmo Gamboa described it: "Mexicans were found in the cranberry bogs at Ilwaco . . . and other coastal communities. Near Seattle and Tacoma, the workers were trained as skillful pruners by blueberry growers in the Puyallup Valley and Cowlitz County. . . . In Oregon, the braceros gathered record-setting potato harvests in Klamath County and, to the east, they were the 'main source of labor' in the pea fields near Pendleton and Umatilla. In southern Idaho they were literally everywhere."[4]

One account suggests what the new, northerly migration stream could entail. Irene Casteñada made the journey in March 1946 to the Pacific Northwest, and her ordeal was similar to the experience of many migrant Mexican braceros and Mexican American workers. Hearing good things about Washington State, she and her husband each paid $25 and an additional $15 for each child to be driven there, bound for Toppenish, in the Yakima Valley. "On the road the truck broke down—who knows how many times. In Utah we had to stay overnight because the road was snowed in. . . . We all slept sitting up with the little ones in our arms because we had no money to rent a motel. We were about twenty-five people in the truck . . . [and with all their items] we looked like sardines. Then a heavy wind came and the tarp on the truck tore in half . . . then the driver lost his way—we almost turned over." Despite the promises, the driver "didn't have housing [for us]—nothing—all lies. . . . He finally found some old sheds . . . and in tents he placed all the people. It was bitterly cold—with wood stoves and wet wood."[5]

Agricultural interest groups wanted to preserve the bracero program after the war because they could exploit the braceros and frequently pay them less than required. At the same time, the number of Mexicans seeking work exceeded the available contracts. The result was a rapid escalation in undocumented Mexicans crossing, braceros not leaving as the contracts mandated, and still others who skipped out on their contracts to find other, better-paying employment or less severe living and working conditions. The numbers of undocumented workers apprehended by the INS leaped from an average of 7,000 per year in the early 1940s to 101,500 in 1946 and nearly 200,000 the next year. Mexican American opponents of the Bracero Program claimed that the Mexicans were, in fact, taking jobs from Americans, such as with the railroads, in factories and smelters. George I. Sanchez described these immigrant workers as "a culturally indigestible peninsula of Mexico" penetrating into the Southwest.

However, the pressures in Mexico were undeniable, as was the enormous gap between conditions there and opportunities north of the border: a reported 31 percent increase in Mexico's population during the 1940s, a five-year drought during the mid- to late-1940s, and inflation and rising unemployment, along with a per capita annual income of $114 in Mexico compared with $1,453 in the United States. Agricultural laborers were earning 69 cents *per day* south of the border and 25 to 50 cents *per hour* north of it. Between 1942 and 1954, three-fourths of those crossing the border were from the states of Durango, Aguascalientes, Guanajuato, Jalisco, Michoacán, and Zacatecas (especially the last three), and they were carving migration channels that remained, becoming deeper and more permanent. Juan Garcia summed up the situation at this time: "When compared to Mexico, plagued by drought, tight agricultural credit, national priority given to industrial investment, over population, and massive unemployment, the United States at least offered a job and a chance to get ahead."

Yet, Ernesto Galarza did point out the flip side in his own 1977 study, namely that the American Farm Bureau Federation viewed braceros as perfect workers because they brought no families and went home after the harvests (or so the growers declared). Therefore, they neither created "difficult social problems" nor became part of the labor movement. Instead, they remained vulnerable to exploitation and abuses. Galarza provides many illustrations, notably that of Francisco Hernandez Caño-Salinas, who would deduct from workers' wages for blankets, medications, insurance fees, and even the ties required to bind their harvested carrots together. Such treatment demonstrated that many could be "cheap and docile" (or so the growers believed). The border was unavoidably, inevitably, and exceedingly permeable, and willing workers were always available.[6]

When Mexico would not agree to a formal extension of the Bracero Program, *Newsweek* magazine reported in late October 1948 that the United States had opened the border—with President Truman's blessing—and then technically arrested those entering, "dried them out" (paroled them), and put them on trucks sent by the Texas Employment Commission. They were expected to "pick 90 percent of the 1948 [cotton] crop" in the Upper Rio Grande Valley.

Between 1947 and 1949 twice the number of workers were reported than had been formally contracted for with Mexico. The situation continued, and with the outbreak of war in Korea in June 1950, demand for contract laborers once more soared. Public Law 78 (July 12, 1951) renewed the Bracero Program (with funding approved August 16) and institutionalized it for the next 13 years— although Mexicans would soon insist on higher wages. Meanwhile, in the five years 1948–1952, some 599,000 braceros were tabulated, not quite as many as the total of temporary foreign workers during the previous five years (ca. 660,000), but that later figure certainly does not include the rising number of undocumented workers.[7]

In the postwar years agriculture was riven by the convergence of conflicting elements, underscoring the struggles still facing immigrants and the children of immigrants in the postwar era. In Texas in 1934 there were reportedly 981,000 laborers, but only 550,000 by 1949. In California in 1954 there were some 123,300 small farms compared with approximately 150,000 in 1935. Nevertheless, western agriculture "represented industrialized farming in its most extreme and unalloyed form." Mechanization, such as with potatoes, corn, beets, asparagus, lemons, rice, cotton, and tomatoes, was reducing labor needs as it increased the demand for skilled workers. On the one hand, that expanded the opportunities for discrimination against black, Mexican, and Filipino workers. On the other, these developments intensified the dramatic confrontations between domestic (American-born) laborers, braceros, and the rapidly growing number of undocumented workers.[8] It was also more than an economic issue. Undocumented Mexicans, "wetbacks," were also being depicted as "a dangerous and criminal social pathogen," which added to the negative stereotypes of Americans of Mexican descent. Locals and undocumented migrants (and undoubtedly braceros, too) were simply lumped together in the public's perception.[9]

At the same time, there was a related convergence of three sets of factors:

a) the contending unions—the National Farm Labor Union (NFLU), UCAPAWA (renamed, shortly before, the Food, Tobacco, Agriculture, and Allied Workers Union, or FTA), and the International Brotherhood of Teamsters (IBT);

b) the massive associations of industrial farm owners, food processors, and canning firms, such as the Arizona Farm Bureau Federation, the California Processors and Growers (CPG), the Kern County Land Company (1.9 million acres in four states), the Spreckels Sugar Company, Standard Oil (2 million acres), the Southern Pacific Railroad (4 million acres in California, Nevada, and Utah), and the DiGiorgio Farms (213,000 acres of cotton); and

c) the federal government, with its enormous military expenditures, support for such industries as aluminum, steel, and synthetic rubber, intermediary role in the Bracero Program, the National Labor Relations Board (NLRB), the

1947 anti-union Taft-Hartley Act, and the government's rather inconsistent enforcement policy against illegal aliens.[10]

UCAPAWA/FTA aspired to represent the diversity of its workers, with meetings in English, Spanish, Japanese, and Chinese and an Executive Board whose nine members included three African Americans and three Latinos.[11] Many women were prominent members and activists and rose to leadership positions in the union as shop stewards and union organizers, espousing "a job-oriented feminism." Nonetheless, the Teamsters prevailed over the FTA in 1945–1946 by signing a sweetheart deal with the CPG, resorting to red-baiting FTA leaders (resulting, for example, in the deportation of five Filipino labor leaders and Guatemalan-born Luisa Moreno), and boycotting goods canned by FTA-affiliated workers. When, in August 1946, more cannery workers voted for the AFL (jointly with the Teamsters) than for the CIO-connected FTA, the latter rapidly declined. Meanwhile, the major processing associations ignored NLRB findings. (Agriculture was exempt from NLRB oversight, but packinghouse workers were classified as industrial labor and, hence, were covered.)

Finally, the NFLU launched a strike against DiGiorgio in central California on August 1, 1947. The conglomerate employed diverse retaliatory tactics, including violence, accusations of subversion and portrayals of the alleged Communist leadership of the union, a fabricated report to members of Congress sabotaging the union film *Poverty in the Valley of Plenty*, and the use of domestic workers from as far away as Texas (then braceros and undocumented migrants) as strikebreakers. The strike limped along until May 9, 1950 — 972 days — but, in the end, the union lacked the resources to match the onslaught from the likes of the DiGiorgio firm. Another generation of workers would have to test its mettle and come forward under significantly different conditions.

The outcome scarcely matched the enormous success of the International Longshoremen's and Warehousemen's Union (ILWU) in Hawaiʻi. Having begun its organizational and racial outreach efforts before the war, the union used its near-labor-monopoly influence to persuade the territorial legislature to enact in 1945 the Hawaiian Employment Relations Act (Hawaiʻi's "Little Wagner Act"), extending the right to organize to plantation workers. The following year a 79-day strike for more money, fewer hours, and an end to plantation paternalism united Japanese and Filipino workers and most of the unions on the Islands. The settlement was written in English, Japanese, and Tagalog. By 1947 the ILWU had 30,000 members, and its 178-day strike in 1949 solidified its position as the labor powerhouse of Hawaiʻi, with immense political as well as economic clout. Already in 1946, 14 of the 15 Democrats endorsed by the union's Political Action Committee were elected. Efforts to label the ILWU as Communist elicited remarks such as this from one worker: "Most of the boys did not know Communism from rheumatism, but they did hate the bosses."[12]

In the mainland West, ethnic workers contended with right-to-work laws, exploitation of braceros who were often confined to squalid conditions—"the small end of the cornucopia," to borrow Ernesto Galarza's phrase—and wages that usually fell between those of domestic and undocumented workers (for example, between 35 and 70 cents per hour). The domino effect of braceros and undocumented migrants convinced more and more Mexican Americans to leave the land and head for the cities. It was not surprising, writes historian Matt Garcia, that Mexican Americans did not view braceros as brothers "but rather as intruders who threatened to take their jobs, lower their wages, or even steal away a potential love interest."

Despite all the labor-related controversies, there was one particular issue involving farmers which did have considerable significance for immigrant groups in the West. In March 1945, Oregon joined a dozen other states forbidding aliens ineligible for citizenship from owning, operating, or controlling land or farm equipment or deeding land to relatives.[13] Two years later, Utah repealed its land law and then, in January 1948, in *Oyama v. State of California*, the U.S. Supreme Court overturned a California decision (based on the cases from 1923) invalidating the right of Fred Oyama's father to purchase eight acres in his son's name and serve as guardian. The state had escheated the land, but the high court declared that such an action, based on a provision of the Alien Land Law, deprived Fred Oyama of the equal protection of the law and his privileges as a U.S. citizen. The court did not declare the law unconstitutional but did conclude, "the rights of a citizen may not be subordinated merely because of his father's country of origin." On March 29, 1949, the Oregon Supreme Court invalidated that state's Alien Land Law, as did California on April 17, 1952. (It was formally repealed by a 2–1 vote for Proposition 13 in November 1956.)[14]

CHAPTER THIRTY-SIX

Immigrants and Ethnics in the Postwar West

W HILE MANY OF THE ECONOMIC, political, and civil rights issues and struggles were obviously not fully resolved during the first half-dozen or so postwar years, other barriers were falling. On July 2, 1946, Congress granted a nominal 100-person quota to Asian Indians, and two days later the president extended the same for Filipinos. A second act on July 2 provided the right of citizenship for both peoples, following the Chinese precedent. Japanese and Koreans would have to wait six more years.[1]

The struggle between restrictionists and liberals (between 1945 and 1952) to reshape immigration law was *initially* won largely by the restrictionists. (The preservation of the National Origins formula was a preeminent concern of theirs.) Although the advocates of more progressive foreign policy strategies and internationalism lacked the votes to implement their policies, the fact remains that the changes in naturalization law, the nominal Asian quotas, and the special legislation for the admission of refugees proved in the long run to be, as a package, a significant turning point, a watershed. In the short run, they offset *some* of the harshness that was incorporated into America's postwar policies that culminated with the McCarran Act (or the Internal Security Act) of 1950 and the McCarran-Walter Immigration and Nationality Act of 1952.

The years following the Second World War marked a significant transition for a number of ethnic groups in the West, with patterns that cut across their boundaries. The rather limited European immigration between 1931 and 1945 (699,383 admitted, compared with the 1920s)[2]—as a result of quotas, the Depression, and war—meant that during the post-1945 period there were fewer newcomers in various stages of adjustment to American life. Instead, an aging first generation's ties to their homelands were waning, for many key sending countries in Europe and Asia were either becoming politically inaccessible or were undergoing recovery programs that were making them less economically needy and their citizens less dependent on remittances from abroad. Their second-generation children were becoming more rapidly Americanized, especially those who had been in the military. Further changes could be seen in the accommodation patterns by traditional ethnic institutions. For example, churches, fraternal organizations, and ethnic community newspapers continued their expanded use of English.

In contrast to the shrinking immigrant generation and rapidly growing second generation among many European and Asian populations—plus the increased numbers of Mexicans and Canadians—these years were marked by dramatic changes among newcomers, especially the new categories of admission, admissions soon based on the mortgaging of future annual quotas. Those categories and mortgages would together become the initial measures leading to the dismantling of the National Origins System in 1965. The new classifications included refugees; displaced persons (although in the West there were far smaller numbers of people in this classification compared with those settling elsewhere in the country); war brides, children, and fiancées of military personnel, including Asians previously ineligible to immigrate; small but significant numbers of Chinese, Asian Indians, and Filipinos admitted under new quotas of 100 per year each, and subsequently the entry of non-quota family members of newly naturalized members of these groups.

In fact, the enactment at last of universal, race-free naturalization qualifications in 1952 constituted a major event in the nation's history, not just for the postwar years. The citizenship reforms between 1940 and 1952 were the key to the process of removing the remaining barriers blocking numerous (mostly Asian) groups that had long been denied the opportunity to legally bring in family members. What then began as a rivulet of newcomers became, within a generation's time, an unanticipated and unprecedented torrent of new immigrants.

The post-1945 years were certainly not free of anti-Asian and anti-Semitic prejudice, as evidenced by the efforts of West Coast mayors and others to bar the return of Japanese Americans, the maneuverings of "restrictionists" in and out of Congress to minimize the entry of Jewish displaced persons, and the discrimination in housing and jobs still experienced by Asians and Jews (as well as by Latinos and Blacks). As the details of the Nazi Holocaust became known, anti-Semitism underwent a dramatic decline between 1946 and 1951, especially in areas of higher education, employment, and the professions. Yet, the influential changes went well beyond the assaults on old prejudices. It has been argued that the war "literally collapsed many of the barriers to greater assimilation, at least for European ethnics." Fostering the new climate of rising expectations for integration and greater job access were the wartime ideological (and propaganda) attacks on Fascism, couched in the portrayal of pluralism and toleration as parts of the American core culture. Keys to that strategy included federal measures challenging employment barriers to ensure fuller participation by minority men and women and the military's authorization of ethnic-based military units (African American, Chinese American, and Japanese American), the success of which became the intermediate step toward the desegregation of the military ordered by President Truman in 1948. The first Freedom Rides organized by the Congress of Racial Equality (CORE) in 1947 symbolized the tidal shift in ethnic-related attitudes and ideological objectives—some well recognized, others not widely known or immediately appreciated.[3]

Those expectations and aspirations were bolstered by new activist ethnic organizations with philosophies and agendas calling for greater equality and by court decisions reassessing the status quo in race relations. They began the unraveling of institutional racism and the crystallization of new racial norms. Three 1948 cases were of particular importance. In January, in *Oyama v. California* (332 U.S. 633), as we have seen, the U.S. Supreme Court found "that the [California] Alien Land Law denies ineligible aliens the equal protection of the laws, and . . . takes [their] property without due process of law." In May, in *Shelley v. Kraemer* (334 U.S. 1), the Court struck down state support for restrictive housing covenants. In October, in *Perez v. Sharp* (32 Cal. 2d 711, 198 P. 2d 17), the California State Supreme Court took steps toward dismantling still another barrier to equality. Taking into account other decisions regarding segregation and discrimination, the court invalidated California's anti-miscegenation law on the grounds that it denied equal protection of the law and the right to freely enter into marriage. Thirty states with such laws gradually began to repeal them, until the high court invalidated all such legislation in 1967's *Loving v. Virginia* (388 U.S. 1).

In his study of Italians in and around San Francisco, Dino Cinel concludes that "the most unexpected force for change was the failure of return migration"— and such was the case, too, among many other European immigrant groups.[4] Initially, as with the Greeks, few immigrants went back during the war to fight for their homelands. But there were opportunities afterward to reconnect with homeland villages (especially if the migrants still possessed lands there), to provide financial assistance to families, and to sponsor long-separated spouses and children, or even to arrange marriages for themselves, as occurred especially among the Chinese, Asian Indians, Filipinos, and several eastern and southern European groups. However, the signs were clear that ties with the old countries had weakened: the immigrants' longer years in America, the impact of their wartime allegiances to America, and their children reaching adulthood and knowing little about the old countries and their ways but a lot about the American ones. It was precisely this adaptation to American culture—its language, customs, education, job mobility, dating, and greater acceptance of marriage with "outsiders"—that increased the distances from their parents' homelands. The onset of the Cold War brought about further changes for European immigrants and then for Asians, creating new barriers to access with their homelands. For example, the Marshall Plan (and formation of the European Union), which launched the economic recovery and prosperity of Western Europe and new opportunities for immigrants to sponsor the admission of long-separated family members, further weakened familial ties with the homelands. These links would increasingly become less transnational and more translocal—periodic, limited, incomplete, more narrowly focused (in effect, less homeland-centered)—with the even more limited connections of their children compounding the fading of transnational bonds. It was not long before "homeland" became an image or association of what scholars come to describe as "symbolic ethnicity."[5]

There were, as noted, the changes in immigrant and ethnic communities. Religious institutions, newspapers, and organizations formalized the shift to English; familiar meeting places, such as the Greek *kaffenion* (coffeehouse) and the afternoon language schools, dwindled in number; children began moving out of the old ethnic neighborhoods—as the Jews did, for example, in moving west from Boyle Heights to mid–Los Angeles and the San Fernando Valley; and discussions began, as they did among Armenians, Japanese, Chinese, and then Jews about homes for the aged for the immigrant parents, marking a most telltale shift in inter-generational family patterns. That venerable tradition of elderly parents residing with their adult children proved mutable in the American environment.

In another aspect of the transitions taking place, whereas new Chinese spouses of Chinese American soldiers frequently settled in Chinese or the newer Chinese American (usually more suburban) communities, the war brides of other ethnicities more often did not reside among their own countrymen and women in America even if such clusters existed (which, for some groups—notably the Australians, French, and English—was rarely the case). Moreover, gulfs developed between postwar newcomers and the older generations of immigrants. Compared to prewar immigrants, newer ones frequently found themselves distanced from the prior generation of immigrants by their different urban backgrounds, higher levels of education and occupation, lower levels of religiosity, often more liberal political orientations, divergent attitudes regarding their homelands, and even the language or dialect used.

While efforts toward these various inter-generational immigrant adjustments were rather apparent among ethnic communities in the Midwest and East, they would also be visible in the West among, for example, Italians, Jews, Filipinos (especially in Hawai'i), Mexicans, Japanese, and Chinese (particularly involving the non-Cantonese who were now arriving). Meanwhile, for others, including Canadians, Scandinavians, and Germans, the processes of integration continued apace, with less friction with newcomers and fewer inter-generational strains either because many of those struggles had been resolved earlier in the Americanizing environment or because the predominantly second, third, and even later generations were far removed from the original homeland origins. In contrast, the inter-generational economic and socio-cultural gulf between Mexicans and Mexican Americans remained more pronounced, even though the number of legal admissions was still comparatively low and some Mexican American community leaders were starting to recognize the commonality of interests and challenges facing the two populations.

Other developments adding stress were visible among a number of other groups where there were considerable postwar in-migrations, such as those veterans and workers from outside the West who had been stationed/employed there and now returned to settle, along with the many veterans who were coming home to their western communities (as we saw with Mexican Americans), and retirees who began relocating there. For example, these returnees and newcomers were especially conspicuous (as were the many refugees) among Jews in various communities from Seattle to Los Angeles to Tucson. In the latter city the numbers of Jews jumped from 480 in 1940 to 4,000 in 1948, and to 4,500 two years later. Other cities, including Denver, Dallas, Houston, San Francisco, and Seattle experienced modest increases, too. In Los Angeles, however, the Jewish population leaped from 130,000 right before the war to 315,000 a decade later. In 1951, almost 45 percent of the city's Jewish households had been present only since 1940. More than 500 Jewish refugee families from Europe were sponsored there by the early 1950s—with one estimate suggesting 10,000 refugees were residing in Los Angeles by 1953. Los Angeles had become home to the second largest Jewish community in the nation.[6]

In that context, and paralleling the earlier generation of Americans who had resettled in Los Angeles from Iowa and elsewhere in the Midwest (and those arriving directly from Europe), these postwar Jewish newcomers established a number of *neolandsmanshaften*—community groups based on city of origin *in America*, such as the Milwaukee Jewish Social Club of Los Angeles and the Jewish Friendship Club of Omaha/Minneapolis.[7]

There were signs of both persistence and change. The Nisei of Cortez, California, were able to resume farming, for those hired to maintain the operations in their absence had done so responsibly. Greek men in Tacoma were receiving photos from home rather than sending their own to the villages, for families eagerly sought grooms in America for sisters, nieces, and cousins. Among Portland Greeks the inter-generational dilemma was described by Tom Doulis, and it was surely not a situation unique to them: "The first generation of Greek immigrants to Oregon had traveled light [bearing few cultural institutions], and the second generation was left to its own devices to bridge the gap between the two cultures." These postwar Greek American children were caught between a clear recognition that their "future was undeniably identified with the United States" and Greek-born after-school instructors who viewed "every adaptation to American life as a sort of apostasy from Hellenism." The children felt they "owed Greece their sentiments, perhaps, but not their loyalties." Meanwhile, one version of the marginality of the children (in this case Italian) was expressed by Dino Cinel, who relates Sam Capelli's comment to his San Francisco social worker after having been arrested twice by age 17: "There is nothing more boring than a Sunday afternoon at North Beach. Life at home is even more boring. My father and uncle get together over the weekend and the topic of conversation is always life in the Old World. For me life begins outside North Beach." Cinel concludes that "the social transformation accelerated by the war, the defeat of Fascism in Italy, the progressive departure from North Beach of the immigrants' children, and the aging of the immigrants themselves hastened the Americanization of the Italians."[8]

These stages, underway earlier among northern European and Scandinavian immigrant communities (especially in Washington and Oregon), were now becoming more and more common among southern and eastern Europeans and Asians (Poles, Czechs, and Japanese in Texas, for example), as well as among Mexican Americans. Harold Nelson focused on the intergenerational strains among Armenian youth in Fresno, be it the young women meeting *odar* (non-Armenian) soldiers while working in the USO (United Service Organizations) or attending USO dances, or those who were now becoming parents themselves. They "neither continue in the same old country manner of their parents, nor have they accepted completely the practices of non-Armenians. They have combined elements of both and arrived at a family pattern which is a synthesis of the old and new; it is neither Armenian nor American."[9] The rich complexity of the situation was apparent not only in the Old World hold on the first generation and the marginality of the second but also the generational overlays that included the younger second-generation children now maturing at the same time that a third generation was appearing and the more prosperous, older, second-generation families were moving out of the "colony." And, all that was to intermesh, if possible, with the postwar arrival of Armenians relocating from the East Coast. Here, too, was a case study that could be readily writ large across many parts of the West.

Or consider Rose Hum Lee, Constance (Jade Snow) Wong, and Mary Lew Gee. They were second-generation Chinese American women who illustrate one further dimension, the many more Chinese and Nisei men and women pursuing college educations and professional careers. Some had reached that stage even prior to the war. Lee, born in Butte, Montana, in 1904, wed a Chinese engineer, went to China until 1939, then returned and attended the University of Chicago, earning her doctorate in 1947. She became the first woman and the first Chinese person to chair a university sociology department (Roosevelt University), and a well-respected scholar on Chinese Americans. Wong, born in San Francisco in 1922, graduated from Mills College in Oakland, California, in 1942. It was wartime, and she found good jobs for women college graduates were scarce. During the war she became a secretary in Sausalito, raised a family, and wrote a classic autobiography, *Fifth Chinese Daughter* (1950). At the same time, she developed a career that made her a recognized artist with ceramics and enamelware. Gee was born in Chico, California, in 1924, where only a handful of Chinese families resided. She became very Americanized, worked in a shipyard during the war, joined the Women's Army Corps (WACs), and afterward became a restaurateur, realtor, and the first Chinese person to buy a home in Pacifica, near Monterey, where she became a community activist.[10]

Other postwar changes involved Filipinos who had planted roots in Alaska, down the Pacific Coast, and out in Hawai'i. In Alaska, these Alaskeros (as they referred to themselves) largely worked in the canneries. Some settled there and married local (usually Native Alaskan) women. During the war they were caught up in the union struggles for control of the cannery workers in a contest that pitted AFL against CIO against the ANB/ANS (Alaskan Native Brothers, Alaskan Native Sisters). The union vote in 1945 was AFL, 301; CIO, 357; and ANB/ANS, 364, with Filipinos generally backing the CIO. The CIO won the NLRB election the following year. Chris Friday described this as "movements of cooperation," where majorities were not clearly present, and the Filipino residents provided the CIO with links to local communities. The fact that whites here were strongly anti-Asian and formed an alliance with Native Alaskan groups (in the form of the Alaska Marine Workers Union) highlighted the contested racial hierarchy. Now, federal policies and national and international market forces reached into the labor controversies, and the relatively small number of Filipinos were able to maintain their presence in the canneries.[11]

On the other hand, in 1951 Thelma Garcia was part of the new wave of Pinays who came to the United States after the war. She obtained a degree from the University of Nevada, Reno, married Jon Buchholdt, and settled in Alaska in 1965. She acknowledged that she missed Filipino foods and "the help we had [in the Philippines]; you know, I didn't know what to do with my clothes, nor how to make a bed." However, she had had role models in missionary schools and a mother who was active in Philippines politics. She herself proved capable enough to become a lawyer and the first Filipina elected to a state legislature, serving in the Alaska State House of Representatives from 1974 to 1983. When she decided to bring Filipino culture to Alaska, she went back to the Philippines in 1968 and relearned the Ilocano language. She remained active in Filipino organizations into the 21st century. Despite her decades in America, she sought to define a balance between her two worlds. She maintained that "If you are born in the Philippines I think you should keep as much of your culture as possible. Now if a child is born here, like my children who are half Filipino, the degree of assimilation should be at least half." But if both parents are Filipinos, "the emphasis should be to keep the culture as much as they can."[12]

Whereas only a few hundred Philippine-born persons lived in Alaska in 1950, almost 61,100 Filipinos (by "race") resided in Hawai'i in 1950—among whom over 33,800 were Philippine born. Aside from the 6,000 men and their 1,361 family members brought in during 1946 for one last effort at plantation recruiting, many who were arriving there after the war were single and better educated than the *sakadas* (temporary migrant workers) had earlier been, and many were students or wives of U.S. citizens, most of whom were or had been in the military. Although 23 percent of the women held jobs, they encountered limited opportunities and had a weak influence on labor matters. Among the ILWU members, two-thirds of the Filipinos were in "travel, hotel and restaurant trades," another one-sixth or more worked in factories, and fewer than one-sixth were unskilled laborers. "The image of Filipinos in Hawai'i was still the lowest among the various ethnic groups. Generally, most local-born Filipino Hawaiians did not take pride in their heritage."[13]

Over 3,800 Filipinos were admitted to the United States between 1946 and 1950 (excluding temporary workers) and another 6,400 between 1951 and 1955. As indicated, many were war brides of U.S. citizens (Filipinos and other Americans), for the old "taboos of liaison with American soldiers and sailors" were now a thing of the past. For example, Asuncion ("Ciony"), who wed Capt. Les De la Cruz, settled in Seattle, became a citizen, went on to organize community activities to win over Americans to their Filipino neighbors, and became Washington State's Mother of the Year in 1973. In 1949 Ying Angeles was the last war bride processed in the Philippines, having married a Filipino medic in the U.S. Army. She labored in a cannery, in a jewelry factory, and as a seamstress. Active in the War Brides Association of Seattle, in 1964 she was named Mother of the Year by the Seattle Filipino community.[14]

Caridad Vallangca points out that in the decade or so following independence 79 percent of the Philippines' college graduates were "an excess of manpower in the fields of education, commerce, and accounting. Lawyers, doctors, and other professionals exceed[ed] the demand . . . [but] there simply was not enough demand for nurses." They came to the United States in a pattern that became well defined, even institutionalized. Yet they would encounter hurdles in licensing and labor laws as well as in the realization "that their spoken English could not be understood by the Americans and that they could not understand the Americans either." In San Francisco, for example, many of the college-educated Filipinos during the late 1940s had to accept jobs as clerks, typists, salespersons, managers of small hotels, and hotel maids. Still, as Pura Zarco Alabastro put it, having arrived in February 1951, "the feeling of wanting to get out" of her homeland outweighed the obstacles she would encounter. Filipinos embraced the American Dream, ultimately building their lives, establishing families in America, and facing the challenges many immigrants were confronting. Said Gloria Baldecano Santiago Clement, wife of army officer William J. Clement (who was a mix of German, French, and black), "the Filipinos that are born in the Philippines and the Filipinos' children that are born in the United States it's just different. They don't get along. . . . I guess the kids born here are just too Americanized," and jealousy comes between them. On the other hand, Alabastro observed, "my children did not have any problems as far as assimilation into the American way. They did not know any other but American culture."[15]

These various examples highlight the full range of ethnic outcomes that could be found among most immigrant groups—before and after the war. The challenges of Americanization continued; the hurdles persisted; the variety of responses could still be seen. But a new set of challenges would also confront ethnic communities during the 1950s Cold War years, prompting many individuals, especially among veterans benefiting from the GI Bill, to distance themselves from the strong ethnic group ties of old and accelerate their integration into mainstream America.

What, then, can we determine about immigrants and ethnic groups in mid-century? On the eve of the passage of the two major bills pushed through by Sen. Pat McCarran, in 1950 and 1952, both of which had such significant consequences for immigrants, what was their place in the West? After all, the early 1950s followed a decade filled with hot wars and the onset of the Cold War, with massive opportunities in the West that held out new possibilities for a rising generation but also rapid demobilization. Laws, wars, and depression had pretty much ensured that the foreign-born population of European origin had plateaued by this time. Meanwhile, doors had reopened for those from the Americas and parts of Asia.[16] As we look back over prior decades of the century, we can see clear patterns of persistence and change.

During the 1940s the United States population grew by 14.4 percent, but once again the growth rate in the West surpassed that elsewhere in the country, this time by triple the amount (34 percent versus nearly 11 percent). The proportion of immigrants who planned to reside in the West had remained rather stable to this point—one fifth of all newcomers in the 1920s, one-fourth during the war, and, between 1946 and 1952, again nearly one-fifth. While nationally the total foreign-born number dropped by 11 percent, most likely due more to attrition than to emigration, the foreign-born population grew in the West, with a difference three times greater than in the rest of the nation—rising 6.7 percent there as it fell over 14 percent elsewhere. However, the West's net foreign-born population had actually risen only in the Southwest—from

Texas to California—while declining in the region's other states and territories. Were the data available, we would likely find that a combination of attrition, population turnover, and declines was offset by significant numbers of arrivals from abroad and from elsewhere in the country (table 4.2).

The long-touted stories of workers and soldiers who labored in or passed through the West and determined to return most likely also held true for many children of immigrants and for immigrants seeking new job opportunities and then more congenial places for retirement. After all, 1.647 million persons sailed out of just San Francisco during the war years, 90 percent of them military personnel, and most of the rest related to the military effort.[17] The number of second-generation white persons in the country (the only figure available) edged up merely 1.8 percent during the 1940s, while jumping by ten times that percentage in the West (thus virtually unchanged in other regions). Significantly, at least half the western states saw that population rise: Texas, Arizona, New Mexico, California, Nevada, Oregon, and Washington—all major areas of employment and military installations during the war (table 4.3).

Taken together, California, Texas, and Washington still anchored the region, for Washington lost nearly 12,200 immigrants but gained 53,800 second-generation persons. Texas had a combined increase of just about 120,500. And, once more, California witnessed a towering jump in its white foreign-stock population by more than 575,400 persons, balancing out losses in other parts of the West. In fact, only about nine immigrant groups experienced increases in the West during the 1940s. Besides Mexicans and Canadians, those particular groups came from countries that had endured some of the worst effects of the Second World War, or soon had members who were beginning to arrive as the spouses of military personnel. They included Austrians, Poles, Greeks, English, French, Dutch, and immigrants from the USSR (see table 4.4).

Furthermore, some of the migration and settlement patterns observed in prior censuses continued to be valid at mid-century, suggesting the tenacity of migration streams and ethnic communities. Half of the foreign-born Norwegians and Finns could still be found in Oregon and Washington, as could well over one-third of Swedes. Over half of all Danes were in California, along with more than seven out of ten French, nine out of ten Portuguese, three-fourths of the Italians, and over one-half of the Canadians (with more than one-third of the latter also in the Northwest). Czechs divided between Texas and California, with just under two-fifths in each state. Mexicans recorded a major shift between Texas and California: 57 percent had been in Texas in 1920 and just one-fifth in California; three decades later 44 percent resided in Texas and two-fifths in California.

Although certain groups continued to be numerous, such as Mexicans in the Southwest, Canadians along the northern border in Idaho and Montana, English in Utah, Japanese in Hawai'i, and Norwegians and Swedes in Washington, the most remarkable presence over time was that of the Germans. Even though their numbers shrank by 10,000 persons—and despite two wars between their homeland and new land—they were still the fifth largest foreign-born group in the West, and among the top five in ten western states.

A few final observations come to mind concerning the immigrant peoples of the West and persistent patterns at mid-century. First, approximately three-fourths of the foreign born lived in urban areas ("approximately" because of the definitional change) compared with over 85 percent elsewhere.

Second, race, recency, and reticence appear to account for the fact that only somewhat over three-fifths of the foreign born (62 percent) had acquired citizenship versus just under three-quarters in the rest of America (73 percent). This can be attributed particularly to the Mexicans' greater resistance (only 45 percent naturalized), the ineligibility of Chinese until 1943 and the Filipinos and Indians until 1946, and the continued ineligibility of Japanese and Koreans for another six years. Quite likely hastened by wartime experiences, Germans' and Italians' citizenship figures now exceeded the national average (79–80 percent), with both continuing to apply in large numbers.

Third, the divergent urban/rural and regional residential patterns between Chinese and Japanese, reflecting their different historical experiences, were most apparent in 1950, even though many Japanese Americans had relocated outside the West. Nonetheless, the West's 298,109 persons of Japanese ancestry represented over 91 percent of that population (with three-fifths in Hawai'i), whereas the region's 102,395 people of Chinese ancestry comprised only two-thirds of that group (with over half in California and just three-tenths in Hawai'i). On the other hand, the census reported 73,127 Philippine-born Filipinos, 46 percent of whom lived in Hawai'i. Most of the others still lived and worked in the mainland West.

Finally, although gender data for the different nationalities at the state level were not available for 1950, overall state trends for the foreign born highlight the shift toward more family migration and greater numbers of female newcomers that began in the mid-1920s. The numerical gap between the West's white foreign-born men and women shrank from 344,200 among whites in 1920 to 190,600 among all foreigners on the eve of war to only 97,000 among the nearly 1.79 million foreign-born whites in 1950. Not surprisingly, the foreign-born gender ratio therefore continued to drop, from 150:100 in 1920 to just 112:100 at mid-century. California, with the greatest numerical growth in the region, saw its white foreign-born gender ratio fall to 107:100. Utah, having a long history of significant Mormon-related and mining-related immigration, achieved virtual equality in gender numbers by 1950. Finally, Hawai'i offers the distinctive contrast of an increasing gender gap between 1930 and 1950, particularly among non-whites (158:100 to 216:100), due to its historical emphasis on labor recruitment. Still, among its relatively small white foreign population (about 6,100–6,200) lived more women than men (91:100) (see table 4.5).[18]

CHAPTER THIRTY-SEVEN

The Cold War Heats Up
The Politics of Immigration, 1950–1952

RECEIVING REPORTS ABOUT conditions in Europe's refugee camps in 1945, President Truman was convinced of the need to take swift action.[1] On December 22, 1945, he issued a Presidential Directive, declaring, "I consider that common decency and the fundamental comradeship of all human beings require us to do what lies within our power to see that our established immigration quotas are used in order to reduce human suffering. . . . The United States shares the responsibility to relieve the suffering. . . . [I]t is essential that we do this ourselves to show our good faith in requesting other nations to open their doors for this purpose." That statement set the nation along a new path for years to come. Truman ordered key federal departments to promptly reestablish consular services in the American zones of occupied Europe, to expedite the issuing of visas "fairly among persons of all faiths, creeds, and nationalities," and to secure the cooperation of welfare organizations (soon called VOLAGS, *vol*untary *ag*encies) to ensure that such individuals did not become public charges and, where possible, to facilitate their reunion with family members in the United States. Noting that between 1943 and 1945 only 5 to 7 percent of the quotas had been used, and reiterating (pragmatically) that he did not wish to change the country's immigration quota system, Truman emphasized the importance of making use of the quotas to achieve his humanitarian objective. Between 1946 and June 25, 1948, about 40,000 displaced persons were admitted under the President's directive.[2]

That precedent-setting action represented one of five that addressed policies concerning immigration during the first seven postwar years. Both the old and the new were being embraced in a dance whose steps would lead the nation in radically new directions, bringing us full circle to our theme of continuity and change. Rejuvenation of immigration was of special concern to Truman and to those groups eager to sponsor long-separated family members and survivors. Indeed, immigration (quota and non-quota) rose from a mere 38,119 in fiscal year 1945 to 188,317 four years later to 265,520 in the year ending June 1952. The quota ceiling was only about 154,300; non-quota persons made up the difference.

As discussed above, one of the major changes that reflected the growing recognition of the intersection of foreign and domestic policies was the expansion of quotas and naturalization privileges to Asians, beginning with the Chinese in 1943 and Asian Indians and Filipinos in 1946.

The nation also recognized its obligation to help resettle well over one million war refugees and the growing numbers now fleeing Communist governments in Eastern Europe. The result was the Displaced Persons Acts of June 25, 1948, and June 16, 1950, as well as the directive permitting those Chinese to remain in America who had become stranded when Nationalist China collapsed in September 1949, many of whom were students and researchers. By the June 30, 1952, expiration of the Displaced Persons laws, 393,542 such persons had been admitted.[3] However, the immediate impact of the legislation on the West was limited, seeing that only 7.5 percent of displaced persons were relocated there (principally Germans, Latvians, Poles, and those from the USSR) and about 10 percent more resettled there following their arrival.[4]

However, two other pieces of legislation certainly had more direct significance for the West. The Act of August 6, 1946, allowed Chinese wives of American citizens (most of whom were Chinese American military personnel) to be admitted as non-quota immigrants. Though time-limited, the Act of July 22, 1947, broadened the War Brides Act of December 28, 1945, which authorized the non-quota admission of spouses and children of U.S. citizens in the military, by providing that alien spouses "shall not be considered inadmissible because of race." During the life of the War Brides Act—from December 28, 1945, to June 30, 1950—there were 119,693 spouses and children of American citizens in the military and those honorably discharged who were admitted, including 5,726 Chinese, 763 Japanese, 467 Asian Indians, 2,485 Filipinos, and 761 others.[5]

The onset of the Cold War turned the nation's preoccupation with national security to possible subversive activities by Fascists, Communists, and any other proponents of totalitarianism—replacing the older fears of ethnic invasion manifested in immigration policy. The Internal Security Act (ISA) (or the McCarran Act) of September 23, 1950, which was enacted just months after the invasion of South Korea and the start of the Korean War, reflected those preoccupations. Its sweeping provisions were felt nationwide, directly impacting groups in the West.

Title I (a foreshadowing of the 2001 USA PATRIOT Act) declared that those "who knowingly and willfully participate in the world Communist movement . . . in effect repudiate their allegiance to the United States." Because "one device for infiltration by Communists" "is procuring naturalization for disloyal aliens," the ISA declared (sec. 22) that "aliens who, *at any time*, shall be or shall have been members" of anarchic, totalitarian, and Communist organizations were to be excluded from admission (including any who advocate, teach, write, or publish such ideas). Also, where "there is reason to believe that such aliens would, *after entry*, be likely" to engage in the prohibited activities, they were also to be barred. Furthermore, sec. 22 (4a) ordered that "Any alien who was *at the time* of entering the United States, or *has been at any time thereafter* a member of any one of the classes of aliens enumerated" shall "be taken into custody and deported"—including "any alien who at any time, *whether before or after* the effective date of this Act, has engaged, or has had a purpose to engage in any of the [enumerated] activities" (emphasis added).[6]

The law not only required annual registration by aliens every January but also excluded from naturalization any alien who advocated, taught, or published such documents or who was affiliated with any Communist organization. These provisions applied to any applicant "who at any time *within a period of ten years immediate preceding* the filing of the petition" was so involved. Additionally, if any person "shall *within five years* . . . following such naturalization" become affiliated with any such organization, "it shall be considered prima facie evidence that such person was not attached to the principles of the Constitution." Such behavior "shall be sufficient . . . to authorize the revocation . . . of the certificate of naturalization." Among the other citizenship requirements, a knowledge of reading, writing, and speaking English and the fundamentals of U.S. history and principles of government was now required.

Not content with all that, Title 2—"Emergency Detention Act of 1950"—indicated that if the president issued a proclamation of emergency due to invasion, war, or insurrection, declaring the existence of an "Internal Security Emergency," he was then "authorized to apprehend and by order detain . . . each person as to whom there is reasonable ground to believe that such person *probably will engage* in . . . acts of espionage or of sabotage," and such persons "shall be confined in such places of detention as may be prescribed by the Attorney General."

The language italicized in this law (much of which is restated in the McCarran-Walter Act, below) unquestionably placed extraordinary discretionary authority in the hands of the president and his attorney general. The impact on immigrants during the 1950s, and the anxieties which the laws engendered among them, would be profound. The precedents would periodically resurface as a threat during the Cold War and reemerge in more drastic form after September 11, 2001. The laws would have a chilling effect on immigrants in the West in particular, for they not only reawakened the hardly dormant Japanese American war time experiences of incarceration and the related Supreme Court decisions, but they also frightened other groups that felt vulnerable, fearing they would be targeted next, especially the Chinese. Robert Divine described the 1950 Act as "the decisive turning point in the post-war debate on American immigration policy," representing "a vital change in attitude toward immigration."[7]

During the decade that followed, 20,585 persons were denied admission to the United States, of whom 1,098 were excluded on the grounds of subversive activities. Of the 129,887 persons deported, only 230 were deported for subversive activities. But, 2,390 persons did lose their U.S. citizenship.[8] However, the psychological impact went beyond these numbers, especially among those from countries then under Communist rule. The effects were akin to what the Issei felt in December 1941, when they hastily destroyed precious heirlooms and valued Japanese religious and cultural possessions for fear that such items would be construed as signs of being pro-Japan, or pro-emperor.

The final development shaping the postwar years reflected the same anxieties as those behind the 1950 Internal Security Act. Pat McCarran had become chair of the Senate Judiciary Committee, and he operated from the position that "immigrants [were] primarily . . . a source of danger to American society." His priorities were the preservation of both national security and the existing ethnic makeup of the nation through the National Origins System.[9] The Immigration and Nationality Act of 1952 (I&NA), known as the McCarran-Walter Act, is a massive omnibus legislation that has technically remained the core of American immigration law for more than half a century, with, as indicated, subsequent legislation representing amendments to this law. Prior to drafting the law, McCarran's Senate committee requested an analysis of existing immigration and naturalization laws, and the staff report included three key recommendations: nominal quotas for Asian nations and, collectively, one for mixed-race persons from that region; second, an emphasis on the primary admission of skilled immigrants as a first preference; and, third, after 162 years (since the first naturalization law in 1790), opening up citizenship to persons of all races—in effect, color-blind naturalizations.

The omnibus bill contained both the components that would preserve the existing National Origins quota system, since it continued to be based on the 1920 census, and the seeds for its thorough revision. Those seeds were the retention of unlimited admission of persons from nations in the Western Hemisphere; the several additional laws providing for the admission of special classes of individuals (notably war brides, fiancées, and refugees) through a formula of either extending (mortgaging country quotas) or sidestepping the quotas by admitting persons as non-quota; and the seemingly minor modifications of quotas for Asians and naturalization rights regardless of race. The three together would ultimately undo the very provisions McCarran so doggedly fought to preserve. The McCarran-Walter Act, as originally enacted, proved to be a relatively short-term victory for restrictionists, notwithstanding Divine's assessment quoted earlier. The law was unnerving, disturbing, and infuriating—but for only 13 more years.

President Truman vetoed the I&NA bill on June 25, 1952. The House immediately overrode the veto, 278–113, and on June 27 the Senate did so, 57–26.[10] The I&N Act of June 27, 1952 (66 Stat. 163), clearly reflected the preoccupations of the Cold War era. Because, as largely revised, it has remained the basic foundation of American law for over a half-century, its initial provisions have affected decades of immigration into, and naturalizations within, the West. The President's Commission on Immigration and Naturalization, reflecting on what shape the laws and policies should take, influenced the legislation that followed, steadily edging the nation in new directions. While the quotas were technically preserved, new grounds for evading them were being enacted.

The National Origins formula for admissions remained, but the law now provided for quotas for most Asian nations, basing all but the Philippines quota on ancestry. For example, Chinese or Asian Indians born anywhere in the world were charged to those minor quotas of 100 each. The exemption of persons born in independent countries of the Western Hemisphere continued (classified as "special immigrants"—non-quota). The preferences within the quotas were shifted. The first 50 percent was reserved for persons with urgently needed skills, followed by 30 percent for parents of citizens, 20 percent for spouses and minor children of resident aliens, and any remaining slots for siblings and adult children of citizens (the latter's spouse and minor children were already non-quota).

Extensive punitive provisions were also included. The clauses denying admission and citizenship to any alien who in any form during the ten years prior to any application had supported Communist or other radical organizations were largely carried over from the 1950 McCarran Act. The I&NA provided that any alien who "is or at any time has been, after entry, a member of" such groups or a supporter of one could be deported, and any "naturalized citizen within a period of ten years *following* his naturalization [who refuses] to testify . . . before a congressional committee concerning his subversive activities," and who has been convicted for that reason, could face the revocation of his or her citizenship. In fact, if, "*within five years next following* such naturalization," a person "become[s] a member of or affiliated with any organization" that would have at the outset precluded that person from receiving citizenship, that person's naturalization would be considered as based on fraud and would be cancelled.[11]

A loophole was inadvertently created. While there remained a vast array of categories of persons, including illiterates, who continued to be denied admission, a provision was added whereby the attorney general could "parole" individuals into the country in cases of emergency or for other compelling public interest reasons. It would prove to be of immense importance in the subsequent admission of various classes of refugees.

In terms of specific provisions with regard to citizenship, all persons were now eligible for naturalization without regard to race, sex, or marital status—the unforeseen core of the coming immigration revolution. The central qualifications for naturalization remained a minimal English language ability, an understanding of American institutions and constitutional principles, five years continuous residence (three for spouses of citizens), good moral character as testified to by two witnesses, and foreswearing all other allegiances. However, the Declaration of Intent was made no longer the obligatory first step to citizenship; persons age 50 and older and present 20 years or more were exempt from the English language requirement; and the government now accepted that conscientious objectors could receive citizenship and would not have to agree to bear arms.

The 1950 and 1952 laws guaranteed that compelling cases for special admissions would continually require bypassing the rigid immigration provisions and that ethnic communities would be sufficiently frightened that the political and cultural environments in many ethnic communities during the 1950s would be strained. Efforts would be made either to mute the groups or hasten their further Americanization—reminiscent of the First World War and the early 1920s. During the 1950s, ethnicity, especially of East European origin, would be downplayed, whereas religion would be seen as setting Americans apart from godless Communists. The nation would pray together and stay together—and ethnic celebrations would have to await another day.

Truman's veto message had declared that "the greatest vice of the present quota system . . . is that it discriminates deliberately and intentionally against many of the peoples of the world." It was also "a slur on the patriotism, the capacity, and the decency of a large part of our citizenry" and fails to present "a true reflection of the ideals we stand for." He emphasized that "In no other realm of our national life are we so hampered and stultified by the dead hand of the past as we are in this field of immigration." He was particularly disturbed by the provisions for denaturalization and deportation. He also urged Congress to pass legislation for the emergency admission of 300,000 additional immigrants over the next three years—which Congress did not do until a new president was in office.[12]

A week after Congress overrode his veto, the president established the Commission on Immigration and Naturalization, which held hearings across America and reviewed the entire I&NA. Its report, *Whom We Shall Welcome*, was submitted to Truman in January 1953. The commission's findings and recommendations differed sharply (but not completely) from the restrictionists' ideological defense of the status quo. Its assessment would materially influence policies directly affecting immigration to the West. It viewed the new law as "a mixture of discriminations based on nationality, and on race irrespective of nationality, and on geography irrespective of any other factor." It placed too much authority in officials' hands and created conditions for a second-class citizenship. The near unanimous view presented by commission members was that the nation "can never again turn its back on the facts of international relations." Thus, regarding asylees and refugees, policies needed to be flexible enough to respond to special circumstances.[13]

Essentially, the commission concluded that the National Origins System, based on the 1920 census, was out-of-date. Between 1925 and 1952, a total of 56 percent of the quotas (2.44 million visas) went unused. Over four-fifths were assigned to northern and western Europe, but not even 39 percent of the total admissions came from those countries, in large part because of the inclusion of both Western Hemisphere persons and non-quota family members of citizens, which together came to 40 percent of the total admitted (1930–1951). On the other hand, emergency refugee legislation mortgaged some country quotas for 60 to 100 years.[14] The commission called for a quota system based on the 1950 census (raising quotas from 154,657 to 251,162) and resting on the principles of the right of asylum, the reunification of families, the requirements of the United States, and the special needs of the free world and general immigration.

In the sphere of naturalization, the report came down especially hard on the second-class status of naturalized persons because of the new provisions that allowed for denaturalization.[15] It especially emphasized that, in general, "the law should not discriminate against naturalized citizens but should place them in the same status as native born citizens." The commission recommended reasonable limits on deportations and denaturalizations but did concur with the exclusion of members of extremist organizations as well as the denaturalization of persons returning for three or more years to their native land.[16]

Over time most of the commission's recommendations would be adopted by the courts and Congress. The foreign policy realities of the Cold War, the growing political empowerment of the second and even third generations, and the ideological consequences of the Civil Rights Movement ultimately proved more compelling than the restrictionists' fears about subversion and anxieties about racial purity. The foreshadowing of events to come, many of which would strongly affect ethnic groups in the West, could be seen in the response of Asians to the color-blind naturalization provisions of the I&NA. Just in fiscal years 1953–1955, there were 6,463 Chinese who acquired citizenship, as did 6,589 Filipinos, 15,017 elderly Japanese, and 583 long-time Korean residents.

That would begin to open doors to the subsequent sponsorship of various classes of family members.

By 1952 all the ingredients were present for an ethnic and immigration revolution in the West in the second half of the 20th century. What had preceded provided the groundwork for further transformations of the region. Few have realized that long-term significance of the new citizenship provisions because immigration law first had to be reformed. So, too, the significance of the legislation reauthorizing the Bracero Program (with 909,100 admitted just between 1953 and 1955) would not be fully grasped until several million had been admitted. At first, the rising numbers of undocumented immigrants that paralleled the Bracero Program would provoke Operation Wetback in 1954, but then the flood of undocumented subsided until the program was terminated in December 1964. Laws, policies, political pressures, foreign affairs, and uncontrolled immigration—all were intertwined, all would affect each other, and all would have a huge impact on the development of the West in the second half of the century.

CHAPTER THIRTY-EIGHT

Dora and the Harbinger of Coming Events

T HE STORY OF DORA SANCHEZ TREVIÑO is a harbinger of events to
come.[1] Dora's story begins with conditions pretty much as they were in the
1950s West. Her experiences embody many of the conditions that become so
prominent from the 1960s onward—uprooting, migration, resettlement, labor
exploitation, concentrations of workers and families that give rise to new communities, women's expanded roles, political mobilization among minorities,
and inter-generational mobility. Dora's life in so many ways expresses social
and economic elements that appear to be unchanging, and yet many changes
do take place and become apparent over the last decades of the century. As the
stories related above in the prelude and part 1 marked continuity and change in
the late nineteenth century, Dora's story compels us to consider the continuities and changes during the late twentieth century—who was now arriving,
where did they go, what roles did they play, what alterations in their lives did
they experience, how much did the region depend on these newcomers, how
much were they exploited, how much could they resist, and to what extent do
these newcomers and their children begin to become a political, even economic and cultural, force in the West?

Quincy is a small community in central Washington State, just east of the
Columbia River and north of Yakima Valley. Mexican workers had been mi-
grating to Yakima Valley since the 1920s, but the completion of the Columbia
Basin Irrigation Project in 1952 provided more job opportunities around
Quincy than the few farms and food-processing plants previously had. During
the postwar years (late 1940s and early 1950s) a small number of Mexicans

began arriving in Quincy mostly from Texas, following established but not deeply rutted migration paths. One Jesse Gonzalez may well have been first, coming with his family in 1948. There were about 800 persons in Quincy at that time, and all but a handful were white Americans. About a dozen years or so later, when Quincy Valley farms expanded with the introduction of labor-intensive crops, more Mexican Americans in Texas, some drawn by labor contractor Rita Puente, proceeded to follow the annual circular stream of agricultural harvest and packingshed workers up to Washington, down through California, and back to Texas. More began to remain in Quincy, around 1,000 by 1970. In the mid-1980s a third phase started, the migration of Mexican nationals, drawn by the agriculture and the prospect of year-round job opportunities. In 1990 the 1,400 Latinos represented 37 percent of Quincy's population, 40 percent by 1996—most of whom were of Mexican origin. This is the setting of Dora's story.

Dora's father, Abel Sánchez, was born in Mexico but was raised in the German community of Lockhart, Texas, near Austin. He had only a second-grade education. Dora's mother, Ignacia, was born either in Seguín or Brownsville, Texas. She had reached the sixth grade but still spoke a limited English. Dora was born in March 1947 in Uvalde, approximately 75 miles west of San Antonio. She was one of ten children, half born in Montana, half in Texas, because between the 1930s and late 1950s her father migrated with his family between farmwork in northeast Montana and, after the sugar beet harvest in October, construction jobs in Texas until the next spring season. Traveling in family groups, the women worked in the fields, too.

Dora's oldest brother established an agricultural machine shop in Quincy and he needed help. To enable her older sister to complete high school, 15-year-old Dora volunteered to go to Quincy in February 1963. She went by bus, alone—and after being blessed by the priest. The rest of the family joined them in Quincy later that year. At the time, Dora recalls, there were about 10 Mexican families living full-time in Quincy, which would normally increase to about 100 during the growing season. Most commonly, she and her high school friends identified themselves as Spanish American, not Mexican American and not Chicana. Nonetheless, since she began high school mid-year and was in fact Mexican American, she was stereotypically labeled as a "migrant" only there for the harvest. And, indeed, family members did seek employment working on the Yoshino Brothers' farm.

Dora and her parents became active in the community, joining the Altar Society of the Catholic Church, then the Latin American Club and soon Community Action, a Great Society program designed to offer migrant children alternatives to a life of farm labor. Her mother had also had an interest in politics and had voted regularly in Texas. When she went to register in Quincy in 1963, she was asked if she was a citizen. Not hearing the question, she asked

Dora in Spanish and responded that she could read and write a little English, but the city clerk concluded she was not fluent enough and refused to register her. She never voted again.

In 1965, Dora graduated from high school—the common scenario of the second generation surpassing the first. She sought a teacher's aide job but went off with a sister to get training as a dental assistant. However, she soon returned to Quincy and applied for a job helping students. She obtained an interim position in a potato-processing warehouse owned by the Yoshinos. The Teamsters were trying to organize the workers, for the women in particular were treated more poorly than the men (e.g., rapid conveyor belts, no bathroom breaks, and standing for long periods, while the men had easier jobs and were paid more). Dora was harassed and then laid off for trying to organize the workers. Eventually, they opted for the union. Yoshino rejected the outcome and sold out, and the plant was unionized under new owners. By that time, however, Dora had acquired a teacher's aide job.

She was now 19, had become pregnant, and married Robert Treviño, who was a very traditional Mexican man. Dora recalled that he was "a very domineering person" who "did not believe women should do something without the husband saying so." He also did not want her "working in the union. Again it [was] that old Mexican tradition where the man rules the household. . . . He felt a wife and woman should not be getting involved with big issues." He was employed in a federally funded community action program until he fell ill. They then tried operating a restaurant for five years. He eventually required full-time medical care and by then had conceded that Dora had the right to return to her job as an elementary school aide. Robert died in June 1978, ending a ten-year illness.

Dora bounced back. She promoted a program to expose migrant children to college life and at some point had another child with a man she had not married. She was appointed to fill a position on the Quincy City Council for a year and a half, and when the first of her children was about to graduate from high school, she moved on to a job with the Department of Social and Health Services as a financial specialist. She played a particularly important role there following the 1986 passage of the Immigration Reform and Control Act (IRCA). By the mid-1990s she had the responsibility for implementing the 1996 welfare reform law.

In the late 1990s Dora remained active in the community, the union, and the Democratic Party. Quincy being a small town, farmers would recognize her, "but they always try to place me as one of their laborers. Instead of recognizing me as a community activist, they stereotype me. They still look at Mexicans as laborers and nothing more." From her vantage point, Dora drew the conclusion that the failure of Anglos to acknowledge this reality stemmed from their unwillingness "to accept the fact that Mexicans are no longer moving back and forth from Mexico or state to state." The 2000 census reported that 65 percent of Quincy's 5,044 persons were Latinos.[2]

However much a disservice that treatment had been to Dora and however regrettable the farmers' failure to recognize her personal contributions to Quincy for several decades, the fact remains that "between the late 1940s and the present, the Chicano labor force contributed significantly to the development of the Columbia Basin, with Chicanos composing a large proportion of the work force"—even though most of the credit for the growth of Quincy is given to its early white settlers. The farmers' myopic view "fails to recognize the equally important contributions of the pioneer Chicano laborers." Jerry Garcia, who compiled Dora's story, concludes that "the economic growth of Quincy was based on two important and related factors," the Irrigation Project, which jump started the area's economic growth, and the "abundant and cheap labor" required to make that growth possible. "Chicano labor met the need."

Garcia's conclusion regarding the contributions of Mexicans to the economic growth of the Quincy area offers the same theme as that throughout this study: the West became what it is because the labor, resources, and entrepreneurialism—the human capital—of the immigrants and the children of immigrants were critical in making that growth possible.

Dora Sanchez Treviño's story captures much about the migration and dispersal, struggles and challenges, survival and adaptation, of Mexicans and Mexican Americans in the Pacific Northwest and how they were perceived and received. Her story is a harbinger of things to come because one can view her family's transplantation as the archetype of what subsequently emerges: a massive influx of Mexican immigrants that will include a skyrocketing number of illegals following the end of the Bracero Program in 1964. Numerically, they will swamp all other immigrant populations in most years beginning in 1960.[3] Even if we confine the significance of Dora's story to that escalation of Mexican American migration and Mexican immigration, that would be sufficient to warrant describing her account as a harbinger of coming events. It would suffice, too, if we add the remarkable dispersal of Mexican workers—men and women— to nearly all sections of the West, from Texas to the Pacific Northwest.

Yet, the story goes further, for it serves as an introduction to a dramatic series of political, economic, and social developments tying Mexico and the United States ever closer, events taking place during the same period covered by her experiences: the growth of the *maquiladoras* (factories along the Mexican side of the border); the unfolding changes in the Mexican economy propelling increasing numbers of both urban and rural men and women to cross the border illegally even as the risks sharply escalated; the passage of the Immigration Reform and Control Act of 1986 (with its amnesty for illegal aliens); the implementation of the North American Free Trade Agreement (NAFTA) beginning in January 1994 (opening markets and reshaping, for example, agricultural production patterns in Mexico); the development of numerous hometown associations (mostly in the United States) and their expanding roles in homeland communities; the reforms by the Mexican legislature permitting thousands of Mexicans in the United States to vote in Mexican elections beginning in 2005; and, finally, the Mexicans' astonishing increases in remittances to more than $13 billion annually, notwithstanding the uncertain legal statuses of many of them and the cost-of-living pressures in the United States.

Taking just these factors with respect to the West—where the majority of persons of Mexican descent still reside—we can see the complex place of Mexicans and Mexican Americans in the West. They have become, as in Quincy, instrumental in the expansion of many job sectors north of the border. However, we also see how they have been putting down roots in the United States in many cases without severing old ones with family and communities south of the border. These patterns became far more extensive in the second half of the twentieth century and not just because of their greater numbers and broader geographical dispersion but to a significant extent because of the unintended consequences of U.S. policies. Instead of working for a time in the United States and periodically returning to Mexico, many more undocumented Mexicans than expected began to assess the costs and dangers of re-crossing the border and have chosen to remain and settle in the States. In so doing, they likewise determined that however dire and precarious the conditions they encountered both in secreting themselves across an ever more perilous border and in coping with the living and working conditions north of the border, the opportunities and wages were more promising than those available in Mexico. Meanwhile, numerous Mexicans and Mexican Americans in Texas came to similar conclusions about that state and migrated to the Midwest and Pacific Northwest. Dora's story represents the struggles of different generations.

Dora's account captures the kinds of experiences and diverse roles Mexican immigrants and their children have been playing in many parts of the West. Her own mobility illustrates the potential for improvement even though negative stereotypes have been slow to fade among Anglos. It is for these reasons that Dora's story provides a narrative transition to the next revolution in American immigration that profoundly affected the West. That revolution has encompassed the major new laws abolishing the quota system, erecting new preference systems and new limits on immigration from nations in the Americas, and creating new policies to provide for different classes of refugees and asylees. Furthermore, in much the same way that we observed how the initial introduction of controls between the 1880s and early 1900s had momentous consequences for immigration and citizenship, so the legislative and policy changes after 1952 have had equally momentous effects—both intended and unintended.

We have seen new groups arrive from new regions around the globe since the end of the Second World War, a vast increase in immigration to the West, many new immigrant communities scattered across the region, and, among the hundreds of thousands of Mexicans entering, many men and women from areas in their homeland that had not previously been major sending ones.

In addition, inseparable from these migration trends but providing a broader context have been the major transformations of the U.S. economy, impacting job opportunities. Economic changes sped through the phase of industrialization to post-industrialization and the departure of many industries that had been for some time crucial avenues for the employment and stability of newcomers and the second generation. The onset of new technological and information- and service-related industries significantly altered many job prospects, particularly due to the educational levels and skills required for many positions. Lacking these and often without even a limited English language competency, many immigrants have had to make do with an array of unskilled and semi-skilled jobs at the lower end of the employment scale, filling countless positions Americans have shunned. Ironically, this has happened to such an extent and in so many locations that it has cumulatively made many Mexicans' contributions so tangible, so widespread, and so substantive that we continue to be justified in moving them to center stage in the history of the American West— along with many other immigrants in comparable situations.

But our theme here and in the next volume goes beyond economics, for the place of immigrants and later generations spans well beyond their jobs. Institutions did change, belief systems and policies were transformed, and certainly socio-cultural as well as economic and technological conditions were altered, all of which necessitated continued adaptations by newcomers. With American society changed as much as it has been since the 1950s, fitting in to it—temporarily or permanently—remained a central concern of the immigrants. Meanwhile, fitting in between the parents' generation and mainstream America continued to be a hurdle confronting the children. Nonetheless, the basic patterns by which ethnic groups and newcomers accommodate to American society have persisted across the decades, although the new technologies have also breathtakingly redefined transportation and communication connections with the immigrants' homelands. And there has been another new dimension added to the equation of such adaptation, one that has been sweeping in its impact, too. The Civil Rights Movement, cutting across at least two decades beginning in 1954, did not affect African Americans alone. Unintended benefits and opportunities came to immigrant peoples of color and their children. While this did mark a major shift in the overall context of reception, American sentiments regarding the admission of immigrants and refugees remained ambivalent, with nativist revivals periodically posing obstacles and threats to immigrant communities. Fitting in meant coping with all this, too.

We can as well look beyond Dora's situation in eastern Washington State for a longer perspective regarding trends framing the events outlined here. We find that economic transformations in both the United States and many sending nations have become very much tied to advances of global capitalism, with U.S. penetration of world markets and vice versa all affecting old and new channels of migration—again, directly affecting the West. And last, as much as U.S. involvement in international affairs beginning in the late nineteenth century had consequences for immigration into the West, so international developments commencing with the start of the Cold War in the late 1940s—and climaxing with the terrorist attacks of September 11, 2001, and U.S. military actions in western Asia—have repeatedly demonstrated that American isolation is a thing of the past. Of importance here is that almost every instance of U.S. involvement abroad has either generated or reinforced migration channels to and within America—from all points and very much to the American West.

In other words, Dora's story stands as a harbinger of events that occurred there and all around her, highlighting the critical place of Mexican immigrants and Mexican Americans but taking us well beyond that to the revolutionary changes in federal laws and their implementation, in the region's economy and culture, in the economic and cultural consequences of globalization, and in the sheer explosion of newcomers spreading throughout the West. New peoples, new economy, new challenges, new laws, new encounters—all the ingredients for examining the extent of continuity and change in America's immigrant West after 1952. Dora's story is the doorway to that discussion.

CHAPTER THIRTY-NINE

Looking Back on America's Immigrant West

*T*HIS STUDY OF 14 western states and territories has incorporated some important approaches to exploring the issues covered here. Economic, social, and demographic realities gradually linking the 14 made it clear that—despite the Census Bureau's definition—the West ought to include Texas as well as the territories of Alaska and Hawai'i.[1] In addition, not content with relying on somewhat broad discussions of groups, I have throughout this volume introduced many stories of men and women whose lives represented in numerous ways the struggles and contributions of immigrants and their children. The accounts make real and human all the larger narratives. It was obvious, too, that no story of America's immigrant West could be told that did not have the double focus on the rural and urban West and how each evolved, grew, and remained so inter-dependent in social, cultural, and, especially, economic terms.

Given that the West has been defined here not just by its environment but also by its diversity, I could only hope to capture some of the breadth of the region's peoples by presenting a selection of Latino, Asian, and European peoples present specifically in the West—groups large and small. Some groups were revisited in different time periods because their presence was continuous albeit changing, which is a central theme of this book. In other cases newer groups were introduced as they entered the story, notably Italians, Greeks, Filipinos, and Japanese.

In fact, one very specific objective here was to make it abundantly clear that Europeans, along with Canadians, continued to be active participants in western history, even though in most accounts many of their stories are generally consigned to the same invisibility as those of peoples of color. Germans, British, and Scandinavians, as well as French, Basques, Italians, Greeks, and other Europeans, populate these pages because they did not as groups disappear, melt, or entirely assimilate. Certainly, individuals did, but nearly all the groups persisted—most of them more and more Americanized but still as groups and communities with organizations.[2] It may be because so many remained in rural occupations. Or perhaps the distinct and visible diversity of the West, with its Latino, Asian, Native American, and small African American populations, drew writers to focus on one or more of them, with little attention given to Europeans who were indeed present—and often interacting (at least economically) with those who were being singled out. That oversight only meant that these major groups, though white, were also being left aside.

Furthermore, if the case for the centrality of immigrants was to be made, it was important to recognize how vital and varied were the roles of the women. The immigrant West was at first unquestionably preponderantly male, but steadily women came, with their number of arrivals exceeding that of males by 1930. Wives were brought in, men settled down, families grew, and women provided vital supporting roles both working in the home and outside of it—single women, wives, and mothers. As we saw, immigrant women built homes, raised families, worked on the farms, labored to support their husbands, fathers, and brothers, created organizations, went out on strike, marched on picket lines, and sought the same dignity for themselves and education and better career opportunities for their children as did so many native-born American women.

And that, in turn, brings us to a vital aspect of this narrative. The immigrant West rather quickly became a west of many first- and second-generation persons, and those children faced the challenge of negotiating the differences between their parents' homeland and their own—America. Many struggled with this marginality but, at the same time, were still critically important to the growth of the West. In fact, census data also make it abundantly clear that many immigrants and their children did not come directly from their homelands but—along with older generations of Americans—had moved westward in steps from (mostly) eastern and midwestern states. They most likely began the Americanization process before arriving at their destinations. By 1920, second-generation Americans—still close to their parents' immigrant experiences—amounted to one-fifth of those "Americans" who resettled in the West.

Consequently, many of the American builders of the West were not rooted in fourth or fifth generations but were men and women who were nearer to their families' foreign roots and who undoubtedly added their outlooks and traditions to regional mixes. (Even local contributions could have a significant cumulative impact.) Taking them together with the immigrants, more than one-third of all those living in the West by 1920 were immigrants and the children of immigrants. A principal aim of this book was to make dramatically clear that immigrants and their children were a critical one-third because the West could not have become the richly diverse, economically powerful region it became by the mid-twentieth century were they not present—men and women as consumers, producers, workers, and community members.

Notwithstanding that the immigrants' economic contributions are at the heart of this story, there were obviously many urban and rural jobs that American-born men performed, although relatively few of their wives worked outside the home until the Second World War (e.g., the Women's Land Army and all those Rosie-the-Riveters). In many types of enterprises these men were initially self-employed or were hired, and many remained as foremen, supervisors, and so on, while others formed businesses and cleared lands for farming. However, it was those immigrant and second-generation men and women who—unable, for example, to start a business or acquire a farm—most often had to accept the jobs at the bottom, providing the labor where native-born (third- and older-generation) Americans had moved on, up, or out. Many of those types of employment often came to be labeled as specifically immigrant jobs (e.g., "Mexican jobs"), reinforcing the gulf between immigrant and American, between white and non-white. Westerners' reliance on such men and women for those jobs remained even as the groups changed.

Furthermore, it is equally evident that infrequently during the decades of this study did the corporate and individual movers and shakers successfully build major portions of the West without the peoples whom they exploited, deprecated, and, at times, feared. Nonetheless, later in the nineteenth and early twentieth centuries, in fleeting moments of candor, Americans in the West acknowledged that most miners were immigrants and most men building the railroads were immigrants. They recognized that immigrants were harvesting most crops, selling fruits and vegetables, constructing roads, streets, and office buildings, leveling forests and operating sawmills and shingle mills, catching or canning fish, turning out garments and myriad consumer products in innumerable factories, and establishing laundries, butcher shops, barbershops, dry goods stores, restaurants, hotels, and confectionaries. Some understood that, from entrepreneurs and vendors to laborers, many of the employees and employers were likely to be immigrants, or the children of immigrants. Even the limited scope of the Dillingham Commission Report on the West made that quite clear. In the final analysis, though, this story is not simply a recounting of the tale of small segments of the population, or just of minority groups—it is an account of the history of the West itself—a West built with a combination of peoples from all points on the globe.

From All Points, Due West—westward bound or heading to the West—was the way I envisioned this study of the American West. It became a destination for a remarkably diverse population. Not surprisingly, it quickly evolved into a stage on which important aspects of the development of America were played out. Yet, paradoxically, many of the "performers" among that myriad assortment of people were not, metaphorically, in the script. Their "lines" were limited but not their labors, for those who wrote the original American script in the 1700s and early 1800s imagined an unfolding West for an expanding new, white American nation. All others were, in the final analysis, not just non-white, partially white, or conditionally white; they were simply not viewed as members of the core society, as recognized participants in the nation building. They were invisible.

The immigrants were invisible in most accounts of the region because those eager to expand the white, Protestant, northern European–based "charter group" of the American nation did not regard many of these workers as those whom they wished would remain. They were an economic variable, taken for granted as docile workers who, it was hoped, would depart when no longer needed. The immigrants' presence was limited to their being entered in the debits and credits of businesses, marginalized, deemed "outsiders." Indeed, Americans' ambivalent response to these "outsiders" was rooted in the fact that this nation was created by a population of northern and western Europeans. They were committed to a body of principles and values (the "civic culture") and an assumption that the norms, values, political practices, customs, and folkways that were held to be synonymous with being a white American would be readily (or, at the very least, eventually) absorbed by newcomers. It was expected that they would come from European communities similar to those from which the founding Americans' own ancestors had come. In other words, it was presumed that this diverse nation—this nation of peoples—would be a nation of descendants of white Europeans, since the blacks, Native Americans, and (later) Asians among them were not regarded as potential citizens. Many immigrants, especially from Scandinavia, Great Britain, and Canada, did rather readily fit in. But upon first meeting, many other new southern and eastern European immigrants did not appear to meet those expectations.[3]

Their stories were also evidently judged less compelling by historians and writers than those of capital investments launching industries, bold entrepreneurial leaders fulfilling the nation's Manifest Destiny, aggressive settlers and soldiers subduing the Indians, federal monies being appropriated for harnessing and exploiting abundant natural resources, and expanding political institutions incorporating new states. With such topics in the forefront, much of the West's history was reframed by white Americans who periodically feared for the nation's homogeneity. And so they plagued with a curse of invisibility those whom they had encouraged to come and work, those whom they initially saw without reason to fear but who became competitors and labor foes, targets of concern and loathing. They may have privately conceded the workers' indispensability, but publicly they mobilized to ensure the workers' powerlessness while ever searching for more dependable, more tractable replace-ments. One is inclined to say that this was done even though many groups were still small and comparatively few in number, but one is also tempted to conclude that this path was taken *because* they were few in number and short on the skills and leverage to effectively resist.

In effect, the nation never prepared for the global diversity which it invited by its open doors and which it witnessed in the West. It was psychologically, cul-turally, and institutionally unequipped to deal with it. And perhaps it could not have been otherwise in the last quarter of the nineteenth and first decades of the twentieth centuries, given the view of nationalities as immutable "races." Instead of embracing the diversity, Americans suspected it, and the more di-verse the population of new immigrants became, the more they were viewed with skepticism.

Since the story of this West is, in key respects, the story of these immigrants and their children who migrated into and within the region, helping it to grow and thrive — with some being welcomed and others marginalized — then there is actually another story that addresses the larger institutional framework within which the basic narrative just outlined was shaped. For nearly a cen-tury the federal government was content to observe the almost entirely unim-peded arrival of newcomers (except for some state regulations). With virtually no limits on the immigrants' entry, borders hardly amounted to boundaries, permeable or not. One can then certainly make the case that, beginning in the 1870s and 1880s, the West was responsible for the critical turnabout in fed-eral policy regarding immigration.

The mounting clamor to curb Chinese immigration and bar their access to citizenship arose principally in the West. Then, at that seminal point in the maturation of the country, national leaders recognized that, having just en-acted controls on the Chinese, an entire administrative machinery to define and implement these controls was essential. It was then no great step to begin viewing borders as boundaries, as a manifestation of a newly appreciated sov-ereignty. The federal government began responding to the escalating numbers of newcomers by asserting its national sovereignty over the whole realm of im-migration.[4]

However, in responding to the demands from the West with unprecedented legislation curbing the admission of a specific class of a specific people — Chinese laborers — the federal government opened up not just the issue of sover-eignty but the entire Pandora's box of federal powers. And once it was opened, an array of local groups and local leaders strongly expressed their vested interests in shaping those federal actions that involved the West.

We then see policies and enforcement machinery directed at illegal Chinese migrants seeking to enter through Canada and Mexico; policies lifting requirements for the importation of temporary (mostly Mexican) workers in both world wars and the Korean War, at one point transforming the U.S. government into a labor employment agency on behalf of the West; policies facilitating the deportation and repatriation of Mexicans and Filipinos (not long after demands that limits on Mexican immigration not be enacted in the late 1920s); and policies launching Operation Wetback and, ironically, then institutionalizing the Bracero Program. All these grew out of pressures from the West.

Time and again, those pressures came from specific interest groups. Economic associations (especially agricultural), chambers of commerce, the Native Sons of the Golden West, the American Legion chapters, branches of the Veterans of Foreign Wars, local political leaders, the press, the media, and many others not so affiliated or affiliated with ad hoc organizations joined the choruses demanding federal action concerning foreigners or non-white groups in the West. For decades many of the major groups among them repeatedly brought pressure to bear in support of those policies. They also continually called for federal action to secure adequate labor supplies and to foil any efforts by labor unions to achieve, via federal recognition, leverage in negotiating with businesses, be they plantations, industrial farms, mines, factories, or canneries. Undoubtedly, however, the incarceration of Japanese Americans was one of the most tragic of all results of the numerous demands for action generated by many groups and leaders along the Pacific Coast. Clearly, the West and the federal government were intertwined over many issues, and a major one revolved around immigration.

Forces of continuity and change run through the West's immigration history as much as who came, where they settled, how well they adapted, and how well they were received. Above all, focusing on this collective story takes the immigrants and their children—men and women, whites and peoples of color—out of the wings and onto center stage of western history, casting aside the veils of invisibility and enabling us to appreciate the full history of the American West.

APPENDIX

TABLE 1.1. RANK ORDER, FOREIGN-BORN POPULATION IN THE AMERICAN WEST, 1890, 1900, AND 1910

1890 TOTAL: 923,866		1900 TOTAL: 1,127,127		1910 TOTAL: 1,765,256	
1. Germans	169,210	1. Germans	185,928	1. Germans	209,956
2. Irish	113,674	2. English	112,282	2. Mexicans	204,655
3. English	113,014	3. Mexicans	100,676	3. English	140,635
4. Chinese	96,178*	4. Canadians	94,729	4. Canadians	140,305
5. Canadians	78,350	5. Irish	90,607	5. Italians	124,677
6. Mexicans	75,740	6. Chinese	86,214*	6. Japanese	123,325 est*
7. Swedes	50,703	7. Japanese	80,204*	7. Swedes	111,521
8. Scots	29,765	8. Swedes	66,363	8. Irish	101,274
9. Italians	27,021	9. Italians	44,648	9. Austrians	82,050**
10. Danes	26,351	10. Danes	31,078	10. Norwegians	64,874
11. Norwegians	21,580	11. Scots	30,803	11. Chinese	58,000 est*
12. French	19,595	12. Norwegians	28,925	12. Russians	50,931
13. Swiss	19,249	13. Austrians	27,840**	13. Danes	44,295
14. Austrians	18,241**	14. Swiss	22,819	14. Scots	42,432
15. Russians	12,205	15. French	19,466	15. Swiss	30,723
16. Welsh	11,141	16. Portuguese	19,252	16. Portuguese	30,429
17. Portuguese	10,509	17. Russians	14,069	17. Finns	29,716
18. Poles	3,304	18. Finns	13,673	18. French	27,257
19. Japanese	1,668	19. Welsh	10,759	19. Poles	19,071
20. Greeks	590	20. Poles	6,697	20. Hungarians	11,049
		21. Greeks	1,106	21. Welsh	9,103

*For 1900 and 1910, figures include Hawai'i. For 1890, with Hawai'i (still a Kingdom) the total would be 112,930; for Japanese the total would be 14,278.

**Austrians could include persons of other ethnicities coming from the Austrian Hungarian Empire.

Sources: Department of Interior, *Compendium of the Eleventh Census: 1890*, Part 1, *Population* (Washington, D.C., 1895), Table 32, 606-9; *Twelfth Census of the United States taken in the Year 1900*, vol. 2, *Population*, Part 2, Table 33 (Washington, D.C., 1902); and *Thirteenth Census of the United States taken in the Year 1910*, vols. 2 and 3, *Population 1910* (Reports by States), Table 1 for each state and territory (Washington, D.C., 1913).

TABLE 1.2. FOREIGN-BORN POPULATION IN THE AMERICAN WEST, BY STATES AND TERRITORIES, 1890, 1900, AND 1910

	1890	1900	1910
U.S. Total:	92,947,714	10,444,717	13,630,073
Pct FB	(14.7%)	(13.7%)	(14.8%)
West Total:	923,866	1,127,127	1,765,256
Pct FB	(17.3%)	(15.4%)	(16.1%)
Alaska	n/a	10,669	20,435
Pct FB	—	(19.9%)	(31.8%)
Arizona	18,795	24,233	48,765
Pct FB	(21.3%)	(19.7%)	(23.9%)
California	366,309	367,240	586,432
Pct FB	(30.2%)	(24.7%)	(24.7%)
Colorado	83,990	91,155	129,587
Pct FB	(20.3%)	(16.9%)	(16.2%)
Hawai'i	n/a	90,780	93,752
Pct FB	—	(58.9%)	(48.9%)
Idaho	17,456	24,604	42,578
Pct FB	(19.7%)	(15.2%)	(13.1%)
Montana	43,096	67,067	94,713
Pct FB	(30.2%)	(27.6%)	(25.2%)
Nevada	14,706	10,093	19,691
Pct FB	(31.1%)	(23.8%)	(24.1%)
New Mexico	11,259	13,629	23,146
Pct FB	(7.0%)	(7.0%)	(7.1%)
Oregon	57,317	65,748	113,136
Pct FB	(18.0%)	(15.9%)	(16.8%)
Texas	152,956	179,357	241,938
Pct FB	(6.8%)	(5.9%)	(6.2%)
Utah	53,064	53,777	65,822
Pct FB	(25.2%)	(19.4%)	(17.6%)
Washington	90,005	111,364	256,241
Pct FB	(25.2%)	(21.5%)	(22.4%)
Wyoming	14,913	17,415	29,020
Pct FB	(23.8%)	(18.8%)	(19.9%)

Source: See table 1.1.

TABLE 3.1. TEN TOP FOREIGN-BORN GROUPS IN THE WEST, 1900 VERSUS 1920

1900		1920	
1. Germans	185,928	1. Mexicans	440,205
2. English	112,282	2. Germans	169,440
3. Mexicans	100,676	3. Canadians	157,708
4. Canadians	94,729	4. English	140,987
5. Irish	90,607	5. Italians	140,552
6. Swedes	66,363	6. Japanese	137,086
7. Italians	44,648	7. Swedes	115,814
8. Danes	31,078	8. Irish	83,209
9. Norwegians	28,925	9. Russians	79,859
10. Swiss	22,819	10. Norwegians	70,170
Total	778,055	Total	1,535,030*
As a percentage of all foreign born in the West	68.9%	As a percentage of all foreign born in the West	74.5%

*Filipinos were nationals and thus not listed in census reports as foreign born. Counting Hawai'i, 99,747 Filipinos were reported by race, including 10,380 second-generation persons in the Islands. In 1920 there were probably few children on the mainland, giving a total of about 89,300 in the United States who were born in the Philippines, over 95 percent of whom were in the West. That placed them eighth in 1920 and increased the total for the top ten to 1,554,160 (omitting Norwegians), or 75.4% of the West's foreign born.

TABLE 3.2. CONCENTRATIONS OF LEADING FOREIGN BORN GROUPS IN THE WEST, 1920

Germans	In top 5 groups in all western states except Nevada (6th there)
English	In top 5 groups in 10 states
Canadians	Among top 5 in 8 western states; leading group in Washington, Oregon, and Montana
Italians	Among top 5 in 8 western states; leading group in Nevada
Mexicans	Comprised 2/3 to 3/4 of foreign born in Texas, Arizona, and New Mexico
Scandinavians	Made up nearly 1/3 of foreign-born in Washington and 1/4 in Oregon
English, Welsh, Scots	1/10 to 1/6 of foreign born in 8 states
Asians (Japanese, Chinese, Koreans)	Over 4/5 of Hawaii's population
French (including French Basques)	Over 3/5 were in California
Czechs	1/2 remained in Texas settlements
Dutch	More than 1/2 in California and Washington

TABLE 3.3. GENDER RATIOS FOR FOREIGN-BORN WHITES IN THE WEST,
1900 VERSUS 1920

LOCATION	1900 WHITE FOREIGN BORN (males: females)	1920 STATE-WIDE IN WEST (males: females)	1920 WHITE FOREIGN BORN (males: females)
All United States	117:100	104:100	122:100
U.S. non-West	114*	103	119**
Total West	157*	113	143**
Alaska	1,227	169	556
Arizona	173	122	134
California	154	112	144
Colorado	158	110	140
Hawai'i	n/a	144	n/a
Idaho	197	118	177
Montana	226	121	165
Nevada	241	148	264
New Mexico	166	112	112
Oregon	170	113	156
Texas	132	107	125
Utah	103	107	121
Washington	191	118	158
Wyoming	232	131	204

*Omits Hawai'i and Alaska from calculation.

**Omits Hawai'i from calculation.

TABLE 3.4. WHITE FOREIGN-BORN URBAN POPULATIONS IN THE WEST, 1920

LOCATION	STATE PERCENTAGE URBAN	PERCENTAGE OF WHITE FOREIGN-BORN URBAN
U.S. Total	51.4	75.5
U.S. Outside the West	52.2	78.6
West, Mainland*	45.7	55.9
Arizona	35.2	37.0
California	68.0	69.3
Colorado	48.2	51.0
Idaho	27.6	28.6
Montana	31.3	35.0
Nevada	19.7	17.6
New Mexico	18.0	19.5
Oregon	49.9	60.2
Texas	32.4	46.6
Utah	48.0	57.2
Washington	55.2	59.9
Wyoming	29.5	33.4

*Data not available for Hawai'i and Alaska.

TABLE 3.5. NATURALIZATION RATES AMONG SELECTED WHITE, FOREIGN-BORN GROUPS IN THE WEST, BY GENDER, 1920

WHITE MALES	PERCENTAGE NATURALIZED	WHITE FEMALES	PERCENTAGE NATURALIZED
1. Irish	71.6%	1. Germans	75.2%
2. Danes	71.4	2. Danes	75.2
3. Germans	71.3	3. Swedes	71.8
4. Swedes	64.6	4. Norwegians	70.1
5. Norwegians	63.7	5. Canadians	68.4
6. Scots	63.2	6. English	67.4
7. English	62.7	7. Irish	66.8
8. Canadians	61.9	8. Scots	64.9
9. Czechs	58.9	9. Czechs	64.6
10. French	55.2	10. Poles	64.4
11. Poles	53.4	11. French	58.4
All Western Foreign born	45.4	*All Western Foreign born*	55.7
12. Russians	43.7	12. Finns	50.3
13. Finns	38.1	13. Russians	47.3
14. Italians	29.6	14. Yugoslavians	43.6
15. Yugoslavians	27.5	15. Italians	33.1
16. Greeks	16.6	16. Greeks	25.1
17. Mexicans	3.3	17. Mexicans	8.7

TABLE 3.6. FOREIGN BORN AND SECOND GENERATION IN WESTERN STATES, 1920

STATE	PERCENTAGE FOREIGN BORN OF TOTAL POPULATION	PERCENTAGE INCREASE TOTAL FOREIGN BORN	PERCENTAGE OF SECOND-GENERATION WHITES IN TOTAL POPULATION	PERCENTAGE INCREASE IN SECOND-GENERATION WHITES
	1920	1900–1920	1920	1900–1920
Total U.S.*	13.2% (14.5)**	34.2%	23.9%	45.1%
Total West*	14.9 (14.9)	102.4	21.2	90.7
Alaska	22.3 (41.6)	96.9	41.4	60.1
Arizona	24.1 (26.8)	232.5	21.3	142.3
California	22.1 (20.9)	106.3	27.7	104.9
Colorado	12.7 (12.7)	30.7	22.1	60.4
Hawai'i	34.1 (21.5)	-3.9	53.6	n/a
Idaho	9.4 (9.2)	65.6	21.7	116.2
Montana	17.4 (17.5)	42.5	30.9	132.3
Nevada	20.7 (20.9)	58.5	27.7	67.4
New Mexico	8.3 (8.9)	118.8	9.6	80.2
Oregon	13.7 (13.3)	63.7	22.0	100.1
Texas	7.8 (9.2)	102.9	11.4	53.9
Utah	13.2 (12.8)	10.1	31.6	20.8
Washington	19.6 (18.9)	138.2	27.1	177.3
Wyoming	13.7 (13.3)	52.6	22.1	71.5

*These figures include Hawai'i and Alaska and, consequently, differ from totals given in census reports, which, in most cases, did not include those two territories but only states.

**Figures in parentheses are the percentage of white foreign born in the total white population.

TABLE 3.7. NATIONAL ORIGINS QUOTA ALLOCATIONS, JULY 1, 1929

Great Britain	65,721	Switzerland	1,707
Germany	25,957	Austria	1,413
Irish Free State	17,853	Belgium	1,304
Poland	6,524	Denmark	1,181
Italy	5,802	Hungary	869
Sweden	3,314	Yugoslavia	845
Netherlands	3,153	Finland	569
France	3,086	Portugal	440
Czechoslovakia	2,874	Greece	307
Russia	2,784	Rumania	295
Norway	2,377	Spain	252

Source: President's Proclamation No. 1872 of March 22, 1929

TABLE 3.8. U.S. IMMIGRANTS ADMITTED AND DEPARTED,
JULY 1, 1930 TO JUNE 30, 1941

YEAR	IMMIGRANTS ADMITTED	IMMIGRANTS DEPARTED	NET SUM
1930	241, 700	50,661	+191,039
1931	97,139	61,882	+ 35,257
1932	35,576	103,295	- 67,719
1933	23,068	80,081	- 57,013
1934	29,470	39,771	- 10,301
1935	34,956	38,834	- 3,878
1936	36,329	35,817	+ 512
1937	50,244	26,736	+ 23,508
1938	67,895	25,210	+ 42,685
1939	82,998	26,651	+ 56,347
1940	70,756	21,461	+ 49,295
1941	51,776	17,115	+ 34,661
Total, 1930–1941	821,907	527,514	+294,393

*Immigrants Admitted refers to quota and non-quota persons admitted to permanent residence in the United States listed by their country of birth, including those born in independent countries of the Western Hemisphere. Immigrants Departed refers to those who had been admitted to permanent residence and then chose to emigrate, most often to their country of birth. In other words, neither column refers to *all* persons arriving and departing, for that would include numerous temporary persons on business, pleasure, government matters, returning citizens, etc.

Source: Annual Reports of Secretary of Labor and, beginning in 1940, the Department of Justice. See, for example, 1935 report, pp. 83–84, and tables 6 and 6a in the *1941 Annual Report*, which are cumulative 1931–1941, admissions and departures.

TABLE 3.9. GERMAN AND AUSTRIAN IMMIGRATION AND EMIGRATION, 1930–1940

	IMMIGRANTS TO U.S BY LAST RESIDENCE		IMMIGRANTS ADMITTED TO PERMANENT RESIDENCE IN U.S. BY COUNTRY OF BIRTH		EMIGRANT DESTINATION	
	Germans/Austrians		Germans/Austrians		Germany/Austria	
1930	26,5691	744	27,119	1,417	4,639	301
1931	10,401	738	10,100	524	3,369	270
1932	2,670	301	2,086	187	5,533	452
1933	1,919	228	1,324	121	5,479	
1934	4,392	310	3,515	229	3,502	158
1935	5,201	829	4,891	641	3,530	154
1936	6,346	677	6,073	569	3,672	147
1937	10,895	480	11,127	409	2,340	105
1938	17,199		17,868		2,270	
1939	33,515		32,759		4,211	
1940	21,520		26,083		1,978	
1941	4,028		13,051		1,758	
1942	2,150		4,883		2	
Totals						
1930–1942:	152,112		164,976		43,870	
1933–1942	109,689		123,543		29,306	

Note: See note for table 3.8.

Source: Compiled from various tables (not all numbered), Annual Reports of Immigration, Department of Labor 1930–1940, and, 1941 on, Department of Justice, 1941–1942.

TABLE 3.10. NATIONALITY GROUPS IN THE UNITED STATES REPORTING UNDER THE ALIEN REGISTRATION ACT, JUNE 30, 1943, BY COUNTRY OF BIRTH AND REGION

REGION OF THE WORLD	
Total, United States	4,593,537*
Total, Europeans	3,251,067 (70.8%)
Total, North and Central Americans,West Indians	1,037,127 (22.6%)
Total, Asians	171,861 (3.7%)
Total, Pacific Region	95,954 (2.1%)
Total, South Americans	28,086 (0.6%)
Total, Africans	4,979 (0.1%)
Total, Other	4,463 (0.1%)

COUNTRY OF BIRTH			
1. Italians	653,359	14. Austro-Hungarians	82,237
2. Canadians	430,315	15. Lithuanians	78,066
3. Mexicans	421,165	16. Greeks	73,761
4. Poles	394,662	17. Portuguese	68,801
5. Russians	324,104	18. Czechoslovaks	63,466
6. Germans	300,064	19. British West Indians	61,539
7. British	266,774	20. Norwegians	59,628
8. Austrians	177,927	21. Yugoslavians	47,718
9. Irish (Eire and Northern)	166,283	22. Finns	44,984
10. Hungarians	106,166	23. Chinese	41,953
11. Japanese	90,928	24. Turks	39,188
12. Swedes	86,395	25. Spanish	37,733
13. Filipinos	84,056	26. French	33,303

*The 1940 census had reported 4.364 million foreign-born resident aliens—those with first papers, none, and not reported, including Hawai'i and Alaska. However, the census does not include non-resident non-immigrants—those temporarily in the country. On the other hand, between 1940 and 1943, some 866,591 persons received their citizenship and would no longer have been required to register.

Source: Unpublished records, Alien Registration 1940 Series AA, table XX, Country of Birth by State of Residence, INS library, Washington, D.C.

TABLE 3.11. ALIEN REGISTRATIONS, 1940 AND 1943, BY STATE OF RESIDENCE

REPORTED LOCATION	1940 REGISTRATIONS	1943 REGISTRATIONS
U.S. Total	4,746,836	4,593,537
Total for the West	961,062 (20.3%)	1,014,773 (22.1%)*
Alaska	n/a	3,651 (3.6%)**
Arizona	30,899 (3.2%)	39,320 (3.9%)
California	528,957 (55.0%)	487, 122 (48.0%)
Colorado	26,689 (2.8%)	27,087 (2.7%)
Hawai'i	n/a	89,578 (8.8%)
Idaho	5,938 (0.6%)	8,532 (0.8%)
Montana	13,639 (1.4%)	11,926 (1.2%)
Nevada	6,219 (0.6%)	5,769 (0.6%)
New Mexico	12,123 (1.3%)	11,348 (1.1%)
Oregon	33,658 (3.5%)	29,287 (2.9%)
Texas	204,450 (21.3%)	208,088 (20.5%)
Utah	10,100 (1.1%)	11,680 (1.2%)
Washington	82,644 (8.6%)	72,828 (7.2%)
Wyoming	5,746 (0.6%)	8,557 (0.8%)

*Percent of U.S. total

**Percent of total for the West

Source: 1940 data in table 13 of the 1941 Department of Justice *Annual Report*; 1943, see note in table 3.10.

TABLE 3.12. FOREIGN-BORN POPULATION IN THE WEST, 1920–1940

LOCATION	1920	1930	1940	PERCENT CHANGE 1920 VERSUS 1940
U.S. Total Population	106,021,837	123,202,624	131,669,275	+24.2%
U.S. Total Foreign Born	14,020,203	14,230,718	11,659,621	-16.8%
U.S. F.B. Outside West	11,958,679	11,965,340	9,868,752	-17.5%
West, Total Population	13,877,148	18,148,551	20,794,816	+49.8%
West, Total Foreign Born	2,061,524	2,265,378	1,790,869	-13.1%
Alaska	12,270	10,569	9,132	-25.6%
Arizona	80,566	65,756	38,693	-52.0%
California	757,625	1,073,964	924,865	+22.1%
Colorado	119,138	99,875	71,564	-40.0%
Hawai'i	87,241	68,537	52,613	-39.7%
Idaho	40,747	32,284	24,712	-39.4%
Montana	95,591	75,903	56,364	-41.0%
Nevada	16,003	15,095	11,041	-31.0%
New Mexico	29,808	24,052	15,402	-48.3%
Oregon	107,644	110,440	90,193	-16.2%
Texas	363,832	362,287	235,528	-35.3%
Utah	59,200	48,015	33,276	-43.8%
Washington	265,292	255,258	210,379	-20.7%
Wyoming	12,270	10,569	9,132	-25.6%

Historical Statistics, rev. ed, C195-227, p. 116; 1930 Census, vol. 2, Population, table 43, p. 35, and table 5, p. 406; 1940 Census, Population, Country of Origin, p. 11, and Non-White Population by Race, table 1, p. 5; 1950 Census, Population by Division and States, tables 13, 14, 17, 24.

TABLE 3.13. CITIZENSHIP IN THE WEST:
NATURALIZATIONS AND FIRST PAPERS BY STATE, 1920 VERSUS 1940*

LOCATION	1920*		1940		Percentage Change	
	NATURALI-ZATIONS	FIRST PAPERS	NATURALI-ZATIONS	FIRST PAPERS	NATURALI-ZATIONS	FIRST PAPERS
United States	46.6%	5.8%	62.4%	7.9%	+12.1%	-24.4%
The West	40.9%	6.8%	53.6%	7.5%	+19.8%	+ .2%
Alaska	60.4%**	18.8%	70.6%	12.4%	+ 1.0%	- 43.2%
Arizona	14.8%	2.4%	31.0%	5.0%	+ .2%	- 1.8%
California	40.2%	6.3%	51.2%	8.7%	+ 56.0%	+68.0%
Colorado	54.3%	8.0%	63.4%	6.3%	- 30.0%	-52.2%
Hawaii	7.7%**	1.2%	10.6%	.8%	+ 5.6%	-52.1%
Idaho	61.3%	8.2%	67.2%	7.1%	-33.5%	-47.2%
Montana	63.0%	9.3%	76.1%	4.6%	-28.7%	-40.5%
Nevada	40.3%	8.9%	53.0%	8.3%	- 9.3%	-36.2%
New Mexico	21.3%	2.8%	37.9%	5.0%	- 8.2%	- 8.3%
Oregon	53.6%	11.4%	63.8%	9.0%	- .3%	- 33.9%
Texas	21.3%	2.8%	32.1%	4.2%	- 2.5%	- 2.5%
Utah	58.4%	6.9%	68.1%	6.2%	- 34.6%	- 49.2%
Washington	52.9%	11.4%	65.3%	8.7%	- 2.1%	- 39.5%
Wyoming	47.6%	9.5%	67.3%	6.3%	- 9.0%	- 57.5%

*U.S. and Western totals do not include Hawaiian and Alaskan data, which were not available.

**Alaskan and Hawaiian data are from 1930 rather than 1920, and percentage changes are for 1940 versus 1930.

Source: 1920 Census, vol. 2, General Report and Analytical tables, tables 1, 5–8, 10 (pp. 804, 807–11, 826–41; 1940 Census, vol. 2, Population, part 1, table 27 (p. 79). Shown are percentages of total foreign-born populations. Percentage changes are the changes in the number of foreigners, 1920 versus 1940, who were naturalized or held declarations of intent, or first papers applying for citizenship.

TABLE 3.14. RANK ORDER OF TOTAL FOREIGN-BORN POPULATION IN
THE UNITED STATES AND THE WEST, 1940

Population: United States		Population: The West	
TOTAL FOREIGN BORN	11,659,621	**TOTAL FOREIGN BORN**	1,790,869
1. Italians	1,623,580	1. Mexicans	338,545
2. Germans	1,237,772	2. Canadians	183,730
3. Canadians	1,065,480	3. Germans	137,612
4. Russians (U.S.S.R.)	1,040,884	4. Italians	137,015
5. Poles	993,479	5. English	125,559
6. Irish	678,447	6. Swedes	92,946
7. English	621,975	7. Russians	90,926
8. Austrians	479,906	8. Japanese	82,844
9. Swedes	445,070	9. Filipinos	68,000*
10. Mexicans	377,433	10. Norwegians	63,320
11. Czechoslovaks	319,971	11. Irish	54,237
12. Scots	279,321	12. Scots	42,624
13. Norwegians	262,088	13. Danes	39,557
14. Greeks	163,252	14. Austrians	33,889
15. Yugoslavs	161,093	15. Swiss	28,304
16. Danes	140,279	16. Poles	26,968
17. Finns	117,210	17. Finns	26,434
18. Dutch	111,067	18. Chinese	25,576
19. French	102,920	19. Yugoslavs	24,651
20. Filipinos	98,132	20. French	24,373
21. Swiss	88,293	21. Greeks	23,844
22. Japanese	84,667	22. Portuguese	21,690
23. Portuguese	52,347	23. Czechoslvks	19,927
24. Syrians	50,859	24. Dutch	18,692
25. Spanish	47,707	25. Spanish	15,633

*Filipinos were technically nationals until 1934 and still not enumerated with other foreign-born groups in 1940. In 1940, some 88,277 were reported by race in the West (90% of all the Filipinos in the U.S.), although in Hawaiʻi it was indicated that 16,791 out 52,569 Filipinos there were second generation. That figure was deducted from the 88,277, leaving 71,486. No second-generation data are available for the mainland, but given the relative recency of arrivals to the mainland, a 14:1 gender ratio in 1930 (15.5 in California, where 83% were reported), and the anti-miscegenation laws in the 1930s, it is presumed that there was not yet a significant number of second-generation Filipino Americans on the mainland in 1940. Considering the small number under age 21 in 1940 and the fact that teenagers had migrated, too, the figure given here can be viewed as a rough approximation of around 68,000 Philippines-born Filipinos in the West in 1940.

Source: 1940 Census, vol. 2, Population, part 1, U.S. Summary, table 14; Population: Characteristics of the Nonwhite Population by Race, table 1.

TABLE 3.15. CHANGES IN MEXICAN IMMIGRANT STATE AND
URBAN POPULATIONS, 1920–1940

	1920 CENSUS	1930 CENSUS	1940 CENSUS
The West	440,205	556,952	338,545
Texas	251,827	266,046	159,266
Texas Urban		142,946	97,983
El Paso		33,654	20,137
San Antonio		33,146	22,530
Houston		6,845	5,035
Dallas		2,990	2,192
California	88,771	199,165	134,312
California Urban		131,954	91,554
Los Angeles		53,573	36,840
San Francisco		6,917	4,729
San Diego		4,694	3,347
Sacramento		2,364	1,285
Oakland		2,159	1,565
Arizona	61,580	48,824	24,902
Arizona Urban		18,292	10,841
Tucson		4,261*	2,874
Colorado	11,037	13,125	6,360
Colorado Urban		4,276	2,512
Denver		1,414	955
New Mexico	20, 272	16,347	8,875
New Mexico Urban		3,078	2,717
Utah	1,166	2,386	1,069
Utah Urban		893	580
Salt Lake City		493	261

Note: The U.S. Census classified most Mexicans as non-whites in 1930, but the 1940 census revised and corrected the 1930 data by re-incorporating Mexicans among foreign-born whites, and the state-level tables containing state and city results for white foreign born do include both 1930 (revised) and 1940 results. Thus, most data used here do come from the 1940 Census, vol. 2, Population by Divisions and States, tables 15, 36–37, and A-40, B-40, C-40 for each state and its cities. Since Mexicans are not included in the table by race, I presume these figures are complete.

*Foreign born in 1920.

TABLE 3.16. SECOND-GENERATION WHITE POPULATION, 1920–1940,
BY REGION AND STATE

LOCATION	1920	1930	1940	PERCENT CHANGE 1920 VERSUS 1940
U.S. Total	22,686,204	25,902,383	23,157,580	+ 2.1%
The West	2,634,929	3,1351,129	3,407,380	+29.2%
Alaska	6,748 est*	18,460 est	30,384 est	+350.3%
Arizona	62,205	103,772 est**	85,980	+38.2%
California	905,094	1,447,607	1,536,100	+69.7%
Colorado	204,108	218,509	189,540	- 7.1%
Hawai'i	23,039 est*	70,815 est	95,840 est	+326.0%
Idaho	92,453	87,280	79,200	- 16.1%
Montana	164,837	161,535	145,020	- 12.0%
Nevada	19,612	22,520 est	22,120	+ 12.8%
New Mexico	32,279	64,172 est	38,800	+ 20.2%
Oregon	169,269	201,846	193,640	+ 14.4%
Texas	445,384	602,100	577,420	+ 29.6%
Utah	139,665	135,333 est	106,440	- 23.8%
Washington	358,016	403,331	388,640	+ 8.6%
Wyoming	42,007	50,124 est	44,480	+ 5.9%

*Due to the way the data are presented for Alaska and Hawai'i, with race rather than ethnicity being used, there may be some small variance in the exact numbers for both territories.

**Because the 1930 census omitted most Mexicans from white foreign-born group data and not all tables were revised and included in the 1940 census, I have used the Mexicans-as-a-race data to compute these figures where revisions were not provided in the 1940 census. That only means there may be small numbers of native-born Mexicans included, but that will not materially affect the resulting percentages.

Source: 1920 Census, vol. 2 Population, tables 5 and 6 (pp. 31–32); 1940 Census, vol. on Country of Origin, table 5 (p. 42), with revised data for 1930. The 1920 and 1930 data are based on full count; 1940 data are based on 5 percent sample (first time used), which is likely to have some impact on the percentage changes.

TABLE 3.17. URBAN AND GENDER TRENDS IN THE WESTERN STATES, 1920 AND 1940, FOR EACH STATE'S TOTAL POPULATION AND FOREIGN-BORN POPULATION

Location	Percent Urban		Gender Ratios	
	1920	1940	1920	1940
Total U.S. Foreign Born*	(75.5%)	(80.0%)	(121.7:100)	(111.1:100)
The West**	44.7%	54.1%	112.1	104.8
Foreign Born	(53.0)	(65.5)	(150.0)	(123.8)
Alaska	N/A	N/A	168.5	145.7
Foreign Born	(N/A)	(N/A)	(N/A)	(361.7)
Arizona	35.2%	34.8%	121.9	107.1
Foreign Born	(36.9)	(45.4)	(135.8)	(106.5)
California	68.0%	71.0%	112.4	103.7
Foreign Born	(67.6)	(74.6)	(153.2)	(120.9)
Colorado	48.2%	52.6%	110.3	102.6
Foreign Born	(50.8)	(56.6)	(141.5)	(127.0)
Hawai'i	37.4%***	42.4%	152.8***	137.6
Foreign Born	(37.4)	(43.2)	(158.4)	(171.0)
Idaho	27.6%	33.7%	118.2	111.4
Foreign Born	(29.0)	(34.6)	(181.9)	(151.2)
Montana	31.3%	37.8%	120.5	114.8
Foreign Born	(35.0)	(40.5)	(167.2)	(147.1)
Nevada	19.7%	39.3%	148.4	125.4
Foreign Born	(17.5)	(38.8)	(282.7)	(204.2)
New Mexico	18.0%	33.2%	112.1	104.6
Foreign Born	(19.3)	(40.4)	(139.7)	(127.1)
Oregon	49.9%	48.8%	113.4	106.8
Foreign Born	(60.5)	(60.5)	(163.5)	(133.9)
Texas	32.4%	45.4%	106.9	100.9
Foreign Born	(46.5)	(61.0)	(125.9)	(109.1)
Utah	48.0%	55.5%	106.8	102.6
Foreign Born	(56.0)	(69.2)	(126.7)	(107.5)
Washington	55.2%	53.1%	118.1	109.1
Foreign Born	(60.0)	(59.6)	(162.3)	(132.9)
Wyoming	24.5%	37.3%	131.3	116.7
Foreign Born	(33.7)	(42.0)	(212.5)	(163.4)

* U.S. data is for white foreign-born persons.

** 1920 summary data for the West for 1920 do not include Hawaiian or Alaskan data.

***Hawaiian data not available for 1920; 1930 data used here.

Source: 1940 Census, vol. 2, Population, parts 1–6, Divisions and States, tables 4 and 5 for each state. 1940 results based on sample data.

TABLE 3.18. POPULATION TRENDS: SELECTED WESTERN CITIES AND SELECTED IMMIGRANT GROUPS, 1920–1940

	SEATTLE	PORTLAND	SAN FRANCISCO	LOS ANGELES	OAKLAND	SAN DIEGO	DENVER	SALT LAKE CITY	HOUSTON	SAN ANTONIO	HONOLULU
Mexicans											
1920:	122	104	3,793	21,598	1,026	2,741	1,390	217	3,946	28,444	—
1930:	100	148	6,917	53,648	2,159	4,694	1,414	493	6,845	33,146	—
1940:	96	62	4,729	36,848	1,565	3,347	955	261	5,035	22,530	—
Canadians											
1920:	14,063	6,491	7,083	13,741	3,785	1,904	3,102	758	357	398	—
1930:	15,886	8,382	9,682	30,978	5,286	3,025	2,562	583	581	456	—
1940:	12,666	7,061	8,694	27,896	4,582	2,894	1,855	631	566	321	—
British											
1920:	11,675	6,104	14,133	14,937	6,360	2,317	5,076	6,919	932	943	—
1930:	12,169	6,820	18,392	32,452	8,713	3,937	4,638	5,684	1,312	879	—
1940:	9,026	5,008	13,541	28,080	6,698	3,497	3,053	3,823	1,129	574	—
Irish [Erie]											
1920:	3,455	1,969	18,257	4,932	3,656	724	3,221	574	373	509	—
1940:	1,482	785	10,271	4,194	1,911	552	1,297	186	355	186	—
Germans											
1920:	4,827	5,384	18,513	10,563	4,661	1,427	4,664	2,033	1,619	2,564	—
1930:				18,094							
1940:	3,581	3,947	14,977	17,528	3,682	1,815	2,829	2,053	1,702	2,132	—
Norwegians											
1920:	9,118	2,915	3,121	1,669	1,163	279	536	870	59	53	—
1930:				3,747							
1940:	8,436	3,025	2,951	3,435	1,259	426	391	599	138	32	—

(Table 3.18, continued)

	SEATTLE	PORTLAND	SAN FRANCISCO	LOS ANGELES	OAKLAND	SAN DIEGO	DENVER	SALT LAKE CITY	HOUSTON	SAN ANTONIO	HONOLULU
Swedes											
1920:	10,253	5,060	6,468	4,998	2,663	731	3,953	2,258	159	94	—
1930:				8,917							
1940:	7,670	3,622	5,278	7,844	2,562	946	2,427	1,260	269	78	—
Danes											
1920:	2,228	1,315	3,389	2,003	1,764	298	922	1,611	115	82	—
1930:				3,536							
1940:	1,514	1,069	2,760	3,138	1,529	391	669	971	136	44	—
Finns											
1920:	2,256	258	1,810	530	390	43	110	75	13	6	—
1940:	1,740	1,078	2,068	1,049	359	84	117	50	30	10	—
Italians											
1920:	3,094	2,847	23,924	7,930	5,094	749	2,871	496	1,290	575	—
1930:	3,457		27,311	12,685	6,350						
1940:	3,055	2,658	24,036	13,256	5,707	1,315	2,339	469	1,346	427	—
Russians											
1920:	3,348	5,161	5,752	9,691	1,062	329	5,333	430	1,096	732	—
1940:	2,371	3,932	7,380	25,595	1,087	641	3,657	210	1,129	572	—
Greeks											
1920:	1,399	896	3,204	1,036	928	201	768	548	177	145	—
1940:	924	744	3,508	1,905	765	271	418	661	419	136	—
Chinese											
1920:	896	1,237	4,450	1,260	2,596	171	147	24	117	N/A	9,574
1940:	830	611	7,114	2,196	1,075	191	47	54	72	211	3,228

(Table 3.18, continued)

	SEATTLE	PORTLAND	SAN FRANCISCO	LOS ANGELES	OAKLAND	SAN DIEGO	DENVER	SALT LAKE CITY	HOUSTON	SAN ANTONIO	HONOLULU
Japanese											
1920:	6,011	1,072	4,175	8,519	1,924	601	398	326	12	N/A	24,522
1930:				11,865							
1940:	2,876	725	2,276	8,726	655	327	112	153	20	14	13,790
Total Foreign Born											
1920:	80,976	49,778	149,195	122,131	45,895	13,295*	38,230	19,897	12,088	36,646	N/A
1930:	78,342	50,228	171,641	247,135	54,931	21,586	32,857	18,094	17,937	40,712	26,930
1940:	63,470	40,005	140,023	227,237	44,531	20,113	24,982	13,560	15,464	28,296	22,718**

*This figure for San Diego indicates the total white foreign born.

**This figure for Honolulu includes 2,604 Koreans but not 6,887 Filipinos who were nationals, not foreign born, prior to 1934 but still appeared as non-foreign born in 1940 in Hawai'i.

TABLE 4.1. APPREHENSION AND INTERNMENT OF ENEMY ALIENS IN WORLD WAR II

APPROX.DATE OF REPORT	TOTAL & STATUS OF POPULATION	JAPANESE ALIENS	GERMANS ALIENS	ITALIANS ALIENS
Priort to 12/7/41[1]	1,662 "taken in"	—	667	995
Dec. 8, 1941[2]	1,717 "taken in"	1,212	—	77
Dec. 10,1941[3]	2,295 "in custody"	1,291	857	147
Dec. 15,1941[4]	2,798 "arrested"	1,430	1,153	215
Feb. 16,1942[5]	3,849 "in custody"	2,192	1,393	264
Feb. 1942[6]	5,151 "arrested"	3,250	1,532	369
June, 1942[7]	8,500 "arrested"	—	—	277
June 30, 1942[8]	9,405 "arrested," FBI	4,764	3,120	1,521
June 30,1942[9]	7,469 "taken in," INS	4,092	2,384	794
Oct. 12 1942[10]				228[11]
Dec. [31] 1942[12]	3,632 "still interned"	1,974	1,448	210
May 30,1943[13]	362 Italians apprehended			151
June [30] 1943[14]	14,800 "taken in"	5,300	6,000	3,500
June 30,1943[15]	9,220 "in INS custody"			
Oct. 1943[16]	14,807 "taken in"	5,307	5,977	3,503
June 30. 1944[17]	6,238 "interned"	3,136	2,971	86
June 30,1945[18]	7,364 "interned"	5,211	2,107	25
FBI Final Rept, 1945[19]	16,062 "apprehended"	5,428	7,043	3,591[20]
June 30,1946[21]	1,539 "being held"	982	555	1
June 30,1947[22]	587 "being held"	384	203	—

1. Culley, "Enemy," 144.

2. Culley, "Enemy," 141. Dept of Justice *Report*, Appendix C.I lists 74 Italians, Dec. 7–10. Compare Lothrop, "Unwelcome," 517, with Lothrop, "Shadow," 209.

3. Pozzetta, 85.

4. Culley, "Trouble", n2.

5. Dept of Justice *Report*, Appendix B. 4.

6. Nagler. 77. Fox (164) reports that on Feb. 16, 1942, there were 1393 Germans and 264 Italians in custody.

7. Lothrop, 525.

8. Pozzetta, 85.

9. Pozzetta, 276n21, says 7270, but Congressional Research Service, 49. Added in 199 "Others."

10. Lothrop, 525.

11. The Dept of Justice *Report* lists 418 who were interned (Appendix D), but lengths of time not reported.

12. Pozzetta, 85. Refers only to those in INS custody at that time.

13. Dept. of Justice, *Report*. 7. The 151 refers to the number interned out of those appre-hended.

14. Fox, 151, and Congressional Research Service, 50. Cumulative no. apprehended in first 18 months.

15. INS *Annual Report 1943*, 14.

16. Culley, "Trouble," n2. Similar data reported by Fox, note 11.

17. INS, *Annual Report 1944*, 22, Refers only to those in IKS custody at that time.

18. INS, *Annual Report 1945*, 26, and Congressional Research Service, 50. Refers to those then in custody.

19. Nagler, 77. Total number of persons taken in by FBI since December 7, 1941.

20. Dept of Justice *Report* lists 1,881 names of Italians taken into custody, plus 418 interned, and 74 initially apprehended, for a total of 2,373, but that is not considered complete (Appen-dix C.2).

21. INS, *Annual Report 1946*, 30. Refers to those in custody in INS facilities at that time.

22. INS, *Annual Report 1947*, 27. Refers to those in INS custody at that time.

TABLE 4.2. WHITE FOREIGN-BORN POPULATION IN THE WEST, 1940–1950

LOCATION	1940	1950	PERCENT CHANGE
U.S. Total Population	131,669,275	150,697,361	+14.4
U.S. Total White Population	118,701,558	134,478,365	+13.3
U.S. Total White Foreign born	11,419,138	10,173,778	-10.9
Non-west White Foreign born	9,774,351	8,386,470	-14.2
Total Population West,	20,793, 943	27,901,156	+34.2
Total White Population West,	18,980,060	25,508,566	+34.4
Total White Foreign born, West,	1,674,787	1,787,308	+ 6.7
Alaska	8,786	6,476	-26.3
Arizona	36,837	45,594	+23.8
California	870,893	985,333	+13.1
Colorado	70,471	58,987	-16.3
Hawai'i	7,929	6,134	-26.7
Idaho	24,116	19,407	-19.5
Montana	55,642	43,119	-22.5
Nevada	10,599	10,530	-0.7
New Mexico	15,247	17,336	+13.7
Oregon	87,639	83,612	-4.6
Texas	234,388	276,645	+18.0
Utah	32,498	29,844	-7.6
Washington	203,163	191,001	-6.0
Wyoming	16,779	13,290	-20.8

Sources: Data are based on 1950 Census, vol. 2, Characteristics of Population, pt. 1, U.S. Summary, table 49, pts. 3–50, table 14, the individual state reports for 1940 and 1950, and Special Report on Nativity and Parentage, table 12.

TABLE 4.3. SECOND-GENERATION WHITE POPULATION, 1940–1950,
BY REGION AND STATE

LOCATION	1940	1950	PERCENT CHANGE
U.S. Total	23,157,580	23,578,375	+1.8
U.S. Non-West	19,750,200	19,553,970	-1.0
The West	3,407,380	4,024,405	+18.1
Alaska	30,384 est*	n/a	n/a
Arizona	85,980	110,805	+28.9
California	1,536,100	1,997,055	+30.0
Colorado	189,540	185,910	-2.0
Hawai'i	95,840 est*	108,979 est*	+13.0
Idaho	79,200	69,020	-12.7
Montana	145,020	125,005	-13.8
Nevada	22,120	24,265	+9.7
New Mexico	38,800	43,485	+11.6
Oregon	193,640	225,430	+16.4
Texas	577,420	655,635	+13.5
Utah	106,440	105,315	-1.1
Washington	388,640	442,420	+13.8
Wyoming	44,480	40,200	-9.6

*May include some third-generation persons.

Source: 1940 census, vol. on Country of Origin, table 5 (p. 42) (5 sample), and 1950, Special Report on Nativity and Parentage, table 13 (pp. 3A-75-78) (20 sample).

**TABLE 4. 4. RANK ORDER, TOTAL WHITE FOREIGN-BORN POPULATION
IN THE WEST, 1940–1950**

Population: The West, 1940		Population: The West, 1950	
Total White Foreign Born	1,674,787	Total White Foreign Born	1,787,308
1. Mexicans	338,545	1. Mexicans	404,658
2. Canadians	183,730	2. Canadians	208,292
3. Germans	137,612	3. Italians	136,375
4. Italians	137,015	4. English/Welsh	127,309 est*
5. English/Welsh	125,559	5. Germans	126,549
6. Swedes	92,946	6. U.S.S.R.	102,445
7. U.S.S.R.	90,926	7. Japanese	75,337est*
8. Japanese	82,344	8. Swedes	74,698
9. Filipinos	71,486	9. Norwegians	56,173
10. Norwegians	63,320	10. Filipinos	53,236 est*
11. Irish (Eire)	43,284	11. Chinese	47,900 est*
12. Scots	42,624	12. Irish	42,824
13. Danes	39,557	13. Scots	41,490 est*
14. Austrians	33,889	14. Austrians	36,820
15. Swiss	28,304	15. Poles	36,395
16. Poles	26,968	16. Danes	33,525
17. Finns	26,434	17. French	25,612
18. Chinese	25,576	18. Greeks	25,542
19. Yugoslavs	24,651	19. Yugoslavs	24,719
20. French	24,373	20. Swiss	24,224
21. Greeks	23,844	21. Finns	21,663
22. Portuguese	21,690	22. Dutch	21,608
23. Czechoslovaks	19,927	23. Czechoslovaks	19,372
24. Dutch	18,692	24. Portuguese	16,980
25. Spanish	15,633	25. Spanish	15,061

*Data are based on white foreign born, but, for comparisons, estimates have been included for Chinese and Japanese by combining the U.S. foreign-born figure in the Census Bureau's West Special Report, tables 28 and 29, plus Hawai'i and an estimate for Texas; hence, these are estimates. Yet the Japanese figure is also exactly the percentage of the whole "race" residing in our West, 91.3%. Because the Filipino data have not been provided by state, the percentage in the West is unavailable, and the percentage from the 1940 data was used to estimate a 1950 total. Scots data are not broken out for Alaska and Hawai'i, and I am estimating 400 Scots in those two territories, plus 41,090 in the 12 states. English data are combined with Welsh and Scots in Hawai'i and Alaska also, but in addition different tables based on sampling have different state totals only for the English/Welsh. That total in the West may be 126,321 or somewhere around 128,296. Although the correct figure is probably the former, I am taking the average of the two and adding 1,000 for Alaska and Hawai'i for this estimate.

Note: This table is of white foreign born; Asians and Filipinos are included for comparison purposes. Data are based on vol. 2, Characteristics of Population, pts. 3–50, table 14 of the individual state reports for 1940 and 1950.

TABLE 4.5. GENDER TRENDS AMONG THE FOREIGN BORN IN THE WESTERN REGION, MALE TO FEMALE RATIO, 1920–1950

LOCATION	1920	1930	1940	1950
U.S. Total Population	104.0:100	102.5:100	100.7:100	98.6:100
Total Foreign Born	121.7	115.8	111.1	n/a [103.9]**
The West	112.1	108.5	104.8	102.2
Foreign Born	(150.0)*	(135.0)	(123.8)	(116.6)[111.5]***
Alaska	168.5	152.1	145.7	161.3
Foreign Born	(N/A)	(456.0)	(361.7)	(246.7)[235.21
Arizona	121.9	113.2	107.1	102.3
Foreign Born	(135.8)	(125.2)	(106.5)	(107.9){105.4]
California	112.4	107.6	103.7	100.1
Foreign Born	(153.2)	(133.8)	(120.9)	(112.5)[107.4]
Colorado	110.3	105.1	102.6	100.8
Foreign Born	(141.5)	(131.7)	(127.0)	(113.4)[113.6]
Hawai'i	N/A	152.8	137.6	121.2
Foreign Born	N/A	(158.4)	(171.0)	(215.6)[90.8]*
Idaho	118.2	114.3	111.4	106.2
Foreign Born	(181.9)	(170.1)	(151.2)	(123.2)[1130.1]
Montana	120.5	120.0	114.8	109.9
Foreign Born	(167.2)	(163.6)	(147.1)	(128.2)[130.7]
Nevada	148.4	137.6	125.4	113.3
Foreign Born	(282.7)	(257.5)	(204.2)	(148.1)[1159.9]
New Mexico	112.1	107.4	104.6	104.2
Foreign Born	(139.7)	(131.8)	(127.1)	(134.2)[127.6]
Oregon	113.4	110.0	106.8	103.2
Foreign Born	(163.5)	(147.3)	(133.9)	(118.5)[117.2]
Texas	106.9	103.8	100.9	100.4
Foreign Born	(125.9)	(115.1)	(109.1)	(110.2)[111.5]
Utah	106.8	104.9	102.6	101.9
Foreign Born	(126.7)	(119.9)	(107.5)	(102.4)[100.2]
Washington	118.1	112 .1	109.1	106.0
Foreign Born	(162.3)	(142.3)	(132.9)	(116.0)[113.7]
Wyoming	131.3	123.8	116.7	114.1
Foreign Born	(212.5)	(181.9)	(163.4)	(149.1)[146.9]

*Data for total foreign born for each year are in parentheses.

**U.S. total for 1950 is for white foreign born; total foreign-born data are not available.

***Square bracketed: white foreign born, 100% count. In parentheses: total foreign born but based on only a 20% sample.

NOTES

Preface

1. This paragraph and the two that follow are drawn from my article "Turning Turner on His Head? The Significance of Immigration in Twentieth-Century American Western History," *New Mexico Historical Review* 77.1 (Winter 2002): 58–64. Note, too, the earlier work by Earl Pomeroy and Moses Rischin, discussed in the article.

2. Both state propositions were efforts to bar undocumented aliens from receiving public benefits from each state. Although most of California's 187 was struck down by the courts, the more narrow provisions of Arizona's proposition have, as of mid-2006, been upheld by the courts.

3. As described below, the term *West*, as used in this work, includes 14 states and territories: Alaska, Arizona, California, Colorado, Hawai'i, Idaho, Montana, Nevada, New Mexico, Oregon, Texas, Utah, Washington, and Wyoming.

Introduction

1. Oscar Handlin, *The Uprooted: The Epic Story of the Great Migrations That Made the American People* (New York: Grosset and Dunlap, 1951), 3. In addition, even before Handlin penned his famous opening line, Marcus Lee Hansen had made a most important observation in this regard, although he was relating it to the frontier's retreat across the continent and confining it to Europeans: "Without the influx of millions of Europeans, this clocklike progression across the continent could not have occurred. The population would not have been so mobile. There would have been a frontier, to be sure, but not the kind of frontier that produced the now accepted historical consequences." Hansen, *The Immigrant in American History* (New York: Harper and Row, 1964 [1940]), 64.

2. Some valuable exceptions are works by Ronald Takaki, *Strangers from a Different Shore: A History of Asian Americans* (Boston: Little, Brown, 1989); Sucheng Chan, *Asian Americans: An Interpretive History* (Boston: Twayne, 1991); Neil Foley, *The White Scourge: Mexicans, Blacks, and Poor Whites in Texas Cotton Culture* (Berkeley: University of California Press, 1997); and especially Walter Nugent, *Into the West: The Story of Its People* (New York: Alfred Knopf, 1999); Gunther Peck, *Reinventing Free Labor: Padrones and Immigrant Workers in the North American West, 1880–1930* (Cambridge: Cambridge Univer-

sity Press, 2000); and Arnoldo DeLeon, *Racial Frontiers: Africans, Chinese, and Mexicans in Western America, 1848–1890* (Albuquerque: University of New Mexico Press, 2002).

3. Carey McWilliams, *Southern California Country: An Island on the Land* (New York: Duell, Sloan and Pearce, 1946), 106.

4. Quoted by Earl Pomeroy, *The Pacific Slope: A History of California, Oregon, Washington, Idaho, Utah, and Nevada* (Seattle: University of Washington Press, 1965), 262.

5. The region was "new" in that most of the territory encompassed by the states covered here had not been incorporated into the United States until between 1845 and 1898, except for small portions that had been part of the 1803 Louisiana Purchase.

6. See Barkan, "Turning Turner on His Head?" 57–88.

7. Brian W. Dippie, "American Wests: Historiographical Perspectives," in *Trails: Toward a New Western History*, ed. Patricia Nelson Limerick, Clyde Milner II, and Charles E. Rankin (Lawrence: University Press of Kansas, 1991), 116; and Gerald D. Nash, "Epilogue: Sharpening the Image," in *The Twentieth Century West: Historical Interpretations*, ed. Gerald D. Nash and Richard W. Etulain (Albuquerque: University of New Mexico Press, 1989), 408. See also Limerick's "What on Earth Is the New Western History?" in *Does the Frontier Experience Make America Exceptional?* ed. Richard W. Etulain (Boston: Bedford/St. Martin's Press, 1999), 110.

8. Walter Nugent did a survey on precisely this question. See "Where Is the American West?" *Montana, the Magazine of Western History* 42 (Spring 1992): 2–23, reprinted as "Where Is the American West? Report on a Survey," in *Major Problems in the History of the West*, 2nd ed., ed. Clyde Milner II, Anne Butler, and David Rich Lewis (New York: Houghton Mifflin, 1997), 15–41.

9. John Findlay, "A Fishy Proposition: Regional Identity in the Pacific Northwest," in *Many Wests: Place, Culture, and Regional Identity*, ed. David Wrobel and Michael Steiner (Lawrence: University of Kansas Press, 1997), 33, 38. Quotations by William Cronon, George Miles, and Jay Gitlin, "Becoming West: Toward a New Meaning for Western History," in *Under an Open Sky: Rethinking America's Western Past*, ed. Cronon, Miles, and Gitlin (New York: W. W. Norton, 1992), 8–9; and by Richard White, *"It's Your Misfortune and None of My Own": A History of the American West* (Norman: University of Oklahoma Press, 1991), 539.

10. Up to 1950 most census tables for the United States actually included only data drawn from the states and contiguous territories, omitting Alaska, Hawai'i, and other, smaller possessions (such as Puerto Rico) because the constitutional mandate for the census was reapportionment of the House of Representatives. Consequently, wherever possible, totals for "the West" presented here include more than the Census Bureau's configuration of the West (which also omits Texas). The figures shown will almost always be greater than the "official" totals for the United States and for the bureau's subdivision of the West. Since 1960, and Alaskan and Hawaiian statehood, the U.S. totals have been the same as officially shown, but totals for "the West" continue to be greater in this work because Texas is here considered part of the West. Indeed, Walter Nugent showed that most discussions of the West actually included parts of Texas notwithstanding the Census Bureau's breakdown.

11. Nugent, *Into the West*, 8; Japanese quoted by Gordon B. Dodds, *The American Northwest: A History of Oregon and Washington* (Arlington Heights, Ill.: Forum Press, 1986), 121; Dippie, "American Wests," 130, 135; quotation from McWilliams, *Southern California*, 105. A half-century later, David Rieff observed that "Southern California was and remains the most heavily mythologized place in America." Rieff, *Los Angeles: The Capital of the Third World* (New York: Simon and Schuster, 1991), 44.

12. San Diego quotation is from McWilliams, *Southern California*, 123; Arthur John Brown, "Means of Promoting Immigration to the Northwest and Washington, to 1910"

(master's thesis, University of Washington, 1942), 63; Carl Abbott, "The American West and Three Urban Revolutions," in *Old West/New West: Quo Vadis*, ed. Gene M. Gressley (Worland, Wyo.: High Plains, 1994), 99; Patricia Limerick, *Legacy of Conquest: The Unbroken Past of the American West* (New York: W. W. Norton, 1987), 24; Limerick, "Layer upon Layer of Memory in the American West," *Chronicle of Higher Education*, March 3, 2000: 5; Michael P. Malone, "Beyond the Last Frontier: Toward a New Approach to Western American History," in *Trails*, ed. Limerick, Milner, and Rankin, 148, 155; Clyde Milner II, "Introduction: America Only More So," in the *Oxford History of the American West*, ed. Clyde Milner II, Carol A. O'Connor, and Martha A. Sandweiss (New York: Oxford University Press, 1994), 2; Donald Worster, "Beyond the Agrarian Myth," in *Trails*, ed. Limerick, Milner, and Rankin, 18; Michael P. Malone and Richard W. Etulain, *The American West: A Twentieth-Century History* (Lincoln: University of Nebraska Press, 1989), 134; and Roger W. Lotchin, "The Impending Urban Past: An Essay on the Twentieth Century West," in *Researching Western History: Topics in the Twentieth Century*, ed. Gerald D. Nash and Richard W. Etulain (Albuquerque: University of New Mexico Press, 1997), 61–62. In the same work, Gerald Nash also discussed the emergence of a multicultural urban society in the West, in "Epilogue: Sharpening the Image," 409. Walter Nugent, however, argues for the imminent disappearance of older European ethnic groups due to assimilation, in *Into the West*, 361.

13. Frederick Luebke, "Ethnic Minorities in the American West," in *Historians and the American West*, ed. Michael P. Malone (Lincoln: University of Nebraska Press, 1983), 393; Dennis M. Ogawa, *Kodomo no tame ni: For the Sake of the Children: The Japanese American Experience in Hawaii* (Honolulu: University of Hawai'i Press, 1978), 89; Yukiko Kimura, *Issei: Japanese Immigrants in Hawaii* (Honolulu: University of Hawai'i Press, 1988), xiii–xiv.

14. Although the more recent migrations did not course their way as strongly or as evenly to and within the Secondary West, there has actually been some new in-migration there, too, notably into Utah, Colorado, and Nevada. The Salt Lake City, Denver, and Las Vegas CMSAs (Consolidated Metropolitan Statistical Areas) were among the top 25 in the nation in terms of the number of immigrants received during the late 1990s. William H. Frey, "Metropolitan Magnets for International and Domestic Migrants" (Washington, D.C.: Brookings Institution, October 2003), table in appendix B.

15. Milner, "Introduction," 6. Among the various challenges to a conception of "A West," Richard Etulain suggested that a case could be made that Idaho and Arizona do not fit into a cultural definition of the West. He wrote, "One might also center on Arizona and Idaho, cultures perched on international boundaries, surrounded by states so unlike them culturally." However, from the standpoint of immigration, earlier in the twentieth century Idaho was the scene of considerable immigration by several different groups (linking it to nearby states). With regard to Arizona, as its agricultural economy continued to expand thanks to irrigation, it became progressively more important as a destination of immigrants crossing the border and especially from other southwestern states. Richard W. Etulain, "Research Opportunities in Twentieth-Century Western Cultural History," in *Researching Western History*, ed. Nash and Etulain, 156.

16. John Bodnar, Roger Simon, and Michael Weber remind us of an important dimension to the adjustment process at this point: "Immediate problems of leaving home, moving to a strange city, finding work, and maintaining families loomed so large as to obscure the larger concerns of scholars—status, success, and succession." Bodnar, Simon, and Weber, *Lives of Their Own: Blacks, Italians, and Poles in Pittsburgh, 1900–1980* (Urbana: University of Illinois Press, 1982), 3.

17. Quoted by William A. Douglass and Jon Bilbao, *Amerikanuak: Basques in the New World* (Reno: University of Nevada Press, 1975), 265.

18. See Act of March 26, 1790: An Act to Establish a Uniform Rule of Naturalization, reprinted in *U.S. Immigration and Naturalization Laws and Issues: A Documentary History*, ed. Michael LeMay and Elliott Robert Barkan (Westport, Conn.: Greenwood Press, 1999), 11. In his seminal study *White over Black: American Attitudes toward the Negro, 1550–1812* (Chapel Hill: University of North Carolina Press, 1968), Winthrop Jordan made the point that white Americans had rejected mulattos as a third party in a system built for two.

19. Peck, *Reinventing Free Labor*, 68; Foley, *White Scourge*, 6–7; and Matthew Frye Jacobson, *Whiteness of a Different Color: European Immigrants and the Alchemy of Race* (Cambridge, Mass.: Harvard University Press, 1998), 57. The last quotation is from Peter Kolchin, "Whiteness Studies: The New History of Race in America," *Journal of American History* 89.1 (June 2002): 155.

Jacobson juxtaposed the Irish and Chinese in the same manner, emphasizing "that whiteness could emerge by its contrast with non-whiteness (as seems to have been the case with Celts in California during the anti-Chinese campaign of the 1870s for instance." In other words, to be anti-Chinese (as anti-black) was to be *not of them*, or even in association with them, which could lower one's status.

20. Peck, *Reinventing Free Labor*, 2, 166; Kolchin, "Whiteness Studies," 155; Foley, *White Scourge*, 6–7, 40; and Peter LaChapelle, "At the Crossroads of Whiteness: Anti-Migrant Activism, Eugenics, and Pop Culture in Depression Era California," in *Moving Stories: Migration and the American West, 1850–2000*, ed. Scott E. Casper and Lucinda M. Long (Reno: Nevada Humanities Committee and Halycon, 2001), 145–46, 144.

21. The first quotation is from Peck, *Reinventing Free Labor*, 2; also, Foley, *White Scourge*, 7; Richard White, "Trashing the Trails," in *Trails*, ed. Limerick, Milner, and Rankin, 29; Karen Brodkin, quoted by Kolchin, *Whiteness Studies*, 159–60; Peck, *Reinventing Free Labor*, 168, 167, 220.

22. Peck, *Reinventing Free Labor*, 167, 220, 221 n, 170; Jacobson, *Whiteness of a Different Color*, 48, 158, 73–74. Emphasized among those qualities, Matthew Jacobson stressed, was not being disqualified for being one who was "unfit for self-government" or who had "no conception of representative and free institutions."

23. Jacobson, *Whiteness of a Different Color*, 174–76; Leo Pap, *The Portuguese Americans* (Boston: Twayne, 1981), 114; Peck, *Reinventing Free Labor*, 234; John Higham, *Strangers in the Land: Patterns of American Nativism, 1860–1925*, 2nd ed. (New Brunswick, N.J.: Rutgers University Press, 1988 [1955]), 3–4, 52–54, 66–67, 92–94.

24. Eduardo Obregón Pagán, *Murder at the Sleepy Lagoon: Zoot Suits, Race and Riot in Wartime L.A.* (Chapel Hill: University of North Carolina Press, 2003), 14–18.

25. Elliott R. Barkan, "America in the Hand, Homeland in the Heart: Transnational and Translocal Immigrant Experiences in the American West," *Western Historical Quarterly* 35.3 (Autumn 2004): 331–354.

26. For a discussion of the use of adaptation and accommodation as part of a whole model of assimilation, see Elliott R. Barkan, "Race, Religion, and Nationality in American Society: A Model of Ethnicity—From Contact to Assimilation," *Journal of American Ethnic History* 14.2 (Winter 1995): 38–75, 95–101.

27. Immigrants' military participation is not being overlooked here; this segment is focusing on economic issues.

28. David Tyack, "School for Citizens: The Politics of Civic Education from 1790 to 1990," in *E Pluribus Unum? Contemporary and Historical Perspectives on Immigrant Political Incorporation*, ed. Gary Gerstle and John Mollenkopf (New York: Russell Sage Foundation, 2001), 331–370.

29. Barkan, "Race, Religion," 46–49, 55–58.

Prelude

1. Gail M. Nomura, "Tsugiki, a Grafting: A History of a Japanese Pioneer Woman in Washington State," in *Women in Pacific Northwest History*, rev. ed., ed. Karen J. Blair (Seattle: University of Washington Press, 2001), 284–307.

2. The two quotations are from Matthew Frye Jacobson, *Barbarian Virtues: The United States Encounters Foreign Peoples at Home and Abroad, 1876–1917* (New York: Hill and Wang, 2000), 61, 68.

3. Pomeroy, *Pacific Slope*, 262–63.

4. Richard D. Scheuerman, "Washington's European American Communities," in *Peoples of Washington: Perspectives on Cultural Diversity*, ed. Sid White and S. E. Solberg (Pullman: Washington State University Press, 1989), 50–51; and Marvin Slind and Fred Bohm, *Norse to the Palouse: Sagas of the Selbu Norwegians* (Pullman, Wash.: Norlys Press, 1990), 35.

5. Michael J. Piore, *Birds of Passage: Migrant Labor and Industrial Societies* (Cambridge: Cambridge University Press, 1979), 52; Patricia Limerick, *Legacy of Conquest: The Unbroken Past of the American West* (New York: W. W. Norton, 1987), 248; and David Montgomery, *The Fall of the House of Labor: The Workplace, the State, and American Labor Activism, 1865–1925* (Cambridge: Cambridge University Press, 1987), 48.

6. The following account is drawn from Nomura, "Tsugiki, a Grafting."

7. This account is based on Angelo Noce's pamphlet, "Columbus Day in Colorado" (Denver: author, 1910), Huntington Library Archives, doc. no. 257279.

8. This account is drawn from Bernard Marinbach, *Galveston: Ellis Island of the West* (Albany: State University of New York Press, 1983), 161–65.

9. This synopsis is based on Murray K. Lee, "Ah Quinn: One of San Diego's Founding Fathers," in *The Chinese in America: A History from Gold Mountain to the New Millennium*, ed. Susie Lan Cassel (Walnut Creek, Calif.: Altamira Press, 2002), 308–28.

10. This account is drawn from Slind and Bohm, *Norse to the Palouse*, 14–24.

11. This account is based on Berge Bulbulian, *The Fresno Armenians: History of a Diaspora Community* (Fresno: Press at California State University, Fresno, 2000), 17–25, 46.

12. Estelle Hudson, *Czech Pioneers of the Southwest* (Dallas: Southwest Press, 1934), 260–66.

13. Levy's biography appears in Charles Henry Carey, *History of Oregon*, 3 vols. (Chicago and Portland, Ore.: Pioneer Historical, 1922), 2: 448, 451.

14. One example of the kind of technological revolutions wherein immigrants were both producers and beneficiaries in the West was the extension of electricity and telephone service. Both fostered insatiable demands for immigrant labor, notably for the mining of copper and the production of wire and other related products (and most likely for the installations as well).

15. Richard White, "Trashing the Trails," 39.

16. Alejandro Portes and Rubén Rumbaut elaborate on this concept of "Context of Reception" in *Immigrant America: A Portrait*, 3rd ed. (Berkeley: University of California Press, 2006), 92–101.

17. Moreover, although it is easy to identify Swedish urban experiences in Tacoma and Norwegian ones in Ballard, there is no shortage of rural ethnic experiences, such as those Valerie Matsumoto so effectively captured for the Japanese/Japanese-American farming community in Cortez, in California's San Joaquin Valley; as did Linda Tamura for the Japanese in Oregon's Hood River Valley; Ronald Takaki for the plantation workers in Hawai'i; Gertrude Singelstad for Norwegians in Silverton, Oregon; and Gilbert Benjamin for the Germans in Texas.

See Valerie J. Matsumoto, *Farming the Home Place: A Japanese American Community in California, 1919–1982* (Ithaca, N.Y.: Cornell University Press, 1993); Linda Tamura, *The Hood River Issei: An Oral History of Japanese Settlers in Oregon's Hood River Valley* (Urbana: University of Illinois Press, 1993); Ronald Takaki, *Pau Hana: Plantation Life and Labor in Hawaii, 1835–1920* (Honolulu: University of Hawai'i Press, 1983); Gertrude Tingelstad, *Scandinavians in the Silverton Country: Their Arrival and Early Settlement* (Corvallis, Ore.: Silverton Appeal Tribune, 1978); and Gilbert Giddings Benjamin, *The Germans in Texas: A Study in Immigration* (Austin: Jenkins, 1974).

18. Frederick Leubke, *European Immigrants in the American West*, (Albuquerque: University of New Mexico Press, 1998), vii; U.S. Department of Labor, "Report of the Bisbee Deportations: U.S. Presidential Mediation Commission, November 16, 1917" (Washington, D.C.: 1918), Huntington Library File no. 265875; and Katherine Benton-Cohen, "Vigilantism as Corporate Policy: Before and After the Bisbee IWW Deportation of 1917," paper presented at the Western Historical Association meeting, Las Vegas, October 15, 2004.

19. Richard White, *"It's Your Misfortune,"* 539.

20. Nugent, *Into the West*, 161.

Introduction to Part 1

1. Malone and Etulain, *American West*, 5.

1. Immigrant Stories from the West

1. Kristine Leander, ed., *Family Sagas: Stories of Scandinavian Immigrants* (Seattle: Scandinavian Language Institute, 1997), 127–29.

2. Harriet Rochlin and Fred Rochlin, *Pioneer Jews: A New Life in the Far West* (New York: Houghton Mifflin, 1984), 94–96.

3. Helen Papanikolas, *A Greek Odyssey in the American West* (Lincoln: University of Nebraska Press, 1997 [1987]), synthesized from the whole book.

4. Ibid., 109.

5. Drawn from Judy Yung's *Unbound Voices: A Documentary History of Chinese Women in San Francisco* (Berkeley: University of California Press, 1999), 9–95. On Chin Lung's economic achievements, see also Sucheng Chan, *This Bittersweet Soil: The Chinese in California Agriculture, 1860–1910* (Berkeley: University of California Press, 1986), 207–209.

6. The three quotations are in Yung, *Unbound Voices*, 23, 101, 98.

7. Barkan, "America in the Hand," 331–54.

2. The Draw of the Late-Nineteenth-Century West

1. The total was 24 percent excluding Texas. That figure varies from other sources but is based on the figures in the 1890 census table for 1880–1890. The total for the West with Texas was actually only 15 percent. In 1880 only 6 states and territories out of 12 (omitting Alaska and Hawai'i) listed any urban populations, with none reported for Montana, Wyoming, Arizona, New Mexico, Idaho, and Washington. The figure some use of 30 percent urban for 1880 is based on the percentage urban in just 5 states (California, Utah, Colorado, Nevada, and Oregon). See table titled "Urban Population: 1880

and 1890," in Department of the Interior, Census Office, *The Miscellaneous Documents of the House of Representatives for the First Session of the Fifty-Second Congress, 1891–1892*, vol. 50, part 8 (of the Eleventh Census, 1890) (Washington, 1895), lxviii; and Carl Abbott, *The Metropolitan Frontier: Cities in the Modern American West* (Tucson: University of Arizona Press, 1993), xvii.

In 1890 the figure was 28.1 percent urban for the West (and 32.9 percent without Texas), based on the revised data appearing in the 1900 and 1910 censuses. See *Thirteenth Census of the United States Taken in the Year 1910*, vols. 2 and 3, *Population 1910 (Reports by States . . .)* (Washington, 1913), table 1 for each state and territory. For a brief discussion of some of the problems with the 1890 census, see Gerald D. Nash, "The Census of 1890 and the Closing of the Frontier," *Pacific Northwest Quarterly* 71.3 (July 1980): 98–100.

2. Nugent, *Into the West*, 57, 95, 131; Sarah Deutsch, "Landscape of Enclaves: Race Relations in the West, 1865–1990," in *Under an Open Sky*, ed. Cronon, Miles, and Gitlin, 113; Richard White, *"It's Your Misfortune,"* 246; Abbott, *Metropolitan Frontier*, xviii; Carol O'Connor, "A Region of Cities," in the *Oxford History of the American West*, ed. Clyde Milner II, Carol A. O'Connor, and Martha A. Sandweiss (New York: Oxford University Press, 1994), 535–36. On the nativist issues, see John Higham, *Strangers in the Land: Patterns of American Nativism, 1860–1925*, 2nd ed. (New Brunswick, N.J.: Rutgers University Press, 1988 [1955]), chapters 3–4; Dale T. Knobel, *"America for the Americans": The Nativist Movement in the United States* (New York: Twayne, 1996), chapter 6; and Limerick, *Legacy of Conquest*, 247.

3. Quoted by Janet E. Rasmussen, *New Land, New Lives: Scandinavian Immigrants to the Pacific Northwest* (Seattle: University of Washington Press and the Norwegian American Historical Association, 1993), 176. Kuwala migrated to the American West in 1910.

4. Joseph Stipanovich, "Falcons in Flight: The Yugoslavs," in *The Peoples of Utah*, ed. Helen Zeese Papanikolas (Salt Lake City: University of Utah Press, 1976), 379.

5. The heading of one chapter in a promotional work for the Northern Pacific Railroad (NPRR), read "Our Mild Winters—Rains Not so Bad as Stated—Preferable to Eastern Weather." Quoted by Arthur John Brown, "Means of Promoting Immigration to the Northwest and Washington, to 1910" (M.A. thesis, University of Washington, 1942), 39.

6. Oscar O. Winther, "English Migration to the American West, 1865–1900," in *In the Trek of the Immigrants*, ed. O. Fritiof Ander (Rock Island, Ill.: Augustana College Library, 1964), 120–21; William G. Robbins, Robert J. Frank, and Richard E. Ross, *Regionalism in the Pacific Northwest* (Corvallis: Oregon State University, 1983), 232; Richard D. Scheuerman, "Washington's European American Communities," in *Peoples of Washington: Perspectives on Cultural Diversity*, ed. Sid White and S. E. Solberg (Pullman: Washington State University Press, 1989), 49; Carlos Schwantes, *Radical Heritage: Labor, Socialism, and Reform in Washington and British Columbia, 1885–1917* (Moscow: University of Idaho Press, 1994 [1979]), 9; Paul G. Merriam, "The 'Other Portland': A Statistical Note on Foreign-Born, 1860–1910," *Oregon Historical Quarterly* 80 (February 1979): tables 1 and 2; Calvin F. Schmid, *Social Trends in Seattle*, University of Washington Publications in the Social Sciences, 14 (October) (Seattle: University of Washington Press, 1944), 4; William Issel and Robert W. Cherny, *San Francisco, 1865–1932: Politics, Power, and Urban Development* (Berkeley: University of California Press, 1986), 24; John Findlay, "A Fishy Proposition: Regional Identity in the Pacific Northwest," in *Many Wests: Place, Culture, and Regional Identity*, ed. David Wrobel and Michael Steiner (Lawrence: University Press of Kansas, 1997), 48; and Arthur John Brown, "Means of Promoting Immigration," 30–31. The Seattle and Palouse quotations are from *Experiences in a Promised Land: Essays in*

Pacific Northwest History, ed. G. Thomas Edwards and Carlos A. Schwantes (Seattle: University of Washington Press, 1986), xiv, and 80–81.

7. San Francisco, whose population in 1870 exceeded that of Oregon, Washington, and Idaho *combined*, would continue to dominate the economy of the Pacific Northwest until the beginning of the twentieth century and the Yukon gold rush—a key event used to great commercial advantage by Seattle.

8. Arthur John Brown, "Means of Promoting Immigration," 49–50, 52, 61, 65; Nugent, *Into the West*, 92. Earlier, in 1842, the Texas legislature had authorized land grants for "empresarios" who would bring people to Texas. A year later, Henri Castro, a French Jew, organized such a settlement of 300 persons from the Rhine region. Castroville had 2,143 people by 1847. The German Emigration Company and Society for the Protection of German Immigrants sent their agent, Prince Carl of Solms-Braunfels, to acquire lands north of San Antonio. Early in 1845 he founded New Braunfels and, the following year, Fredericksburg. Texas soon repealed the law. Rupert N. Richardson, Adrian Anderson, Cary D. Wintz, et al., *Texas, the Lonestar State*, 8th ed. (Upper Saddle River, N.J.: Prentice Hall, 2001), 149–51.

9. Principally, they were the Great Northern, Northern Pacific, Union and Central Pacific, Southern Pacific, and the Atchison, Topeka, and Santa Fe Railroads. The most notable connections completed at this time were to Portland, Tacoma, Los Angeles, and Seattle; that to San Francisco had been completed by 1870.

10. Baker, quoted by Carlos Arnaldo Schwantes, *The Pacific Northwest: An Interpretive History*, rev. ed. (Lincoln: University of Nebraska Press, 1996), 291, and George Sánchez, *Becoming Mexican American: Ethnicity, Culture and Identity in Chicano Los Angeles, 1900–1915* (New York: Oxford University Press, 1993), map 1, p. 21. The railroad data are from Montgomery, *Fall of the House of Labor*, 63, and Richard White, "*It's Your Misfortune*," 252. Part of the railroad empires were the steamship companies operating out of Galveston, San Francisco, Portland, Seattle, and soon Los Angeles, plus the railroad links with Mexico and Canada.

11. See Arthur John Brown, "Means of Promoting Immigration," 85–86; Abbott, *Metropolitan Frontier*, xviii; Schwantes, *Radical Heritage*, 16; and O'Connor, "Region of Cities," 535.

12. No urban population was reported for Alaska or Idaho even in the revised tables, and we must presume that neither had any appreciable urban centers (by Census standards) in 1890. See also Theodore Saloutos, "The Immigrant in Pacific Coast Agriculture, 1880–1940," *Agricultural History* 49.1 (January 1975), 182–201.

13. Schwantes, *Pacific Northwest*, 329–30; Montgomery, *Fall of the House of Labor*, 51–52; Richard Maxwell Brown, "Violence," in the *Oxford History of the American West*, ed. Milner, O'Connor, and Sandweiss, 396; Michael J. Piore, *Birds of Passage: Migrant Labor and Industrial Societies* (Cambridge: Cambridge University Press, 1979), 31–32.

14. This and the next two paragraphs make use of the following: Montgomery, *Fall of the House of Labor*, 52, 73; Piore, *Birds of Passage*, 17, 52, 59–60; Portes and Bach, *Latin Journey*, 30–34; Dino Cinel, *From Italy to San Francisco: The Immigrant Experience* (Stanford, Calif.: Stanford University Press, 1982), 103; and Nora O. Solum, "Oregon and Washington Territory in the 1870's, as Seen through the Eyes of a Pioneer Pastor," in *Norwegian-American Studies and Records*, vol. 16 (Northfield, Minn.: Norwegian-American Historical Association, 1950), 67–72.

15. Given the scarcity of Jewish women in the West, a strategy used by Jewish men was to go back East to find—or be put in touch with—a woman willing to accept the challenges of raising a family in the West.

16. Robert E. Levinson, "Julius Basinski: Jewish Merchant in Montana and the Pacific Northwest," reprinted in *The Northwest Mosaic*, ed. James A. Halseth and Bruce Glasrud (Boulder, Colo.: Pruett, 1977), 179–90; Rochlin and Rochlin, *Pioneer Jews*, 61.

17. Rochlin and Rochlin, *Pioneer Jews*, 45, 52–55, 57–58, 61, 64–66, 112. They do emphasize that there "were the thousands of less visible Jewish merchants and artisans who arrived in the Far West lacking one or more of these keys to success"—most often capital (61). The Pomeroy quotation is from Earl Pomeroy, "On Becoming a Westerner: Immigrants and Other Migrants," in *Jews of the American West*, ed. Moses Rischin and John Livingston (Detroit: Wayne State University Press, 1991), 192.

18. David M. Emmons, *The Butte Irish: Class and Ethnicity in an American Mining Town, 1875–1925* (Urbana: University of Illinois Press, 1989), 6–7, 20 (quotation), 23, 36 (quotation), 63, 147, 157, 187, 25–29 (quotations), 69, 224 (quotation).

19. Emmons, *Butte Irish*, 188–89, 78 (quotation), 70–71.

20. Strain's story is based upon an oral history of Leonora Pierotti, his granddaughter, May 6, 1974, California State University, Fullerton, Oral Document Program, no. OD 73, and photos in the Thomas Strain folder, no. 17, nos. 311 and 315.

21. The premise that step migration leads to easier subsequent acculturation is explored in my model in Barkan, *Asian and Pacific Islander Migration to the United State: A Model of New Global Patterns* (Westport, Conn.: Greenwood Press, 1992), 95–152.

22. See, for example, Margaret K. Holden, "Gender and Protest Ideology: Sue Ross Keenan and the Oregon Anti-Chinese Movement," *Western Legal History* 7 (Summer/Fall 1994): 223–43, reprinted in *Major Problems in the History of the American West*, 2nd ed., ed. Clyde Milner II, Anne M. Butler, and David Richard Lewis (New York: Houghton Mifflin, 1997), 295–301.

23. Hawai'i's multi-racial environment would fully emerge in the twentieth century, although tolerance of intermarriage had already been demonstrated by the royal family and was starting to become evident among some Chinese. (The census for 1900 listed 7,857 part-Hawaiians, but with no breakdown until 1910, when there were 3,734 Asian Hawaiians among the 12,506 part Hawaiians).

24. Many western communities would be shaped by myriad events involving immigrants as well as by those involving native-born minority populations. In Texas, for example, the most populated state in the West in 1880, its 7.2 percent foreign born was small percentage-wise but represented the second highest number in any western state (114,616), behind just California (292,874). Along with southern whites and blacks moving into east Texas, clusters of European settlers—among them French, German, Polish, and Czech farmers—had been settling in central and southern Texas since the 1850s, and Mexicans would move back and forth across the ill-defined border. The outcome of this multi-racial convergence would have lasting consequences.

In neighboring New Mexico, which had the fifth largest population total in 1880 (nearly 120,000), the population was overwhelmingly Latino, comprised predominantly of the descendants of those Spanish and Mexicans who had arrived nearly three centuries earlier and established Santa Fe and surrounding villages. For that very reason, as we shall see, they were regarded as a conquered people, and many of them directly confronted the exploitation, displacement, and massive land frauds that undermined their multi-century communities.

3. Where in the West Were They?

1. About 19,250 Swiss and 18,740 "Austrians" were also reported, and their settlement patterns were similar to those of the Germans. However, we have no breakdown for either group (German Swiss or French Swiss? Austrian or a minority within the Austro-Hungarian Empire? Until after World War One many of the latter were apparently labeled simply as Austrian.) We infer that many of the Swiss and Austrians were German,

based on destination preferences in California and Texas, as well as Washington. More "Austrians" were in Colorado, and most likely included South Slavs, such as Croatian and Slovenian miners. Washington, Colorado, and Oregon each had 12,000–15,000 Germans.

2. In 1890, there were 6,648 Irish in Montana and nearly 4,900 in Oregon. Along with the 20,900 English in Utah were 6,400 Welsh and Scots. There were slightly more than 9,000 Canadians in Montana and 6,460 in Oregon.

3. The 1890 U.S. Census figures for Chinese foreign born conflict with the figures by race, making it difficult to determine how many second-generation children were present, or which numbers are the accurate ones.

4. There are no data for Alaska until 1900, at which time there were 3,116 Chinese, mostly working in the canneries.

5. The Atchison, Topeka and Santa Fe Railroad to Los Angeles initially drew many native-born Americans from the Midwest.

6. Eleanor C. Nordyke, *The Peopling of Hawai'i*, 2nd ed. (Honolulu: University of Hawai'i Press, 1989), table 3-1, pp. 178–79; and Wilson D. Wallis, *Fresno Armenians (to 1919)*, ed. Nectar Davidian (Lawrence, Kans.: Coronado Press, 1965), 32–36. The 1890 census is inconsistent regarding the Japanese (as it similarly is with the Chinese), reporting 2,039 by race (table 12, p. 474) but 2,292 foreign born (table 32, p. 608).

7. Moses Rischin, "The Jewish Experience in America," in *Jews of the American West*, ed. Rischin and Livingston, *Jews of the American West*, 33, 35; Rochlin and Rochlin, *Pioneer Jews*, 44, 61, 84–85, 110–11, 243; Norton B. Stern, "The Founding of the Jewish Community in Utah," *Western States Jewish Historical Quarterly* 8.1 (October 1975): 65–69; and Lee Micklin, "Seattle Sephardim: Early Beginnings," HistoryLink Data Output (Seattle Public Library), http://www.historylink.org/output.cfm?file_id=864. See also note 26 in chapter 4, below.

4. Targets of Racism

1. Randall E. Rohe provides an excellent map of the West showing the movements of the Chinese to various mining locations. See "Chinese Mining in the Far West, 1850–1890," *Montana Magazine of History* 32 (Autumn 1982): 2–19, reprinted in Milner's *Major Problems*, 1st ed., 331.

2. Limerick, *Legacy of Conquest*, 265; Don Conley, "The Pioneer Chinese of Utah," in *The Peoples of Utah*, 259–60; Fern Coble Trull, "The History of the Chinese in Idaho, from 1864 to 1910" (M.A. thesis, University of Oregon, June 1946), 23–27, 59–60.

3. Conley, "Pioneer Chinese of Utah," 254; Larry D. Quinn, "Chink, Chink China-man: The Beginning of Nativism in Montana," *Pacific Northwest Quarterly* April 1967: 87.

4. Rochlin and Rochlin, *Pioneer Jews*, 145; Shi Shan Henry Tsai, *The Chinese Experience in America* (Bloomington: Indiana University Press, 1986), 67–71; Chan, *Asian Americans*, 45; Andrew Gyory, *Closing the Gate: Race, Politics, and the Chinese Exclusion Act* (Chapel Hill: University of North Carolina Press, 1998), 287n4.

5. Stanford Lyman, "Strangers in the City: The Chinese in the Urban Frontier," in *Roots: An Asian American Reader*, ed. Amy Tachiki, Eddie Wong, and Franklin Odo (Los Angeles: UCLA Asian American Studies Center, 1971), 166.

6. Kevin Starr, *Endangered Dreams: The Great Depression in California* (New York: Oxford University Press, 1996), 11; Takaki, *Strangers from a Different Shore*, 240; Joan B. Trauner, "The Chinese as Medical Scapegoats in San Francisco, 1870–1905," *California History* 57.1 (Spring 1978): 73; Benson Tong, *The Chinese Americans* (Westport, Conn.:

Greenwood Press, 2000), 35–40; Chan, *Asian Americans*, 94–95; Tsai, *Chinese Experience in America*, 38–39; and Gyory, *Closing the Gate*, 79, 84. Regarding efforts against the Chinese elsewhere in California, see Gyory, *Closing the Gate*, 266n8, and on the queue ordinance, 283–84n8.

7. This and the next paragraph are based on Chan, *This Bittersweet Soil*, 1, 4–7, 56, 59–62, 68–71, 107, 114–15, 193–96, 224; and McWilliams, *Southern California*, 88. See also Stanford M. Lyman, "Social Demography of the Chinese and Japanese in the U.S. of America," in *The Asian in the West*, by Lyman, Social Science and Humanities Publication no. 4 (Reno and Las Vegas: Desert Research Institute, University of Nevada, 1971), 65–80, which provides a great deal of statistical data for the period up to 1930. The Chan quotation is on 78. In *This Bittersweet Soil* (70–71), Chan lists the various products being manufactured by the Chinese in San Francisco, among them candles, gum, soap, sugar, jute, and flour. She also details the many different craftsmen there, including printers, masons, bakers, carpenters, as well as some of the types of professionals, such as linguists, teachers, photographers, and lawyers.

8. In 1870, three-fifths of the 3,536 Chinese women in California listed their occupations as prostitutes; the figure was 71 percent in San Francisco. The March 1875 Page Law was explicitly targeting the Chinese, among whom the sex ratio was nearly 19–1 in 1860 and peaked at almost 27–1 in 1890. The combination of the Page Law and Exclusion Laws reduced the number of women who were allowed to enter, while, as we saw with Leong Shee, the wives of merchants increased. By 1900 the gender ratio was "only" 19–1 and would steadily narrow as more wives were brought in and the number of second-generation daughters rose.

See Takaki, *Strangers from a Different Shore*, 41; Yung, *Unbound Voices*, 20n.; "A Chinese American Woman Details Life as a Prostitute in America, 1898," in *Major Problems in American Immigration and Ethnic History*, ed. Jon Gjerde (New York: Houghton Mifflin, 1998), 250–52; Judy Yung, *Unbound Feet: A Social History of Chinese Women in San Francisco* (Berkeley: University of California Press, 1995), 33–37; Louise A. Littleton, "Worse Than Slaves," in *Unbound Voices*, 164–70, as well as 201–10 for Wong Ah So's story after 1900; Sucheng Chan, "The Exclusion of Chinese Women, 1870–1943," in *Entry Denied: Exclusion and the Chinese Community in America, 1882–1943*, ed. Sucheng Chan (Philadelphia: Temple University Press, 1991), 105–109; Lucie Cheng, "Free, Indentured, Enslaved: Chinese Prostitutes in Nineteenth Century America," in *Labor Immigration under Capitalism: Asian Immigrant Workers in the United States before World War II*, ed. Lucie Cheng Hirata and Edna Bonacich (Berkeley: University of California Press, 1984), 402–34.

9. In the 1882 law, Congress intended to resolve explicitly the issues raised in the *In re Ah Yup* case (U.S. District Court, April 1878), which were in part a consequence of confusion arising from the initial accidental omission of the phrase "free white person" when the naturalization laws were codified and reprinted in 1875. See Charles J. McClain, *In Search of Equality: The Chinese Struggle against Discrimination in Nineteenth-Century America* (Berkeley: University of California Press, 1994), 70–73; and Matthew Frye Jacobson, *Barbarian Virtues: The United States Encounters Foreign Peoples at Home and Abroad, 1876–1917* (New York: Hill and Wang, 2000), 194–95.

10. Gyory, *Closing the Gate*, 169–76; Lyman, "Social Demography," 165; Roy Wortman, "Denver's Anti-Chinese Riot in 1880," *Colorado Magazine* 42 (1965): 275–91; and McClain, *In Search of Equality*, chapter 7; and "Chinese Accounts of the Killings at Rock Springs, 1885," in *Major Problems in the History of the American West*, 1st ed., ed. Clyde A. Milner II (Lexington, Mass.: D.C. Heath, 1989), 316–19.

11. It was alleged that Weisbach was a liquor dealer with a limited knowledge of

English and a family still in Germany to whom he regularly sent remittances. If true, the standards that applied to the Chinese did not apply to all. See the pamphlet by S. L. Baldwin, "Must the Chinese Go?" (New York: H. B. Elkins, 1890), Huntington Library, manuscript item 17525.

12. Schwantes, *Radical Heritage*, 24; Schwantes, in *Experiences in a Promised Land*, 182–89; Halseth and Glasrud, eds., *Northwest Mosaic*, 73–86, 132; Dodds, *American Northwest*, 118–20; Oscar Osburn Winther, *The Great Northwest: A History*, 2nd ed. (New York: Knopf, 1960), 423.

13. Quinn, "Chink, Chink Chinaman," 83, 84, 86, 87; Conley, "Pioneer Chinese of Utah," 265; tourism quotation from Chris Friday, "There are Chinese and Chinese: Regional Variations in Imaging the 'Other': An Illustrated Essay and Review," *Pacific Northwest Quarterly* 89.2 (Spring 1998): 98; Colquhon quotation from Thomas E. Sheridan, *Arizona: A History* (Tucson: University of Arizona, 1995), 169.

14. Erika Lee, "Enforcing the Borders: Chinese Exclusion along the U.S. Borders with Canada and Mexico, 1882–1924," *Journal of American History* 89.1 (June 2002): 54–86. The U.S. government pressured both nations to recognize the U.S. exclusion and to control their own admissions and their borders accordingly. By 1923 Canada had indeed revised its laws to match those of the United States. Mexico was less willing to cooperate; Lee, "Enforcing the Borders," 74–78.

15. Chris Friday, *Organizing Asian American Labor: The Pacific Coast Canned Salmon Industry, 1870–1942* (Philadelphia: Temple University Press, 1994), 2, 23–24, 26–27, 31, 56–59, 68; Friday, "Chinese, Chinese," 101; Robert Schwendinger, "Chinese Sailors: America's Invisible Merchant Marine," *California History* 57.1 (Spring 1978): 58–67.

16. A comparison of tables from the 1890 census, though flawed at the state level, suggests there might have been by this time almost 800 second-generation children of Chinese ancestry, nearly all of them in the West. See Department of Interior Census Office, *Compendium of the Eleventh Census: 1890*, Part 1: *Population* (Washington, D.C., 1892), table 12 (p. 474) and table 32 (p. 609). The 1890 census figures for Chinese foreign born also conflict with those by race, making it difficult to determine how many second-generation children were present, or which numbers are the accurate ones.

17. The various Exclusion Laws were those of May 6, 1882, July 5, 1884, the Scott Act of September 13, 1888, as amended October 1, 1888, the Geary Act of May 5, 1892, the McCreary Amendment of November 3, 1893, and the Acts of April 29, 1902, and April 27, 1904.

18. Funding had also been provided to establish a federal inspection station on Ellis Island in New York City harbor to replace Castle Garden. It opened in January 1892.

19. Yung, *Unbound Feet*, 23; and Chan, "Exclusion of Chinese Women," 110–12. Charles J. McClain discusses the case but says nothing about the wives; see *In Search of Equality*, 160–61. Hyung-chan Kim errs in saying that the law "also denied entry to the wives of laborers already in the United States." See Kim, *A Legal History of Asian Americans, 1790–1990* (Westport, Conn.: Greenwood Press, 1994), 61. McClain's chapters 6 and 8 discuss these various laws and the surrounding cases. Kim does, too, on pp. 60–62 and 70–86.

20. Tsai, *Chinese Experience in America*, 73. The actual texts of the laws and several related cases and other relevant documents may be found in *U.S. Immigration and Naturalization Laws and Issues: A Documentary History*, ed. Michael LeMay and Elliott Robert Barkan (Westport, Conn.: Greenwood Press, 1999), 33–40, 49–54, 60–75.

21. LeMay and Barkan, eds., *U.S. Immigration*, 82–85; Kim, *Legal History of Asian Americans*, 94–95; and McClain, *In Search of Equality*, 163–65. Kim referred to the 50 "major" cases brought before the U.S. Supreme Court to challenge the new laws between 1882 and 1921 (p. 70). Jacobson writes of over 7,000 cases within the first decade but is not

more specific; see *Barbarian Virtues*, 195. Basically, the Fourteenth Amendment declared that "all persons born or naturalized" in the United States are American citizens.

22. LeMay and Barkan, eds., *U.S. Immigration*, 86–88.

23. During the 1890s, Hawaiian sources only listed persons by race and, therefore, we cannot determine how big a proportion of that Chinese increase was due to births.

24. As a result, production shot up from less than 9,400 tons in 1870 to over 298,540 tons in 1900, and nearly 560,000 in 1920. To achieve that, the number of plantations jumped from 20 to 52 by 1910, hence the enormous pressures to attract immigrant labor and to encourage them to remain after their contracts expired. By the 1890s, plantations were already beginning to introduce voluntary contracts, which became mandatory after 1900. Non-contract workers were paid more. Illustrating the dual wages, Portuguese were paid one-fourth more than the Chinese. See Takaki, *Pau Hana*, 19–20; John M. Liu, "Race, Ethnicity and the Sugar Plantations: Asian Labor in Hawaii, 1850–1900, in *Labor Immigration under Capitalism*, 186, 193, 195–98, 202; and Katherine Coman, *The History of Contract Labor in the Hawaiian Islands* [1903] (New York: Arno Press, 1970), 23, 28, 31, 35–36, 40.

25. Nordyke, *Peopling of Hawai'i*, table 3.1 (178–79); Kimura, *Issei*, 6–9; Takaki, *Pau Hana*, 23–39; Ogawa, *Kodomo no tame ni*, 13–17. Despite the conditions, between 1885 and 1897, Ogawa reported, 37,451 Japanese came on three-year contracts, and less than one-third returned home (36).

26. After 1900, additional peoples would be sought from Korea, Puerto Rico, the Philippines, and several South Pacific islands. Moreover, as part of their calculated effort to maintain a segmented labor force, the planters made sure white men were supervisors, managers, and overseers and that a multiple wage scale was in place, with different groups paid significantly different monthly wages.

27. Lawrence Fuchs, *Hawaii Pono: A Social History* (New York: Harcourt, 1961), 19–25, 37–38, 52, 86; Takaki, *Pau Hana*, 23–39; Victoria Wyatt, "Alaska and Hawai'i," in *Oxford History*, 583–85; Wayne Paterson, *The Korean Frontier in America: Immigration to Hawai'i, 1896–1910* (Honolulu: University of Hawai'i Press, 1988), 4–13. In 1890 the Chinese constituted 18.6 percent of the population, Portuguese and Japanese each 14 percent, and other Caucasians 6.9 percent. Such diversity would continue and would profoundly reshape Hawaiian society and culture. Takaki, *Pau Hana*, 28.

28. See, for example, Speech of George F. Hoar (R-MA), March 1, 1882, before the U.S. Senate, reprinted in *Racism, Dissent, and Asian Americans from 1850 to the Present*, ed. Philip S. Foner and Dan Rosenberg (Westport, Conn.: Greenwood Press, 1993), 54–55; and *U.S. Immigration*, 77–79.

5. *The Scandinavians and Step Migration*

1. Toskey, quoted by Marvin G. Slind and Frederick C. Bohm, *North to Palouse: Sagas of the Selbu Norwegians* (Pullman, Wash.: Norlys Press, 1990), 10; Thomas O. Stine, *Scandinavians on the Pacific* [1900] (San Francisco: R & E Research Associates, 1968), 30–33; Leola Nelson Bergmann, *Americans from Norway* (Westport, Conn.: Greenwood Press, 1950), 111.

2. Lottie Roth, *History of Whatcom County*, 2 vols. (Chicago: Pioneer Historical, 1926), 2: 134–35.

3. Step migration was common among Scandinavians who had already migrated to America and in many parts of Europe, including in Sweden. There, reports Harald Runblom, "substantial numbers of Swedes spent five or more years in Stockholm before leaving for North America." That may not have hastened their adjustment in America,

but it did familiarize them with the uprooting effects of migration. *From Sweden to America: A History of the Migration,* ed. Harald Runblom and Hans Norman (Minneapolis: University of Minnesota Press, 1976), 138.

4. Stine, *Scandinavians on the Pacific,* 154, 43–44; Salvon, quoted by Rasmussen, *New Land, New Lives,* 300.

5. Jorgen Dahlie, "Old World Paths in the New Scandinavia: Finding a Familiar Home in Washington," in *Experiences in a Promised Land,* 100, 106, and Dahlie, "A Social History of Scandinavian Immigrants, Washington State, 1895–1910" (Ph.D. dissertation, Washington State University, 1967; New York: Arno Press, 1980), vi. Orm Øverland has provided an interesting exploration of Norwegian efforts to confirm their legitimacy in the minds of Americans, which echoes some of Dahlie's points. *Immigrant Minds, American Identities: Making the United States Home, 1870–1930* (Urbana: University of Illinois Press, 2000).

6. Teacher, quoted by Slind and Bohm, *North to Palouse,* 10. Swedish quotation in Dahlie, "Old World Paths," 106. On the other hand, Danish converts to Mormonism, and other converts no doubt, were particularly eager to learn English, the language of their new church and *The Book of Mormon.*

7. Mormon missionaries capitalized on the religious dissent and social unrest in Denmark. Danes proved to be the most receptive of Nordics to Mormonism and began migrating to Utah in the early 1850s. By 1900 there were 24,751 persons of Danish foreign stock in Utah, compared with 14,578 Swedes and 4,554 Norwegians (totaling 43,883). Scandinavians equaled one-third of the foreign born and almost one-sixth of the whole state population in 1900. See William Mulder, "Scandinavian Saga," in *The Peoples of Utah,* 141, 145–46, 154.

8. Dodds, *American Northwest,* 120; George R. Nielsen, *The Danish Americans* (Boston: Twayne Books, 1981), opening page, no number; Patsy Adams Hegstad, "Citizenship, Voting, and Immigrants: A Comparative Study of the Naturalization Propensity and Voter Registration of Nordics in Seattle and Ballard, Washington, 1892–1900" (Ph.D. diss., University of Washington, 1992), 285, 292–94, 152.

9. Mulder, "Scandinavian Saga," 154, 146, 158, 179, 182, 184.

10. Gertrude Tingelstad, *Scandinavians in the Silverton Country: Their Arrival and Early Settlement* (Corvallis, Ore.: Silverton Appeal Tribune, 1978), 6–7, 10.

11. Finns are sometimes grouped with Scandinavians as Nordics because of the geographical proximity of their countries and the significant proportion of Swede Finns in the Finnish population. For convenience I am discussing them here.

12. Nielsen, *Danish Americans,* 60–64, 168; Leona Nelson Bergmann, *Americans from Norway,* 108.

13. Lucille McDonald, *Coast Country: A History of Southwest Washington* (Portland, Ore.: Binford and Mort, 1966), 106–109, 147; Norman C. Clark, *Washington: A Bicentennial History* (New York: Norton, 1976), 138.

14. Occasional efforts were made to create combined Scandinavian churches, such as Our Savior, in Oakland, California, in 1879, but this "pan-Scandinavian" effort faded when Norwegian nationalism was sparked by independence in 1905. The push, then, as in Utah, was to establish their own churches and social organizations, singing groups, etc. See John Jenswold, "The Rise and Fall of Pan-Scandinavianism in Urban America," in *Scandinavians and Other Immigrants in Urban America: Proceedings of a Research Conference, October 26–27, 1984,* ed. Odd S. Lovoll (Northfield, Minn.: St. Olaf College Press, 1985), 162. Rasmussen, *New Land, New Lives,* 300–301; Jerry Schofer, "Urban and Rural Finnish Communities in California, 1860–1960" (San Francisco: R & E Research Associates, 1975), 76, 17.

15. Hegstad, "Citizenship, Voting, and Immigrants," 156–59; Arlow W. Andersen, *Norwegian Americans* (Boston: Twayne Books, 1975), 145–47; Stine, *Scandinavians on the Pacific*, 86–87; Hans Bergmann, *History of Scandinavians in Tacoma and Pierce County* (Tacoma, Wash.: n.p., 1926), 55–79; Dahlie, "Social History," 156–69. See, too, Iverne Dowie and Ernest M. Espelie, eds., *The Swedish Immigrant Community in Transition: Essays in Honor of Dr. Conrad Bergendoff* (Rock Island, Ill.: Augustana Historical Society, 1963), 153, 170. Among these varied organizations there were also the Scandinavian Democratic and Republican Clubs. One of the founders of the Swedish Club in 1892 was John Nordstrom, who started the Nordstrom department store chain.

16. Stine, *Scandinavians on the Pacific*, 52–54. "Andrew Chilberg," King County Biographies, http://freepages.genealogy.rootsweb.com/~jtenlen/achilberg.txt (accessed September 1, 2002).

6. The German Presence

1. "Arthur Breyman," in *The History of Oregon*, by Charles Henry Carey, 3 vols. (Chicago: Pioneer Historical, 1922), 2: 582–83.

2. The following discussion of Germans is based on the following sources as well as those in the next several endnotes: Carey's history of Oregon; Richard Scheuerman's "Washington's European American Communities," in White and Solberg's collection on the peoples of Washington; Ronald K. Dewsnup, "The Waves of Immigration," *Utah Historical Quarterly* 52.4 (Fall 1984): 384, 350, 352–56; Issel and Cherny, *San Francisco*, 16, 27, 56–58, 65, 105, 200; McWilliams, *Southern California*, 29–35; Merriam, "'Other' Portland," 266–68; Glenna Matthews, "Forging a Cosmopolitan Civic Culture: A Regional Identity of San Francisco and Northern California," in *Many Wests*, 214, 216–17; Oscar Osburn Winther, *The Great Northwest: A History*, 2nd ed. (New York: Knopf, 1960): 48; Stephen Erie, *Rainbow's End: Irish America and the Dilemma of Urban Machine Politics, 1840–1985* (Berkeley: University of California Press, 1988), 45–46, 64, 75; and Brian J. Godfrey, *Neighborhoods in Transition: The Making of San Francisco's Ethnic and Non-conformist Communities* (Berkeley: University of California Press, 1988), 72–73, 77, 80–82.

3. The actual quotation is by Christiane Harzig, discussing Conzen's views in her H-Ethnic, online book review of *The German American Encounter: Conflict and Cooperation between Two Cultures, 1800–2000* (New York: Berghahn Books, 2001). H-Ethnic @H-Net.MSU.edu, September 3, 2002.

Harzig sums up Conzen's contention that Germans held to a "colonizing vision"—to populate America and contribute to it by imbuing it with some "culture." That culture would consist of 1) "self-contained fragments of the homeland" in rural communities; 2) urban neighborhood communities with institutions and organizations ("thus inventing the institutionalized ethnic community"); and 3) resistance to seeing America unified around one "common set of religious beliefs and cultural values," rather than a more diverse one with Germanness as a part of the whole.

4. Terry G. Jordan, "Germany," *The Handbook of Texas Online*, www.tsha.utexas .edu/handbook/online/articles/view/GG/png2.html (accessed April 19, 2005); and Gilbert Giddings Benjamin, *The Germans in Texas: A Study in Immigration* (Austin, Texas: Jenkins, 1974), 1–64, 115–18, 122–32. The quotations are from pp. 24 and 55. The population figures are cited on p. 65. See census figures on p. 66 of the text.

5. Census Report for 1910, vol. 1, *Population*, part 2, state reports, Texas, table 5, p. 799. In 1910 German foreign stock made up 28.5 percent of all such persons in Texas,

dominating the European populations. Mexicans, however, constituted 38.7 percent. Jordan suggests that San Antonio was only one-third German by 1880.

6. Allan Kent Powell, "The German-Speaking Immigrant Experience in Utah," *Utah Historical Quarterly*, 52.4 (Fall 1984): 311–21.

7. Kenneth W. Rock, "'Unsere Leute': The Germans from Russia in Colorado," *Colorado Magazine* 54.2 (Spring 1977): 155–65.

8. Matthews, "Forging a Cosmopolitan Civic Culture," 217.

9. Germans constituted 14.2 percent of the foreign born in all California in 1870 and were, like the Irish—who made up 25.9 percent—concentrated in San Francisco. However, by 1900, the German percentage of the white foreign stock in the state had steadily risen to 19.7 percent, whereas the Irish figure plummeted during the depression decade of the 1890s to merely 12.1 percent. The occupational differences between the two in San Francisco—with the Irish far more concentrated in semi-skilled and construction-related jobs versus the Germans, who were more commonly merchants, shopkeepers, and artisans, may well have enabled the Germans to weather the downturn and thereby remain in the city. See Issel and Cherny, *San Francisco*, 56–58.

10. Issel and Cherny, *San Francisco*, 56–58, Rochlin and Rochlin, *Pioneer Jews*, 34–35, 54–56, 80–81, 133, 177–78; and Martin A. Meyer, *Western Jewry: An Account of the Achievements of the Jews and Judaism in California* (San Francisco: Emanu El and California Press, 1916), 91–94.

11. James Rawls and Walton Bean, *California: An Interpretive History*, 6th ed. (New York: McGraw-Hill, 1993), 171, 194, and David Igler, *Industrial Cowboys: Miller & Lux and the Transformation of the Far West, 1850–1920* (Berkeley: University of California Press, 2001).

12. Meyer, *Western Jewry*, 25–70; Rochlin and Rochlin, *Pioneer Jews*, 151–65, 195–221. Scott Cline calculated that three-fourths of the Jews in Portland in 1880 were German or Austrian. He also noted that the modal age among all the males in 1880 was 21–25 (50 out of 413). Cline, "The Jews of Portland, Oregon: A Statistical Dimension, 1860–1880," *Oregon Historical Quarterly* 88.1 (Spring 1987): 6–9, 22; William Toll, *The Making of an Ethnic Middle Class: Portland Jewry over Four Generations* (Albany: State University of New York Press, 1982), 16, 41 (Toll's figure for Jews in Portland in 1880 was only 490 versus Cline's 768.)

7. Proximity of Homeland

1. Manuel Gonzales offers a total of about 94,000 Mexicans, but the time period varies from 11,000 in Texas and 60,000 in New Mexico in the late 1840s to 8,000 in Tucson in the late 1870s and 15,000 in California in the late nineteenth century. Thus, any count can only be approximate. *Mexicanos: A History of Mexicans in the United States* (Bloomington: Indiana University Press, 1999), 91, 93, 98, 106.

2. Linda Gordon, *The Great Arizona Orphan Abduction* (Cambridge: Harvard University Press, 1999), 22.

3. Manuel Gonzales, *Mexicanos*, 96–97.

4. Carey McWilliams, *North from Mexico*, 104–109, 184–86, and Rodolfo Acuña, *Occupied America: A History of Chicanos*, 4th ed. (New York: Longman, 2000), 70–79, 365.

5. See Erika Lee's discussion of the border/boundary issue in "Enforcing the Borders," 54–86; Limerick, *Legacy of Conquest*, 222, and newspaper article quoted, 253; and Meinig, quoted by William Robbins, in "Laying Siege to Western History," in *Trails*, ed. Limerick, Milner, and Rankin, 194.

I originally discussed the concept of proximity of homeland and the impact of nearby homelands on migrants and ethnic groups—using as examples Mexicans and French Canadians (and, secondarily, Native Americans and Puerto Ricans)—in "Proximity and Commuting Immigration: An Hypothesis Explored via the Bi-polar Ethnic Communities of French Canadian and Mexican Americans," 163–83, in *American Ethnic Revival*, ed. Jack Kinton (Aurora, Ill.: Social Science and Sociological Resources, 1977).

Lee does describe how the United States pressured Canada to curb more effectively Chinese immigration and the latter's use of Canada as a conduit to the United States, but overall "border control" has far more often referred to actions along the U.S.-Mexican line.

6. See note 14 of chapter 4, above. I am leaving aside the more complicated and detailed aspects of border crossings by groups moving southward, fleeing U.S. military or Texas Rangers, such as Juan Cortina, and some of the social bandits discussed in the literature of the Southwest, as well as those moving northward, fleeing Porfirio Diaz's regime, notably Ricardo Flores Magón, or, later, crossing during Mexico's civil war, particularly Pancho Villa. Regarding the monitoring of the border (principally to apprehend illegal Chinese) prior to the creation of the Border Patrol in 1924, see Erika Lee, *At America's Gates: Chinese Immigration during the Exclusion Era, 1882–1943* (Chapel Hill: University of North Carolina Press, 2003), 184–87.

7. My total comes from table 33, p. 734, U.S. Census Office, *Twelfth Census of the United States Taken in the Year 1900*, Census Reports, vol. 2: *Population*, part 1 (Washington, 1902). George Sánchez, *Becoming Mexican American*, 19, uses a U.S. total of 103,393. The immigration figure can be found in table 4.1, p. 41, in Richard Griswold del Castillo and Arnold De León, *North to Aztlán: A History of Mexican Americans in the United States* (New York: Twayne, 1997).

8. For an intense discussion of the expansion of capitalism in pre-1910 Mexico and its consequences, see chapter 2, "Empire and the Origins of Twentieth-Century Migration from Mexico to the United States," in *A Century of Chicano History*, by Gilbert G. Gonzalez and Raul A. Fernandez (New York: Routledge, 2003), as well as chapter 1 of George J. Sánchez's *Becoming Mexican American*.

9. Arnoldo De León, "Region and Identity: Topographical Identities in Texas," in *Many Wests*, 263–66, and his excellent analysis in *They Called Them Greasers: Anglo Attitudes toward Mexicans in Texas, 1821–1900* (Austin: University of Texas Press, 1983); Foley, *White Scourge*, 41, 44; Gordon, *Great Arizona Orphan Abduction*, 103–104; Albert Camarillo, *Chicanos in a Changing Society: From Mexican Pueblos to American Barrios in Santa Barbara and Southern California, 1848–1930* (Cambridge, Mass.: Harvard University Press, 1996 [1979]), 16.

10. Camarillo, *Chicanos in a Changing Society*, 43–45, 49–50, 87–91; Foley, *White Scourge*, 37; Richard White, "*It's Your Misfortune*," 324; Acuña, *Occupied America*, 45, 106, 156; McWilliams, *North from Mexico*, 161; Richard Griswold del Castillo, *The Los Angeles Barrio, 1850–1890: A Social History* (Berkeley: University of California Press, 1979), 150–59 and 60. Acuña's chapters 3–6 cover in great detail the period from 1848 to 1900 for Texas, New Mexico, Arizona, and California, respectively.

11. Acuña, *Occupied America*, 92–94, 100–101; Sarah Deutsch, "Landscape of Enclaves: Race Relations in the West, 1865–1890," in *Under an Open Sky*, 110–111. Deutsch develops this story of the New Mexican villagers much more fully in *No Separate Refuge: Culture, Class, and Gender on an Anglo Hispanic Frontier in the American Southwest, 1880–1940* (New York: Oxford University Press, 1987). See also Frederick Nolan, *The Lincoln County War: A Documentary History* (Norman: University of Oklahoma Press, 1992).

12. In many areas, such as in Arizona, barrios began as *colonias* on the outskirts of towns that were eventually enveloped, or surrounded, by urban expansion, thus becoming barrios.

13. Acuña, *Occupied America*, 96–97, 122–23; Manuel Gonzales, *Mexicanos*, 105–106; and Roberto R. Calderón, "Unión, Paz, y Trabajo [Union, Peace, and Work]: Mutual Aid Societies, 1890s," in *Mexican Americans in Texas History*, ed. Emilio Zamora, Cynthia Orozco, and Rodolfo Rocha (Austin: Texas State Historical Association, 2000), 63–77.

14. Camarillo, *Chicanos in a Changing Society*, 53, 79, 101; Griswold, *Los Angeles Barrio*, chapter 5; Gordon, *Great Arizona Orphan Abduction*, 99; and quotation from Gamio, in Limerick, *Legacy of Conquest*, 245.

15. Foley, *White Scourge*, 107; Acuña, *Occupied America*, 76; *In re Rodriguez*, 81 F 337; 1897 U.S. Dist Court, W.D. Texas. A portion of the decision is in *U.S. Immigration*, 79. Most of the treaty can be found in LeMay and Barkan, eds., *U.S. Immigration*, 25–26. A complete version is in *Major Problems in Mexican American History*, ed. Zaragosa Vargas (New York: Houghton Mifflin, 1999), 136–40. See also Acuña, *Occupied America*, 54.

16. Manuel Gonzales, *Mexicanos*, 82.

8. In the Year 1903

1. The following three paragraphs are based on Acuña, *Occupied America*, 126, 128n, 138; Allan Kent Powell, "The 'Foreign Element' and the 1903–04 Carbon County Coal Miners' Strike," *Utah Historical Quarterly* 43 (1985): 125–54; David G. Gutiérrez, *Walls and Mirrors: Mexican Americans, Mexican Immigrants and the Politics of Ethnicity* (Berkeley: University of California Press, 1995), 100–101; McWilliams, *North from Mexico*, 136; and especially Gordon, *Great Arizona Orphan Abduction*, 220–45.

2. There was a fifth strike, the major confrontation at Cripple Creek, Colorado, beginning in March 1903 and dragging on until the violent summer of 1904. For that reason it is discussed at length in part 2.

3. Jacobson, *Barbarian Virtues*, 246–65; Thomas E. Sheridan, *Arizona*, 172.

9. Foreshadowing Twentieth-Century Patterns

1. Stat. 1213; 8 USC and 32 Stat. 1222. The text of these two laws is in LeMay and Barkan, eds., *U.S. Immigration*, 90–93. The naturalization law is incorporated as sec. 39 of the codified law of that year.

Introduction to Part 2

1. W. E. B. DuBois, *The Souls of Black Folk*, introduction by Henry Lewis Gates Jr. (New York: Bantam Books, 1989 [1903]), 10.

10. Immigrant Stories and the West in the 1900s

1. "Oral memoirs of Agyris B. Karahal," Texas Economic History Project, Baylor University, 1971.

2. "The Denmark District as Seen by Andy Sorenson," Oral History Collection. KITTITAS Project, KIT 75 –9sa, Washington State Archives, March 20, 1975.

3. "You Had to Kind of Turn the Penny." Interview with Nina Kanyer, Oral History collection. KITTITAS Project, KIT 76 –73sa, Washington State Archives, June 24, 1976,

4. "An Italian Immigrant Coal-Miner's Wife." Interview with Camilla Saivetto. Oral History Collection, KITTITAS Project. KIT 76–69sa, Washington State Archives, April 20, 1976.

5. Jessie Bloom interview, Jewish American History Project, University of Washington, Seattle, February 1970, February 1976, and March 1976, accession no. 2623.

6. Of course, it is possible that more Jewish-related matters were discussed prior to this interview, for Bloom refers to previous interviews.

7. Odd Lovoll, *The Promise of America: A History of the Norwegian American People*, rev. ed. (Minneapolis: University of Minnesota Press, 1999), 246 (p. 162 in the first edition [1984]); and Leola Nelson Bergmann, *Americans from Norway*, 123–24. The Web site of the town of Petersburg, Alaska, is www.petersburg.org (accessed June 22, 2003). Lovoll and Bergmann spell his name Buschmann; the Web site says Bushmann. There is a small discrepancy in dates as well.

8. "The Life History as a Social Document," by Chotoku Toyama, May 27, 1924, William C. Smith Collection, University of Oregon, Box 1, Folder 12.

9. See, for example, the data summarized by Mark Wyman, in *Round-Trip to America: The Immigrants Return to Europe, 1880–1930* (Ithaca, N.Y.: Cornell University Press, 1993), 10–12.

11. Who Came?

1. Joaquin Miller, "The Chinese and the Exclusion Act," *North American Review* 173 (December 1901): 785–89, reprinted in *Racism, Dissent, and Asian Americans*, ed. Foner and Rosenberg, 124.

2. Slightly more than one-fourth of all the Chinese immigrants resided in Hawai'i, compared with almost half of the Japanese.

3. Until the last decade of the twentieth century the first decade remained the peak in terms of immigrants admitted. The figures are based on an analysis of various tables in the 1910 and 1920 census reports. Data for 1900 were taken mostly from those two subsequent reports. While the tables mostly provide totals for the lower 48 states and territories (or totals for all U.S. territories), I have incorporated available data from Alaska and Hawai'i into my totals for the United States and the West because they are part of the definition of the West used in this study. *Thirteenth Census of the United States Taken in the Year 1910*, vol. 1, *Population, General Report*, tables 22, 24, 25, 36, and 39, and vols. 2 and 3, *Population, Reports by States*, table 1 for each state (Washington, 1913); *Fourteenth Census of the United States Taken in the Year 1920, vol. 2, Population 1920, General Reports*, tables 5, 6, 10, and 11, and vol. 3, *Population 1920, Composition and Characteristics of the Population by States*, table 12 for each state, and the subsections on Alaska and Hawaii, tables 1–6. Several tables in 1920 have revised data for 1910, which were used.

The West grew by 48 percent compared with 18 percent elsewhere in the years 1900 to 1909 and increased by another 26.4 percent versus 13.4 percent during the 1910s. For the foreign born it was 56.3 percent versus 27.4 percent in the years 1900 to 1909 and 16.8 percent versus 0.79 percent during the 1910s.

4. For census data on this period, see tables in appendix, particularly tables 3.1, 3.3, 3.4, and 3.6.

5. This is not meant to overlook the Native Americans, but they, like African Americans at this time, comprised small percentages of the population in most places, and their

impact on the region's culture, economy, and politics was as yet still rather limited (or was more indirect). The point here is that 1.09 million of all second-generation persons in 1920 had resettled in the West (41.4 percent of that population). Of that 1.09 million, over 207,000 had come from another western state (19 percent), and I suggest that they contributed to the weave linking western states together. Thus, over one-third of whites came from another state, of whom more than one-fifth were second generation and constituted 40 percent of all such second-generation persons in the West. Of the *whole* white population in the West, one-fifth were second-generation persons (combining both those born in their state of residence and out of state).

6. Idaho, 73.1 percent increase; Montana, 41.2 percent; Wyoming, 66.6 percent; and Colorado, 42.2 percent. Hawai'i's total foreign-born population grew by a mere 3.3 percent, but that of the Japanese rose by 6 percent, and that of the Portuguese by 16 percent, together with the arrival of two important new peoples — Koreans and Filipinos.

7. By percentage, Utah had the largest second-generation population in 1910, at 35.2 percent of all persons; Texas and New Mexico had the lowest at 9.3 percent and 8 percent, respectively. However, as mentioned, Utah's second generation was in decline during this period because its wave of immigration preceded most other states and then was slowed by the Mormon Church early in the new century.

8. Data available only for white foreign-born populations. In most places the Asian populations were too small for meaningful ratios. White foreign-born gender ratios were Alaska 9.8:1, Wyoming 2.9:1, and Nevada 3.3:1, as well as Montana 2.4:1 and Idaho 2.3:1, compared with Utah (1.3:1). In comparison to the Chinese, the figures for the Japanese were 2.2:1 (Hawai'i), 5.6:1 (California), and 10.6: 1 (Oregon).

12. *The Dillingham Commission and the West*

1. Oscar Handlin, introduction to the Arno Press edition, U.S. Senate, *Reports of the [Dillingham] Immigration Commission: Abstracts of the Reports of the Immigration Commission*, 61st Cong., 3rd sess. (New York: Arno Press, 1970 [1911]), 1: viii–ix.

2. Cheryl Shanks, *Immigration and the Politics of American Sovereignty, 1890–1990* (Ann Arbor: University of Michigan Press, 2001), 34. Desmond King provides a useful overview, although he understates the extent to which the volumes on the West amply discuss Asians. King, *Making Americans: Immigration, Race, and the Origins of the Diverse Democracy* (Cambridge, Mass.: Harvard University Press, 2000), 58–81. See also Alan M. Kraut, *The Huddled Masses: The Immigrant in American Society, 1880–1921*, 2nd ed. (Wheeling, Ill.: Harlan Davidson, 2001), 209, and Matthew Jacobson's comments, in *Whiteness*, 79–80.

3. Despite Desmond King's erroneous conclusion about "the Dillingham Commission's exclusive concern with new immigrants from southern and eastern Europe" (*Making Americans*, 80), part 25 of the Dillingham Report is titled *Japanese and Other Immigrant Races in the Pacific Coast and Rocky Mountain States*. It consists of three volumes: vol. 23, "Japanese and East Indians"; vol. 24, "Agriculture"; and vol. 25, "Diversified Industries." The full citation is U.S. Senate, *Reports of the [Dillingham] Immigration Commission. Abstracts of the Reports of the Immigration Commission*, 2 vols.; and *Part 25: Japanese and Other Immigrant Races on the Pacific Coast and Rocky Mountain States*, 3 vols., vol. 23: *Japanese and East Indians*, 61st Cong., 3rd sess. (New York: Arno Press, 1970 [1911]).

4. The quotations are from *[Dillingham] Immigration Commission*, 23: 63, 67–68. The remittance table is on 140, illustrating that Japanese saved — for farms or businesses — rather than send a lot of their earnings home.

5. Ibid, 23: 43, 40.

6. Ibid., 24: 151, 15, 19, 377.

7. Ibid., 24:3, 21.

8. Ibid., 24: 31, 50, 58, 110.

9. Ibid., vol. 1, "Abstracts of Reports of the Immigration Commission," including "Immigration Conditions in Hawaii," 709, 716. Thousands of Asians either went to the mainland prior to 1907 or returned home. For example, 111,137 Japanese arrivals were reported, but only 79,675 appear in the 1910 census. Wayne Patterson indicates that 27,000 Japanese went to the mainland between 1903 and 1907, during which time 1,087 Koreans did so. Patterson, *The Korean Frontier in America: Immigration to Hawaii, 1896–1910* (Honolulu: University of Hawai'i Press, 1988), 173.

10. *[Dillingham] Immigration Commission*, 24: 592, and 419, 471, 420, 548.

11. Ibid., 25: 80–81, and 232. Among northern Europeans, 60–70 percent were naturalized versus 4.5–8.5 percent among Italians and Mexicans.

12. Ibid., 25: 156, 217, 214 (quotation).

13. Ibid., 25: 356. In addition to the foreign born in the 3,430 sample, nearly one-fifth more were second-generation workers, and that figure continued to rise.

14. The commission reported that, of the members of the Fisherman's Protective Union, 22 percent of the total were Norwegian, 17 percent Swedish, 14 percent Finnish, and 3.4 percent Danish, but this may have been overstated because only 3,000 of the 6,775 members were Scandinavian in 1908. (See note 49 in chapter 15.)

13. The Continuing Evolution of Immigration and Naturalization Issues and Policies

1. Jacobson, *Barbarian Virtues*, 61.

2. Erika Lee, "The Chinese Exclusion Example: Race, Immigration, and American Gatekeeping, 1882–1924," *Journal of American Ethnic History* 21.3 (Spring 2002): 37, 40. See also Erika Lee, "The Keepers of the Gate," chapter 2 in *At America's Gates: Chinese Immigration During the Exclusion Era, 1882–1943* (Chapel Hill: University of North Carolina Press, 2003).

3. Joan B. Trauner, "The Chinese as Medical Scapegoats in San Francisco, 1870–1905," *California History* 57.1 (Spring 1978): 70–85.

4. *North American Review* (November 1901): 663–76, Huntington Library accession no. 209.

5. "Proceedings, California Chinese Exclusion Convention," San Francisco, November 21–22, 1901, Huntington Library accession no. 241795.

6. On this phenomenon of the paper sons at that time, see chapter 6 of Erika Lee, *At America's Gates*.

7. Erika Lee, "Enforcing the Borders," 55, 57, 58, 59, 70, 71. Much of this essay is in chapter 5 of Lee's book.

8. Janet Leung Larson, "The Chinese Empire Reform Association (Baohuanghui) and the 1905 Anti-American Boycott: The Power of Voluntary Association," pp. 195–216 in *The Chinese in America: A History from Gold Mountain to the New Millennium*, ed. Susie Lan (New York: Rowman and Littlefield, 2002).

9. Huntington Library accession no. 1644.

10. "In re Hom Chee Fong," July 21, 1913, National Archives RG 85, 53560/225, pp. 27–28. This particular exchange took place in Boston but was identical to those conducted at Angel Island.

11. Poem no. 35 in *Island: Poetry and History of Chinese Immigrants on Angel Island, 1910–1940*, ed. Him Mark Lai, Genny Lim, and Judy Yung (San Francisco: Hoc Doi, Chinese Culture Foundation, 1986), 84.

12. There is much confusion about the various figures. Ronald Takaki gave the number of women admitted in San Francisco as rising from 219 in 1910 to 1,893 in 1924 (p. 235), but Erika Lee's table 5 (*At America's Gates*, 118) indicates 172 to 983. Lee's table 1 on total admissions into San Francisco's Angel Island (p. 83) gives a total of 182,440 for 1913–1924, whereas unpublished INS data on ports of entry provided to this author indicate a total of only 109,990 for 1905–1924 (including 1911–1912, which Lee reported as unavailable). In addition, Takaki suggested that about 10,000 Chinese females were admitted between 1907 and 1924, whereas Lee's table 2 (p. 98) indicates 9,565 admitted from 1910 to 1924. However, that figure includes U.S. citizens, students, teachers, and returning laborers. All the other categories total just 7,300. Inconsistencies exist in the data on gender and classes admitted (Lee's tables 2–5), but the author notes that the discrepancies were due to the different ways early Bureau of Immigration officials kept records. The results were "consistently inconsistent." E-mail, Erika Lee to the author, July 1, 2003.

Finally, another table of historical abstracts lists only 51,650 Chinese admitted between 1905 and 1924. U.S. Department of Commerce, Bureau of the Census, *Historical Statistics of the United States, Colonial Times to 1970, Part 1* (Washington, D.C., 1975), International Migration and Naturalization, Series C 89–119, Immigrants by Country: 1820–1970, p. 107. See also Tsai, *Chinese Experience in America*, 101.

13. Fern Coble Trull, "The History of the Chinese in Idaho from 1864 to 1910" (Ph.D. diss., University of Oregon, June 1946), 58–128; Tsai, *Chinese Experience in America*, 135–36; and Takaki, *Pau Hana*, 416. See also Huping Ling, *Surviving in Gold Mountain: A History of Chinese American Women and Their Lives* (Albany: State University of New York Press, 1998). For the women in San Francisco, see Yung, *Unbound Feet*, chapters 1–2.

Erika Lee reports on the Confession Program that between 1959 and 1965, there were 30,530 Chinese who were implicated by others. The INS *Annual Reports* for 1959–1965 report results for 1957–1965, with the 1959 report providing a total for 1957–1959. The program involved persons who confessed and, by doing so, implicated others who had entered falsely. In addition, those confessing identified "slots" for future false admissions, which were then cut off. The total in the six reports of those confessing and those implicated equals 30,440 rather than 30,530. In addition, at least 8,181 "slots" were closed down as a result of the confessions, but no "slots" figure is given for 1957–1959. (*Annual Reports of the INS*, 1959 [p. 8], 1960 [p. 8], 1961 [p. 9], 1962 [p. 10], 1963 [p. 12], 1964 [p. 11], and 1965 [p. 12]), and Lee, *At America's Gates*, 191.

14. Carlos Bulosan, *America Is in the Heart: A Personal History* (Seattle: University of Washington Press, 1946), vii.

15. The Page Law, of March 3, 1875, barred the admission of prostitutes in general but also specifically mentioned the exclusion of Asian women being transported under contract for "lewd and immoral purposes." Doc. 28 in LeMay and. Barkan, eds., *U.S. Immigration*.

16. A small number of Barbadians and some other West Indians soon entered along the East Coast. See Takaki, *Pau Hana*, 270, 29; Won Moo Hurh, *The Korean Americans* (Westport, Conn.: Greenwood Press, 1998), 34; Karen Isaksen Leonard, *The South Asian Americans* (Westport, Conn.: Greenwood Press, 1997), 42; and Wayne Patterson, *The Ilse: First Generation Korean Immigrants in Hawai'i, 1903–1973* (Honolulu: University of Hawai'i Press, 2000), 5. Prior to 1908, some 1,087 of the 7,500 Koreans relocated to the mainland; between 1910 and 1924, the United States admitted 951 Korean picture brides. In 1920 there were 1,677 Koreans on the mainland and 4,950 in Hawai'i (slightly up from 4,533 in 1910). Filipinos began entering in late 1906. There were 2,361 in 1910

and 21,031 by 1920. U.S. Department of Commerce, Bureau of the Census, *Fourteenth Census of the United States Taken in the Year 1920*, vol. 3, *Population 1920: Composition and Characteristics of the Population by States*, "Hawaii," table 1, p. 1171.

17. Takaki reports twenty strikes in Hawai'i in 1900, mostly by Japanese, but one confrontation involved Chinese and Japanese and another Japanese and Portuguese. See *Strangers from a Different Shore: A History of Asian Americans* (Boston: Little, Brown, 1989), 149.

18. By 1910, just in California, where 57 percent of the Japanese resided, they owned 17,035 acres, leased 139,866, and worked another 37,898 by contract. See Matsumoto, *Farming the Home Place*, 32. Takaki reported 16,980 acres owned (*Strangers*, 188). However, although Masao Suzuki cites for 1910 (table 2, p. 44) the same 16,980 acres owned as does Takaki and the same 37,898 under contract as provided by Matsumoto, she gives 156,843 for the number of acres leased (her source being Ichioka, 150). See Suzuki, "Impotent or Important? Taking Another Look at the 1920 California Alien Land Law," Working Paper no. 1999.13 (Public Policy Institute of California, October 1999).

19. Roger Daniels referred to it as the Asiatic Exclusion League as of May 14, 1905, and most others have followed that. However, Herbert B. Johnson, a prominent social activist, wrote in 1907 "Discrimination against Japanese in California: A Review of the Real Situation" (Berkeley: Courier, 1907), Huntington Library accession no. 258590. In it he referred to the new group as the Japanese and Korean Exclusion League and its formation meeting on May 7, 1905. Even more indicative, A. E. Yoell sent a letter to Congressman Everis Anson Hayes on May 1, 1906, in which he identified himself as "Secretary of the Japanese and Korean Exclusion League, San Francisco," and wrote, "As it is now nearly one year since the organization of the Japanese and Korean Exclusion League, I venture to write." Letter reprinted on the Web site of the Museum of the City of San Francisco under the title "Asiatic Coolie Invasion," www.sfmuseum.org/1906.2/invasion.html (accessed September 15, 2003). Daniels, *Politics of Prejudice: The Anti-Japanese Movement in California and the Struggle for Japanese Exclusion* (New York: Atheneum, 1968), 27–28.

20. Quoted by Herbert B. Johnson, "Discrimination against Japanese," 15, 26–27. See also Issel and Cherny, *San Francisco*, 84, 86, 154–55. David A. Takami reports that the Kings County (Seattle) Republican Club had already called for Japanese exclusion in April 1900. See Takami, *Divided Destiny: A History of Japanese Americans in Seattle* (Seattle: University of Washington Press, 1998), 23.

21. "Japanese Exclusion: Speech of the Hon. Everis Anson Hayes (California Member of Congress) in the House of Representatives, March 13, 1906" (Washington, D.C., 1906), Huntington Library accession no. 2146.

22. Herbert B. Johnson, "Discrimination against Japanese," 15, 26; Daniels, *Politics of Prejudice*, 31–35.

23. Herbert B. Johnson, "Discrimination against Japanese," 29.

24. Takaki, *Pau Hana*, 150–52. The quotation is on 153.

25. Ian F. Haney Lopez, *White by Law: The Legal Construction of Race* (New York: New York University Press, 1996), 9, 26, and appendix A, 203–206.

14. Miners, Merchants, and Entrepreneurs

1. Peck, *Reinventing Free Labor*, 129–30.

2. Helen Geracimos Chapin, "The Greeks of Hawai'i: An Odyssey from Kingdom to Statehood," *Hellenic Journal of San Francisco*, February 17, 1983: 12, March 3: 12, and March 17: 5, 12; Chapin, "From Sparta to Spencer Street: Greek Women in Hawai'i,"

Hawaiian Journal of History 13 (1979): 140-42; and Chapin, "The Greeks of Hawai'i," in *New Directions in Greek American Studies*, ed. Dan Georgakas and Charles Moskos, 62–64, 68 (New York: Pella, 1991).

3. Peter W. Dickson, "The Greek Pilgrims: Tsakonas and Tzintzinians," in *New Directions in Greek*, 35–54.

The Camarinos brothers also established a thriving business shipping refrigerated pineapples (a pioneering venture) and importing meat and fresh produce into Hawai'i (Letter from Helen Chapin to author, July 27, 2003).

4. Papanikolas, *Greek Odyssey*, 10, 141, 146, 148, 151–56, 159–61; Helen Papanikolas, "The Exiled Greeks," in *New Directions*, ed. Georgakas and Moskos, 412–13; Papanikolas, "Life and Labor among the Immigrants of Bingham County," *Utah Historical Quarterly*, 33 (1969): 305–7; Nugent, *Into the West*, 160 (quotation); Peck, *Reinventing Free Labor*, 31–32, 97–99, 152, 160, 167, 204, 211–17; Peck, "Crisis in the Family: Padrones and Radicals in Utah, 1908–1912," in *New Directions*, 72, 85–93.

Images of Greeks, Gunther Peck points out, stressed that they were "lawless, dirty, lewd, and lazy"—stereotypes akin to those used against African Americans in the South (*Reinventing Free Labor*, 118).

5. Dean P. Talagan, "Faith, Hard Work, and Family: The Story of *Wyoming Helenes*," in *Peopling the High Plains: Wyoming's European Heritage*, ed. Gordon Olaf Hendrickson, 149–68 (Cheyenne, Wyo.: State Archives and Historical Department, 1977). The quotation is from G. James Patterson, "Greek and Romanian Immigrants as Hyphenated Americans: Toward a Theory of White Ethnicity," in *New Directions*, 158.

6. "Fictive kin" refers to individuals regarded as relatives—with the corresponding benefits and responsibilities—but who are not actually related.

7. Robert James Theodoratus, "A Greek Community in America: Tacoma, Washington" (Sacramento, Calif.: Sacramento State College Anthropological Society, 1971), 4, 7, 15, 109; Thomas Doulis, *A Surge to the Sea: Greeks in Oregon* (n.p.: Jack Lockie and Associates, 1977), 7, 8, 15, 17; Peck, *Reinventing Free Labor*, 163–64, 181; 1910 *Census, Population*, vol. 3, *Reports by States*: Washington, tables 1, 12; 1920 *Census, Population*, vol. 2, table 6, p. 697.

Helen Chapin points out, regarding Greek girls, that "Without a dowry it simply did not matter how beautiful or pure the girl was . . . she could not marry." Thomas Doulis notes that one alternative was to bring the sister to America to marry a Greek here, in which case dowries were far less relevant or were even dispensed with. That option was more palatable to the women. The men preferred it to marriage with non-Greek women, for that isolated them from their community unless the women adapted to the Greek culture. Chapin, "From Sparta," 138, and Doulis, *Surge to the Sea*, 29.

8. Theodoratus, "Greek Community," 7, 9, 12–18, 157, 188–203; Scheuerman, "Washington's European American Communities," 61; Theodore Saloutos, "Greeks," in *Harvard Encyclopedia of American Ethnic Groups*, ed. Stephen Thernstrom and Ann Orlov (Cambridge, Mass.: Harvard University Press, 1980), 434–35; Dodds, *American Northwest*, 130–32.

9. Among the few groups for which there is scant information of such patterns are the Canadians and the English, which is significant in view of the fact that in 1910 140,305 of the 1.2 million Canadian-born persons in the United States lived in the West (principally Washington and California and secondarily in Montana, Oregon, Colorado, and Idaho). Nearly the same number of English (140,635 out of nearly 878,000 nationwide) were reported in the West (chiefly in California, Washington, Utah, and Colorado, followed by Montana, Texas, and Oregon).

10. Elizabeth Jameson, *All That Glitters: Class, Conflict, and Community in Cripple*

Creek (Urbana: University of Illinois Press, 1998), 25, 29, 141. Several examples of works that deal with the Chinese in the West into the early twentieth century (besides others already cited and several covering urban areas, addressed below) are Don C. Conley, "The Pioneer Chinese of Utah," in *The Peoples of Utah*, ed. Helen Z. Papanikolas (Salt Late City: University of Utah Press, 1976), 251–77; Trull, "History of the Chinese"; Dodds, *American Northwest*, 119–20; Randall Rohe, "Chinese Miners in the Far West," originally published 1982, reprinted in *Major Problems in the History of the American West*, 1st ed., ed. Clyde A. Milner II (New York: D. C. Heath, 1989), 328–43; "Henry Sienkiewicz Appraises Chinese Labor in California, 1880," in *Major Problems in California History*, ed. Sucheng Chan and Spencer Olin, 172–74 (Boston: Houghton Mifflin, 1997); and Chan, *Asian Americans*, chapter 2.

11. Jameson, *All That Glitters*, 49–59, 76, 119–39, 141–42.

12. Ibid., 143, 144, 148–49, 153.

13. Ibid., 208, 236, 212, 213–22; Carroll D. Wright, U.S. Commissioner of Labor, "Class Conflict in Colorado," from the Official Report, Sen. Doc. 122, 58th Cong., *Kayland's Monthly* (Girard, Kans.), no. 84: April 1907, Huntington Library accession no. 247125. The Bell quotation is in Wright, 43.

Historian Elizabeth Jameson recently stressed that "Who set the dynamite and who paid them remains hotly debated. . . . I don't think anyone really knows what happened." Jameson, "High-Grade and Fools' Gold: The Cripple Creek Strike of 1903–1904 in History and Memory," paper presented at the Western Historical Association meeting, Las Vegas, October 15, 2004, 2.

14. Jameson, *All That Glitters*, 234, 236, 245, 247–51.

15. Emmons, *Butte Irish*, 20, 25, 27, 29, 30, 36, 18, 133–34, 181–82.

16. Ibid., 41, 63, 64, 259; Jameson, *All That Glitters*, 306n6, 310 n. 8–9, 311n14, 312n18. See also Michael P. Malone, Richard B. Roeder, and William L. Lang, *Montana: A History of Two Centuries*, rev. ed. (Seattle: University of Washington Press, 1991), 85, 91, 204–07.

17. Emmons, *Butte Irish*, 184, 187, 197, 259, 312, 341–48, 361.

18. Ibid., 224, 256, 258, 237, 244, 266–69, 272–73, 365–66, 400, 367.

19. Laurie Mercer, *Anaconda: Labor Community and Culture in Montana's Smelter City* (Urbana: University of Illinois Press, 2001), 14, 22, 30; Mercer, "'We Are Women Irish': Gender, Class, Religion, and Ethnic Identity in Anaconda, Montana," in *Writing the Range: Race, Class, and Culture in the Women's West*, ed. Elizabeth Jameson and Susan Armitage (Norman: University of Oklahoma Press, 1997), 311–33.

20. Matjaz Klemenčič, "Slovene Miners in Leadville and the Colorado Labor Movement," paper presented at the Organization of American Historians meeting, Washington D.C., April 2002, 7.

21. Alan Kent Powell, "The 'Foreign Element' and the Carbon County Coal Miners' Strike," *Utah Historical Quarterly* 43 (1975): 125–26, 133, 138, 144–45.

22. Helen Zeese Papanikolas, "Life and Labor among the Immigrants of Bingham Canyon," *Utah Historical Quarterly* 33 (1969): 290, 298, 292, 305–07, 310–11. Among the Greeks, 800 were in the union and voted to strike.

23. Earl Stinneford, "Mines and Miners: The East Europeans in Wyoming," in *Peopling the High Plains: Wyoming's European Heritage*, ed. Gordon Olaf Henrickson (Cheyenne: Wyoming State Archives and Historical Department, 1977), 121, 123, 131; Dee Garceau, "'I Got a Girl Here, Would You Like to Meet Her?' Courtship, Ethnicity, and Community in Sweetwater County, 1900–1925," in *Writing the Range*, 277, 280, 293, 296; and Joseph Stipanovich, "Falcons in Flight: The Yugoslavs," in *The Peoples of Utah*, 363, 377–79, 370–71, 368–69.

24. Roberto R. Calderón, *Mexican Coal Mining Labor in Texas and Coahuila, 1880–1930* (College Station: Texas A & M University Press, 2000), 11–12, 101, 103, 133, 78, 9, 11, 10.

25. Thomas E. Sheridan, *Arizona*, 168–70, and Philip Mellinger, "'The Men Have Become Organizers': Labor Conflict and Unionization in the Mexican Mining Communities of Arizona, 1900–1915," in *The American West: The Reader*, ed. Walter Nugent and Martin Ridge, 203–24 (Bloomington: Indiana University Press, 1999). The information on Jerome comes from the displays in the Jerome Historical Museum, Jerome, Arizona.

26. Gordon, *Great Arizona Orphan Abduction*, 101–105; Thomas E. Sheridan, *Arizona*, 177–78.

27. Thomas E. Sheridan, *Arizona*, 171–72; Mellinger, "'Men Have Become Organizers,'" 203–24. The quotation is on 224.

28. Annie M. Cox, "History of Bisbee, 1877–1937," (M.A. thesis, University of Arizona, 1938), Huntington Library acquisition no. 286700, and U.S. President's Mediation Committee, Department of Labor, "Report of the Bisbee Deportations, November 6, 1917" (Seattle: University of Washington, 1918), Huntington Library acquisition no. 265875. The estimate regarding Mexicans in Bisbee is from Nugent and Ridge, *American West*, 203. The Schwantes quotation is from "Wage Earners and Wealth Makers," 432. See also Acuña, *Occupied America*, 181–82.

29. Katherine Benton-Cohen, "Vigilantism as Corporate Policy: Before and After the Bisbee IWW Deportation of 1917," paper presented at the Western Historical Association meeting, Las Vegas, October 15, 2004, concluding quotation, 11.

30. Nugent, *Into the West*, 159, and 57, 117, 119, 120, 154–55, and Walter Nugent, "The People of the West since 1890," in *The Twentieth Century West: Historical Interpretations*, ed. Gerald Nash and Richard Etulain, 47–48 (Albuquerque: University of New Mexico Press, 1989).

31. Montgomery, *Fall of the House of Labor*, 343–45; Dean J. Saitta, Randall McGuire, and Philip Duke, "Working and Striking in Southern Colorado, 1913–1914," 1999 Society for Historical Archeology meeting, Salt Lake City, www.cdpheritage.org/heritage/ludlow/working.html (accessed July 2, 2003; available May 1, 2006, at www.du.edu/anthro/ludlow/working.html); Stephen Millies, "The Ludlow Massacre and the Birth of Company Unions," *Workers World*, January 26, 1995, www.hartford-hwp.com/archives/45b/030.html (accessed July 2, 2003); Carlos Schwantes, "Wage Earners and Wealth Makers," 443.

15. *Land, Labor, and Immigrant Communities*

1. Carey McWilliams, *Factories in the Field: The Story of Migratory Farm Labor in California* (n.p.: Archon Books, 1969 [1939]), 103–104; and Winther, *Great Northwest*, 425.

2. Matt Garcia, *A World of Its Own: Race, Labor, and Citrus in the Making of Greater Los Angeles, 1900–1970* (Chapel Hill: University of North Carolina Press, 2001), 40–41. The quotation is from Garcia.

3. Dodds, *American Northwest*, 121; Montgomery, *Fall of the House of Labor*, 85; and Fuchs, *Hawaii Pono*, 42.

4. Fuchs, *Hawaii Pono*, 54, Kimura, *Issei*, 102; Wayne Patterson, *Korean Frontier*, 98, 171–73, 232 n. 45; Fred Cordova, *Filipinos: Forgotten Asian Americans* (New York: Kendall Hunt, 1983), 29. See also Wayne Patterson, *Ilse*, 2000), chapter 1, for an excellent detailed account. A brief account, with slightly different figures, is Linda Pomerantz, "The Background of Korean Emigration," pp. 277–315, in *Labor Migration under Capitalism: Asian Workers in the United States before World War Two*, ed. Lucie Cheng and Edna

Bonacich (Berkeley: University of California Press, 1984). Almost 10 percent of the initial Korean migrants were women and children (299).

5. Wayne Patterson, *Korean Frontier*, 174–75; Fuchs, *Hawaii Pono*, 52–53; and Pap, *Portuguese Americans*, 77. However, the number of second-generation Portuguese did continue to rise, from 9,163 in 1900 to 21,208 in 1920.

In a 1906 report, William F. Blackman raised the question of the ability of white laborers to adapt to working in the tropics. He reported that the 1896 Hawaiian census showed — in addition to 15,191 Portuguese foreign stock (44 percent of them female) — 2,250 British, 1,432 Germans, 378 Norwegians, 101 French, and 3,086 Americans, together with 24,407 Japanese, 21,616 Chinese, and 455 South Sea Islanders. Moreover, by 1896, some 2,112 children had a European father and a Hawaiian mother, and 1,464 had a Chinese or Japanese father and a Hawaiian mother. Blackman, *The Making of Hawaii: A Study in Social Evolution* (New York: Macmillan, 1906), 185–86, 206–07, 246–47. Huntington Library accession no. 334796.

6. The Alcantara quotation is in Cordova, *Filipinos*, 28. The quotation from the HSPA's president is in Miriam Sharma, "Labor Migration and Class Formation among the Filipinos in Hawaii, 1906–1946," in *Labor Migration*, ed. Cheng and Bonacich, 582. See also Cordova, *Filipinos*, 140, 143; Edna Bonacich, "Asian Labor in the Development of California and Hawaii," in *Labor Migration* 178, 181; Fuchs, *Hawaii Pono*, 49; Takaki, *Pau Hana*, 23; and Nordyke, *Peopling of Hawaii*, table 3–12 (224). See also Alan Moriyama, "The Causes of Immigration: The Background of Japanese Emigration to Hawaii, 1885–1894, in *Labor Migration*, 248–76; and John M. Liu, "Race, Ethnicity, and the Sugar Plantation System: Asian Labor in Hawaii, 1850–1900," in *Labor Migration*, 186–210.

In 1916 a Hawaiian commissioner of labor noted, "Plantations have to view laborers primarily as instruments of production. Their business interests require cheap, not too intelligent, docile unmarried men." Quoted by Teresa Ammott and Julie Matthaei, *Race, Gender, and Work: A Multi-Cultural Economic History of Women in the United States*, 2nd ed. (Boston: South End Press, 1996), 236.

7. Kimura, *Issei*, 102–3, 106–7; Fuchs, *Hawaii Pono*, 248–49; and Ogawa, *Kodomo no tame ni*, 190. Full citation for Dillingham Report is in note 3 of chapter 12, above.

The Dillingham Commission (1709) analyzed data for the period between June 14, 1900, and June 30, 1910. It reported that during this period 3,850 Chinese men, women, and children entered Hawai'i, but 13,920 left, for a net loss of 10,070; yet, a drop of only 4,064 appears in the census. Similarly, the commission found that 77,421 Japanese men, women, and children had entered, but 75,186 left, for a modest increase of only 2,235. However, the census reports a jump of 18,548. Both cases would suggest significant increases in Hawaiian-born children during that period. See the tables in Nordyke, *Peopling of Hawaii*, confirming this.

Yukiko Kimura reports that when the Japanese first organized the joint stock Washington Pineapple Company in Oahu, the Caucasian canning company refused to buy their crop, which they then had to dump, for a loss of $32,500. Kimura, *Issei*, 37.

8. Takaki, *Pau Hana*, 84–89; Wayne Patterson, *Korean Frontier*, 122; Coman, *History of Contract Labor*, 46.

9. Ogawa, *Kodomo no tame ni*, 77–78; Takaki, *Pau Hana*, 202; Kimura, *Issei*, 15, 142, 143; Wayne Patterson, *Korean Frontier*, 173; Nordyke, *Peopling of Hawaii*, table 3–3b and 3c (186, 188). Many tales have been told about the picture bride experiences, for the men often resorted to subterfuges to hide their age and true financial situation or employment. Woo Hong Pong Yun, age 23, met her new husband, age 36, and recalled, "When I see him, he skinny and black. I no like. No look like picture. But no can go home." On the Islands, resorting to *kakeochi* (desertion) was even more difficult than on the main-

land. Takaki, *Pau Hana*, 123; Ammott and Matthaei, *Race, Gender, and Work*, 223; and Ogawa, *Kodomo no tame ni*, 77.

10. One particularly demeaning treatment they received was by the *lunas* (foremen), who would address them only by their numbers (*bangos*) rather than by their names. See Takaki, *Pau Hana*, 89 and 138–39. See chapter 3, regarding the paternalism and rules that were supported by police and consuls; chapter 4, for conditions on the plantations and the rising inter-ethnic interaction; and chapter 5 on the violence toward workers, prompting many to "walk away" from their contracts. Takaki sums this up in *Strangers*, 133–42. William Carlson Smith also lists the changes after 1920, in *Americans in Process: A Study of Our Citizens of Oriental Ancestry* (New York: Arno Press, 1970 [1937]), 48–49.

11. The quotation is from Takaki, *Pau Hana*, 153, plus 153–63. See also Ogawa, *Kodomo no tame ni*, 135–77; Kimura, *Issei*, 89; and Fuchs, *Hawaii Pono*, 55, 119.

12. Dillingham Commission Report, quoted by Miriam Sharma, "Labor Migration," 601.

13. The overall situation during the strike was aggravated by the influenza epidemic that had killed nearly 1,000 persons in Hawai'i during the prior year. During the 1920 strike, more than 2,000 workers fell ill, and 100 died. Chan, *Asian Americans*, 85.

14. Kimura, *Issei*, 97–101; Fuchs, *Hawaii Pono*, 223; Takaki, *Pau Hana*, 174, 179 (quotation); and Takaki, *Strangers*, 150–55.

15. Glen Grant and Dennis M. Ogawa, "Living Proof: Is Hawaii the Answer?" *Annals AAPSS* 530 (November 1993): 137–54; and William Carlson Smith, *Americans in Process*, 20–25, 39. The following table is based upon Smith's data. Among other things, the data make it clear that in December 1941 most Hawaiian Nisei were still teenagers (Smith, 41–43).

		Mainland		Hawai'i	
		NATIVE BORN	THIRD GENERATION	NATIVE BORN	THIRD GENERATION
Chinese	1920	18,532	2,391	12,342	1,303
	1930	30,868	4,325	19,711	4,582
Japanese	1920	29,672	212	48,586	326
	1930	68,357	839	91,185	4,289

16. Nordyke, *Peopling of Hawaii*, table 3–1 (178–79); Kimura, *Issei*, 36, 112, 124–25, 170, 178, 199; Ogawa, *Kodomo no tame ni*, 43, 70, 141; and Fuchs, *Hawaii Pono*, 111. Takaki offers a most interesting description of the multiculturalism on and off the plantations, in *Strangers*, 155–76. William Carlson Smith's census data for 1920 and 1930, in the previous endnote, are quite relevant here, too.

17. Kimura, *Issei*, 15–16, 40, 196; Fuchs, *Hawaii Pono*, 97–98.

18. Richard White, "*It's Your Misfortune*," 443–44.

19. McWilliams, *Factories*, 156–63; Acuña, *Occupied America*, 180–81; and Starr, *Endangered Dreams*, 39–40.

20. Matt Garcia, *World of Its Own*, 3, 43, 61.

21. Saburo Tanaka was the father of Akemi Kikumura, who describes her early life and his role as a contractor in *Through Harsh Winters: The Life of a Japanese Immigrant Woman* (Novato, Calif.: Chandler and Sharp, 1981), 40–42. Daigoro Hashimoto worked in Los Angeles and then in Salt Lake City. See Helene Zeese Papanikolas, "Japanese Life in Utah," in *The Peoples of Utah*, 337–39.

22. Chan, *This Bittersweet Soil*, 207–209, 269; Yung, *Unbound Voices*, 13–14, 89, 356; McWilliams, *Southern California Country*, 89–90; and McWilliams, *Factories*, 109.

23. McWilliams, *Factories*, 111–13; Matsumoto, *Farming the Home Place*, 31, 32–34, 37–38.

24. Tamura, *Hood River Issei*, 20, 44, 71, 102, and Marvin Gavin Pursinger, "The Japanese Settle in Oregon: 1880–1920," *Journal of the West* 5 (1966): 255, 257. Shortly after World War One the American Legion was already pushing for an anti-Japanese resolution and the formation of the Hood River Anti-Alien Association (Tamura, 89–90).

25. Gerald N. Hallberg, "Bellingham, Washington's Anti-Hindu Riot," *Journal of the West* 12 (1973): 163–75; Rajanmi Kanta Das, *Hindustani Workers on the Pacific Coast* (Berlin: Walter de Gruyter, 1923), 1–15, 18–36, 45–59, 68–78; McWilliams, *Factories*, 117–18; Takaki, *Strangers*, 296–98.

26. Sucheta Mazuma, "Punjabi Agricultural Workers in California, 1905–1945," 549–78 in *Labor Migration*, in particular 563–66; and Takaki, *Strangers*, 306–11. Karen Isaksen Leonard estimated that 85 percent of the first groups were Sikh. *The South Asian Americans* (Westport, Conn.: Greenwood Press, 1997), 42.

27. Das, *Hindustani Workers*, 80, 89–90, and Karen Isaksen Leonard, *South Asian Americans*, chapter 2, with its extended discussion of the early farmers and the Punjabi-Mexican, or "Mexican-Hindu," marriages and families. The first couples involved two partners, aged 36 and 37, who wed sisters, 18 and 21. See, too, Takaki, *Strangers*, 300–01.

28. Thomas K. Walls, *The Japanese Texans* (San Antonio: University of Texas Institute of Texas Cultures, 1987), 40–79, 119–20, 124–27, and Diana J. Kleiner, "Saibara, Seito," *The Handbook of Texas Online*, www.tsha.utexas.edu/handbook/online/articles/SS/fsagp.html (accessed April 19, 2005).

29. Pap, *Portuguese Americans*, 73, 134–35. In 1940, for example, there were 80 boats engaged in tuna fishing in San Diego, half of which were owned by Portuguese.

30. Ibid., 145, 152, 226, 231. The quotation is on 226.

31. Leo Pap reports 24,963 arrivals but notes that for a time Madeirans were not included. In fact, given the multiple origins that fell under the Portuguese umbrella and the uneven data keeping, the total was probably significantly higher (45). The 1920 census for California lists 24,609 Portuguese by country of birth (vol. 2, table 6, p. 698) and 34,388 second generation (vol. 2, table 8, p. 925). About 44 percent of those of Portuguese origin in the United States were in California in 1920 (vol. 2, table 1, 897).

32. In 1910 there were 7,585 foreign-born Portuguese in Hawai'i, along with 14,716 of Portuguese descent. Of the former, 3,700 still worked on the sugar plantations, many as *lunas* (supervisors or foremen); few went to the pineapple plantations. By 1926 only 1,341 first-born Portuguese were still employed in Hawai'i. At the end of that decade a majority were living in Honolulu or Hilo. Pap, *Portuguese Americans*, 45, 53, 68, 75–76, 149–51, 227.

33. Berge Bulbullian, *The Fresno Armenians: History of a Diaspora Community* (Fresno: Press at California State University, Fresno, 2000), 5; Wilson D. Wallis, *Fresno Armenians (to 1919)*, ed. Nectar Davidian (Lawrence, Kans.: Coronado Press, 1965), 54; and Mark Arax, "Recalling Armenian Genocide," *Los Angeles Times*, April 20, 2005.

34. Bulbullian, *Fresno Armenians*, 148.

35. M. Vartan Malcom, *The Armenians in America* (Boston: Pilgrim Press, 1919), 61, 64–67, and Bulbullian, *Fresno Armenians*, 9–10. The quotation is from Malcom, 88. The 1920 census data is from vol. 2, table 5, p. 699. Because no second-generation data are given, and some island populations were not always included, there is no doubt that the group's totals in the country and specifically in California were much higher, although probably not 70,000, given the recency of arrival of so many.

36. Wallis, *Fresno Armenians*, 40–41; Bulbullian, *Fresno Armenians*, 54–61; Mc-Williams, *Factories*, 186–90; and Malcom, *Armenians in America*, 89–94.

37. Malcom, *Armenians in America*, 45, 71; Bulbullian, *Fresno Armenians*, xi–xii, 35, 63, 65–66.

38. Wallis, *Fresno Armenians*, 52; Malcom, *Armenians in America*, 5, 14–18, 125–26; and Bulbullian, *Fresno Armenians*, 106–15. The quotation is on p. 116. Harold Nelson's dissertation also provides a number of valuable insights into the adaptation of Armenian family life to American culture, the culture clashes between the generations due to the inescapable influences of the surrounding American culture and the earlier prejudice against Armenians including residentially. Nelson, "The Armenian Family: Changing Patterns of Family Life in a California Community" (Ph.D. diss., University of California, Berkeley, Anthropology, 1954), v, 1–63. For a brief discussion of the small Armenian and Middle Eastern community in Utah at this time, see Robert F. Zeidner, "From Babylon to Babylon: Immigrants from the Middle East," in *Peoples of Utah*, 385–408.

39. Rasmussen, *New Land, New Lives*, 24–25, 200–203, 110.

40. Kristine Leander, ed. *Family Sagas: Stories of Scandinavian Immigrants* (Seattle: Scandinavian Language Institute, 1997), 39–40.

41. Ibid., 83–84.

42. Kendric Charles Babcock, *The Scandinavian Element in the United States* (New York: Arno Books, 1969 [1914]), 67. The Dillingham Commission Report's table for persons arriving between 1899 and 1910 gave 151,774 for Finns, including 17,189 repeaters, for a net new migration of 134,585, which was rather close to the figures given by Jerry Schofer in "Urban and Rural Finnish Communities in California: 1860–1960" (San Francisco: R & E Research Associates, 1975), 8–10. The U.S. Bureau of Immigration included Finns with Russians until after the First World War, when the Finns acquired their independence. Dillingham, *Statistical Review of Immigration*, table 37.

43. Arlow Andersen, *The Norwegian Americans* (Boston: Twayne, 1975), 111; Rasmussen, *New Land, New Lives*, 272; and Kenneth O. Bjork, *West of the Great Divide: Norwegian Migration to the Pacific Coast, 1847–1893* (Northfield, Minn.: Norwegian American Historical Association, 1958), 528, 544. See also Elliott R. Barkan, "French Canadians," in *Harvard Encyclopedia of American Ethnic Groups*, ed. Stephen Thernstrom and Ann Orlov (Cambridge, Mass.: Harvard University Press, 1980), 388–401. The immigration data are from the Dillingham Commission Report, vol. 3, *Statistical Review of Immigration*, table 27, 289–92.

44. Patsy Adams Hegstad, "Sailor, Sawyer, Laborer, Lawyer: Occupations of Nordic Immigrants in Seattle and Ballard, 1892–1900," in *Scandinavian and Other Immigrants in Urban America*, ed. Lovoll, 69, and Bjork, *West of the Great Divide*, 152–53, 596–98, 600.

45. The Dillingham Commission, as a case in point, reported 28,044 Scandinavians departed the United States between 1908 and 1910. *Statistical Review of Immigration*, table 48.

46. Ibid., 60–63. Hegstad, for example, reported that in 1900 in Seattle, 23 percent of Swedes were laborers, 21 percent of Norwegians, and 20 percent of Danes.

47. Danes had the highest percentage of "housewives" among Scandinavians in 1900, about 70 percent.

48. Rasmussen, *New Land, New Lives*, 200–204.

49. Jorgen Dahlie, "Old World Paths in the New: Scandinavians Find a Familiar Home in Washington," in *Experiences in a Promised Land*, ed. Edwards and Schwantes, 105; Dahlie, *A Social History of Scandinavian Immigrants, Washington State, 1895–1910* (Ph.D. diss.; New York: Arno Press 1980 [1967]), 58; Odd Lovoll, *Promise of America*, 1st ed., 156, 159, 161; and Hans Bergmann, ed., *History of Scandinavians in Tacoma and Pierce County* (Tacoma, Wash.: Hans Bergmann, 1926), 123.

50. Bjork, *West of the Great Divide*, 12, 569, 583–86; Hegstad, "Sailor," 65; Nielsen, *Danish Americans*, 161–63, 166–67; Rasmussen, *New Land, New Lives*, 173; Hans Bergmann, *History of Scandinavians*, 108–9, 117–18, 121–22. See Frederik Madsen's experience with the Folk School in Solvang, in Rasmussen, 292–98. His conclusion: "Because I am a Dane and have gone to folk schools, I think I am a better American" (298).

51. Rasmussen, *New Land, New Lives*, 217–22.

52. Jorgen Dahlie, "Old World Paths," 51.

53. Bjork, *West of the Great Divide*, 544, 550–52, 556–65; Hans Bergmann, *History of Scandinavians*, 123.

54. Hans Bergmann, *History of Scandinavians*, 124–25; Hegstad, "Sailor," 67–68.

55. Dahlie, *Social History*, 61, and Dahlie, "Old World," 51–52.

56. Dahlie, "Old World," 51, 53, 54; Dahlie, *Social History*, vi, 62, 64–65, 95, 107–110 (quotation is on 110). Based on my analysis of Thomas Osterson Stine's biographies from 1900 and nearly half of Lottie Roeder Roth's mammoth 1,000-page collection of biographies, I estimate that three-fourths of the foreign born in Washington State had come from elsewhere in the United States, as had so many native-born Americans. Ernst Skarstedt's 1908 collection of 372 Swedish biographies in Seattle, Tacoma, and Spokane found only five foreign born who had come directly to Washington. Those findings help us to understand A. G. Overn's letter to "Amerika," March 1892, urging readers to go west and not be scared away "even if they are called Missourians or whatever else." See Stine, *Scandinavians on the Pacific*; Roth, *History of Whatcom County*, 1:1–449; and Skarstedt, as cited by Dahlie, "Old World," 52. The quotation from the letter appears in Gertrude Tingelstad, *Scandinavians in the Silverton Country: Their Arrival and Early Settlement* (Silverton, Ore.: Silverton Appeal Tribune, 1978), 8.

57. Rasmussen, *New Land, New Lives*, 51, 167–68, 283; Nielsen, *Danish Americans*, 87; and Lovoll, *Promise of America*, 1st ed., 195, 209, 327–38.

58. This list is gleaned from the following sources: Patsy Adams Hegstad, "Citizenship, Voting, and Immigrants: A Comparative Study of the Naturalization Propensity and Voter Registration of Nordics in Seattle and Ballard, Washington, 1892–1900" (Ph.D. diss., University of Washington, 1982), 156–61; Rasmussen, *New Land, New Lives*, 304; Nielsen, *Danish Americans*, 168, 173–75; Lovoll, *Promise of America*, 1st ed., 183–86; Dahlie, *Social History*, 83, 156–59; Bjork, *West of the Great Divide*, 125, 163, 171,189, 616–17; Hans Bergmann, *History of Scandinavians*, 85; Frederick Hale, ed., *Danes in North America* (Seattle: University of Washington Press, 1984), xvii; Steve J. Forslund, *The Swedes in Tacoma and the Pugent Sound Country, 1852–1976*, ed. Doris Gunstrom King (Ogden, Utah: Brigham Young University, 1976), 111, 113, 136, 141, 150.

59. Babcock's earlier work refers to this matter. See pp. 94 and 129 and note 43.

60. Richard White, *"It's Your Misfortune,"* 453; and Rasmussen, *New Land, New Lives*, 232. For a brief discussion of changing attitudes regarding working wives during the 1910s, see Maurine Weiner Greenwald, "Working-Class Feminism and Family Wage Ideal: The Seattle Debate on Married Women's Right to Work, 1914–1920," in *Women in Pacific Northwest History*, ed. Blair, 94–134.

61. Bjork, *West of the Great Divide*, 14, 16; Tingelstad, *Scandinavians*, 25, 36–39, 55; Nielsen, *Danish Americans*, 64, 86–89; John R. Jenswold, "The Rise and Fall of Pan-Scandinavianism in Urban America," in *Scandinavians and Other Immigrants*, 162.

62. Dahlie, *Social History*, 151; Slind and Bohm, *Norse to Palouse*, 44–45, 54–55, 73; Forslund, *Swedes in Tacoma*, 56, 73, 84; Lovoll, *Promise of America*, 1st ed., 209; Rasmussen, *New Land, New Lives*, 144–45; Hans Bergmann, *History of Scandinavians*, 63; and Nielsen, *Danish Americans*, 150–51.

63. These sources refer to this and the next three paragraphs. Hegstad, "Citizenship," 148; Rasmussen, *New Land, New Lives*, 124, 300–301; Schofer, "Urban and Rural"; and

Lucile McDonald, *Coast Country: A History of Southwest Washington* (Portland, Ore.: Binfords and Mort, 1966); and three of the essays in the collection edited by Ralph J. Falkanen, *The Finns in North America: A Social Symposium* (Hancock, Mich.: Michigan State University Press for Suomi College, 1969): Reino Kero, "The Background of Finnish Emigration," 55–69; Tauri Aaltio, "A Survey of Emigration from Finland to the United States and Canada," 63–69; and David T. Halkola, "Finnish Language Newspapers in the United States," 73–90. See also Timothy Egan, "Nordic Culture Thrives as Young Seek Out Roots" (dateline: Astoria, OR), *New York Times*, May 12, 2002: 12. Apparently, in another edition of the *Times* for the same day the title appears as "Lutefisk (uff da) Reigns in Revival of Nordic Roots." See http://select.nytimes.com/search/restricted/article?res=F70D15FA3D5DOC718DDDAC08 (accessed June 14, 2006). Mary Murphy briefly discusses Finntown in Butte, Montana, in *Mining Cultures: Men, Women, and Leisure in Butte, 1914–41* (Urbana: University of Illinois Press, 1997), 13–14. The dispersal of Finns could be appreciated by the fact that a community developed in Redwood Valley, not far from the California coast, but there was little contact with Finns along that stretch of coast, or even in Fort Bragg, where they were concentrated.

64. Sandra Johnson Witt, "The Lasting Legacy of the Deep River Finns," http://sydaby.eget.net/emig/deep_river.htm (accessed April 21, 2005), and "Deep River and Its Finns, Wahkiakum County, Washington," Pioneer Series (Portland: Finnish American Historical Society of the West) 24.1 (December 1997): 8.

65. McDonald, *Coast Country*, 106–09, 147.

66. Hegstad, "Citizenship," 121; e-mail message, August 21, 2002, from Jonathan Ratila, *Raivaaja* business manager; and Web site: "Antti Oskari Tokoi," compiled by June Ilona Rantanen, Finnish Center at Saima Park, Fitchburg, Mass., June 10, 2003: www.saima-park.org/admin/park/oskari_tokoi.htm (accessed July 10, 2003). Throughout her study, Hegstad offers more information on Finns in Seattle in the 1890s and 1900. Several other works on mining communities have passing references to the presence of Finns.

67. Anna Guttormsen Hought, *Anna*, with Florence Ekstrand (Seattle: Welcome Press, 1986).

68. Rasmussen, *New Land, New Lives*, 189, 195, 202–204, 274 (the quotation). Ralph Strom, an immigrant, especially commented on the effects of the increasingly multi-ethnic environments that were more and more difficult to ignore. The changes could be dramatic or subtle, but they did take place. He describes the impact of World War One and afterward in Alaska. He had arrived from Sweden in 1912 and became a boilermaker in Seattle. "I wasn't around Swedes all the time. The kind of people that came to this country at that time, they were good people from all over the world. I had a lot of Greek friends in Seattle and Czechoslovaks and Russians, and everything you can think of" (Rasmussen, 193).

16. Newcomers, Old and New

1. Philip Notarianni, "Italianita in Utah: The Immigrant Experience," in *Peoples of Utah*, 322, 321, 306–307, 310–11, 331, 320.

2. David Kathka, "The Italian Experience in Wyoming," in *Peopling the High Plains*, 67–94.

3. In addition, they were the sixth largest foreign-born group in Idaho, Texas, and Utah. By 1910 they had thus become one of the top immigrant populations in 10 of the 13 mainland western states and territories.

4. Nugent, "People of the West," 163. See also 118, 162, and 209. In terms of white foreign stock, only the Irish and Germans outnumbered the Italians in San Francisco in 1920.

5. Andrew Rolle, *Westward the Immigrants: Italian Adventurers and Colonists in an Expanding America* (Niwot: University Press of Colorado, 1999 [originally published as *The Immigrant Upraised*, 1968]), 265–66, 276.

6. A 1910 San Francisco ordinance banned the hiring of aliens, such as the Italians, unless labor shortages could be shown to exist. Three hundred persons were fired after it was enacted. See Paola A. Sensi-Isolani and Phylis Cancilla Martinelli, eds., *Struggle and Success: An Anthology of the Italian Immigrant Experience in California* (Staten Island, N.Y.: Center for Migration Studies, 1993), 28.

7. Dino Cinel, *From Italy to San Francisco: The Immigrant Experience* (Stanford: Stanford University Press, 1982), 13, 21, 114; and Sensi-Isolani and Martinelli, eds., *Struggle and Success*, 3–4, 12–13, 24–27. The foreign-born totals are derived from the state population totals in the 1910 and 1920 censuses. By this time the Mexican population (440,205) was more than triple that of the Italians.

8. Rolle, *Westward the Immigrants*, 176–79, 200, 202, 206–07, 210, 212–14, 218, 226, 228, 246, 267, 270, 272–76, 278. According to the list of names on the Ludlow Massacre memorial plaque, possibly ten victims were Italian (six of whom were children) and four most likely Mexican. See "The Ludlow Massacre," www.members.tripod.com/~RedRobin2/index-29.html (accessed September 30, 2003) and Wikipedia, "Ludlow Massacre," http://www.reference.com/browse/wiki/Ludlow_Massacre (accessed December 5, 2005). The family names included Pedregone, Petrucci, Bartolotti, Costa, Rubino, and Valdez.

9. Rolle, *Westward the Immigrants*, 274; Kevin Starr, *Inventing the Dream: California through the Progressive Era* (New York: Oxford University Press, 1985), 231–32; Cinel, *From Italy*, 236–39; Deanna Paoli Gumina, "Andrea Sbarboro, Founder of the Italian-Swiss Colony Wine Company: Reminiscences of an Italian American Pioneer," in *Struggle and Success*, ed. Sensi-Isolani and Martinelli, 95–106; and Felice Bonadio, "A. P. Giannini and the Bank of Italy: California's Mixed Multitudes," in *Struggle and Success*, 107–23.

10. Rosalind Giardina Crosby, "The Italians of Los Angeles, 1900," in *Struggle and Success*, 40; Gilbert G. Gonzalez, "Factors Relating to Property Ownership of Mexican Americans and Italians Americans in Lincoln Heights, Los Angeles," in *Struggle and Success*, 222; and Rolle, *Westward the Immigrants*, 264.

11. Paola A. Sensi-Isolani, "Tradition and Transition in a California Paese," in *Struggle and Success*, 58–75; and William C. Richardson, "Fishermen of San Diego: The Italians," *Struggle and Success*, 84–94.

12. However, Cinel notes (*From Italy*, 212), with San Francisco's Italian fishermen controlling 80 percent of California's fishing and 90 percent of San Francisco's, they proved that "a group could isolate itself almost totally from the larger society, recreating patterns of economic and social organization almost entirely from the Old World." Parenthetically, by the early 1920s that dominance in fishing began to slip, at least in the tuna-fishing center of San Diego, where half the crews were Japanese by that time, and only 30 percent were Italian. There were also a number of highly successful Portuguese, as discussed earlier. See Donald H. Estes, "Silver Petals Falling: Japanese Pioneers in San Diego's Fishery" (n.d.), www.jahssd.org/cgi-bin/page2.cgi?donarticle3 (accessed September 30, 2003).

13. Sensi-Isolani and Martinelli, *Struggle and Success*, 16–17, 2, 50, 70; Joseph Giovinco, "'Success in the Sun?' California's Italians during the Progressive Era," in *Struggle*

and Success, 33–34; Cinel, *From Italy,* 199–203, 242–45; Starr, *Inventing,* 232; Rolle, *Westward the Immigrants,* 303, 207.

14. Jeronima Echeverria, "*Euskaldun Andreak:* Basque Women as Hard Workers, *Hoteleras,* and Matriarchs," in *Writing the Range,* ed. Jameson and Armitage, 300; William A. Douglass and Jon Bilbao, *Amerikanuak: Basques in the New World* (Reno: University of Nevada Press, 1975), 301–02; Annick Foucrier, *La rêve californien: Migrants français sur la côte Pacifique xviiᵉ–xxᵉ siècles* (Paris: Belin, 1999), 282. David A. Cookson points out that there are seven main provinces with Basque populations: three in France—Laboud, Basse Navarre, and Soule—and four in Spain—Vizcaya, Navarra, Guipuzcoa, and Alvara. Less than 10 percent of the population resided in the French portion. See "The Basques in Wyoming," in *Peopling the High Plains,* ed. Henrickson, 96. Foucrier also relates an interesting account of Paul de Longpré, a prominent Frenchman in what was then the rural Hollywood area of the early 1900s (344–45).

15. Carol W. Hovey, "Pedro and Bernardo Altube: Basque Brothers of California and Nevada," in *Portraits of Basques in the New World,* ed. Richard W. Etulain and Jeronima Echeverria, 57–79 (Reno: University of Nevada Press, 1999); John Bieter, "John B. Archabal: A Portrait of an Immigrant Success Story," in *Portraits of Basques,* 83–96; Peck, *Reinventing Free Labor,* 35; William A. Douglass, "Calculating Ethnicity through the U.S. Census: The Basque Case," unpublished paper, n.d., 267.

16. Douglass, "Calculating Ethnicity," 270, 268.

17. Echeverria, in *Writing the Range,* 303. See also Echeverria, "California's Basque Hotels and Their Hoteleros," pp. 297–316, in *Essays in Basque Social Anthropology and History,* ed. William Douglass, Basque Studies Program Occasional Papers no. 4 (Reno, Nev.: University of Reno, 1989).

18. Douglass, "Calculating Ethnicity," 233–35, 301–2; Echeverria, "*Euskaldum,*" 300–1; Carlos A. Schwantes, *In Mountain Shadows: A History of Idaho* (Lincoln: University of Nebraska Press, 1991), 127; Cookson, 99–108; David Britton and Gordon Irving, "The Continental Inheritance," in *Peoples of Utah,* 226, 235; see also Helen Papanikolas's introduction to *Peoples of Utah,* 8.

19. Douglass, "Calculating Ethnicity," 242–44, 252, 282–85, 239; Schwantes, *In Mountain Shadows,* 128; and Richard W. Etulain, "Basque Beginnings in the Pacific Northwest," pp. 57–67 (latter quotation) in *The Northwest Mosaic: Minority Conflicts in Pacific Northwest History,* ed. James Halseth and Bruce A. Glasrud (Boulder, Colo.: Pruett, 1977 [*Idaho Yesterdays,* Spring 1974]). The Etulain quotation is on p. 62.

20. This and the next paragraph are based upon Foucrier, *La rêve californien,* 188–347.

21. Foucrier, *La rêve californien,* 270–71, 281, 350; Brian J. Godfrey, *Neighborhoods in Transition: The Making of San Francisco's Ethnic and Non-Conformist Communities* (Berkeley: University of California Press, 1988), 81.

22. Douglass, "Calculating Ethnicity," 5–6.

23. Acuña, *Occupied America,* 5th ed. (2004), 152. Nonetheless, by 1960 Mexico would surpass all others to become the leading source of legal and undocumented immigrants to the United States, and that would remain true for most of the remaining years of the century. Few areas of the West by the year 2000 would be untouched by the waves of Mexicans that started spilling across the 2,000-mile-long border in the first three decades of the century.

24. For data on the volume of migration between 1904 and 1929, see Gilbert G. Gonzalez and Raul A. Fernandez, *A Century of Chicano History: Empire, Nations, and Migration* (New York: Routledge, 2003), 44.

25. Carl Abbott, "The Federal Presence," in *Oxford History,* 495.

26. For a provocative view of these developments, see Gonzalez and Fernandez, chapter 2 (33–34), in which they emphasize the factor of the on-going "U.S. economic domination over Mexico . . . during the twentieth century" (47).

They also contend that the pre-1900 struggles (Mexicans versus Anglos) had "faded" by the new century due to the small number of Latinos who had been present earlier and the cultural disintegration that had taken place. For them, the post-1900 migrants represented "a completely new period in the history of the Spanish speaking people in the Southwest" (13). On the other hand, the violent reaction in Texas to El Plan de San Diego in 1915 and the anxieties stirred by the Zimmerman Note two years later suggest that the historical memory had actually not faded entirely.

27. Gonzalez and Fernandez also maintain that "The recent regional development of the Southwest has depended on massive east-to-west U.S. migration and south-to-north Mexican migration" (13). They make a strong case for their argument that "the Mexican American migrants to the United States have also been central to the construction of the national economy of the United States for more than a hundred years" (xiii, and 13, 38, 58, 181–82). On the persistent stereotyping, see Gonzalez and Fernandez, *Century of Chicano History*, 75–78.

28. Sánchez, *Becoming Mexican American*, 70, 44, 34–35, 64, 66; Richard White, "*It's Your Misfortune*," 446–47; and Gonzalez and Fernandez, *Century of Chicano History*, 38–43. To illustrate this point further, in 1911 some 60 percent of the workers in Arizona smelters and 43 percent of the miners were Mexican. Sánchez's data are based on a sample of only those who had applied for citizenship and, therefore, may or may not be representative of those who did not apply, or of those who did not remain in the country.

29. Albert Camarillo, *Chicanos in a Changing Society*, 31, 100, 167, 93, 155–57, 101, 49.

30. Ricardo Romo, "The Urbanization of Southwestern Chicanos in the Early Twentieth Century," in *New Directions in Chicano Scholarship*, ed. Ricardo Romo and Raymund Paredes, 184–89, table 1 (Santa Barbara: Center for Chicano Studies, University of California, Santa Barbara, 1984); Camarillo, *Chicanos in a Changing Society*, 127, 211.

31. Gonzalez and Fernandez, *Century of Chicano History*, 131–39, on citrus and vegetable crops and the central role of Mexican workers.

32. Camarillo, *Chicanos in a Changing Society*, 157, 213, 167, 165, 179–81, 215, 182, 221, 225–28.

33. Clement, quoted by McWilliams, *Factories*, 126.

34. Matt Garcia, *World of Its Own*, 61, 3–4, 37, 59.

35. Ibid., 69–70, 57–58, 75–76, 71–72, 98–99 (Hanna).

36. Ibid., 91–92 (Shuler), 94 (McWilliams, *Factories*), 38.

37. There are significant differences in the figures cited regarding Mexican population in the early years because their numbers did fluctuate, with many migrating as well as returning to Mexico in patterns of circular migration. Others were simply not counted. Thus, estimates will give higher figures, especially when authors are trying to calculate those beyond the second generation, not enumerated separately by ethnicity. (In 1910, some 163,000 Mexican American "whites" were enumerated and 583,442 in 1930; these are undoubtedly incomplete totals.). The figures in the text are from Griswold and De León, *North to Aztlán*, 61, 64, 65, and Foley, *White Scourge*, 42n5.

38. The Torres and Mares quotations are from Manuel Gamio, *The Mexican Immigrant: His Life Story* (New York: Arno Press, 1969 [1931]), 58, 139. Also, Camarillo, *Chicanos in a Changing Society*, 189, Sánchez, *Becoming Mexican American*, 69, David G. Gutierrez, *Walls and Mirrors: Mexican Americans, Mexican Immigrants, and the Poli-*

tics of Ethnicity (Berkeley: University of California Press, 1995), 59; and McWilliams, *North from Mexico*, 79.

39. Meinig, quoted by Limerick, *Legacy of Conquest*, 194; Oscar J. Martinez, *Troublesome Border* (Tucson: University of Arizona Press, 1988), and *Border People: Life and Society in the U.S.-Mexico Borderlands* (Tucson: University of Arizona, 1994), xviii, 16, 19, 35, 87.

40. Mario T. Garcia, *Mexican Americans: Leadership, Ideology, and Identity, 1930–1960* (New Haven, Conn.: Yale University Press, 1989), 178–82.

41. For example, during 1913, supporters of General Victoriano Huerta battled those of Venustiano Carranza and Pancho Villa, with all having troops and weapons in El Paso, which they also used as their respective base of operations. By April 1914, General John Pershing had brought 6,500 troops to the city to guard against attacks by Villa. Instead, Villa attacked Columbus, New Mexico (west of El Paso), on March 9, 1916, killing 18 and wounding many. By summer, 65,000 U.S. troops were present in the El Paso area, with Mexican Americans pledging loyalty to the United States and Mexicans doing likewise with various Mexican factions. See Mario T. Garcia, *Mexican Americans*, 183–96, and Michael C. Meyer and William L. Sherman, *The Course of Mexican History*, 5th ed. (New York: Oxford University Press, 1995), 539–41.

42. Mario Garcia, *Mexican Americans*, 4, 8, 66, 88, 65, 54, and Oscar J. Martinez, *Troublesome Border*, 45, 92.

43. David Montejano, *Anglos and Mexicans in the Making of Texas, 1836–1986* (Austin: University of Texas Press, 1987), 60–64, 104, 83–90, 109–14.

44. Arnoldo De Leon, "Region and Identity: Topographical Identities in Texas," 259–66 in *Many Wests*; quotations from Paul S. Taylor, *Mexican Labor in the United States: Dimmit County WGD, South Texas* (Chicago: University of Chicago Press, 1930), 1:335, 339, 338; Montejano, *Anglos and Mexicans*, 196. The Winter Garden District included Dimmit, Maverick, and Zavela Counties.

45. Mario Garcia, *Mexican Americans*, 41–43, 108–09; Gamio, *Mexican Immigrant*, 136, 139.

46. Benjamin H. Johnson, *Revolution in Texas: How a Forgotten Rebellion and Its Bloody Suppression Turned Mexicans into Americans* (New Haven, Conn.: Yale University Press, 2003), 1–5, 20, 126. Johnson stresses that leaders of the insurgency included Mexicans and *tejanos*. He also suggests that, with the considerable immigration taking place, the U.S. government decided to determine the exact size of the Mexican population, prompting its ill-fated effort to distinguish Mexicans by race in the 1930 census (apart from whites). The newly formed League of United Latin American Citizens spearheaded the campaign to get that classification reversed in the 1940 census.

In contrast to Johnson's thesis, Charles H. Harris III and Louis R. Sadler argue that El Plan de San Diego was hatched by Mexico's president Venustiano Carranza in order to halt the support being given to Pancho Villa. Harris and Sadler, *The Texas Rangers and the Mexican Revolution: The Bloodiest Decade, 1910–1920* (Albuquerque: University of New Mexico Press, 2004). See also the review of Johnson's book by Victoria Hennessey Cummins, "Review: Cummins on Johnson, *Revolution in Texas*," www.h-net.org/reviews/showrev.cgi?path=134461094059083, September 1, 2004.

47. Montejano, *Anglos and Mexicans*, 117–19, 135–51, 160, 195, 162; Paul S. Taylor, *Mexican Labor*, 390; and Foley, *White Scourge*, 44.

48. Central Texas: Dallas to the north, Corpus Christie to the south, Houston to the east, and San Antonio to the west (Foley, *White Scourge*, 15).

49. Patricia Limerick stated (*Legacy of Conquest*, 244) that "the Southwest depended on Mexican labor." Largely true but certainly not throughout the West. Vicente Mayer quotes Santo Cabrera in Utah, where there were so few Mexicans early in the century

that, "when you saw a Mexican woman, it was like seeing your mother." Not until the Revolution and the war would their numbers edge upward there. Until then, southern European immigrants (Greeks and Italians, especially) were the chief source of labor. In fact, as late as 1916 the Mexican consul in Salt Lake City was a Japanese labor contractor, Edward Daigoro Hashimoto. See Vicente Mayer, "After Escalante: The Spanish Speaking People of Utah," in *The Peoples of Utah*, 439–40.

50. Foley, *White Scourge*, 9, 13, 72, 87, 117, 140; Pomeroy, "On Becoming a Westerner," 280–81; Sarah Deutsch, "Landscape of Enclave Race Relations in the West, 1865–1990," pp. 110–11 in *Under an Open Sky: Rethinking America's Western Past*, ed. William Cronon, George Miles, and Jay Gitlin (New York: W. W. Norton, 1992). Deutsch reports that the sugar beet industry in Colorado recruited about 20,000 workers each year, mainly among Hispanos in southern Colorado and New Mexico. See Deutsch, *No Separate Refuge: Culture, Class, and Gender on an Anglo-Hispanic Frontier in the American Southwest, 1880–1940* (New York: Oxford University Press, 1987), 128–29. As mentioned above, German Russians were another major cohort of sugar beet harvest workers.

17. The First World War and Americanization

1. Acuña claimed (*Occupied America*, 181; 5th ed., 164–65) that many of the victims of the Ludlow attack were Mexicans, yet the brass plaque commemorating the event lists the names of the victims: Petrucci (2), Pedresone (2), Rubino, Costa (4), Bartolotti, Valdez (4), Tikas, Fyler, and Snyder. Maybe the Valdezes (three children and a mother) were Mexican, but most were Italian. See http://members.tripod.com/~RedRobin2/ index-29.html (accessed September 6, 2003). Regarding other events, see Schwantes, "Wage Earners," 445, 444, and Norman H. Clark's superb work, *Mill Town: A Social History of Everett, Washington* (Seattle: University of Washington Press, 1970), 79 (the quotation), 128, 131–84. Clark says only four were killed (214).

2. Mary Murphy, *Mining Cultures: Men, Women, and Leisure in Butte, 1914–1941* (Urbana: University of Illinois Press, 1997), 23–32; Malone, *Montana*, 272; Dodds, *American Northwest*, 203–204; Emmons, *Butte Irish*, 364–77; McWilliams, *Factories*, 182; Schwantes, "Wage Earners," 431–32, 446–47; Michael Malone and F. Ross Peterson, "Politics and Protest," in the *Oxford History of the West*, 512.

3. Higham, *Strangers in the Land*, 196, 198, 203–4, 205, 210–11, 213–16, 219–20, 227, 231. The Act of February 1917 is discussed below.

4. Nancy Gentile Ford, *Americans All! Foreign-Born Soldiers in World War I* (College Station: Texas A & M University Press, 2001), 17–22, 28–29, and Emmons, *Butte Irish*, 340–49, 354, 360–64.

5. Quotation in Frank Van Nuys, *Americanizing the West: Race, Immigrants, and Citizenship, 1890–1930* (Lawrence: University Press of Kansas, 2002), 1; Malone and Peterson, "Politics and Protest," 512; Higham, *Strangers in the Land*, 286–91.

6. Ford, *Americans All!* 41, 53–56, 61, 67–77, 80, 81, 137–38. Ford concentrated on camps in the eastern half of the country and did not furnish for the West in particular specific numbers enlisted or drafted or other instances of the plan's implementation, but she indicated that it was most likely done in other military installations in the region, given the extensive number of foreign-born men there. Ford, two e-mail messages to author, September 24, 2003. (Possibilities might include Camp Kearny, California, and Camps Del Rio and Kelly Field, in Texas.)

7. The following episodes are drawn from Malone and Peterson, "Politics and Protest," 511; Chris Cook, "The History of Hawai'i: Kelemania—Germans in Hawai'i," www.islander-magazine.com/germans.html (accessed September 2002); Dodds, *Ameri-*

can Northwest, 199; Don Hodgson and Vivien Hills, "Dream and Fulfillment: Germans in Wyoming," Peopling the High Plains, 56; Malone and Peterson, 511; T. Lindsay Baker, The First Polish Americans: Silesian Settlements in Texas (College Station: Texas A & M University Press, 1979), 125; "German and Austro-Hungarian Internment during World War One in the United States," http://www.people.memphis.edu/~kenichls/2602WWOneInternment.html; "The System of Arrest and Internment in the West 1917–1920," http://netfiles.uiuc.edu/rcunning/www/system.htm; and "The Western United States in World War One—Chronology of Events," http://netfiles.uiuc.edu/rcunning/www/westchr.htm (all three accessed April 28, 2005).

In late 2005 law students at the University of Montana began a movement to get the 64 sedition convictions reversed. See "The Montana Sedition Project," a University of Montana web site, which says 64 were convicted. http://www.umt.edu/journalism/student_resources/class_web_sites/media_law/sedition_project/faq.html. Reporter Maurice Possley then stated that 74 were convicted. See Possley, "Sedition Project Aims for Posthumous Pardons," Los Angeles Times, December 30, 2005: 36–37. However, in May 2006 Montana governor Brian Schweitzer actually pardoned 75 men and 3 women (and one other person had already been pardoned after the war) who had been convicted of sedition in 1918. Forty of the men and one of the women served time in state prison. See Jim Robbins, "Silence Broken, Pardons Granted 88 Years after Crimes of Sedition," New York Times, May 3, 2006: 1, 19; and John M. Barrows and Lynn Marshall, "War Critics Pardoned, Nearly 9 Decades Later," Los Angeles Times, May 4, 2006: 5.

A 1922 Oregon law against foreign language parochial schools was struck down, but by 1930 most such German language schools had changed or closed in that state. See Walter D. Kamphoefner, "German Americans: Paradoxes of a 'Model Minority,'" in Origins and Destinies: Immigration, Race and Ethnicity in America, ed. Silvia Pedraza and Rubén G. Rumbaut (Belmont, Calif.: Wadsworth, 1996), 158.

8. Emmons, Butte Irish, chapter 10; Acuña, Occupied America, 4th ed., 175–77 (5th ed., 180–81). The Los Angeles Times took to describing the Brown Scare with such inflammatory lines as "Sedition conspiracy and plots in the very air. . . . Los Angeles is headquarters for this vicious system, and it is here that the deals between German and Mexican representatives are frequently made." Limerick, Legacy of Conquest, 252; Romo, "Urbanization," 96, 106; McWilliams, North from Mexico, 111–12.

In contrast to Acuña's assessment regarding the emergence of Mexican Americans, George Sánchez claimed that "A more generic form of Chicano identity . . . began to dominate Mexican American cultural life" in the 1920s, and then, during the 1930s, one could see in Los Angeles "the rapid transformation of the population from a community dominated by the Mexican-born to one centered around the American-born" (146, 228).

9. Van Nuys, Americanizing the West, 2, 4–6, 8, 12, 15, 17, 18–19, 24–25, 99, 105. The quotations are on pp. 4–5, 18, 24, 15, 17. See also Sánchez, Becoming Mexican American, chapter 4, regarding the program efforts during the 1920s.

10. Van Nuys, Americanizing the West, 59, 61, 65–67 (quotation), 104–107, 109 (quotation), 191 (quotation).

18. State and Federal Laws and Decisions, 1917–1920

1. Daniels, Politics of Prejudice, 44, 58–62, 87–92. Suzuki, "Impotent or Important?" 9–10; Takaki, Strangers, 27, 46, 203–08; Yuji Ichioka, The Issei: The World of the First

Generation Japanese Immigrants, 1885–1924 (New York: Free Press, 1988), 71–72, 227–28. Alaska, Hawai'i, Nevada, and Colorado did not enact Alien Land Laws.

2. Daniels, *Politics of Prejudice*, 47–63, with quotations on 55 and 61.

3. Ichioka, *Issei*, 226–43, Chan, *Asian Americans*, 95–96, and Takaki, *Strangers*, 205. Ichioka reported a 2-1 vote (p. 225) in favor of the 1920 Proposition 1, but Suzuki put it at 3-1 (p. 10), and she is correct. The vote was 668,483 to 222,086 (74.1 percent to 24.9 percent). The 1923 amendment forbids ineligible aliens to "acquire, possess, enjoy, use, cultivate, occupy, and transfer real property."

4. Suzuki, "Impotent or Important?" 17. The crops included grapes, fruits, nuts, berries, cantaloupes, vegetables, potatoes, and onions. Because many non-farm occupational avenues remained closed to the Issei, by the eve of the Second World War more than half of Issei workers were still in agriculture.

5. Van Nuys, *Americanizing the West*, 19–20; Takaki, *Strangers*, 203; and Rechs Ann Pedersen, "Alien Land Laws" (2001), http://www.santacruzpl.org/history/ww2/9066/land.shtml (accessed July 7, 2003). For a discussion of court cases challenging the Alien Land Acts, see Hyung-chan Kim, *A Legal History of Asian Americans, 1790–1990* (Westport, Conn.: Greenwood Press, 1994), 126–31.

6. Reed Ueda observes that the exemptions included an alien's father and grandfathers over 55 and mother, wife, grandmothers, and unmarried sisters, thus ensuring that the new literacy requirement would not hinder family reunification. One can also see that as a stepping-stone to non-quota categories in subsequent immigration laws. See Ueda, "Historical Patterns of Immigrant Status and Incorporation in the United States," pp. 302–303 in *E Pluribus Unum?* ed. Gerstle and Mollenkopf.

7. Mark Reisler, *By the Sweat of Their Brow: Mexican Immigrant Labor in the United States, 1900–1940* (Westport, Conn.: Greenwood Press, 1976), 27–38, and Acuña, 5th ed., 175–76. Arizona cotton growers used 30,000 workers between 1918 and 1921. Sugar beet growers were especially responsible for getting the program extended beyond the war.

Reed Ueda points out that the immigrant temporary worker programs implemented during both world wars and then from the Korean War to December 1964 represented a unique departure in that these workers were admitted "only to serve as labor and . . . were excluded from a position within civil society." They could not remain, nor could they qualify for citizenship. See Ueda, "Historical Patterns," 303.

8. Chris M. Sterba, *Good Americans: Italian and Jewish Immigrants during the First World War* (New York: Oxford University Press, 2003), 57, 71. Sterba points out that, in response to the Selective Service Act of May 18, 1917, there were 487,434 immigrants drafted, including some 200,000 who waived exemptions. About 280,000 applied for expedited citizenship.

19. The Early 1920s

1. Van Nuys, *Americanizing the West*, 58; Kraut, *Huddled Masses*, 206–11; Higham, *Strangers in the Land*, 242–299, 305–06 (quotation is from 269); and Elliott R. Barkan, *And Still They Come: Immigrants and American Society, 1920 to the 1990s* (Wheeling, Ill.: Harlan Davidson, 1996), chapter 1. Higham also noted—in response to the flood of Jewish immigrants and the fact that many political activists were Jewish—a widespread surge of anti-Semitism promoted by the KKK and such hostile leaders as Henry Ford and his *Dearborn Independent*. They were portrayed as the "symbol of foreign radicalism" (279).

2. Higham, *Strangers in the Land*, 311.

3. Barkan, *And Still They Come*, 11–12. Figures are from table 2.1; Desmond King, *Making Americans*, 295.

4. See Ichioka, *Issei*, 219–24, and 226 (newspaper quotation), and Takaki, *Strangers*, 208.

5. Takaki, *Strangers*, 299, and Hyung-chan Kim, *Legal History*, 119–22.

Introduction to Part 3

1. Kazuo Ito, *Issei: A History of Japanese Immigrants in North America*, trans. Shinichiro Nakamura and Jean S. Gerard (Seattle: Japanese Community Service, Executive Committee for Publication of *Issei*, 1973), 624–25. The quotation comes from a new immigrant's experience in a store when trying to request a "bag."

2. Herman Feldman, *Racial Factors in American Industry* (New York: Harper and Brothers, 1931), 133, 137; McWilliams, *Factories in the Field*, 103–104; Celler, quoted by Cheryl Shanks, *Immigration and the Politics of American Sovereignty, 1890–1990* (Ann Arbor: University of Michigan Press, 2001), 67; McWilliams, *Southern California Country*, 143.

3. Starr, *Americans*, 443.

4. Richard White, *"It's Your Misfortune,"* 432–33. Some four decades ago Dorothy O. Johansen suggested that many easterners had also moved to the Midwest before going on to the Pacific Northwest and, therefore, the Midwest was truly a "crucible in which the population of the Pacific Northwest was molded." This was part of her thesis that persons of different geographical origins going to the same location will be more similar than those of the same origins going to different destinations because the former are responding to similar pull factors—which are then combined with comparable motives and expectations among those who follow. Oregon, she posited, drew people who saw it as "safely American"—respectable, sober, modest, conservative; they were less often risk takers than others going westward. Johansen, "A Working Hypothesis for the Study of Migrations," *Pacific Historical Review*, February 1967, reprinted in *Experiences in a Promised Land*, ed. Edwards and Schwantes, 43–46.

20. A World of Peoples

1. Oral interview with Mrs. Maria Abastilla Beltran, "Filipino Pioneer: A Woman's Experience," Washington State Archives, Olympia, Filipino-King Project, FIL-KNG 75—9ck, May 5, 1975.

2. As discussed below, in 1935 the U.S. government offered to pay the travel costs for Filipinos willing to return to their homeland, but this free offer was seen as a ploy to bar them from easily returning to the United States. Accepting it was also regarded, except by students, as an admission of having failed in America.

3. Oral interview with Zacarias M. Manangan. "Filipino Pioneer: Union Organizer in Auburn, Washington," Washington State Archives, Olympia: Filipino-King Project, FIL-KNG 75 –30ck, September 30, 1975.

4. "Life History and Social Document of Andrew Kan, Seattle, Washington, August 22, 1924," University of Oregon, Eugene, William C. Smith Collection, Box 1, Folder 25, File no. 178A.

5. Oral Memoirs of George Moses Fadal, July 23, 1977," Baylor University, Waco, Institute for Oral History, 1994.

6. "Interview with Florence Flaks, July 16, 1975," University of Washington, Seattle, Jewish Archives Project, Accession no. 2519.

7. "Interview with Mr. T. Torikai, July 8, 1924," Eugene: University of Oregon, William C. Smith collection, Box 1, Folder 22, File no. 156. No first name was given. The typed text says "K. Torikai," and I am assuming the text had the correct first initial.

8. The following excerpts are from Gamio, *Mexican Immigrant*, 89–91, 14–19, 146–49, 159–62, 79–86, 131–33, 67, 96, 181–82.

9. See also attitudes regarding citizenship expressed by Fernando Sanchez, Gonzalo Plancarte, and Vincente Gaumer. Gamio, *Mexican Immigrant*, 67, 96, 181–82.

10. Roger Daniels, *Guarding the Golden Door: American Immigration Policy and Immigrants since 1882* (New York: Hill and Wang, 2004), 46, 49. Hundreds of Asians and Filipinos in the Armed Forces in 1917–1918 were entitled to citizenship but had to wait until Congress reaffirmed that any person who had served was eligible regardless of race (Act of June 24, 1935): "any alien veteran of the world war heretofore ineligible to citizenship because not a free white person or of African nativity or of African descent may be naturalized under this act."

11. Nugent, *Into the West*, 165, 218, 133. For sure, the refusal in 1905 of Anglo-dominated Arizona to join with its multicultural, multi-racial New Mexico neighbor as one large, new state symbolized some of the existing divisions. Malone and Etulain, *American West*, 61.

12. Owen Edwards, "Antique Road Show," *Smithsonian*, November 2003: 32, 34.

13. Sarah Deutsch, "Landscape of Enclaves: Race Relations in the West, 1865–1990," in *Under an Open Sky: Rethinking America's Western Past*, ed. William Cronon, George Miles, and Jay Gitlin (New York: W.W. Norton, 1992), 123; Richard White, "*It's Your Misfortune*," 284; Richard White, "Western History," rev. ed. (Washington: American Historical Association, 1997), 5; Sarah Deutsch, George I. Sánchez, and Gary Okihiro, "Contemporary Peoples/Contested Places," in *Oxford History of the American West*, ed. Milner, O'Connor, and Sandweiss, 639–41.

14. Different Asian groups may have lived in proximity to one another there, but the dynamics of ethnic interaction in such instances were quite apparent. Various peoples would interact for economic or commercial reasons, recalled one resident, but they otherwise "just never intermingled." Dorothy Bintang Fujita Rony, "You Got to Move Like Hell: Trans-Pacific Colonialism and Filipina/o Seattle, 1919–1941" (Ph.D. diss., Yale University, 1996), 140–42, and Nomura, "Tsugiki, a Grafting," 140.

15. Nugent, *Into the West*, 153, 158, 171, and Donald Worster, *Rivers of Empire: Water, Aridity, and the Growth of the American West* (New York: Pantheon Books, 1985). Regarding mechanization, even where it was incorporated, not all of the agricultural production could be mechanized; the need for laborers remained strong.

16. Malone and Etulain, *American West*, 49.

17. Abbott, *Metropolitan Frontier*, and Carol O'Connor, "A Region of Cities," in *Oxford History*, 535–63. Nugent refers to the years 1901–1913 as the "golden years" of home-steading, including the Desert Land Act of 1907, granting 640 acres if the land was irrigated within three years. See Nugent, *Into the West*, 154. Carl Abbott referred to the 1900–1920 decades as "the era of the federally sustained frontier" ("Federal Presence," 495). At the same time, during that period the centrality of the West's urban centers became indisputable.

18. Nugent, *Into the West*, 129–32, concluded that the transformation from rural society to metropolitan society, which plays a critical role in the economic integration of the West, "was the major change in American history" (129). See, too, Malone and Etulain, *American West*, 31–37.

19. Erika Lee points out that the Immigration Service began recording entries and inspecting aliens along the Mexican border in 1903. However, that "did not apply to

Mexicans at all," but rather to the Chinese. Lee, "Enforcing the Borders," 71–72. The Act of May 28, 1924 (43 Stat. 240; 8 U.S.C 118) was entitled "Act Creating Border Patrol."

20. Abbott, "Federal Presence," 474–79, 482.

21. Starr, *Inventing the Dream*, chapter 10; Stephen Kinzer, "Rescuing the First Cowboy Movie Star from a Canyon of Obscurity [Max Aronson]," *New York Times* July 17, 2003; and "Jewish Stars over Hollywood," http://100777.com/node/179?PHPSESSID =328252414368881b5c9696a5cbob5d7 (accessed May 1, 2005).

22. Malone and Etulain, *American West*, 31–43; Ford, *Americans All!* and Chris M. Sterba, *Good Americans: Italian and Jewish Immigrants during the First World War* (New York: Oxford University Press, 2003).

23. Schwantes, *Radical Heritage*, 213–16. See also Van Nuys, *Americanizing the West*, passim; Robert A. Divine, *American Immigration Policy, 1924–1952* (New Haven: Yale University Press, 1957), 6–8; Higham, *Strangers in the Land*, chapters 8 and 9; Robert F. Zeidel, *Immigrants, Progressives, and Exclusion Politics: The Dillingham Commission, 1900–1927* (DeKalb: Northern Illinois University Press, 2004), 147; and Shanks, *Immigration and the Politics*, 81–82.

24. The quotations are from Bill Ong Hing, *Defining America through Immigration Policy* (Philadelphia: Temple University Press, 2004), 60–61. "Tribal Twenties" is John Higham's title for his chapter 10 on the 1920s in *Strangers in the Land*.

21. Demographic Trends

1. The following section has been adapted from 28 tables in the 1920 Census: Department of Commerce, Bureau of the Census, *Fourteenth Census of the United States Taken in the Year 1920*, vol. 2, *Population, General Report and Analytical Tables* (Washington, D.C.: Government Printing Office, 1922), chapter 1 (Race), tables 10 (p. 36), 11 (37), 12 (46); chapter 2 (Population), table 5 (114); chapter 5 (State of Birth), tables 18 (635), 21 (646), 22 (651); chapter 6 (Country of Birth), tables 2 (693), 3 (694), 4 (695), 6 (697), 10 (722); chapter 7 (Year of Immigration), tables 1 (779), 4 (782), 6 (785); chapter 8 (Citizenship), tables 1 (804), 2 (805), 6 (808), 7 (809), 8 (816), 9 (818), 10 (826); chapter 9 (Foreign White Stock), tables 1 (897), 5 (902), 8 (905); and vol. 3, *Population, Composition . . . by States* (including Hawaii and Alaska), 1158–89.

2. There were 2.06 million foreign born and 2.79 million second generation, totaling 4.85 million foreign stock in the West. Alternatively, there were 1.87 million white foreign born and 2.66 million second generation for a white foreign stock total of 4.54 million. Thus, about 310,000 were foreign stock peoples of color.

3. John Palmer Gavit, *Americans by Choice* (New York: Harper & Brothers, 1922), 210, 215, 216, 226, 241. The 26,284 petitions he analyzed were drawn from 28 federal and state courts, of which only three were in the West (Portland and Seattle). Length of residence was based on 13,849 petitions of men who were 21 or older upon arrival. While there is no way to be certain if his statistical findings were fully applicable to those in the West, I do believe his conclusions regarding residence and income constituted primary factors there, too.

4. All of these figures are somewhat provisional. The 1900 census, which reported 58 percent of all foreign-born males (21 and older) were naturalized, had 14.9 percent non-reporting. That is too great to make the figures entirely reliable. In 1910 that figure declined to 11.7 percent, meaning that one in nine was never counted for this census variable, likewise casting some doubt on the figures' reliability. By 1920 the rate of non-response had fallen to 5.2 percent among males and 6.7 percent among females.

5. Usually, a Declaration of Intent to become a citizen ("first papers") was required

for persons seeking a homestead (and for some occupations, too). The changes in the homestead laws during this period, as described earlier in Anna Hought's life story, for example, enticed many to apply for one—which could also account in part for the spike in the number of applications for first papers. The recency of arrival (nearly 1.25 million of those in the 1920 census had entered between 1914 and 1919, with almost 347,000 of them in the West) and the pressures for demonstrations of loyalty by both the Americanization movement and the general wartime sentiments likely provided additional incentives. When the war ended and the pressures were reduced, not all would follow through with petitions for naturalization. Using data from 1908–1918, Gavit found that 35 percent of those filing first papers had not gone on to petition for naturalization within the seven years allotted for petitioning (221).

6. See notes 3 and 4 of chapter 21, above. Gavit reported that more than two-thirds of the men filing petitions in his sample were married (247). A comparison of the men and women also suggests the presence of many single men who were yet to initiate such actions. For example, in Idaho, Utah, and Washington, the percentages of naturalized men were 60.7, 56.9, and 53.9, respectively, whereas the women's figures were 75.8, 71.7, and 65.1.

7. Yukiko Kimura points out that prior to 1905 some 50 Japanese had been naturalized in various state courts, including Tomizō Katsunuma, who went on to become a U.S. immigration inspector in Hawai'i. See Kimura, *Issei*, 16. Regarding Asians who served in the U.S. Armed Forces during World War One and their eligibility for citizenship, see note 10 of chapter 20, above.

22. *Institutionalizing the Quota System*

1. Quotations are from Desmond King, *Making Americans*, 77; Zeidel, *Immigrants, Progressives*, 3, 115; and Shanks, *Immigration and the Politics*, 34. For a succinct summary of the Dillingham Commission recommendations, see King, *Making Americans*, 76–77, as well as Zeidel's discussion of the Progressive roots of the commission in his first chapter.

2. Kristofer Allerfeldt, *Race, Radicalism, Religion, and Restriction: Immigration in the Pacific Northwest, 1890–1924* (Westport, Conn.: Praeger, 2003), 115, 117, 121.

3. Divine, *American Immigration Policy*, 13, 24. John Higham had written that, with the depression of 1920–1921, the expenditures for Americanization projects no longer seemed worthwhile (*Strangers in the Land*, 261–62). The crusade was also falling apart by 1921 because of the collapse of the Red Scare. Once the fear of a Bolshevik revolution dissipated, "fear of a radical danger" gave way to "a racial bias." To that, Cheryl Shanks adds, "a crisis (World War One) made an idea (that ethnic heterogeneity would tear apart the country) seem plausible" (*Immigration and the Politics*, 29).

Allerfeldt, among others, also noted that developments in workplace technology reduced "the requirements for itinerant laborers. . . . By 1924 the need for a 'casual', itinerant, floating labor force in the [Pacific Northwest] region was vastly [lessened] from what it had been in 1890" (*Race, Radicalism*, 102). While that ultimately did not prove to be the case, for a time that perception softened business communities' opposition to general immigration restrictions.

4. Divine, *American Immigration Policy*, 6–8, 10, 13–14, 16–17, 24–25. Mae M. Ngai, "The Architecture of Race in American Immigration Law: A Reexamination of the Immigration Act of 1924," *Journal of American History* 86.1 (June 1999): 80. Divine had concluded, too, that the four "keys to an understanding of American immigration policy" were "economic, social (racial), and nationalistic aspects and considerations of foreign policy" (25).

5. Principally, *Porterfield et al. v. Webb* (263 U.S. 225) and *Terrace et al. v. Thompson* (263 U.S. 197), both November 12, 1923.

6. As Jun Kitahara [pseudonym by Michio Kitahara] succinctly put it in his book *Naze Taiheiyō Sensō ni natta no ka* (Why did the Pacific War break out?) (Tokyo: TBS-Britannica, 2001), "Masanao Hanihara, Japanese Ambassador to the United States at that time, wrote an official letter dated April 10, 1924, to Secretary of the State [Charles Evans] Hughes, stating that the new immigration law would result in extremely grave consequences." Congressional leaders took those ill-chosen words as a threat. Excerpted in "Why Did Japan Attack Pearl Harbor?" http://p-h.ifrance.com/japan_ph.php?lang=en (accessed December 15, 2005).

7. Orlando Patterson maintains that those who appeared to be white sought acceptance "within the Caucasian chalk circle" and "were usually welcomed as long as they could prove that they had no African "blood." "Non-blackness" was becoming a "powerful unifying force." Quoted by Desmond King, *Making Americans*, 23.

8. See Ngai, "Architecture of Race," 70, Desmond King, *Making Americans*, 14; and Ian F. Haney Lopez, *White by Law: The Legal Construction of Race* (New York: New York University Press, 1996), 171. Shanks (262) provides a chart detailing the quota allocations versus the proportion of the world's population and nation states in the various regions. For example, 55 percent of the world's population then was in the Asiatic Barred Zone, which received 0.5 percent of the allotments.

9. Section 11 (d) of the Act explicitly omitted from the calculations of the nation's "origins" those persons native to the Western Hemisphere, descendants of slaves (mostly from a wide band of kingdoms and then colonies across central and west Africa), and groups ineligible for citizenship. While an overall Hemisphere ceiling of 120,000 was enacted in 1965, no country quotas were set aside for those born in or native to the Western Hemisphere, nor would any be imposed until 1976. Nonetheless, the inference went beyond the allocation of immigrant slots to the assumption that such classes of people were not part of America's founding peoples.

The preference system, along with the 20,000 per country limit, was extended to the Americas effective in 1978. See David M. Reimers, *Still the Golden Door: The Third World Comes to America*, 2nd ed. (New York: Columbia University Press, 1985), 84–87.

10. The exception would be Chinese, who, under the Act of December 17, 1943, became the first Asian people eligible for citizenship. Others were added in 1946 and 1950, and all persons were made eligible in 1952.

11. For additional details, see Daniels, *Guarding the Golden Door*, 49–58, and Mae M. Ngai's excellent chapter on the background and impact of the 1924 law in *Impossible Subjects: Illegal Aliens and the Making of Modern America* (Princeton, N.J.: Princeton University Press, 2004), chapter 2.

12. The following are specific numbers and percentages for the topics discussed in the next few pages.

First, during the second half of the 1920s (1925–1929 versus 1920–1924), southern and eastern European immigration fell by 76.1 percent, that of Asians by 70.2 percent, whereas northern and western European numbers rose by 22.2 percent. Admissions of Canadians increased by nearly 12 percent (to 924,515 for 1921–1930) and that of Mexicans by 28.5 percent (for a decade total of 459,287).

Second, during the 1920s the West's foreign-born percentage of the total population dropped from 14.9 percent to 12.5 percent, although the actual number went up 9.9 percent (203,854). Because the number of native-born Americans in the West jumped by 30.8 percent (427,367), we see this decline in the *percentage* of foreign born.

Third, in the West the second-generation population leaped by 41 percent (1.092

million) during the 1920s, while elsewhere the growth was only 12 percent (2.401 million). Still, the fact that the entire native-born population in the West jumped 34.4 percent (compared with 16.1 percent outside the West) accounts for the comparatively small rise in the *percentage* of second generation among the West's native born, from 21.2 percent to just 22.78 percent (24.1 percent outside the West). See Barkan, *And Still They Come*, table 2.1 (p. 197). Immigration data drawn from *Annual Reports of the Commissioner of Immigration*, 1911–1924, table 9; 1925–1927, table 24; 1928–1931, table 28. Ports of entry data were derived from unpublished tables provided to the author from the INS's Statistics Division. Census data were adapted from the Census Bureau, U.S. Department of Commerce, *Fifteenth Census of the United States: 1930* (Washington, D.C.: GPO, 1932); vol. 2, *Population, General Report*, tables 4, 6, 11, 12, 17, 18, 20, 21, 22, 35, table 9 (281), tables 4–11 (498–511); and vol. 3, part 1, *Population, Alabama-Missouri*, tables 26, 27, 37, 40, 41.

13. The term legislatively "curtail" refers to the fact that administrative procedures and requirements now existed and could be enforced along the border, which would, in effect, curb admissions without having to resort to any new law specifically targeting Mexicans. Herman Feldman noted, regarding a 1930 bill to limit Mexican immigration, that the U.S. Department of Agriculture opposed the measure because of the labor needs of land reclamation projects and agriculture, "both of which rest heavily upon the shoulders of Mexican labor" (108). Also opposed were key pressure groups, such as the Arizona Cotton Growers Association. In addition, the administration's desire to promote a good neighbor policy (a phrase earlier used by President Theodore Roosevelt), the extensive capital investments in the Americas, and the reality that about one-third of the nation's foreign trade was with the Americas all combined to discourage any policy that could have negative international consequences, especially in economic terms.

See Wayne Patterson, *Korean Frontier*, 174, and Hing, 122, 125. Regarding Bogardus's statement, see *The Mexican in the United States* (New York: Arno Press, 1970 [USC Press, 1934]), 88.

14. In addition, the number of foreign born departing from outside the West did decrease more dramatically than among those emigrating from the West.

15. The relocation by Mexicans may have been particularly relevant here, since many were migratory and subsequently headed for the Midwest. For example, 385,929 persons said they were headed for Arizona or Texas (1920–1929), but in the 1930 census only 111,567 persons in those two states reported that they had arrived in those same years, a difference of 71 percent (274,362). That alone equaled 57 percent of the gap between the immigration and census data.

16. In 1930 the Census Bureau separated Mexicans from whites, sparking a firestorm of protest by Mexicans. In 1940 they were reintegrated with other white populations, and many of the 1930 tables were recalculated and included in the 1940 reports. My inclusion of Mexicans is therefore based on 1940 tables that included the revised 1930 data.

17. In 1930 the percentage of western immigrants living on farms was most apparent among six groups: Czechs (48 percent), Swiss (36 percent), Germans (25 percent), Danes (22 percent), Finns (21 percent), and Norwegians (nearly 19 percent).

18. The data in this and the prior paragraph are derived from the *Annual Report to the Commissioner General of Immigration*, 1926 (table 82) and 1930 (table 91), and from the Department of Labor, 1930 *Census*, vol. 2, *Population: General Reports*, table 11, p. 508. See also Sánchez, *Becoming Mexican American*, table 8, p. 66.

The figures reported here rest on the assumption that both the immigration and census data were reasonably accurate. The number during the 1920s who came to California and left (or never arrived there) was only 35,300 versus the 217,600 figure for

Texas, reaffirming the Mexican patterns of entering and moving on to other work sites, such as in the Midwest and Southwest. (Also see note 15, above.)

23. Divided Yet Interlinked: The Rural West

1. "Interview with Inder Singh (Hindu [Sikh?—nearly all persons named Singh were actually Sikhs rather than Hindus])—El Centro, May 31, 1924," William C. Smith Collection, University of Oregon, Eugene, Box 1, Folder 35, File no. A237. In addition, Karen Isaksen Leonard found that 304 such Punjabi-Mexican marriages took place, mostly in Southern California, beginning in 1916. Seventy-four others included marriage with African American women, nine of them in Northern California. Leonard, *South Asian Americans*, 51.

2. Willard A. Schnurr, "Hindus in Los Angeles," William C. Smith Collection, Box 1, Folder 41, File no. 273 (n.d. but circa 1923–1924). Regarding his population figures, Karen Isaksen Leonard's table (70), lists 1,720 in California in 1920, down from 1,948 in 1910.

3. "Mr. Chand's Statement," William C. Smith Collection, Box 1, Folder 35, File no. 235.

4. Chloe Holt, "Japanese in Orange County, January 1925," William C. Smith Collection, Box 1, Folder 42, File no. 274.

5. See Ogawa, *Kodomo no tame ni*, 223–25, regarding the efforts to recruit second-generation workers. See also Edward D. Beechert, *Working in Hawaii: A Labor History* (Honolulu: University of Hawai'i Press, 1985), 241–43, 253, and William Carlson Smith, *Americans in Process*, 60.

6. Montgomery, *Fall of the House of Labor*, 85, and Pursinger, "Japanese Settle in Oregon," 260.

7. Rasmussen, *New Land, New Lives*, 41; Nielsen, *Danish Americans*, 11; and Dodds, *American Northwest*, 126.

8. Takami, *Divided Destiny*, 20; Starr, *Endangered Dreams*, 62, 63; Teresa Amott and Julie Matthaei, *Race, Gender, and Work: A Multi-cultural Economic History of Women in the United States*, rev. ed. (Boston: South End Press, 1996), 226; Tamura, *Hood River Issei*, 87, 76; Pursinger, "Japanese Settle in Oregon," 257; Ito, *Issei*, 459; McWilliams, *Factories*, 109; Irwin Tang, "Japanese Americans in the Lone Star State," *AsianWeek* April 22, 2004: 12–13; and Howard Lindsay, "Texans Mark 100 Years of Japanese Texan Pioneers," [JACL] *Pacific Citizen*, May 7, 2004: 5. Seito Saibara had his wife and son bring him 300 pounds of the superior Shinriki rice seed.

9. The two quotations are from Ito, *Issei*, 437, 446.

10. Ito, *Issei*, 157–63, 430–58; Department of Commerce, Bureau of the Census, *Fourteenth Census of the United States Taken in the Year 1920*, vol. 5, *Agriculture: General Report and Analytical Tables* (Washington, D.C.: GPO, 1922), table 22, p. 310; Suzuki, "Impotent or Important?" table 2; and McWilliams, *Factories*, 116.

Valerie Matsumoto reports that 46 percent of employed Japanese in 1925 were still in agriculture (*Farming the Home Place*, 11). In 1932 in California, Japanese farmers owned 38,000 acres and leased 250,000, but a decade later, on the eve of their incarceration, they owned 69,000 acres yet leased only 163,000 acres (Suzuki, "Impotent or Important?" table 2). Matsumoto also noted that at least two of the agricultural colonies established near Livingston, California, by Abiko Kyutaro—Yamato and Cortez— survived both the Depression and the relocation (Matsumoto, 10–12).

Ronald Takaki enumerated the states that also enacted alien land acts, including, in addition to California, "Washington, Arizona, Oregon, Idaho, Nebraska, Texas, Kansas,

Louisiana, Montana, New Mexico, Minnesota, and Missouri," as well as Florida (*Strangers*, 206–207).

11. Matsumoto, *Farming the Home Place*, 33–34, and Pursinger, "Japanese Settle in Oregon," 255. In 1928 there were 208 Issei and 265 Nisei children in the Hood River Valley (Tamura, *Hood River Issei*, 102).

12. The two quotations are from Winther, *Great Northwest*, 425, and Evelyn Nakano Glenn and Rhacel Salazar Parreñas, "The Other Issei: Japanese Immigrant Women in the Pre-World War Two Period," in *Origins and Destinies: Immigration, Race, and Ethnicity in America*, ed. Silvia Pedraza and Rubén G. Rumbaut (Belmont, Calif.: Wadsworth, 1996), 128–29.

13. Matt Garcia, *World of Its Own*, 91–92.

14. "Interview with L. C. Lee of El Centro, California, June 1924," William C. Smith Collection, Box 1, Folder 17, File no. 93.

15. "Interview with W. S. Fawcett, El Centro, California," William C. Smith Collection, Box 1, Folder 14, File no. 72.

16. Cletus Daniel, "Communist Organizers in the Imperial Valley," excerpt from *Bitter Harvest: A History of California Farmworkers, 1870–1941* [1981], in *Major Problems in California History*, ed. Sucheng Chan and Spencer Olin (Boston: Houghton Mifflin, 1997), 288.

17. Section 3 of the 1917 Act denied admission to immigrants over age 16 who could not read in English or their native language except those entering who were the fathers or grandfathers of U.S. citizens and over 55 and the mothers, grandmothers, wives, or unmarried or widowed daughters of U.S. citizens. Except during the 1917–1921 period, this applied also to Mexicans seeking admission, which contributed to the decision many made to begin entering illegally.

18. Pomeroy, *Pacific Slope*, 90; McWilliams, *Factories*, 90; Paul S. Taylor, "Mexican Labor in the United States: Dimmit County, Winter Garden District, South Texas," in Taylor's *Mexican Labor in the United States*, vol. 1 (Berkeley: University of California Press, 1930), 378, 349; and Matt Garcia, *World of Its Own*, 89. The reverse perception to that quoted here was also true regarding Mexicans returning to Mexico, noted Camille Guerin-Gonzalez. Hacendados reported that those who worked in the United States "soon became unmanageable and of little use." Camille Guerin-Gonzales, *Mexican Workers and American Dreams: Immigration, Repatriation, and California Farm Labor, 1900–1939* (New Brunswick, N.J.: Rutgers University Press, 1994), 36.

19. Bogardus, *Mexican in the United States*, 85–86 n.; Montejano, *Anglos and Mexicans*, 178; Guerin-Gonzalez, *Mexican Workers*, 45, 44; Matt Garcia, *World of Its Own*, 39; and Thomas E. Sheridan, *Arizona*, 215, 214. At this time Mexican workers were also establishing a significant presence in the sugar beet industry and in various factories in the Midwest. The Teague quotation is from Matt Garcia, 93. See also Starr, *Inventing the Dream*, 173.

20. McWilliams, *Factories*, 198; Matt Garcia, *World of Its Own*, 59–60, 69–70, 88; Paul S. Taylor, "Dimmit," 379; Mario T. Garcia, *Mexican Americans*, 13–14; Foley, *White Scourge*, 38–39; and Feldman, *Racial Factors*, 113, 104. Gonzalez and Fernandez emphasize the same point about the influence of Mexican stereotypes on perceptions of Mexicans and Mexican Americans in the United States. See *Century of Chicano History*, 73–78 and 84–88.

In Helen Papanikolas's account of her father's life, recounted earlier (Yoryis Zeese), she noted that money would be sent home to improve life there, "and those who would come after would never know the horrible, debasing poverty that had sent the young immigrants into voluntary exile." Such a description could well apply to many others, Mexican peasants in particular. Papanikolas, *Greek Odyssey*, 174.

21. Starr, *Endangered Dreams*, 236–39. Keith Windschuttle offers a counter perspective to that put forth by John Steinbeck's *Grapes of Wrath* and echoed by Starr. Windschuttle maintains that 315,000 Okies went to California during the 1930s, following 250,000 who had come before the Depression (1920s) and preceding double the 1930s figure who will arrive during the 1940s. Black Sunday, the epic dust storm, occurred on April 14, 1935, and of those entering between 1935 and 1940, only 36 percent had come from farms. Half were from urban areas with decidedly non-rural occupations. Overall, about 100,000 went to Los Angeles and 250,000 to San Francisco and San Diego. The San Joaquin and San Bernardino and Imperial Valleys drew most of the agricultural workers (7,000 and 20,000, respectively), many of whom already had relatives in California.

Moreover, he adds, and contrary to the stereotypes, many of those who had farmed had come from areas that had not been affected by dust storms, which were worst in Oklahoma's western panhandle, but were tenants evicted by landowners encouraged by the 1933 Agricultural Adjustment Act subsidies to curb production. The economic boom of the 1940s drew the greatest number from the south central states. Whatever the original push factor, Okies who had taken farm labor jobs in California were quick to leave the fields and seek urban employment even before the wartime economy had fully unleashed huge job opportunities. Keith Windschuttle, "Steinbeck's Myth of the Okies," *New Criterion* 20.10 (June 2002): 3–4, 6, www.newcriterion.com/archive/20/jun02/steinbeck.htm (accessed December 15, 2005). See Elizabeth Royte's review of Timothy Eagan's *The Worst Hard Time: The Untold Story of Those Who Survived the Great American Dust Bowl*, in *New York Times Book Review*, December 25, 2005: 9.

22. Starr, *Endangered Dreams*, 61. Although Starr mentions 10,000 Volga Germans and 75,000 Portuguese, these are likely exaggerations because the 1920 census listed only 59,356 Portuguese foreign white stock for all of California. Germans from Russia were not listed separately and can only be estimated based on German mother tongue and birthplace (e.g., 82,000 Germans, Austrians, and Swiss in California, but 94,800 persons with a German mother tongue, and 27,225 persons born in Russia but only 14,000 with a Russian mother tongue). If ten thousand of the latter were present just in Fresno County (ignoring Russian-born, Yiddish mother-tongue persons), it would have been almost entirely during harvest time. More likely the number was in the thousands but less than 10,000, whereas such a number did live in Colorado, their principal location in the West. See 1920 Census, vol. 2, *Population*, table 5, p. 904, and table 10, p. 1001.

23. Because of the Census Bureau's reconfiguration of Mexicans as a small number of whites and most classified as a non-white race, there is no complete breakdown of all second-generation Mexican Americans. Hence, the figure in the text here includes some third or even later generations along with all other white, second-generation persons. At this time the figure for native born of native parents for Mexicans was still relatively small and largely concentrated in New Mexico and Texas. In 1940 the Bureau recombined the figures for Mexicans but did not recalculate all the 1930 tables. Using the 1930 Mexican "race" figure of 1.423 million and deducting 556,952 foreign born, it appears that half of the native-born Mexican Americans in the West were living in rural areas compared with 44.5 percent of the foreign born. 1930 census, vol. 2, *Population*, table 22 (p. 66).

24. William Carlson Smith, *Americans in Process*, 61; Takaki, *Strangers*, 316–18; Barbara M. Posadas, *The Filipino Americans* (Westport, Conn.: Greenwood Press, 1999), 15; Nugent, *Into the West*, 217. Posadas (23) points out that the U.S. Navy had early on begun recruiting Filipinos (as did the army fighting in the Philippines), and by 1922 over 5,000 had enlisted, although that number would decline to 3,922 a decade later. In addition, perhaps as many as 14,000 were still attending educational institutions into the 1930s.

25. Takaki, *Strangers*, 331–33; "Filipino American Elders, through the Decades of

the 1900s," a publication of the Stanford Geriatric Education Center, 1999. See http://www.gasi.org/diversity/cohort/filipino_am_cohort.htm (accessed January 3, 2004). William Carlson Smith reported (65) that the HSPA had also had a policy of paying for the return passage of Filipinos who had completed their contracts and that between June 1932 and June 1934 the number of Filipinos on the sugar plantations fell by 5,600, and even more so on the pineapple plantations.

The U.S. government would deflect pressures to legislate restrictions against Mexicans, as it would do with Filipinos, by strictly enforcing provisions against the admission of those "Likely to become a Public Charge" (LPC). The net effect on both groups was a drastic drop in admissions.

26. Manuel Buaken, *I Have Lived with the American People* (Caldwell, Idaho: Caxton Printers, 1948), 194, 199.

27. Pomeroy, *Pacific Slope*, 282.

28. The Federal Unemployment Tax Act also excluded farmworkers—here defined to include women packinghouse employees—except in Hawai'i. Under the Workmen's Compensation Act, 29 states likewise omitted farmworkers. See *Cannery Captives: Women Workers in the Produce Processing Industry*, comp. Daniel C. McCurry, in the *American Farmers and the Rise of Agribusiness: Seeds of Struggle* series (New York: Arno Press, 1975). The legislation is covered in the 1940 study by the U.S. Women's Bureau, "Application of Labor Legislation to the Fruit and Vegetable Canning and Preserving Industries."

29. Devra Anne Weber, "Mexican Farm Workers on Strike," in Chan and Olin, 289, 291.

30. Paul S. Taylor, *Mexican Labor in the United States*, vol. 1, part 1: "Imperial Valley," 45–54, and Starr, *Endangered Dreams*, 66–67.

31. The California Criminal Syndicalism Act defined "criminal syndicalism" as "any doctrine or precept advocating, teaching or aiding and abetting the commission of crime, sabotage . . . , or unlawful acts of force and violence or unlawful methods of terrorism as a means of accomplishing a change in industrial ownership or control, or effecting any political change," and anyone who promoted it or any members of organizations promoting it might be guilty of a felony. From the summary of the U.S. Supreme Court decision in *Whitney v. People of State of California* (274 U.S. 357, 1927), http://caselaw.lpfindlaw.com/scripts/getcase.pl?navby=case&court=us&vol=274&invol=357 (accessed June 11, 2006).

32. Karl Yoneda, "A Partial History of California Japanese Farm Workers," in *Racism, Dissent, and Asian Americans*, ed. Foner and Rosenberg, 200–202, and Acuña, *Occupied America*, 4th ed., 208–11.

33. Devra Weber, "Raiz Fuerte: Oral History and Mexicana Farmworkers," in *Working People of California*, ed. Daniel Cornford (Berkeley: University of California Press, 1995), 209–24, and editor's introduction, 208–209; McWilliams, *Factories*, 220–24; and Acuña, *Occupied America*, 229–37. Acuña put the strike force at between 10,000 and 12,000 (230).

34. McWilliams, *Factories*, 224; Starr, *Endangered Dreams*, 81–82, and Fuchs, *Hawaii Pono*, 237.

35. Deanna Paoli Gumina, "Andrea Sbarboro, Founder of the Italian Swiss Colony Wine Company: Reminiscences of an Italian American Pioneer," in *Struggle and Success*, ed. Sensi-Isolani and Martinelli, 99–100; Starr, *Endangered Dreams*, 158–63; and McWilliams, *Factories*, 153, 233–36, 261–66. McWilliams gives a powerful illustration of the forces arrayed against the workers. In April 1936, some 2,000 workers launched the Venice, California, celery strike. Fifteen hundred vigilantes were recruited, and they gassed and beat the strikers, breaking the strike (243–44). See note 6, chapter 25, below.

24. Filipinos

1. John S. Whitehead, "Noncontiguous Wests: Alaska and Hawai'i," in *Many Wests*, ed. Wrobel and Steiner, 328.

2. Carey McWilliams, introduction to Carlos Bulosan's *America in the Heart: A Personal History* (Seattle: University of Washington Press, 1946), viii. However, Posadas (*Filipino Americans*, 15) does provide a total migration figure for 1909–1934 of 118,556 *sakadas* (contract workers) to Hawai'i, of whom 15,043 were women and children.

3. Rony, "You Got to Move Like Hell," 99.

4. Bulosan, *America in the Heart*, 102, 177, 253; and Buaken, *I Have Lived*, 88.

5. Rony, "You Got to Move Like Hell," 109. Rony's dissertation was published as *American Workers, Colonial Power: Philippine Seattle and the Transpacific West, 1919–1941* (Berkeley: University of California Press, 2003). The episode quoted appears on p. 101.

6. Despite the Washington Alien Land Laws of 1921 and 1923, Filipinos made arrangements with Native Americans on the Yakima reservation to lease farm land, but in November 1927 white Americans drove the Filipinos from Toppenish and then in Wapato attacked Filipino farmers and those Japanese farmers who hired Filipino workers. In 1937 Washington State amended the Alien Land Law to include Malays, but Filipino labor contractor Pio de Cano persuaded Philippine authorities and the Yakima tribal council to urge changes in the law barring Asians from leasing reservation lands. He brought a lawsuit in 1940, and the Washington Supreme Court did in fact overturn that part of the law. In 1942 Filipinos were at last able to lease farmlands on the reservation; see Rony, "You Got to Move Like Hell," 94–95, 129–30.

7. Bulosan, *America in the Heart*, 135, 109, 146, 188–89, and one quotation in Richard White, *"It's Your Misfortune,"* 129–30.

8. Rony, "You Got to Move Like Hell," 105, 122–23, 201–3, 213; Cordova, *Filipinos*, 73, and Buaken, *I Have Lived*, 208. See also Friday, *Organizing Asian American Labor*, 127–28, for another such migratory account.

9. Manuel Buaken reported that students continued to be prominent among Filipino workers, with about 1,300 attending school in the 1930s and earning $300 per season during the summer. As opposed to the early *pensionados* in the first wave of Filipinos (up to 1906), the "school boys" in the second wave (1906–1934) had to support themselves. In the early 1920s some 2,000 received the *Filipino Students Bulletin*; a decade later that number had fallen by over two-thirds. In 1932, the Filipino Students Association at the University of Washington put in a bid to supply workers for the Alaskan canneries. The CWFLU achieved changes in work conditions that reduced the leverage of the contractors and foremen, because, at the outset, it had excluded contractors and foremen from membership in the CWFLU. Buaken, *I Have Lived*, 125–27; Friday, *Organizing Asian American Labor*, 130–31, 135; and Cordova, *Filipinos*, 130–31. Regarding Chris Friday's point that many white cannery workers were fishermen's wives, see "Competing Communities at Work: Asian Americans, European Americans, and Native Alaskans in the Pacific Northwest, 1938–1947," in *Over the Edge*, 308.

10. Friday, *Organizing Asian American Labor*, 126–27; Buaken, *I Have Lived*, 205.

11. In the overall peak year of 1929, of the 16,080 shoremen in the Alaska canneries, 5,824 were white, 4,010 Filipino, 1,902 Alaskan Native, 1,341 Japanese, 944 Chinese, and 1,787 Mexican.

12. The tables with the distribution of workers can be found in Buaken, *I Have Lived*, 206–10, although the totals shown are added incorrectly. See also Cordova, *Filipinos*, 66–70. The quotation is on p. 66. Mexican data are from the Bureau of Immigration,

Annual Report, 1930, 14–15. Eventually commercial aircraft were chartered to and from Seattle in lieu of steerage in order to shorten the time-consuming 600-mile journey.

13. Buaken, *I Have Lived,* 217, 226–27.

14. Nugent, *Into the West,* 217; Starr, *Endangered Dreams,* 63–64; McWilliams, *Factories,* 137–38; H. Brett Melendy, "Filipinos," in the *Harvard Encyclopedia of American Ethnic Groups,* ed. Stephen Thernstrom and Ann Orlov (Cambridge, Mass.: Harvard University Press, 1980), 361. Nugent points out that the new Deportation Act of March 4, 1929, was used by government officials as a union-busting strategy in the Southwest during the 1930s through the provision that made reentry of a deported individual a felony (236). Gail Nomura also discusses the struggles by Filipinos in agriculture and canneries, focusing on Washington State, in "Washington's Asia/Pacific American Communities," in *Peoples of Washington: Perspectives on Cultural Diversity,* ed. Sid White and S. E. Solberg (Pullman: Washington State University Press, 1989), 124, 129, 137–39.

15. Takaki, *Strangers,* 330; Melendy, "Filipinos," 360. Although not classified as whites, most Native Americans were previously awarded citizenship when receiving land allotments. The rest received it with the Act of June 2, 1924. The Los Angeles County data and the Visco-Salas marriage are discussed by Allison Varzally in "Romantic Crossings: Making Love, Family, and Non-Whiteness in California, 1925–1950," *Journal of American Ethnic History* 23.1 (Fall 2003): 19–21.

16. Buaken, *I Have Lived,* 71. The Rohrback quotation is in Buaken and in Cordova, *Filipinos,* 116. See Cordova, 115–18, Varzally, "Romantic Crossings," 8, and Arlene De Vera, "The Tapia-Saiki Incident: Inter-ethnic Conflict and the Filipino Response to the Anti-Filipino Exclusion Movement," pp. 201–14 in *Over the Edge: Remapping the American West,* ed. Valerie Matsumoto and Blake Allmendinger (Berkeley: University of California Press, 1999).

17. Quotation is from Weber, "Raiz Fuerte," 204; also, Buaken, *I Have Lived,* 110–12, 115, 169; and Bulosan, *America in the Heart,* 143. Filipino mixed marriages were made illegal in California, Arizona, and Nevada, compelling Filipinos and white fiancées to go to Utah to marry.

18. The quotations are from Rony, "You Got to Move Like Hell," 91, and McWilliams, *Factories,* 133.

19. Feldman, *Racial Factors,* 103; Nomura, "Washington's Asia/Pacific American Communities," 137; Cordova, *Filipinos,* 186 (quotation); Posadas, *Filipino Americans,* 151; Rony, "You Got to Move Like Hell," 187, 182. Despite Feldman's sympathetic comment, quoted here from his 1931 book, he also stated (102), regarding American-born Filipinos, that they were "unwelcome here and are lacking ties to *their* own land" (emphasis added), namely the Philippines—the kind of sentiment frequently associated with both Issei and Nisei. In other words, no matter where they were born, their loyalty to Japan was racially based, and the same was implied concerning Filipinos. Amusing then is the anecdote about the Visayan mother who opposed her daughter's marriage to an Ilocano man. (Besides language differences and origins on different islands, Filipino stereotypes of Ilocano men ridiculed their appearance and dress.) The internal splits were certainly not unique to Filipinos but suggested that homeland ties were by no means unified at this time. They would be even less so among the second generation.

Dr. José Rizal was a leader of the Philippines independence movement who was executed by the Spanish on December 30, 1896. That is the date of Rizal Day and has since been celebrated as a national holiday (Posadas, *Filipino Americans,* 54–55).

20. Rony, "You Got to Move Like Hell," 88, 189, 228, 275; Cordova, *Filipinos,* 102, 149, 180, 181, 202; Bulosan, *America in the Heart,* 285; Buaken, *I Have Lived,* 62; and Chan, *Asian Americans,* 77. Regarding the discrimination, see also Takaki, *Strangers,* 324–31.

21. Takaki, *Strangers*, 188, 212–14; Rony, "You Got to Move Like Hell," 28–29; and Cordova, *Filipinos*, 83–87, 99. Despite the thrust of this legislation, the U.S. Supreme Court, in *Toyota v. the United States* (268 U.S. 402; June 25, 1925), had affirmed that the Act of May 9, 1918 ("Naturalization of Aliens with Military Service"), had granted to Filipinos—since they are "not aliens and owe allegiance to the United States"—the right to submit a declaration of intention and petition for naturalization without having resided in the United States for five years, and who had served in the U.S. Navy for at least three years and had been (or would be) honorably discharged.

22. Beechert, *Working in Hawaii*, 217–32. On the Philippines labor background, see Greg Bankoff, "Wants, Wages, and Workers: Laboring in the American Philippines, 1899–1908," *Pacific Historical Review* 74.1 (February 2005): 73–75.

23. Friday, *Organizing Asian American Labor*, 135–38, and Cordova, *Filipinos*, 73–74.

24. Friday, *Organizing Asian American Labor*, 136–47, 150–58, 162–71, 180–81; Rony, "You Got to Move Like Hell," 201–16; Friday, "Competing Communities," 307–28.

25. Cordova, *Filipinos*, 119–20; Rony, "You Got to Move Like Hell," 79 (Bogardus quotation), 93; other quotations from Buaken, *I Have Lived*. 163–65; and Robert Vallangca, *Pinoy: The First Wave (1898–1941)* (San Francisco: Strawberry Hill Press, 1977), 26. Also, Buaken, 156; Nugent, *Into the West*, 238; Takaki, *Strangers*, 332–34. There were 45,208 Filipinos reported on the mainland in 1930 and 45,563 in 1940. However, 63,052 (all generations) were recorded in Hawai'i in 1930 but only 52,569 in 1940.

26. Carlos Bulosan wrote about arriving with his traveling companions, being quickly cheated of their money by Filipino gamblers, and having no funds to pay for their hotel room until a short, fat Filipino, Jake, came in, paid for their room, and took them to work in the salmon canneries. Then, "we were sold for five dollars each to work in the fish canneries in Alaska, by a Visayan from the island of Leyte to an Ilocano from the province of La Union" (6).

25. Divided Yet Interlinked: The Urban West in the Interwar Years

1. Since this figure includes white foreign stock and all non-white foreign-born races (thus omitting Native Americans and African Americans), plus all Mexicans, some third- and later-generation persons are included, but those would not significantly influence these percentages.

2. Outside the West the net foreign-born population remained rather static between 1910 and 1930—at between 11.86 and 12.12 million—whereas that of the West rose nearly 10 percent during the tumultuous 1920s. However, that figure actually masks the full impact of California's role. California's foreign-born population rose by 316,339 during the 1920s (to 1.07 million), whereas the total increase for the entire West was only 203,854, indicating that there had been an attrition of 112,485 elsewhere in the West, undoubtedly due to a combination of deaths, out-migration to other regions, and emigration from the country. Among just the white foreign born, the figures were down 82,731 for the West versus up 319,718 in California.

3. The immigration data are derived from table 82 in the 1926 *Annual Report of the Commissioner General of Immigration* and table 91 in the 1930 *Annual Report*. The situation appears to have been still more complex. The 1930 census reported 203,854 more foreign-born persons in the West in 1930; however, government immigration reports indicate that 867,965 persons had been admitted between July 1, 1920, and June 30, 1929, giving a western state or territory as their destination. Even without considering in-migration from other states and other variables, it would appear that over 664,100 foreigners

who said they were going to the West either did not go there or did not remain until the next census count (or, most likely, some combination thereof). The most conspicuous case involved Texas, which experienced a small, 1,545-person decline in foreign born by 1930, but over 333,864 were supposed to have entered and moved there, for a discrepancy or out-migration of 335,409.

4. Nugent, *Into the West*, 129 (the earlier quotation regarding metropolitization), 228. Richard White discusses the political fallout of such changes in these "peripheral" regions, in *"It's Your Misfortune,"* 430–31.

5. Quotation is from Baker, *First Polish Americans*, 163. See also Hodgson and Hills, "Dream and Fulfillment," 35–65. Many other works have been cited on this theme, but two other personal accounts dramatically recounted the rural experiences and some of the overlap with urban life: Akemi Kikumura, *Through Harsh Winters: The Life of a Japanese Immigrant Woman* (Novato, Calif.: Chandler and Sharp, 1981), and Mary Paik Lee, *Quiet Odyssey: A Pioneer Korean Woman in America*, ed. Sucheng Chan (Seattle: University of Washington Press, 1990).

6. There were many agricultural, plantation, and cannery strikes during the 1920s and 1930s, to which one could add the strike by Mexican and Filipino celery pickers begun on April 17, 1936, against Japanese growers in Venice, California. The Southern California Farm Federation, composed of some 800 Japanese farmers, rejected the workers' demands. The strike escalated until early June, when about 1,500 Mexicans suddenly accepted a lower-wage offer and no union recognition, ending the strike. The general farm workers' struggle for union recognition would continue, illustrating the reality that, even in the throes of the Depression, the oppressive conditions and surplus labor pools did not dissuade workers from striking when conditions and wages became intolerable. See Nobuya Tsuchida, "Japanese Gardeners in Southern California, 1900–1941," pp. 458–59 in *Labor Migration under Capitalism: Asian Workers in the United States before World War Two*, ed. Lucie Cheng and Edna Bonacich (Berkeley: University of California Press, 1984), and McWilliams's account of the 1936 clash (*Factories*, 84).

7. Vicki L. Ruiz, *Cannery Women, Cannery Lives: Mexican Women, Unionization, and the California Food Processing Industry, 1930–1950* (Albuquerque: University of New Mexico Press, 1987), 14–18. She points out that often the "extra" money was used to purchase "items perceived as conferring American respectability" (18). However, Ruiz also notes that Mexican women in the canneries and packinghouses were being paid $2.30–$2.70 per day, whereas the men earned $3.50–$4.50 (15). See Daniel McCurry's collection of studies of Pacific Northwest women workers during the 1920s for further details.

8. Walter Nugent points out that the bridge construction across the San Francisco Bay area had a similar effect, accelerating population dispersion just as highways were doing in so many other areas. See Nugent, *Into the West*, 254.

9. Phrase is from Richard White, *"It's Your Misfortune,"* 319. See also Nugent, *Into the West*, 222, and Allerfeldt, *Race, Radicalism*, 103. Allerfeldt cites the example of Multnomah County, Oregon, where Portland sits, and the jump in car registrations from fewer than 10,000 in 1920 to about 90,000 before the decade ended (103).

10. During the 1920s other foreign-born groups actually rose in number in the West, led by Italians (12,300), Dutch, Yugoslavians, Poles, Russians, and Norwegians. Seven declined, the Japanese foremost (22,400), followed by Chinese, Greeks, Portuguese, and Austrians. (The drop in the latter, 14,700, may have largely reflected peoples from the former Austro-Hungarian Empire re-identifying their origins with newly independent homeland nations, especially Yugoslavia.) See Pomeroy, *Pacific Slope*, 264.

11. Issel and Cherny, *San Francisco*, 77–79. Seattle's Japanese population highlights one of the complex developments of this period because their total population rose by

38 percent between 1910 and 1930 (6,127 to 8,448) before falling 17 percent during the 1930s (to 6,276). While some of the attrition was due to deaths, the reaction to the new immigration laws prompted a great number of Issei to depart. In his study, Shotaro Frank Miyamoto may have captured in the words of an older Issei the sentiment many felt: "I still feel a longing to go back to Japan. Here in this country, I am an alien because I have no citizenship, and my world feels small because it is restricted at certain points. When I walk around among the Americans, I have a feeling that I don't belong here."

Between 1920 and 1940, the total Issei population fell by 54,242 (to 82,844), including Hawai'i, with 31,236 more departing during the 1930s (11,486 from the mainland) than were entering. Issei losses were reported in Oakland (by 347), in Sacramento (468), in San Francisco (970), and in Seattle (1,472). The second generation was rapidly increasing (although less so during the Depression years). Some of the population changes in the West were also due to Nisei moving to the East, particularly to pursue a college education. Issei migration data drawn from Paul R. Spickard, *Japanese Americans: The Formation and Transformation of an Ethnic Group* (Boston: Twayne, 1996), 47–49, and tables 2, 3, and 10. See also Shotaro Frank Miyamoto, *Social Solidarity among the Japanese in Seattle*, University of Washington Publications in the Social Sciences 11.2 (December 1939): 67–68 (quotation); and Calvin Schmid, *Social Trends in Seattle*, University of Washington Publications in the Social Sciences 14 (October 1944): 131, 135–36.

12. Cinel, *From Italy*, 139–40. The Japanese came to play a major role in coastal fishing, especially out of San Pedro and San Diego. They built a colony on Terminal Island, in what became Los Angeles Harbor. By 1940 there were 500 fishermen there, 150 merchants, and 450 women and children. Chinese, Mexicans, Italians, and Yugoslavians joined the Japanese there. In 1923–1924, some 48 percent of those applying for commercial fishing licenses in Los Angeles were Japanese. Although nearly one-third were Japanese in 1933–1934, they included only 4 Nisei (William Carlson Smith, *Americans in Process*, 89). That would change after the war, especially among the tuna fleets out of San Diego. Meanwhile, the Issei were establishing a major role in the tuna industry in San Diego. While they would be unable to return to Terminal Island after the war, they resumed that leadership in San Diego. See McWilliams, *Southern California*, 322, and William C. Richardson, "Fisherman of San Diego: The Italians," in *Struggle and Success*, ed. Sensi-Isolani and Martinelli, 86.

13. Miyamoto reported that 75 percent of employed Japanese in Seattle in 1935 were in trades or domestic and personal services, and the fact that so many were in business created an "identity of interest" that was "a major factor in the solidarity of this group" (71–72). A measure of the reputation of Seattle's Nihonmachi (Japanese community) was evident in the selection of James Sakamoto as national president of the new Japanese American Citizens League (JACL). In Seattle, he had launched the *Japanese-American Courier*, an English language paper, and had been involved in converting the Seattle Progressive Citizens League into a chapter of the JACL. JACL's first national meeting was held in Seattle (Dodds, *American Northwest*, 247).

14. Glenn and Parreñas, "Other Issei, 132–33; Portes and Bach, *Latin Journey*, 43–47; and Chapin, "From Sparta," 145–47.

Portes and Bach point out that already by 1919 the Japanese owned 47 percent of the hotels and one-fourth of the groceries in Seattle (*Latin Journey*, 43). Glenn and Parreñas noted, besides the increasing demand for Japanese language teachers and midwives, the fact that job openings differed among different cities due to the varied opportunity structures. For example, in 1940 many more business-related openings were available for Japanese women in Seattle, whereas in San Francisco half the women were employed in domestic services (133–34).

15. On the various migrations, see Nugent, *Into the West*, 243–49.

16. McWilliams, *Southern California*, 345, and Richard White, *"It's Your Misfortune,"* 427–28.

17. Philip K. Hitti, *The Syrians in America* (New York: G. H. Doran, 1924), 98–99, 100, 120.

18. Quotation from Takami, *Divided Destiny*, 26. George Sánchez's discussion is in chapters 4 and 5 of *Becoming Mexican American*.

Harold Nelson well documented the inter-generational strains among Fresno Armenians. By the 1930s, the parents were older and less controlling, while daughters were straining against the bonds of convention (and their parents' preoccupation with their daughters' virtue). Older siblings were often called upon to interpret for their parents external events and demands by younger siblings, further eroding old guidelines. Family unity was being strained as this inter-generational cultural gap widened. Compounding the problem, the children would soon reach marriage age, and some girls began to select *"odars"*—foreigners, non-Armenians (especially during the 1940s with soldiers nearby). Nelson, "Armenian Family," 66–67, 81–85, 91–92, 99–100, 259–60.

19. Varzally, "Romantic Crossings," 4–5, 6–17, 20.

20. Walter Kamphoefner, "German Americans: Paradoxes of a 'Model Minority,'" in *Origins and Destinies*, ed. Pedraza and Rumbaut, 158. While there were numerous church mergers among Scandinavian Lutherans, such blending did not always cross ethnic lines. For example, a Polish pastor in Texas rejected a proposal to join with German Catholics on the grounds that "we Poles have our own saints in heaven" (Baker, *First Polish Americans*, 138–39).

21. Valerie Matsumoto, "Japanese American Women and the Creation of Urban Nisei Culture in the 1930s," pp. 300–302 in *Over the Edge*.

22. Kimura, *Issei*, 101.

23. See, for example, the model laying out a spectrum of possible ties by immigrants with their homelands—from disengaged to regular, ongoing involvement in various homeland activities—in Barkan, "America in the Hand," 127–54.

24. Adapted from Baker, *First Polish Americans*, 170.

26. Urban Landscapes and Ethnic Encounters

1. Malone and Etulain, *American West*, 81–83; Dodds, *American Northwest*, 216–19; Edwards and Schwantes, eds., *Experiences in a Promised Land*, 262; Richard White, *"It's Your Misfortune,"* 384 (quotation); Pomeroy, *Pacific Slope*, 226, 285; Van Nuys, *Americanizing the West*, 68–69; Papanikolas, 430–31 (quotation) in *The Peoples of Utah*, ed. Helen Z. Papanikolas (Salt Late City: University of Utah Press, 1976); Talagan, "Faith, Hard Work, and Family," 151; Kamphoefner, "German Americans," 158; Norman C. Clark, *Washington: A Bicentennial History* (New York: Norton, 1976), 188 (quotation); and especially Eckard V. Toy Jr., "The Ku Klux Klan in Tillamook, Oregon," *Pacific Northwest Quarterly* 53 (1962): 60–64 (quotations), and reprinted in *Northwest Mosaic*, ed. Halseth and Glasrud, 106–15, and in *Experiences in a Promised Land*, ed. Edwards and Schwantes, 268–86. Toy does point out that "For a decade, the majority of municipal, county, and state officials elected in Tillamook were Klansmen or former Klansmen" (Edwards and Schwantes, 274; Halseth and Glasrud, 111).

Carl Abbott argued that the Klan tapped into the frustrations of Westerners "who found its attacks on foreigners and city-bred life styles the only convenient way to strike back at the increasing scale and complexity of American life" ("American West," 86).

2. "Assyrian Situation at Turlock, California," by William Carlson Smith, plus in-

terview by Nettie J. Pride, August 14, 1924, William C. Smith Collection, Box 1, Folder 12, University of Oregon.

3. This account is distilled from the Smith Collection, Box 1, Folder 40, item 266 (copies of news stories, flyers, and correspondence); William Carlson Smith, *Americans in Process*, 189–92, 330–32; Steve Fugita, "John Fugue Aiso," in *Distinguished Asian Americans: A Biographical Dictionary*, ed. Hyung-chan Kim (Westport, Conn.: Greenwood Press, 1999), 15–17; "Veteran Profiles: Aiso, John," Military Intelligence Service Research Center, www.njahs.org/misnorcal/profiles/profile.php?id=2000 (accessed February 20, 2004). In a tragic conclusion to such a sterling career, Aiso was killed by a mugger in December 1987. In the Little Tokyo area of Los Angeles, San Pedro Street between First Street and Temple was renamed Judge John Aiso Street in his honor.

4. This account is derived from a number of documents in the William C. Smith Collection, most in Box 1, Folder 11, including copies of the *Hollywood Citizens*, April 17, 18, 23, 24, 27, 1923; the *Hollywood News*, May 15, 17, 1923, and January 15, 17, 1924; *the Los Angeles Examiner*, April 22, 24, 1923, May 18, 25, 1924; Smith's interview with R. R. Bowles, April 3, 1924, plus handbills, photographs, and correspondence from Horikoshi and the Presbyterian Church from the papers of E. S. Bickford. See also Box 1, Folder 34, no. 231.

5. An 8.3 earthquake struck Tokyo just before noon on September 1, 1923, killing between 100,000 and 140,000 persons.

6. Interview with Mr. and Mrs. Sessions, William C. Smith Collection, Box 1, Folder 39, item 255A, and interview with Mrs. S., item 256A and 257A.

7. "Case Study: Buddhist Temple in Pasadena," William C. Smith Collection, Box 1, Folder 38, item 238F.

8. The following account is drawn from William C. Smith Collection, Box 1, Folder 17, item 111, which included "A Report sent in to the Methodist Headquarters . . . [regarding] Pico Heights," around September 1923, and "Interview with Dr. Byron Wilson . . . July 15, 1924." The Pico Heights area was bounded roughly by Olympic and Pico Boulevards and by Vermont and Normandie Avenues.

9. "From *Los Angeles Ledger* . . . Sept. 28, 1923" (with Fitzpatrick letter), "Interview with Mr. T. M. McClellan . . . July 1924," along with "Conflict at Pico Heights . . . July 9, 1924," included with William C. Smith Collection, Box 1, Folder 17, item 111.

10. Quotations are by Pomeroy, *Pacific Slope*, 162, McWilliams, *Southern California*, 160, 124, and Nugent, *Into the West*, 183. See also Pomeroy, 306, O'Connor, "Region of Cities," 550–51, Richard White, *"It's Your Misfortune,"* 416, and Malone and Etulain, *American West*, 30–36.

11. Montgomery, *Fall of the House of Labor*, 460, Richard White, *"It's Your Misfortune,"* 441.

12. Rochlin and Rochlin, *Pioneer Jews*, 167, 225; Ellen Eisenberg, "From Cooperative Farming to Urban Leadership," in *Jewish Life in the American West*, ed. Ava F. Kahn (Seattle: University of Washington Press and the Autry Museum of Western Heritage, 2002), 113–31; and Robert A. Goldberg, "Zion in Utah: The Clarion Colony and Jewish Agrarianism," in *Jews in the American West*, ed. Moses Rischin and John Livingston (Detroit: Wayne State University Press, 1991), 66–91.

13. Data drawn from the 1920 Census, vol. 2, *Population by States*, tables 7, 8, 12, 13, 26, Supplementary volume on *Outlying Territories and Possessions* for Alaska and Hawai'i (table 2); 1930 Census, vol. 2, *Characteristics of Population*, tables 8, 11, 26, 27; 1940 Census, vol. 2, *Population*, Parts 1–6, *Divisions and States*, tables 36 and 37 and A40, B40, C40 by State. As noted, Seattle and Salt Lake City fairly closely paced their respective states, rising 16 percent and 19 percent, respectively, while Washington increased by 15 percent and Utah by 13 percent.

14. In smaller communities, Fresno grew by 16 percent during the 1920s, although its white foreign born fell by 7 percent. Stockton had, overall, a 19 percent increase but a 1 percent slippage in its white foreign born. Drops in the white foreign-born populations in Phoenix, Tucson, and Pueblo (Colorado) cannot be taken at face value because Mexicans had largely been removed from the white counts in the 1930 census and not reincorporated in any 1940 census report revising 1930 urban data. In all five cases had data on Mexicans and foreign-born non-whites been available, the declines would have been less dramatic or even reversed. However, both Spokane and Tacoma also had 10–11 percent increases, yet in both cities the foreign-born populations decreased by 4–6 percent. Both cities had few Mexicans.

15. The 15 principal groups were Austrians, Canadians (French and others), Danes, British, French, Germans, Greeks, Irish, Italians, Mexicans, Norwegians, Russians, Swedes, Japanese, and Chinese.

16. As noted above, in note 10 of chapter 25, this could be a function of peoples no longer being required to identify with Austria due to the split up of the Austro-Hungarian Empire. In addition, since only small numbers were returning to Europe, mortality and relocation outside the West may also have played a role in the Austrian reductions. During the 1920s that population declined in Oakland, Denver, Dallas, El Paso, San Antonio, Salt Lake City, Spokane, and Tacoma.

Germans, who had been well established in at least 10 major cities (Oakland, San Francisco, Denver, Portland, Dallas, El Paso, San Antonio, Seattle, Spokane, and Tacoma), did not regain the pre-war levels in many cities where they had long been established. On the other hand, increasing numbers of Canadians were reported in 11 main cities: Los Angeles, San Diego, Oakland, San Francisco, Portland, Dallas, El Paso, Houston, San Antonio, Seattle, and Tacoma. Regarding Norwegians, it was in Seattle, Portland, San Francisco, and especially Los Angeles where more Norwegians settled during the 1920s—in fact, tripling their population in the latter city. So, too, Swedes were being drawn away from the Northwest to San Francisco, Oakland, and especially Los Angeles, where their population experienced a 78 percent growth after 1920. Russians (including Russian Jews) flocked to San Francisco and Los Angeles. Even the British population noticeably increased in all the main California cities, along with Portland, Houston, and Seattle.

17. The Hawaiian census provided only such city data by race; hence, these figures include first- and second-generation persons. The Japanese went from 12,093 to 47,468; Chinese from 9,574 to 19,334; Koreans from 460 to 2,604; Filipinos from 87 to 4,776; and Portuguese from 6,147 to 12,097. Asians and Asian Hawaiians together comprised 58 percent of Honolulu's population.

18. marie rose wong, "The Urban Pattern of Portland, Oregon's First Chinatown," pp. 416–33 in *The Chinese in America: A History from Gold Mountain to the New Millennium*, ed. Susie Lan Cassel (Walnut Creek, Calif.: AltaMira Press, 2002). One of the first studies to examine the idea of ethnicity without community involved Poles in Los Angeles. See Neil C. Sandberg, *Ethnic Identity and Assimilation: The Polish-American Community, A Case Study of Metropolitan Los Angeles* (New York: Praeger, 1974).

19. Harry T. Getty, "Interethnic Relationships in the Community of Tucson," Ph.D. diss. (University of Chicago, 1950; New York: Arno Press, 1976). See Acuña, *Occupied America*, 116, 122–23. The Getty quotations are from pp. 54, 172, 59.

20. This discussion of Jews is drawn from Carl Abbott, "American West," 80; Toll, *Making of an Ethnic Middle Class*, 129, 138–48; Max Vorspan and Lloyd P. Gartner, *History of the Jews of Los Angeles* (San Marino, Calif.: Huntington Library, 1970), 102, 103 (quotation), 114, 127, 139, 145 (quotation), 164 (quotation), 222–23; Jeanne Abrams,

"Chasing the Cure in Colorado: The Jewish Consumptives' Relief Society," in *Jews in the American West*, ed. Rischin and Livingston, 92–115; Leonard Dinnerstein, "From Desert Oasis to the Desert Caucus: The Jews of Tucson," in *Jews in the American West*, ed. Rischin and Livingston, 142–43; Richard White, "*It's Your Misfortune*," 378–79; Dodds, *American Northwest*, 251, 132–33; Issel and Cherny, *San Francisco*, 206; Rochlin and Rochlin, *Pioneer Jews*, 157–63; and Carl V. Hallberg, "Jews in Wyoming," *Annals of Wyoming* 16.1 (Spring 1989): 26–27.

Dinnerstein claims that between 1910 and 1940 "every Jew who came to Tucson did so because a family member was afflicted with arthritis or a respiratory disease." In all of Arizona there were 1,150 Jews in 1920 and 1,847 Jews 17 years later. Yet, beginning in the 1920s Phoenix and Tucson became "the January suburb of the Mid-West." Between just 1910 and 1940, Phoenix's total population grew from 11,134 to 64,414 and Tucson from 13,193 to 35,752. A Conservative congregation was established in Tucson in 1930, but it still had only 20–25 families in September 1939 (Dinnerstein, "From Desert Oasis," 142–43).

21. Rochlin and Rochlin, *Pioneer Jews*, 227; Deborah Dash Moore, "Jewish Migration in Postwar America: The Case of Miami and Los Angeles," *Studies in Contemporary Jewry* 8 (1992): 105; Vorspan and Gartner, *History of the Jews*, 287; Hallberg, "Jews in Wyoming," 26; and Ava F. Kahn and Marc Dollinger, "The Other Side," in *California Jews*, ed. Kahn and Dollinger (Hanover, N.H.: University Press of New England, 2003), 1–16 and, regarding Hollywood in particular, 14–15, as well as Felicia Herman, "Jewish Leaders and the Motion Picture Industry," in Kahn and Dollinger, 95–109.

22. Carey McWilliams made the observation that "the east-side Jewish districts [principally Boyle Heights] are Yiddish and radical; the west-side elements are prosperous and liberal" (McWilliams, *Southern California*, 322).

23. Vorspan and Gartner, *History of the Jews*, 113–17, 118 (quotation), 203–204, 217 (quotation); George Sánchez, "The Agony of Whiteness: How Jews Moved Out of the Eastside and What Difference That Makes for Race in Los Angeles," seminar paper presented at the Autry Museum of Western Heritage, February 13, 2003, and Bruce Phillips, "The Challenge of Family, Identity, and Affiliations," in *California Jews*, ed. Kahn and Dollinger 19 (quotation on Boyle Heights). The FHA quotation is from Deutsch, Sánchez, and Okihiro, "Contemporary Peoples/Contested Places," 641. Carey McWilliams noted that there were in Boyle Heights "Russians [Molokans], Armenians, Russian-Armenians, Poles, Mexicans, [and] Jews, particularly Russian-Jewish groups," (McWilliams, *Southern California*, 322). And we know Asians soon moved there, too. For an interesting description of the distinctive Jewish community in beachside Venice, California, see Amy Hill Shevitz, "Jewish Space and Place in Venice," pp. 65–76, in Kahn and Dollinger.

24. "Boyle Heights Project: The Power of Place," Oral Histories, www.janm.org/exhibits/bh/ (accessed May 20, 2006).

25. Portes and Bach, *Latin Journey*, 41, and Starr, *Inventing*, 283–336. Although we here identify the movie industry as synonymous with Hollywood, in actuality some of the major studies were located in Culver City, east of Venice Beach, beginning in 1915. By the mid-1920s, under the management of Louis B. Mayer, Metro-Goldwyn-Mayer was the major studio there. http://www.culvercity.org/cityinfo/history/10202.html (accessed May 9, 2005).

26. Crosby, "Italians of Los Angeles," 38–57; Sensi-Isolani and Martinelli, "Part Three: Social and Political Experience," in *Struggle and Success*, ed. Sensi-Isolani and Martinelli, 146–59; Gloria Ricci Lothrop, "The Italians of Los Angeles," *The Californians*, May/June 1987: 28–43; and Lothrop, "Shadow on the Land: The Impact of Fascism on Los Angeles Italians," in *Fulfilling the Promise of California: An Anthology of Es-*

says on the Italian American Experience in California, ed. Gloria Ricci Lothrop (Spokane, Wash.: Arthur H. Clarke, 2000), 189–214. The quotation is from Lothrop's "Shadow," 196.

27. Fuchs, *Hawaii Pono*, 39.

28. Ronald Takaki, *Pau Hana: Life and Labor in Hawaii, 1835–1920* (Honolulu: University of Hawai'i Press, 1983), 109–19; William Carlson Smith, *Americans in Process*, 23; Ogawa, *Kodomo no tame ni*, xx–xxi. The quotation is from Fuchs, *Hawaii Pono*, 42.

29. Pap, *Portuguese Americans*, 93; Fuchs, *Hawaii Pono*, 66; Nordyke, *Peopling of Hawai'i*, table 3.1. The student quoted by William C. Smith (*Americans in Process*, 162) was Korean, but the attitude expressed was widely shared among the young Asian Americans in Hawai'i.

30. Fuchs, *Hawaii Pono*, 86, 105, 86–105.

31. Ibid., 119–21, 122–23, 190; Kimura, *Issei*, 103, 107; Ogawa, *Kodomo no tame ni*, 190; Sharma, "Labor Migration," 585–87. Ogawa gave the urban figures as 10 percent in 1900 and 22.4 percent in 1920 (190). See also Miriam Sharma, "The Philippines: A Case Study of Migration to Hawaii, 1906–1946," in *Labor Migration*, ed. Cheng and Bonacich, 337–58.

32. This discussion of the Uchinanchu is extensively treated in *Uchinanchu: A History of Okinawans in Hawaii*, compiled by the Ethnic Studies Oral History Project and the United Okinawan Association of Hawaii (Honolulu: University of Hawai'i at Manoa, 1981). In particular, see the preface by Mitsugu Sakihara (xxi–xxiv), the "History of Okinawa" by Sakihara (3–22), and "Okinawans in Hawaii" by Masanori Higa (37–49). See also Ryan Masaaki Yokota, "A Brief History of the Uchinanchu" on the website of the Okinawan Peace Network of Los Angeles, www.uchinanchu.org/uchinanchu/history_of_uchinanchu.htm (accessed June 24, 2004).

One taunt directed at the Uchinanchu by Naichi children was "*Okinawa ken, ken, buta kau kau*" (Okinawans eat pig; 41). Relations may have improved since 1945, but contemporary Japanese Americans remember that teasing phrase and the stereotype of Okinawan men as exceptionally hairy.

33. Ogawa, *Kodomo no tame ni*, 23, 26, 191, 230; Kimura, *Issei*, xiii–iv (quotation), 22, 23, 26, 27 (quotation), 30, 49, 52.

34. Kimura, *Issei*, 124–25, 137, 170, 178, 187–91, 199; Ogawa, *Kodomo no tame ni*, 70, 142–44, 176 (quotation), 147 (quotation), 192–94.

35. Fuchs, *Hawaii Pono*, 127–29, 176–81, 276; William Carlson Smith, *Americans in Process*, 122. Smith found that there was a total of 7,000 Japanese of voting age on the mainland in September 1934 versus the nearly 13,100 in Hawai'i in 1930.

36. Cordova, *Filipinos*, 32 (quotation), 29; Sharma, "Labor Migration," 585, 591–92, 594 (quotation), 602. Lawrence Fuchs (*Hawaii Pono*, 141–42) also emphasized that returning was the Filipinos' great obsession, but, he observed, during the interwar years the *sakadas* "were overwhelmed by frustration" because they had little family in the Islands and a homeland that was neither independent nor able to afford much protection.

37. William Carlson Smith, *Americans in Process*, 38–39. The Portuguese, struggling to gain their own recognition as haoles—that is, as part of the Caucasian population—did express some prejudice against Asians, who had often been employed under the supervision of Portuguese *lunas* on the plantations.

27. From "Reoccupation" to Repatriation

1. Gregg Jones, "Apology Sought for Latino 'Repatriation' during the '30s," *Los Angeles Times*, July 15, 2003: B1+.

2. Oscar J. Martinez, *Border People*, xvii–xviii; Limerick, *Legacy of Conquest*, 194; Barkan, "Proximity and Commuting Immigration," 163–83; and Barkan, "French Canadians," in *Harvard Encyclopedia*, 388–401.

3.Vicki L. Ruiz, *From Out of the Shadows: Mexican Women in Twentieth-Century America* (New York: Oxford University Press, 1998), 35; Limerick, *Legacy of Conquest*, quotations, 194, 222; and Oscar J. Martinez, *Border People*, 222.

4. Mario T. Garcia, *Desert Immigrants*; and Paula Gunn Allen, "Cuentos de la Tierra Encontada: Magic and Realism in the Southwest Borderlands," in *Many Wests*, ed. Wrobel and Steiner, 342–60.

5. Allen, "Cuentos," 346–47, 349–50, 354, 357; Gavin quotation from Limerick, *Legacy of Conquest*, 346, and 245; McWilliams, *Southern California*, 319; William Deverell, "Privileging the Mission over the Mexican: The Rise of Regional Identity in Southern California," in *Many Wests*, ed. Wrobel and Steiner. 243.

6. Camarillo, *Chicanos in a Changing Society*, 191; Ruiz, *From Out of the Shadows*, 16 (Weber quotation); Clare Sheridan, "Contested Citizenship: National Identity and Mexican Immigration Debates of the 1920s," *Journal of American Ethnic History* 21.3 (Spring 2002): 4, 24; Mario T. Garcia, *Desert Immigrants*, 214.

7. Haines, quoted by Ricardo Romo, in "Mexican Americans: Their Civic and Political Incorporation," p. 90, in *Origins and Destinies*, ed. Pedraza and Rumbaut; Forster, quoted by Thomas Muller and Thomas Espenshade, *The Fourth Wave: California's Newest Immigrants* (Washington, D.C.: Urban Institute, 1985), 32–33; and Montejano, *Anglos and Mexicans*, 181–82. Quotations from Clare Sheridan, "Contested Citizenship," 23; Foley, *White Scourge*, 59–61; Guerin Gonzalez, *Mexican Workers*, 68; Richard White, "*It's Your Misfortune*," 451.

8. Bogardus, *Mexican in the United States*, 17, 21, 23, 49–50, 52, 43, 53, 63, 83 n.

9. Quotation from Camarillo, *Chicanos in a Changing Society*, 189; Limerick, *Legacy of Conquest*, 246; Deutsch, "Landscape of Enclaves" 110–111; Oscar J. Martinez, *Border People*, 95–96; Romo, "Mexican Americans," 93; quotation from Mario Garcia, *Mexican American*, 25–34, 296; Guerin-Gonzalez, *Mexican Workers*, 2, 6–7.

10. Montejano, *Anglos and Mexicans*, 243–44, and Mario Garcia, *Mexican Americans*, 46–49.

11. Thomas A. Guglielmo, "Fighting for Caucasian Rights: Mexicans, Mexican Americans, and the Struggle for Civil Rights Legislation in World War Two Texas," paper presented at the conference "Immigration History and the University of Minnesota: Where We Have Been, Where We Are Going," Minneapolis, May 12, 2005, 10–11. In February 1944, a Texas Appeals Court ruled that the resolution was not an enforceable law (14).

12. Mario Garcia, *Mexican Americans*, 62–73, 78; Gutierrez, *Walls and Mirrors*, 69–71; Foley, *White Scourge*, 13; and Montejano, *Anglos and Mexicans*, 224, 246, 251.

13. Gutierrez, *Walls and Mirrors*, 85–88; Montejano, *Anglos and Mexicans*, 244; Mario Garcia, *Desert Immigrants*, 127, 235.

14. Gordon, *Great Arizona Orphan Abduction*, 99, 178–7; Nugent, *Into the West*, 208; Sánchez, "Agony of Whiteness," 70–71 and chapter 3. See also Arnoldo DeLeon, "Region and Identity: Topographical Identities in Texas," in *Many Wests*, ed. Wrobel and Steiner, 259–74.

15. Among the many types of employment were—in addition to nearby agricultural enterprises—steel, iron, and tire factories; cement and tile producers; construction; meatpacking firms; canneries; various needle trades; railroad maintenance; street paving; laundries; bakeries; and domestic services.

16. Ricardo Romo, "Urbanization," 183–207 in *New Directions in Chicano Scholarship*, ed. Romo and Raymond Paredes (La Jolla: University of California, San Diego,

Chicano Studies Program, 1978), and Sánchez, *Becoming Mexican American*, 44, 64, 66. Sánchez's demographic data are based on a sample of Declarations of Intent and Petitions for Citizenship, which may or may not be representative of the vast majority of Mexicans who at this time did not apply for citizenship and who often did not remain in Los Angeles.

17. For example, for Santa Barbara teamsters: Anglos earned $4 per day, Mexicans received $2 to $2.50 per day. In El Paso, Anglo saleswomen in 1919 were paid $33.50 to $40 per week, Mexicans $10 to $20.

18. Romo, "Urbanization," 185–94; Camarillo, *Chicanos in a Changing Society*, chapter 9, especially 210–13, and 215 (quotation); Ruiz, *From Out of the Shadows*, 75–77; Mario Barrera, "Class Segmentation and the Political Economy of the Chicano, 1900–1930," in *New Directions in Chicano Scholarship*, ed. Romo and Paredes, 172–73, 175. See also McWilliams, *North from Mexico*, 175.

19. Julia Kirk Blackwelder, *Women of the Depression: Caste and Culture in San Antonio, 1929–1939* (College Station: Texas A&M University Press, 1984), 94–96, 98, 105, 141–43; McWilliams, *North from Mexico*, 177; Ruiz, *From Out of the Shadows*, 79–80. A synopsis of Tenayuca's life can be found in Roberto R. Calderon and Emilio Zamora, "Manuela Solis Sager and Emma Tenayuca: A Tribute," pp. 269–79 in *Between Borders: Essays on Mexican/Chicana History*, ed. Adelaide R. Del Castillo (Encino, Calif.: Floricanto Press, 1990). She went on to become a teacher in San Antonio. See interview with Emma Tenayuca in Texas, "If the Principles Are Gone," http://www.texancultures.utsa.edu/memories/htms/tenayuca_transcript.htm (accessed May 2, 2005).

20. Ruiz, *From Out of the Shadows*, 10; Nugent, *Into the West*, 202; Montejano, *Anglos and Mexicans*, 160–61, 198–99, 200; Foley, *White Scourge*, 52–53; and Paul S. Taylor, *Mexican Labor in the United States*, "Imperial Valley," 70, 91.

21. Foley, *White Scourge*, 139–40; Montejano, *Anglos and Mexicans*, 196; Francisco E. Balderrama and Raymond Rodriguez, *Decade of Betrayal: Mexican Repatriation in the 1930s* (Albuquerque, University of New Mexico Press, 1995) 80, 82; Ruiz, *From Out of the Shadows*, 29 (Garis quotation); and Acuña, *Occupied America*, 4th ed., chap 9, 5th ed., 203–210.

22. Mae Ngai points out that the legislation of March 4, 1929, converted illegal immigration — in that case, a person who had been deported and returns illegally — from a misdemeanor to a felony. First entering the country illegally through a non-designated entry was a misdemeanor. See Ngai, *Impossible Subjects*, 90 n., 90–91; Guerin Gonzalez, *Mexican Workers*, 73–74; Nugent, *Into the West*, 236; "40. Act of March 4, 1929 (45 Statutes-at-Large 1551)," http://uscis.gov/graphics/shared/aboutus/statistics/legishist/475.htm (accessed January 2, 2006); Muller and Espenshade, *Fourth Wave*, 30; Matt Garcia, *World of Its Own*, 113–14. An expanded version of Ngai's article appears as her first chapter in *Impossible Subjects*. Balderrama and Rodriguez reported that more than 17,600 were deported in 1929 from the Lower Rio Grande Valley of South Texas. See *Decade of Betrayal*, 59.

23. Nugent, *Into the West*, 236; Camarillo, *Chicanos in a Changing Society*, 144; Deverell, "Privileging the Mission," 248; Barkan, *And Still They Come*, table 2.1 (p. 197); and Daniels, *Guarding the Golden Door*, 51 and 59–60. Balderrama and Rodriguez found that between 1930 and 1939 over 46 percent of all those deported from the United States were Mexican (*Decade of Betrayal*, 53).

24. Balderrama and Rodriguez, *Decade of Betrayal*, 79.

25. Acuña, *Occupied America*, 4th ed., 211–12, 220–25; McWilliams, *North from Mexico*, 176–77; Manuel Gonzales, *Mexicanos*, 148–49; and Balderrama and Rodriguez, *Decade of Betrayal*, 79–80.

26. Balderrama and Rodriguez, *Decade of Betrayal*, 120; Guerin-Gonzalez, *Mexican Workers*, 77–78; and Sánchez, *Becoming Mexican American*, 211, 221–24. Sánchez's chapter 10 is devoted to the impact of the repatriations on the Los Angeles Mexican and Mexican American community. Guerin-Gonzalez devotes chapters 2 to 4 to this, including the use of repatriation as a strike-breaking weapon (113). In addition, especially note Balderrama and Rodriguez, 99–121, from which several quotations have been taken (99, 101, 105, 121–22).

27. Balderrama and Rodriguez, *Decade of Betrayal*, 117.

28. Matt Garcia, *World of Its Own*, 49–52; Camarillo, *Chicanos in a Changing Society*, 170–82, 205; McWilliams, *North from Mexico*, 176; and Acuña, *Occupied America*, 4th ed., 208–11, 225–52, which includes other labor organizations and workers' efforts besides those outlined here. McWilliams's actual statement says "By 1930," but it is part of a discussion about events during the 1930s, and it would appear that "1930" was typed in error for "1940."

29. Robert Alvarez Jr., "The Lemon Grove Incident: The Nation's First Successful Desegregation Case," *San Diego History* 32.2 (Spring 1986), http://www.sandiegohistory.org/journal/86spring/lemongrove.htm (accessed May 5, 2005); Leonel Sanchez, "Before Brown," *San Diego Tribune*, May 18, 2004, http://www.signonsandiego.com/uniontrib/20040518/news_1n18grove.html (accessed May 5, 2005). See also Lothrop, "Shadow on the Land" regarding the Italians' experiences.

28. Darker Turns during the Interwar Years

1. "Pedro and Cresencia Ponce: The Striker and the Healer," pp. 107–19 in *Hanahana: An Oral History Anthology of Hawaii's Working People*, ed. Michi Kodama Nishimoto, Warren S. Nishimoto, and Cynthia A. Oshiro (Honolulu: Ethnic Studies Oral History Project [ESOHP], University of Hawai'i, Manoa, 1984). This version is based on the transcript of the Ponce interview, pp. 28off in *The 1924 Filipino Strike on Kuaui*, vol. 1 (ESOHP, June 1979). See also Beechert, *Working in Hawaii*, 218–22.

2. Beechert, *Working in Hawaii*, 224–25, 232, 238–43, and 247 (quotation). On pp. 250–51 Beechert notes the kinds of wage gaps that existed in the late 1930s, including white waitresses receiving $40/month and non-whites $35; one-seventh of women earning less than 10 cents an hour, while men got an average of 23 cents; and at tourist hotels Filipinos in the kitchen receiving $50.10/month, Japanese housekeepers and kitchen help $56.30, and white desk clerks and supervisors $102.90.

3. Beechert, *Working in Hawaii*, 256–67, 278–79. See also Ruiz, *Cannery Women*, 55–81, and Patricia Zavella, *Women's Work and Chicano Families: Cannery Workers of the Santa Clara Valley* (Ithaca, N.Y.: Cornell University Press, 1987), 33, 35, 40, 42–48.

4. Beechert, *Working in Hawaii*, 285; William Carlson Smith, *Americans in Process*, 204–5. Smith's book was published in 1937.

5. Divine, *American Immigration Policy*, 84. See also Daniels, *Guarding the Golden Door*, 59–71 on the Mexican and Filipino episodes. Divine called these 1931 efforts "the high point of the restrictionist tide in the 1930s," but surely the obstinate refusal to allow Jewish refugees to enter more readily, especially the passengers on the SS *St. Louis* in 1939, should rank as the high point.

6. Ibid., 73.

7. Ibid., 73–80. However, Daniels's table (78) mistakenly includes quota and non-quota German immigrant totals based on country of last residence. The annual tables, based on quota immigrants by country of birth yield the total given here. Moreover,

between 38,000 and 40,000 Germans also departed the United States for Germany between 1930 and 1940, according to the immigration service's annual reports. U.S. Department of Labor, *Annual Report of the Secretary of Labor* from 1933 onward. Prior to that the title was *Annual Report of the Commissioner General of Immigration* (tables not always numbered).

8. Data on emigration from Germany from the Chronology in *Exiles and Émigrés: The Flight of European Artists from Hitler*, ed. Stephanie Barron (Los Angeles: Los Angeles County Museum of Art, 1997), 386–95; Daniels, *Guarding the Golden Door*, 79 (quotation); Divine, *American Immigration Policy*, 99–101; Maxine Schwartz Seller, *To Seek America: A History of Ethnic Life in the United States*, rev. ed. (n.p.: Jerome S. Ozer, 1988), 259 (quotation).

9. Taylor quotation, November 3, 1939, in Shanks, *Immigration and the Politics*, 103. On visas issues, see Divine, *American Immigration Policy*, 97, 102–103, and Daniels, *Guarding the Golden Door*, 79–80. See also Barkan, *And Still They Come*, 50–53.

10. David Brody, "American Jewry, the Refugees and Immigration Restriction (1932–1942)," (June 1956), reprinted in *America, American Jews, and the Holocaust*, ed. Jeffrey Gurock (New York: Routledge, 1998), 181–209. Quotations from pp. 200, 205.

11. Quotation from Martin Jay, "The German Migration: Is There a Figure in the Carpet?" in *Exiles and Émigrés*, ed. Barron, 326; Lawrence Weschler, "Paradise: The Southern California Idyll of Hitler's Cultural Exiles," in Barron, 343–45 (with paradise quotation); and Vorspan and Gartner, *History of the Jews*, 115, 196, 204. Nugent (*Into the West*, 239) cites the Starr data versus Vorspan and Gartner, *History of the Jews*, 197. See also the map of Los Angeles with the residences of leading refugees, in Barron, 359–61.

A U.S. Census Survey in 1936 reported 42 congregations with 82,000 "members," and Vorspan and Gartner estimated that there were 50 in 1941, with about 5,000 children getting some Jewish education. In addition, following the August 1937 organizational merger, 92 organizations would affiliate with the UJC, and that number would rise to 156.

12. Toll, *Making of an Ethnic Middle Class*, 180–86; Dodds, *American Northwest*, 252; Goodman, "Jews in Utah," pp. 16–18 in Papanikolas, *Peoples of Utah*.

13. Weschler, "Paradise," 341. See also Cecilia Rasmussen, "'Castle by the Sea' Became a Haven for Intellectuals," *Los Angeles Times*, March 20, 2005, regarding Villa Aurora, the home of Lion and Marta Feuchtwanger, and popular gathering place for German émigrés during the war.

14. Weschler, "Paradise," 346, 344.

15. Toll, *Making of an Ethnic Middle Class*, 160–62, 187–89, 192; Vorspan and Gartner, *History of the Jews*, 115, 205–6, 214–15; Dodds, *American Northwest*, 251–52. Some Jewish groups were certainly defense organizations or had incorporated that role with other basic community services. The Nazi threat was real and did add some poison to national sentiments regarding Jews, although the surge of American anti-Semitism pre-dated the Nazis in power. Still, in light of unfolding events in Europe, these groups could not be ignored. For example, the League of the Friends of New Germany, established in May 1933 and advocating German National Socialism, was operated by the Nazi Party through Nazi centers in Los Angeles, San Francisco, the East, and the Midwest. By 1934 there were reported to be 22,000 members, allegedly German Americans who hated "U.S. Jewry." The League of the Friends of New Germany was led by Heinz Spanknoebel and sought to "Hitlerize" the 45,000 members of the German American Alliance in Southern California. The Whites Shirts group, actually established in 1930, was led by George W. Christiano and by the end of 1933 had become "a major problem in Idaho, Oregon, and Washington." Moreover, Father Charles Coughlin's harsh, right-wing radio programs had a national audience. Both Spanknoebel and Christiano sought a Fascist

revolution in American, which each hoped to lead. Furthermore, William Dudley Pelley
had formed the Silver Shirts, with followers at least in California and Utah. See Vorspan
and Gartner, *History of the Jews*, 208–13 and 222–24. This paragraph's German material is
also based on Neil McMillen, "Pro-Nazi Sentiment in the United States, March 1933–
March 1934" [1963], 246–49 and passim, in Gurock, *America, American Jews*.

16. Weschler, "Paradise," 353, 356.

29. Aliens and Race Issues on the Eve of the Second World War

1. See Richard White, *"It's Your Misfortune,"* 496–99.

2. Drawn from "Honolulu Boat Builder," in *Hanahana*, ed. Nishimoto, Nishimoto, and Oshiro, 58–71.

3. Greg Robinson, *By Order of the President: FDR and the Internment of Japanese
Americans* (Cambridge, Mass.: Harvard University Press, 2001), 257, 7, 12, 19, 23, 26, 31,
34–35, 38, 40–42. Homer Lea's two books are *Valor of Ignorance* (1909) *and Day of the
Saxon* (1914).

4. Robinson, *By Order of the President*, 49–52, 55–57, 58.

5. Ibid., 59, 61–62, 63–67, 69. A separate FBI report in November 1941 acknowledged that the majority of Japanese belonged to numerous societies but were not seen
as a security threat.

6. Ibid., 70, 72. Also, Margo Anderson, *The American Census: A Social History* (New
Haven, Conn.: Yale University Press, 1988), 193–94. Anderson and William Seltzer provide an analysis of the evidence that the Census Bureau cooperated with various war-
related government agencies in providing "mesodata" on the location of Japanese Americans—by race and not just by the registration of "enemy aliens"—down to the block
level. See "After Pearl Harbor: The Proper Role of Population Data Systems in Time of
War" (draft dated March 28, 2000), 5, 7, 15, 20, 27, http://www.uwm.edu/~margo/govstat/
newpaa.htm (accessed November 19, 2003).

7. Roger Daniels's comments can be found in *The Decision to Relocate the Japanese
Americans* (Malabar, Fla.: Robert E. Krieger, 1975), 3–13.

8. Quoted by Beechert, *Working in Hawaii*, 285.

30. Interwar or Interlude?

1. However, the immigrants in 1940 continued to be over-represented in the labor
force: 10.6 percent, referring to just those classified as white.

2. If the number of aliens fell by a higher percentage than the number for those with
citizenship, then the proportion of the latter goes up even if their actual number declined.

3. Yet, events of the period were well mirrored in the Canadian case, for there were
157,700 Canadians in the West in 1920, a figure that jumped by one-fourth (to over
197,400) by 1930 and then fell during the 1930s to just over 183,700.

4. In 1940, for the first time, the Census Bureau introduced sampling. These data sets
are based on a 5 percent sample, whereas prior years were 100 percent counts. Consequently, they are not entirely comparable data sets.

5. The figures for Alaska and Hawai'i also appear to be higher by 126,224, for a total
increase in the 10 states and territories of 949,751 (I use the term "appear" because data are
presented differently in Alaska and Hawai'i). For all 14, the net increase in 1940 was
868,888 more second-generation persons over the 1920 figure—of which 72 percent took
place in California. While there was a jump in these figures in the West during the 1930s,

they fell elsewhere in the country by 1.5 percent. In Idaho, Montana, and Utah these numbers were declining during the 1920s as well. Data are available for only white persons.

6. Bogardus, *Mexican in the United States*, 88.

31. *Voices from America on the Eve of War*

1. This and the following accounts are adapted from the synopses and oral histories in *An Era of Change: Oral Histories of Civilians in World War II Hawai'i*, 5 vols., Center for Oral History, Social Science Research Institute (Honolulu: University of Hawai'i, April 1994). The Lindley account is in vol. 1:lii.

2. Ibid., 1:lvii.

3. Ibid.

4. Ibid., 1:lxi–lxii, 2:1305–19.

5. Ibid., 1:lvi–lvii, 2:164ff, 166, 168, 179–82, 188.

6. The University of Hawai'i's Center for Oral History reported that about 1,400 were held on Sand Island, and in the Haseyama story 1,466 were mentioned. Many were subsequently released, and Roger Daniels reports that 1,118 were eventually sent from Hawai'i to camps and detention centers on the mainland. See ibid., 1:xliii, and Roger Daniels, "The Forced Migrations of West Coast Japanese Americans, 1942–1946: A Quantitative Note," p. 74 in *Japanese Americans: From Relocation to Redress*, rev. ed., ed. Roger Daniels, Sandra C. Taylor, and Harry H. L. Kitano (Seattle: University of Washington Press, 1991). See also Dennis M. Ogawa and Evarts C. Fox Jr., "Japanese Internment and Relocation: The Hawaiian Experience," 135–38 in *Japanese Americans*.

7. *An Era of Change*, 1:xliii–xliv, 5:1723–52.

8. This account is adapted from Teresa Watanabe's "Déjà Vu" [The Story of the Watanabe Family], *Los Angeles Times Magazine*, June 8, 2003: 16–20, 46.

9. *Sokuku* actually means "fatherland;" "motherland" in Japanese is *bokoku*.

10. See chapter 9, "Minidoka Relocation Center, Idaho," in "Confinement and Ethnicity: An Overview of World War II Japanese American Relocation Sites," by J. Burton, M. Farrell, F. Lord, and R. Lord, for the National Park Service, http://www.cr.nps.gov/history/online_books/anthropology74/ce9.htm (accessed July 9, 2004).

11. Adapted from Interview with Suma Tsuboi Bullock in Dallesport, Washington, May 18, 1989, Oregon Historical Society, Accession no. 315.

12. Suma recalled this as taking place during or following Japan's invasion of Manchuria, which occurred in 1931.

13. Between May 7 and July 23, 1941, over 4,800 persons from all three coastal states were held there. From "Pinedale Assembly Center, California," chapter 16, in "Confinement and Ethnicity," http://www.cr.nps.gov/history/online_books/anthropology74/cet.htm (accessed July 7, 2004).

14. Adapted from Interview with Anthony Yturri, November 9, 1990, Oregon Historical Society, Accession no. 1134.

15. Her first name was not given, but her maiden name was obviously Elorriaga, for she was the sister of John A. Elorriaga's father. John—who was Anthony's cousin and who had also been born in Jordan Valley—went on to become president of United States Bankcorp and, for many years, board chairman and CEO of the U.S. National Bank of Oregon. On November 13, 1994, five years before Yturri's death, he and Elorriaga attended the 13th annual Basque Hall of Fame awards ceremony, organized by the Society of Basque Studies in America and held at John Ascuaga's hotel, the Nugget, in Sparks, Nevada. There, Yturri introduced Elorriaga, a recipient of one of the society's awards for

his outstanding contributions in banking, philanthropy, and other humanitarian endeavors. See "Basque Studies Program Newsletter," no. 49, 1994, http://basque.unr.edu/09/9.3/9.3.49t/9.3.49.04.fame.htm (accessed July 6, 2004).

16. Interview with Remedios "Reme" Yturri, March 16, 2002. *Oroitzapenak*—the Basque Oral History Project. http://www.basquemuseum.com/oralhistory/Yturri_Reme/Yturri_Reme.htm (accessed July 7, 2004).

17. Oral Memoirs of Angel Noe Gonzalez, August 26, 1972, Institute for Oral History, Baylor University. I have provided extensive descriptions of perceptions of Mexicans that corroborate Gonzalez's assessment of what he encountered. See Paul Taylor's study of Mexican labor in Dimmit County, *Mexican Labor in the United States*, 378; Mario Garcia's study of El Paso and the paucity of education for Mexican Americans, *Desert Immigrants*, 123–26; and David Montejano's description of the school segregation, *Anglos and Mexicans*, 167–68.

32. War

1. Geoffrey S. Smith, "Racial Nativism and Origins of Japanese American Relocation," pp. 79–80 in *Japanese Americans*, ed. Daniels, Taylor, and Kitano.

2. Stan Flewelling, *Shirakawa: Stories from a Pacific Northwest Japanese American Community* (Auburn and Seattle, Wash.: White River Valley Museum and the University of Washington Press, 2002), 170–72, 176, 184–85; Roger Daniels, "Words Do Matter: A Note on Inappropriate Terminology and the Incarceration of Japanese Americans," in *Nikkei in the Pacific Northwest: Japanese Americans and Japanese Canadians in the Twentieth Century*, ed. Louis Fiset and Gail M. Nomura (Seattle: Center for the Study of the Pacific Northwest in association with the University of Washington Press, 2005). The other phrase (rudderless) comes from Louis Fiset's outstanding work on Iwao and Hamaye Matsushita, *Imprisoned Apart: The World War II Correspondence of an Issei Couple* (Seattle: University of Washington Press, 1997), 33.

3. Fiset, *Imprisoned Apart*, 6–8. Daniels notes that it "may never be" possible "to give precise figures for either the total number of persons interned or how many there were of each nationality." However, the data presented here have been provided by Marian L. Smith, historian, U.S. Citizenship and Immigration Services, Department of Homeland Security—via Josef Barton's e-mail to H-ETHNIC, titled "Query: WWII Japanese & German Americans," November 3, 1999. For the many sources I used, see the footnotes to table 4.1.

4. In the 1940 Alien Registration process, 91,858 alien Japanese registered versus 314,715 non-citizen Germans and 695,363 non-citizen Italians. The census that year had reported 84,781 foreign-born Japanese residing in the entire United States (including Hawai'i and Alaska) compared with 1,237,772 Germans and 1,623,580 Italians. In the 14 western states and territories, there were 82,845 Issei, 137,612 foreign-born Germans, and 137,015 foreign-born Italians. *1940 Census of Population*, vol. 2, *Characteristics of the Population*, pts. 3–50, table 24.

Note that the Alien Registration Act required individuals to register who were not residents formally admitted into the country but who were in the United States 30 days or more. Therefore, there would likely be a difference between Alien Registration figures and census figures.

5. Robert C. Sims, "Japanese Americans in Idaho," p. 105 in *Japanese Americans*, ed. Daniels, Taylor, and Kitano.

6. Claus M. Naske, "The Relocation of Alaska's Japanese Residents," *Pacific Northwest Quarterly* 74.3 (July 1983): 125.

7. Hugh Carter, LeRoy B. DePuy, and Ernest Rubin, U.S. Department of Justice and Immigration and Naturalization Service, Office of Research and Educational Services, "Administrative History of the Immigration and Naturalization Service during World War II," August 19, 1946: 309–310 (unpublished manuscript; my thanks to Marian Smith for this document); Naske, "Relocation of Alaska's Japanese," 125.

8. Naske, "Relocation of Alaska's Japanese," passim. It was not made clear why Kimura could not acquire citizenship because the issue of World War One service as a qualification without regard to race had been resolved seven years before.

9. Lon Kurashige, *Japanese American Celebration and Conflict: A History of Ethnic Identity and Festival in Los Angeles, 1934–1990* (Berkeley: University of California Press, 2002), 68, 79, 80, 86. See also Betty Mitson, "Look Back in Anguish: Oral History and Japanese American Evacuation," in *Voices Long Silent: An Oral Inquiry into the Japanese American Evacuation*, ed. Arthur Hansen and Betty Mitson, Oral History Program, Japanese American Project (Fullerton: California State University, 1974), 23n37. Mitson notes that Heimusha-Kai was at first devoted to raising funds for war relief, but it "soon also went into raising a war chest for the Japanese government." The JACL and the strategy and complications facing the JACLers is discussed in Arthur Hansen and David A. Hacker, "The Manzanar 'Riot': An Ethnic Perspective," in *Voices Long Silent*, 42, 47, 49, 56–59, and Arthur Hansen, "Political Ideology and Participant Observation: Nisei Social Scientists in the Evacuation and Resettlement Study, 1942–1945," in *Guilt by Association: Essays on Japanese Settlement, Internment, and Relocation*, ed. Mike Mackey (Powell, Wyo.: Western History, 2001), 123–25.

10. Flewelling, *Shirakawa*, 175, 168, 126; Mary Paik Lee, *Quiet Odyssey: A Pioneer Korean Woman in America* (Seattle: University of Washington Press, 1990), 94–95 and 77 and 87.

11. Daniels, *Decision to Relocate*, 8.

12. Ibid., 11–12, 18; William Seltzer and Margo Anderson, "After Pearl Harbor: The Proper Role of Population Data Systems in Time of War," March 28, 2000 draft, 5, 7, 8, 10, 11, http://www.uwm.edu/~margo/govstat/newpaa.htm (accessed July 15, 2004); Lynette Clemetson, "Homeland Security Given Data on Arab Americans," *New York Times*, July 30, 2004: A10.

In the aftermath of September 11, 2001, the Census Bureau repeated this serious compromise of its pledge of confidentiality, notwithstanding its formal apology in 2000 "for allowing its statistical data to be used to round up Japanese Americans for internment during World War II," wrote reporter Lynette Clemetson. Kenneth Prewitt, former census director, acknowledged that during the war there was an issue of principle as well as law. "In World War II we violated our principles even if we didn't violate the law, and we assured people we wouldn't do it again." Yet, Clemetson here noted, "The Census Bureau has provided special tabulated population statistics on Arab-Americans to the Department of Homeland Security, including detailed information on how many people of Arab backgrounds live in certain ZIP codes." Arab-American advocacy groups quickly likened it "to the Census Bureau's compilation of similar information about Japanese-Americans during World War II." See Clemetson's "Homeland Security Given Data on Arab-Americans," *New York Times*, July 30, 2004: A10, and Clemetson's "Census Policy on Providing Sensitive Data Is Revised," *New York Times*, August 31, 2004: A12.

13. Daniels, *Decision to Relocate*, 12–15, 21–23; Geoffrey S. Smith, "Racial Nativism," 80; Bill Tonelli, "Thriller Draws on Oppression of Italians in Wartime in U.S.," *New York Times*, August 2, 2004: Arts 1; and U.S. Department of Justice, *Report to the Congress of the United States: A Review of the Restrictions on Persons of Italian Ancestry during World War II*, November 2001, accessed via U.S. House of Representatives, Committee on the Judiciary, "News Advisory: Sensenbrenner Releases Justice Department Report on Treat-

ment of Italian-Americans during World War II," November 27, 2001, http://www.house.gov/judiciary/news112701.htm (accessed August 2, 2004).

14. Dept. of Justice, *Report*, 80; Daniels, *Decision to Relocate*, 23, 26, 41. A few days later, on February 14, the Department of Justice reduced the number of zones to 117: 68 in California, 24 in Oregon, 18 in Arizona, and 7 in Washington (Dept. of Justice, *Report*, appendix B).

15. War Department, Office of the Chief of Staff, "Notes on Evacuation of Japanese from Hawaiian Islands," n.d., but grouped with February 1942 documents under "Archival documents, February 20, 1942–March 19, 1942," in *American Concentration Camps: A Documentary History of the Relocation and Incarceration of Japanese Americans, 1942–1945*," ed. Roger Daniels, 9 vols. (New York: Garland Press, 1989), vol. 3 (not paginated). Martial law was declared in Hawai'i from December 7, 1941, to October 24, 1944 (Fuchs, *Hawaii Pono*, 299–300). For a brief description of the efforts to control or screen suspect groups, see Ogawa and Fox, "Japanese Internment and Relocation." Regarding the congressional members' actions, see Dept. of Justice, *Report*, appendix B. Morton Grodzins provides an extended coverage of the mounting calls for evacuation, in *Americans Betrayed: Politics and the Japanese Evacuation* (Chicago: University of Chicago Press, 1949), 21, 30, 34, 35, 48, 68, 103, 109, 110–12, 119, 127. He also noted the few voices in opposition to precipitous action, but most, he pointed out, came after evacuation was a "fait accompli": 92, 181–202. In fall 1943, Emmons replaced De Witt at the head of the Western Command.

16. Daniels, *Decision to Relocate*, 24–26, 31, and Stephen Fox, *The Unknown Internment: An Oral History of the Relocation of Italian Americans during World War II* (Boston: Twayne, 1990), 51–52, 63, 54. As noted above, zone "B" would largely correspond to Biddle's Restricted Areas, where enemy aliens could remain but be subject to a 9 P.M.–6 A.M. curfew, which De Witt later expanded to 8 P.M. to 6 A.M. While earlier information cited 1,875 Japanese removed to the mainland, the more recent figure is about 1,500 (see note 6 of chapter 31, above).

17. Daniels, *Decision to Relocate*, 27, 31, 34–38, and Pomeroy, *Pacific Slope*, 286–87.

18. Pomeroy, *Pacific Slope*, 36–43, 47–48; Geoffrey S. Smith, "Racial Nativism," 81–82. The Olson quotation, as related by Togo Tanaka, who was present, is from Betty E. Mitson, "Look Back in Anguish," 40. The Daniels quotation is in *Decision to Relocate*, 40–41.

19. Daniels, *Decision to Relocate*, 82; Roger Daniels, "Relocation, Redress, and the Report: A Historical Appraisal," in *Japanese Americans*, ed. Daniels, Taylor, and Kitano, 7–8; "Chronology of Japanese American History," in *Japanese Americans*, xvi–xvii; F. Alan Coombs, "Congressional Opinion and War Relocation, 1943," in *Japanese Americans*, 91; and Daniels, *Decision to Relocate*, 40–41, 44, 48–51. It is quite relevant that most of DeWitt's subsequent public proclamations and exclusion orders were justified on the explicit grounds of military necessity. However, Chief of Staff George C. Marshall had concluded that relocation "was *not* a rational military precaution," but he was compelled to accept that political decision, although it did not originally include incarceration (quoted by Daniels, "Relocation, Redress," 8). Ultimately, it was precisely the unjustified nature of those claims of military necessity on which the congressional Commission on Wartime Relocation and Internment of Civilians (CWRIC) concentrated its harshest criticism.

20. Excerpts from the congressional debates leading to the Act of March 21, 1942, and its text appear in "Congressional Record, selected papers," in Daniels, *American Concentration Camps*, vol. 3 (unpaginated), Stephen Fox, *Unknown Internment*, 106–107; and note 23 of chapter 32, below.

21. The *Los Angeles Times* articles of February 23, 1942, are quoted by Arthur Verge, in "The Impact of the Second World War on Los Angeles," in *American West*, ed. Nugent

and Ridge, 239. Millikin's quotation is from David A. Takami, *Divided Destiny: A History of Japanese Americans in Seattle* (Seattle: University of Washington Press, 1998), 45. Curry's letter is reprinted in Daniels, *American Concentration Camps*, vol. 3, "Archival documents, March 20, 1942–March 31, 1942," n.p.

 For other examples of fear-inducing rumor mongering, see the *Coos Bay Times*, on Oregon's central coast, and the *Oregonian* in G. Thomas Edwards, "The Oregon Coast and Three of Its Guerrilla Organizations, 1942," in *The Pacific Northwest in World War Two*, ed. Carlos Schwantes (Manhattan, Kans.: Sunflower University Press, 1986), 25, 30.

 22. That figure of 4,889 is reported in the U.S. Supreme Court case *Ex Parte Endo* (323 U.S. 283; December 18, 1944), 288 n. 2. The Court's source was the U.S. Department of War, *Final Report: Japanese Evacuation from the West Coast, 1942* (New York: Arno Press, 1978 [G.P.O. 1943]), chapter 9, which also reported that over 10,300 indicated they planned to relocate, but only the 4,889 were able to do so. Eastern Washington and Oregon as well as Idaho were other prominent destinations. Over four-fifths had migrated from California, and 70 percent were Nisei (107–13). (See, too, Louis Fiset, "Thinning, Topping, and Loading: Japanese Americans and Beet Sugar in World War Two," *Pacific Northwest Quarterly* 90.3 [Summer 1999]: 125.) Sandra Taylor cited the figure of voluntary resettlers moving to Denver, in "From Incarceration to Freedom: Japanese Americans and the Departure from the Concentration Camps," in *Alien Justice: Wartime Internment in Australia and North America*, ed. Kay Saunders and Roger Daniels (St. Lucia: University of Queensland, Australia, 2000), 211. Regarding the University of Washington, see Takami, *Divided Destiny*, 46.

 Army statistics had indicated that at the outset 117,116 Japanese Americans were "eligible" for incarceration, but only 110,723 were taken in. It is likely that a good part of that difference can be attributed to those who left voluntarily. See Roger Daniels, "Forced Migrations," 72–73. Discussions of the proclamations can be found in Daniels, *Decision to Relocate*, 23, 26, 43, 53, 124–25 (text of Proclamation No. 3). DeWitt's original Military Areas A and B are shown in Daniels, *American Concentration Camps*, 1:320, and Michi Weglyn, *Years of Infamy: The Untold Story of America's Concentration Camps*, rev. ed. (Seattle: University of Washington Press, 1996), 16). A map of the final six Military Areas in the seven western states is in *Final Report*, 87. The proclamations, exclusion orders, and the government's other detailed maps are reprinted in Daniels, *American Concentration Camps*, 1: "Official proclamations and other public documents, December 7, 1941–April 20, 1942," appendix.

 23. Jason Scott Smith, "New Deal Public Works at War: The WPA and Japanese American Internment," *Pacific Historical Review* 72.1 (2003): 72. Public Proclamation No. 4 and Civilian Exclusion Order No. 1 are reprinted in Daniels, *American Concentration Camps*, 1:331–34. The quotation is from the latter document.

 24. Roger Daniels, "Western Reaction to the Relocated Japanese Americans: The Case of Wyoming," in *Japanese Americans*, ed. Daniels, Taylor, and Kitano, 114.

 25. Timeline, in *Japanese Americans*, ed. Daniels, Taylor, and Kitano, xviii–xix.

 26. Two of many Internet sites providing details on the Battle of Midway, marking it as a vital turning point in the war, are "Battle of Midway, June 4-7, 1942—Overview and Special Image Selection," www.history.navy.mil/photos/events/wwii-pac/midway/midway .htm, and "Battle of Midway—Part 1," www.sunwest-emb.com/wiseman/bmidway.htm (both accessed July 12, 2004).

 Kevin Starr, in his recent study of California in the 1940s, suggests the evolution of thinking during the first half of 1942. The capture of the Philippines in April was viewed as a calamity second only to the Pearl Harbor attack, followed by the Japanese occupation of three outer Aleutian Islands in June. He poses the question: In view of the earlier shelling of Santa Barbara by Japanese submarine I-17 on February 23, could these setbacks not confirm the possibility of an invasion, and if so, could not that scenario also suggest that espionage and sabotage by Japanese along the coast were a real possibility? Starr concludes, "As racial hatred against the Japanese surfaced into respectability . . . [it] became a vehement proof of patriotism," and whiteness was even more identified with the war effort. However, Starr's collapsing of events over a critical four-month period confuses the evolution of public opinion, for the March public opinion poll already demonstrated that widespread support for the removal of the Japanese had materialized—before Bataan and before Midway and the Aleutian invasion. Starr, *Embattled Dreams: California in War and Peace, 1940–1950* (New York: Oxford University Press, 2002), 90, 98 (quotation).

27. Roger Daniels, introduction to "Effects of Incarceration Analyzed," part 6 of *Japanese Americans,* ed. Daniels, Taylor, and Kitano, 149, as well as the essays in that section by Harry Kitano, Sandra Taylor, and Gary Okihiro and David Drummond.

28. James Ricci, "Accentuating the Positive: Mary Nomura Is Still 'Preaching' as the Songbird of Manzanar," *Los Angeles Times,* July 13, 2004: E1, E9. Quotation is from Ricci.

29. Sarah Kershaw, "Japanese Americans Relive Barbed Era," *New York Times,* June 30, 2003: A14; and Steve Hymon, "Finally Sharing Manzanar's Bitter Tale," *Los Angeles Times,* April 25, 2004: A1, A30–31. There are numerous accounts now of the relocation/incarceration experiences. For example, besides others cited herein, see Yoshiko Uchida, *Desert Exile: The Uprooting of a Japanese-American Family* (Seattle: University of Washington Press, 1982); Richard S. Nishimoto, *Inside an American Concentration Camp: Japanese American Resistance at Poston, Arizona,* ed. Lane Ryo Hirabayashi (Tucson: University of Arizona Press, 1995); Sandra C. Taylor, *Jewel of the Desert: Japanese American Internment in Topaz* (Berkeley: University of California Press, 1993); and Gary Y. Okihiro, *Storied Lives: Japanese American Students and World War II* (Seattle: University of Washington Press, 1999).

30. In 1944, J. Edgar Hoover reported that by that time 14,807 enemy aliens had been taken into custody, but Daniels believes that the exact number will never be known, and he "guesstimates" that the actual number interned was "something under 11,000, broken down as follows: Japanese, perhaps 8,000; Germans, perhaps 2,300 . . . , and only a few hundred Italians." Others had been held only for a short time. The INS *Annual Report* for 1944 indicates (22) that at the end of that fiscal year (June 30), 6,238 persons were in custody, down from 9,220 the prior year. That 1944 interned population included 2,971 Germans, 3,136 Japanese, and 86 Italians. See table 4.1 in appendix.

Furthermore, under the original 1940 alien registration, there were, in the United States, 695,363 Italians, 314,715 Germans, and 91,858 Japanese, plus others from Alaska, Hawai'i, and Latin America. In 1943 there were 653,359 Italians, 300,064 Germans, and 90,928 Japanese registered. In addition, 2,264 Japanese were brought chiefly from Peru, plus 1,058 Germans, and 288 Italians from 15 Latin American countries. Regarding the terminology, see Daniels, "Words Do Matter," 7, 4.

31. Flewelling, *Shirakawa,* 38–40, 98–100, 104, 121–23, 181, 170, 190–92, 194–95, 231, 235. Jeanne Wakatsuki Houston and James D. Houston also present an account of her father's interrogation that is both poignant and amusing. See *Farewell to Manzanar* (New York: Houghton Mifflin, 1973), 43–46.

32. Naske, "Relocation of Alaska's Japanese," 130. The INS did provide an option for family members who wished to remain in their detention centers with those being formally held. These "voluntary internees" were most commonly housed in the Crystal City, Texas, facility, beginning in December 1942. Thus, for example, among the 6,238 in custody at the end of June 1944, some 1,045 were voluntary. A year later, out of 7,364, there were 1,120 who were voluntary. In June 1946, with the Pacific war ended for over 10

months and that in Europe terminated 14 months earlier, 1,539 remained in INS custody, among whom there were still 146 voluntary internees. See INS *Annual Report, 1944,* 22; *1945,* 26; *1946,* 30; Carter, DePuy, and Enbin, "Administrative History," 312–14; and Thomas K. Walls's description of the INS camps in Texas, in *The Japanese Texans,* chapter 7.

33. Daniels, "Words Do Matter," 12, 14, 16, 19; Kurashige, *Japanese American Celebration,* 75, 85–86; and Daniels, "Relocation, Redress," 6–7.

34. For example, the 431 Japanese Americans evacuated from Hood River Valley, Oregon, in early May were given six days' notice, and each was allowed to take 70 pounds in luggage. Tamura, *Hood River Issei,* 166–67.

Individuals going from Los Angeles to the Manzanar "Reception Center," as were others going to other locations, were instructed to bring linens, toilet articles, clothing, silverware, and "essential personal effects"—all of which had to be securely packaged. "The size and number of the packages is limited to that which can be carried by the individual or family group." The government offered storage for big items (not vehicles) "at the sole risk of the owner." CEO No. 3 (March 30, 1942) and CEO No. 9 (April 20, 1942), in Daniels, *American Concentration Camps,* 1: "Official proclamations"—appendix, 336, 344. See also *Final Report,* chapter 11, "Protection of Property of Evacuees."

35. After working for the WRA for nine months, Iwao taught at the university for two years, entered a B.A. program, graduating in 1951 with honors in Far Eastern studies, and in 1952 was hired by the University of Washington's Far Eastern Library until he retired a decade later. But the recovery part of his story was not yet complete. With the change in U.S. law in 1952, Iwao became a U.S. citizen on March 22, 1954; two years later, he became a principal in the reopened Japanese language school. In February 1965, Hanaye died of cancer, not living to see Iwao Matsushita honored by the Japanese government in 1969 and again in 1974. He died five years later.

This account of the Matsushitas is drawn from Louis Fiset's exceptional work *Imprisoned Apart,* part 1, with principal quotations from 65–66, 71–72, 77, 79.

36. Naske, "Relocation of Alaska's Japanese," 130, 128–29.

37. Ngai discusses the WRA perspective on social engineering in the camps (*Impossible Subjects,* 177–81). Regarding the nationalistic groups, see Arthur A. Hansen, "Cultural Politics in the Gila River Relocation Center, 1942–1943," *Arizona and the West* 27.4 (Winter 1985): 327–62, and John J. Culley, "The Santa Fe Internment Camp and the Justice Department Program for Enemy Aliens," 57–71 in *Japanese Americans,* ed. Daniels, Taylor, and Kitano. See also Lane Ryo Hirabayashi, "The Impact of Incarceration on the Education of Nisei School Children," 44–51 in *Japanese Americans;* and Amy Iwasaki Mass, "Psychological Effects of the Camps on Japanese Americans," in *Japanese Americans,* 159–67; and chapter 20 in Bill Hosokawa, *Nisei: The Quiet Americans* (New York: William Morrow, 1969). Three interesting, early collections of photographs on the internment experience are in *Life* magazine's spread on "Tule Lake: At This Segregation Center Are 18,000 Japanese Considered Disloyal to U.S.," photographs by Carl Mydan, 20 March 1944, 25–35; Maisie and Richard Conrat, *Executive Order 9066: The Internment of 110,000 Japanese Americans* ([San Francisco]: California Historical Society, 1972); and Ansel Adams's photos in John Armor and Peter Wright, *Manzanar* (New York: New York Times Books, 1988).

38. This and the next two paragraphs are drawn from Susan L. Smith, "Caregiving in Camp: Japanese American Women and Community Health in World War II," in *Guilt by Association,* ed. Mackey, 191; Sandra Taylor, "From Incarceration to Freedom," 217; and Hansen, "Cultural Politics" and the segment by Kurashige on the December 1942 Manzanar "uprising," 85–94. The quotation regarding the fences is from Valerie Matsumoto, "Japanese-American Women during World War II," in *Impact of the Second*

World War, ed. Nugent and Ridge, 255. The Mike quotation is from Takami, *Divided Destiny,* 59–60.

Given these many negative aspects of the camp experiences, one must still acknowledge, as several authors have, that for the many Issei women who had labored for years raising families and toiling in the fields—arduous dual lives of productive and reproductive labor—the camp period gave them (involuntarily) a time for relaxation and leisure they had not known before: "a well earned and highly deserved holiday," as one put it. See, for example, Tamura, *Hood River Issei,* 207, and Matsumoto, "Japanese-American Women," 263.

Robert Spence, writing about the Gila River camp in Arizona, noted: "To the people, the area seemed a forbidding wasteland. Above all, the heat remained oppressive, reaching at times 120 degrees Fahrenheit. Small children and the elderly were particularly adversely affected. Deaths were not uncommon among these groups but they . . . were given little administrative attention." "Gila in Retrospect," in *Views from Within: The Japanese American Evacuation and Resettlement Study,* ed. Yuji Ichioka (Los Angeles: UCLA Asian American Studies Center, 1989), 161.

39. In 1940 there were still 5,135 Issei and Nisei farm operators just in California and 6,118 in the three coastal states, with 258,674 acres valued at $72.64 million.

40. Chan, *Asian Americans,* 128; Sandra Taylor, "Evacuation and Economic Loss: Questions and Perspectives," in *Japanese Americans,* ed. Daniels, Taylor, and Kitano, 165; Matsumoto, "Japanese-American Women, 267–68; Hosokawa, *Nisei,* 355–56; Fiset, *Imprisoned Apart,* 124–26, 128–30, 133, 134, 136–37, and notes 68 and 82; and Sims, "Japanese Americans in Idaho," 104, 107–8.

41. Quotations are from Daniels, "Words Do Matter," 20–21, 24, and "Further Thoughts on the Japanese American Cases" *OAH Magazine of History* 17 (January 2003): 53, 55. The Manzanar "revolt" is described by Arthur Hansen and David Hacker, in "The Manazanar 'Riot': An Ethnic Perspective," in *Voices Long Silent,* ed. Hansen and Mitson, 41–79. See also the episode as described by Hansen in "Cultural Politics" and the segment in the 1945 INS *Annual Report,* 30. Takami wrote about the JACLers' opposition to those who did not go along with the evacuation, noting that Mike Masaoka even urged that they not support Min Yasui's legal challenge to the curfew (*Divided Destiny,* 56).

42. Daniels, "Forced Migrations," 72–74. Bill Hosokawa reported (296) that the Kibei, who studied for three or more years in Japan, comprised 12.2 percent of the Nisei. His chapter 23 covers the military achievements of the 442/100 as well as Aiso and the MISLS (*Nisei,* 394–400). The presumption here is that 45 percent remained in the camps until 1945. Kurashige indicates that in Manzanar 51 percent left only after restrictions were canceled on returning to the coast (103, 108–110). In addition, the FBI's Final Report in 1945 indicates that, overall, 5,428 Japanese had been apprehended and held in custody by the INS (not WRA) and that approximately 5,200 were actually interned by that agency, including 1,416 transferred from Tule Lake in early 1945. Prior to that the maximum number of Japanese in INS facilities was 3,136 in June 1944 (table 4.1.) Regarding Nisei who transferred to colleges outside the West, see Allan W. Austin, *From Concentration Camp to Campus: Japanese American Students and World War II* (Urbana: University of Illinois Press, 2005). Meanwhile, Okinawans from Hawai'i, who had been ridiculed for not speaking the prevalent Japanese dialect among the migrants, Chūgoku-ben, were asked to play a major role when the U.S. military reached Okinawa; they were called in to persuade the enemy on the Ryukyu Islands to surrender (Kimura, *Issei,* 72).

43. Sandra Taylor, "From Incarceration to Freedom," 206, and Bill Hosokawa, *Nisei,* 417. Jeanne Wakatsuki Houston related her experience as people began to return in

early 1945. "Ominous reports of their reception began trickling back," and she briefly recounts episodes in Los Angeles, Fresno, San Jose, and Seattle. However, most "resettled without suffering bodily harm." Psychological harm was another matter. See Houston's *Farewell to Manzanar*, 93.

44. Starr, *Embattled Dreams*, 94–95.

45. Chan, *Asian Americans*, 131–32; Spickard, *Japanese Americans*, 118–20; "Japanese Americans and World War II: The Heart Mountain Fair Play Committee," session at the Organization of American Historians, Boston, March 27, 2004, with Frank Emi, one of the founders of the FPC; William Hohri, "Redress as a Movement towards Enfranchisement," in *Japanese Americans*, ed. Daniels, Taylor, and Kitano, 196–97. Regarding the draft quota see Weglyn, *Years of Infamy*, 143–44. She says there was a quota of 3,000, and 1,181 came forward; Chan (133) suggests the quota was closer to 4,000 but agrees on the number who came forward. Much of Weglyn's book is devoted to the widespread resistance within the camps that was for so long minimized. There is a brief discussion of this episode and the number drafted and the number refusing to be screened in *Personal Justice Denied: Report of the Commission on Wartime Relocation and Internment of Civilians* (Seattle: University of Washington Press, 1997), chapter 9.

There is, however, inconsistent information regarding the number who did not respond in 1943 to the two questions or responded negatively, setting themselves apart from others as the "disloyals." Bill Hosokawa (*Nisei*, 365) indicated that "some 11 percent of those eligible to register—about 7,600 evacuees—gave 'No' or qualified answers to the loyalty questions. At Tule Lake, some 3,000 refused to register." Sucheng Chan states (131) that "Altogether 78,000 individuals were required to register. . . . Over 4,000 of the latter [Nisei males 17–37] refused to answer the two questions or gave negative or qualified answers." Paul Spickard, discussing the controversy over the two questions, went on to state (*Japanese Americans*, 119) that "For whatever reasons, about 12,000 inmates declared themselves 'disloyal' to the United States" and were subsequently sent to Tule Lake." I am suggesting here that the latter is probably a combination of those who answered negatively and those who refused to answer.

46. Tono's statement appears in John Tateishi's *And Justice for All: An Oral History of the Japanese American Detention Camps* (Seattle: University of Washington Press, 1984), 169–75. The 2000 JACL ceremony was discussed at the OAH session cited in endnote 45, above. In addition, the recent episode, including the formal apology in 2000 and the ceremony in 2002, was described by Andy Noguchi in "The Nisei Draft Resisters and the JACL," *Pacific Citizen Holiday Issue*, December 2003: 32, 81. See also chapter 23 in Hosokawa and chapter 10 in *Personal Justice* regarding the 442/100.

47. About 3,700 were also in the Pacific theater, mostly with the military intelligence service, a story kept classified for years (Hosokawa, *Nisei*, 398).

48. Richard Goldstein, "Yukio Okutsu, 81, Soldier Who Led Attack on Germans," *New York Times*, September 14, 2003; Cecilia Rasmussen, "World War II Soldier's Heroism Sent a Message about Prejudice," *Los Angeles Times*, July 4, 2004; and Hosokawa, *Nisei*, 398. Regarding the Lost Battalion episode, also see http://www.goforbroke.org/ history/history_historical_campaigns_rescue.asp (accessed July 15, 2004).

49. Many of the points quoted in this and the next paragraph are drawn from Howard Ball's outstanding essay, "Judicial Parsimony and Military Necessity Disinterred: A Reexamination of the Japanese Exclusion Cases, 1943–44," in *Japanese Americans*, ed. Daniels, Taylor, and Kitano, 176–85.

50. Matt Bai recounts that Ernest Besig, executive director of the American Civil Liberties Union for Northern California, was seeking a test case to challenge the government's removal of Japanese Americans, although Bai incorrectly states that the case even-

tually filed dwelt on internment. Actually, as described here, the court's decision focused only on the evacuation orders. Bai also describes the negative reaction among Japanese Americans to Korematsu's action and court case and the ultimate vindication that came with Peter Irons's challenge in federal court four decades later. Bai, "He Said No to Internment," *New York Times Magazine*, December 25, 2005: 38.

51. The decision pointed out, in its footnote 19, that by the end of July 1944 there were 28,911 persons on indefinite leave, with 61,002 remaining in nine relocation centers and another 18,684 in the Tule Lake camp (108, 597).

52. Omitting all states where there were WRA camps or INS facilities, plus the four states with military zones, the number of Japanese in all other states (by race) rose from 5,092 in 1940 to 28,083 in 1950, to 59,162 in 1960. In the four Western states in which evacuations took place (California, Arizona, Oregon, Washington), the Japanese population (by race) fell from 112,985 in 1940 to 99,090 in 1950, rebounding thereafter to 180,486 in 1960. At least in the short run, the percentage of all those of Japanese descent in the mainland West did fall from 95.6 percent in 1940 to 79.9 percent in 1950. See Spickard, appendix, tables 2 and 3.

53. *Japanese Americans*, ed. Daniels, Taylor, and Kitano, xxi. The 1946 INS *Annual Report* (30) indicates that, previously, 1,416 "troublesome" Japanese Americans had been transferred to an INS center (1945 *Report*, 26) and then 4,320 were placed in the Tule Lake camp after it was officially closed, at which time it was placed under INS control but was maintained by WRA staff. Many of these were individuals who had filed for repatriation to Japan. The Issei quotation is from Ichioka, *Issei*, 260. Quite interesting is the story about Tule Lake, run by *Life* in March 1944 (note 37 in chapter 32, above).

54. *Personal Justice*, 251–52. Following the debacle of questions 27 and 28 and the desire expressed by some Nisei to renounce their American citizenship, Congress passed the Act of July 1, 1944, "In Respect to Loss of Nationality" (58 Stat. 677), which provided that, "in a state of war," Americans *within the United States* could submit "a formal written renunciation of nationality" that would not be "contrary to the interests of national defense." This new provision enabled the Nisei to proceed, and nearly 5,800 did so. However, regarding most of those 1,900 noted separately in the text, since they were actually Nisei minors, dependents of Issei applying for repatriation, technically most had not individually renounced their citizenship and "requested" expatriation, as did the 1,100 adult Nisei. Of the 5,800 who initially filed for renunciation, 3,186 subsequently requested hearings to reverse their renunciation decisions, and 2,737 were granted (Weglyn, *Years of Infamy*, 260, 258).

Mae Ngai argues that the Nisei renunciants "held complicated divided loyalties" that could have included "patriotic sympathies with Japan." She concludes that their actions were "at once principled and pragmatic" (*Impossible Subjects*, 200–201). That may hold for many Kibei, but it is more problematic for other Nisei, many of whom had either renounced their dual citizenship earlier or had never been registered at birth with the consulate.

55. *Personal Justice*, chapter 4; Teresa Watanabe, "Donor to Fund UCLA Chair on WWII Internment," *Los Angeles Times*, February 15, 2004; "UCLA Gets $500,000 to Study World War II Internments," *AsianWeek*, February 19, 2004; Roger Daniels, introduction to "Effects of Incarceration Analyzed," part 6 of *Japanese Americans*, ed. Daniels, Taylor, and Kitano, 148–49; Sandra Taylor, "Evacuation and Economic Loss: Questions and Perspectives, *Japanese Americans*, 163–67.

56. The quotation was the title of an NBC TV special in 1972, cited by Roger Daniels, in "The Exile and Return of Seattle's Japanese," *Pacific Northwest Quarterly* 88.4 (Fall 1997): 168.

57. Quoted by Roger Daniels from an interview with Black, in "Korematsu v. United States Revisited, 1944 and 1983," in *Race on Trial: Law and Justice in American History*, ed. Annette Gordon-Reed (New York: Oxford University Press, 2002), 148.

58. Sucheng Chan emphasizes that Roosevelt wanted no action taken regarding the camps until after the 1944 election, "even though his staff had repeatedly told him from late 1943 onward that there was no longer any military necessity to keep the Japanese" in the camps (138).

59. Ball, "Judicial Parsimony," 184.

60. Ngai's statement is in *Impossible Subjects*, 8. For more recent episodes along this line, see "Guantánamo Farce," Editorial, *Los Angeles Times*, September 2, 2004: B12, and Rich B. Schmitt, "U.S. Erred in Terror Convictions," editorial, *Los Angeles Times*, September 2, 2004: A1, A17.

33. *The Second World War's Other Enemy Aliens*

1. Stephen Fox, *Unknown Internment*, 1, and George E. Pozzetta, "Alien Enemies or Loyal Americans? The Internment of Italian Americans," in *Alien Justice*, ed. Saunders and Daniels, 81.

2. The accounts in this and the next paragraph are drawn from Stephen Fox, *Unknown Internment*, 10–11, 19, 15–16. See also Carol McKibben, *Beyond Cannery Row: Cicilian Women, Immigration, and Community in Monterey, California, 1915–1999* (Urbana: University of Illinois Press, 2006), 106–107, 115–16. McKibben points out that because it was so common for the women not to seek citizenship (men who had not become citizens were considered "lazy" and "stupid"), "Few families were immune" from the orders to evacuate. Many did feel that the lack of citizenship marked them as "uncultured" and, hence, not fully sharing in American "whiteness," although legally they were white (85–87).

3. Pozzetta, "Alien Enemies," 82; Jörg Nagler, "Internment of German Enemy Aliens in the United States during the Second World War," in *Alien Justice*, ed. Saunders and Daniels, 75; Gloria Ricci Lothrop, "Unwelcome in Freedom's Land: The Impact of World War II on Italian Aliens in Southern California," *Southern California Quarterly* 81.4: 510–516; Lothrop, "Shadow on the Land," 206, 209; Monterey quotations are from McKibben, *Beyond Cannery Row*, 76–77; Mario Valdastri Jr., "Two Men in Suits," in *Una Storia Segreta: The Secret History of Italian American Evacuation and Internment during World War II*, ed. Lawrence DiStasi (Berkeley, Calif.: Jeyday Books, 2001), 153–54; and Dept. of Justice, *Report*, 4–5, on the FBI's early apprehensions, possibly including two dozen Italians, December 7–8, 1941.

4. In the Department of Justice's 2001 *Report*, it listed 1,881 Italians who were apprehended, in addition to the 418 who were interned (lengths of time unknown) and the 74 arrested in early December 1941. That totaled 2,373 brought in by the FBI, although the report notes that its lists of names may not be complete.

The figures cited in this section have been culled from numerous sources in order to determine with some consistency what the different totals were and just what they represented. Table 4.1 contains what I have unearthed. The sources include Nagler, "Internment," 77; Pozzetta, "Alien Enemies," 85, 276 n. 21; Stephen Fox, *Unknown Internment*, 151, 164; Fiset, *Imprisoned Apart*, 72; Lothrop, "Unwelcome in Freedom's Land," 519, 523–25; John Joel Culley, "Enemy Alien Control in the United States during World War II: A Survey," in *Alien Justice*, ed. Saunders and Daniels, 141, 144; and Culley, "Trouble at the Lordsburg Internment Camp," *New Mexico Historical Review* 60 (1985): 244n2; Rose

D. Scherini, "Executive Order 9066 and Italian Americans: The San Francisco Story," in *Fulfilling the Promise*, ed. Lothrop, 217; and the INS's *Annual Reports* for 1945, 26; 1946, 30; and 1947, 27. My thanks to Marian Smith, historian, Immigration Library, Dept. of Homeland Security, for providing the latter three sources. See also Dept. of Justice, *Report*, appendixes C.2 and D.

An example of the challenge presented by these reported figures can be seen in comparing, first, Pozzetta ("Alien Enemies") with Scherini ("Executive Order 9066," 222) and, second, Lothrop's data in "Unwelcome in Freedom's Land" (517) with her similar statement in "A Shadow on the Land" (209). However, Lothrop more specifically notes that during the whole duration of the war, merely 6 Italians were apprehended in San Diego, 458 in San Francisco, and 142 in Los Angeles ("Unwelcome in Freedom's Land," 517n24).

5. Quoted in Lothrop, "Unwelcome in Freedom's Land," 139. To add some perspective, in America in 1940 there were 3.49 million persons of German foreign stock, 4.043 million of Italian foreign stock and, on the mainland, just 126,947 persons of Japanese ancestry. In Washington, Oregon, and California, there were 398,240 persons of German foreign stock, 278,847 of Italian stock, but only 112,353 persons of Japanese descent. In San Francisco alone there were 39,000 of German and Italian foreign stock. Officials undoubtedly found such numbers politically and economically daunting.

6. Daniels, *Decision to Relocate*, 15, 23–24; Stephen Fox, *Unknown Internment*, 51–52, 63; Scherini, "Executive Order 9066," 218–20. The figure on Italian aliens in Military Area One is in Dept. of Justice, *Report*, 26.

7. Scherini, "Executive Order 9066," 218, and Stephen Fox, *Unknown Internment*, 59–61. The Dept. of Justice reports that the FBI entered 2,900 Italian homes across the country and arrested 442 for violations of the curfews and contraband requirements. It appears most were usually given warnings. *Report*, 22.

8. Stephen Fox, *Unknown Internment*, 63–64, 70–71, 81; McKibben, *Beyond Cannery Row*, 88, 90–91; Dept. of Justice, *Report*, 5:27.

9. Dept. of Justice, *Report*, 5:55, 105, 11, 133, 127; Pozzetta, "Alien Enemies," 89; and Scherini, "Executive Order 9066," 219–221.

10. Stephen Fox, *Unknown Internment*, 101.

11. Ibid., 132; McKibben, *Beyond Cannery Row*, 88.

12. Angelo de Guttadauro, "Exclusion Is a Four-Letter Word, in *Una Storia Segreta*, 158; Dept. of Justice, *Report*, 5:10–13. The list of prohibited areas throughout the United States is on p. 159.

13. Starr, *Embattled Dreams*, 91.

14. Nagler, "Internment," 78–79, 70.

15. Nationally, 82.4 percent of Germans in 1940 were citizens or had first papers versus 69.8 percent of Italians and 72.4 percent among all white foreign born.

16. Allen Kent Powell, "The German-Speaking Immigrant Experience in Utah," *Utah Historical Quarterly* 52.4 (Fall 1984): 304–45, especially 336–38, 335–36; Pozzetta, "Alien Enemies," 87; Fiset, *Imprisoned Apart*, 136, 139n82; Grodzins, *Americans Betrayed*, 97; and a number of observations by Richard D. Scheuerman, "Washington's European American Communities," in *Peoples of Washington*, ed. Sid White and Solberg, 67. Scheuerman tells of Albert Weirich, who, as a POW, labored on truck farms in western Washington and returned with his wife in 1953 to establish his own orchard.

17. Drawn from Fox, *Unknown Internment*, 164–65.

18. There were many legal struggles regarding land ownership, inheritance, marriage, and guarantees of citizenship legislated for any World War One veterans honorably discharged, but the latter was not confirmed until 1935. The total number of naturalizations

in 1944 was just under 442,000, a total not exceeded until 1995, when 488,000 became citizens.

19. Evelyn Nakano Glenn, *Unequal Freedom: How Race and Gender Shaped American Citizenship and Labor* (Cambridge, Mass.: Harvard University Press, 2002), 52, 54.

20. Mai Ngai provides a useful, brief review of many recent studies on this topic in *Impossible Subjects*, 5–7, 276–77. However, Ngai adds to the oversight of others by stating (276n9) that "eligibility for citizenship was limited to" free white persons and persons of African origin and descent "until the McCarran-Walter Immigration and Naturalization Act of 1952," thus omitting Mexicans and the key liberalization measures in 1940, 1943, and 1946.

It is astonishing how, for many years, immigration scholars focused so little attention on the critical place of the right to acquire and preserve citizenship in the lives of immigrants, other minority persons, and American-born women. As we move the immigrant/ethnic story to center stage, the long-fought struggles to acquire equal citizenship are being more appreciated.

21. Again, to add more perspective, by December 1940 over five million aliens had registered. By the end of fiscal year 1944 that figure dropped to 3.83 million (3,828,658), and the INS estimated that in June 1945 there were only slightly more than 3 million (3,050,803). Regarding the 1940 total, compare Donald Perry and Edward Hutchison's figure (5,009,857) with the INS 1941 *Annual Report*, table 13 (4,746,836), and the 1945 INS *Report* (p. 16) figure for 1940 of 4,889,770. See Donald R. Perry and Edward P. Hutchinson, "New Alien Registration Data," *Monthly Review* 2.7 (January 1945): 91–93.

22. Nagler, "Internment," 66–67.

34. *The Homefront in Wartime*

1. Gerald D. Nash, *The American West Transformed: The Impact of the Second World War* (Bloomington: Indiana University Press, 1985), 14; Pomeroy, *Pacific Slope*, 297; Abbott, *Metropolitan Frontier*, xiii, 4, 6, 26; Nugent, *Into the West*, 240; Malone and Etulain, *American West*, 119; and Paul Hendrickson, "Saving Pie Town," *Smithsonian*, February 2005, 76. Into this isolated New Mexican community on the Continental Divide families flocked from Kansas, Oklahoma, and West Texas, but within a few years, as crops failed and urban industries mushroomed, most relocated "to cities, to jobs in defense plants and airplane factories" from Albuquerque to Los Angeles.

2. Nugent, *Into the West*, 257–59; Nugent, "People of the West," 53–61; Richard White, *"It's Your Misfortune,"* 508; Schwantes, *Radical Heritage*, 7 (including Boeing quotation), 12; Malone and Etulain, *American West*, 115, 125–26; Edwards, "Oregon Coast," 65; Winther, *Great Northwest*, 431–32; McWilliams, *Southern California*, 324–25; Nash, *American West Transformed*, 121; Verge, "Impact of the Second World War," 240; Pomeroy, *Pacific Slope*, 298 n. 9. Regarding federal funding, see also Abbott, "Federal Presence," 471–73, and Jonathan Dembo, "Dave Beck and the Transportation Revolution in the Pacific Northwest," in *Experiences in a Promised Land*, ed. Edwards and Schwantes, 340–41, 350.

Various works focus on growth during the war years or during the decade. During the war years Seattle grew from 368,300 to 530,000; Richmond jumped from 23,600 to 150,000; a whole new community of Vanport, near Portland, rose up to 40,000 and then virtually disappeared with the war's end. By the end of the decade Bremerton went from 15,000 to 75,000, Tacoma from 109,400 to 140,000, Portland from 200,000 to 360,000, Vallejo from 20,000 to 100,000, Richmond from 23,600 to 150,000 and back down to

71,850, San Diego from 202,000 to 510,000, and Tucson from 48,000 to over 90,000. Between 1940 and 1960 Phoenix jumped from 65,000 to 439,000, El Paso from 99,000 to 277,000, and Albuquerque from 35,000 to 201,000.

3. Verge, "Impact of the Second World War," 240, 237, 244; Malone and Etulain, *American West*, 110, 245–46; Schwantes, *Radical Heritage*, 7; Richard White, *"It's Your Misfortune,"* 503; Carl Abbott, "The Metropolitan Region: Western Cities in the New Urban Era," in *Twentieth Century West*, ed. Nash and Etulain, 71; Thomas E. Sheridan, *Arizona*, 270–71; Winther, *Great Northwest*, 432–33; Cordova, *Filipinos*, 23, 29.

4. Schwantes says that west of the Mississippi the African American population rose from 171,000 to 620,000 (*Radical Heritage*, 12), and Malone and Etulain report that in California their numbers rose from 124,000 in 1940 to 462,000 in 1950 (*American West*, 146). See also Kevin Allen Leonard, "'In the Interest of All Races': African Americans and Interracial Cooperation in Los Angeles during and after World War II," in *Seeking El Dorado: African Americans in California*, ed. Lawrence de Graaf, Kevin Mulroy, and Quintard Taylor (Seattle: University of Washington Press, 2001), 311–13.

5. Verge, "Impact of the Second World War," 240; Nugent, *Into the West*, 256–57; Nugent, "People of the West," 53–58; Abbott, "Metropolitan Region," 17–19, 26; Schwantes, *Radical Heritage*, 7, 12; and Malone and Etulain, *American West*, 109, 129–30, 146–47. During the war Washington's net population rose by 533,000, Oregon's by 194,000. The shipyard quotation is from Nash, *American West Transformed*, 40. Kevin Starr's description of California in 1940, in chapter 1 of *Embattled Dreams*, is outstanding.

6. David Rieff, *Los Angeles: Capital of the Third World* (New York: Simon and Schuster, 1991), 163; Abbott, "Metropolitan Region," 6–7; Nugent, *Into the West*, 255–56.

7. Pomeroy, *Pacific Slope*, 395, and Nugent, *Into the West*, 257. At its peak, Boeing had 55,000 employees, of whom 46 percent were women. Schwantes, *Pacific Northwest*, 11.

8. McWilliams, *Southern California*, 326, 328.

9. Nash, *American West Transformed*, 214–15, 127.

10. Ibid., 125–26.

11. Eduardo Obregón Pagán, *Murder at the Sleepy Lagoon: Zoot Suits, Race, and Riot in Wartime Los Angeles* (Chapel Hill: University of North Carolina Press, 2003), 14–15.

12. Quite illuminating is Kevin Starr's description of the climate of opinion at this time, the behavior of these young persons compared with Anglo teens, and the widespread concerns about juvenile delinquency in the wartime American society of the early 1940s (*Embattled Dreams*, 99–103).

13. Many details of the murder are presented in Eduardo Obregón Pagán's recent study (*Murder at the Sleepy Lagoon*). His reassessment of the events, based on testimonies that were generally overlooked, appears in the epilogue, 224–26.

14. Ibid., 76, 78, 203.

15. Sánchez, *Becoming Mexican American*, 266–67; Acuña, *Occupied America*, 268–71; and Gutierrez, *Walls and Mirrors*, 124–27.

16. *People v. Zammora*, 66 Cal. App. 2d 166, October 4, 1944, http://login.findlaw.com/scripts/callaw (accessed August 26, 2004). See also "People and Events: Alice McGrath (1917–[since deceased])," American Experience, Zoot Suit Riots, http://www.pbs.org/wgbh/amex/zoot/eng_peopleevents/p_mcgrath.html (accessed August 26, 2004); Hector Tobar, "Sleepy Lagoon Victims Laud Their Champion" [Alice McGrath's birthday], *Los Angeles Times*, April 20, 1997: A1; Frank O. Sotomayor, "Patron Saint of Lost Causes: The Notorious Sleepy Lagoon Trial Inspired Alice Greenfield McGrath to Crusade Got Social Justice," *Los Angeles Times*, February 2, 2002: A1+; and Frank Sotomayor, "Obituary: Ysmael Parra; Defendant in 'Sleepy Lagoon' Trial," *Los*

Angeles Times, May 21, 2001: B9. An excellent summary of the Sleepy Lagoon event and McGrath's relationship with the convicted boys can be found on the PBS American Experience Web site for the documentary "Zoot Suit Riots." See "People & Events" listing at the beginning of this note.

17. The following analysis is based on Pagán, *Murder at the Sleepy Lagoon,* 11–17; Starr, *Embattled Dreams,* 104–109; and Stuart Cosgrove, "An Interpretation of the Causes of the Zoot Suit Wars," excerpted in *Major Problems in Mexican American History,* ed. Zaragosa Vargas (Boston: Houghton Mifflin, 1999), 316–23. See also Jonathan Kirsch's book review of Pagán's book, "When Music, Fashion, and Politics Clashed," *Los Angeles Times,* November 30, 2003: R2; Susan King, "A City at War with Itself," *Los Angeles Times,* February 10, 2003: *Los Angeles Times,* TV3 (regarding a PBS documentary by Joe Tovares, "Zoot Suit Riots"); Frank Sotomayor, "Zoot Suits Set Off Rage of Vigilante Servicemen," *Los Angeles Times,* October 25, 1999: B4; Daniel Yi, "Zoot Suits Dress Up His Memories of War Time," *Los Angeles Times,* June 2, 2003: B4; and Kirsch, review of *The Bad City in the Good War,* by Roger W. Lotchin, *Los Angeles Times,* August 17, 2003: R2.

18. This account relies on Pagán, *Murder at the Sleepy Lagoon,* chapters 7 and 8; Cosgrove, "Interpretation"; Sánchez, *Becoming Mexican American,* 267; Gutierrez, *Walls and Mirrors,* 124–25; Acuña, *Occupied America,* 4th ed., 271–73; Nugent, *Into the West,* 284; Richard White, *"It's Your Misfortune,"* 509; Vargas, *Major Problems,* 303; and Mauricio Mazón, *The Zoot Suit Riots: The Psychology of Symbolic Annihilation* (Austin: University of Texas Press, 1984), 73–74, 85. The quotation is from Mazón, 75.

19. The continued funding bonanza until the 1990s prompted Carlos Schwantes's comment that "In a real sense, World War Two never ended" for the West. See Schwantes's article "Wage Earners and Wealth Makers," in *Oxford History of the American West,* ed. Milner, O'Connor, and Sandweiss, 435–36.

20. George I. Sanchez, "Pachucos in the Making," reprinted in *A Documentary History of Mexican Americans,* ed. Wayne Moquin, with Charles Van Doren (New York: Praeger, 1971), 316–20.

21. Getty, "Interethnic Relationships."

22. Mario Garcia, *Mexican Americans,* 114, 118. See also Rieff, *Los Angeles,* 71, comparing Los Angeles of 1920s and 1990s, which fits so well for the 1940s, too.

23. Gutierrez, *Walls and Mirrors,* 136–38; Sánchez, *Becoming Mexican American,* 255–57; Acuña, *Occupied America,* 255; and Richard Griswold del Castillo and Arnoldo De León, *North to Aztlán: A History of Mexican Americans in the United States* (Boston: Twayne, 1997), 93.

24. Matt Garcia, *World of Its Own,* 212, 22, 234–35, 255; Mario Garcia, *Mexican Americans,* 101–6; Acuña, *Occupied America,* 314–15; Matt S. Meier and Margo Gutierrez, eds., *Encyclopedia of the Mexican American Civil Rights Movement* (Westport, Conn.: Greenwood Press, 2000), 132–33, 239.

25. Gutierrez, *Walls and Mirrors,* 171 (quotation) and 168–72; Acuña, *Occupied America,* 314–15; and Ricardo Romo, *East L.A.: A History of a Barrio* (Austin: University of Texas Press, 1983), 168.

26. Jose Gardenas, "History of World War 2 Gets the Latino Perspective," *Los Angeles Times,* May 27, 2002: B1.

27. Lianne Hart, "Dispatch from Three Rivers, Texas: World War Two Dispute Again Divides Town," *Los Angeles Times,* May 31, 2004: A11; Acuña, *Occupied America,* 280; Meier and Gutierrez, *Encyclopedia of the Mexican American Civil Rights Movement,* 10–11, 132; Gutierrez, *Walls and Mirrors,* 154.

28. *Westminster School District of Orange County et al. v. Mendez et al.,* 161 F. 2d

774; 1947 U.S. App. (April 14, 1947); Meier and Gutierrez, *Encyclopedia of the Mexican American Civil Rights Movement* 72, 144–45.

29. *Delgado v. Bastrop Independent School District*, "The Handbook of Texas Online," http://www.tsha.utexas.edu/handbook/online/articles/print/DD/jrd1.html (accessed August 12, 2004).

35. *Wartime and Postwar Agricultural Issues*

1. Exemption from the head tax, literacy test, prohibitions of contract labor, and the registration now required under the 1940 Alien Registration Act.

2. Nash, *American West Transformed*, 49–50, 51, 52; Nash and Etulain, *Twentieth Century West*, 133; Ngai, *Impossible Subjects*, 138–40; Richard B. Craig, *The Bracero Program: Interest Groups and Foreign Policy* (Austin: University of Texas Press, 1971), 63–64; Deutsch, "Landscape of Enclaves," 128; Juan Ramon Garcia, *Operation Wetback: The Mass Deportation of Mexican Undocumented Workers in 1954* (Westport, Conn.: Greenwood Press, 1980), 23–24; Rich Connell and Robert J. Lopez, "Mexico to Look into Missing Missions Saved for Braceros," *Los Angeles Times*, January 28, 2001: A1, A9; "Give Braceros Back Their Money," editorial, *Los Angeles Times*, February 6, 2001; and James F. Smith, "Ex-Migrants Sought for Class-Action [regarding 'money set aside as savings for "braceros"']," *Los Angeles Times*, March 15, 2001.

Smith reported that a 1984 Tulane University study suggested that, at 10 percent withheld from braceros' earnings, $34.7 million was put aside by mid-1946 and perhaps $28.5 million was paid out, but others maintain that as much as $60 million was actually withheld and less than half that was paid out. Connell and Lopez cited similar statistics, based on Mexican government documents. Smith and Connell and Lopez conclude that perhaps all but $6 million had, in fact, been refunded, but a class action lawsuit was filed, challenging the figure and claiming that even something close to that amount would be worth much more today due to compounded interest. See "Mexican Report Contradicts Claims That '40s War Workers Weren't Paid," *Los Angeles Times*, March 30, 2001: A3.

3. During the war, 74 percent of agricultural braceros were Mexican; however, for the whole period 1946–1952, over 85 percent were Mexican. See notes 2 and 4 of this chapter for more details and sources.

4. Craig, *Bracero Program*, 50–52; Schwantes, *In Mountain Shadows: A History of Idaho* (Lincoln: University of Nebraska Press, 1991), 230 (quotation); Carlos Gil, "Washington's Hispano American Communities," in *Peoples of Washington*, ed. Sid White and Solberg, 169, 170 (quotation); Nugent, *Into the West*, 303; Gutierrez, *Walls and Mirrors*, 139, 145; Montejano, *Anglos and Mexicans*, 264; Matt Garcia, *World of Its Own*, 164–68; Congressional Research Service, "History of the Immigration and Naturalization Service," Report to the Committee on the Judiciary, U.S. Senate, 96th Cong, 2d sess. (Washington, D.C.: GPO, 1980), 51; and Erasmo Gamboa, *Mexican Labor and World War II* (Seattle: University of Washington Press, 2000[1990]), xviii, 59 (quotations). Nugent points out that braceros would, in fact, displace other workers over time, such as cotton workers in north Texas during the 1950s and Mexican Americans in south Texas. Indeed, braceros soon equaled three times the number of Mexican American workers in south Texas (Nugent, *Into the West*, 300–301).

An unpublished INS manual on the history of the agency includes a section on "The Importation of Foreign Workers" during the war. In it they indicate 163,000 Mexican agricultural workers were admitted during the war as well as 127,000 Mexican railway laborers, plus 42,000 agricultural and 7,000 non-agricultural workers from Jamaica; 900 agricultural workers and 7,000 non-agricultural workers from Barbados; 10,000 agricultural workers from the Bahamas; 1,300 non-agricultural workers from British Honduras, and 1,800 agricultural workers from Newfoundland. In June 1945, there remained in the United States about 70,000 Mexican agricultural workers, 65,000 non-agricultural Mexicans; 22,000 agricultural and 5,000 non-agricultural Jamaicans; 1,100 Newfoundlanders; 6,000 Bahamians; 1,000 British Hondurans; 6,000 non-agricultural Barbadians; 5,700 Canadian woodsmen; and even 500 Chinese cooks from Mexico (157–166).

5. Account presented by Gil, "Washington's Hispano American Communities," 162.

6. Juan Ramon Garcia, *Operation Wetback*, 3, 7, 11 (quotation), 30; and Ernesto Galarza, *Farm Workers and Agribusinesses in California, 1947–1960* (Note Dame, Ind.: University of Notre Dame Press, 1977), 32, 211–12; Ngai, *Impossible Subjects*, 140–49; and Pomeroy, *Pacific Slope*, 287.

7. "Farming: The Mexican Wetbacks," *Newsweek*, October 25, 1948: 44–45; Acuña, *Occupied America*, 4th ed., 285–89; Craig, *Bracero Program*, 89; Richard White, *"It's Your Misfortune,"* 528.

8. Braceros (1946–52: over 730,000 entered), and the rapidly growing number of un-documented workers (1946–52: 2,280,474 apprehended).

9. The Congressional Research Service's "Report" indicates that between 1946 and 1952, of the 2,280,474 illegal aliens apprehended, 95 percent departed voluntarily (54). The number apprehended jumped fivefold between 1946 and 1951 and more than doubled by 1954, to 1.089 million. Bracero data were drawn from the Report's table 30 and included only agricultural workers (65). The non-Mexicans were, for the most part, essentially British West Indians, Bahamians, Canadians, and a small number of Newfoundlanders. The quotation is from Ngai, *Impossible Subjects*, 149.

10. The prior two paragraphs are based on Malone and Etulain, *American West*, 111–13; Montejano, *Anglos and Mexicans*, 273; Galarza, *Farm Workers*, 21–23, 74, 98; Zavella, *Women's Work*, 49–51; Thomas E. Sheridan, *Arizona*, 276–77; Ruiz, *Cannery Women*, 82, 92, 98, 104, 120; and Matt Garcia, *World of Its Own*, 159–61.

11. This and the following paragraphs draw on Matt Garcia, *World of Its Own*, 160–61; Galarza, *Farm Workers*, 16 (quotation), 98–114; Ogawa, *Kodomo no tame ni*, 358 (quotation), 510–12; and Fuchs, *Hawaii Pono*, 355, 358.

12. Meanwhile, the push for right-to-work laws that would undermine unions on the mainland continued, especially in the Southwest. In Arizona, for instance, grievances among members of the International Union of Mine, Mill and Smelter Workers (IUMMSW) in Clifton-Morenci were increasing, and returning veterans were unwilling to accept segregation and dual wage systems. A 104-day strike, beginning September 22, 1946, led to substantial gains in pay, benefits, and promotions from Phelps Dodge. However, by 1950, in neighboring New Mexico the indignities and inequities in working and living conditions, the job preferences for Anglos, and the dual wage arrangements finally provoked the IUMMSW's 1,400 members (90 percent of whom were Mexican American) to launch a 15-month strike against Empire Zinc and Grant County in Bayard (near Silver City) between October 1950 and January 1952. An injunction against miners picketing led to a women's auxiliary taking over the task, which at one point resulted in the arrest of 45 women, 17 children, and a baby. The strike yielded few gains but did inspire the now classic, documentary-style film *Salt of the Earth* (1954). It featured a leading Mexican actress, Rosaura Revueltas, who was deported before the filming was completed as part of the efforts to squelch what was regarded as a Communist-leaning project. It may be the only Hollywood film ever blacklisted, revealing much about the polarized political climate at that time. See Acuña, *Occupied America*, 5th

ed., 290, and "Salt of the Earth," http://en.wikipedia.org/wiki/Salt_of_the_Earth and http://film.society.tripod.com/nzffs/bib-_Salt_of_the_Earth (both accessed June 12, 2006).

13. Oregon's action may well have grown out of a controversy in Hood River Valley, where Japanese farmed quite successfully. In November 1944, the local American Legion removed the names of 16 Nisei from its war memorial. Five months later, threatened by the national office with the loss of its charter, the post restored all but one name.

14. Tamura, 249; Taylor, 166; Weglyn, *Years of Infamy*, 274–76; Hyung-chan Kim, *Asian Americans and the Supreme Court: A Documentary History* (Westport, Conn.: Greenwood Press, 1992), 617–19. For the Oyama case, see also 332 U.S. 633, 68 Sup. Ct. 269 (1948).

36. Immigrants and Ethnics in the Postwar West

1. The two July 2, 1946, laws regarding Indians and Filipinos are 60 Stat. 416; 8 U.S.C. 212b, 212c. One provided an immigration quota for Asian Indians, the other extended naturalization to both Asian Indians and Filipinos, along with the Chinese. Presidential Proclamation 2696, July 4, 1946, also part of the package, extended a comparable immigration quota to Filipinos. See also Divine, *American Immigration Policy*, 153–54; Peter Wallenstein, *'Tell the Court I Love My Wife': Race Marriage and Law — An American History* (New York: Palgrave, 2002), 192–99.

In support of the earlier proposal to grant those rights to the Chinese, Roosevelt, acknowledging the intersection of foreign affairs and domestic policies, had told Congress on October 4, 1943, "By the repeal of the Chinese exclusion laws we can correct a historic mistake and silence the distorted Japanese propaganda." The foreign policy dimensions were a significant factor — along with the efforts of Richard Walsh and the Citizens Committee to Repeal Chinese Exclusion plus the enormous impact made by Madame Chiang Kai-shek's 1943 speaking tour from Boston to New York to Washington, D.C., to San Francisco and Los Angeles. The Roosevelt quotation is from Divine, *American Immigration Policy*, 148. See, too, Elaine Woo, "Mme Chiang Kai-shek: Charismatic, Feared Emissary of China's Nationalist Regime," *New York Times*, October 25, 2003: A1, A10.

2. Congressional Research Service "Report," 43, 49. That immigration figure is not adjusted for emigrants who departed the country during those years. Hence, this is the gross number, not net number of new admissions.

3. The shift in America's ideological orientation to include pluralism in its core culture is discussed most effectively by Philip Gleason, in "American Identity and Americanization," pp. 47–50 in the *Harvard Encyclopedia of American Ethnic Groups*, ed. Stephen Thernstrom, Ann Orlov, and Oscar Handlin (Cambridge, Mass.: Harvard University Press, 1980). Quoted from Leonard Dinnerstein, *Anti-Semitism in America* (New York: Oxford University Press, 1994), 150–56, esp. 151, Mario Garcia, *Mexican Americans*, 297, and the account of the mayors' efforts against the Japanese and the campaign by the Civic Unity Commission to defuse those proposals are in Howard A. Droker, "Seattle Race Relations during the Second World War," in *Experiences in a Promised Land*, ed. Edwards and Schwantes, 362, 365.

4. Cinel, *From Italy*, 257.

5. Barkan, "America in the Hand," 331–54. The takeover of mainland China by the Communists in September 1949 produced comparable responses among many Chinese, especially since so many had supported Chiang Kai-shek and the Kuomintang (Guomindang: KMT), who fled to Formosa, soon renamed Taiwan.

6. Vorspan and Gartner, *History of the Jews*, 225–28; L. Sandy Maisel and Ira N. Forman, *Jews in American Politics: Essays* (New York: Rowman and Littlefield, 2004), tables on 316–18.

7. Vorspan and Gartner, *History of the Jews*, 235–36.

8. The observations in this and the next paragraph are drawn from Theodoratus, "Greek Community," 114–15; Doulis, *Surge to the Sea*, 43, 55; Cinel, *From Italy*, 125–26, 197; and Talagan, "Faith, Hard Work, and Family," 154–56.

9. Nelson, "Armenian Family," 110.

10. Yung, *Unbound Voices*, 464–66, 473, 480.

11. Chris Friday, "Competing Communities at Work: Asian Americans, European Americans, and Native Alaskans in the Pacific Northwest, 1938–1947," in Matsumoto's *Over the Edge*, 307–28.

12. Caridad Concepcion Vallangca, *The Second Wave: Pinay and Pinoy (1945–1960)* (San Francisco: Strawberry Hill Press, 1987), 82–85.

13. Bureau of the Census, *Census of the Population: 1950*, vol. 2, *Characteristics of the Population, Territories and Possessions* (Washington, D.C.: GPO, 1952), Hawaii, table 8 (p. 52–53); Cordova, *Filipinos*, 29; and Vallangca, *Second Wave*, 185.

14. Vallangca, *Second Wave*, 32, 34–38, 59.

15. Ibid., 63, 138, 145, 149, 186.

16. The data presented in this section, drawn largely from the 1940 and 1950 censuses, are complicated because the Census Bureau introduced sampling, using a 20 percent sample, especially for questions regarding age, the second generation, and rates of naturalization. Consequently, many figures for the same groups vary from table to table, including four different totals for the U.S. foreign-born population. Thus, for some tables there was no longer a 100 percent count, making comparisons with earlier data somewhat imperfect. The 1950 census also introduced a new definition of urban population that included unincorporated urban population clusters, further complicating comparisons. Moreover, since immigration had declined so much, many earlier tables were no longer employed, making it difficult, for example, to trace internal migrations by foreign-stock populations. Finally, foreign-born Asian groups by state could not be located, necessitating a reliance on the listing for Chinese and Japanese "races."

17. Starr, *Embattled Dreams*, 84.

18. The total Issei population was about 83,100, only 1,600 below that of 1940. In 1940 there were 200,300 Nisei (and a number of Sansei, third generation), and that sum grew to 243,300 a decade later. Among the Chinese in 1950, about 75,450 were immigrants, roughly 33,300 above that reported in 1940. The total "race" figure suggests that the Chinese American population had risen from about 64,200 to approximately 74,500. These figures are derived from the 1950 census, vol. 2, *Characteristics of Population*, part 1, *United States Summary*, table 59, as well as part 52, *Hawaii*, tables 8 and 18, and the Special Report on *Nonwhite Population by Race*, tables 17 and 28 on Japanese, 18 and 29 on Chinese, and 19 and 30 on Filipinos. The gender data are derived from tables 14 and 54 in each of the individual state sections of vol. 2 along with Alaska's table 6 and Hawai'i's tables 8 and 32. See also Barkan, *And Still They Come*, 21.

In a unique development, appearing for the first time in the 1950 census, table 12 of the Special Report on "Nativity and Parentage" (3A-71) enumerates foreign-born white persons and includes 4,650 white immigrants from Japan, 11,985 born in China, 13,445 born in the Philippines, 5,370 born in India, and 1,215 born in Korea. Speculations suggest the figures include some of the 868 Asian children accompanying war brides but primarily the children of missionaries now able, or wishing, or needing to return to America following the war.

37. *The Cold War Heats Up*

1. Barkan, *And Still They Come*, 74.

2. "President Truman's Statement and Directive on Displaced Persons," from the *New York Times*, December 22, 1945, reproduced on www.sunsite.unc.edu/pha/policy/post-war/451222a.html and www.ess.uwe.ac.uk/documents/displace.htm (accessed August 23, 2004); and Congressional Research Service, 54.

Leonard Dinnerstein points out that only 13,000 or so slots were set aside for East European Displaced Persons, while 26,000 quota places were reserved for Germans. He later notes that by June 30, 1947, a total of 22,950 visas had been issued under the directive, with 15,478 (67.4 percent) going to Jews, compared with only 16 percent of those later admitted under the Displaced Persons Act. Dinnerstein, *America and the Survivors of the Holocaust* (New York: Columbia University Press, 1982), 113, 165, 287.

3. *Memo to America: The D P Story—The Final Report of the U.S. Displaced Persons Commission* (Washington, D.C.: GPO, 1952), table 2, 366; Divine, *American Immigration Policy*, 193–94.

4. Data from tables 4 and 9, 10–13 in *Memo to America.*

5. The laws regarding Asian spouses were extended to March 1952 (by the Acts of August 19, 1950, and March 19, 1951). The War Brides Act provided visas for 114,691 wives, 333 husbands, and 4,669 children. See the INS *Annual Report* for 1950, table 9A; and Divine, *American Immigration Policy*, 154.

6. Mai Ngai provides a good discussion of the evolution of deportation in American immigration law, especially as expanded in 1917 and 1924. The 1950 legislation went further. See Ngai's *Impossible Subjects*, 57–60.

7. Divine, *American Immigration Policy*, 163, 164.

8. All emphases in the above quotations have been added by the author. Data on the impact of the law can be found in table 31 of the 1980 Congressional Research Service "Report" (67). The controversy over the USA PATRIOT Act has revived memories of episodes during the Cold War and the impact of the McCarran Act. See, for example, "Detained without Details," *Los Angeles Times*, November 1, 1993: A1, A16.

9. Divine, *American Immigration Policy*, 135.

10. McCarran attacked the veto as Communistic and un-American. Divine, *American Immigration Policy*, 184–85. A new study of McCarran is Michael Ybarra's *Washington Gone Crazy: Senator Pat McCarran and the Great American Communist Hunt* (Hanover, N.H.: Steerforth Press, 2004), reviewed by David Greenberg, "Nativist Son," *New York Times Book Review*, October 31, 2004: 8–9.

11. Emphasis added by author.

12. The veto message is appended to *Whom We Shall Welcome: Report of the President's Commission on Immigration and Naturalization* (Washington, D.C.: GPO, 1953), 275–84.

13. Ibid., 16, 19, 46–47, 70–71.

14. Ibid., 102–3, 104, 106–7, 108–9.

15. Ibid., 236–37.

16. Ibid., 240, 264–66.

38. *Dora and the Harbinger of Coming Events*

1. This account is based on Jerry Garcia's exceptional essay "A Chicana in Northern Aztlán: An Oral History of Dora Sanchez Treviño," in *Women in Pacific Northwest History*, ed. Blair, 195–236.

2. Tables P1 and P4, on the Census Bureau's American Fact Finder Internet site (http://factfinder.census.gov/home/saff/main.html?_lang=en) give one set of figures for Quincy, 3,264 Latinos in a population of 5,044, but table P10 reports 3,374 Latinos in a population of 5,188. The latter may have slightly higher numbers because of multiple ethnic/racial choices. Thus, I used the first statistics. See Census 2000 Summary File 1 (SF 1), 100–Percent Data, Selection by Place, Washington State, Quincy, tables P1, P4, P10 (accessed August 30, 2004).

3. Over one-fifth of *all* immigrants legally admitted, 1961–2000, were from Mexico. The next highest were Filipinos, at just over 6 percent of the total. Three-fourths of those granted amnesty under the 1986 Immigration Reform and Control Act were Mexican. The vast majority of undocumented aliens continue to be Mexican.

39. *Looking Back on America's Immigrant West*

1. The constitutionally mandated purpose of the decennial census is to provide for reapportionment of members of the House of Representatives. Since territories do not have representation, Alaska and Hawai'i were, logically, not included in almost all population charts (except for separate volumes on possessions) until they received statehood in 1959. The qualification here chiefly applies to Texas, especially central, southern, and western Texas, which I find to be culturally and economically much closer to the Southwest. To provide the most complete portrait of the West as defined here beginning in 1870, Texan and Alaskan data were added to the tables. Pre-1893 (the year it was taken over by a coup by American businessmen) Hawaiian data are referred to, but Hawai'i itself is generally included in the tables only beginning in 1900.

2. Canadians are an exception because they so easily fit into American society that the non-French scarcely formed any organized communities in the West that would have been a marker of Canadian ethnicity. Despite their considerable numbers, their virtual invisibility was a choice they made.

3. A thoughtful essay that explores some of these ideas is Desmond King's "Making Americans: Immigration Meets Race," in *E Pluribus Unum?* ed. Gerstle and Mollenkopf, 143–72. In the same collection, Reed Ueda also explores the founding Europeans as the "charter group" and the consequences of those persons in terms of both immigration and naturalization policies. Ueda, "Historical Patterns of Immigrant Status and Incorporation in the United States," *E Pluribus Unum?* 292–327.

4. In addition to works already cited by Shanks and Lee, on this topic of sovereignty and state actions, see T. Alexander Aleinikoff, "Policing Boundaries: Migration, Citizenship, and the State," *E Pluribus Unum?* ed. Gerstle and Mollenkopf, 267–91.

THE LIBRARY
TOWER HAMLETS COLLEGE
POPLAR HIGH STREET
LONDON E14 0AF
Tel: 0207 510 7763

SELECT BIBLIOGRAPHY

Abbott, Carl. *The Metropolitan Frontier: Cities in the Modern American West.* Tucson: University of Arizona Press, 1993.

Acuña, Rodolfo. *Occupied America: A History of Chicanos.* 5th ed. New York: Pearson Longman, 2004.

Allerfeldt, Kristofer. *Race, Radicalism, Religion, and Restriction: Immigration in the Pacific Northwest, 1890–1924.* Westport, Conn.: Praeger, 2003.

Austin, Allan W. *From Concentration Camp to Campus: Japanese American Students and World War II.* Urbana: University of Illinois Press, 2005.

Balderrama, Francisco E., and Raymond Rodriguez. *Decade of Betrayal: Mexican Repatriation in the 1930s.* Albuquerque: University of New Mexico Press, 1995.

Barkan, Elliott Robert. "America in the Hand, Homeland in the Heart: Transnational and Translocal Immigrant Experiences in the American West." *Western Historical Quarterly* 35.3 (Autumn 2004): 331–354.

———. *And Still They Come: Immigrants and American Society, 1920 to the 1990s.* Wheeling, Ill.: Harlan Davidson, 1996.

———. "Race, Religion, and Nationality in American Society: A Model of Ethnicity— From Contact to Assimilation." *Journal of American Ethnic History* 14.2 (Winter 1995): 38–75 and 95–101.

———. "Turning Turner on His Head? The Significance of Immigration in Twentieth-Century American Western History." *New Mexico Historical Review* 77.1 (Winter 2002): 57–88.

Barkan, Elliott Robert, ed. *A Nation of Peoples: A Sourcebook on America's Multicultural Heritage.* Westport, Conn.: Greenwood, 1999.

Barron, Stephanie, ed. *Exiles and Émigrés: The Flight of European Artists from Hitler.* Los Angeles: Los Angeles County Museum of Art, 1997.

Beechert, Edward D. *Working in Hawaii: A Labor History.* Honolulu: University of Hawai'i Press, 1985.

Benjamin, Gilbert Giddings. *The Germans in Texas: A Study in Immigration.* Austin, Tex.: Jenkins, 1974.

Bjork, Kenneth O. *West of the Great Divide: Norwegian Migration to the Pacific Coast, 1847–1893.* Northfield, Minn.: Norwegian American Historical Association, 1958.

Blackwelder, Julia Kirk. *Women of the Depression: Caste and Culture in San Antonio, 1929–1939.* College Station: Texas A & M University Press, 1984.

Blair, Karen J., ed. *Women in Pacific Northwest History*. Rev. ed. Seattle: University of Washington Press, 2001.

Bogardus, Emory. *The Mexican in the United States*. New York: Arno Press, 1970 [USC Press, 1934].

Boyle Heights Project: The Power of Place. "Oral Histories: Selected Excerpts of Oral History Interviews. www.janm.org/exhibits/bh/ (accessed May 20, 2006).

Buaken, Manuel. *I Have Lived with the American People* [Filipino]. Caldwell, Idaho: Caxton Printers, 1948.

Bulbulian, Berge. *The Fresno Armenians: History of a Diaspora Community*. Fresno: California State University, Fresno, Press, 2000.

Bulosan, Carlos. *America Is in the Heart: A Personal History*. Seattle: University of Washington Press, 1946.

Camarillo, Albert. *Chicanos in a Changing Society: From Mexican Pueblos to American Barrios in Santa Barbara and Southern California, 1848–1930*. Cambridge, Mass.: Harvard University Press, 1996 [1979].

Center for Oral History. *An Era of Change: Oral Histories of Civilians in World War II Hawai'i*. 5 vols. Honolulu: University of Hawai'i, Social Science Research Institute, Center for Oral History, 1994.

Chan, Sucheng. *Asian Americans: An Interpretive History*. Boston: Twayne, 1991.

——. *This Bittersweet Soil: The Chinese in California Agriculture, 1860–1910*. Berkeley: University of California Press, 1986.

Chen, Yong. *Chinese San Francisco, 1850–1943: A Trans-Pacific Community*. Stanford, Calif.: Stanford University Press, 2000.

Cinel, Dino. *From Italy to San Francisco: The Immigrant Experience*. Stanford, Calif.: Stanford University Press, 1982.

Clark, Norman H. *Mill Town: A Social History of Everett, Washington*. Seattle: University of Washington Press, 1970.

Cordova, Fred. *Filipinos: Forgotten Asian Americans*. Dubuque, Iowa: Kendall Hunt, 1983.

Cronon, William, George Miles, and Jay Gitlin, eds. *Under an Open Sky: Rethinking America's Western Past*. New York: W. W. Norton, 1992.

Dahlie, Jorgen. "Old World Paths in the New: Scandinavians Find a Familiar Home in Washington." In *Experiences in a Promised Land: Essays in Pacific Northwest History*, ed. G. Thomas Edwards and Carlos A. Schwantes. Seattle: University of Washington Press, 1986.

——. *A Social History of Scandinavian Immigrants, Washington State, 1895–1910*. Ph.D. diss.,Washington State University, 1967. Reprint, New York: Arno Press, 1980.

Daniels, Roger, ed. *American Concentration Camps: A Documentary History of the Relocation and Incarceration of Japanese Americans, 1942–1945*. 9 vols. New York: Garland, 1989.

——. *The Decision to Relocate the Japanese Americans*. Malabar, Fla.: Robert E. Krieger, 1975.

——. *Politics of Prejudice: The Anti-Japanese Movement in California and the Struggle for Japanese Exclusion*. New York: Atheneum, 1968 [1962].

Daniels, Roger, Sandra C. Taylor, and Harry H. L. Kitano, eds. *Japanese Americans: From Relocation to Redress*. Rev. ed. Seattle: University of Washington Press, 1991.

de Graaf, Lawrence, Kevin Mulroy, and Quintard Taylor, eds. *Seeking El Dorado: African Americans in California*. Seattle: University of Washington Press, 2001.

DeLeon, Arnoldo. *Racial Frontiers: Africans, Chinese, and Mexicans in Western America, 1848–1890*. Albuquerque: University of New Mexico Press, 2002.

———. *They Called Them Greasers: Anglo Attitudes toward Mexicans in Texas, 1821–1900*. Austin: University of Texas Press, 1983.

Deutsch, Sarah. *No Separate Refuge: Culture, Class, and Gender on an Anglo Hispanic Frontier in the American Southwest, 1880–1940*. New York: Oxford University Press, 1987.

Dinnerstein, Leonard. *America and the Survivors of the Holocaust*. New York: Columbia University Press, 1982.

DiStasi, Lawrence, ed. *Una Storia Segreta: The Secret History of Italian American Evacuation and Interment during World War II*. Berkeley, Calif.: Heyday Books, 2001.

Divine, Robert A. *American Immigration Policy, 1924–1952*. New Haven, Conn.: Yale University Press, 1957.

Dodds, Gordon B. *The American Northwest: A History of Oregon and Washington*. Arlington Heights, Ill.: Forum Press, 1986.

Douglass, William A., and Jon Bilbao. *Amerikanuak: Basques in the New World*. Reno: University of Nevada Press, 1975.

Edwards, G. Thomas, and Carlos A. Schwantes, eds. *Experiences in a Promised Land: Essays in Pacific Northwest History*. Seattle: University of Washington Press, 1986.

Eisenberg, Ellen. "From Cooperative Farming to Urban Leadership." In *Jewish Life in the American West*, ed. Ava F. Kahn, 113–31. Seattle: University of Washington Press and the Autry Museum of Western Heritage, 2002.

Emmons, David M. *The Butte Irish: Class and Ethnicity in an American Mining Town, 1875–1925*. Urbana: University of Illinois Press, 1989.

Ethnic Studies Oral History Project and the United Okinawan Association of Hawai'i, comps. *Uchinanchu: A History of Okinawans in Hawaii*. Honolulu: University of Hawai'i, 1981.

Etulain, Richard W., and Jeronima Echeverria, eds. *Portraits of Basques in the New World*. Reno: University of Nevada Press, 1999.

Fiset, Louis, and Gail M. Nomura, eds. *Nikkei in the Pacific Northwest: Japanese Americans and Japanese Canadians in the Twentieth Century*. Seattle: University of Washington Press, 2005.

Flewelling, Stan. *Shirakawa: Stories from a Pacific Northwest Japanese American Community*. Auburn, Wash.: White River Valley Museum, 2002. Distributed by the University of Washington Press.

Foley, Neil. *The White Scourge: Mexicans, Blacks, and Poor Whites in Texas Cotton Culture*. Berkeley: University of California Press, 1997.

Foucrier, Annick. *La rêve californien: Migrants français sur la côte Pacifique xviie–xxe siècles*. Paris: Belin, 1999.

Fox, Stephen. *The Unknown Internment: An Oral History of the Relocation of Italian Americans during World War II*. Boston: Twayne, 1990.

Friday, Chris. *Organizing Asian American Labor: The Pacific Coast Canned Salmon Industry, 1870–1942*. Philadelphia: Temple University Press, 1994.

Fuchs, Lawrence. *Hawaii Pono: A Social History*. New York: Harcourt, Brace and World, 1961.

Galarza, Ernesto. *Farm Workers and Agribusinesses in California, 1947–1960*. Notre Dame, Ind.: University of Notre Dame Press, 1977.

Gamio, Manuel. *The Mexican Immigrant: His Life Story*. New York: Arno Press, 1969 [1931].

Garcia, Juan Ramon. *Operation Wetback: The Mass Deportation of Mexican Undocumented Workers in 1954*. Westport, Conn.: Greenwood, 1980.

Garcia, Mario T. *Desert Immigrants: The Mexicans of El Paso, 1880–1920*. New Haven, Conn.: Yale University Press, 1981.

———. *Mexican Americans: Leadership, Ideology, and Identity, 1930–1960*. New Haven, Conn.: Yale University Press, 1989.

Garcia, Matt. *"A World of Its Own": Race, Labor, and Citrus in the Making of Greater Los Angeles, 1900–1970*. Chapel Hill: University of North Carolina Press, 2001.

Getty, Harry T. *Interethnic Relationships in the Community of Tucson*. Ph.D. diss., University of Chicago, 1950. Reprint, New York: Arno Press: 1976.

Glenn, Evelyn Nakano. *Unequal Freedom: How Race and Gender Shaped American Citizenship and Labor*. Cambridge, Mass.: Harvard University Press, 2002.

Glenn, Evelyn Nakano, and Rhacel Salazar Parreñas. "The Other Issei: Japanese Immigrant Women in the Pre–World War Two Period." In *Origins and Destinies: Immigration, Race, and Ethnicity in America*, ed. Silvia Pedraza and Rubén G. Rumbaut, 125–40. Belmont, Calif.: Wadsworth, 1996.

Goldberg, Robert A. "Zion in Utah: The Clarion Colony and Jewish Agrarianism." In *Jews in the American West*, ed. Moses Rischin and John Livingston, 66–91. Detroit, Mich.: Wayne State University Press, 1991.

Gonzalez, Gilbert G., and Raul A. Fernandez. *A Century of Chicano History*. New York: Routledge, 2003.

Gordon, Linda. *The Great Arizona Orphan Abduction*. Cambridge: Harvard University Press, 1999.

Gordon-Reed, Annette, ed. *Race on Trial: Law and Justice in American History*. New York: Oxford University Press, 2002.

Grodzins, Morton. *Americans Betrayed: Politics and the Japanese Evacuation*. Chicago: University of Chicago Press, 1949.

Guerin-Gonzales, Camille. *Mexican Workers and American Dreams: Immigration, Repatriation, and California Farm Labor, 1900–1939*. New Brunswick, N.J.: Rutgers University Press, 1994.

Gurock, Jeffrey, ed. *America, American Jews, and the Holocaust*. New York: Routledge, 1998.

Gutiérrez, David G. *Walls and Mirrors: Mexican Americans, Mexican Immigrants and the Politics of Ethnicity*. Berkeley: University of California Press, 1995.

Gyory, Andrew. *Closing the Gate: Race, Politics, and the Chinese Exclusion Act*. Chapel Hill: University of North Carolina Press, 1998.

Halseth, James A., and Bruce Glasrud, eds. *The Northwest Mosaic*. Boulder, Colo.: Pruett, 1977.

Hansen, Arthur, and Betty Mitson, eds. *Voices Long Silent: An Oral Inquiry into the Japanese American Evacuation*. Oral History Program, Japanese American Project. Fullerton: California State University, 1974.

Hegstad, Patsy Adams. "Citizenship, Voting, and Immigrants: A Comparative Study of the Naturalization Propensity and Voter Registration of Nordics in Seattle and Ballard, Washington, 1892–1900." Ph.D. diss., University of Washington, 1992.

Hendrickson, Gordon Olaf, ed. *Peopling the High Plains: Wyoming's European Heritage*. Cheyenne, Wyo.: State Archives and Historical Department, 1977.

Hing, Bill Ong. *Defining America through Immigration Policy*. Philadelphia: Temple University Press, 2004.

Hirata, Lucie Cheng, and Edna Bonacich, eds. *Labor Immigration under Capitalism: Asian Immigrant Workers in the United States before World War II*. Berkeley: University of California Press, 1984.

Houston, Jeanne Wakatsuki, and James D. Houston. *Farewell to Manzanar*. New York: Houghton Mifflin, 1973.

Hsu, Madeline Y. *Dreaming of Gold, Dreaming of Home: Transnationalism and Migration between the United States and South China, 1882–1943*. Stanford, Calif.: Stanford University Press, 2000.

Hurh, Won Moo. *The Korean Americans*. Westport, Conn.: Greenwood, 1998.

Ichioka, Yuji. *The Issei: The World of the First Generation Japanese Immigrants, 1885–1924*. New York: Free Press, 1988.

Ichioka, Yuji, ed. *Views from Within: The Japanese American Evacuation and Resettlement Study*. Los Angeles: UCLA Asian American Studies Center, 1989.

Issel, William, and Robert W. Cherny. *San Francisco, 1865–1932: Politics, Power, and Urban Development*. Berkeley: University of California Press, 1986.

Jacobson, Matthew Frye. *Barbarian Virtues: The United States Encounters Foreign Peoples at Home and Abroad, 1876–1917*. New York: Hill and Wang, 2000.

———. *Whiteness of a Different Color: European Immigrants and the Alchemy of Race*. Cambridge, Mass.: Harvard University Press, 1998.

Jameson, Elizabeth. *All That Glitters: Class, Conflict, and Community in Cripple Creek*. Urbana: University of Illinois Press, 1998.

Jameson, Elizabeth, and Susan Armitage, eds. *Writing the Range: Race, Class, and Culture in the Women's West*. Norman: University of Oklahoma Press, 1997.

Johnson, Benjamin H. *Revolution in Texas: How a Forgotten Rebellion and Its Bloody Suppression Turned Mexicans into Americans*. New Haven, Conn.: Yale University Press, 2003.

Kikumura, Akemi. *Through Harsh Winters: The Life of a Japanese Immigrant Woman*. Novato, Calif.: Chandler & Sharp, 1981.

Kim, Hyung-chan. *A Legal History of Asian Americans, 1790–1990*. Westport, Conn.: Greenwood, 1994.

King, Desmond. "Making Americans: Immigration Meets Race." In *E Pluribus Unum? Contemporary and Historical Perspectives on Immigrant Political Incorporation*, ed. Gary Gerstle and John Mollenkopf, 143–72. New York: Russell Sage Foundation, 2001.

Kurashige, Lon. *Japanese American Celebration and Conflict: A History of Ethnic Identity and Festival in Los Angeles, 1934–1990*. Berkeley: University of California Press, 2002.

Lai, Him Mark, Genny Lim, and Judy Yung, eds. *Island: Poetry and History of Chinese Immigrants on Angel Island, 1910–1940*. San Francisco: Hoc Doi, Chinese Culture Foundation, 1986.

Lan, Susie, ed. *The Chinese in America: A History from Gold Mountain to the New Millennium*. New York: Rowman and Littlefield, 2002.

Le May, Michael, and Elliott Robert Barkan, eds. *U.S. Immigration and Naturalization Laws and Issues: A Documentary History*. Westport, Conn.: Greenwood, 1999.

Leander, Kristine, ed. *Family Sagas: Stories of Scandinavian Immigrants*. Seattle: Scandinavian Language Institute, 1997.

Lee, Erika. *At America's Gates: Chinese Immigration during the Exclusion Era, 1882–1943*. Chapel Hill: University of North Carolina Press, 2003.

———. "Enforcing the Borders: Chinese Exclusion along the U.S. Borders with Canada and Mexico, 1882–1924." *Journal of American History* 89.1 (June 2002): 54–86.

Lee, Mary Paik. *Quiet Odyssey: A Pioneer Korean Woman in America*. Ed. Sucheng Chan. Seattle: University of Washington Press, 1990.

Leonard, Karen Isaksen. *The South Asian Americans*. Westport, Conn.: Greenwood, 1997.

Limerick, Patricia. *Legacy of Conquest: The Unbroken Past of the American West*. New York: W. W. Norton, 1987.

Limerick, Patricia, Clyde Milner II, and Charles E. Rankin, eds. *Trails: Toward a New Western History*. Lawrence: University Press of Kansas, 1991.

Lopez, Ian F. Haney. *White by Law: The Legal Construction of Race*. New York: New York University Press, 1996.

Lothrop, Gloria Ricci. "The Italians of Los Angeles." *The Californians*, May/June 1987: 28–43.

——. "Shadow on the Land: The Impact of Fascism on Los Angeles Italians." In *Fulfilling the Promise of California: An Anthology of Essays on the Italian American Experience in California*, 189–214. Spokane, Wash.: Arthur H. Clarke, 2000.

——. "Unwelcome in Freedom's Land: The Impact of World War II on Italian Aliens in Southern California." *Southern California Quarterly*, 81.4: 510–516.

Lovoll, Odd. *The Promise of America: A History of the Norwegian American People*, Rev. ed. Minneapolis: University of Minnesota Press, 1999.

Malone, Michael P., and Richard W. Etulain. *The American West: A Twentieth-Century History*. Lincoln: University of Nebraska, 1989.

Marinbach, Bernard. *Galveston: Ellis Island of the West*. Albany: State University of New York Press, 1983.

Martinez, Oscar J. *Border People: Life and Society in the U.S.-Mexico Borderlands*. Tucson: University of Arizona Press, 1994.

——. *Troublesome Border*. Tucson: University of Arizona Press, 1988.

Matsumoto, Valerie J. *Farming the Home Place: A Japanese American Community in California, 1919–1982*. Ithaca, N.Y.: Cornell University Press, 1993.

Matsushita, Iwao, and Hamaye Matsushita. *Imprisoned Apart: The World War II Correspondence of an Issei Couple*. Ed. Louis Fiset. Seattle: University of Washington Press, 1997.

McClain, Charles J. *In Search of Equality: The Chinese Struggle against Discrimination in Nineteenth-Century America*. Berkeley: University of California Press, 1994.

McKibben, Carol. *Beyond Cannery Row: Sicilian Women, Immigration, and Community in Monterey, California, 1915–1999*. Urbana: University of Illinois Press, 2006.

McWilliams, Carey. *Factories in the Field: The Story of Migratory Farm Labor in California*. N.p.: Archon Books, 1969 [1939].

——. *North from Mexico: The Spanish-Speaking People of the United States*. Updated by Matt S. Meier. New York: Praeger, 1990 [1948].

——. *Southern California Country: An Island on the Land*. New York: Duell, Sloan, and Pearce, 1946.

Mellinger, Philip. "'The Men Have Become Organizers': Labor Conflict and Unionization in the Mexican Mining Communities of Arizona, 1900–1915." In *The American West: The Reader*, ed. Walter Nugent and Martin Ridge, 203–24. Bloomington: Indiana University Press, 1999.

Mercer, Laurie. *Anaconda: Labor Community and Culture in Montana's Smelter City*. Urbana: University of Illinois Press, 2001.

Milner, Clyde, II, Carol A. O'Connor, and Martha A. Sandweiss, eds. *Oxford History of the American West*. New York: Oxford University Press, 1994.

Montejano, David. *Anglos and Mexicans in the Making of Texas, 1836–1986*. Austin: University of Texas Press, 1987.

Murphy, Mary. *Mining Cultures: Men, Women, and Leisure in Butte, 1914–41*. Urbana: University of Illinois, 1997.

Nash, Gerald D., and Richard W. Etulain, eds. *The Twentieth Century West: Historical Interpretations*. Albuquerque: University of New Mexico Press, 1989.

Nelson, Harold, "The Armenian Family: Changing Patterns of Family Life in a California Community." Ph.D. diss., University of California, Anthropology, 1954.

Ngai, Mae M. *Impossible Subjects: Illegal Aliens and the Making of Modern America*. Princeton, N.J.: Princeton University Press, 2004.

Nielsen, George R. *The Danish Americans*. Boston: Twayne Books, 1981.

Nishimoto, Michi Kodama, Warren S. Nishimoto, and Cynthia A. Oshiro, eds. *Hana-hana: An Oral History Anthology of Hawaii's Working People*. (Honolulu: Ethnic Studies Oral History Project [ESOHP], University of Hawai'i, Manoa, 1984.

Nordyke, Eleanor C. *The Peopling of Hawai'i*. 2nd ed. Honolulu: University of Hawai'i Press, 1989.

Nugent, Walter. *Into the West: The Story of Its People*. New York: Alfred Knopf, 1999.

Ogawa, Dennis M. *Kodomo no tame ni: For the Sake of the Children: The Japanese American Experience in Hawaii*. Honolulu: University of Hawai'i Press, 1978.

Okihiro, Gary Y. *Storied Lives: Japanese American Students and World War II*. Seattle: University of Washington Press, 1999.

Øverland, Orm. *Immigrant Minds, American Identities: Making the United States Home, 1870–1930*. Urbana: University of Illinois Press, 2000.

Pagán, Eduardo Obregón. *Murder at the Sleepy Lagoon: Zoot Suits, Race and Riot in Wartime L.A.* Chapel Hill: University of North Carolina Press, 2003.

Pap, Leo. *The Portuguese Americans*. Boston: Twayne, 1981.

Papanikolas, Helen. *A Greek Odyssey in the American West*. Lincoln: University of Nebraska Press, 1997 [1987].

———, ed. *The Peoples of Utah*. Salt Late City: University of Utah Press, 1976.

Paterson, Wayne. *The Ilse: First Generation Korean Immigrants in Hawai'i, 1903–1973*. Honolulu: University of Hawai'i Press, 2000.

———. *The Korean Frontier in America: Immigration to Hawai'i, 1896–1910*. Honolulu: University of Hawai'i Press, 1988.

Peck, Gunther. *Reinventing Free Labor: Padrones and Immigrant Workers in the North American West, 1880–1930*. Cambridge: Cambridge University Press, 2000.

Pomeroy, Earl. *The Pacific Slope: A History of California, Oregon, Washington, Idaho, Utah, and Nevada*. Seattle: University of Washington Press, 1965.

Portes, Alejandro, and Rubén Rumbaut. *Immigrant America: A Portrait*. 2nd ed. Berkeley: University of California Press, 1996.

Rasmussen, Janet E. *New Land, New Lives: Scandinavian Immigrants to the Pacific Northwest*. Northfield, Minn.: Norwegian American Historical Association, and Seattle: University of Washington Press, 1993.

Reimers, David M. *Still the Golden Door: The Third World Comes to America*. 2nd ed. New York: Columbia University Press, 1985.

Rieff, David. *Los Angeles: The Capital of the Third World*. New York: Simon and Schuster, 1991.

Robinson, Greg. *By Order of the President: FDR and the Internment of Japanese Americans*. Cambridge, Mass.: Harvard University Press, 2001.

Rochlin, Harriet, and Fred Rochlin. *Pioneer Jews: A New Life in the Far West*. Boston: Houghton Mifflin, 1984.

Rohe, Randall E. "Chinese Mining in the Far West, 1850–1890," *Montana Magazine of History* 32 (Autumn 1982): 2–19.

Rolle, Andrew. *Westward the Immigrants: Italian Adventurers and Colonists in an Expanding America.* Boulder: University Press of Colorado, 1999 [originally published as *The Immigrant Upraised,* 1968].

Romo, Ricardo, and Raymund Paredes, eds. *New Directions in Chicano Scholarship.* Santa Barbara: Center for Chicano Studies, University of California, Santa Barbara, 1984.

Rony, Dorothy Bintang Fujita. *American Workers, Colonial Power: Philippine Seattle and the Transpacific West, 1919–1941.* Berkeley: University of California Press, 2003.

Ruiz, Vicki L. *From Out of the Shadows: Mexican Women in Twentieth-Century America.* New York: Oxford University Press, 1998.

Saloutos, Theodore. "The Immigrant in Pacific Coast Agriculture, 1880–1940." *Agricultural History* 49.1 (January 1975): 182–201.

Sánchez, George. *Becoming Mexican American: Ethnicity, Culture and Identity in Chicano Los Angeles, 1900–1915.* New York: Oxford University Press, 1993.

Sandberg, Neil C. *Ethnic Identity and Assimilation: The Polish-American Community; A Case Study of Metropolitan Los Angeles.* New York: Praeger, 1974.

Schiesl, Martin, and Mark M. Dodge, eds. *City of Promise: Race and Historical Change in Los Angeles.* Claremont, Calif.: Regina Books, 2006.

Schmid, Calvin F. *Social Trends in Seattle.* University of Washington Publications in the Social Sciences 14 [October 1944]. Seattle: University of Washington Press, 1944.

Schofer, Jerry. "Urban and Rural Finnish Communities in California: 1860–1960." San Francisco: R & E Research Associates, 1975.

Schwantes, Carlos A. *The Pacific Northwest: An Interpretive History.* Rev. ed. Lincoln: University of Nebraska Press, 1996.

———. *Radical Heritage: Labor, Socialism, and Reform in Washington and British Columbia, 1885–1917.* Moscow: University of Idaho Press, 1994 [1979].

Sensi-Isolani, Paola A., and Phylis Cancilla Martinelli, eds. *Struggle and Success: An Anthology of the Italian Immigrant Experience in California.* Staten Island, N.Y.: Center for Migration Studies, 1993.

Shanks, Cheryl. *Immigration and the Politics of American Sovereignty, 1890–1990.* Ann Arbor: University of Michigan Press, 2001.

Smith, William Carlson. *Americans in Process: A Study of Our Citizens of Oriental Ancestry.* New York: Arno Press, 1970 [1937].

Spickard, Paul R. *Japanese Americans: The Formation and Transformation of an Ethnic Group.* Boston: Twayne, 1996.

Starr, Kevin. *Americans and the California Dream, 1850–1915* New York: Oxford University Press, 1973.

———. *Embattled Dreams: California in War and Peace, 1940–1950.* New York: Oxford University Press, 2002.

———. *Endangered Dreams: The Great Depression in California.* New York: Oxford University Press, 1996.

———. *Inventing the Dream: California through the Progressive Era.* New York: Oxford University Press, 1985.

Tachiki, Amy, Eddie Wong, and Franklin Odo, eds. *Roots: An Asian American Reader.* Los Angeles: UCLA Asian American Studies Center, 1971.

Takaki, Ronald. *Pau Hana: Plantation Life and Labor in Hawaii, 1835–1920.* Honolulu: University of Hawai'i Press, 1983.

———. *Strangers from a Different Shore: A History of Asian Americans.* Boston: Little, Brown, 1989.

Takami, David A. *Divided Destiny: A History of Japanese Americans in Seattle.* Seattle: University of Washington Press, 1998.

Tamura, Linda. *The Hood River Issei: An Oral History of Japanese Settlers in Oregon's Hood River Valley.* Urbana: University of Illinois Press, 1993.

Tateishi, John. *And Justice for All: An Oral History of the Japanese American Detention Camps.* Seattle: University of Washington Press, 1984.

Taylor, Paul S. *Mexican Labor in the United States: Dimmit County WGD, South Texas.* Vol. 1. Chicago: University of Chicago Press, 1930.

Thernstrom, Stephen, and Ann Orlov. *Harvard Encyclopedia of American Ethnic Groups.* Cambridge: Harvard University Press, 1980.

Toll, William. *The Making of an Ethnic Middle Class: Portland Jewry over Four Generations.* Albany: State University of New York Press, 1982.

U.S. Bureau of Immigration. *Annual Reports, 1923–1939.* Washington, D.C.: Government Printing Office.

U.S. Census Bureau. *Decennial Reports, 1880–1960.* Washington, D.C.: Government Printing Office.

U.S. Commission on Wartime Relocation and Internment of Civilians. *Personal Justice Denied: Report of the Commission on Wartime Relocation and Internment of Civilians.* Seattle: University of Washington Press, 1997.

U.S. Department of Justice. *Report to the Congress of the United States: A Review of the Restrictions on Persons of Italian Ancestry during World War II,* November 2001. Accessed via U.S. House of Representatives, Committee on the Judiciary, "News Advisory: Sensenbrenner Releases Justice Department Report on Treatment of Italian-Americans during World War II," November 27, 2001. http://www .house.gov/judiciary/news112701.htm (accessed August 2, 2004).

U.S. Displaced Persons Commission. *Memo to America: The D P Story—The Final Report of the U.S. Displaced Persons Commission.* Washington: GPO, 1952.

U.S. Immigration and Naturalization Service. *Annual Reports, 1940–1954.* Washington, D.C.: Government Printing Office.

U.S. President's Commission on Immigration and Naturalization. *Whom We Shall Welcome: Report of the President's Commission on Immigration and Naturalization.* Washington, D.C.: Government Printing Office, 1953.

U.S. Senate. *Reports of the [Dillingham] Immigration Commission.* 61st Cong., 3rd sess. Part 25, *Japanese and Other Immigrant Races in the Pacific Coast and Rocky Mountain States.* Vol. 23, "Japanese and East Indians"; vol. 24, "Agriculture"; and vol. 25, "Diversified Industries." New York: Arno Press, 1970 [1911].

Vallangca, Caridad Concepcion. *The Second Wave: Pinay and Pinoy (1945–1960).* San Francisco: Strawberry Hill, 1987.

Vallangca, Robert. *Pinoy: The First Wave (1898–1941).* San Francisco: Strawberry Hill, 1977.

Van Nuys, Frank. *Americanizing the West: Race, Immigrants, and Citizenship, 1890–1930.* Lawrence: University Press of Kansas, 2002.

Vorspan, Max, and Lloyd P. Gartner. *History of the Jews of Los Angeles.* San Marino, Calif.: Huntington Library, 1970.

Walls, Thomas K. *The Japanese Texans.* San Antonio: University of Texas, Institute of Texas Cultures, 1987.

Weber, Devra. "Raiz Fuerte: Oral History and Mexicana Farmworkers." In *Working People of California,* ed. Daniel Cornford, 209–24. Berkeley: University of California Press, 1995.

Weglyn, Michi. *Years of Infamy: The Untold Story of America's Concentration Camps.* Rev. ed. Seattle: University of Washington Press, 1996.

White, Richard. *"It's Your Misfortune and None of My Own": A History of the American West.* Norman: University of Oklahoma, 1991.

White, Sid, and S. E. Solberg, eds. *Peoples of Washington: Perspectives on Cultural Diversity.* Pullman: Washington State University Press, 1989.

Whitehead, John S. "Noncontiguous Wests: Alaska and Hawai'i." In *Many Wests: Place, Culture, and Regional Identity,* ed. David M. Wrobel and Michael C. Steiner, 315–41. Lawrence: University Press of Kansas, 1997.

wong, marie rose. "The Urban Pattern of Portland, Oregon's First Chinatown." In *The Chinese in America: A History from Gold Mountain to the New Millennium,* ed. Susie Lan Cassel, 416–33. Walnut Creek, Calif.: AltaMira, 2002.

Wrobel, David, and Michael Steiner, eds. *Many Wests: Place, Culture, and Regional Identity.* Lawrence: University of Kansas Press, 1997.

Yung, Judy. *Unbound Feet: A Social History of Chinese Women in San Francisco.* Berkeley: University of California Press, 1995.

———. *Unbound Voices: A Documentary History of Chinese Women in San Francisco.* Berkeley: University of California Press, 1999.

Zavella, Patricia. *Women's Work and Chicano Families: Cannery Workers of the Santa Clara Valley.* Ithaca, N.Y.: Cornell University Press, 1987.

INDEX

ABOUT THE AUTHOR

Elliott Robert Barkan is Professor Emeritus of History and Ethnic Studies at California State University. He is author of *Our Multicultural Heritage: A Guide to America's Principal Ethnic Groups* and *And Still They Come: The Immigrant in American Society, 1920s–1990s*, among other books, and co-editor (with Michael LeMay) of *American Immigration and Naturalization Policy: A Documentary History*.

Barkan's chief research and teaching interest has been the multi-disciplinary, multi-ethnic study of contemporary American ethnicity and race relations. His research has ranged from French Canadians in the Northeast to Mexicans in the Southwest, Scandinavians in the Pacific Northwest, and Asians in Hawai'i. It has also included computer analyses of immigration, naturalization, and census data as well as statewide public opinion polls in California.